Forensic Psychology

Forensic Psychology
Concepts, debates and practice

Second edition

Edited by

Joanna R. Adler and Jacqueline M. Gray

WILLAN
PUBLISHING

Published by

Willan Publishing
2 Park Square
Milton Park
Abingdon
Oxon
OX14 4RN

Published simultaneously in the USA and Canada by

Willan Publishing
270 Madison Avenue
New York
NY 10016

© The editors and contributors 2010

All rights reserved; no part of this publication may be reproduced, stored in a retrieval system, or transmitted in any form or by any means, electronic, mechanical, photocopying, recording or otherwise without the prior written permission of the Publishers or a licence permitting copying in the UK issued by the Copyright Licensing Agency Ltd, Saffron House, 6–10 Kirby Street, London EC1N 8TS.

First published 2010

ISBN 978-1-84392-414-2 paperback
978-1-84392-930-7 hardback

British Library Cataloguing-in-Publication Data

A catalogue record for this book is available from the British Library

Project managed by Deer Park Productions, Tavistock, Devon
Typeset by GCS, Leighton Buzzard, Bedfordshire
Printed and bound by T.J. International, Padstow, Cornwall

Contents

Notes on contributors

Joanna R. Adler is a forensic psychologist and chartered member of the British Psychological Society. She works in the Department of Psychology at Middlesex University where she runs Forensic Psychological Services and is the Postgraduate Programme Leader for the MSc in Forensic Psychology. She has conducted research and published in areas including fear, power, and victimisation in prisons; the effects of fear of crime on psychological well-being; intra-familial violence; the punishment of young offenders; radicalisation of 'at risk youth'; post-genocide survival and hate crimes. Other publications with Willan Publishing include the first edition of this text (2004); *My Brother's Keeper* (2005) with Jonathan Burnside, Nancy Loucks and Gerry Rose; and *Why We Kill* (2010) with Nancy Loucks and Sally Smith Holt.

Laurence Alison is a forensic psychologist, chartered member of the British Psychological Society and Director of the Centre for Critical and Major Incident Research at the University of Liverpool. His core area of interest is social cognition and the processes by which individuals make sense of ambiguous, complex or contradictory information. This has led to involvement of evaluations of expert reports prepared for the police and courts, so-called 'offender profilers' advice and credibility assessments of significant witnesses and victims. His work has attracted attention from many police forces in the UK and abroad and he has contributed to a number of major police inquiries, particularly complex and controversial investigations, including *R.* v. *Stagg*, a review of the behavioural information provided in the Dowler Inquiry. He has been key psychological adviser in several major debriefs, including the recent London Bombings.

Louise Almond is a forensic psychologist, chartered member of the British Psychological Society and Deputy Director of the Centre for Critical and Major Incident Research at the University of Liverpool. Her core area of interest is the criminogenic pathways of violent and sexual offenders. This has led to involvement in examining the content of UK offender profiles and behavioural investigative advice, in addition to how such advice is interpreted and used. In 2001 Dr Almond carried out a project commissioned by the Home Office into arson and arsonists.

Lara Arsuffi is a trainee forensic psychologist. She has worked with children and families involved in child protection proceedings, as well as with adolescent offenders and adult forensic psychiatric patients. During her career, she has practised in a variety of organisations, including social services, education establishments, the National Health Service and the Criminal Justice System. She has experience of providing clinical interventions to individuals, families and groups of clients, as well as providing consultation, conducting research projects and teaching, both to university students and to teams of professionals. Lara is the developer of the Triple C (anger control) programme, which is currently being piloted in two medium secure units with forensic psychiatric patients.

Emma Barrett runs a government research unit that provides training, advice and support to a range of UK law enforcement agencies and government departments. She holds an MSc with distinction in Investigative Psychology (University of Liverpool, 2002) and in 2009 she was awarded a PhD from the University of Birmingham. Emma's PhD thesis explores the psychological mechanisms underlying the acquisition, interpretation and exploitation of information by detectives in complex criminal enquiries, and is based on research funded by the ESRC and supported by a number of police forces throughout the UK. Her current research interests include interview strategies for suspects and informants, investigative decision-making, and terrorist motivation and behaviour.

John Bearchell retired from the Metropolitan Police in 2009 after 32 years' service, reaching the rank of Detective Chief Superintendent. As a career detective, he has investigated a wide spectrum of serious and organised crimes and has enjoyed secondments to the (then) National Criminal Intelligence Service and Home Office Police Standards Unit. At the time of his retirement, he was the OCU Commander for the

Olympic Security Directorate responsible for coordinating across law enforcement agencies and Government departments planning for the security of the London 2012 Olympic Games. John holds a BSc Degree in Policing and an MSc in Criminal Justice from the University of Portsmouth, an LL.M from Greenwich University and an MA in Criminology from Middlesex University, where he is studying towards the award of a PhD. Throughout his academic career he has focused upon the training and field application of investigative interviewing. John is now the senior security manager (Europe) for the Coca-Cola Company.

Ros Burnett is Reader in Criminology at the Centre for Criminology, University of Oxford. She gained her doctorate in social psychology from the University of Oxford in 1986, and was a probation officer before entering academia. She has considerable experience in research, project management and student supervision in the subject areas of recidivism and desistance from crime, rehabilitation and criminal justice services, and has published widely in these areas, including books (*Joined-up Youth Justice* (2003) and *What Works in Probation and Youth Justice* (2004)), policy reports (e.g. *Fitting Supervision to Offenders* (1996), *Racial Incidents in Prisons* (1994), *Reducing Re-offending: Key Practice Skills* (2005)) and numerous articles in practitioner and academic peer-reviewed journals.

Graham M. Davies is Professor Emeritus of Psychology at the University of Leicester and an Honorary Professor of Forensic Psychology at the Universities of Birmingham and Coventry. His research interests focus on the testimony of children and adults and the support of vulnerable witnesses at court, on which topics he has published some six books and over 100 articles in scientific journals. He is a former president of the Society for Applied Research in Memory and Cognition and immediate past president of the European Association for Psychology and Law and continues as Founding Editor of the journal *Applied Cognitive Psychology*. In addition to his academic work, he sits as a magistrate on the Melton, Belvoir and Rutland bench.

Liz A. Dixon is the Hate Crime Co-ordinator for London Probation. She assembled a toolkit called the 'Diversity and Prejudice Pack: A toolkit for working with racist and hate offending'. The toolkit consists of intervention materials to assist with identification, assessment and intervention re offending behaviour. Liz has been developing this work since 2000 and provides consultancy and professional intervention in casework both in the community and in prisons. Liz also worked as a Senior Lecturer in Criminal Justice studies in Brunel University and the University of Hertfordshire. She has a number of publications in peer-reviewed journals and books. She is also on the editorial board of the *Probation Journal*. Liz has more recently been involved in working with those charged under terrorist legislation and is developing interventions to work with different offenders who present with different risk and is developing a typology to assist those working on the frontline with these offenders.

David P. Farrington is Professor of Psychological Criminology in the Institute of Criminology at Cambridge University. He has been President of the American Society of Criminology, the British Society of Criminology and the European Association of Psychology and Law. He has received the Sellin-Glueck and Sutherland awards of the American Society of Criminology and the prize for distinguished scholarship of the American Sociological Association Criminology Section. He has published widely on criminological and psychological topics.

Anna Gekoski worked as a journalist and writer, specialising in crime, before embarking upon doctoral research in forensic psychology at Middlesex University. Her thesis is about the secondary victimisation, by criminal justice agencies and the media, of those bereaved by homicide. Her other research interests include victims of crime, rape, offender profiling and ethical issues in conducting trauma-focused research. She is the author of *Murder by Numbers: British Serial Sex Killers Since 1950* (1998).

Elizabeth A. Gilchrist is a registered forensic psychologist and Professor in Forensic Psychology at Glasgow Caledonian University. Liz's primary research interest is in the area of domestic violence, with particular focus on risk assessment. She has been involved in training postgraduate forensic psychologists since 1996 and has been a member of various forensic and professional committees within the British Psychological Society since then also. She is currently Chair of DFPTC and acting Chair of DFP-Scotland. Liz is also recognised as an expert in the area of domestic violence and child protection; she is a network lead (violence) for the Scottish Centre Crime and Justice Research, a member of the Research Advisory Group and a recognised training provider for the RMA, a part-time psychologist member of the Parole Board for England and Wales and a lay member of the Parole Board for Scotland.

Agnieszka Golec de Zavala is a social psychologist working as a Senior Lecturer in the Department of Psychology at Middlesex University. She has conducted research and published in the areas of psychological factors predicting escalation and de-escalation of intergroup conflict; predictors of intergroup hostility; forms of social identification and group love; collective and national narcissism; predictors of political extremism and radicalism; psychological aspects of terrorism and psychological underpinnings of political beliefs. She is a recipient of scholarships from the Fulbright Commission, the Kosciuszko Foundation, the Stefan Batory Foundation and Netherlands Institute for Advanced Studies. She has published over 20 scientific papers in international peer-reviewed journals.

Anthony H. Goodman is Professor of Criminal and Community Justice Studies in the Department of Criminology and Sociology at Middlesex University. He is the Postgraduate Programme Leader for the MA in Youth Justice, Community Safety and Applied Criminology and recently set up a Masters in Public Protection with London Probation. He has conducted research in probation practice, hate crime, young people, ethnicity and alcohol (Joseph Rowntree Foundation) and currently with the Brunel and Leeds Metropolitan Universities on an ESRC project, 'Negotiating Identity: young people's perspectives on faith values, community norm and social cohesion'. Recent publications include *Social Work with Drug and Substance Misusers* (2nd edition) and *Children as Victims* (edited with Peter Kennison), both published by Learning Matters.

Jacqueline M. Gray is a Senior Lecturer in Forensic Psychology at Middlesex University. Her research interests focus around two main themes: the prosecution of rape, and various aspects of terrorism. In relation to rape trials, she is particularly interested in assessing the effects of rape myths on verdicts, and also on the public understanding of what constitutes consent. Her terrorism research focuses on public understanding of and support for counter-terrorism measures, and she is also interested in terrorist group processes. In addition to these specific research interests, she also teaches and supervises research across a wide range of topics within forensic psychology.

Mark R. Kebbell is a Chief Investigator with the Australian Centre of Excellence in Policing and Security. His expertise and research are in the area of investigative psychology, particularly with regard to the investigation and prosecution of serious crime. Within the Centre, he is the lead Chief Investigator on the Risky People and Intelligence Methods. In addition, he is working on an investigative interviewing project with colleagues Powell and Hughes-Scholes and Victoria Police Service. His previous work has included writing the guidelines for police officers in England and Wales (with Wagstaff) for the assessment of eyewitness evidence. He has worked on more than 70 criminal cases, principally involving murder or serious sexual assault, and has given expert evidence on numerous occasions including uncontested psychological evidence in an Old Bailey appeal case. Academically, the quality of his work has been recognised by the award of a British Academy Postdoctoral Fellowship for Outstanding Younger Scholars. He is the editor, with Professor Graham Davies, of the book *Practical Psychology for Forensic Investigations and Prosecutions* (2006) published by Wiley.

Nicholas LeBoutillier obtained his PhD in 2000. He is currently a Principal Lecturer in Psychology at Middlesex University in the United Kingdom. His research interests include creativity, mental imagery and altered states of consciousness. He has published in internationally recognised journals and has advised at a local capacity in these areas.

Lucy Lemanski is a graduate of the MSc in Forensic Psychology at the University of Surrey, where she is currently employed. She has previously worked on research in aggression and psychopharmacology, and disruptive airline passenger behaviour. Her research interests lie in a number of areas of forensic psychology, notably terrorist bomb attacks and single-issue extremism. She is currently working with Margaret Wilson on research funded by the National Consortium for the Study of Terrorism and Responses to Terrorism (START), a US Department of Homeland Security Center of Excellence at the University of Maryland.

Alex Lord joined Broadmoor Hospital in 2002 where he has worked with complex one-to-one formulations, delivering risk and need assessments as well as individual and group therapies, including a group for sexual offenders. He contributed to setting up the DSPD pilot unit, chairs the Risk Management Advisory Group and has contributed to designing, running and evaluating the Understanding Personality Disorder group for patients with this diagnosis. He also co-convenes Broadmoor Hospital's modules on the MSc in Forensic Psychology at the University of Surrey and he is a member of the editorial board of the *British Journal of Forensic Practice*. Previously he worked as a forensic psychologist in HM Prison Service for nine years, including working with young offenders and personality-disordered/disruptive prisoners.

Nancy Loucks is the Chief Executive of Families Outside, a national Scottish voluntary organisation that specialises in advocacy and support for families affected by imprisonment. Prior to this, she worked as an independent criminologist, specialising in research on prison policy and comparative criminology. She received her M.Phil and PhD from the Institute of Criminology at the University of Cambridge and has conducted extensive research into human rights issues in prison, female and young offenders, prison violence and protests, addiction, suicides and self-harm, violence risk assessment and management, the experience of offenders with learning difficulties and learning disabilities, homelessness among ex-prisoners, and the maintenance of prisoners' family ties. She was a Trustee for the Visitors' Centre at HMP Edinburgh for six years and an invited member of the National Advisory Body on Offender Management for the Scottish Cabinet Secretary for Justice.

Beverly Love studied substance misuse and offender rehabilitation during her MSc in Forensic Psychology whilst at Middlesex University and is currently undertaking a PhD at Surrey University researching the psychological health of substance misusing offenders. She has worked within the field since 2003. He work has included helping to implement a national treatment and rehabilitation programme for substance misusing offenders.

Sarah Marsden is currently undertaking a doctorate in International Relations at the University of St Andrews, UK, examining the relative success of groups which use terrorism. She has carried out a variety of research, including looking at those who engage with terrorist offenders, issues of disenfranchisement and radicalisation in community contexts, and the assessment of success and failure in terrorism and counter-terrorism, with a particular focus on al-Q'aeda and Global Jihad. Sarah is also an Associate Lecturer in Forensic Psychology for the Open University.

Lisa Marzano is a postdoctoral researcher at the Centre for Suicide Research, University of Oxford. She started researching suicide and self-harm in prisons in 2000. Since then, she has conducted extensive work on self-injury among male prisoners, near-lethal suicide attempts in women's prisons, and on the impact on staff of prisoner self-harm.

Barbara Masser is a Senior Lecturer in Psychology at the University of Queensland. Her research interests lie in the area of applied social psychology, with a specific focus on gender, sexism and stereotyping.

Blake McKimmie is a Senior Lecturer in Psychology at the University of Queensland. A social psychologist by training, his research focuses on the influence of stereotypes in the courtroom, the validity of jury simulations, group processes and decision-making, group processes in organisational settings, and attitude–behaviour relations.

Becky Milne is a Reader in Forensic Psychology at the Institute of Criminal Justice Studies at the University of Portsmouth. She is the course leader of the FdA Investigation and Evidence, a distance-learning degree programme specifically for investigators. A forensic psychologist and scientist and Associate Fellow of the British Psychological Society, she has worked closely with the police and other criminal justice organisations (in the UK and abroad) through training of the Enhanced Cognitive Interview, Witness Interview Advising and also in the interviewing of vulnerable groups (Tiers 3 and 5). Becky was part of a writing team who developed the national guidance document *Achieving Best Evidence* (Home Office 2007) that outlines the best ways to interview witnesses and victims for legal purposes. In April 2009 Becky was given the Tom Williamson Award by ACPO for her outstanding achievements in the field of investigative interviewing.

Terrie E. Moffitt studies how genetic and environmental risks work together to shape the developmental course of abnormal human behaviours and psychiatric disorders. Her particular interest is in antisocial and criminal behaviour, but she also studies depression, psychosis and substance abuse. She is associate director of the MRC-funded Dunedin Longitudinal Study, which follows 1,000 people born in 1972 in New Zealand. She also directs the MRC-funded Environmental-Risk Longitudinal Twin Study, which follows 1,100 British families with twins born 1994–1995. Currently, Moffitt is a member of the working party for childhood disruptive disorders and ADHD for the DSM-V, forthcoming from the American Psychiatric Association in 2012. She works at Duke University, North Carolina, USA; at the Institute of Psychiatry, King's College, London, UK; and at the Dunedin School of Medicine, New Zealand. She is a licensed clinical psychologist, who completed her clinical hospital training at the UCLA Neuropsychiatric Institute in 1984.

Pamela Ormerod is a practising magistrate with considerable experience of chairing adult, youth and family courts. She has used her knowledge of the judicial system and her interest in psychology to complete a doctoral thesis at Middlesex University. This was directed towards understanding what factors influence magistrates in their sentencing choices and whether there are individual differences which affect those choices.

Alex R. Piquero is Professor in the College of Criminology & Criminal Justice at Florida State University and co-editor of the *Journal of Quantitative Criminology*. His research interests include criminal careers, criminological theory, and quantitative research methods.

Sam Poyser is a Senior Lecturer in Criminology, Criminal Justice and Policing at the Institute of Law and Criminal Justice Studies, Canterbury Christchurch University, Kent. Her main research interest lies in the issue of miscarriages of justice in England and Wales which she has extensively researched, particularly in relation to media involvement in this area. She is currently engaged in doctoral research on miscarriages of justice and has published in this area and in the areas of crime prevention and policing.

Stephen P. Savage is Professor of Criminology and Director of the Institute of Criminal Justice Studies, University of Portsmouth, which he founded in 1992. He has published widely on policing and the politics of criminal justice policy, including *Police Reform: Forces for Change* (Oxford University Press, 2007) and (with Nathan Hall and John Grieve) *Policing and the Legacy of Lawrence* (Willan Publishing, 2009). He has recently researched and published on miscarriages and justice, and his current research is on the independent investigation of complaints against the police.

Lorraine Sheridan is a forensic psychologist, chartered member of the British Psychological Society and an international expert on stalking and harassment. She completed Europe's first PhD on stalking and has so far published four books and more than 40 papers on the subject. She is a police-accredited offender profiler and compiles psychological reports related to offenders, highlighting the risks posed by known or unknown suspects. After a long stint as a senior academic at the University of Leicester, England, Lorraine is now a part-time Senior Research Fellow at Heriot Watt University, Edinburgh. She is a board member of the Division of Forensic Psychology of the British Psychological Society and a founder member of the Association of European Threat Assessment Professionals.

Graham Towl was formerly Chief Psychologist at the Ministry of Justice. Currently he is a Professor of Psychology and Principal of St Cuthbert's Society at Durham University. He is a recipient of the British Psychological Society (BPS) Award for Distinguished Contributions to Professional Practice and a Fellow of the BPS. He is widely published in the forensic field.

Brandon C. Welsh is an Associate Professor in the College of Criminal Justice at Northeastern University, Boston, Massachusetts and Senior Research Fellow at the Netherlands Institute for the Study of Crime and Law Enforcement at Free University in Amsterdam.

Rachel Wilcock is a Senior Lecturer in Psychology at London South Bank University and Course Director of the MSc Investigative Forensic Psychology course. Her major area of research interest is eliciting accurate eyewitness evidence from adults aged 60 years and over. She has worked with a number of police forces across England and Wales, collecting data on the identification decisions made by older witnesses, as well as investigating methods of improving older mock witnesses' performance in a laboratory setting. She has published widely in international peer-reviewed journals and presented at a number of national and international conferences.

Tom Williamson was a visiting professor at the Institute of Criminal Justice Studies, University of Portsmouth until his death in March 2007. A chartered forensic psychologist, he had a doctorate from the University of Kent for his research into investigative interviewing. He was one of the founders of the PEACE method of interviewing. A former police officer, he retired from the post of Deputy Chief Constable of the Nottinghamshire Police in 2001 and was previously a Commander at New Scotland Yard.

Margaret A. Wilson is a forensic psychologist, chartered member of the British Psychological Society and is currently Course Director for the MSc in Forensic Psychology at the University of Surrey. She has a range of interests in the area but is best known for her work on the psychology of terrorism. Her current research on terrorist bombing campaigns is funded through the National Consortium for the Study of Terrorism and Responses to Terrorism (START), a centre of excellence of the US Department of Homeland Security based at the University of Maryland.

Introduction

Joanna R. Adler and Jacqueline M. Gray

The first edition of *Forensic Psychology: concepts, debates and practice* was well received. This was both gratifying and encouraging as it showed that the contributors had addressed matters of interest and relevance to our discipline, to students and to related practitioners. It is intended that this second edition will again be of interest to practitioners and students who want, and need, to go beyond introductory texts. The contributors have raised questions for research and posed problems for practice. We intend to provide the reader with evidence of success and examples of where forensic psychology has clarified procedures and practice within criminal justice. As such, we aim this second edition at an audience that is much the same as the first one and we have endeavoured to update, revise and expand this edition. We hope that academics, students and practitioners will find this worthwhile. The text is again rich in content and style. It develops further the picture of diversity and depth of forensic psychology that has been built over the past few years.

There continue to be a number of forensic psychology textbooks on the market. Some are more legal in focus, others concentrate on treatment and therapeutic jurisprudence, while still others look at such matters as the aetiology and prevention of offending or address specific topics from within the discipline. With expansion of the field and growth of sub-disciplines, it is increasingly rare to see a textbook that is accessible, broad based enough to tackle the whole field, and aimed at anything other than an introductory level. We do not intend that this book be a handbook of practice, nor the definitive textbook for students, and we do not claim that it will provide the reader with a complete overview to the field of criminological psychology. This second edition does cover more than the first in the legal domain but, again, we do not promise any student that this one stop will fulfil all syllabus requirements for legal psychology.

This book provides a contextual setting and explanation for the theoretical and practical developments in forensic psychology, particularly in Britain but drawing on international contexts where possible. We devote more space than most to consideration of the societal and political contexts in which forensic psychologists work. This is largely a book that assumes knowledge of at least some basic ideas in either the practice or theory of forensic psychology and we do not seek to rehearse them all here. Rather, the authors have again generated material that considers the development of our discipline and provides pointers for ongoing evolution and change.

As editors, we are delighted about the diversity of contributors to this text. We are heartened by how many people have been able to revise and update their initial contributions and pleased to welcome several authors who have newly joined us in this edition.[1] The authors are drawn from a wide variety of settings: from eminent theoreticians and chairs of psychological and criminological associations, to major employers of forensic psychologists and those who both make and implement policy. Contributors are based in the United Kingdom, elsewhere in Europe, the United States of America and Australia, and range from people who have been practising for more than 40 years, to those who are at the outset of their careers. As editors, we think that this talented, enthusiastic and capable group of people have brought together some interesting, insightful and innovative material. We hope that you agree.

Outline of the book

This second edition of *Forensic Psychology: Concepts, Debates and Practice* is a revised, longer and more broad-based collection of contributions than the first edition. We have retained much from the scope of the original book and the structure and broad organising principles are the same.

In the opening chapter of this edition, we set forensic psychology in a broader context. Joanna R. Adler and Jacqueline M. Gray have considered some of the ways in which the discipline has progressed in the past five years. They touch on matters relating to the uses of risk assessment and the roles of forensic psychology practice, in different jurisdictions. They discuss the ethics of practice, considering human rights obligations, and begin to explore the needs for training and ongoing statutory regulation of psychologists. We move from this introductory chapter on to a section on investigation and prosecution.

Section 1: Investigation and Prosecution

The four chapters of this section reflect both revision and broadening of the second edition in comparison to the first. In Chapter 2, Becky Milne, Sam Poyser and Steve Savage have revised the chapter initially written by Tom Williamson. Tom's loss was a blow to us all and it was important to us that his work on miscarriages of justice be properly continued. We are thus delighted that the team with whom Tom worked so closely were able to take the original chapter and reshape it for the current collection.

In Chapter 3, Laurence Alison, Emma Barrett and Louise Almond provide an updated review and critical exploration of the interpretation and utilisation of offender profiles. Drawing on debate about the reliability and validity of various offender profile techniques, they point to ways to maximise both and to build on the intellectual rigour and practical utility of such investigative approaches.

John Bearchell's work in Chapter 4 builds on each of the preceding two chapters to look at police interviewing. He considers the relationships between public confidence in the police, the evidence they elicit and the means by which it is gained. The previous needs for legislative intervention and subsequent impact of changes to police procedure are explored. John then moves to an in-depth assessment of the impact of improved interviewing styles, and proper consideration of the purposes of the interviews.

The last chapter in this section is by Jacqueline M. Gray and Anna Gekoski. In Chapter 5, Jackie and Anna consider the developments in the way rape is dealt with, from initial reporting through to court and beyond. Their review encompasses the impact of criminal justice system responses and low conviction rates and it explores the likely impact of the most recent changes in the way consent is to be considered by the courts.

Section 2: Testimony and Evidence

This section is another where we have widened the scope of the book. We have retained our ambition to move beyond the materials routinely considered in an introductory textbook. So, rather than a chapter on eyewitness evidence per se, there are two considering the uses of testimony from a more developed perspective. Similarly, in the first chapter in this section, Blake McKimmie and Barbara Masser move beyond basic considerations of how jurors reach their decisions to look at the roles played by 'extra legal factors' in jury processes. In particular, they explore the impacts of gender in the courtroom.

Chapter 7 is by Pamela Ormerod and Joanna R. Adler. Pamela is a magistrate with three decades of experience and is chair of a youth panel. She has bolstered this direct experience with a body of psychological research exploring how magistrates make decisions. This chapter provides the reader with an outline of the official guidance provided to magistrates and their training. It then moves to an assessment of the processes involved in reaching sentencing disposals and what the implications are for the implementation of justice.

Having considered how jurors and magistrates reach decisions, we move to more direct consideration of the processes at play in the way witnesses' evidence is brought into court and used. In Chapter 8, Mark R. Kebbell and Elizabeth A. Gilchrist provide an updated and revised version of their chapter on how evidence is elicited from witnesses. They consider some of the strategies used by lawyers in an adversarial system to construct the narratives necessary for their version of the case. The impact of these strategies is then explored both in terms of how it affects witnesses themselves and the potential issues of reliability of the information elicited.

The cognitive interview is a technique considered in a number of the chapters in this book and it again makes an appearance in Chapter 9. Here, Rachel Wilcock considers the impact of the cognitive interview and other means of gaining evidence from witnesses. This time, the focus is on the impact of ageing on eyewitness evidence and its reliability. In evaluating the research evidence, Rachel raises questions of how best to work with and for older witnesses so that we can maximise the utility of their testimony and best serve the interests of justice.

The last chapter in this section is by Graham M. Davies and he looks at the impact of procedures adopted to improve the position of vulnerable witnesses. Graham's research has been pivotal to changes made in courtroom procedure. His assessment of the 'special measures' now available in court includes case examples and a clear appraisal of how far we have come and what is still to be done, both in the courtroom and beyond.

Section 3: Serious and Persistent Offending

This section is a mixture of old and new. In the first two chapters, we present the original contributions from Alex Piquero and Terrie Moffitt and Lorraine Sheridan and Graham M. Davies. In each of these chapters we have provided updated reading lists at the end, but the body of each text remains unaltered from the first edition. Alex and Terrie's consideration of life course persistent offenders provides a comprehensive summary of the many studies in this area for Chapter 11. In Chapter 12, Lorraine and Graham share their insight on the impacts of stalking on victims and how responses can be improved.

Chapter 13 is a new chapter from Margaret A. Wilson and Lucy Lemanski, which considers how forensic psychology can help in understanding and responding to terrorism, by examining the parallels and differences that exist between terrorism and other forms of crime and between terrorists and other types of offender. This burgeoning field of work has been neglected by many forensic psychological textbooks and we welcome their internationally recognised work here.

The subsequent chapter, by Agnieszka Golec de Zavala and Joanna R. Adler examines another often neglected field of endeavour. In this case, they explore how social psychology and forensic psychological understanding can be brought to bear in consideration of genocide. Their chapter sets genocide within its societal context and helps us to understand better the warning signs that should signal intervention. In each of these chapters, the impact for both individual victims and societies can be enormous, yet little forensic psychological attention has traditionally been paid to the aetiology of such offending.

Section 4: Treatment as Intervention

This section moves us back to what is potentially more familiar forensic psychological terrain as we consider ways to treat offenders who present with mental or personality disorder and/or substance abuse histories. In Chapter 15, Alex Lord draws on his extensive clinical and forensic experience in assessing the impact of interventions with Dangerous and Severe Personality Disordered Offenders. As noted in the first edition, this classification is a legal term, not clinical. Ways to treat or manage such offenders appropriately have been controversial. Alex assesses the impact of the interventions currently adopted, both for the client group and those who work with them.

In Chapter 16, Lara Arsuffi considers how best to intervene with offenders who are inpatients in secure psychiatric settings and have also been assessed as being in need of anger management. She considers the standard therapeutic and criminogenic interventions available, then moves to an explanation and assessment of an anger management tool that she has designed. This chapter should be of interest to anyone concerned with whether standardised tools are used appropriately when adopted in a wider setting than that for which they were initially designed, as well as those specifically interested in dual diagnosis issues.

The next and final chapter in this section moves to a consideration of the diversionary schemes and treatments available for substance misusing offenders. In Chapter 17, Nicholas LeBoutillier and Beverly Love draw on academic, practitioner and real case histories to assess the impact of recent government shifts in intervention with this group of offenders.

Section 5: Intervention and Prevention

The next section of our text picks up on ways to intervene with offenders and elucidates ways to prevent recidivism in a number of key areas. In Chapter 18, Elizabeth A. Gilchrist and Mark R. Kebbell provide a significantly revised, updated and broadened chapter on Intimate Partner Violence. They evaluate the changes to the field and what is still to be done, providing the reader with both a useful contextual summary and practical advice on intervention.

Chapter 19 is a revised and updated chapter by Brandon Welsh and David Farrington in which they look at the various interventions adopted to prevent delinquency. Drawing on international, longitudinal studies and evaluations of policy and practice, they show how much we have learnt and how much influence previous research (both their own and others') has had on policy. They are clear about the need for rigorous evaluation and ongoing policy review and point to steps for future improvement in practice.

In the following chapter, Anthony H. Goodman and Joanna R. Adler look in more depth at the impact of parenting programmes on those who attend them. Tony and Joanna look more closely at the political climate in which parenting programmes have come about. They draw on psychological and sociological literature in taking a more participant-centred view of parenting programmes and considering the effects of parenting training as punishment.

The last chapter in this section is by Liz A. Dixon and Joanna R. Adler and its focus is hate crimes. This is again an area of neglect within forensic psychological literature. In this chapter, Liz and Joanna consider the importance of definition to our recognition and prosecution of a crime. They remind us that how a crime is defined will have subsequent effects not just on levels of reporting and prosecution, but also on how intervention can be conducted.

Section 6: Punishment and Corrections

In the final section of this book, we move from the community into prison. We open this section with a consideration of the purposes of punishment and deterrence. In Chapter 22, Sarah Marsden considers the philosophy and societal contexts in which punishments are implemented. She raises ethical, practical and theoretical concerns and gives us a comprehensive historical and legislative set of perspectives on the uses of deterrence. Sarah demonstrates how deterrence has been moulded and its scope widened, alongside shifts in our understanding of offending behaviour and the ways in which society has responded to criminality.

In Chapters 23 and 24, Nancy Loucks and Lisa Marzano explore some of the effects of imprisonment, considering women prisoners and those who self-harm, or commit suicide. Nancy's chapter is a revised and updated assessment of her chapter in the first edition. This update reflects regression away from some of the more hopeful statements on women's imprisonment that were being made when we first published. The chapter considers the impact and implications of imprisoning more women.

In the next chapter, Lisa Marzano picks up on some of the themes discussed in Chapter 23 and moves to an assessment of the issues around self-harm in prisons. She provides a nuanced understanding of the impact of prison on prisoners and staff and how both suicide and self-harm can have ramifications far wider than directly for those men and women who harm themselves.

In Chapter 25, Ros Burnett moves us forward from prison to a consideration of how prisoners can be reintegrated into society on release. She looks at how approaches to reintegration have shifted and how they have been received by offenders. Ros reminds us again of the importance of understanding the impact of shifts in policy on offenders and offending behaviour, again highlighting the importance of social context and available support.

This interaction between social policy and forensic psychology is something that we reprise as we close the book. In Chapter 26, Graham Towl gives us an assessment of the roles that forensic psychologists can and should have within the prison and probation services, revisiting some of the themes from the opening chapter. He reiterates the importance of listening to offenders in trying to understand how best to prevent recidivism and develops a cogent case that professional bodies and employers need to work more closely to help further our discipline.

Note

1 A selection of chapters from the first edition that are not included within this collection can be found at www.willanpublishing.co.uk/cgi-bin/indexer?product=9781843924142

Chapter 1

Forensic psychology: some concepts and debates about practice

Joanna R. Adler and Jacqueline M. Gray

The first edition of this book was published in 2004. In the past six years, much has stayed the same. There are still fundamental differences in what is meant by 'forensic psychology' across jurisdictions; there is still intense interest in the study of forensic psychology or psychology and law among students, and the uses of risk assessment tools are still both pervasive and controversial.

Much though has changed; in Britain, there has been a gradual move towards greater recognition of forensic mental health needs and we are beginning to see greater development of work relating to terrorism prevention. Terrorist incidents of the past 10 years such as those in New York (2001), Bali (2002), Madrid (2004) and London (2005) led to fundamental shifts in legislation, policy and practice. For decades, psychologists had been working alongside academics and practitioners from international relations, social policy and criminology regarding terrorism in multiple domains. However, the massive shift in policy and funding reflected in the European and American anti-terrorism strategies has found us evaluating strategies to prevent violent extremism, understanding terrorist group processes, dealing with hate crimes and working with probation colleagues to manage 'radical offenders' as they are released from prison.

In the intervening years, we have also gone from an era of unprecedented spending on forensic psychological and correctional interventions to one of public spending cutbacks. This edition is published at a time of uncertainty and with higher graduate unemployment than any of us would have predicted. Yet in England and Wales, it is also a time when the discipline, indeed psychology as a whole, is recasting itself in the wake of new arrangements whereby the profession has been put onto a statutory footing.

Readers familiar with the first edition may notice some changes. Firstly, one editor has become two. We have worked together on teaching and research for several years and it was both a natural and logical progression for us to edit this second edition together. Secondly, this book is 10 chapters longer than the first edition, yet some of the original chapters are not reflected in this second edition. This indicates both the growth in the discipline and a shift in our thinking about what to prioritise. Those chapters that were included in the first edition have been revised and updated for this collection. In most cases, this involved significant rewriting. However, the authors of Chapters 11 and 12 were so heavily committed to other projects that we have only been able to update the reading lists. More details on each of the chapters and the structure of the book are provided in the Introduction. We are very grateful to all the contributors.

In many parts of the world today, it is possible to find psychology being practised with a forensic twist. Forensic psychologists evaluate offender behaviour programmes, design risk assessments, aid investigative processes, support victims, provide treatment and generally try to facilitate justice. Psychological testimony is now fairly commonplace in the courts themselves. It may be given in cases ranging from the prosecution of war crimes to an adoption hearing. Most people would concur that forensic psychology is a discipline concerned with providing psychological information to people, agencies and systems involved directly, and sometimes indirectly, in the implementation of justice (Dushkind 1984). There are some who define forensic psychology more narrowly, as work provided solely for use by the courts (Gudjonsson and Haward 1998). Yet even these definitions can be used differently. So, for example, in their assessment of American forensic psychology trainee experiences, Morgan *et al.* (2007) distinguish between correctional and forensic psychology as follows:

> correctional psychology is the application of psychological principles to individuals convicted of a crime and sentenced to serve time in a correctional setting (including community corrections), whereas forensic psychology (specifically, criminal forensic psychology for purposes of this article) is the application of psychological principles to individuals charged with a crime but who remain in the judicial process (i.e., have not been

convicted of the crime with which they are charged). (Morgan *et al.* 2007: 96)

The definitional differences partly arise as there are no particular skill sets that definitively separate a forensic psychologist from any other type of psychologist. Rather, it is the context within which we practise and apply our knowledge that makes it forensic (Blackburn 1996). Furthermore, there are increasing roles for other kinds of psychologists within forensic settings so even this definition is limited in utility. For those practising as forensic psychologists, licensing or statutory registration are relatively recent innovations. The American Psychological Association (APA) and the British Psychological Society (BPS) each have divisions concerned with forensic psychology that were only fully established within the past 30 years. In England and Wales, statutory registration for applied psychologists offering services to the public came into force in July 2009.[1]

Within the British Psychological Society, the Division of Forensic Psychology is still responsible for nearly all training of forensic psychologists and there has been protracted debate as to how people should best acquire and demonstrate necessary knowledge and skills for full membership. In part, the debate reflects individuals' very different understandings of what makes a forensic psychologist. In part, it is a debate about how best to interpret competency-based criteria that were painstakingly drawn up over many years of consultation. Unfortunately, this debate has also led to a qualification bottleneck, with trainees lacking clarity, guidance and support from their learned society that is only now beginning to be properly addressed. As the borders come down across the European Union and its membership expands, professions are expected to make welcome their counterparts from elsewhere in the confederation of states. Differences in training, practice and professional expectations have the potential to cause border disputes along the parameters of a discipline and to endanger the public through mismatches in expectations and needs.

Potential problems are clear but the solutions are far from simple. This may be demonstrated by a brief exploration of our transatlantic cousins' certification procedures. In the USA, board certification is controlled by State not Federal regulations. Firstly, there has arisen something of a divide between 'legal psychologists' and 'forensic psychologists', with the latter being cast more as practitioners, often with a clinical expertise, and the former as consultants/academics. This is an oversimplification but the labels do matter. Not least, they matter because without appropriate certification from the State concerned, psychologists cannot testify directly to the courts. Thus, an expert from one State with many years' knowledge and experience, both in research and evidentiary matters, is not necessarily able to give advice to the courts, nor be called by interested parties in another State. In England and Wales, we now have legally binding protection over specific titles such as Registered or Practitioner Psychologist or, indeed, Forensic Psychologist. However, the generic title psychologist is not protected in law.[2] The qualifications necessary as an expert to provide evidence to the courts are not regulated and largely come down to experience and ability to add something of probative value to the court hearing (British Psychological Society 2009).

Even when evidence can be given to the courts, by the best available people, we do not always agree as to what to say. Nor do we agree about the relative merits of the research studies on which much of the evidence is based. Like other social scientists, forensic psychologists have argued long and hard regarding generalisability and ecological validity of approaches to research and how robust the findings may be, when applied to the 'real world'. There is lively discussion about when and where laboratory-based research is appropriate and how such findings should be interpreted within the contexts of police practice, court decision-making, and the implementation of justice. It is easy to see why one may want to impose rigorous experimental control into designs trying to assess exactly how cognitive processes might be operating, for example. It is equally easy to see why one might seek to investigate the possibility of improving policy or practice in more realistic settings than the eponymous research cubicle. Without rigorously controlled research designs, alternative explanations for findings will abound, requiring us to equivocate our advice. Yet, if we wish to pass commentary on criminal justice systems, then we need to ensure that our work is going to be as meaningful, and contextually appropriate, as any other piece of applied psychology.

With this emphasis on the problems of self-definition, it would be understandable to think of forensic psychology as a social scientific neophyte. Yet, for as long as psychology has been dealt with as a separate area of endeavour, the enterprise has encompassed the forensic realm. For well over a hundred years, psychological practice and research have been directed at ways of improving the implementation of justice, explaining and minimising criminal behaviour and the ramifications of crime (Gudjonsson 1991). The courts' use of evidence that we might now classify as psychological and/or criminological go back somewhat further than the turn of the last century. Beccaria and Lombroso had been working on explanations for crime and criminal behaviour for several years before the end of the nineteenth century. Similarly, insanity rules have been a feature of various jurisdictions for generations. A broad-reaching excuse to culpability was introduced to France in 1810. In England, the later, more narrow rules based on the case of Daniel M'Naghten, have been largely unchanged for 150 years, although they have been supplemented, most recently by the Mental Health (Amendments) Act 2007.

The first person generally acknowledged to have written specifically about the use of expert evidence in court is Münsterberg, whose book has become a classic text (Münsterberg 1908). As such, he should be credited with much of the establishment and popularising of the use of psychology in courts. Even at the start of the twentieth century, the use of psychological evidence was not without controversy, and had its detractors (Wigmore 1909). We can also see that, from the start, psychological tools were being utilised to bring about justice beyond the confines of the courtroom. By 1916, Terman had revised Binet and Simon's intelligence test (Binet and Simon 1905) and was advocating its use in the selection of police and fire officers. He also gathered together studies on potential relationships between criminal behaviour and intelligence, thereby applying psychology to criminal behaviour itself.

Terman wrote at a time when there were related publications and statistics coming from elsewhere in North America and the rest of the world. For example, in Britain, Charles Goring was making similar arguments (Goring 1913). Like Goring, Terman took issue with Lombroso's conclusions about the physical differences between offenders and the law-abiding, which were themselves derived from Lavater in 1789 and Lauvergne in 1848 (Walsh 2003). Drawing on a series of studies conducted in reformatories, Terman concluded that intelligence tests

> have demonstrated, beyond any possibility of doubt, that the most important trait of at least 25 per cent of our criminals is mental weakness. The physical abnormalities which have been found so common among prisoners are not the stigmata of criminality, but the physical accompaniments of feeble-mindedness. They have no diagnostic significance except in so far as they are indications of mental deficiency. Without exception, every study which has been made of the intelligence level of delinquents has furnished convincing testimony as to

> the close relation existing between mental weakness and moral abnormality. (Terman 1916)

That statement neatly encapsulated one side of an argument regarding criminality, intelligence, moral development and the associated issues of both culpability and treatment that continues to this day.

Differences in opinion regarding intelligence run deep. When taken in conjunction with the difficulties in defining our profession as a distinct group, they help to demonstrate that the forensic field is replete with complex theoretical and practical dimensions. We have, however, managed to make some significant collaborative inroads with other disciplines and in tackling specific problems thrown up by the practices of justice systems and agencies. In much of Europe, the relationship between criminology and psychology has become strengthened in recent years with the growth of 'effective practice' initiatives. Applied psychology has generally expanded and given greater credence to sociological theories. Likewise, applied sociological disciplines have been able to consider contributions made by psychology. This can be seen in the increasing prominence of leading psychologists within criminological texts, such as the fourth edition of the *Oxford Handbook of Criminology* (Maguire *et al.* 2007).

This is not to claim that all is rosy in our collaborative gardens. If, within disciplines, there is debate as to what constitutes a proper approach and who is the most qualified to conduct work, so it is that outwith the disciplines, we still sometimes strive to show that we have a right to be present at the table. At the American Society of Criminology annual meetings, it is not uncommon for presenters drawing on forensic psychological theory to predicate their work with explanations of and justifications for the very discipline itself, even in symposia clearly marked as being psychological in orientation. Within psychology there is a similar problem with recognition of the value of applied disciplines in general. Within universities, the apparent sidelining of applied psychology in general and forensic psychology in particular has been considered as a manifestation of the progress of academic monitoring and assessments of research value that are directly linked to the monies gained by university departments. So, Brown (2009) argues that the Research Assessment Exercise in Britain contributed directly to an impoverishment in the discipline through departmental cuts and implicit guidance as to which parts of psychology were to be most valued.

One area in which forensic psychologists have been active alongside people working in related disciplines is in the 'What Works?' debate.

We have been involved in designing and evaluating programmes targeted at reducing recidivism, often in violent, sexual and/or mentally disordered offenders. Increasingly, we are to be found working in multi-agency settings and are finding ways to integrate psychology within service user approaches to multidisciplinary working (e.g. Gudjonsson and Young 2007). Alongside that work, much effort has been expended on risk assessments, both in their design and conduct (Bonta *et al.* 1998; Harris *et al.* 1993; Quinsey *et al.* 1995; Sreenivasan *et al.* 2000). In England and Wales, as elsewhere, the merits of different sorts of risk assessment are not only a source of contention, but a good example of how psychological tools may be used by legislative authorities. At the time of writing, the Ministry of Justice was pilot testing a new risk matrix to be used with 'radical offenders' due for release from prison, and risk assessments are routinely used as prisoners are considered for licence/parole or moves from one level of security to another.

Modern prisons policies in North America and much of Europe have been characterised by swings from rehabilitative to punitive and back again. Regimes for women, young offenders, and members of religious or ethnic minorities have made few concessions that they are in any ways different from the majority white, adult, male offending population. The experiential and evaluative commentary from ex-prisoners, sociologists, criminologists, philosophers and even a few psychologists, posed questions that were never fully answered. Essentially, what is the prime purpose of imprisonment, how can we assess whether its espoused aims have been met and does it disproportionately affect some more than others? In reality, such basic questions can only be answered in a dynamic way and never definitively. Policy and therapeutic aims shift with time, resources, public opinion and political will. On this occasion, it seems that forensic psychologists are at the forefront of the debate.

As Stephenson has pointed out, forensic psychologists have sometimes seemed to publish in something of a social vacuum (Stephenson 1992). We have described phenomena, labelled behaviours and people without always acknowledging the contextual realities of their lives or the social infrastructures around them. We have learnt from other disciplines, for example the *anti-psychiatry* movement including the work of Szasz (1963). Yet, our conduct as ethical, professional practitioners is still something worth consideration. Despite our accountability and responsibility to our professional bodies and the general public, there has been very little recent consideration of the roles of forensic psychologists within the parameters of human rights law.

In a cogent, rigorously sourced piece, Birgden and Perlin (2008) draw on international norms on the treatment of prisoners, and professional codes of conduct alongside theoretical and practitioner research to question the lack of materials considering prisoners' human rights and our responsibilities as practitioners when working with them. They suggest that the intersection of therapeutic jurisprudence (e.g. Wexler and Winick 1996 or, more recently, Petrucci *et al.* 2003) and human rights laws may offer us a route to proceed. Ward *et al.* (2009) also provide a comprehensive review of human rights laws, again via the United Nations conventions. In addition, they look more directly at the APA ethical code, providing a worked-through case example to highlight how we should consider the core principles of human rights within our practice: namely the application of *Beneficence and Nonmaleficence; Fidelity and Responsibility; Integrity; Justice and Respect for People's Rights and Dignity* to the involuntary treatment of sex offenders (Ward *et al. ibid.*). We believe that ethical, properly informed practice needs to be cogniscant of international human rights as well as jurisdiction-specific legislation and appropriate professional conduct guidelines. Indeed, we would concur with Ward *et al.* (*ibid.*) that these understandings reflect the 'kind of ethical sensitivity that is essential in dealing with the nuances of forensic practice and in grasping how values and skills acquisition are interrelated' (Ward *et al.* 2009: 144).

This brings us from definitional concerns, through to practice issues and back to definitional matters. This time, we move to consider more directly the process of training. In various guises, forensic psychologists are practitioners, be that practice in the courts, prisons, secure hospitals, youth justice, policy, education, research or the other diverse settings in which forensic psychologists may be found. In all of these settings, individuals apply, share and develop advanced knowledge of forensic psychological theory and research. What differs in practice is the aspect, or aspects, that they use regularly, their specialist areas. For example, a prison psychologist may undertake risk assessment or facilitate a treatment programme, whereas a forensic psychologist working in developing policy on court procedures may apply knowledge of the effects of witness testimony or jury decision-making. Indeed, most expert psychological witnesses in the UK, as elsewhere in the world, do more civil court work than criminal (Gudjonsson 2007) so it is those areas of work on which they concentrate. What is evident is that no practitioner could be reasonably expected to bring in-depth, practical expertise in the full range of areas covered by the discipline. While training should no doubt cover a breadth of experiences, exactly what these experiences should be needs to be considered with a level of nuance and flexibility that is not always demonstrated among the participants of membership qualification committees. Concomitantly, the need to protect the public and conform to codes of conduct must mean that fitness to practice in any one domain needs to be demonstrable through ongoing continued professional development and reflective practice.

Most practitioners, whatever their specific enterprise, focus predominantly on a few areas of practice, and are regulated by professional bodies, with increasing statutory oversight. Without wishing to claim expertise on the qualification practices for forensic psychologists in all countries in the world, we can say that a common approach is to have a period of academic training followed by a period of supervised practice (see for example the training requirements of the American Psychological Association, the Australian Psychological Society and the Division of Forensic Psychology of the British Psychological Society). There are debates in both the UK and the USA as to whether this training should be more closely allied to the doctoral model of other disciplines (e.g. Clements and Wakeman 2007 in comparison with Zaitchik *et al.* 2007). However, there is concordance over the idea that both academic and supervised practice components should be included. This allows trainee forensic psychologists to gain an advanced theoretical academic understanding, which they then build on in developing the practice expertise that they will need. A fundamental issue that needs consideration, particularly in Britain, is what the supervised practice stage of training should entail.

The Division of Forensic Psychology of the British Psychological Society (BPS) requires forensic psychology trainees to demonstrate competency across a wide range of areas of practice. The same qualifying criteria are also employed by the Health Professions Council (HPC) which now regulates the practice of applied psychology, including forensic. The professional standards are now monitored and enforced by both the learned society, BPS, and the regulatory authority, HPC. This means that psychologists face disciplinary and potential legal action if they practise beyond their competence, or outside of their expertise. It may therefore be questioned how much actual practical experience in any particular domains outside one's areas of practice is required. Clearly, some knowledge and perspectives about the range of psychological practice are desirable but how much, and in what depth, as well as breadth, is still a matter in need of more rigorous consideration. As argued by Towl (this volume), the current training procedures in Britain have seen a substantial decline in the numbers of forensic psychologists completing their training, which will in turn lead to fewer recognised forensic psychologists able to train future practitioners, both academically and through supervised practice. A means of recognising the value of the different facets of forensic psychological practice would contribute to reversing this trend. This may require a shift away from core skills and competencies demonstrated across domains, back to more fundamental demonstrations of competence to understand and apply theory in a variety of contexts.

While the above example may seem parochially British, the implications are important and bring us back to the fundamental question: what is a forensic psychologist? It seems, at least in the academic domain, that forensic psychology has grown to encompass many new topics. This edition includes chapters on terrorism, hate crime and genocide that were not included in the first edition of this text, and similar expansion of the topic can be seen in other publications. There are also chapters representing many of the more traditional topics from forensic psychology, which again show the diversity of the discipline. Should a practising forensic psychologist have practical expertise across all of these areas? It seems that such a requirement would be impossible to achieve, which therefore means that agencies responsible for the training of forensic psychologists have to find ways of realistically recognising the diversity of the professional practice that they represent.

A key issue to consider is whether any particular areas of practice should be privileged over others, in determining whether someone is a forensic psychologist. Maybe it is necessary to design and implement interventions with offenders to be considered a forensic psychologist. On the other hand it may be that an essential component is that the individual must be able to provide advice to the courts. Those wishing to emphasise working with the police, informing policy or educating future forensic psychologists could also surely make claims for centrality. As the conceptualisation of forensic psychology has expanded over the years, the actual practice of this discipline has also moved on and the sometimes narrow definitions of practice considered by regulatory bodies to be core also need to move on.

We recognise that such change would be fraught with complexity and difficulties of its own. However, without reassessment of the conditions of training now, it seems likely that 'prison psychologists', 'police psychologists', 'court psychologists' and 'academic forensic psychologists' will evolve as trainees and their employers give up on the notion of them becoming registered practitioners and fail to see the value in claiming the generalised *forensic psychologist* protected title. Paradoxically, the lack of protection over the generic *psychologist* leaves this route to diverse, unprotected and unregulated titles open and may thus leave the public with a split discipline and less protected.

This book is partly designed to show that we can look at context, using it to inform our theories and using our theories to influence that context in turn. The contributors to this text have been selected to reflect a wide diversity of approaches, and the topics chosen because they reflect current issues of concern. As with the first edition, not every one of the authors would call him or herself a forensic psychologist. Every one of the chapters does, however, concern the aetiology or ramifications of crime, offending and the implementation of justice, and every one of them utilises well-established psychological techniques in their consideration of the problems posed. There is something of a deliberate bias away from laboratory studies and towards analysis of real offenders, patients, victims, witnesses, archives and legal cases and materials. The chapters are here because they deal with areas of research and policy that relate to the practice of forensic psychology, to the running of criminal justice and to the ways of tackling and preventing offending behaviour within society today.

This book is bigger than the first edition but it is still not an encyclopaedic compendium. We have compiled instead a series of selected snapshots of current debates, within which we have sought to include issues of theoretical as well as practical importance. Many of those debates have been with us since Münsterberg, others are more recent responses to policy or political or social events. We have tried to set the work within an appropriate historical frame. However, there is insufficient space in a volume such as this to devote anything other than a fleeting glance at the history of forensic psychology. Fortunately, there are several other good sources of information (for example, Bartol and Bartol 1999; Gudjonsson 1996; Ogloff and Finkelman 1999). In this chapter, we have highlighted some issues that we feel to be of particular importance to the field of forensic psychology, and which provide an underlying rationale for the topics included in the text. Matters of risk assessment, ethical practice in the context of human rights and the roles of forensic psychologists that we have discussed herein are clearly interrelated, and speak to the significance of theoretically grounded practice.

This text concentrates on criminological and legal psychology as related to crime. We are aware, of course, that forensic psychologists also have a distinguished commitment to civil justice and indeed did try to include contributions in this arena. However, other commitments intervened and it was not possible: maybe it will be third time lucky. Another area that we feel to be under-represented within this collection is that of cross-cultural and multicultural perspectives on forensic psychology. We agree with Powell and Bartholomew (2003) as to why such matters must be considered within training and practice. We have drawn on information from different jurisdictions and do have a range of authors from Europe, America and Australia. Similarly, although there is little direct consideration of theoretical matters of equality and diversity, we do have chapters considering very real matters of concern regarding gender and ethnicity inequity. So, having got in some of the brickbats first, let us turn now to the bouquet.

Note

1 www.hpc-uk.org/aboutregistration/professions/index.asp?id=14#prof (details accessed December 2009).
2 See www.bps.org.uk/the-society/statutory-regulation/stat.reg_home.cfm. accessed December 2008, for more information.

References

Bartol, C.R. and Bartol, A.M. (1999) 'History of forensic psychology', in A.K. Hess and I.B. Weiner (eds), *Handbook of Forensic Psychology* (2nd edn). London: John Wiley and Sons.

Binet, A. and Simon, T. (1905). 'Upon the necessity of establishing a scientific diagnosis of inferior states of intelligence', in W. Dennis (ed.), *Readings in the History of Psychology*. New York: Appleton Century Crofts.

Birgden, A. and Perlin, M. (2008) 'Tolling for the luckless, the abandoned and forsaken: Therapeutic jurisprudence and international human rights law as applied to prisoners and detainees by forensic psychologists', *Legal and Criminological Psychology*, 13 (2): 231–43.

Blackburn, R. (1996) 'What is forensic psychology?', *Legal and Criminological Psychology*, Feb; Vol 1(Part 1): 3–16.

Bonta, J., Law, M. and Hanson, R.K. (1998) 'The prediction of criminal and violent recidivism among mentally disordered offenders', *Psychological Bulletin*, 123: 123–42.

British Psychological Society (2009) (2nd edn) *Psychologists as Expert Witnesses Guidelines and Procedure for England and Wales. Report commissioned by the Professional Practice Board (PPB) and Research Board (RB) of the British Psychological Society. Produced by the British Psychological Society Expert Witness Advisory Group*. Leicester: BPS. Available from http://www.bps.org.uk/publications/guidelines-for-practitioners/guidelines-for-practitioners.cfm (accessed November 2009).

Brown, J. (2009) 'The narrowing focus of UK psychology?', *The Psychologist*, 22 (10): 818–19.

Clements, C. and Wakeman, E. (2007) 'Raising the bar: the case for doctoral training in forensic psychology', *Journal of Forensic Psychology Practice*, 7 (2): 53–63.

Dushkind, D.S. (1984) 'Forensic psychology – a proposed definition', *American Journal of Forensic Psychology*, 2 (4): 171–72.

Goring, C. (1913) *The English Convict: A Statistical Study*. London: His Majesty's Stationery Office.

Gudjonsson, G. (2007/8) 'Psychologists as expert witnesses: the 2007 BPS survey', *Forensic Update*, 92: 23–29.

Gudjonsson, G. (1991) 'Forensic psychology – the first century', *Journal of Forensic Psychiatry*, 2 (2): 129.

Gudjonsson, G.H. (1996) 'Forensic psychology in England – one practitioner's experience and viewpoint', *Legal and Criminological Psychology*, 1(Part 1): 131–42.

Gudjonsson, G.H. and Haward, L.R.C. (1998) *Forensic Psychology: A guide to practice*. London: Routledge.

Gudjonsson, G. and Young, S. (2007) 'The role and scope of forensic clinical psychology in secure unit provisions: A proposed service model for psychological therapies', *Journal of Forensic Psychiatry and Psychology*, 18 (4): 534–56.

Harris, G.T., Rice, M.E. and Quinsey, V.L. (1993) 'Violent recidivism of mentally disordered offenders: the development of a statistical prediction instrument', *Criminal Justice and Behavior*, 20: 315–35.

Maguire, M., Morgan, R. and Reiner, R. (eds) (2007) *The Oxford Handbook of Criminology* (4th edn). Oxford: Oxford University Press.

Morgan, R.D., Beer, A.M., Fitzgerald, K.L. and Mandracchia, J.T. (2007) 'Graduate students' experiences, interests, and attitudes toward correctional/forensic psychology', *Criminal Justice and Behavior*, 34 (1): 96–107.

Münsterberg, H. (1908) *On the witness stand – Essays on psychology and crime.* New York: Doubleday Page.

Ogloff, J.R.P. and Finkelman, D. (1999) 'Psychology and law: an overview', in R. Roesch, S.D. Hart and J.R.P. Ogloff (eds), *Psychology and Law: The State of the Discipline*. New York: Kluwer Academic Press.

Petrucci, C.J., Winick, B.J. and Wexler, D.B. (2003) 'Therapeutic jurisprudence: an invitation to social scientists', in R. Bull and D. Carson (2nd edn), *The Handbook of Psychology in Legal Contexts*. Chichester: Wiley.

Powell, M.B. and Bartholomew, T. (2003) 'The treatment of multicultural issues in contemporary forensic psychology textbooks', *Psychiatry, Psychology and Law*, 10 (1): 254–61.

Prins, H. (1991) 'Is psychopathic disorder a useful clinical concept? A perspective from England and Wales', *International Journal of Offender Therapy and Comparative Criminology*, 35 (2): 119–25.

Quinsey, V.L., Rice, M. and Harris, G. (1995) 'Actuarial prediction of sexual recidivism', *Journal of Interpersonal Violence*, 10: 85–105.

R v. M'Naghten (1843–1860) All ER 229.

Sreenivasan, S., Kirkish, P., Garrick, T., Weinberger, L.E. and Phenix, A. (2000) 'Actuarial risk assessment models: a review of critical issues related to violence and sex-offender recidivism assessments', *The Journal of the American Academy of Psychiatry and the Law*, 28: 438–48.

Stephenson, G.M. (1992) *The Psychology of Criminal Justice*. Oxford: Blackwell.

Szasz, T. (1963) *Law, Liberty and Psychiatry*. New York: Macmillan.

Terman, L.M. (1916) *The Uses of Intelligence Tests*. (Classics in the History of Psychology, Internet Resource http://psychclassics.yorku.ca/Terman/terman1.htm). Boston: Houghton Mifflin.

Walsh, A. (2003) 'The holy trinity and the legacy of the Italian school of criminal anthropology: review of "Born to Crime: Cesare Lombroso and the Origins of Biological Criminology"', by Mary Gibson, 2002 Praeger Press. *Human Nature Review*, 3(15th January): 1–11.

Ward, T., Gannon, T. and Vess J. (2009) 'Human rights, ethical principles, and standards in forensic psychology', *International Journal of Offender Therapy and Comparative Criminology*, 53 (2): 126–44.

Wexler, D.B. and Winick, B.J. (1996) 'Introduction', in D.B. Wexler and B.J. Winick (eds), *The law in a Therapeutic Key: Developments in therapeutic jurisprudence* (pp. xvii–xx). Durham, NC: Carolina University Press.

Wigmore, J.H. (1909) 'Professor Münsterberg and the Psychology of Testimony – being a report of the case of Cokestone v. Münsterberg', *Illinois Law Review*, 3: 399–445.

Zaitchik, M., Berman, G., Whitworth, D. and Platania J. (2007) 'The time is now: the emerging need for master's-level training in forensic psychology', *Journal of Forensic Psychology Practice*, 7 (2): 65–71.

Section I

Investigation and Prosecution

A sound and thorough investigation is the foundation on which all later stages of the criminal justice process are built. Without a rigorous and sound investigation, there will almost inevitably be no prosecution, and hence no offender brought to justice, no 'payment' to the victim or society through punishment, and the public perception of an effective criminal justice system may be damaged. Also closely associated with the perception of justice being seen to be done, is the way in which cases are handled by the courts.

Research has made extensive and ongoing contributions to the investigation of crime, as evidenced by the development of the interviewing techniques used in the UK with both witnesses and suspects. This material is considered in the following chapters. Similarly important contributions have been made in other areas of investigation, such as offender profiling. However, despite these developments, it should be noted that not all jurisdictions choose to follow the same models, as can be seen in Chapter 2. Here, Becky Milne, Sam Poyser, Tom Williamson and Steve Savage draw comparisons between the UK and the USA. As well as differences in the practical application of research, there are still theoretical and empirical debates regarding the most valid and effective ways to proceed in various areas. It is the aim of this section to present some of the key areas of practice and academic literature pertaining to the investigation of crime, and moving into the issue of prosecution, which is picked up again in the next section. The following four chapters highlight areas of progress, debate, aspects where further research is needed as well as those where developments in practice could lead to greater justice.

This section contains contributions from authors from practice and research backgrounds who have expertise in the investigation and prosecution of crime in the UK. Chapters 2 to 4 focus on aspects of investigation, starting (in Chapter 2) by considering miscarriages of justice, including those that occur when evidence arising from witnesses and victims is missed, as well as the more traditional consideration of the consequences of poor interviewing practices with suspects. This is followed (in Chapter 3) by a critical review of the literature concerned with 'traditional' approaches to offender profiling, in which Laurence Alison, Emma Barrett and Louise Almond provide a 'reality check' regarding the frequently shared understanding of offender profiling. The investigation aspect of this section ends with an account from John Bearchell in Chapter 4 of the development of procedures used by the UK police in the interviewing of suspects, including recent data evaluating police interviewing practice. This section ends with Jacqueline M. Gray and Anna Gekoski's consideration in Chapter 5 of the specific issue of rape, encompassing both the investigation and prosecution of this crime and the particular difficulties faced by victims.

Chapter 2

Miscarriages of justice: what can we learn?

Rebecca Milne, Sam Poyser, Tom Williamson and Stephen P. Savage

Introduction

Past miscarriage of justice cases have invariably drawn attention to police incompetence, inaction, and sometimes to police corruption (Macpherson 1999). Research examining such cases and investigation processes (e.g. Ask and Granhag 2005) has made significant contributions to identifying what the investigatory processes are, drawing attention to their potential weaknesses, and making recommendations for their improvement (Jones *et al.* 2008). This should in turn minimise the risk of wrongful conviction. Indeed some jurisdictions have taken such research on board and have incorporated the outcomes into attempts to professionalise the investigative process (e.g. UK Police Service, Professionalising the Investigative Process initiative, see Stelfox 2007). There are, however, no grounds for complacency and plenty for continued vigilance.

This chapter will consider miscarriages of justice primarily in the United Kingdom and the response by its government and criminal justice agencies. We will examine:

- what constitutes a miscarriage of justice;
- concerns about police competence in criminal investigations;
- the over-reliance on confession evidence in adversarial systems of justice;
- UK legislation regulating custodial questioning;
- the new genre of miscarriages in the UK: witness interviewing practices;

- factors contributing to miscarriages of justice in the USA;
- USA/UK responses to miscarriages of justice;
- opportunities for greater involvement of forensic psychologists in the future to minimise miscarriages of justice.

What is a miscarriage of justice? A definition

When the term 'miscarriages of justice' is used, it usually refers to what are called 'wrongful (or questionable) convictions' (or what could be termed 'doing the wrong thing'). Walker (1999: 52–5) summarises the 'recurrent forms of miscarriage of justice' from which we might take the following as being causes of questionable convictions in the past: fabrication of evidence; unreliable identification of an offender by the police or witnesses; unreliable expert evidence; unreliable confessions resulting from police pressure or the vulnerability of suspects; non-disclosure of evidence by the police or prosecution; the conduct of the trial (due mainly to the judge's role in the proceedings); and problems associated with appeals procedures (including limited access to legal funds) (Savage *et al.* 2007). It is important to note, however, that the reduction of miscarriages of justice to purely 'wrongful convictions' or questionable convictions is only partially adequate (Savage and Milne 2007).

The term 'miscarriages of justice' can also apply to circumstances where there is *no action, inaction* or *questionable actions,* whereby an offence has taken place but no action or insufficient action or intervention has followed. This can be described as failure to act in response to victimisation or 'not doing anything or not doing enough' (Walker 1999: 36). Whilst much of the research on miscarriages of justice has focused on 'wrongful convictions', miscarriages based on what have been termed *questionable actions* should also be noted (Savage and Milne 2007). 'Questionable actions' include police malpractice and incompetence (failures to investigate effectively; poor treatment of victims and their families), inadequate prosecution processes (poor communication with the police; 'risk avoidance'), and problematic trial practices (such as hostile cross-examination of witnesses; weak presentation of the prosecution case). More specifically, questionable actions embrace the failure of the police to identify suspects and to press charges, the failure of the prosecution to mount a case, the collapse of the prosecution case during the trial and, throughout all of these, the failure of the agencies involved to inform or support victims and their families. To this, one can also add miscarriages of justice that relate to the failure of the authorities to *protect* citizens from a known danger or dangers. An example of such a case is that of Jonathan Zito, who was killed by Christopher Clunis, who had just been released from hospital having been deemed safe to the community (see Zito Trust, n.d.). Lastly, it is important to note that except in the cases whereby someone is convicted for an offence which never happened (a death, for example, that was the result of an accident or natural causes, rather than murder), each time a questionable conviction is exposed, another 'miscarriage of justice' is simultaneously exposed, as this leaves an offence for which no one has been brought to justice.

Miscarriages of justice: a history. Concerns about police competence

The role of the police in criminal investigations: criminological research

The Royal Commission on Criminal Procedure (Philips 1981) was appointed amid growing concern about the police role in the investigation of offences, and concerns about police competence and corruption are recurring themes in criminological research. The Police and People in London series revealed that several types of serious misconduct by the police were believed to occur. The Police Studies Institute Report found:

> The use of threats and unfair pressure in questioning is the kind of misconduct that is thought to be most widespread. About half of informants think it happens at least occasionally, but perhaps more important, one-quarter think that it often happens – that it is a usual pattern of behaviour by police officers. The other kinds of misconduct are thought to happen at least occasionally by a substantial proportion of Londoners, while about one in ten Londoners think police officers fabricate evidence, and use violence unjustifiably on people held at police stations. These findings suggest that there is a complete lack of confidence in the police among at least one in ten Londoners, and that about half of Londoners have serious doubts about the standards of police conduct, though in most cases they do not think there is a pattern of frequent or usual misconduct. (Smith 1983: 325)

One third of young white people thought the police often used threats or unreasonable pressure during custodial questioning whereas 62 per cent of young people of West Indian descent believed they did so. The Islington Crime Survey also found that the public were more critical of the police where they had a high degree of contact with the police or they were subject to a high level of victimisation (Jones *et al.* 1986).

This kind of research provides a rich picture of the nature and quality of the relationship between the citizen and the police. It provides evidence of the areas of dissatisfaction with policing practice and performance that forms the basis for a relationship of reciprocity between citizens and State in a democratic country (Wright 2002). It seems that a lot of this dissatisfaction stemmed from the investigation and interview processes specifically. This undoubtedly is partially due to the highly publicised miscarriage of justice cases where a central concern in the acquittals in all these cases was the police interview with the suspect (e.g. Guildford Four and Birmingham Six). However, this raises the question of whether this dissatisfaction was representative of *actual* investigation practices.

The pre-PACE primacy of interrogation in detecting offences

The Royal Commission on Criminal Procedure (1981) commissioned a series of research studies including one that examined the police role in the investigation of offences (Steer 1981). In a study of detectives in the Thames Valley Police, Steer found that the majority of offenders were detected in circumstances that did not involve the exercise of detective skills. Only 40 per cent of offenders were detected following an investigation and of those, 17 per cent were one of a small group of people who could have committed the offence, 11 per cent were detected as a result of intelligence or forensic evidence such as a fingerprint, and an accomplice implicated 12 per cent during an interrogation. This points to the importance of interrogation in detecting offences. The conclusions of Mawby (1979) and Bottomley and Coleman (1980) further indicate that interrogation of suspects was the most important means of detecting offences at that time.

In an observational study for the Royal Commission of how police interrogations were conducted in four police stations, it was found that about 60 per cent of suspects made a full confession or a damaging admission (Softley 1981). The emphasis on confession evidence prior to the introduction of PACE was also identified by

Irving (1981) and Baldwin and McConville (1981) (see Chapter 4 of this volume for further discussion of this issue).

At this point in the history of criminal investigation in the United Kingdom, it seems that the police role in detecting offences was primarily one of interrogation rather than enquiry, and the investigation tended to focus wholly upon attaining a confession, promulgating narrowly steered investigative mindsets. To understand why a confession was so important it is necessary to consider the operation of various systems of justice.

A search for the truth or getting a conviction?

The adversarial system is not a search for the truth (Zander 1994). Zander argues that:

> the common law system has never made the search for the truth, as such, its highest aim. It is not that there is any objection to the truth emerging. But, centuries ago it was appreciated that the truth is many-sided, complex, and difficult to ascertain. Even when all the relevant evidence is admissible, we commonly do not know for sure whether the defendant was, or, was not, innocent or guilty. The common law system does not ask whether the defendant is guilty or innocent but rather the more manageable question – can it be proved beyond a reasonable doubt that he is guilty?

The Royal Commission on Criminal Procedure 1993 addressed this issue. In an adversarial system, the judge is considered to be a neutral umpire who leaves the presentation of the case to the prosecution and defence, who prepare their case, call, examine and cross-examine witnesses. The 'inquisitorial' system purports to be a search for the truth. Here, the judge is not neutral but will play a major part in the presentation of the evidence at the trial. It is the judge who calls and examines the defendant and the witnesses while the lawyers for the prosecution and defence can only ask supplementary questions. The Royal Commission argued that 'It is important not to overstate the differences between the two systems: all adversarial systems contain inquisitorial elements, and vice versa' (Runciman 1993: 12).

Over the past hundred years within adversarial systems of justice, it is the police who have developed the responsibility for discharging this inquisitorial function. The manner in which the product of the investigation is then dealt with in court led the Royal Commission to acknowledge 'But, we do recognise the force of the criticisms which can turn a search for the truth into a contest played between opposing lawyers according to a set of rules which the jury does not necessarily accept or even understand' (*op. cit.*).

The Commission was against the fusion of the functions of investigation and prosecution found in inquisitorial systems. It regarded as fundamental the principle that the prosecution in an adversarial system had to establish the guilt of the defendant beyond all reasonable doubt. The burden of proof lay with the prosecution. The court was not interested in the truth per se, it simply had to decide whether guilt had been established beyond all reasonable doubt.

Given this context, it is not surprising that confession evidence assumed primacy and was relied upon too much within the investigation process. The focus of investigators was simply to attain a confession, allowing the investigation team to move on to the next case. Analysis of the police role indicates that it was aimed at successful prosecution of a suspect rather than an impartial investigation or a search for the truth. Getting a conviction largely depended on getting a suspect to confess, and as the Police and Londoners Survey (*op. cit.)* had found at that time, many Londoners believed that the police used force to obtain a confession, or if that did not succeed they fabricated it.

An independent prosecution system

McConville and Hodgson (1993) examined the way in which a prosecution case was prepared. They argued that the investigation was not a search for the truth and that the investigative process relied too heavily on the role of interrogation. Custodial detention placed, and still places, the suspect in a hostile environment where custodial questioning takes place on police terms. Rarely would the suspect have the benefit of legal representation at that time and Irving (1981) in his study of interrogations at a Brighton police station showed how the police could easily manipulate the decision-making of suspects.

The US Supreme Court in the case of *Miranda* v. *Arizona* addressed the vulnerability of suspects facing custodial questioning. The Supreme Court considered custodial questioning to be inherently coercive and ensured that no statement made during police questioning and no evidence discovered as a result of that statement can be admitted in evidence at trial unless suspects are first warned of, among other things, their right to consult with and to have counsel present during questioning. If unable to afford a lawyer, one will be provided at public expense. Any waiver to the right has to be made explicitly by the suspect.

In the UK, the members of the Royal Commission on Criminal Procedure (1981) were clearly influenced by the Miranda rules in relation to the proposals that they made for regulating custodial interviews in England and Wales. Their recommendations were included in the Police and Criminal Evidence Act 1984 and the Codes of Practice issued under Section 66. In addition, an independent prosecution service was created in 1986 as a result of the Prosecution of Offences Act 1985 separating the role of investigation from that of prosecution.

Miscarriages of justice as a driver for change

Miscarriage of justice cases played a role in bringing about the Royal Commission on Criminal Procedure 1981. The Government of the United Kingdom had previously been taken before the European Court of Human Rights by the Government of Ireland in a landmark case in which it was alleged that suspects had been subjected to torture, cruel, inhuman and degrading treatment or punishment. It became known as the 'hooded men' case as the men were subjected to military interrogation practices.[1] The decision of the court that the men had experienced degrading treatment led to a Government inquiry into interrogation practices in Northern Ireland (Bennett 1979).

At about the same time, another Government inquiry had examined the convictions of three youths for the murder of a male transvestite (Fisher 1977). All three youths had made admissions in the presence of their parent or guardian. Yet, one of the youths was proved to have been attending a Salvation Army youth club at the time of death and so his confession was unreliable. The subsequent Inquiry identified that all three youths had various forms of psychological vulnerabilities; indeed, one had learning difficulties and had attended a special needs school. Irving, a psychologist, gave evidence to the Inquiry drawing attention to these factors.

Although these cases led to the need for a Royal Commission on Criminal Procedure being identified, there has since been a continuous stream of miscarriages of justice from which we can continue to learn. Indeed, Gudjonsson (2003) identifies 22 landmark British Court of Appeal cases of disputed confession since 1989. Psychological evidence relating to suggestibility and compliance was considered seriously by the Court in each of these cases (Gudjonsson 2003).[2]

Since 2001 further cases have come to light where a disputed confession is at the heart of the quashing of a conviction and these include:

2002	Frank Johnson	
2002	Robert Brown	
2002	Patrick Irvine	
2002	Thomas Green (Belfast)	
2003	Anthony Steele	
2005	Paul Blackburn	
2006	Patrick Nolan	(Innocent 2008)

It seems that there continues to be a disturbing number of people that have been affected by poor police questioning (see Savage and Milne 2007).

The Police and Criminal Evidence Act 1984

One way that the government and associated organisations reacted to these cases was to legislate against such police practices, resulting in the Police and Criminal Evidence Act 1984 (PACE), which provides a legislative framework for the regulation of custodial questioning. Under Section 76 of PACE, it was no longer up to the defence to show that *something had* happened in the interrogation that would render the statement unreliable, it was up to the prosecution to show that *nothing* had happened to make the statement unreliable (as all interviews were now recorded and open to scrutiny). Under Section 78 of the Act, the trial judge can exclude anything that is deemed 'unfair' such as deception by the interviewing officers or providing misleading information. In *R.* v. *Heron* the judge acquitted the defendant when, *inter alia*, the interviewing officers misled the accused regarding identification evidence in a homicide case.[3]

Section 66 of the Act provides for a Code of Practice which covers a number of areas of police activity, one being the detention, treatment and questioning of persons by police officers. The Act entitled suspects to free legal advice and also provided for the digital recording of interviews with suspects. Effective representation for suspects at public expense has also contributed to a growth in professionalism of the interview process and the Law Society has created training courses, while an accreditation system for legal advisers has ensured that legal representation is of a good quality (Bridges and Choongh 1998; see also Shepherd 1996).

The Police and Criminal Evidence Act provides various rights for detainees. They have the right to inform someone of their arrest (Section 5), and to consult privately with a legal representative (Section 6), which can only be waived with the authority of a Superintendent. This waiver only applies where there is fear of immediate harm, so in practice, it is rarely exercised. Detainees have a right of access to the Codes of Practice, the custody officer dealing with their detention must provide a written notice of their rights, and they must be informed of the grounds for their detention. The codes also contain provision for special groups of detainees. Interpreters must be provided for those who only speak a foreign language or have English as a second language or communicate through facilitated communication methods (e.g. sign language). Juvenile detainees must have a parent or guardian informed of their detention and like detainees with a mental disorder (those deemed 'at risk') have the right to have someone who is experienced in dealing with such vulnerabilities, called an 'Appropriate Adult', attend the interview in addition to the person providing legal advice (see Pearse and Gudjonsson 1996 regarding the effectiveness of such a provision).

The conditions under which detainees are held are also regulated. There must only be one person per heated, cleaned and ventilated cell, which must have light. There must be access to washing and toilet facilities. Detainees must be provided with two light meals and one main meal per day. Dietary and religious needs must be observed. Detention is a documented process and complaints and requests for medical attention and medicines are to be recorded and actioned.

The duration for which the police can detain a person is strictly regulated. A detained person can make representation to an inspector regarding detention for more than eight hours and to a superintendent after 24 hours. Suspects can only be detained after 72 hours on the order of a magistrates' court. Whatever the length of the detention, they must be charged as soon as the police have sufficient evidence to prosecute and there must be no further questioning after charge.

Changes in interviewing suspects, victims and witnesses

Early research into the quality of the police interviews, which was possible through the analysis of video and audio tape recordings post the implementation of PACE, revealed that interviewing skills were generally poor (Baldwin 1992), where the role of the police in the investigation of offences was still one of persuading suspects to confess rather than engaging in a process of inquiry, which was a search for the truth (see Chapter 4 for more on the historical development of police interviewing). The reliance on confession evidence also meant that witnesses and victims were frequently overlooked, not seen as an integral part of the investigation process, thus were not interviewed thoroughly and so were unable to provide all the information they were capable of giving as evidence.

In an analysis of over one thousand tape-recorded interviews in London *et al.* (1992) found that there was a strong correlation between the strength of the evidence and the outcome of the interview. Where the evidence was weak, 77 per cent of suspects denied the allegation and where the evidence was strong, 67 per cent of suspects made admissions. Indeed, subsequent research has repeatedly demonstrated that the most likely factor to help encourage someone to give a comprehensive account of their transgressions is the weight of evidence. However, it is only through thorough investigation (e.g. good witness interviewing) that one can attain such weighty and persuasive evidence in the first place (e.g. Kebbell and Daniels 2005).

Clearly, there was a need for a change of investigative culture to meet the aspirations of the new legislation and to prevent challenges to the evidence obtained through questioning. This resulted in the creation of a national committee on investigative interviewing that involved police officers, lawyers and psychologists. The outcome was the birth of the PEACE interviewing model (Milne *et al.* 2007).

What then occurred is an amazing testament to the commitment of the British Police Service to improving its interviewing standards across the board. In 1993 a large-scale operation began in England and Wales to train all officers (i.e. over 120,000) in the PEACE framework of interviewing (Milne *et al.* 2007). In addition, the initial working party, when examining what PEACE training should consist of, looked at what academia had to offer. Indeed, two models of interviewing emerged as best practice: (i) conversation management (CM; Shepherd 1993) which was deemed useful for interviewing the more resistant interviewee, and (ii) the cognitive interview (CI; Fisher and Geiselman 1992) which was more useful for interviewing the more co-operative interviewee, being an interviewee who is willing to speak (however truthful; for a fuller description see Milne and Bull 1999; Shepherd 2007; Fisher and Geiselman 1992). PEACE training started to be rolled out to forces in England and Wales in 1993 as a week-long course for interviewers. This then continued at varying degrees of thoroughness across the UK for over 10 years. The PEACE process was later developed into a five-tiered structure that aims to provide a developmental approach to interview training across a police officer's career, dependent on their ability (see Griffiths and Milne 2005 and Chapter 4 this volume for more on this development).

Clarke and Milne (2001) conducted a national evaluation of PEACE, and also examined officers' ability to interview witnesses to and victims of crime. Officers from across the country were asked to tape-record their interviews, including all offence types, over a period of time. What was revealed was a disturbing state of affairs with interviews being mainly police led, dominated by poor questioning, and the interview being mainly focused upon the statement taking process as opposed to trying to gain as much information from the interviewee about what had happened (Savage and Milne 2007). Indeed Clarke and Milne concluded that the standard of interviews of witnesses and victims of crime was far worse than the interviews of those suspected of crime. The Clarke and Milne report concluded with a number of recommendations to improve interviewing standards which have subsequently been taken up by the Association of Chief Police Officers (ACPO) and developed further into the 'ACPO Investigative Interviewing Strategy: a National Initiative' (see Appendix). Thus it can be seen that miscarriage of justice cases and responses to research can help and have helped change national policy and practice in the UK (see Grieve 2007).

Criminal Cases Review Commission

The Criminal Appeal Act 1995 created the Criminal Cases Review Commission whose function is to review all allegations of miscarriages of justice. So far, over 356 cases have been referred to the Court of Appeal. The Commission has reviewed over 10,500 cases and at the time of writing had 442 cases under review. A similar review commission has been established in Scotland. This organisation acts as a further safeguard against miscarriage of justice cases in the UK.

Safer UK justice?

It is argued that the combined effect of the Police and Criminal Evidence Act 1984 with the Codes of Practice, the introduction of an independent Crown Prosecution Service, legal representation for suspects at public expense, and the introduction of the Criminal Cases Review Commission should lead to safer criminal justice in the UK and to fewer miscarriages of justice. A Parliamentary Home Affairs Select Committee examined the conduct of investigations into past cases of abuse in children's homes. It dealt with allegations of physical and sexual abuse when the adult complainants were children resident in the homes. It was not within the remit of the Committee to examine individual cases, but a large number had been drawn to its attention. It concluded, 'We share the general view that a significant number of miscarriages of justice have occurred' (HASC 2002: para. 1.35). They were particularly concerned that the interviews with complainants had not been recorded. They also found that the test for referring alleged miscarriages to the Court of Appeal was too narrow, as the legislation required that there had to be new evidence. They recommended that the test should be broadened, in line with the Scottish Criminal Review Commission, to make a referral where the Commission believed that a miscarriage of justice may have occurred. In the evidence of one solicitor specialising in such cases, 'in excess of 100 care workers and teachers have been wrongly convicted' (Saltrese p. Ev.105 *op. cit.*). Safer justice? Yes, for some. A total of 21 recommendations were made by the Select Committee to plug the loopholes in legislation that the inquiry had uncovered. Thus, in the UK at least, there is a new genre of miscarriages of justice, those that involve witnesses and victims of crime.

Miscarriage of justice cases: witnesses and victims

As noted above, the Clarke and Milne report (2001) concluded that the treatment of witnesses was far poorer than the treatment of those suspected of crime and thus it seems that the focus of attention in the UK should turn to the interviewing of witnesses to and victims of crime. This is even more important when considering the fact that due to the interviewing of suspects having improved dramatically over the past 30 years, rendering such interviews as more ethical and lawful, the defence focus has had to change also, i.e. to find a new target. What is emerging is that the interviews of victims and witnesses are seeing increased attention from the criminal justice system. Unfortunately, research (Griffiths and Milne 2008) has consistently shown that such interviews are somewhat lacking. Furthermore, the process of recording interviews with adult witnesses and victims through handwritten statements has also been highly criticised (e.g. Milne and Bull 2006; Milne and Shaw 1999; Heaton-Armstrong 1995).

Such handwritten records have been seen to be full of inaccuracies (Rock 2001), as they rely on the interviewer's memories of what was said, and memory is not a perfect process (Conway 2008). Thus the interviews lack quality (Clarke and Milne 2001), the resultant reports lack detail and are inaccurate, and tend to misrepresent what the interviewee has actually said (McLean 1995; Lamb *et al.* 2000). There urgently needs to be transparency in this vital part of the investigation and criminal justice process.

Miscarriages of justice in the United States of America

Using the English system as a template and applying it to the justice system in the United States, it will be seen that similar lessons can be learned from a study of miscarriages of justice in that country.

The United States has a federal constitution and so there is no equivalent of PACE covering the whole of the country. Laws relating to investigation, where they exist, are passed at the local or State level. The American constitution guarantees its citizens certain rights. The US Supreme Court set out in *Miranda* v. *Arizona* the rights of citizens who were being questioned by the police. However, the US Supreme Court has consistently watered down the rights articulated therein. In *Gideon* v. *Wainwright*, under the Sixth Amendment to the Constitution, indigent defendants have a right to a lawyer to provide 'effective assistance' in trials for serious offences. Effective assistance has been considered by the courts to include lawyers who are drunk, asleep, on drugs, or who in capital cases were unable to name a single Supreme Court decision on the death penalty (Cole 1999; Scheck *et al.* 2000).

The standards of 'effective defence' can be gauged from death penalty cases in the State of Alabama. Death penalty cases last four days on average and the death penalty phase only 3.5 hours. In *Schlup* v. *Delo* (1995) 115 S. Ct. 851 the trial lasted two days. The lawyer spent a total of 75 minutes with his client, who was convicted. A review found that there was a videotape of the defendant in a cafe when the homicide occurred and there were 20 witnesses to this, who the lawyer had failed to interview. It is particularly worrying that procedural faults of this kind and omissions of the defence lawyer are visited on their clients. Good representation is possible in the US but it is based on class and income. This class-based disparity falls disproportionately on minorities because they are the poorest.

Race and the death penalty

In 1972, the Supreme Court declared the death penalty unconstitutional because it was 'arbitrary and capricious'. This was reversed in 1976 reflecting widespread public support for the death penalty. Between 1976 and 1998 six white men were executed for killing black victims whereas 115 black men were executed for killing white victims. In a study by Baldus *et al.* (1994) of 2,000 murder cases in Georgia it was found that where the attack had been by a black person on a white person the death penalty was given in 22 per cent of cases but where the attack was by a white person on a black person the death penalty was given in only 3 per cent of cases. In a review of 28 death penalty studies the US Government concluded that in 82 per cent of cases the race of the victim was related to the death penalty.[4]

In *McClesky* v. *Kemp* (1987) 481 US 279.327, it was argued that the strong statistical evidence of racial bias in death penalty cases should lead to the abolition of the death penalty. The court said that the statistical evidence on its own was not sufficient and that there would have to be an admission of racial bias. While this was unlikely, the Court did concede that the statistics represent a 'challenge to the validity of capital punishment in a multi-cultural society', but considered that this issue was best addressed by legislation.

There are now at least 110 people who were on death row who have been released and totally exonerated as a result of new DNA forensic evidence showing that they could not have committed the offence. In April 2002, Governor Ryan of the State of Illinois reported on a review of the death penalty in Illinois. It was found that almost half of the defendants should not have been convicted. The commission made a total of 80 recommendations including the creation of a State-wide panel to review prosecutor requests for the death penalty; banning death sentences on the mentally retarded (*sic*); significantly reducing the number of death eligibility factors; videotaping interrogations of homicide suspects; and controlling the use of jailhouse informants. The members of the committee were split over the issue of abolition of the death penalty but made a series of recommendations which they argued would make the death penalty safer and be applied more scrupulously.

On examination of these miscarriage of justice cases where the defendants in 74 cases are actually innocent, it is possible to identify the causes leading to wrongful convictions. These appear to be the main contributory factors:

- 81 per cent mistaken ID
- 69 per cent 'junk' forensic science
- 50 per cent police misconduct
- 45 per cent misconduct by prosecutor
- 22 per cent false confessions
- 20 per cent false witnesses
- 19 per cent informants

(Scheck *et al.* 2000: 361)

Although 'junk' science was a factor in the Court of Appeal decision in the case of the 'Birmingham Six', there has been much less criticism of forensic science in Britain than in the USA. In England and Wales, the forensic science laboratories have been removed from the control of the police and are now a stand-alone government agency.

USA and UK similarities and differences

The public mindset in both countries appears to be becoming more punitive and less tolerant. This constrains what politicians and elected officials can achieve through reform of the existing system. This is particularly true in the United States where judges, prosecutors and senior law enforcement officials are elected and so reflect public attitudes to punishment. There are fewer opportunities for ethical leadership.

The response in Britain to miscarriages of justice has been through legislation to put in place a rigorous regulatory regime, which has been strictly enforced by the judges. Technology has been adopted to ensure that custodial questioning is open, transparent and that what is said during questioning is said freely and recorded accurately. In the USA, reaction to miscarriages of justice is still in the denial phase and has not yet created the pressure necessary for reform.

Within the US Federal Constitution, there is no means of providing national legislation or delivering training to improve investigative standards to a national standard. There is also an absence of public high-profile champions for change in the USA, whereas research in the UK suggests that, here, there have been a number of champions, particularly within the media (Poyser, forthcoming). In the USA the tide may be changing as President Obama said in his speech to the CIA in April 2009, when talking about interrogation tactics used in

Guantanamo Bay, that he will put an end to the old interrogation methods and that 'power of values including the law' is important.

The retention by the USA of the death penalty marks a significant difference between the two jurisdictions. Had Britain retained the death penalty, there is little doubt that the Guildford Four, the Birmingham Six and Judith Ward would probably have been executed. The lack of safeguards in the criminal justice system presents powerful evidence for abolition of the death penalty, a step that had been taken by the end of 2000 by 75 countries and territories. A further 13 countries had abolished it for all but exceptional crimes such as wartime crimes. At least 20 countries were abolitionist in practice: they had not carried out any executions for the past 10 years or more and were believed to have an established practice of not carrying out executions (Amnesty International 2001).

Minimising miscarriages of justice

There would appear to be a number of steps that societies can take in order to minimise miscarriages of justice. Good pre-trial investigation and custodial questioning processes will reduce the over-reliance on confession evidence and encourage a search for the truth. Making better use of forensic evidence and more thorough questioning of victims and witnesses to enable them to give their best evidence will be more likely to enable courts to reach the truth. Greater sensitivity in interviewing those who are vulnerable would prevent many future miscarriages of justice.

Still there are important safeguards. Formal systems for reviewing alleged miscarriages of justice are an important investment. Independent status for forensic science laboratories should prevent some of the 'junk' science that has been a feature in miscarriage of justice cases. Given the propensity for error in adversarial systems of justice it is important to continue challenging the validity of capital punishment. There needs to be greater recognition that truth and justice suffer when criminal justice systems become too adversarial. As Stephenson (1992) identified, many of the current systems are fundamentally flawed. This should provide an incentive and broad range of opportunities for forensic psychologists to continue to identify the weaknesses and propose reform based on scientific research of the kind that has been so valuable in minimising miscarriages of justice.

Notes

1 *Ireland* v. *United Kingdom* 1978 2 EHRR 25.
2 Gudjonsson (2003) provides a comprehensive analysis of these cases. See also Mullin, C. (1990) *Error of Judgement: The Truth About the Birmingham Bombings* (revised edn). Dublin: Poolbeg; and Victory, P. (2002) *Justice and Truth. The Guildford Four and Maguire Seven*. London: Sinclair-Stevenson.
3 Unreported, Leeds Crown Court, 18 October 1993.
4 US Gen. Accounting Office, *Death Penalty Sentencing: Research Indicates Pattern of Racial Disparities*, 6 (1990).

References

Amnesty International (2001) *Annual Report for 2001*. London: Amnesty International Publications.

Ask, K. and Granhag, P.A. (2005) 'Motivational sources of confirmation bias in criminal investigations: the need for cognitive closure', *Journal of Investigative Psychology and Offender Profiling*, 2: 43–63.

Baldus, D.C., Woodworth, G. and Pulaski, C.A. Jr (1994) *Reflections on the 'Inevitability' of Racial Discrimination in Capital Sentencing and the 'Impossibility' of its Prevention, Detection and Correction*. 51 Wash. and Lee L. Rev. 359.386 n.115 (1994).

Baldwin, J. and McConville, M. (1981) *Confessions in Crown Court Trials*. Research Study No. 5 Royal Commission on Criminal Procedure (1981). Cmnd 8092. London: HMSO.

Baldwin, J. (1992) *Video taping police interviews with suspects – an evaluation*. Police Research Series Paper 1. London: Home Office.

Bennett, H.G., QC (1979) *Report of the Committee of Inquiry into Police Interrogation Procedures in Northern Ireland*. Cmnd 7497. London: HMSO.

Bottomley, A.K. and Coleman, C.A. (1980) 'Police effectiveness and the public: the limitations of official crime rates', in R.V.G. Clarke and J.M. Hough (eds), *The Effectiveness of Policing (1980)*. Farnborough: Gower.

Bridges, L. and Choongh, S. (1998) *Improving Police Station Legal Advice*. London: jointly by Legal Aid Board and Law Society.

Clarke, C. and Milne, R. (2001) *National Evaluation of the PEACE Investigative Interviewing Course*, Police Research Award Scheme, PRAS/149. London: Home Office.

Cole, D. (1999) *No Equal Justice. Race and Class in the American Criminal Justice System*. New York: The New Press.

Conway, M.A. (2008) *Guidelines on Memory and the Law: Recommendations from the Scientific Study of Human Memory*. Leicester: British Psychological Society.

Fisher, H., Sir (1977). *Report of an Inquiry by the Hon. Sir Henry Fisher into the circumstances leading to the trial of three persons on charges arising out of the death of Maxwell Confait and the fire at 27, Doggett Road, London SE6*. London: HMSO.

Fisher, R. and Geiselman, R. (1992). *Memory-enhancing Techniques for Investigative Interviewing: The cognitive interview.* Springfield, Ill: Thomas.

Grieve, J. (2007) 'Behavioural science and the law: investigation', in D. Carson, R. Milne, F. Pakes and K. Shalev (eds), *Applying Psychology to Criminal Justice*. Chichester: Wiley.

Griffiths, A. and Milne, R. (2005) 'Will it all end in tiers: Police interviews with suspects in Britain', in T. Williamson (ed.), *Investigative Interviewing: Rights, research, regulation*. Cullompton: Willan Publishing.

Griffiths, A. and Milne, R. (2008) 'Is omni-competence possible? Comparing skills of advanced interviewers in real life suspect and witness interviews.' Paper presented at Third International Investigative Interviewing Conference, Quebec, Canada.

Gudjonsson, G.H. (2003) *The Psychology of Interrogations and Confessions. A Handbook*. Chichester: Wiley.

Heaton-Armstrong, A. (1995) 'Recording and disclosing statements by witnesses – law and practice', *Medicine, Science and the Law*, 35: 136–43.

Home Affairs Select Committee (2002) *The Conduct of Investigations into Past Cases of Abuse in Children's Homes.* HC 836-1. London: House of Commons.

Innocent (2008) www.innocent.org.uk/ (accessed 15 November 2008).

Irving, B. (1981) *Police Interrogation. A case study of current practice.* Research Study No. 2 Royal Commission on Criminal Procedure (1981). Cmnd 8092. London: HMSO.

Jones, D., Grieve, J. and Milne, R. (2008) 'A case to review murder investigations', *Policing: A Journal of Policy and Practice*, 2: 470–80.

Jones, T., MacLean, B. and Young, J. (1986) *The Islington Crime Survey, Crime Victimization and Policing in Inner-City London*. London: Gower.

Kebbell, M. and Daniels, T. (2005) *Mock suspect decisions to confess: The influence of eyewitness statements and identifications.* Paper presented at the 15th European Psychology and Law Conference, Vilnius, Lithuania, July.

Lamb, M.E., Orbach, Y., Sternberg, K.J., Hershkowitz, I. and Horowitz, D. (2000) 'Accuracy of investigators' verbatim notes of their forensic interviews with alleged child abuse victims', *Law and Human Behavior, 24*(6), 699–708.

Macpherson of Cluny, Sir W. (1999) *The Stephen Lawrence Inquiry,* Cm 4262-1. London: HMSO.

Mawby, R. (1979) *Policing the City*. Farnborough: Saxon House.

McConville, M. and Hodgson, J. (1993) *Custodial Legal Advice and the Right to Silence*. London: HMSO.

McLean, M. (1995) 'Quality investigation? Police interviewing of witnesses', *Medicine, Science and the Law*, 35: 116–22.

Milne, R. and Bull, R. (1999) *Investigative Interviewing: Psychology and Practice.* Chichester: Wiley.

Milne, R. and Bull, R. (2006) 'Interviewing victims, including children and people with intellectual disabilities', in M. Kebbell and G. Davies (eds), *Practical Psychology for Forensic Investigations*. Chichester: Wiley.

Milne, R. and Shaw, G. (1999) 'Obtaining witness statements: Best practice and proposals for innovation', *Medicine, Science and the Law*, 39: 127–38.

Milne, R., Shaw, G. and Bull, R. (2007) 'Investigative interviewing: The role of psychology', in D. Carson, R. Milne, F. Pakes and K. Shalev (eds), *Applying Psychology to Criminal Justice*. Chichester: Wiley.

Moston, S., Stephenson, G.M. and Williamson T.M. (1992) 'The effects of case characteristics on suspect behaviour during police questioning', *British Journal of Criminology*, 32 (1): 23–40.

Mullin, C. (1990) *Error of Judgement. The Truth about the Birmingham Bombings*. Dublin: Poolbeg.

Pearse, J. and Gudjonsson, G. (1996) 'How appropriate are appropriate adults?', *Journal of Forensic Psychology*, 7: 570–80.

Philips, C., Sir (1981) *The Royal Commission on Criminal Procedure*. Cmnd 8092. London: HMSO.

Poyser, S. (forthcoming) 'Miscarriages of justice: the media and their investigations', *Criminology and Criminal Justice.*

Rock, F. (2001) 'The genesis of a witness statement', *Forensic Linguistics*, 8: 44–72.

Runciman, Viscount, of Doxford, CBE, FBA (1993) *The Royal Commission on Criminal Justice*. Cm 2263. London: HMSO.

Ryan, G.H. (2002) *The Governor's Commission on Capital Punishment*. Office of the Governor, State of Illinois, USA (www.idoc.state.il.us/ccp).

Savage, S., Grieve, J. and Poyser, S. (2007) 'Putting wrongs to right: campaigns against miscarriages of justice', *Journal of Criminology and Criminal Justice*, 7 (1): 83–105.

Savage, S. and Milne, R. (2007) 'Miscarriages of justice – the role of the investigative process', in T. Newburn, T. Williamson and A. Wright (eds), *Handbook of Criminal Investigation*. Cullompton: Willan Publishing.

Scheck, B., Neufeld, P. and Dwyer, J. (2000) *Actual Innocence. Five days to execution, and other dispatches from the wrongly convicted*. New York: Doubleday.

Shepherd, E. (1993) 'Ethical interviewing', in E. Shepherd (ed.), *Aspects of Police Interviewing. Issues in Criminological and Legal Psychology, No. 18.* Leicester: BPS.

Shepherd, E. (1996) *Becoming Skilled*. London: Law Society.

Shepherd, E. (2007) *Investigative Interviewing: The conversation management approach*. Oxford: Oxford University Press.

Smith, D.J. (1983) *Police and People in London. I. A Survey of Londoners.* London: Policy Studies Institute.

Softley, P. (1981) *Police Interrogation: an observational study in four police stations.* Research Study No. 4 *Royal Commission on Criminal Procedure* (1981). Cmnd 8092. London: HMSO.

Steer, D. (1981) *Uncovering Crime: the Police Role*. Research Study No. 7 *Royal Commission on Criminal Procedure* (1981). Cmnd 8092. London: HMSO.

Stelfox, P. (2007) 'Professionalizing criminal investigation', in T. Newburn, T. Williamson, and A. Wright (eds), *Handbook of Criminal Investigation*. Cullompton: Willan Publishing.

Stephenson, G.M. (1992) *The Psychology of Criminal Justice.* Oxford: Blackwell.

Walker, C. (1999) 'Miscarriages of justice in principle and practice', in C. Walker and K. Starmer (eds), *Miscarriages of Justice: A Review of Justice in Error*, pp. 31–62. London: Blackstone.

Wright, A. (2002) *Policing: An Introduction to Concepts and Practice*. Cullompton: Willan Publishing.

Zander, M. (1994) 'Ethics and crime investigation by the police', *Policing*, 10 (1): 67–86.

Zito Trust (n.d.). http://www.zitotrust.co.uk/home.html (accessed 4 December 2008).

Appendix

March 2008

National Investigative Interviewing Strategy

The Principles of Investigative Interviewing

4.1 The principles of investigative interviewing, which have generally stood the test of time, have been revised. The *Principles of Investigative Interviewing 2007* are:

i. The aim of investigative interviewing is to obtain accurate and reliable accounts from victims, witnesses or suspects about matters under police investigation.

ii. Investigators must act fairly when questioning victims, witnesses or suspects. Vulnerable people must be treated with particular consideration at all times.

iii. Investigative interviewing should be approached with an investigative mindset. Accounts obtained from the person who is being interviewed should always be tested against what the interviewer already knows or what can reasonably be established.

iv. When conducting an interview, investigators are free to ask a wide range of questions in order to obtain material which may assist an investigation.

v. Investigators should recognise the positive impact of an early admission in the context of the criminal justice system.

vi. Investigators are not bound to accept the first answer given. Questioning is not unfair merely because it is persistent.

vii. Even when the right of silence is exercised by a suspect, investigators have a responsibility to put questions to them.

Note: these points were reiterated in the 2009 strategy, Section 1.4, page 6 http://www.npia.police.uk/en/docs/National_Investigative_Interviewing_Strategy_09.pdf accessed December 2009.

Chapter 3

The interpretation and utilisation of offender profiles: a critical review of 'traditional' approaches to profiling*

Laurence Alison, Emma Barrett and Louise Almond

In this chapter, one of the most prominent approaches to constructing 'offender profiles' is reviewed and the social psychological reasons for its continued but, we argue, largely unwarranted popularity are explored. It is important to emphasise at the outset that this review considers the type of profiling that has been most prominent in the past decade and has attracted the most media attention. The profiling we review involves the extrapolation of lists of characteristics of offenders, based upon an evaluation of a 'type' of offender as derived from a profiler visiting a crime scene. Hereafter, we refer to this as the 'traditionalist' perspective. Other recent papers consider the many positive steps forward in behavioural investigative advice (Almond *et al.* 2007; Alison *et al.* 2004; Bennell and Canter 2002; Fritzon and Ridgway 2001; Hanfland *et al.* 1997) but we do not concentrate on this activity here. The interested reader will find that these and a number of other papers highlight different approaches to the provision of advice, recognising the need for systematic research, justification of the claims made and the requisite ethical standards. Indeed, ACPO (Association of Chief Police Officers) requirements in the UK (ACPO 2000) have resulted in significant restrictions on the way in which advice is provided to and employed by the police, thereby making traditional profiling methods more and more difficult to apply in

*Support for the preparation of this chapter was provided by Economic and Social Research Council Grant PTA-030-2002-00482, awarded to the second author.

practice. Why then is it important to review a form of profiling that is probably in 'recession'?

Firstly, in the mind of the public, and indeed many practitioners, profiling is typically associated with an approach in which typologies of offenders are derived from observations of a crime scene (Douglas *et al.* 1986). Yet there is, as we show, a lack of evidence for the utility of this type of advice, as well as a host of theoretical reasons why it is likely to prove unproductive (Alison *et al.* 2002). In this chapter, we consider why such profiles nevertheless hold so much appeal for police and public alike. Canter and Youngs (2003) have termed this the 'Hollywood Effect' and it is clear that its seduction extends to students who are eager to learn about profiling. We therefore hope that this chapter will serve as a 'reality check' for students who might otherwise hold unrealistic views both of the present state of profiling and of what is taught on forensic and investigative psychology courses.

Secondly, we suggest that much of the advice contained within traditional perspectives is ambiguous, unverifiable and contains many erroneous 'lay' beliefs about the consistency of human behaviour and the ability to classify individuals into discrete 'types' (Alison *et al.* 2003a). As such, it affords us the opportunity to highlight some interesting psychological phenomena that relate to the way in which individuals perceive human behaviour.

Finally, enquiries in which profiles are sought are, by definition, serious and complicated cases. When faced with complex and ambiguous investigative data, investigators tend to engage in the generation of one or more narratives to make sense of the data (Innes 2002). We suggest that profiles, by offering plausible 'explanations' of an offender's actions by reference to the supposed psychological aetiology of such behaviour, and by providing otherwise elusive hints as to an offender's characteristics, help to fill important gaps in these narratives. Furthermore, these explanations and hints are particularly compelling because they tend to be consistent with generally held beliefs about behavioural consistency and the lay perception that behaviour can be explained by reference to types, despite the empirical evidence that context has a strong impact upon behaviour (Cervone 1999). The creative interpretation of a profile may thus lead to a more favourable assessment of ambiguous, unverifiable and potentially erroneous accounts than is warranted by the evidence (Alison *et al.* 2003b). We further suggest that lay beliefs concerning the 'types' of offenders, their motivations and behaviours, may be highly influential in many other decisions in criminal investigations.

The content and structure of such beliefs is therefore an appropriate and important area for further psychological enquiry.

The plausibility of traditional approaches to offender profiling

Offender/behavioural/investigative/criminal profiling has variously been referred to as 'a technique for identifying the major personality and behavioural characteristics of an individual based upon an analysis of the crimes he or she has committed' (Douglas *et al.* 1986: 405); the 'process of inferring distinctive personality characteristics of individuals responsible for committing criminal acts' (Turvey 1999: 1) where, according to Pinizzotto and Finkel (1990), an offender profile 'focuses attention on individuals with personality traits that parallel traits of others who have committed similar offences' (p. 216) and where the 'interpretation of crime scene evidence can indicate the personality type of the individual(s) who committed the offence' Rossmo (2000: 68). According to Douglas *et al.* (1992), 'The crime scene is presumed to reflect the murderer's behavior and personality in much the same way as furnishings reveal the homeowner's character' (p. 21).

However, as Alison *et al.* (2002) have pointed out, the concept that reliable 'personality traits' of an offender(s) are based on observations of a crime scene is at odds with contemporary conceptualisations of personality and behaviour, where, in contrast, behaviour is explained in terms of conditional patterns that depend on the individual and his or her specific situation (Shoda *et al.* 1994).

Assumptions underlying traditional approaches to profiling

Some of the most widely recognised and oft-employed experts in the USA, the UK and several other European countries have previously made claims that clusters of behaviours can be derived from crime scenes and converted into some taxonomic framework. Further, from this classification, background characteristics may be derived (Åsgard 1998; Boon 1997; Douglas *et al.* 1992; Douglas *et al.* 1986; Britton 1992). It has been argued that the inferential process can be represented in the question series, 'What to Why to Who?' (Pinizzotto and Finkel 1990). Based on the crime scene material (What), a particular motivation for the offence behaviour is attributed to the perpetrator (Why). This, in turn, leads to the description of the perpetrator's likely characteristics (Who). This simple 'What to Why to Who' inference assumes that the supposed specific motivations that drive the initiation of the offence are consistently associated with specific types of background characteristics of the offender (e.g., '... if motivation X then characteristics A, B, C and D').

The idea of inferring background characteristics from crime scene actions relies on two central assumptions about offence behaviour. The first is the assumption of *behavioural consistency*: the variance in the crimes of serial offenders must be smaller than the variance occurring in a random comparison of different offenders. This is exemplified in the definitions of profiling outlined at the outset of this chapter and in statements such as 'profiling rests on the assumption that at least certain offenders have consistent behavioural traits. This consistency is thought to persist from crime to crime and also to affect various non-criminal aspects of their personality and lifestyle, thus making them, to some extent, identifiable' (Homant and Kennedy 1998: 328). Similarly, the traditional view of personality dispositions leads to the assumption that 'individuals are characterised by stable and broadly generalised dispositions that endure over long periods of time and that generate consistencies in their social behaviour across a wide range of situations' (Mischel 1990: 112).

However, as Mischel (1968) points out, there is little evidence to support this notion. As long ago as 1928, a number of studies examining behavioural consistency (tested by observing people's social behaviour as it occurred across a variety of natural settings) demonstrated that inter-correlations among behaviours comprising a particular trait concept tend to be low (Dudycha 1936; Hartshorne and May 1928; Newcomb 1929). This led many theorists to question not only popular trait theories (e.g., Mischel 1968; Peterson 1968; Vernon 1964), but the concept of personality itself (Epstein 1979). More recently, studies such as the often-cited Carleton College study also failed to allow predictions of behaviour across specific situations (Mischel and Peake 1982).

In terms of consistency in offence behaviour, a number of studies have revealed some evidence, albeit rather weak in most cases, that offenders are somewhat consistent. Most of this research has been conducted on samples of rapists (Bennell 1998; Grubin *et al.* 1997; Mokros 2000) although there is also some evidence of behavioural consistency in other offences such as domestic burglary (Goodwill 2000). What is most revealing about these studies though is the finding that individual behaviours are subject to some fluctuation from crime to crime, due perhaps, as many of the authors argue, to situational influences and the dynamic features of re-offending. The most significant aspect of behavioural consistency appears to relate to location, with proximity being the most effective element for linking and the actual behaviours occurring within the crime, the least effective.

The second assumption is the *homology assumption* (Mokros and Alison 2000). In its most basic form, the assumption is that the more similar two offenders are in terms of characteristics, the more similar their behavioural style during the commission of the offence. Thus, two rapists who are, for example, both married, have pre-convictions for robbery and a history of alcohol abuse should be more likely to commit an offence in the same way than if their offence style was compared with an offender who is unmarried, has no pre-convictions and no history of alcohol abuse.

Davies *et al.* (1998) had some success in linking specific actions to particular characteristics. For example, they found that rapists who break into a victim's house are five times more likely to have a previous conviction for burglary than those who do not enter a victim's house by force. However, Davies *et al.*'s attempt to integrate sets of crime scene variables into logistic regression models in order to predict the characteristics of rapists was unsuccessful. Similarly, House (1997) generated four thematic foci (*aggression, criminality, pseudo-intimacy* and *sadism*) from a sample of 50 rapists and, while achieving some success in linking particular behaviours to particular actions, was unable to develop lists of probable characteristics (specifically pre-convictions) of offenders based on the thematic foci. Neither study tested whether particular configurations of crime scene actions are associated with particular configurations of characteristics other than pre-convictions.

In Knight *et al.*'s (1998) clinically oriented classification scheme (the Massachusetts Treatment Center Rapist Typology Version 3; MTC: R3), typologies are derived on the basis of primary motivations. Motivations include *opportunity*, *pervasive anger*, *sexual gratification* and *vindictiveness*. These are further differentiated through the degree of social competence and the amount of sadism implicit in the offence. While these have been used productively for clinical interventions, Knight *et al.* concede that one of these data sets contains 'extensive coding of crime-scene information but minimal offender data', while the other one comprises 'extensive offender data but minimal crime-scene data' (Knight *et al.* 1998: 46). So, for clinical reasons and as a result of its focus on motivation, the taxonomy does not consider the types of characteristics commonly outlined in offender profiles. For example, it does not link actions to age, socio-demographic status or previous convictions – all characteristics that are most likely to be of use in actual investigations (Annon 1995; Ault and Reese 1980; Grubin 1995; Homant and Kennedy 1998).

In an attempt to investigate the homology assumption Mokros and Alison (2002) conducted a study on a sample of rapists (N = 100), for whom they had access to details both of the behaviours in the offence and the background characteristics of offenders. In terms of support for the homology assumption, results were not encouraging: neither age, socio-demographic features, nor previous convictions could be reliably linked to themes within offence behaviour.

In summary, there seems to be little evidence for the consistency and homology assumptions. Why, then, does 'offender profiling' in this form appear to enjoy such public and investigative attention?

The evaluation of profiles

Evaluations of offender profiling have commonly focused on police officers' claims of satisfaction with the advice received (Britton 1992; Copson 1995; Douglas 1981; Goldblatt 1992; Jackson *et al.* 1993). These reviews concluded that there was some perceived utility in using such reports but that they rarely led to the identification of the offender.

In a US study, Pinizzotto (1984) examined 192 profiled cases, 88 of which had been solved. Of these, a profile was perceived to have helped in the identification of a suspect in 15 cases (17 per cent). In a number of other cases, the responding agencies reported that profiling helped to focus the investigation or to locate or prosecute a suspect. Over a decade later, Bartol (1996) conducted a survey of 152 police psychologists. In this study, 70 per cent of the police psychologists did not feel comfortable with profiling and seriously questioned its validity and usefulness. Another study examined UK police officers' perceptions of usefulness of profiles and found that fewer than a quarter were judged as being of any assistance in solving the case, and profiles were perceived as opening new lines of enquiry in fewer than one in five cases (Copson 1995). Despite this, in over 60 per cent of cases, profiles were perceived as furthering officers' understanding of the offender and in over half of the cases they reassured the officers' own judgements about the offender. There is, therefore, mixed evidence from these studies: while police officers may not regard profiling as crucial to their investigations, a high number appear to find the advice of profilers useful.

In order to investigate the validity and therefore accuracy of offender profiling, several studies have examined whether profilers produced qualitatively superior reports to those produced by other occupational groups, e.g. students or investigators. Kocsis and colleagues (see Kocsis 2003 for a review of validity studies) conducted several comparative studies; from these studies Kocsis identified four major conclusions important to the validity of profiling. First, he claimed that profilers made a greater number of correct predictions than any of the other occupation groups. Profilers were better at identifying psychological processes, physical characteristics, lifestyle characteristics, social history and offending behaviours than the other groups. However, psychologists were better at determining personality characteristics of the offender. Second, he argued that the poor performance of police officers fails to support the arguments that investigative experience is a key skill necessary for proficient profiling. Third, he states that logical reasoning is crucial to success in profiling. Fourth, he states that there is little support for the use of psychics and the intuition they represent. To summarise, Kocsis and his colleagues concluded that professional profilers can produce more accurate predictions about an unknown offender in comparison with police officers, psychologists, students and psychics.

More recently it has been argued that the conclusions reached by Kocsis and his colleagues are too premature. Bennell *et al.* (2006) conducted a critique of Kocsis and his colleagues' studies. First, they argued that Kocsis's measure of profile accuracy was unsound and highly dependent on the interpretation of the respondent. Second, they criticised Kocsis for not actually assessing his participant groups to ascertain whether they possessed the skills he attributed to them. Finally, Bennell *et al.* (2006) argued that Kocsis's data collection procedures and methods of analysis were biased. The number of profilers sampled by Kocsis across his studies was low and not representative of profilers in general and the participant groups were not tested under the same conditions.

The content of profiles has also received criticism. Alison *et al.* (2003a) applied Toulmin's (1958) philosophy of argument as an evaluation process to 21 profiles produced from 1997–2001. They found that 80 per cent of the approximately 4,000 claims made in the profiles they sampled were unsupported. The claims lacked appropriate *grounding* in psychological knowledge, contained no *warrants* (specific examples of supportive research), were provided with no estimation of their *veracity* (e.g. probability) and less than a third were *falsifiable*. However, a contemporary study conducted by

Almond *et al.* (2007) of behavioural investigative reports produced by the National Policing Improvements Agency (NPIA) found that there was a very large positive difference between this contemporary sample and previous non-NPIA expert advice in terms of the substantiveness of their arguments. They found that contemporary NPIA behavioural investigative advice has clearer boundaries around the claims made and they present material in a more coherent and evidence-based format than previous expert advice.

The interpretation of profiles

Alison *et al.* (2003b) have argued that a contributory factor in the perception of usefulness of traditional profiles, despite evidence to the contrary, concerns the psychological processes involved in interpreting the information. Even when the identity of an offender is unambiguously determined, there exists a distinctly subjective element in deciding how well any given person fits an offender profile. In a small sample of non-NPIA profiles, Alison *et al.* (2003a) demonstrated that 24 per cent of the profiling predictions were ambiguous and open to subjective interpretation (such as, 'the offender will have poor heterosocial skills'). This figure was 13 per cent for a sample of contemporary NPIA profiles (Almond *et al.* 2007). Further, 55 per cent of statements in non-NPIA profiles would be extremely difficult to verify, even if the offender was caught (for instance, 'the offender will have fantasised about the act in the weeks leading up to offence'). This figure was 21 per cent in the NPIA sample. Alison *et al.* (2003a) suggested that one of the possible dangers of such ambiguous and unverifiable information is that it facilitates 'creative interpretation' on the part of the investigator.

To explore this notion, Alison *et al.* (2003b) conducted two pilot studies. Participants included police officers, individuals involved in the legal profession and forensic clinicians. The participants in the first study were all police officers. A profile was constructed that contained ambiguous and unverifiable information and was provided to participants who were to imagine that they were investigating a murder. Participants were given details of an actual offence,[1] the constructed profile and a suspect. Two groups of participants each received the same profile but different suspects. In one group, participants received a brief outline of the actual offender (genuine suspect), while in the other group participants were given a hypothetical suspect constructed for the study (bogus). The bogus suspect was constructed so as to be quite different on key demographic features while still enabling him to be a possible suspect (the suspect had to be male and of an age where it was physically possible to have committed the offence). Participants were asked to rate the accuracy of the profile based on the suspect that they were given. Despite being given quite different suspects (one was twice as old as the other, one had many pre-convictions, the other none, one had a history of psychiatric problems, the other did not, etc.), the mean accuracy rating for both groups was 5.3 (where 1 = very inaccurate and 7 = very accurate). The median for both groups was 6; the mode for the genuine suspect was 5, and for the bogus suspect it was 6. Over 40 per cent (9 of the 22) of the 'genuine' group rated the profile as a generally–very accurate fit, while just over 50 per cent (13 of the 24) in the 'bogus' group rated the profile as generally–very accurate. None of the participants rated the profile as either generally or very inaccurate. Alison *et al.* also examined the qualitative justifications for the scores given. One group (genuine offender) focused on relationship issues and the offender's sexuality (as mentioned in the profile), while relationship issues and the motivation of the offender appeared to justify scores given in the other group (bogus offender).

In a second exploratory study, involving police officers and individuals involved in the legal profession, Alison *et al.* employed a profile used in an actual enquiry. In this study, they also asked whether the profile would be useful in an enquiry. Twenty-nine of the 33 participants in study two stated that the profile would be useful if they were investigating the crime, with the most common justification relating to the idea that the profile could narrow down a suspect search. Using a similar design (two suspects: one bogus, one genuine, different demographic features in each) overall mean accuracy scores were 5.4 for the genuine offender and 5.2 for the fabricated offender with no differences between ratings for the two contrasting suspects.

Both studies indicated that the majority of participants rated the profile as at least somewhat accurate despite the distinctly different suspects that they were given. Of course, there are many limitations of this type of study, including the questionable ecological validity of paper and pencil tests of this sort, the fact that there is a non difference between groups, the relatively low numbers in each group and so on. However, Alison *et al.* argue that these preliminary studies highlight the need to conduct further research to test more comprehensively the hypothesis that participants were selectively noting aspects of the profile that can be easily applied to the suspect, ignoring those aspects that are not applicable, and constructing meaning from ambiguity. If this is the case, then such 'creative interpretation' of ambiguous information is reminiscent of the so-called 'Barnum Effect' in which people tend to accept vague and general personality descriptions as being specific to themselves (Forer 1949; Furnham and Schofield 1987; Meehl 1956).

Previous research has examined the role of the Barnum Effect in how individuals interpret feedback from psychometric tests, horoscopes, as well as handwriting analysis (Dickson and Kelly 1985; Fichter and Sunerton 1983; Snyder *et al.* 1976). The effect is particularly prominent when the information provided is ambiguous, vague, difficult to verify and comes from an authoritative source. This effect, and the closely related process of 'personal validation' in which individuals classify information that could be applied to anyone as being particularly descriptive of their own qualities, has much in common with processes of attribution theory (Ross 1977); the notion of scripts and schemas (Schank and Abelson 1977, 1995) and narrative approaches to personality (McAdams 1993). In each case, researchers argue that in attempting to make the world more predictable, individuals rely on pre-existing, case-based experiences when interpreting new information. Incoming information is thus structured according to familiar patterns and beliefs that have been informed by personal experiences, social cultural norms and the media, and which include beliefs about the regularity of human behaviour. Beyond the application of these processes to profiling, we believe that such issues may be of significance to the wider arena of investigative decision-making.

Marshall and Alison (2007) went on to explore how offender profiles might influence the way in which individuals interpret investigative information dependent on its congruence with the investigator's own beliefs. This study comprised an online questionnaire and involved participants receiving a profile which was either congruent or incongruent with an atypical or stereotypical suspect. In an additional condition, the participants were presented with the suspect details either before or after the profile. Participants appeared to use several different cognitive strategies when interpreting the investigative information. The two main strategies identified were *representativeness*, which refers to judgements based on the suspects' resemblance to a preconceived stereotype, and *cognitive elaboration*, which refers to a preference for generating causal links between chunks of information in order to justify the basis for a particular judgement.

Individuals relying on the representativeness strategy were more influenced by a profile challenging their views (incongruent) than one supporting them (congruent). Whilst individuals who invested more cognitive effort, i.e. cognitive elaborators, were more resistant to changing their views in light of an incongruent profile, this is tentative evidence to suggest a confirmation bias is occurring. Marshall and Alison (2007) also found that a profile was perceived as more influential when it was presented before the suspect description than after. They suggest that the risk of decision-making errors such as belief persistence and confirmation bias might be minimised by presenting an offender profile early in an investigation.

Thus far, our studies have focused on the use of traditional profiles in isolation, as one particular source of information available to investigators engaged in a complex criminal investigation. However, we believe that similar processes are at work as investigators attempt to make sense of a whole range of complex, ambiguous and incomplete information in the course of their enquiries. In the following section, we present evidence from a range of psychological research dealing with the cognitive mechanisms by which individuals deal with complex information. This evidence indicates that the general mechanism by which individuals make sense of such information, in particular, social information, is one of story generation. The creative interpretation of offender profiles by investigators may be a specific application of a more general story generation mechanism, employed as a heuristic strategy for dealing with ambiguous and complex information.

The process of investigation

The idea that people use stories both to store and to explain information about the world has received much attention from researchers in a variety of fields, including cognition (e.g. Schank and Abelson 1995), social psychology (e.g. Read 1987; Wyer and Radvansky 1999) and personality psychology (e.g. McAdams 1993). The discussion here is largely confined to the notion of story generation as a cognitive heuristic employed when attempting to comprehend an otherwise confusing situation.

The suggestion that individuals construct stories as a means of understanding a situation has also received support from the study of Naturalistic Decision Making (NDM), an area of research concerned with the ways in which individuals and teams use their experience to make meaningful decisions in dynamic, uncertain and often time-pressured situations (Zsambok 1997). According to one of the most prominent and widely tested NDM models, Klein's Recognition-Primed Decision Model, when tackling complex and ambiguous problems, a decision-maker engages in story building to create a mental representation of the problem situation, drawing on existing case-specific, domain-specific and general knowledge from long-term memory, and integrating it with perceived information (Klein 1999).

A number of researchers have argued that story generation is a particularly useful tool for understanding social information. For instance, in his approach to causal reasoning, Read argues that in order to comprehend the behaviours of others, individuals need to have an understanding of how conditions initiate particular goals and how people's actions are performed as part of plans to achieve those goals (Read 1987; Read and Miller 1993, 1995).

There is good reason to believe that people rely on story construction to help them understand complicated information, both in general and in the more specific case of information about crimes and criminals, because stories summarise important data about the development of other people's goals and the execution of their plans, and help us understand what underlies conflicts between individuals with differing goals and plans. As such, story generation can be thought of as an heuristic strategy by which we make sense of complex and ambiguous information. Despite the focus on 'biases' in Kahneman and Tversky's well-known 'heuristics and biases' programme (e.g. Kahneman *et al.* 1982), heuristic strategies should not be seen as inherently irrational (Gigerenzer and Todd 1999). Indeed, there is a significant body of work that suggests that the use of heuristic strategies is essentially adaptive. Story generation is a good example of an adaptive heuristic: in general, events follow one another in an understandable sequence, outcomes have causes, and, in a general sense, people often do predictable things in well-defined circumstances. Thus far, the evidence suggests that 'people's decisions based on heuristics are pretty good, pretty often' (Markman and Medin 2002: 424).

While heuristic use has important benefits, it can also have significant costs: stories may be helpful vehicles for understanding social information, but they are not necessarily always accurate. If the perception of new information is faulty, or if the existing knowledge with which it is combined is unsound or incomplete, flawed mental models of the situation will result. Equally, defective social situation models may result if the comprehender holds biased or erroneous views on the meanings of particular behaviours, or if they fail to take account of important factors such as situational variables (e.g. Cervone 1999).

Stories and profiles

Our argument has important implications for our understanding of the cognitive processes that often lead investigators to hold a favourable view of traditional offender profiles, despite a lack of evidence for their utility. Firstly, the readiness to believe that psychologists, popularly believed to be 'experts' in the study of human behaviour, may have something to offer in a police investigation probably owes a lot to police officers' recognition that the understanding of the behaviour of others is crucial in an investigation. Believing a source of information to be both credible and useful is, of course, likely to predispose officers favourably towards the information itself.

Secondly, the use of a 'story generation' heuristic strategy may be an inevitable consequence of the complexity of the task at hand. Bringing coherence to the sort of intricate and ambiguous material available in a criminal investigation involves significant cognitive effort. Thus, it may be unsurprising that investigators will tend to fill gaps with assumption-based reasoning and to rely on the informed speculation of others, particularly those considered 'experts', to bring coherence to an otherwise confusing situation. These suggestions have some empirical support: for instance, Horowitz *et al.* (2001) report that when presented with trial-like information of increasing complexity, mock jurors appear less able to process such information systematically.

Thirdly, it is possible that the overly positive view individuals hold of the type of profiles and profilers frequently mentioned in the press is, in part, influenced by the use of 'technical' psychological terms in such profiles. Horowitz *et al.*'s participants seemed to find expert witnesses to be more credible when the language they used was more technical, probably because such language use conforms to lay expectations about the nature of expert testimony.

Fourthly, there is some evidence that highly stressful, highly ambiguous situations tend to promote superstitious beliefs and the readiness to invoke simplistic views of behaviour (Vyse 1997).

Finally, it should be acknowledged that there are pragmatic reasons why police might commission profiles even if they believe them to have little or no value. In the UK, the Criminal Procedure and Investigations Act 1996 imposes on the police a statutory responsibility to pursue 'all reasonable lines of enquiry'. Add to this the public pressure that is so often brought to bear on the police in high-profile cases and it is perhaps understandable that the police often make significant efforts to be seen to have employed every possible investigative resource, no matter how sceptical they might be in private about the efficacy of a particular technique.

Case-based reasoning in criminal investigation: novice and expert

Thus far we have made no clear distinction between experienced and novice investigators when considering their interpretation of information from profiles, and, indeed, other investigative information. Further research is needed to determine whether and in what ways experienced investigators' greater store of domain-relevant information may facilitate effective processing of complex forensic information. For instance, the acquisition of experience may allow investigators to develop a richer and more diverse set of stereotypes upon which they rely heuristically when processing investigative material, thus reducing the need to rely on untested expert information when doing so. Equally, greater experience may lead to an increased ability to resist the temptation to interpret investigative material (including profiles) creatively, and to recognise flaws in assumption-based reasoning.

However, experience is not necessarily synonymous with expertise: as Yates points out, it is quite possible for an individual to achieve 'experienced incompetence' (2001: 24) by repetitive use of poor strategies. What, then, does it mean to be an expert in an investigative context? An increased ability to think critically about investigative material, including profiles, may not be a natural consequence of an increase in domain-relevant experience but may depend in part on the development of a particular set of meta-cognitive skills. Indeed, there is evidence from related fields that experts operating in highly pressured and ambiguous situations undergo a process of critiquing the stories that they generate to help them understand such situations (Cohen *et al.* 1998). By correcting unreliable assumptions and filling gaps with carefully considered evidence, as opposed to speculation, such experts construct more reliable and accurate stories, which allow them to take more effective action.

To summarise, we suggest that investigators attempt to generate a mental representation of an investigative problem situation, consisting of a coherent, convincing and evidentially sound story explaining the circumstances of the crime. Such a story consists of a series of episodes in which are embedded arguments about the actors (offenders, victims and witnesses) and their motivations and plans, their actions and the cause–effect relationships between them. An investigator's mental model, the narrative of the crime, must be complete and coherent. Where arguments are based on assumptions, they must be valid, and robust enough to withstand the scrutiny of the court. Where they exist, alternative stories should be shown to be implausible, incoherent or unreliable. The process of constructing such a representation is the process of investigation.

The clearer the incoming investigative data, and the more skilled the investigator at interpreting such information, the more effective the process is likely to be. Returning to the principal topic of this chapter, ambiguous and unverifiable information is particularly dangerous when it masquerades as scientific fact. Therefore, the concerns that have arisen in the past few years with regard to clarity in profiles and the increasing recognition that offenders cannot be neatly fitted into types based on an analysis of the crime scene is a welcome development. Work is gradually emerging within the social sciences that will contribute to our understanding of criminal behaviour for the purpose of assisting investigations. This now burgeoning field, which has begun to embrace both experience and systematic research as a way forward, promises stronger links between practitioners and academics and a stronger footing upon which advice may be provided (Alison *et al.* 2004). However, it is important to articulate clearly the reasons why the type of profiles that have had a very lengthy media honeymoon have been so successful. Such knowledge may help inform subsequent research into investigative decision-making and into the guidelines for constructing investigative advice.

Note

1 The offence involved the abduction, sexual assault and murder of a male youth in the 1970s.

References

ACPO (2000) (Association of Chief Police Officers) *ACPO Crime Committee, Behavioural Science Sub-committee.* Internal report.

Alison, L., Bennell, C., Mokros, A. and Ormerod, D. (2002) 'The personality paradox in offender profiling: A theoretical review of the processes involved in deriving background characteristics from crime scene actions', *Psychology, Public Policy and Law*, 8 (1): 115–35.

Alison, L., Smith, M., Eastman, O. and Rainbow, L. (2003a) 'Toulmin's philosophy of argument and its relevance to offender profiling', *Psychology, Crime and Law*, 9 (2): 173–83

Alison, L., Smith, M. and Morgan, K. (2003b) 'Interpreting the accuracy of offender profiles', *Psychology, Crime and Law*, 9 (2): 185–95.

Alison, L. J., West, A. and Goodwill. A. (2004) 'The academic and the practitioner: Pragmatists' views of offender profiling', *Psychology, Public Policy and Law*, 10 (1): 71–101.

Almond, L., Alison, L.J. and Porter, L. (2007) 'An evaluation and comparison of claims made in Behavioural Investigative Advice reports compiled by the National Policing Improvements Agency in the United Kingdom', *Journal of Investigative Psychology and Offender Profiling*, 4 (2): 71–83.

Annon, J.S. (1995) 'Investigative profiling: A behavioural analysis of the crime scene', *American Journal of Forensic Psychology*, 13 (4): 67–75.

Åsgard, U. (1998) 'Swedish experiences in offender profiling and evaluation of some aspects of a case of murder and abduction in Germany', in Case Analysis Unit (BKA) (eds), *Method of Case Analysis: An international symposium* (pp. 125–30). Wiesbaden: Bundeskriminalamt Kriminalistisches Institut.

Ault, R.L. and Reese, J.T. (1980) 'A psychological assessment of crime profiling', *FBI Law Enforcement Bulletin*, 49: 22–25.

Bartol, C. (1996) 'Police psychology: then, now and beyond', *Criminal Justice and Behavior*, 23 (1): 70–89.

Bennell, C. (1998) *Linking Serial Sex Offences.* Unpublished MSc thesis, Department of Psychology, University of Liverpool.

Bennell, C. and Canter, D. (2002) 'Linking commercial burglaries by modus operandi: tests using regression and ROC analysis', *Science and Justice*, 42 (3): 153–64.

Bennell, C., Jones, N. Taylor, P. and Snook, B. (2006) 'Validities and abilities and criminal profiling: A critique of the studies conducted by Richard Kocsis and his colleagues', *International Journal of Offender Therapy and Comparative Criminology*, 50 (1): 1–18.

Boon, J. (1997) 'Contribution of personality theories to psychological profiling', in J.L. Jackson, and D.A. Bekarian (eds), *Offender Profiling: Theory, research and practice* (pp. 43–59). Chichester: Wiley.

Britton, P. (1992) *Review of Offender Profiling.* London: Home Office.

Canter, D. and Youngs, D. (2003) 'Beyond "offender profiling": the need for an investigative psychology', in R. Bull and D. Carson (eds), *Handbook of Psychology and Legal Contexts* (pp. 171–206). West Sussex: Wiley and Sons.

Cervone, D. (1999) 'Bottom-up explanation in personality psychology: The case of cross-situational coherence', in D. Cervone and Y. Shoda (eds), *The Coherence of Personality: Social-cognitive bases of personality consistency, variability, and organization*. New York: Guilford Press.

Cohen, M.S., Freeman, J.T. and Thompson, B. (1998) 'Critical thinking skills in tactical decision making: A model and a training strategy', in J.A. Cannon-Bowers and E. Salas (eds), *Making Decisions under Stress*. Washington, DC: American Psychological Association.

Copson, G. (1995) *Coals to Newcastle? Part One: A Study of Offender Profiling.* Police Research Group Special Interest Series (Paper no.7). London: Home Office Police Department.

Davies, A., Wittebrood, K. and Jackson, J.L. (1998) *Predicting the Criminal Record of a Stranger Rapist.* London: Home Office, Policing and Reducing Crime Unit.

Dickson, D.H. and Kelly, I.E. (1985) 'The "Barnum Effect" in personality assessment: A review of the literature', *Psychological Reports*, 57 (2): 367–82.

Douglas, J.E. (1981) *Evaluation of the (FBI) Psychological Profiling Programme.* Unpublished manuscript.

Douglas, J.E., Burgess, A.W., Burgess, A.G. and Ressler, R.K. (1992) *Crime Classification Manual: A standard system for investigating and classifying violent crime.* New York: Simon and Schuster.

Douglas, J., Ressler, R., Burgess, A. and Hartman, C. (1986) 'Criminal profiling from crime scene analysis', *Behavioural Sciences and the Law*, 4 (4): 401–21.

Dudycha, G.J. (1936) 'An objective study of punctuality in relation to personality and achievement', *Archives of Psychology*, 204 (1): 1–319.

Epstein, S. (1979) 'The stability of behavior I: On predicting most of the people most of the time', *Journal of Personality and Social Psychology*, 37 (6), 1097–1126.

Fichter, C.S. and Sunerton, D. (1983) 'Popular horoscopes and the "Barnum Effect"', *Journal of Psychology*, 114 (1): 123–24.

Forer, B. (1949) 'The fallacy of personal validation: A classroom demonstration of gullibility', *Journal of Abnormal and Social Psychology*, 44 (1): 118–23.

Fritzon, K. and Ridgway, J. (2001) 'Near death experience: the role of victim reaction in attempted homicide', *Journal of Interpersonal Violence*, 16 (7): 679–96.

Furnham, A. and Schofield, S. (1987) 'Accepting personality test feedback: a review of the Barnum Effect', *Current Psychological Research and Reviews*, 6 (2), 162–78.

Gigerenzer, G. and Todd, P.M. (1999) 'Fast and frugal heuristics: the adaptive toolbox', in G. Gigerenzer, P.M. Todd and the ABC Research Group (eds), *Simple Heuristics that Make Us Smart.* New York, NY: Oxford University Press.

Goldblatt, P. (1992) *Psychological Offender Profiles: How psychologists can help the police with their enquiries.* Unpublished manuscript.

Goodwill, A. (2000) *Suspect Prioritisation in Linking Burglary Offences.* Dissertation for MSc Investigative Psychology. Internal Document: University of Liverpool.

Grubin, D. (1995) 'Offender profiling', *Journal of Forensic Psychiatry and Psychology*, 6 (2): 259–63.

Grubin, D., Kelly, P. and Ayis, S. (1997) *Linking Serious Sexual Assaults.* London: Home Office Police Research Group.

Hanfland, R., Keppel, R. and Weiss, J. (1997) 'Case management for missing children homicide investigation: Executive summary.' Olympia: Office of the Attorney General.

Hartshorne, H. and May, M.A. (1928) *Studies in the Nature of Character (Volume 1): Studies in deceit.* New York: Macmillan.

Homant, R.J. and Kennedy, D.B. (1998) 'Psychological aspects of crime scene profiling: validity research', *Criminal Justice and Behavior*, 25 (3): 319–43.

Horowitz, I.A., Bordens, K.S., Victor, E., Bourgeois, M.J. and Forster-Lee, L. (2001) 'The effects of complexity on jurors' verdicts and construction of evidence', *Journal of Applied Psychology*, 86 (4): 641–52.

House, J.C. (1997) 'Towards a practical application of offender profiling: the RNC's criminal suspect prioritization system', in J.L. Jackson and D.A. Bekerian (eds), *Offender Profiling: Theory, research and practice* (pp. 177–90). Chichester: John Wiley and Sons.

Innes, M. (2002) 'The "process structures" of police homicide investigations', *British Journal of Criminology*, 42 (4): 669–88.

Jackson, J.L., Van Koppen, P.J. and Herbrink, C.M. (1993). *Does the Service Meet the Needs: An evaluation of consumer satisfaction with specific profile analysis and investigative advice as offered by the Scientific Research Advisory Unit of the National Criminal Intelligence Division (CRI), The Netherlands.* Unpublished manuscript.

Kahneman, D., Slovic, P. and Tversky, A. (eds) (1982) *Judgement Under Uncertainty: Heuristics and biases.* Cambridge: Cambridge University Press.

Klein, G. (1999) *Sources of Power: How people make decisions*. Cambridge, MA: MIT Press.

Knight, R., Warren, J., Reboussin, R. and Soley, B. (1998) 'Predicting rapist type from crime scene characteristics', *Criminal Justice and Behavior*, 25: 46–80.

Kocsis, R.N. (2003) 'Criminal psychological profiling: validities and abilities', *International Journal of Offender Therapy and Comparative Criminology*, 47 (2): 126–44.

Markman, A.B. and Medin, D.L. (2002) 'Decision making', in D.L. Medin and H. Pashler (eds), *Stevens Handbook of Experimental Psychology (3rd edn), Volume 2* (pp. 413–66). New York: John Wiley and Sons.

Marshall, B. and Alison, L. (2007) 'Stereotyping, congruence and presentation order: interpretative biases in utilizing offender profiles', *Psychology, Crime and Law*, 13 (4): 285–303.

McAdams, D. (1993) *The Stories We Live By.* New York, NY: The Guilford Press

Meehl, P.E. (1956) 'Wanted – A good cookbook', *American Psychologist*, 11 (6): 263–72.

Mischel, W. (1968) *Personality and Assessment*. New York: John Wiley and Sons.

Mischel, W. (1990) 'Personality dispositions revisited and revised: A view after three decades', in L. Pervin (ed.), *Handbook of Personality: Theory and research* (2nd edn) (pp. 111–34). New York: Guilford Press.

Mischel, W. and Peake, P.K. (1982) 'Beyond déjà vu in the search for cross-situational consistency', *Psychological Review*, 89 (6): 730–55.

Mokros, A. (2000) *The centroid as a grouping variable for offences: A cluster-analytical approach.* Unpublished internal document, Department of Psychology, University of Liverpool.

Mokros, A. and Alison, L. (2002) 'Is profiling possible? Testing the predicted homology of crime scene actions and background characteristics in a sample of rapists', *Legal and Criminological Psychology*, 7 (1): 25–43.

Newcomb, T.M. (1929) *Consistency of Certain Extrovert-Introvert Behavior Patterns in 51 Problem Boys.* New York: Columbia University, Teachers College, Bureau of Publications.

Payne, J.W., Bettman, J.R. and Johnson, E.J. (1993) *The Adaptive Decision Maker*. Cambridge: CUP.

Peterson, D.R. (1968) *The Clinical Study of Social Behavior.* New York: Appleton-Century-Crofts.

Pinizzotto, A.J. (1984) 'Forensic psychology: criminal personality profiling', *Journal of Police Science and Administration*, 12 (1): 32–40.

Pinizzotto, A.J. and Finkel, N.J. (1990) 'Criminal personality profiling: an outcome and process study', *Law and Human Behavior*, 14 (3): 215–33.

Read, S.J. (1987) 'Constructing causal scenarios: a knowledge structure approach to causal reasoning', *Journal of Personality and Social Psychology*, 52 (2): 288–302.

Read, S.J. and Miller, L.C. (1993) 'Rapist or "regular guy": explanatory coherence in the construction of mental models of others', *Personality and Social Psychology Bulletin*, 19 (5): 526–41.

Read, S.J. and Miller, L.C. (1995) 'Stories are fundamental to meaning and memory: for social creatures, could it be otherwise?', in R.S. Wyer (ed.), *Advances in Social Cognition: Volume 8. Knowledge and Memory: The real story*.Hillside, NJ: Lawrence Erlbaum Associates.

Ross, L. (1977) 'The intuitive psychologist and his shortcomings: distortions in the attribution process', in L. Berkowitz (ed.). *Advances in Experimental Social Psychology* (vol. 10). Academic Press: New York.

Rossmo, D.K. (2000) *Geographic Profiling*. Boca Raton: CRC Press.

Schank, R.C. and Abelson, R.P. (1977) *Scripts, Plans, Goals and Understanding.* Hillside, NJ: Laurence Erlbaum Associates.

Schank, R.C. and Abelson, R.P. (1995) 'Knowledge and memory: the real story, in R.S. Wyer (ed.), *Advances in Social Cognition: Volume 8. Knowledge and Memory: The real story*. Hillside, NJ: Lawrence Erlbaum Associates.

Shoda, Y., Mischel, W. and Wright, J.C. (1994) 'Intra-individual stability in the organization and patterning of behavior: incorporating psychological situations into the idiographic analysis of personality', *Journal of Personality and Social Psychology*, 67 (4): 674–87.

Simon, H. (1990) 'Invariants of human behavior', *Annual Review of Psychology*, 41 (1): 1–19.

Snyder, C.R., Larsen, D.K. and Bloom, L.J. (1976) 'Acceptance of personality interpretations prior to and after receiving diagnostic feedback supposedly based on psychological, graphological and astrological assessment procedures', *Journal of Clinical Psychology*, 32 (2): 258–65.

Toulmin, S. (1958) *The Uses of Argument*. Cambridge: Cambridge University Press.

Turvey, B. (ed.) (1999) *Criminal Profiling: An introduction to behavioural evidence analysis*. New York: Academic Press.

Vernon, P.E. (1964) *Personality Assessment: A critical survey*. New York: Wiley.

Vyse, S. (1997) *Believing in Magic: The Psychology of Superstition*. Oxford: Oxford University Press.

Wyer, R.S. and Radvansky, G.A. (1999) 'The comprehension and validation of social information', *Psychological Review*, 106 (1): 89–118.

Yates, J.F. (2001) '"Outsider": Impressions of naturalistic decision making', in E. Salas and G. Klein (eds), *Linking Expertise and Naturalistic Decision Making*. Mahwah, NJ: Lawrence Erlbaum Associates, Inc.

Zsambok, C.E. (1997) 'Naturalistic decision making: where are we now?', in C.E. Zsambok and G. Klein (eds), *Naturalistic Decision Making*. Mahwah, NJ: Lawrence Erlbaum Associates, Inc.

Chapter 4

UK police interviews with suspects: a short modern history

John Bearchell

The eliciting of information through the interviewing of victims, witnesses and suspects of crime is seen by many as a core function of policing. However, history shows that public confidence in the criminal justice system can be seriously undermined if malpractice is uncovered in the form of a miscarriage of justice (see Chapter 2 of this volume). Such malpractice has been found to exist, and even flourish, where confession-focused interviewing strategies (with admissions being seen as the best evidence) are prevalent and represent the primary aim of a police interview with a suspect. An alternative strategy approaches the interview as a 'search for the truth', which is considered as part of an overall criminal investigation, or even the start of such, rather than an end in its own right (Williamson 2006).

Given the importance of interviewing to the policing function, it may be rather surprising that no formalised national police interview training programme existed until the early 1990s, before which officers learned by watching other, more experienced colleagues. Shepherd (1988) referred to this haphazard training of police interviewers as learning from 'sitting by Nellie'. He highlights that 'on-the-job' training in the police service was almost totally unsystematic and that the identity of 'Nellie' could be 'somebody, anybody or nobody' (*op. cit.* 179).

This chapter will focus particularly on the police–suspect interview interaction, and in doing so, it will briefly highlight some of the infamous miscarriages of justice to emerge during the 1980s–1990s. These helped shape society's opinion of the police at that time and fuelled the drive for legislation that enshrined ethical practice at the heart of police treatment of suspects of crime. Furthermore, it will consider some of the key academic research studies which informed the development of the first investigative interviewing training, and how later studies have driven the evolution of such. Finally, it will present some emerging research findings as to whether, after more than a decade of structured, ethical investigative interviewing training, officers approach an interview with a suspect as an opportunity to 'harvest facts', rather than to secure a confession.

Drivers for change in police interviewing practices

> When smacking a fag out of a suspect's mouth do not burn your hand ... the trick is to aim for the cheek rather than the gob. Slap them hard in the face and the cigarette will fly out sure enough. (DCI Hunt [*sic*] 1973: 91)

> It is sometimes helpful to slap a suspect around the face when interviewing them. (Walkley 1987: 89)

The first of the quotations above comes from the fictional 1970s Detective Chief Inspector Gene Hunt, a character in the immensely popular UK television series *Life on Mars*. However, it seems that this is to some extent reflective of the reality of policing as it was in the 1970s and early 1980s, with the latter quotation being a statement circulated to police officers as part of a research questionnaire, to which some 50 per cent of the questionnaire respondents agreed (Walkley 1987). Evidence also indicates that this was reflected in public attitudes towards the police at that time. A survey circulated among Londoners in the same year illustrated that a significant percentage of the public felt that threat and intimidation during police interrogation were widespread; furthermore, that the police routinely fabricated evidence (Smith 1983). However, it would seem that society had not always been so mistrusting of their police service. Reiner (1986) points out that in the 1950s–1960s 'the police were accepted throughout British society, to the extent of becoming symbols of national pride' (p. 261).

Indeed, a national opinion survey conducted on behalf of the Royal Commission on the Police (1960) documented an overwhelming vote of public confidence in the police. The authority the police enjoyed to exercise exclusive control over the conditions in which suspects were detained and interrogated, shielded their activities from immediate external scrutiny. Crucially, this also meant that the images of the police, their work, their competence, their interactions with suspects and the effectiveness of the controls to which they were subject could only be obtained through the records they alone prepared. These records provided the external audience, such as solicitors, magistrates, barristers, juries and judges, with a single and ostensibly reliable source of information on the investigation process, and then only when a prosecution had been instituted. A study of 400 cases presented before the courts revealed that they almost exclusively (98.5 per cent) relied upon unverifiable police accounts presented in the handwritten statements of individual police officers (McConville and Baldwin 1981: 53).

Official confirmation that the police did not follow the rules to the letter came in 1977, when former High Court judge, Sir Henry Fisher, reported on the events leading to the trial of three youths charged with the murder of Maxwell Confait. Three suspects, aged 14, 15 and 18 years, were interrogated by police and, on the basis of signed confession evidence, were subsequently convicted of offences ranging from arson to murder. All three of these youths were psychologically vulnerable, but despite this no legal advisers or independent parties were present for crucial periods of the interrogations (Gudjonsson 1992).

In October 1975 the Court of Appeal freed the three youths when scientific evidence showed that they could not have committed the offences and therefore their confessions could not have been true. This case, perhaps more than any other of that time, was used to illustrate that it was possible 'for a prosecution based wholly (or almost wholly) on uncorroborated confessions to proceed to trial without proper steps having been taken to seek evidence to support or contradict the evidence of confession' (Fisher Report 1977: 19). Sir Henry's report also stated that there existed a great deal of misunderstanding regarding the (then) Judges' Rules pertaining to the treatment and interviewing of suspects of crime: and that this existed at a senior level within the police and even among some members of the legal profession. Fisher (1977) recommended that the Judges' Rules be backed up with workable sanctions, and that any breach of the Rules should constitute grounds for the trial judge to exclude the confession evidence as unreliable.

The Maxwell Confait case was by no means the only high-profile miscarriage of justice to arise following the (sometimes) nefarious interviewing tactics employed by the police in the 1970s, even though it took some defendants two decades before they could finally clear their names. Two of the most significant appeals to come before the Court of Appeal concerned terrorist atrocities arising from the Irish conflict, and became separately known as the Guildford Four and the Birmingham Six. The former case was successfully prosecuted in 1975 and, following years of campaigning, the appellants were finally released in 1989 when the original interview confessions put forward by the police were demonstrated to be unreliable. This case was followed in 1991 by the acquittals of the Birmingham Six. Once again the appeal was based upon the unreliability of the police interview evidence, showing that in some cases it was the result of police coercion. Gudjonsson argues that these two cases were the worst examples of police interview malpractice of the last century. However, he points out that these cases were by no means exceptional, listing 22 such cases of the period from the Court of Appeal (2003: 439). See Chapter 2 of this volume for a fuller discussion regarding miscarriages of justice.

Throughout the late 1970s and into the 1980s there were increasing numbers of allegations of police brutality, discrimination and malpractice, and a body of evidence showing routine abuse of existing police powers. It was in this climate that a Royal Commission on Criminal Procedures (RCCP) was set up in June 1977 under the Chair of Sir Cyril Phillips. One of the primary roles of the RCCP was to review the existing regulatory framework of police interviews with suspects which, rather than being enshrined in statute law, was governed by a set of administrative guidelines, the Judges' Rules, and a collection of Home Office directives, the efficiency of which had been previously challenged in the Fisher Report (1977). The RCCP stated: 'Police training on interviewing should be developed in ways which will not only improve their interview techniques but also bring home to them the powerful psychological forces that are to play upon the suspect and the dangers that are attendant upon these' (*ibid.*: para. 2: 18–24).

The Police and Criminal Evidence Act 1984 (PACE), together with associated Codes of Practice (introduced in January 1986), altered the previous legal position where the police acted as the sole unmonitored, and possibly inadequately regulated, narrators of what had transpired during the interrogation of a suspect, by the introduction of measures for internal supervision, contemporaneous (tape) recording, and the strengthening of a suspect's rights. See Chapter 2 of this volume for further details of this legislation.

Early research on the impact of PACE by Irving and McKenzie (1989) showed indications that the introduction of the role of Custody

Sergeant had a regulating effect on those officers who sought to 'stretch' the new rules in order to secure a confession. However, other research suggested that the introduction of the PACE regulations concerning the interviewing of suspects merely led to nefarious police questioning practices outside of the authentication procedures. McConville *et al.* (1991) quote how one officer 'got around' the requirements of a contemporaneous interview 'by trying to have a few words that aren't on the record, i.e. on the way in [to the police station], in the car, on the way to the cell – give them something to think about – or before the start of the interview' (*ibid.*: 58).

However, even with the additional safeguards introduced under PACE, the tape recording of the interview and the presence of a solicitor, police interrogation practices continued to attract adverse publicity through further miscarriages of justices. In *R.* v. *Paris, Abdullahi and Miller* (1993), which has become widely known as the 'Cardiff Three', the (then) Lord Chief Justice, Lord Taylor, delivered one of the clearest judgements to date on the concept of 'oppression'. The judgement of their Lordships was highly critical in respect of not only the behaviour and performance of the interviewing police officers, but also the attendant solicitor: 'The officers … were not questioning him so much as shouting at him what they wanted him to say. Short of physical violence, it is hard to conceive of a more hostile and intimidating approach by officers to a suspect. It is impossible to convey on the printed page the pace, force and menace of the officers' delivery' (97 Cr. App. R. 99).

In a further, post-PACE case, *R.* v. *Heron* (1993), the defendant was charged with the abduction and murder of a seven-year-old girl. The officers were accused of deliberately misrepresenting the strength of evidence against Heron (Williamson 1994). Critically, a description of a man seen with the victim shortly before she disappeared was 'overplayed' by the interviewing officers as being that of Heron. The Court also disapproved of the interviewing officers' repeated accusations of Heron's guilt, and their continued persuasive suggestions that it was in his best interests to admit his guilt. During the hearing the defence contested that admissions secured during police interrogations should not be admitted as evidence because they had been obtained by oppression. This was supported by the trial judge, Mr Justice Mitchell, and the prosecution case collapsed. Unlike the case of the 'Cardiff Three' there had been no shouting, hectoring or aggressive behaviour on the part of the police investigators. However, Justice Mitchell stated: 'Oppression may take more insidious forms … which contain two elements, continuity and injustice. Where these elements are combined and are systematically visited upon the suspect there is prima facie evidence of oppression' (*R.* v. *Heron* 1993). Commentators suggest that Mr Justice Mitchell marked the end of an era in British police interrogation by taking a stance against not just interrogation (threat of) violence, but also some kinds of 'softer', persuasive interrogation methods (Clark 1994).

The past three decades have seen a number of studies aimed at shedding academic light on the previously shadowy interaction of police interrogations with suspects of crime. Irving (1980) carried out the first of three observational studies at Brighton police station, in which he observed 60 police interviews with suspects. During later studies in 1986 and 1987, Irving observed a further 68 such interviews in each study. The Irving studies are important in the field of academic research relating to police interviewing of suspects as they allow comparison before and after the introduction of PACE. After his first study Irving (1980) concluded that custodial interrogations (interviews conducted by police with a person who is under arrest) were inherently coercive and that police officers were prone to adopt a number of manipulative and persuasive tactics to secure the desired admission.

Softley (1980) also carried out pre-PACE observational studies of custodial interviews in four police forces. He identified at least one discernible coercive tactic in 60 per cent (n=187) of the interviews he observed. Pointing out contradictions was most common (22 per cent), followed by bluffing or hinting at further evidence (15 per cent), and stressing overwhelming evidence (13 per cent). In only 11 per cent of interviews were efforts made by the police officers to establish any type of rapport with the suspect, although it is not clear if this was only done at the outset of the interview or was present throughout.

Moving on to post-PACE evaluations of police investigative interviewing, it is evident that while there had been some improvement there was no room for complacency. A study by Moston *et al.* (1990) reviewed some 1,067 taped (post-PACE) interviews of suspects from 10 Metropolitan Police stations. This study illuminated the preoccupation of many police interviewers with securing a confession, often at the cost of missing opportunities to secure good corroborative evidence. Although in 42 per cent of the interviews reviewed the suspects had made confessions, this had more to do with the weight of available evidence and the advice of their solicitors than any perceived interviewing skills by the officers. The researchers concluded that the police interviewers involved generally considered that an admission of guilt was regarded as the desired end to the investigative process rather than one element of it, often ideally a starting point. The researchers emphasised the need for training, but stressed that any such training would need to set the interview into the context of the overall investigation and not treat it as an event aimed at gaining confession evidence, set apart from the overall investigation process.

The concerns regarding the quality of police interviewing of suspects, including the apparent lack of supervision of such, were being expressed both within and externally to the police service. In 1990, the Home Office, in partnership with the Association of Chief Police Officers (ACPO), commissioned the extension of a pilot study carried out by Baldwin on the evaluation of videoing police interviews with suspects. This proved to be the first of a number of independent studies carried out on behalf of the newly formed Home Office Police Research Group.

In 1992, Baldwin published the study and concluded that when it came to interviewing the suspects of crime, most police interviewers contrive to make exceedingly heavy weather of it. He exploded the myth that police interviews were lengthy, tense confrontations, reporting that 'most were short and surprisingly amiable discussions in which it seemed the officers were rather tentative in putting the allegations to the suspect' (Baldwin 1992: 331). During the course of his report, Baldwin summed up what he felt to be the thrust of the change needed in police interviewing practices at that time. He highlighted the need for police to adopt the notion that a professional interview is not just the one which elicits a confession, but one in which the suspect is given the unhurried opportunity to state their position without harrying or coercive questions from un-listening officers. Furthermore, any account given by the suspect should be tested with information already possessed by the police with firmness, fairness and integrity. Baldwin concluded his work with several recommendations. He noted that senior members of the police service (at that time) did not accept that the problem existed; therefore, he proposed that they be routinely required to view random selections of interviews and he suggested that training courses should include practical testing of interview skills.

The situation, as it existed, gave the police service the opportunity to establish for the first time a national standard for police interviewing training. A steering group was set up by the Association of Chief Police Officers in the early 1990s in response to the mounting concerns over the ethics and reliability of police methods of interviewing. The terms of reference of the group recognised the need for a standardised training course in which best interviewing practice would be applied equally to the interviewing of victims, witnesses and suspects.

The concept of investigative interviewing was established and was intended to encourage a non-oppressive, non-coercive approach, with the emphasis on information gathering rather than obtaining a confession per se; it presents an opportunity to 'shift the police service from its traditional prosecution orientation and to encourage it to see its task as a search for the truth' (Williamson 1994: 111). In 1992 a one-week national training course in investigative interviewing skills for police officers, supported by two national booklets produced by the Central Policy Training Unit (CPTU), was introduced for a trial period. The *Interviewer's Rule Book* (CPTU 1992a) focused upon the legal requirements of interviewing, while the *Guide to Interviewing* (CPTU 1992b) gave an overview of the wider concepts of good interviewing. These publications were distributed to all police officers in England and Wales in line with the earlier recommendation made by Baldwin (1992).

The Police Research Group commissioned a review of the investigative interviewing training pilot sites by three academics, McGurk, Carr and McGurk (1993). The research covered the design of the course and established a series of performance indicators, which together tested four out of the five stages of an interviewing model which was known by the mnemonic PEACE. The one element excluded from the research was 'evaluation'. The PEACE mnemonic is derived from the following elements: Preparation and Planning, Engage and Explain, Account, Closure and Evaluate. The research concluded that the results from the four pilot sites were encouraging, with the students' knowledge being shown to increase post-course, and this increase being maintained over a six-month period. The skills associated with a successful interview were significantly enhanced in both the simulated and real-life interviews.

The introduction of the investigative interviewing (PEACE) training course

The National Investigative Interviewing Training Course was introduced via the Home Office Circular 7/93, which contained information relating to police interviews with victims and witnesses, as well as suspects, of crime. At the same time, research was being published regarding the supervision of police interviews with suspects (Stockdale 1993). This work was again commissioned by the Police Research Group, and went some way towards addressing concerns raised in earlier works regarding the levels of effective supervision in this area (Baldwin 1993; Baldwin and Bedward 1991; Evans 1993; McConville and Hodgson 1993). The fundamental objective of Stockdale's research was to determine the most practical way of ensuring that police supervisors were operating effective quality control of interviewing. This is a prerequisite if unethical interviewing methods are to be appropriately addressed by internal police sanctions as prescribed under PACE.

Stockdale (1993) suggested that there was considerable room for improvement in the standard of police investigative interviewing. Most officers held a clear idea about what features constituted good interviewing practice, and those indicative of a poor one. However, there was a noted reluctance on the part of the officers to admit to a deficiency in their own performance, even when interviewing caused them a problem. Stockdale (*ibid.*) made recommendations split into two areas of interview supervision: officers responsible for direct supervision and monitoring; and officers responsible for the management of interview quality. The core of her recommendations was the same for both groups, stressing the need for development of appropriate competencies by way of self-learning packages that demanded the active participation of the supervisor in exercises and backed up by locally based training seminars.

Continuing the series of evaluations of police interviewing, Mortimer (1994) researched the attitudes of 150 police officers with regard to evidence contained in five simulated volume crime files of the type they would be expected to investigate. The files were constructed so that they did not contain overwhelming amounts of evidence against the suspects. The officers were asked to review the files and prepare an interview strategy for each suspect, and after reading the papers they were asked to complete a questionnaire. Some 75 per cent believed that the suspects they were about to interview were guilty of the allegations and 66 per cent believed the purpose of the interview was to secure a confession.

In 1996 a revised package, *Investigative Interviewing: A Practical Guide*, was circulated to all police services in England and Wales by the National Crime Faculty at Bramshill police college. This contained practical guidance to interviewing officers and greater emphasis on the importance of the principles of investigative interviewing. Gathering evidence and obtaining information are outlined as the primary goals for the police officer, and the publication reinforces the need to plan and prepare for an interview as well as how to expand, clarify and challenge where appropriate (National Crime Faculty 1996).

In 2001 the National Investigative Interviewing Steering Group commissioned a 'root and branch' evaluation of the PEACE model (Clarke and Milne 2001) that found that interviews with suspects of crime had improved since the implementation of the national investigative interview training, although similar improvements had not been found in the interviewing of witnesses to crimes. In 2002 an updated national interviewing strategy was introduced to police forces within the United Kingdom. This latest evolution was driven by changes in legislation, together with evidence from academic research, and developed the single, or one size fits all, interviewing model into a more comprehensive five-tier strategy. The five-tier strategy and training was designed to equip officers with the interviewing skills appropriate to their role and the type of crimes they would be involved in investigating. Tier one of the training is undertaken while the officer is undergoing recruit training and is designed to give an introduction to the legal requirements and basic strategies for interviewing both witnesses and suspects of crime. Tier two is designed for those officers who are expected to deal with investigations into volume crimes, while tier three is aimed at 'advanced interviewing' for those specialist investigators handling more complex and complicated investigations such as homicide and terrorist activities. Tier four provides training designed for those expected to supervise the conduct of interviews with suspects, while tier five created a role of specialist interview co-ordinators based at a force or regional level.

Emerging findings of attitudes to police interviews of suspects

This research draws upon earlier work carried out by Soukara and Bull (2002) which included the responses of 38 police officers from a rural police force to a number of questions presented in a structured interview by the primary researcher. The current research (Bearchell, in preparation) reflects some of the original questions and involves a structured questionnaire which has been electronically circulated to all police officers receiving tier two investigative interviewing training, between January 2005 and December 2006, in the Metropolitan Police Service (a large urban police force). These dates reflect the initial two years of the current tier two training package and represent some 1,265 contactable officers from whom 741 (59 per cent) anonymous responses were recorded. Furthermore, the questionnaire, with some slight personal descriptive changes, was circulated to 100 members each of the Crown Prosecution Service (CPS), National Offender Management Service (NOMS) and legal representatives, who attend police stations to dispense legal advice to, and are present during the interviewing of, suspects of crime. Response rates of 52 per cent, 44 per cent and 52 per cent respectively were recorded. Six key questions from the questionnaire have been selected as being particularly pertinent to this chapter as they seek to establish the participants' attitudes towards the importance of securing a confession during the police interviewing of a suspect, the ethics of manipulating the psychological environment of the interview to encourage such a confession and whether the requirements of PACE are seen as an inhibitor to such.

The question was posed that the interviewer's individual style of interviewing exerted an influence as to whether the suspect made a confession. A significant number of respondents within the sample groups agreed (or strongly agreed) with this notion; police (42 per cent), CPS (39 per cent) and NOMS (48 per cent). However, the legal representatives sample recorded only 8 per cent of respondents in agreement with this notion, with 69 per cent in disagreement and a further 8 per cent strongly disagreeing. Legal representatives are the only non-police sample group that are present during police interviews of suspects, and their ability to influence their clients' responses and behaviour may account, to some degree, for such results. The CPS sample, who regularly review (at least) summaries of post-event police interviews with suspects, recorded 46 per cent of respondents disagreeing with the notion, with 15 per cent holding mixed views on this particular question.

When the question of how important it was for the interviewing officer to secure a confession from the suspect was posed, some 5 per cent of the police sample signified this was very important, with a further 19 per cent stating that it was important; 50 per cent had mixed views. None of the remaining sample groups felt this was very important or important, with the exception of 10 per cent of the NOMS sample who considered this to be important. Only 26 per cent of the police sample felt that the securing of a confession from a suspect was unimportant (24 per cent) or very unimportant (2 per cent). This would suggest that almost a quarter of police interviewers enter into an interview with a suspect placing a high degree of importance upon the securing of a confession as, at least, part of the outcome and a further half place some importance upon such an outcome within their mixed views response. This is in sharp contrast to the views of the other participant groups in which the majority of respondents stated that the securing of a confession was either unimportant or very unimportant: CPS (8 per cent and 92 per cent), legal representatives (44 per cent and 50 per cent) and NOMS (52 per cent and 27 per cent).

Participants were also asked to consider whether the purpose of the interview with a suspect is to secure the 'facts of the incident', and there were high levels of agreement across the four sample groups. The police sample recorded 27 per cent of respondents strongly agreeing and 46 per cent agreeing with this notion; 16 per cent held mixed views, 10 per cent disagreed, and a further 1 per cent strongly disagreed. In effect, some 27 per cent of the police respondents did not agree (at least in part) that the purpose of the interview with a suspect of crime was to gather 'facts of the incident'. The remaining samples responded entirely in the two 'agreement' categories: CPS (87 per cent strongly agree and 13 per cent agree); legal representatives (73 per cent strongly agree and 23 per cent agree); NOMS (86 per cent strongly agree and 14 per cent agree).

A further item presented participants with the question of whether the securing of corroborative evidence of an incident was more important than securing the suspect's confession to the crime. Strong support for this notion was found across the sample groups with the police sample recording 20 per cent strongly agreeing and 40 per cent agreeing; the CPS sample recorded 90 per cent strongly agreeing and 10 per cent agreeing; the legal representatives sample recorded 71 per cent strongly agreeing and 29 per cent agreeing; while the NOMS sample recorded 91 per cent strongly agreeing and 9 per cent agreeing. This left the police sample with a substantial 35 per cent holding mixed views and a further 5 per cent disagreeing with the notion. These findings suggest that within the police sample (as with the remaining three sample groups) there is strong support for the idea that it is of limited importance to secure a confession within an interview, and that the focus should be the securing of facts of an incident and corroborative evidence. However, there remains a substantial minority of police respondents who hold mixed views, or disagree with this question.

The remaining two questions in this section relate to the perceived effects that PACE has on the ability of the interviewer to secure a confession (Q.5) and the acceptability of the interviewer to (lawfully) manipulate the psychological environment to encourage the suspect to make a confession (Q.6). The police sample for Q.5 recorded responses of 6 per cent strongly agreeing, and 14 per cent agreeing, that PACE has negatively affected their effectiveness within the interview situation, and a further 7 per cent strongly agreeing, with 31 per cent agreeing, that it is acceptable for the interviewer to manipulate the psychological environment to encourage the suspect to make a confession. Some 42 per cent and 34 per cent respectively held mixed views on these points, with 38 per cent either strongly disagreeing or disagreeing with the former and 22 per cent strongly disagreeing and 6 per cent disagreeing with the latter. Interestingly, some 54 per cent of the CPS respondents either strongly agreed (4 per cent) or agreed (50 per cent) that PACE had negatively affected the police interviewers' effectiveness within the suspect interview environment. Similar support for this notion was found within the NOMS sample, with 5 per cent strongly agreeing and 59 per cent agreeing with the notion. A notable difference was found with the responses from the legal representatives sample, where no responses were recorded in either of the agreement categories. However, some 56 per cent disagreed and a further 40 per cent strongly disagreed that PACE had limited police effectiveness in interviewing suspects. The question as to whether it was acceptable for the police interviewer to manipulate the psychological environment of the interview (Q.6) found significantly less support within the non-police sample groups. Some 17 per cent disagreed and 54 per cent strongly disagreed with this within the CPS sample group, 15 per cent disagreed and 83 per cent strongly disagreed within the legal representatives sample group and 30 per cent disagreed and 56 per cent strongly disagreed within the NOMS sample group.

It can be seen from these preliminary findings that there are some areas of agreement across the agencies questioned, but importantly there also seem to be some discrepancies. The aim of the research, of which these findings form a part, is to investigate whether police have moved from a confession focus to an information gathering approach to interviewing suspects. Whilst these findings have not yet been fully analysed, it can be seen that they are suggesting that there are still some police officers who appear to be hanging on to the old confession focus, despite having recently received modern interview training. Fortunately, these officers are in the minority across all of these questions, but in some cases the minority is still quite substantial, suggesting that there is still some way to go to eradicate these long-established police attitudes.

Conclusion

Since the early 1990s much police time, effort and resources have been dedicated towards the professionalising of interviewing of victims and witnesses, and particularly with the suspects of crime. This has been driven partly as a result of previous miscarriages of justice, and the legislative changes that were brought in to protect against such, and partly by the desire within the Police Service to move away from a confession-focused interaction to one which is seen more as an opportunity to gather reliable evidence that contributes to an overall investigation (Williamson 2006). Evidence exists that through the medium of investigative interview training, officers make significant improvements in interviewing style and legal compliance and that these improvements are transferred into the workplace (Clarke and Milne 2001; Griffiths 2008). This, along with a lack of miscarriages of justice arising from unethical interviewing practices within that time, can rightly be seen as a successful return on the investments of the past 15 years. However, whether the training has influenced the attitudes of interviewing officers – in terms of the role and underlying purpose of the police interview with a suspect – is less clear-cut. Whilst Bearchell (in preparation) has found high levels of agreement among police officers that the purpose of a suspect interview is to secure the facts of the incident, a not inconsiderable number, it would seem, feel that such facts are best secured in the form of a confession to the alleged incident.

It therefore seems appropriate to conclude at this time that while there has been notable progress in the practice of police interviewing of suspects, there is still some way to go before a confession focus can be considered to be a concern of the past. The introduction of PACE, the PEACE method of interviewing and the five-tier training system have clearly facilitated a change in most officers' orientation with regard to obtaining a confession and the ethical conduct of interviews. However, while there remain officers who see confession as the most important goal of an interview, there remains the risk of future miscarriages of justice.

References

Baldwin, J. (1992) *Video-taping of Interviews with Suspects – An Evaluation*. London: Home Office.

Baldwin, J. (1993). 'Police interview techniques. Establishing truth or proof?', *British Journal of Criminology,* 33: 325–52.

Baldwin, J. and Bedward, J. (1991) 'Summarising tape recordings of police interviews', *The Criminal Law Review,* 671–79.

Bearchell, J. (2004) *The move from harvesters of confessions, to gatherers of facts: A longitudinal study of the quality of taped interviews with suspects of crime within the Metropolitan Police Service.* Unpublished MA dissertation, Middlesex University.

Bearchell, J. (in preparation) *Have the Police successfully moved from a culture of 'confession focused' suspect interviewing to being 'harvesters of facts', through the use of the Investigative Interview Training Programme?* Unpublished PhD thesis, Middlesex University.

CPTU (1992a) *The Interviewer's Rule Book*. Harrogate: Central Planning and Training Unit.

CPTU (1992b) *A Guide to Interviewing*. Harrogate: Central Planning and Training Unit.

Clark, M. (1994) 'The end of an era', *Police Review,* 29 July: 22–4.

Clarke, C. and Milne, R. (2001) *National Evaluation of PEACE Investigative Interviewing Course*. Police Research Award Scheme Report No. 149. London: Home Office.

Evans, R. (1993) *The Conduct of Police Interviews with Juveniles*. Royal Commission for Criminal Justice Report. London: HMSO.

Fisher, Sir Henry (1977) *Report of an Inquiry by the Hon. Sir Henry Fisher into the circumstances leading to the trial of three persons on charges arising out of the death of Maxwell Confait and the fire at 27 Doggett Road, London, SE6.* London: HMSO.

Gudjonsson, G.H. (1992) *The Psychology of Interrogations, Confessions and Testimony* (1st edn). Chichester: Wiley.

Gudjonsson, G.H. (2003) *The Psychology of Interrogations, Confessions and Testimony. A Handbook.* Chichester: Wiley.

Griffiths, A. (2008) *An examination into the efficiency of police advanced investigative interview training*. Unpublished PhD thesis, University of Portsmouth.

Home Office (1978) *Judges' Rules and Administrative Directions to the Police.* Circular No. 89/1978. London: Home Office.

Home Office (1984) *Police and Criminal Evidence Act 1984.* London: Home Office.

Home Office (1993) *Training for Investigative Interviewing*. Circular No. 7/1993. London: Home Office.

Hunt, G. (2007) *The Rules of Modern Policing: 1973 edition*. London: Bantam Press.

Irving, B. (1980) *Police Interrogation: A case study of current practice*. Royal Commission on Criminal Procedure, Research Study No. 2. London: HMSO.

Irving, B. and McKenzie, I. (1989) *Police Interrogation: the effects of the Police and Criminal Evidence Act, 1984*. London: The Police Foundation.

McConville, M. and Baldwin, J. (1981) *Courts, Prosecutions and Convictions*. Oxford: Oxford University Press.

McConville, M., Sanders, A. and Leng, R. (1991) *The Case for the Prosecution*. London: Routledge.

McConville, M. and Hodgson, J. (1993) *Custodial Legal Advice and the Right to Silence*. London: HMSO.

McGurk, B.J., Carr, M.J. and McGurk, D. (1993) *Investigative Interviewing Courses for Police Officers: an evaluation*. Rep. No. 4. London: Home Office Police Research Group.

Mortimer, A. (1994) 'Asking the right questions', *Policing*, 10: 111–24.

Moston S., Stephenson, G.M. and Williamson, T.M. (1990) *Police Interrogation Styles and Suspect Behaviour.* Report to the Police Requirements Support Unit. Canterbury: University of Kent.

National Crime Faculty (1996) *Investigative Interviewing: A Practical Guide*. London: Home Office.

Philips, Sir Cyril (1981) *Royal Commission on Criminal Procedure*. Report (Cmnd 8092). London: HMSO.

Reiner, R. (1986) *The Politics of the Police*. Oxford: Oxford University Press.

Royal Commission on the Police (1960) London: HMSO.

Shepherd, E. (1988) 'Developing interviewing skills: a career span perspective', in P. Southgate (ed.), *New Directions in Police Training*. London: HMSO.

Smith, D. (1983) *Police and People in London (I): A survey of Londoners*. London: Policy Studies Institute.

Softley, P. (1980) *Police Interrogation. An observational study in four police stations*. Home Office Research Study No. 61. London: HMSO.

Soukara, S. and Bull, R. (2002) 'Police detectives' aims regarding their interviews with suspects: any change at the turn of the millennium', *International Journal of Police Science and Management*, 4: 100–14.

Stockdale, J. (1993) *Management and Supervision of Police Interviews*. Rep. No. 4. London: Home Office.

Walkley, J. (1987) *Police Interrogation. A Handbook for Investigators*. London: Police Review Publication.

Williamson, T. (1994) 'From interrogation to investigative interviewing; strategic problems in police questioning', *Journal of Community and Applied Social Psychology*, 3: 89–99.

Williamson, T. (2006) 'Towards greater professionalism: minimising miscarriages of justice', in T. Williamson (ed.), *Investigative Interviewing: Rights, Research and Regulation*. Cullompton: Willan Publishing.

Chapter 5

The investigation and prosecution of rape

Jacqueline M. Gray and Anna Gekoski

Introduction

The subject of rape is one that regularly brings forward strong, but often conflicting, views from the public, legal professionals, victims and perpetrators. There exist organisations that promote the welfare and rights of victims, as well as those that argue that many men are falsely accused of rape and seek to protect their rights and freedom. The potential sentences for a conviction of rape show that it is considered to be a very serious crime, yet victims' complaints of rape are often not believed unless the rape meets a very narrow range of characteristics, which will be discussed in this chapter. Any attempt to balance these conflicting views and concerns ultimately leads us to a consideration of the overarching issue of how we obtain justice for both complainants and defendants of rape, while serving justice for the wider society.

Feist *et al.* (2007) identified that 13 per cent of the cases 'crimed' resulted in a conviction, which is higher than the rate of around 6 per cent that has previously been found (Home Office 2005a and b). However, the higher figure includes cases where the conviction was for a 'lesser' crime such as sexual assault, and the convictions for rape was 6 per cent, as in the earlier research. Whilst some of the legal professionals interviewed by Temkin and Krahé (2008) considered that the low conviction figure was spurious, as seen above, repeated research findings have found low conviction rates (also see Harris and Grace 1999; Walby and Allen 2004). Another relevant finding, suggesting that justice is not currently being served, is the ongoing low level of reporting of rape to the police, which has been found to be around 15 per cent (Walby and Allen 2004) to 20 per cent (Myhill and Allen 2002). It seems evident that a conviction rate for rape cases reported to the police of less than 6 per cent, or even 13 per cent if lesser convictions are included, cannot represent justice for either complainants or for society as a whole.

The purpose of this chapter is to provide an overview of a number of factors that have been identified as potentially influencing this very low conviction rate, focusing particularly upon the likely impact of commonly held attitudes around rape for complainants. Consideration will also be given to legislative and procedural changes that have been introduced to improve the situation for rape victims and the chapter will conclude with a discussion of some outstanding issues that need to be addressed by researchers and practitioners in the field. While victims of rape are not exclusively women, they still represent by far the greatest proportion of victims of rape and other sexual assaults (Coleman *et al.* 2007). Hence, the focus of this chapter is on female victims, although some of the issues discussed may also be pertinent to male victims of rape and sexual assault.

The legal context

Over the past 30 years or so there have been a number of legislative changes made that have sought to improve the situation for rape victims, both in terms of making their experience of the Criminal Justice System (CJS) less aversive and with the aim of increasing the conviction rate. A comprehensive review of the legislation is not within the remit of this chapter, but there are two particular pieces of legislation that are especially pertinent to the following discussion. Sections 41–43 of the Youth Justice and Criminal Evidence Act 1999 replaced section 2 of the Sexual Offences (Amendment) Act 1976 and sought to limit the use of sexual history evidence by removing judicial discretion in the matter. This Act is intended to exclude the use by the defence of evidence regarding the complainant's sexual history, although there are limited situations set out in the Act under which, following a written application, such an application can be allowed by the judge (see Kelly *et al.* 2006 for a review). The other legislation of particular interest for this chapter is the Sexual Offences Act 2003. This Act sets out four categories of sexual offence including rape and assault by penetration, both of which carry maximum penalties of life imprisonment. Rape now includes acts of penetration of the vagina, anus or mouth with a penis. As such, the gender of the victim is not restricted, but it is a crime for which a penis is necessary to the perpetrator. Assault by penetration covers the same acts but carried out with an object other than a penis, and can therefore be committed by any gender. As noted by Temkin and Ashworth (2004), for both rape and assault by penetration, the prosecution has to prove that the penetration was intentional, that the complainant did not consent, and that there was not a reasonable belief of consent on behalf of the defendant. The 2003 Act also sets out a number of circumstances where consent is presumed to be absent (see Temkin and Ashworth 2004 and Temkin and Krahé 2008 for useful reviews).

The problem of attrition

It has been seen above that the conviction rate for rape is very low, meaning that between an offence occurring and a small number of cases obtaining a conviction, events unfold which lead to many cases being 'lost' from the system. This reduction in cases through the CJS is known as attrition.

Harris and Grace (1999) note that between 1985 and 1997 there was a substantial increase in the number of rapes recorded by the police, and that this reflects an increase in the number of cases reported in that period. However, while the number of reported rapes has increased, the number of convictions has remained fairly static (Kelly *et al.* 2005), suggesting that those extra cases reported are not necessarily obtaining a conviction, particularly if they are of the type traditionally found to be difficult for the CJS.

The majority of rapes do not conform to the traditional or 'real rape' stereotype (i.e. that rape is carried out by a stranger, in an isolated outdoor location, using or threatening violence) (Temkin 2002). In these cases, where it is likely that there has been some degree of acquaintance prior to the assault, the issue of importance to the CJS for determining guilt is not usually whether sexual intercourse occurred, but whether or not the complainant consented. It is thus not something that can be evidenced solely by forensic assessments such as DNA analysis, and there are unlikely to be direct witnesses other than the defendant and complainant, meaning that it is more difficult for the prosecution to prove their case. Whilst the nature of these cases does pose some particular challenges for the CJS, it will be seen that there are a number of factors that may further contribute to the low conviction rate in rape.

Before moving on to consider some underlying reasons for the high level of attrition in rape cases, it is worthwhile highlighting the main stages that have been identified as key points at which cases drop out of the system. The first, and largest, point of attrition occurs because victims decide not to report the assault to the police (Myhill and Allen 2002; Walby and Allen 2004). Of those that are reported to the police a substantial number will be 'no crimed', appropriately or not (Kelly *et al.* 2005). Feist *et al.* (2007) set out the conditions under which cases should be 'no crimed' and identify that 15 per cent of the cases that they examined were 'no crimed' and that 17 per cent of these 'no crimed' cases did not meet the established criteria (3 per cent of the total sample).

If a reported rape is recorded by the police, the next stage of attrition occurs during the investigation, and in the study by Feist *et al.* 70 per cent of the cases they examined were lost between recording and charge, a figure similar to that reported by Kelly *et al.* (2005). Both of these studies found that the most common reasons for a charge not being made were that the victim withdrew the complaint or that there was insufficient evidence. Victims withdraw their complaints for a number of reasons, but often cited are concerns about how the courts will respond to them and fears about the ways in which they will be treated in court and by the wider criminal justice system (Feist *et al.* 2007; Kelly *et al.* 2005).

Feist *et al.* (2007) and Kelly *et al.* (2005) both identify that once a defendant has been charged the rate of attrition decreases, although some cases are discontinued by the CPS and there are a few victim withdrawals. For the relatively small proportion of cases that reach court, around half of the convictions are due to the defendant pleading guilty. If the defendant pleads not guilty, then the verdict is most likely to be an acquittal (Feist *et al.* 2007; Kelly *et al.* 2005). It can be seen that the two recent studies into attrition in rape cases in the UK have shown a fairly consistent pattern of attrition. Of particular note is that although most of the cases where the victims withdraw their complaints occur prior to charge, frequently cited reasons for such withdrawal relate to fear of being disbelieved, fear of the trial and other aspects of the CJS. Thus, beliefs about the later stages of the process seem to be impacting upon decision-making at earlier stages.

Rape myths in court

The term rape myth is used to encompass a range of stereotypical beliefs around rape, its victims and perpetrators. While the exact definition of this set of attitudes has evolved with time, a recent definition that highlights both the content and function of rape myths is:

> Rape myths are descriptive or prescriptive beliefs about rape (i.e., about its causes, context, consequences, perpetrators, victims, and their interaction) that serve to deny, downplay or justify sexual violence that men commit against women. (Gerger *et al.* 2007: 423)

Other authors have also identified the widespread nature of these beliefs (Payne *et al.* 1999), which means that rape victims face the possibility of a sceptical response if they tell friends and family, aside from the potential impact of such beliefs on the operation of the CJS.

The prevalence of rape myth acceptance is clearly demonstrated in a study commissioned by Amnesty International UK (2005) of a representative sample of over 1000 members of the general public, which identified six behaviours that may be demonstrated by a woman that could mean that she was considered to be at least partially to blame if she was raped. These included behaving in a flirtatious manner, wearing revealing clothing or being drunk. If a woman had failed to say 'no' clearly, then 37 per cent of respondents felt that she was either partially or totally to blame for being raped. Perhaps somewhat surprisingly, the situations in which blame was least commonly attributed to the woman were if she had had many sexual partners, or if she was alone in a deserted or dangerous area, with 22 per cent of respondents attributing total or partial blame to the woman. Victim blaming myths are widely supported, and Temkin and Krahé (2008) suggest that these myths, together with those around the 'real rape' stereotype, are particularly influential in decision-making undertaken at various stages of the CJS.

It has been seen that one of the major elements in the high level of attrition in rape cases is that complainants withdraw their support for the case (Feist *et al.* 2007; Kelly *et al.* 2005). Rape victims have long reported that the experience of the trial, particularly cross-examination, is very difficult and upsetting for them (Adler 1987; Lees 1996, 2002), and it remains evident from recent research that concerns about the criminal justice process figure prominently in many victims' decisions to withdraw (Feist *et al.* 2007; Kelly *et al.* 2005). Victims have also specifically identified the likelihood of evidence regarding their sexual history being used against them as a reason for not reporting their victimisation to the police (Kelly *et al.* 2006).

As in all criminal cases in England and Wales, the defendant in a rape trial is presumed to be innocent unless proven by the prosecution to be guilty. It is therefore up to the prosecution to present a case that convinces the jury of his guilt, beyond reasonable doubt. Thus, as noted by Carson and Pakes (2003), the defence will be successful if they can lead the jury to have a reasonable doubt as to the defendant's guilt. In a rape trial, the defence frequently seeks to achieve this by using a variety of means to undermine the credibility of the complainant or to suggest that either she (or he) did consent or that the defendant could have reasonably believed that the complainant consented (Temkin 2002). It is during this cross-examination that the heavy reliance upon rape myths can be seen in practice.

As noted above, the Youth Justice and Criminal Evidence Act 1999 included provisions to restrict the use of sexual history evidence in rape trials, although Kelly *et al.* (2006) found that the use of such evidence, either within or outside the framework of Section 41 applications, is still widespread. This type of evidence is used by defence counsel to undermine the credibility of the complainant and to suggest to the jury that there is a question over whether or not the complainant consented (Kelly *et al.* 2006; Lees 2002). The defence therefore suggests to the jury that if the complainant has consented to sex previously, the claim not to have consented this time is less credible, showing how these two concepts of consent and credibility are intertwined. Although the 1999 Act was intended to restrict the use of sexual history evidence, there are a range of other rape myths that the defence can draw upon to undermine the credibility of the complainant as a witness or to make her seem to be in some way to blame for her victimisation.

A number of common rape myths operate around how a 'genuine' victim of rape is supposed to behave and prescribe the effects that the rape will have upon her. Examples of such rape myths are that she will report the assault to the police immediately, will present with an outward display of emotion, will be traumatised, will have signs of physical violence having been used and will have tried to escape from the assailant (Temkin and Krahé 2008). These characteristics, together with the expectations of the 'real rape' stereotype, serve to provide a severely limited picture of a credible rape. Therefore the defence may seek to show that the victim or the rape does not conform to one or more of these stereotypical expectations to make her complaint seem less credible to the jury. This is despite ample evidence that rape and rape victims frequently do not conform to these stereotypes (e.g. Feist *et al*. 2007; Lees 2002; Myhill and Allen 2002).

The other tactic commonly employed by the defence is to draw upon rape myths that suggest that the victim is in some way to blame for the assault, thereby reducing the culpability of the defendant. The types of myth commonly drawn on to achieve this include those regarding the victim's appearance or behaviour and are used to indicate to the jury that this was causative of the rape and hence that the victim is in some way deserving of what has happened. Lees (2002) provides vivid examples of some of the subject matter of this type of cross-examination, including that the complainant was wearing a short skirt, the nature of her underwear, that she had consumed alcohol or was wearing make-up. Other rape myths of this type include those that blame victims who invite a man into their home, accept a lift or are attacked in an isolated location. Given modern society, it can be seen that many of these myths are predicated upon behavioural norms which, if they were ever valid in the first place, are now clearly outdated (Lees 2002).

Temkin (2000) and Temkin and Krahé (2008) report interview-based studies which provide evidence that as well as using these myths as tools in the defence of rape, there are prosecution and defence barristers, as well as judges, who subscribe to such stereotypical beliefs themselves. This means that, while not a universal problem, there will be cases where those responsible for the conduct of the trial are unlikely to challenge the reliance on rape myths by the defence as they too hold these views.

It can be seen that rape myths are prevalent in society, and that they pervade all aspects of the CJS, from a victim's decision whether to report a rape through to the courtroom. The barrier that these attitudes create for victims of rape in obtaining justice has been recognised in legislation, in procedural changes that have been introduced in the courts and in how police deal with rape victims. The specific changes regarding the use of sexual history evidence brought in by the Youth Justice and Criminal Evidence Act 1999 have been reviewed above, and we now turn to a consideration of other measures that have been introduced to attempt to reduce secondary victimisation throughout the CJS experienced by rape victims.

Secondary victimisation

Rape myths that operate within the CJS and serve to undermine the credibility of the rape complainant not only contribute to attrition by influencing police and prosecutor decision-making and victim withdrawal, but may also lead to the secondary victimisation of the rape complainant. Secondary victimisation can be broadly defined as the inadequate, insensitive or inappropriate responses to, and treatment of, victims of crime by the CJS (Maguire and Pointing 1988). More specifically, in the context of rape, secondary victimisation may be seen as the result of a group of attitudes and behaviours that serve to blame or judge rape complainants, subject them to disbelief or scorn, or deny them assistance. Research has found that such negative experiences with the CJS are a reality for nearly three-quarters (72 per cent) of rape victims (Ullman and Townsend 2007) and may be experienced as a 'second rape' (Madigan and Gamble 1991). This can have a significant impact on victims' subsequent recovery, magnifying feelings of shame, disempowerment and guilt, and leading to an increase in post-traumatic stress disorder (PTSD) symptoms (Orth and Maercker 2004). In recognition of the phenomenon of secondary victimisation and in an attempt to curtail attrition rates and boost convictions, there have been numerous changes within the CJS over recent years designed to assist the rape victim through the reporting, investigation and prosecution process. The main changes that have been implemented over the past 10 years by three criminal justice agencies – the police, the medical system, and the courts – will be briefly considered here.

Public criticism of the way in which the police handled rape cases was sparked in 1982 after the BBC filmed Thames Valley police officers harshly interrogating a rape victim as if she were the perpetrator, rather than victim, of a crime. Academic research in the 1980s and 1990s reaffirmed the typicality of this incident, with police officers voicing concerns about false reporting, and rape victims complaining of police officers displaying sceptical, hostile, unsympathetic and disbelieving attitudes (for example, see Chambers and Millar 1983; Blair 1985; Victim Support 1996; Temkin 1997, 1999). Other complaints highlighted by these studies included rape victims being dealt with by male officers, not being provided with sufficient information about their case, poor facilities in police stations and inadequate investigation. In the worst instances, victims' dealings with the police could be so distressing as to replicate 'the violation felt in the rape itself' (Jordon 2001: 679).

In a bid to make the experience of reporting rape to the police easier and to curtail attrition rates at this stage of proceedings, in 2001 the Metropolitan Police Service (MPS) set up Operation Sapphire, a new initiative to deal with rape in London. As part of their new duty of care to rape victims, the MPS pledged that:

> If you have been sexually assaulted, whoever you are, we promise to: be kind, sensitive and polite; explain everything so you can be sure you understand what is happening; and make you as comfortable as possible. (www.met.police.uk/sapphire)

Victims' initial statements are now taken in dedicated private suites at police stations by specially trained 'SOIT' officers (who have completed the Sexual Offences Investigative Techniques course), who are available 24 hours a day in every London borough. In addition to taking a statement, these officers can arrange, and accompany a victim to, a medical and forensic examination, and explain the case to the doctor to avoid the victim having to relive the details of the rape again. After the initial reporting phase, victims are then guaranteed a specially trained chaperone who can, if the victim wishes, contact a support group on their behalf, make hospital appointments, talk to employers and discuss future personal safety arrangements. The chaperone should also keep them up to date with what is happening in the investigation, including information regarding court appearances, delays, arrangements for bail, the results of the court case, and the appeals process.

Exemplary as these guidelines might appear, as Temkin (1999) noted, inadequate police responses to rape are rarely about the presence or absence of policy and standards of good practice, but are more often attributable to police culture in general, and individual officers' attitudes towards women and rape specifically. Thus, while Operation Sapphire's duty of care to rape victims is certainly admirable in intention, in the absence of any formal evaluation of the project, it still remains to be seen whether such guidelines are being adequately and consistently implemented at a grass-roots level.

The medical system is the second area in which changes have been implemented to reduce secondary victimisation. Concern about the way in which rape victims were treated, specifically by police surgeons or forensic medical examiners (FMEs), first began to emerge in the 1970s and early 1980s in response to criticism from women's groups and emerging academic research (Temkin 1996). Complaints included: police surgeons not being sufficiently skilled in performing examinations, potentially leading to the loss of vital forensic evidence; examinations being conducted in police stations; the absence or inadequacy of advice concerning pregnancy and sexually transmitted infections (STIs); examinations being carried out by male doctors; unfamiliarity with Rape Trauma Syndrome and the effects of rape; doctors behaving in a hostile and unsympathetic manner; and doctors displaying disbelieving attitudes (see, for example, Chambers and Millar 1983; Corbett 1987; Lees and Gregory 1993; Temkin 1996).

In response to such criticisms, a number of Sexual Assault Referral Centres (SARCs) were set up across the UK. After referral by the police or through self-referral in the aftermath of rape, SARCs offer victims forensic and medical examinations conducted by a team of specially trained female examiners, counselling, screening for sexually transmitted infections (STIs) including HIV, prescription of post-coital contraception and pregnancy testing, and 24-hour telephone information and support (Lovett *et al.* 2004). The first UK SARC was established in Manchester in 1986, two further SARCs in Northumbria and West Yorkshire were set up in the 1990s and, by 2009, there were 28 centres nationwide, with a government pledge to have one within every police area by 2011 (www.equalities.gov.uk/media/press_releases/ per centC2 per centA316m_for_rape_charities.aspx, accessed December 2009).

In an attempt to discover whether rape victims were experiencing increased satisfaction regarding their medical care in the wake of these changes, a large-scale study was commissioned by the Home Office which compared areas with SARCs to those without, tracking over 3,000 cases of rape prospectively through the CJS (Lovett *et al.* 2004). Although there were still problems reported, such as long delays in seeing a doctor, the study found the greatest satisfaction levels for areas with integrated SARCs, where medical examinations were carried out on the premises rather than outsourced. At integrated SARCs it was found that a greater proportion of women had forensic examinations at all, female medical examiners were the norm, victims were afforded more control over the proceedings, and doctors were more likely to treat the victim with care and sensitivity during the examination. The study concludes by suggesting a model for an 'ideal' SARC, a 'gold standard' that all centres should aspire to, and emphasises the need to establish minimum standards of training for FMEs and to develop national standards for the examinations themselves.

Most research on secondary victimisation and rape concentrates on the last stage of the legal process, the courts, where there have been various important changes made recently. The rape victim, it has been argued, is in a unique position in an adversarial system in that she is frequently treated with as much suspicion, indeed perhaps more, than the defendant (see, for example, Adler 1987; Temkin 1987; Lees 1993). Made to relive every detail of her ordeal in front of a courtroom of strangers and the defendant himself, ruthlessly cross-examined about her sexual history, behaviour and personality, and subjected to suggestions that she was to blame for her own fate, she may be left feeling a victim of 'judicial rape' (Lees 1993).

In order to assist rape victims and other vulnerable and intimidated witnesses (VIWs)[1] to give best evidence, in 1998 the Home Office report *Speaking Up for Justice* made 78 recommendations. These included court visits prior to the trial to familiarise the witness with the courtroom and procedures, liaison officers, pagers, separate waiting areas for witnesses, and having a support person in court. Other recommendations, referred to as 'special measures', requiring legislative action, were implemented in the Youth Justice and Criminal Evidence Act (YJCEA) 1999. In addition to curtailing the circumstances in which sexual history evidence can be used and banning the cross-examination of a rape complainant by the defendant, the YJCEA made other provisions available to adult victims of sexual offences including screens to shield the witness from the defendant, evidence given by live CCTV link, clearing the public gallery, and the removal of wigs and gowns. On the basis of recommendations made in the consultation paper *Convicting Rapists and Protecting Victims* (2006), in 2007 the government recommended that these special measures be further enhanced to include video-recorded evidence-in-chief[2] to be automatically available and allowing expert evidence on the psychological impact of rape.

Early evidence to evaluate the use of special measures introduced in the YJCEA has been generally positive (e.g. Hamlyn *et al.* 2004; Burton *et al.* 2006; Kebbell *et al.* 2007). In a VIW satisfaction survey, Hamlyn *et al.* (2004) found that the vast majority of VIWs who used special measures rated them very highly. Also, a third of VIWs who used any such measure (and 44 per cent of victims of sexual offences in particular) would not have been willing or able to give evidence in the absence of that measure. Overall, VIWs who used special measures were more likely to be generally satisfied with the CJS than those who did not, were less likely to experience anxiety, and were less upset during cross-examination.

However, research has found that there is still 'a huge unmet need' for special measures among VIWs (Burton *et al.* 2006: 69), with only 32 per cent of such witnesses being consulted about their use, due to incorrect classifications, and a lack of information and resources (Hamlyn *et al.* 2004). Given the overwhelmingly positive feedback from VIWs who have utilised special measures, such shortcomings should have been urgently addressed so that their use could be extended to all victims of rape and other VIWs who could benefit from them. (Please see Chapter 10 for further consideration of arrangements for VIWs).

In the past decade, various changes have been made to assist the rape victim through the emotionally fraught process of reporting, investigation and prosecution within the CJS, including the setting up of new police initiatives, sexual assault centres, and changes in the law. Although these are certainly necessary and welcome changes, as long as the more fundamental problem of stereotypical societal attitudes towards women and rape remains, the secondary victimisation of the rape victim is likely to continue.

The problem with consent

There have been a number of changes to the legislation surrounding rape since the Sexual Offences Act 1956, but the aspect of legislation that is of particular interest in the present section of this chapter is the issue of consent, and how this is understood by a jury. As we have seen, in the early 1970s public concern was growing about the way in which rape was investigated and prosecuted. This disquiet reached a peak with the House of Lords ruling in *DPP* v. *Morgan* (1976) that if a defendant honestly, but mistakenly, believed that the victim consented to sexual intercourse that belief did not have to be reasonable.[3] This ruling was widely held as a 'Rapist's Charter' by the public (Adler 1987) and it had been the initial, lower courts' rulings in these trials that prompted the then Home Secretary to appoint an Advisory Group on the Law of Rape (as noted by Lees 2002). Published in 1975, the Heilbron Report endorsed the decisions from the lower courts regarding the Morgan case, but expressed grave concerns about the experience of the rape victim in the legal system and made several recommendations, among which was the need to curtail sexual history evidence and provide a statutory definition of rape.

The Heilbron Report paved the way for the Sexual Offences (Amendment) Act 1976, which was the first legislation to put the notion of consent, as opposed to force, at the heart of rape law.

However, while this was a step forward, there was no indication of how consent should be defined, an issue that was partially addressed by the Criminal Justice and Public Order Act 1994, which ruled that for a rape to have occurred there must have been sexual intercourse without consent, and the defendant must have known that the victim was not consenting or have been reckless as to consent (see Temkin 2002). Further clarifications were made in the Sexual Offences Act 2003, which finally overturned the Morgan ruling and made important provisions regarding the issue of consent. The Act provides a statutory definition of consent in which a person 'agrees by choice, and has the freedom and capacity to make that choice', and a test of reasonable belief in consent. The Act rules that: 'Person A is guilty of rape if they have acted intentionally; if person B has not consented; and if person A does not reasonably believe that person B consented.' The reasonableness of belief takes into account all of the circumstances of the case, which includes, but is not limited to, whether the defendant took measures to establish consent (Temkin and Krahé 2008).

Whilst the judgement of reasonableness has to take into consideration 'all the circumstances', this is still largely subjective, although there also seems to be an element of objectivity as the very notion of 'reasonable' suggests an element of comparison with common understanding. The legal literature shows the complexity of the definitional, evidential and practical consequences of the legislation pertaining to consent (e.g. McEwan 2005, 2006; Temkin and Ashworth 2004). However, a question arising from this legislation of particular interest to psychologists is what circumstances would be considered by the public to indicate that a person's belief in sexual consent was reasonable.

Given the prevalence of rape myths, it is likely that the judgement of reasonableness will be based upon these commonly held stereotypes, with the associated bias against the complainant (Temkin and Ashworth 2004). However, how the reasonableness or otherwise of a defendant's belief in consent should be established is not clear. It is therefore pertinent to consider briefly previous research that has sought to identify how sexual consent is conveyed, to identify the sorts of notion that may be drawn upon to determine whether belief in consent is reasonable. Beres (2007) highlights the complexity of the notion of consent, pointing to the inconsistent definitions in the literature, and that authors frequently rely on a shared understanding that implies that 'we know consensual sex when we see it'.

Research has repeatedly shown that consent is conveyed through a mixture of verbal and non-verbal cues, and that these may be direct or indirect in nature (Beres 2007; Beres *et al.* 2004; Hall 1998; Hickman and Muehlenhard 1999). It has also been noted that sexual activity frequently proceeds as a consensual process, without spoken consent, unless either party says or otherwise indicates that they are withdrawing consent, although explicit consent is more likely for sexual intercourse and oral sex (Hall 1998). Hickman and Muehlenhard (1999) note that the most frequent way consent is communicated is by not resisting, again highlighting the often implicit nature of consent.

It has been suggested that rape is the result of extreme miscommunication between the sexes (Tannen 1990), but subsequent research has highlighted the inadequacy of this approach (O'Byrne *et al.* 2006). More recent research has shown that both men and women do share understandings of how consent to sex is refused that does not generally entail a direct refusal in the oft-prescribed form of 'just saying no'. Kitzinger and Frith (1999) highlight that in social interactions of many types, there are normative ways of refusing that actually make it difficult to actually say 'no'. Whilst Kitzinger and Frith's research was based on a female sample, O'Byrne *et al.* (2006) found that their male participants were well aware of the socially normative ways in which refusals are carried out. Examples of these normative forms of refusal can be seen in the common excuses such as a prior arrangement or illness that may be given to refuse any unwanted invitation. Whatever the situation, sexual or not, it is rare that we actually 'just say no'.

Whilst the above research does provide some understanding of how sexual relationships are negotiated, and the means by which lack of consent might be indicated and understood, it does not provide evidence regarding how a third party might judge such an interaction. If jurors or judges are expected to determine whether the defendant's belief in consent was reasonable, there is a need to investigate what complainant, event and defendant characteristics, and combinations thereof, are likely to lead to belief in consent being considered to be reasonable. The first author of this chapter is currently undertaking research to shed light on what factors would be considered in such a decision, which are most probative, and what a complainant would have to have done to be widely understood as having not consented.

Summary and conclusions

It has been seen that despite a number of legislative changes and substantial amounts of academic research, the conviction rate for rape and serious sexual assault remains alarmingly low. There have been a variety of measures taken across the CJS to improve the experience of rape complainants. Although some of these interventions, such as measures in court for VIWs and the introduction of SARCs, have been evaluated positively by users, there remains a particularly high level of attrition in the prosecution of these offences.

Studies that have examined attrition in rape cases (e.g. Feist *et al.* 2007; Myhill and Allen 2002; Walby and Allen 2004) have identified that a common reason for complainants withdrawing their support from a case is due to fear of the later stages of the process, notably the trial. Changes have been made to the legal definition of rape and restrictions have been introduced to limit the use of sexual history evidence in court, with the intention of closing the 'justice gap' in rape cases. However, it appears that there are still plenty of opportunities for prejudicial beliefs to influence the conduct of rape trials and impact upon decision-making in the courts. Recent proposals to allow expert testimony regarding the reactions of rape victims after an assault may be of some assistance in dispelling some rape myths, but still do not address the host of other rape myths that can be used to undermine the complainant throughout the trial.

The final question addressed in this chapter relates to the issue of consent as it has been framed in the 2003 Sexual Offences Act, particularly whether the defendant's belief in consent was reasonable. That a decision has to be made regarding whether or not the defendant's belief was reasonable implies that there is some shared understanding of what constitutes a reasonable belief, or at least that such a shared understanding can be negotiated. However, it remains unclear whether there is indeed such a shared understanding, and if there is, the nature of what constitutes a reasonable belief in consent.

What emerges from the wealth of literature in this area is that there has been a long-term concern about the ways in which rape is investigated and prosecuted. Whilst successive governments have taken steps to improve the lot of rape complainants it is evident that there still remains a significant problem for victims of rape in obtaining justice. More research is clearly required to disentangle some of the complex assumptions that are brought into rape trials and to inform government policy. However, it also seems that it will be necessary to better engage the public, the legal profession and government in this debate, as well as to ensure the continuing involvement of academics if justice is to be done for victims of rape and society as a whole.

Notes

1 Other VIWs include children under the age of 17, those with physical or mental disabilities and those fearing intimidation.
2 Currently automatically available for witnesses under the age of 17.
3 The accused had been invited to the complainant's house by her husband, who had told them that his wife would enjoy sex with all of them, no matter how much she struggled and protested.

References

Adler, Z. (1987) *Rape on Trial*. London: Routledge and Kegan Paul.

Amnesty International UK (2005) *Sexual Assault Research Summary Report*. Amnesty International. Available from: www.amnesty.org.uk/uploads/documents/doc_16619.doc (accessed 9th December 2008).

Beres, M.A. (2007) ' "Spontaneous" sexual consent: An analysis of sexual consent literature', *Feminism and Psychology*, 17: 93–108.

Beres, M.A., Herold, E. and Maitland, S.B. (2004) 'Sexual consent behaviours in same-sex relationships', *Archives of Sexual Behavior*, 33: 475–86.

Blair, I. (1985) *Investigating Rape: A New Approach for Police*. London: Croom Helm.

Burt, M.R. (1980) 'Cultural myths and supports for rape', *Journal of Personality and Social Psychology*, 38: 217–30.

Burton. M., Evans, R. and Sanders, A. (2006) *Are Special Measures for Vulnerable and Intimidated Witnesses Working? Evidence from the criminal justice agencies*. Home Office Online Report 01/06. Available at: www.homeoffice.gov.uk/rds/pdfs06/rdsolr0106.pdf (accessed 23rd September 2008).

Carson, D. and Pakes, F. (2003) 'Advocacy: Getting the answers you want', in D. Carson and R. Bull (eds), *Handbook of Psychology in Legal Contexts* (2nd edn). Chichester: Wiley.

Chambers, G. and Millar, A. (1983) *Investigating Rape*. Edinburgh: HMSO.

Coleman, K., Jansson, K., Kaiza, P. and Beed, E. (2007) *Homicides, Firearm Offences and Intimate Violence 2005/2006*. Home Office Statistical Bulletin 02/07. London: Home Office. Available at: http://rds.homeoffice.gov.uk/rds/pdfs07/hos60207.pdf (accessed 9th December 2008).

Corbett, C. (1987) 'Victim support services to victims of serious sexual assault', *Police Surgeon*, 32: 6–16.

Cowan, G. and Quinton, W.J. (1997) 'Cognitive style and attitudinal correlates of the perceived causes of rape scale', *Psychology of Women Quarterly,* 21: 227–45.

Feist, A., Ashe, J., Lawrence, J., McPhee, D. and Wilson, R. (2007) *Investigating and Detecting Recorded Offences of Rape.* Home Office Online Report 18/07. London: Home Office. Available at http://rds.homeoffice.gov.uk/rds/pdfs07/rdsols1807.pdf (accessed 9th December 2008).

Gerger, H., Kley, H., Bohner, G. and Siebler, F. (2007) 'The acceptance of modern myths about sexual aggression scale: development and validation in German and English', *Aggressive Behaviour,* 33: 422–40.

Hall, D.S. (1998) 'Consent for sexual behaviour in a college student population', *Electronic Journal of Human Sexuality, 1.* Accessed 1 September 2008 from www.ejhs.org/volume1/consent1/htm

Hamlyn, B., Phelps, A., Turtle, J. and Sattar, G. (2004) *Are Special Measures Working? Evidence from surveys of vulnerable and intimidated witnesses.* Home Office Research Study 283. Available at: www.homeoffice.gov.uk/rds/pdfs04/hors283.pdf (accessed 23rd September 2008).

Harris, J. and Grace, S. (1999) *A Question of Evidence? Investigating and Prosecuting Rape in the 1990s.* Home Office Research Study 196. London: Home Office. Available at http://rds.homeoffice.gov.uk/rds/pdfs/hors196.pdf

Hickman, S.E. and Muehlenhard, C.L. (1999) ' "By the semi-mystical appearance of a condom": How young women and men communicate sexual consent in heterosexual situations', *The Journal of Sex Research,* 36: 258–72.

Home Office (1998) *Speaking Up For Justice.* Report of the Interdepartmental Working Group on the treatment of Vulnerable and Intimidated Witnesses in the Criminal Justice System. Available at: www.homeoffice.gov.uk/documents/sufj.pdf?version=1 (accessed 23rd September 2008).

Home Office (2005a) *Criminal Statistics, England and Wales 2004.* Home Office Statistical Bulletin 19. London: Home Office. 105 (2nd edn). Available at http://rds.homeoffice.gov.uk/rds/pdfs05/hos61905.pdf (accessed 9th December 2008).

Home Office (2005b) *Crime in England and Wales 2004/5.* Home Office Statistical Bulletin 11/05. London: Home Office. Available at http://rds.homeoffice.gov.uk/rds/pdfs05/hos61105.pdf (accessed 9th December 2008).

Home Office (2006) *Convicting Rapists and Protecting Victims – Justice for Victims of Rape.* Available at: www.homeoffice.gov.uk/documents/cons-290306-justice-rape-victims (accessed 23rd September 2008).

Jordon, J. (2001) 'Worlds apart? women, rape and the police reporting process', *The British Journal of Criminology,* 41: 679–706.

Kebbell, M., O'Kelly, C. and Gilchrist, E. (2007) 'Rape victims' experiences of giving evidence in English courts', *Psychiatry, Psychology and Law,* 14 (1): 111–19.

Kelly, L., Lovett, J. and Regan, L. (2005) *A Gap or a Chasm? Attrition in Reported Rape Cases.* Home Office Research Study 293. London: Home Office. Available at http://rds.homeoffice.gov.uk/rds/pdfs05/hors293.pdf (accessed 9th December 2008).

Kelly, L., Temkin, J. and Griffiths, S. (2006) *Section 41: An Evaluation of New Legislation Limiting Sexual History Evidence in Rape Trials.* Home Office Online Report 20/06. London: Home Office. Available at http://rds.homeoffice.gov.uk/rds/pdfs06/rdsolr2006.pdf (accessed 9th December 2008).

Kitzinger, C. and Frith, H. (1999) 'Just say no? The use of Conversation Analysis in developing a feminist perspective on sexual refusal', *Discourse and Society*, 10: 293–316.

Lees, S. (1993) 'Judicial rape', *Women's Studies International Forum*, 16 (1): 11–36.

Lees, S. (1996) *Carnal Knowledge: Rape on Trial.* London: Hamish Hamilton.

Lees, S. (2002) *Carnal Knowledge: Rape on Trial* (revised edn). London: The Women's Press.

Lees, S. and Gregory, J. (1993) *Rape and Sexual Assault: a study of attrition.* London: Islington Council Police and Crime Prevention Unit.

Lovett, J., Regan, L. and Kelly, L. (2004) *Sexual Assault Referral Centres: developing good practice and maximising potential.* Home Office Research Study 285. London: Home Office. Available at http://rds.homeoffice.gov.uk/rds/pdfs04 hors/285.pdf (accessed 23rd September 2008).

Madigan, L. and Gamble, N. (1991) *The Second Rape: society's continued betrayal of the victim.* New York: Lexington Books.

Maguire, M. and Pointing, J. (eds) (1988) *Victims of Crime: a new deal?* Milton Keynes: Open University Press.

McEwan, J. (2005) 'Proving consent in sexual cases: legislative change and cultural evolution', *International Journal of Evidence and Proof*, 9: 1–28.

McEwan, J. (2006) ' "I thought she consented": defeat of the rape shield or the defence that shall not run?', *Criminal Law Review, November*: 969–80.

Metropolitan Police. *Project Sapphire: Our Duty of Care.* Available at: www.met.police.uk/sapphire/advice_booklet_en.htm (accessed 23rd September 2008).

Myhill, A. and Allen, J. (2002) *Rape and Sexual Assault of Women: the Extent and Nature of the Problem.* Home Office Research Study 237. London: Home Office. Available at http://rds.homeoffice.gov.uk/rds/pdfs2/hors237.pdf (accessed 9th December 2008).

O'Byrne, R., Rapley, M. and Hansen, S. (2006). ' "You couldn't say 'no', could you?" Young men's understanding of sexual refusal', *Feminism and Psychology*, 16: 133–54.

Orth, U. and Maercker, A. (2004) 'Do trials of perpetrators retraumatize victims?', *Journal of interpersonal Violence*, 19: 212–27.

Payne, D.L., Lonsway, K.A. and Fitzgerald, L.F. (1999) 'Rape myth acceptance: exploration of its structure and its measurement using the Illinois Rape Myth Acceptance Scale', *Journal of Research in Personality*, 33: 27–68.

Peterson, Z.D. and Muehlenhard, C.L. (2004) 'Was it rape? The function of women's rape myth acceptance and definitions of sex in labelling their own experiences', *Sex Roles*, 51: 129–44.

Sexual Offences Act 2003. Available online at: www.opsi.gov.uk/Acts/acts2003/ukpga_20030042_en_1

Sexual Offences (Amendment) Act 1976. Available online at: www.opsi.gov.uk/RevisedStatutes/Acts/ukpga/1976/cukpga_19760082_en_1

Tannen, D. (1990) *You Just Don't Understand: Women and Men in Conversation*. New York: Ballantine Books.

Temkin, J. (1987) *Rape and the Legal Process*. London: Sweet and Maxwell.

Temkin, J. (1996) 'Doctors, rape and criminal justice', *Howard Journal of Criminal Justice*, 35: 1–20.

Temkin, J. (1997). 'Plus ça change?: reporting rape in the 1990s', *British Journal of Criminology*, 37: 507–28.

Temkin, J. (1999) 'Reporting rape in London: a qualitative study', *Howard Journal of Criminal Justice*, 38 (1): 17–41.

Temkin, J. (2000) 'Prosecuting and defending rape: Perspectives from the bar', *Journal of Law and Society*, 27: 219–48.

Temkin, J. (2002) *Rape and the Legal Process* (2nd edn). Oxford: Oxford University Press.

Temkin, J. and Ashworth, A. (2004) 'The Sexual Offences Act 2003: (1) Rape, sexual assaults and the problem of consent', *Criminal Law Review*, May: 328–46.

Temkin, J and Krahé, B. (2008) *Sexual Assault and the Justice Gap: A Question of Attitude*. Oxford: Hart Publishing.

Ullman, S. and Townsend, S. (2007) 'Barriers to working with sexual assault survivors: a qualitative study of rape crisis centre workers', *Violence Against Women*, 13 (4): 412–43.

Victim Support (1996) *Women, Rape and the Criminal Justice System*. London: Victim Support.

Walby, S. and Allen, J. (2004) *Domestic violence, sexual assault and stalking: findings from the British Crime Survey*. Home Office Research Study 276. London: Home Office. Available at http://rds.homeoffice.gov.uk/rds/pdfs04/hors276.pdf (accessed 9th December 2008).

Youth Justice and Criminal Evidence Act 1999. Available online at: www.opsi.gov.uk/acts/acts1999/19990023.htm

Section 2

Testimony and Evidence

This section moves from investigation and prosecution of crime to consider specific factors that can influence the prosecution of crime. In these chapters, it is possible to see more areas where academic research in general, and psychology in particular, have made substantial contributions to our understanding of processes involved in delivering justice, such as decision-making, stereotyping, memory and cognitive processing. In addition to these issues, this section also considers the effectiveness of particular practices that have been instituted to enhance the quality of evidence that is obtained from witnesses. Thus, the aim of this section is to highlight key areas of debate, developments in practice and to identify areas where evidence is still needed.

This section focuses on the processes that occur in the courts with chapters that address issues relevant to both magistrates' courts and Crown courts. We start with a review from Blake McKimmie and Barbara Masser of the psychological literature regarding the effects of gender in the courtroom, particularly the consequences of cognitive shortcuts commonly employed by trial participants. Continuing the theme of decision-making, Pamela Ormerod and Joanna R. Adler address the decisions made by magistrates in the UK. The second part of this section moves on to issues specific to witnesses in court, starting with an overview of how best to elicit eyewitness testimony, written by Mark R. Kebbell and Elizabeth A. Gilchrist. We then move to a consideration of the specific issues pertaining to the ageing eyewitness from Rachel Wilcock. The section ends with an evaluation by Graham M. Davies of 'special measures', brought into courts to protect vulnerable and intimidated witnesses.

Chapter 6

The effect of gender in the courtroom

Blake M. McKimmie and Barbara M. Masser

Overview

In a perfect legal system, determinations of guilt or not should be made purely on the basis of the facts of the case. However, a substantial body of research has identified a number of extra-legal factors that might be influential in the courtroom. These include, but are not limited to, pre-trial publicity (Ogloff and Vidmar 1994) and the attractiveness, age, gender and ethnicity of the various people involved in the case (see, for examples, Bodenhausen 1990; Dean *et al.* 2000; Gerdes *et al.* 1988; Haegerich and Bottoms 2000; McKimmie *et al.* 2004). Such factors are not legally relevant to the determination of guilt and, as such, there is a desire to reduce their impact as they arguably serve to undermine the fairness of any trial or hearing (but see Franklin and Fearn 2008). While extra-legal factors in general have been the subject of much research attention, and the influence of many individual factors is well documented, in this chapter we focus specifically on the influence of gender in the courtroom.

While the importance of gender in legal settings has been frequently noted (a search of the literature reveals well over 200 papers related to gender in legal settings) and has been the focus of special issues of psychology and law journals (e.g. *Law and Human Behavior*; see Goodman-Delahunty 1998 as an example), we contend that in the courtroom the potential breadth of the influence of gender may be easy to overlook. Gender is a primary basis for categorisation (Mackie *et al.* 1996) and, as such, this categorisation (and associated stereotypes) may be influential for a variety of reasons in a courtroom setting. Further, legally irrelevant stereotypic beliefs about men and women may be erroneously interpreted as reflecting real differences between the genders (Hall and Carter 1999). In this chapter, we aim to look at the possible influence of gender and such stereotypes in the context of pre-trial decisions, jury trials and sentencing hearings.

Gender stereotypes

Gender stereotypes are sets of beliefs associated with males or females that do not necessarily accurately reflect the features of, or differences between, these two categories. For example, women are stereotypically seen as being more caring and nurturing, and less physically aggressive than men (Eagly and Steffen 1986). A feature of stereotypes is that these sets of beliefs are ascribed to the category as a whole, and individuals seen as belonging to that category are seen as being similar in terms of stereotypic dimensions (Doise *et al.* 1978; Tajfel *et al.* 1964). Perceivers tend to maintain stereotypes because they offer one way in which to simplify the social world (Hogg and Abrams 1988), allowing a large amount of information to be dealt with on a day-to-day basis. In the courtroom context, researchers have repeatedly demonstrated that people draw on their existing knowledge, or cognitive schemas, in the form of prototypes (e.g. cognitive representations of the typical features present in a particular crime) and stereotypes to make sense of the information presented to them (e.g. Finkel and Groscup 1997; Jones and Kaplan 2003; Pennington and Hastie 1992; Smith 1991; Wiener *et al.* 2002).

There are a number of reasons why, and circumstances under which, stereotypes might have such an influence. The first of these is related to the ability of stereotypes to allow for the rapid simplification of complex information. Dual process models of persuasion, such as the elaboration likelihood model (Petty and Cacioppo 1986) and the heuristic-systematic model (Chaiken 1980), suggest that cues such as stereotypes will have the greatest influence when perceivers do not have the ability or motivation to process complex information. Ability may be influenced by the complexity, amount or ambiguity of the information, whereas motivation can be influenced by personal involvement with the information (Petty and Cacioppo 1986). Given that it is not uncommon for jury trials to last several days or weeks, it is understandable that the amount of information presented at trial may be somewhat overwhelming. Further, as the nature of the adversarial legal system involves two sides (the defence and prosecution) often arguing for conflicting versions of reality, jurors are frequently asked to make sense of ambiguous information. This, and the addition of complex information in the form of expert testimony or legal rules, may make it difficult for jurors to engage in effortful consideration of all of the trial information, regardless of their level of motivation.

Stereotypes may also be influential when information is limited (Hamilton and Sherman 1996), when concepts are unfamiliar (Fiske and Taylor 1991; see also Pennington and Hastie 1992) or when the content of the stereotype is endorsed (i.e. agreed with), and thus potentially chronically accessible (e.g. Stangor *et al.* 1992), rather than just known. Further, as stereotypes serve a sense-making purpose (e.g. Pennington and Hastie 1992), according to the heuristic-systematic model they may be influential in a courtroom setting even when extensive information processing occurs. A final way in which stereotypes might influence perceptions in the courtroom is by acting as a filter for the encoding and decoding of information. There is a tendency for stereotype-congruent information to be preferentially encoded and recalled (Cohen 1981), although clearly counter-stereotypical information also appears to be especially favoured in recall as it receives a greater amount of attention (Stern *et al.* 1984).

Within this chapter, we consider a range of possible ways in which gender stereotypes might be influential in the courtroom. While there is evidence that women are less likely to be prosecuted for some types of offences and so are less likely than men to reach the courtroom (Bernstein *et al.* 1977; Krohn *et al.* 1983; Spohn *et al.* 1987; Wilczynski 1997; cf. Albonetti 1992; Bishop and Frazier 1984), we focus on the courtroom as this is where most of the research has been conducted. While we emphasise the various ways in which gender may be influential in jury trials, it is also worth considering the impact of gender on pre-trial hearings as well as sentencing hearings, which are held if a defendant is convicted or enters a guilty plea.

Pre-trial hearings

Pre-trial hearings are often heard in lower courts in some jurisdictions (e.g. the magistrates' court in the United Kingdom, Australia, or some parts of the USA) or by grand jury (in some jurisdictions in the USA) with the purpose of deciding whether there is sufficient evidence to commit a defendant to stand trial. Hearings may also be held once the defendant is so committed, to determine whether the defendant should be remanded in custody or let out on bail. At both of these points the gender of the defendant may be influential, and this influence may have far-reaching consequences in the criminal justice process. For example, Katz and Spohn (1995) explicitly note the well-documented relationship between pre-trial decisions with regard to bail and detention and the likelihood of conviction at trial and the severity of the sentence imposed if the defendant is found guilty. Defendants who are detained pre-trial are more likely to be convicted and more likely to receive a harsher sentence (Farrall and Swigert 1986; Wheeler and Wheeler 1980).

While there is very little data that speak to the possible influence of gender at the committal stage, there are a number of studies examining the decision to remand the defendant in custody, and the results of these suggest that: (a) men are more likely than women to be remanded, although this difference may disappear once other predictors of remand decision-making such as prior record, age, race and employment are taken into account (e.g. Daly 1989; Demuth and Steffensmeier 2004; Goldkamp and Gottfredson 1979; Katz and Spohn 1995; Kruttschnitt 1984; Nagal 1969); (b) when bail is set, higher amounts are set for men compared with women (Kruttschnitt 1984). While the evidence that being female confers an advantage at the pre-trial stage is rather clear, the relationship between gender and outcomes becomes somewhat more complex once a defendant is before a jury.

Jury trials

Juries serve an important function in adversarial legal systems such as those in place in Australia and other Commonwealth jurisdictions (e.g. Canada, New Zealand, and the United Kingdom), and the United States of America. The jury's primary role is to find the facts[1] of a case based on the evidence presented at trial, uninfluenced by bias or preconceived ideas that they may have about the defendant's character, ethnicity or social class. A significant body of social science research has, however, questioned the extent to which juries are able to achieve this goal (e.g. Arkes and Mellers 2002). In this section, we focus on how the gender of various participants in the trial, namely the gender of defendants, victims, expert witnesses and the jurors themselves, might influence outcomes.

Defendants

Research suggests that being a female defendant can be beneficial in terms of perceptions and outcomes in the courtroom, but that paradoxically it can also result in more negative perceptions and harsher judgements. Stereotypes about gender can influence how a defendant's defence is perceived, what occurs during deliberations, as well as the final verdict. For example, in terms of defendants relying on the defence of battered women syndrome in cases where a woman has killed her spouse, the extent to which such women are perceived as being battered women has been found to be dependent on gender stereotypic aspects of their physical appearance (see Gula and Yarmey 1998; Yarmey and Kruschenske 1995). Further, women may be up to three times more likely to succeed, compared with men, in claiming the defence of insanity in cases of murder (Breheney *et al.* 2007).

In line with this, in a consideration of legal and medical documents in 129 London Crown Court cases focusing on homicide, arson and assault, Allen (1986, cited in Allen 1987) noted that female offenders tended to be 'medicalised' and their actions viewed as a result of external pressures rather than conscious intent (see also Godfrey *et al.* 2005). In a similar analysis of homicide case files from Victoria (Australia), Armstrong (1999) documented a similar 'medicalisation' bias for women, that was moderated by the relationship of the offender to the victim. Armstrong (1999) noted that for women, but not for men, a more moderate approach in terms of charge and chance of custodial sentence was taken if a female offender killed a family member (spouse or child) rather than a non-family member. In these instances the gender of the defendant may influence the perception of the incident, with violent acts by women being viewed as more isolated incidents reflecting a temporary loss of control (Faulstich and Moore 1984). Alternatively the context of the crime (i.e. within the home or against family) may result in the (female) defendant being viewed as less of a threat to the community compared with men who engage in the same crimes (Breheney *et al.* 2007).

There is further evidence to suggest that verdicts are influenced by gender. For example, Dean *et al.* (2000) found that male defendants were more likely to be found guilty than female defendants in cases where either assault or theft were alleged to have occurred. It is important to note though, that such findings do not seem to simply reflect a general bias towards convicting male defendants. Although Mazzella and Feingold's (1994) meta-analysis of 80 studies found a slight tendency to favour convicting male defendants compared with female defendants, they found that the advantages of being a female defendant did not apply universally across all types of crime; in fact, it was only significantly beneficial in cases of theft. Other researchers have also observed more favourable impressions of female perpetrators in cases of sexual assault, but primarily among male jurors when the victim was a boy (Quas *et al.* 2002), and cases of murder (Forsterlee *et al.* 2004). In this latter type of case, the difference in evaluations of male and female defendants disappeared when a victim impact statement was introduced which had the effect of inducing mock jurors to perceive the female defendant as more deviant. Other research by McKimmie and colleagues (e.g. McKimmie *et al.* 2006) suggests that female defendants charged with either armed robbery or murder of a home invader also receive more lenient judgements.

Within this literature, the match between the gender of the offender and the gender of the stereotypical offender for that specific crime seems to be key. Building on Eagly *et al.*'s (1992) explanation for why women receive more negative evaluations in leadership roles, for crime the extent to which the context and the person are stereotypically congruent may moderate evaluations of the target. That is, when the gender of the defendant is congruent with the gender of the stereotypical offender, the defendant may be evaluated more in line with that stereotype. In terms of leadership positions, women are evaluated more negatively because they do not fit the stereotypical characteristics of leaders. In terms of crimes that are characterised as stereotypically male, women may be seen as less guilty (or less responsible: Allen 1987; Armstrong 1999) because they do not fit the characteristics of the stereotypical offender. Thus, in these cases female defendants benefit from gender stereotypes, as they are seen as unlikely to be guilty due to appearing to be dissimilar to the typical offender (Bishop and Frazier 1984). For other, perhaps more minor offences (e.g. drug use), the mismatch between the 'gender' of the stereotypical offender and the defendant is less pronounced and differences in perceived guilt as a function of gender may be less evident.

Other research has suggested that gender not only has an influence on verdicts, but also affects what information gets considered during jury deliberations. McKimmie *et al.* (2006) used a 20-page written transcript of a murder case to examine the way in which defendant gender impacted on verdicts and group discussion among mock jurors. In this study, participants read about a case where a burglar was killed by a homeowner after assaulting the homeowner when he/she unexpectedly returned home. The homeowner, who was either male or female, claimed that he/she was acting in self-defence because of his/her fear for their life. Thus, jurors had to decide the intent of the defendant's actions that led to the burglar's death in order to decide whether to accept the defence. To this end, 20 mock juries of between five and seven people deliberated for up to an hour while being videotaped to try and reach a unanimous verdict. Not only did mock juries tend to find the male defendant guilty more often than the female defendant after deliberation, but the mock juries' verdicts were more influenced by discussion of elements of the offence when the defendant was male, and more influenced by discussion of the defendant's gender when the defendant was female.

While the preceding discussion seems to suggest that when there are differences related to gender it is beneficial to be a female defendant, there are, however, certain circumstances under which female defendants are perceived more negatively due to the influence of gender-related stereotypes. In particular, female defendants may be seen as particularly out of place in the legal setting (Worrall 1981, 1990), and so their behaviour may be seen as abnormal (Allen 1987; Armstrong 1999) or more extreme than similar behaviours performed by a male defendant. Such a possibility fits with research looking at how categorisation by gender influences the perceived aggressiveness of behaviour performed by children. In a study by Condry and Ross (1985), the same rough play behaviour attributed to either two boys, two girls, or a combination of one boy and one girl was seen as relatively more aggressive when at least one girl was involved in the interaction. Such a contrast effect may occur because men are expected to be, and also tend to actually be, more aggressive than women, especially when the aggressive behaviour has the potential to produce pain or physical injury rather than psychological harm (Eagly and Steffen 1986). Thus when a woman behaves in an equally aggressive manner as a man, she is seen to be relatively more extreme in terms of aggressiveness because expectations for aggressiveness are lower for women. This type of effect has been labelled a shifting standard (Biernat *et al.* 2003).

Women may also be evaluated negatively not because of some category contrast effect, but due to perceivers' more general gender-related beliefs. In a study examining perceptions of Myra Hindley, who, in conjunction with her partner, abducted and murdered a number of children in England, Viki *et al.* (2005) found that people who scored higher on a measure of benevolent sexism had more negative evaluations of Hindley. Benevolent sexism is the component of the ambivalent sexism inventory (Glick and Fiske 1996) which assesses ostensibly positive attitudes about women. These positive beliefs tend to be prescriptive in nature, however, and set out a constrained role for women in society based around traditional gender roles. Thus, for perceivers higher on benevolent sexism, a woman will be evaluated positively as long as she conforms to that traditional gender role. Viki *et al.* argued that it was because Myra Hindley deviated from this traditional role, which includes nurturing and caring, that she lost the protection of the paternalistic benevolent beliefs and was evaluated more negatively.

Victims

Although some research has characterised any effect of characteristics of victims on jurors' verdicts as minimal (e.g. Mazzella and Feingold 1994), gender is one feature of victims that does influence verdicts. In their meta-analysis of 80 studies, Mazzella and Feingold found that defendants were more likely to be found guilty when the victim of their alleged behaviour was a woman compared with a man. This may be in part because the victim's claims about the alleged offence are more likely to be believed when they are female compared with male (e.g. Haegerich and Bottoms 2000). It may also be because women are seen as more likely to be victimised in assault cases, even if they are more likely to be blamed for their victimisation (Howard 1984b). This perception is stronger the more perceivers' attitudes towards women are consistent with traditional gender stereotypes (Howard 1984a). A similar pattern has been observed in cases of opposite sex sexual assault, with male victims being seen as more likely to have initiated, encouraged and enjoyed the sex acts compared with female victims (Smith *et al.* 1988).

The role of individual beliefs such as benevolent sexism and traditional gender stereotyping on evaluations of victims has been highlighted by a number of researchers, particularly those looking at cases of sexual assault (e.g. Abrams *et al.* 2003; Taylor and Joudo 2005). Sexual assault is a physically and psychologically heinous crime for which reporting, prosecution and conviction rates remain disproportionately low in numerous jurisdictions (e.g. Australia: Australian Bureau of Statistics 2005; Canada: Du Mont *et al.* 2003; UK: Gregory and Lees 1996; USA: Frazier and Haney 1996; see Chapter 5 of this volume for a discussion of factors influencing the conviction rate in rape cases). Convictions for sexual assault are often dependent on circumstantial evidence as there is typically little corroborating evidence (Office of the Director of Public Prosecutions and Australian Federal Police 2005). Because of the lack of other evidence, stereotypes about female victims of sexual assault can have a significant impact on jurors' decisions (Taylor and Joudo 2005): for example, when victims are perceived to violate expectations of female victims of sexual assault, they are blamed more for their assault and their assailants blamed less (Krahé 1988) than when this is not the case.

Negative evaluations of victims of sexual assault have differentially been attributed to violations of victim stereotypes (i.e. beliefs about how genuine victims of sexual assault should be; Lees 1996) and violations of more general gender stereotypes. For example, Abrams *et al.* (2003) found that the more strongly people endorsed benevolent sexism (a belief system that prescribes a restrictive traditional role for women; Glick and Fiske 1996), the more they blamed victims of acquaintance rape for their assault. In addition, jury-simulation research (e.g. Taylor and Joudo 2005) has shown that traditional gender-based stereotypes can impact on jurors' reactions to female victims of sexual assault.

To date, research in this area has typically relied on scenarios (e.g. Abrams *et al.* 2003; cf. Taylor and Joudo 2005) focusing on the victim's behaviour at the time of the assault and the relationship between the victim and alleged perpetrator (Anderson and Doherty 2008). One limitation of such an approach is that it can confound different schemas that jurors may activate – i.e. their offence prototypes (beliefs about offences), victim stereotypes (beliefs about victims) and gender stereotypes (beliefs about men and women; Masser *et al.* in press). As such, attempts to manipulate victim stereotypes have typically involved scenarios that simultaneously vary both offence prototypicality (i.e. whether the assailant is known to the victim) along with aspects of the victim's behaviour (i.e. whether she invites the man in for coffee; Du Mont *et al.* 2003). Further, victim stereotypes have also been confounded with gender stereotypes. Not only do 'genuine' victims of sexual assault not invite a man in for coffee (because 'genuine' victims should not engage in actions that might be viewed as precipitating the offence; Stewart *et al.* 1996), 'nice', or gender stereotypical, women do not behave in this way either (Abrams *et al.* 2003).

As such, it is not clear from research to date what unique role, if any, gender stereotypes may play in influencing perceptions of sexual assault victims. Arguably, the results of much research in this area can be explained by offence, victim or gender-related schemas. The more prototypical the offence, the more the victim seems like the stereotypical victim and the more that the woman is seen in terms of positive traditional stereotypes, the less a juror will blame her (and not the offender; Viki *et al.* 2004) for her assault. Further, the precise interrelationship between these schemas is not clear from the literature, but research suggests that it may be complex (McKimmie *et al.* 2007). In the context of sexual assault though, understanding precisely which schemas influence perceptions and how they do so is an obviously critically important first step to the identification of a means to overcome the influence of these stereotypes in sexual assault trials.

Jurors

While research seems to suggest that juror characteristics such as ethnicity seem to have relatively little influence on their verdicts (Baldwin and McConville 1979), gender does have an influence and is believed to be influential by observers. In a consideration of jury selection, Norton *et al.* (2007) found that in a case of a woman charged with murdering her abusive husband, participants acting as prosecutors were more likely to enact peremptory challenges for female rather than male jurors. The authors proposed that this occurred because the participants believed that female jurors would be sympathetic to the defendant; however, participants provided non-gender-related reasons for their dismissal of the female jurors. Further, a number of studies have documented that female jurors are more likely to convict in cases involving allegations of rape (e.g. Hans and Vidmar 1982) or sexual abuse (Crowley *et al.* 1994). It has been suggested that in these cases, this finding is most likely due to differences between men and women in receptiveness to allegations of sexual assault, with women being more likely to believe such allegations (Haegerich and Bottoms 2000).

Such differences in the extent to which allegations of sexual assault are believed do not appear to reflect the influence of socially conservative attitudes, sexism, or attitudes towards homosexuality (Quas *et al.* 2002), although there is some evidence that belief in a just world might contribute to differences in how male and female jurors evaluate cases (Whatley and Riggio 1993). Belief in a just world (Lerner 1980) is the belief that good things happen to good people and bad things happen to bad people, so if some criminal act is committed against a victim, it is seen as being due to some flaw of the victim's character or behaviour. Such beliefs are self-protective in that they make uncontrollable negative events appear controllable; as long as you are good, nothing bad will happen to you. In Whatley and Riggio's (1993) study, male participants blamed a victim of sexual assault more for the assault than female participants, even when the victim was male, and this effect was greater when the victim was 'bad' (had prior arrests) compared with 'good' (no prior arrests). They attributed this to the observation that their male participants scored higher than the female participants on a measure of belief in a just world.

While the effect of juror gender on perceptions in cases involving sexual assault is rather consistent, most of the studies examining juror gender have relied on transcript-based methodology. When jury deliberation is taken into account, however, these effects appear to diminish (Brekke and Borgida 1988), suggesting that the effect of juror gender may not be a substantial concern in actual trials. In addition, there is some evidence that other variables may moderate the effect of juror gender. For example, the attractiveness of the defendant can reverse the effect of defendant gender. In a study that examined perceptions of a female defendant charged with vehicular homicide, female jurors treated an unattractive defendant more harshly than an attractive defendant, whereas male jurors evaluated an attractive defendant more harshly (Abwender and Hough 2001).

Combined effects of gender

The previous sections have considered the various effects of victim gender, defendant gender, and juror gender independently; however, there is some evidence that these effects interact with each other. For example, as noted before, female perpetrators are evaluated more leniently compared with male perpetrators by male jurors when the victim of the alleged child sexual assault was male (Quas *et al.* 2002). Furthermore, Wayne *et al.* (2001) found that female sexual harassers were evaluated more negatively than male sexual harassers when their victim was of the opposite gender, and that harassers who harassed someone of the same gender were evaluated most negatively. Conversely, when the domain of a case threatens mock jurors because of their gender (e.g. cases of sexual discrimination for female jurors, and cases involving child custody disputes for male jurors), mock jurors favour same-gendered plaintiffs (Elkins *et al.* 2002). Part of this effect has been attributed to a gender similarity bias, whereby jurors favour plaintiffs of the same gender due to greater similarity (Elkins *et al.* 2001). The observation that this bias was stronger when evidence was uncertain (Elkins *et al.* 2001) suggests that gender similarity is, in effect, a decisional short cut.

Expert witnesses

Expert testimony is often admitted at trial to assist jurors to understand complex evidence that is outside that of which it would be reasonable to expect a layperson to have knowledge. While expert testimony can be helpful in assisting jurors to understand complex information (e.g. psychological conditions relevant for defences; Schuller *et al.* 2004; Schuller and Rzepa 2002), there is evidence that the gender of an expert serves to trigger stereotypes that then influence how that expert's testimony is evaluated (e.g. McKimmie *et al.* 2004; Schuller *et al.* 2001, 2005). In some cases, such as those involving the issue of child custody, a female expert will have greater persuasive impact compared with a male expert (Swenson *et al.* 1984). It has been argued that these gender effects are likely to follow the lines of gender-role stereotypes (e.g. Schuller and Cripps 1998) and, more generally, that the extent to which the context and the person are stereotypically congruent may moderate evaluations of the target. That is, when congruent with the stereotype, the target is evaluated more positively (e.g. Eagly *et al.* 1992).

To examine the possibility that judgements about the credibility of an expert in a legal context are dependent on gender congruency of the expert and the case domain, Schuller *et al.* (2001) varied the gender of the expert testifying and the gender orientation of the case. They found that in a male-oriented domain (e.g. the construction industry), a male expert was more persuasive than a female expert. In a female-oriented domain (e.g. clothing industry), however, a female expert did not enjoy as large an advantage over a male expert in terms of persuasiveness (see also McKimmie *et al.* 2004). McKimmie *et al.* found that this effect was driven by evaluations of the expert, as these evaluations mediated the extent to which gender-domain congruence influenced participants' decisions. Schuller *et al.* (2005) demonstrated that the effects of gender of expert were stronger under conditions in which it would be expected that peripheral cues such as gender stereotypes would influence jurors' decisions, namely when testimony was complex and difficult for participants to understand.

While there is a growing body of literature identifying the influence of expert gender, there are examples of some case domains where, even though it is reasonable to expect that there are gender-relevant stereotypes that might come into play, no differences are observed in mock jurors' reactions to expert testimony based on expert gender. For example, Couch and Sigler (2002) found that the gender of the expert witness who was an auto engineer did not impact on participants' perceptions of that expert's testimony in a civil case involving a car accident. This suggests that there may be important moderators of the effect of expert gender that need to be identified in further research. For example, research shows that perceivers have clear expectations about the type of language that men and women stereotypically use (Strand 1999; Quina *et al.* 1987; Wiley and Eskilson 1985), and so it might be that expert gender is only influential when experts communicate in a gender-congruent manner.

Sentencing

At the conclusion of a criminal trial, should the defendant plead or be found guilty, the sentencing hearing is held. At this stage, the judge will take into account a range of factors to determine the appropriate sentence to be imposed. For example, judges may take into account reports about the offender's background, prospects of rehabilitation, evidence of good character, remorse or psychiatric state, the nature of the crime, the maximum penalty, any sentencing precedents, any aggravating or mitigating factors and so on. The sentencing process also involves taking into account community expectations to some extent, as noted by Justice McHugh in *Markarian* v. *The Queen* 'for the sake of criminal justice generally, judges attempt to impose sentences that accord with legitimate community expectations'. The question arises whether taking into account these factors results in similar sentences being given to defendants, regardless of their gender. As research has consistently demonstrated that the same factors that influence jurors' perceptions also impact on judges' perceptions (Guthrie *et al.* 2001; Landsman and Rakos 1994), it is perhaps not unexpected that there are differences in sentencing as a function of offender gender.

Within the sentencing literature, two types of decision are commonly considered – whether the offender should be given a custodial sentence or not, and for those who are given a custodial sentence, the length of sentence handed down. For these decisions, when examining the effect of defendant gender, the evidence is mixed and complex. Gender effects typically remain even when a sophisticated range of analytic strategies are employed to control for an increasing number of legally relevant variables (Steffensmeier *et al.* 1993). However, because of the difficulties of designing a study to control for all possible alternative contributing factors, the 'pure' effect of gender (uncontaminated by variations in all legally relevant factors) remains somewhat ambiguous (e.g. Farrington and Morris 1983; Franklin and Fearn 2008; Heidensohn 1996; Rodriguez *et al.* 2006). With regard to the decision to commit the offender to custody, the vast majority of studies find that female offenders are generally less likely to be given custodial sentences than male offenders (e.g. Daly and Bordt 1995; Farnworth and Teske 1995; Hedderman 2004; Hedderman and Gelsthorpe 1997; Hedderman and Hough 1994; Jeffries *et al.* 2003; Kruttschnitt and Green 1984; Mustard 2001; Spohn 1999; Spohn and Holleran 2000) and where no gender differences have been found (e.g. Curry *et al.* 2004) this has been attributed to sample specific characteristics (i.e. a large proportion of the sample being convicted of offences for which non-custodial sentences were not an option). Further, Steffensmeier *et al.* (1993) noted that this effect was moderated by offence type, such that the difference in the likelihood of a custodial sentence based on gender was greater for violent and serious offences (e.g. robbery) than for less serious offences such as drug offences. Somewhat contrary to this, Rodriguez *et al.* (2006) in a consideration of 7,729 convicted felons in Texas found that female offenders were less likely to be incarcerated than male offenders for property and drug offences, whereas the risk of incarceration for violent crime did not differ by offender gender.

The impact of defendant gender on the length of sentences handed down is somewhat more variable. On the one hand, a number of studies have found that female offenders receive more lenient sentences compared with male offenders (e.g. Curry *et al.* 2004; Jeffries *et al.* 2003; Kruttschnitt 1984; Mustard 2001; Wilczynski 1997) while others find no differences (e.g. Crew 1991), or that females are treated more harshly (e.g. Cowen 1995). Rodriguez *et al.* (2006) provide a comprehensive discussion of the diversity of these findings. Further, with regard to mandatory or structured sentencing, research indicates that men are significantly more likely to receive mandatory sentences (Ulmer *et al.* 2007) and significantly less likely than female offenders to receive sentencing departures below the standard range (Engen *et al.* 2003). Overall, the literature suggests that female offenders receive shorter sentences. Similar to the decision to give a custodial sentence or not, there is also evidence of some moderation by offence type. While Rodriguez *et al.* (2006) found that female offenders tended to receive shorter average sentences than male offenders, this difference was maximised for violent crimes, for which male offenders received sentences that were on average 4.49 years longer than those handed down to female offenders.

Why does gender have such an impact?

Pre- and post-trial judgements

So what is to be made of the possible effect of gender in the courtroom? While the evidence is complicated, it does seem that there is a relatively consistent effect of gender, or at least gender stereotypes, in the courtroom. At the pre- and post-trial (i.e. sentencing) stage, men and women are treated differently. Men are somewhat more likely to be remanded and are subject to higher amounts of bail if released. At the sentencing stage, female offenders are generally less likely to be given custodial sentences than male offenders. In addition, where female offenders are remanded, they are typically given shorter sentences than male offenders. Katz and Spohn (1995) suggest that these latter effects are unlikely to be independent of the pre-trial decisions. Further at the sentencing stage, some evidence of moderation by crime type is apparent, with the discrepancy between men and women in terms of whether they are given a custodial sentence being largest for minor crimes, while the sentencing discrepancy for men and women is largest for violent crimes.

In considering why discrepancies occur at the pre-trial and sentencing stages, Steffensmeier *et al*. (1993; see also Steffensmeier 1980; Steffensmeier and Demuth 2000) and others (e.g. Albonetti 1992; Curry *et al*. 2004) have suggested that women are treated more leniently because gender may be used by judges as a proxy to provide information, sometimes on legally relevant considerations, in situations when information is limited. As such, because female offenders are less likely to have a prior record (Albonetti 1992) they may be judged as less blameworthy; because their serious offending is seen to typically take place in specific circumstances, they may be judged as less of a risk to the community (Albonetti 1992; Steffensmeier *et al*. 1993); and because they are more likely to have responsibilities for children it may be judged as more practical or 'morally right' (Steffensmeier 1980; Kruttschnitt 1984), as well as being legally valid mitigating circumstances, to give them a noncustodial sentence (Daly 1987, c.f., Spohn 1999). While male defendants seem to benefit to an extent when they also have family responsibilities (Kruttschnitt and McCarthy 1985), Daly (1987) suggests that women benefit to a greater extent, potentially due to the stereotypical traditional nurturing role associated with women. However, Steffensmeier *et al.* (1993) suggest, arguing against the influence of extra-legal factors such as stereotypes, that should a male and female offender present with the same characteristics, they would receive similar treatment (see Farrington and Morris 1983).

Thus, apparent differences between the genders in terms of offending-relevant features appear on one level to provide an adequate account for sentencing disparities. Such a conclusion is further supported by the observation that the increased likelihood of male versus female offenders receiving the death sentence can largely be attributed to sexual nature of homicides committed by men (Williams *et al.* 2007). Further, the differences in sentence length may actually reflect differences in victim gender and the pleas utilised by defendants of different gender. Male offenders receive longer sentences especially when their victims are females (Curry *et al.* 2004); female defendants tend to rely on psychiatric pleas while male defendants rely on normal pleas and so each are sentenced accordingly (Allen 1987; Armstrong 1999; Wilczynski 1997).

Despite these apparently objective reasons for differences in sentences as a function of gender, there remains the possibility that such differences cannot be attributed purely to case differences. Objective explanations for what appear to be gender-driven differences may appear attractive because the base rate of offending is highly skewed towards males, thus it might seem logical to assume that a male defendant is more likely to be guilty or more likely to reoffend. The problem with this assumption is that base rates are only valid if random sampling from the population has taken place, and this is unlikely to be the case with defendants. The importance of gender in these post- (and potentially pre-) trial decisions is underpinned by a recent examination by Karamouzis and Wood Harper (2007) of American offenders who had all been sentenced to death. Karamouzis and Wood Harper (2007) trained an artificial intelligence system to identify the factors that best predicted whether the death sentence would be carried out. All of the offenders who were included in the study had been convicted of a capital offence and given the death sentence, and so any differences in pleas or victim characteristics were no longer relevant. The system was over 90 per cent accurate in predicting the fate of inmates, and the most important factor turned out to be the gender of the inmates, with women rarely being executed in comparison with men. This is an interesting finding because the researchers did not have access to measures of the strength of evidence presented at trial (in particular whether DNA evidence was admitted), nor to measures of the skill of the defence lawyer. The features of the cases used to reliably predict whether the inmate would be executed were all extra-legal in nature. Such a finding suggests that offender gender may well play an inappropriate role in sentencing if it has such an effect on whether sentences are carried out.

Trial decisions

In the context of a trial, the evidence suggests that gender and gender stereotypes influence evaluations, from what is considered by the jury, evaluations of the defendant and expert witnesses, to evaluations of defences that are raised and accepted. On the whole these stereotypes appear to result in an apparent leniency towards typically 'traditional' women, especially when perceivers hold prescriptive stereotypic beliefs (e.g. Viki *et al.* 2005) and/or the crime committed matches gender-related expectations. The types of crimes that this leniency is manifested for remains somewhat unclear, although potentially it is related to the 'gendered' nature of the offence (Eagly *et al.* 1992). Further, male perpetrators of crimes against women are more likely to be found guilty than female perpetrators of crime against men, with female victims seemingly cast as passive rather than active agents within the offence (Smith *et al.* 1988). However, an exception is observed in the case of sexual assault where counter-stereotypical victims may be blamed more for their assault than stereotypical victims, particularly by those holding prescriptive gender stereotypic or associated beliefs (e.g. belief in a just world). Further, in some instances, juror gender may impact directly, with jurors favouring plaintiffs of the same gender due to perceived similarity (Elkins *et al.* 2001).

At this stage of the courtroom process, and because of the type of decisions jurors are asked to make, stereotypes are more likely to act as a filter or as a mechanism that allows for the rapid simplification of complex or limited information in a situation where concepts are unfamiliar. For judgements relating to offenders and victims, this process appears to concur broadly with the selective chivalry/ paternalism account of the influence of gender stereotypes in legal settings (e.g. Rodriguez *et al.* 2006). Here women are stereotyped as weak, passive and in need of protection. As such those women who offend but who adhere to traditional gender stereotypes will be afforded leniency in comparison with men (Franklin and Fearn

2008; Rodriguez *et al.* 2006), and those men who offend against (stereotypical) women (rather than men) will be punished most severely (Franklin and Fearn 2008). This perspective proposes that gender counter-stereotypical female offenders will be treated similarly to men who commit comparable crimes (Belknap 2007; Belknap and Holsinger 2006; Bernstein *et al.* 1977; Koons-Witt 2002; Smart 1977; Viki *et al.* 2005; cf. Godfrey *et al.* 2005). Alternatively, it could be argued that these 'deviant' women may be 'medicalised' if that option is available (Allen 1987; Armstrong 1999; Wilczynski 1997).

The influence of gender and gender stereotypes at this stage of the criminal justice process is, however, broader than that suggested by the selective chivalry/paternalism account. Gender determines what is considered in the jury deliberations that lead to verdicts (McKimmie *et al.* 2006) and, potentially through the influence of shifting standards (Biernat *et al.* 2003), how actions of the defendant may be viewed and evaluated (Worrall 1981, 1990). Further, gender and gender stereotypes have been repeatedly demonstrated to influence how expert testimony is evaluated in trials (McKimmie *et al.* 2004; Schuller *et al.* 2001, 2005; cf. Couch and Sigler 2002).

Challenges and conclusions

Although a substantial body of research now exists documenting the influence of gender in the courtroom, one of the challenges facing researchers is making a convincing argument that the findings of experimental research conducted in a courtroom or jury context are relevant for legal practice. Due to the methods often used by researchers, which allow for high levels of control over independent variables through the use of scenarios or transcripts in low-fidelity simulations, many experiments lack ecological validity and so may seem to be irrelevant to practitioners. Thus, despite attempts to argue that the method of studying jury decision-making largely does not impact on the validity of the findings (e.g. Bornstein 1999), the findings of such research may have little impact because they do not accurately approximate what actually happens in a courtroom. Further, some researchers have suggested that the comparison between low-fidelity simulations and more realistic trials may actually show that there are real differences in the conclusions that can be drawn (Bermant *et al.* 1974; see also MacCoun 2005). Arguably, it may be that low-fidelity simulations underestimate some of the effects of gender because such cues become more salient in face-to-face interactions (Ratneshwar and

Chaiken 1991), such as in the courtroom. Problematically, research that uses real trials to counter such a criticism suffers from low levels of internal validity, making it difficult to conclude much about the causal processes that influence perceptions in the courtroom. It should also be acknowledged that in many jurisdictions (e.g. UK and Australia) there are often legal restrictions which make speaking to actual jurors and exerting control over the jury context to explore the influence of various variables very difficult, if not impossible. Further, research using more realistic trial recreations is often prohibitively time-consuming and expensive.

Another challenge that limits the impact of findings such as those reported in this chapter is that often such research is perceived by those working in the legal system as a criticism of jurors or judges. Such a reaction is perhaps understandable, especially given that researchers have previously characterised people as 'mental sluggards' or 'cognitive misers' (Fiske and Taylor 1991). Thus, researchers could be perceived as casting jurors, and even possibly judges, as being of less than optimal cognitive ability and not up to the task before them. While understandable, this conclusion is perhaps a misreading of the literature on two fronts. First of all, when developing models of social cognition, researchers have not singled out any one profession but rather have attempted to develop models that can explain social thinking in general for all perceivers, including themselves.

Second, recent researchers have been keen to emphasise the point that while stereotypes might be influential, perceivers can be best thought of as 'cognitive optimisers' who are motivated to obtain the most information possible from a social situation, and stereotypes assist with this goal as information load increases (Sherman *et al.* 1998). Recent research has emphasised the point that while stereotypes may be influential, the most influential part of the trial for jurors is the evidence (Vidmar 2005). On this point, it is not reasonable to expect jurors or judges to somehow develop superhuman cognitive abilities that elevate them above the influence of the generally useful cognitive strategies (i.e. stereotypes and heuristics) that help people get through their day-to-day lives. Rather than viewing the literature reviewed in this chapter as suggesting that jurors and judges are irredeemably biased by stereotypes and cognitive short cuts, it is more constructive to view it as suggesting that there are simply some limits to human cognition, and that the use of stereotypes provides a marker of when those limits are reached. By utilising stereotype-driven effects to identify the features of trials that impair perceivers' abilities to focus on the facts, it may be possible to suggest changes that make perceivers' tasks more cognitively manageable. While the research in this area should certainly be subject to robust critique, a general rejection of the relevance of the literature may mean some useful opportunities to assist perceivers in the legal system are lost.

Some positive moves have been made to take into account the influence of gender in the courtroom, for example the 'reasonable woman' test introduced in cases of sexual harassment which recognises that men and women have different definitions of what constitutes sexual harassment (Blumenthal 1998). Further, researchers appear to be trying to come to grips with the issues surrounding the ecological validity of their studies (see Anderson and Doherty 2008). Hopefully, researchers will now also start to move beyond describing the influence of stereotypes in the courtroom and draw on the rich body of descriptive research that exists collectively in sociology, criminology and psychology (and other disciplines) to work systematically to identify ways in which such an influence might be reduced.

Note

1 Guidance on the function of the jury is mixed. For example, in England and Wales, the stated purpose of the jury is to decide, on the evidence, whether the person charged is guilty or not (Her Majesty's Court Service (HMCS): *Your Guide to Jury Service*), which is a different task to finding the 'facts', which is the stated aim in other jurisdictions (e.g. USA).

References

Abrams, D., Viki, G.T., Masser, B. and Bohner, G. (2003) 'Perceptions of stranger and acquaintance rape: the role of benevolent and hostile sexism in victim blame and rape proclivity', *Journal of Personality and Social Psychology*, 84 (1): 111–25.

Abwender, D.A. and Hough, K. (2001) 'Interactive effects of characteristics of defendant and mock juror on U.S. participants' judgment and sentencing recommendations', *The Journal of Social Psychology*, 141 (5): 603–15.

Albonetti, C.A. (1992) 'Charge reduction: an analysis of prosecutorial discretion in burglary and robbery cases', *Journal of Quantitative Criminology*, 8: 317–33.

Allen, H. (1987) *Justice Unbalanced.* Milton Keynes, UK: Open University Press.

Anderson, I. and Doherty, K. (2008) *Accounting for Rape: Psychology, Feminism and Discourse Analysis in the Study of Sexual Violence.* New York, NY, US: Routledge/Taylor and Francis Group.

Arkes, H.R. and Mellers, B.A. (2002) 'Do juries meet our expectations?', *Law and Human Behavior*, 26 (6): 625–39.

Armstrong, I. (1999) 'Women and their "uncontrollable impulses": the medicalisation of women's crime and differential gender sentencing', *Psychiatry, Psychology and Law*, 6: 67–77.

Australian Bureau of Statistics (2005) *Personal Safety Survey Australia.* Canberra: Commonwealth of Australia.

Baldwin, J. and McConville, M. (1979) *Jury Trials.* Oxford: Clarendon Press.

Belknap, J. (2007) *The Invisible Woman: Gender, crime, and justice* (3rd edn). Belmont, CA: Wadsworth/Thompson.

Belknap, J. and Holsinger, K. (2006) 'The gendered nature of risk factors for delinquency', *Feminist Criminology*, 1: 48–71.

Bermant, G., McGuire, M., McKinley, W. and Salo, C. (1974) 'The logic of simulation in jury research', *Criminal Justice and Behavior*, 1 (3): 224–33.

Bernstein, I.N., Kick, E., Leung, J.T. and Schulz, B. (1977) 'Charge reduction: an intermediary stage in the process of labeling criminal defendants', *Social Forces*, 56: 363–84.

Biernat, M., Kobrynowicz, D. and Weber, D.L. (2003) 'Stereotypes and shifting standards: some paradoxical effects of cognitive load', *Journal of Applied Social Psychology*, 33 (10): 2060–79.

Bishop, D.M. and Frazier, C.E. (1984) 'The effect of gender on charge reduction', *Sociological Quarterly*, 25: 358–36.

Blumenthal, J.A. (1998) 'The reasonable woman standard: a meta-analytic review of gender differences in perceptions of sexual harassment', *Law and Human Behavior. Special Issue: Gender and the Law*, 22 (1): 33–57.

Bodenhausen, G.V. (1990) 'Stereotypes as judgmental heuristics: evidence of circadian variations in discrimination', *Psychological Science*, 1 (5): 319–22.

Bornstein, B.H. (1999) 'The ecological validity of jury simulations: is the jury still out?', *Law and Human Behavior*, 23 (1): 75–91.

Breheney, C., Groscup, J. and Galietta, M. (2007) 'Gender matters in the insanity defense', *Law and Psychology Review*, 31: 93–123.

Brekke, N. and Borgida, E. (1988) 'Expert psychological testimony in rape trials: a social-cognitive analysis', *Journal of Personality and Social Psychology*, 55 (3): 372–86.

Chaiken, S. (1980) 'Heuristic versus systematic information processing and the use of source versus message cues in persuasion', *Journal of Personality and Social Psychology*, 39(5): 752–66.

Cohen, C.E. (1981) 'Person categories and social perception: testing some boundaries of the processing effect of prior knowledge', *Journal of Personality and Social Psychology*, 40(3): 441–52.

Condry, J.C. and Ross, D.F. (1985) 'Sex and aggression: the influence of gender label on the perception of aggression in children', *Child Development*, 56: 225–33.

Couch, J.V. and Sigler, J.N. (2002) 'Gender of an expert witness and the jury verdict', *The Psychological Record*, 52 (3): 281–87.

Cowen, B. (1995) 'Women and crime', in L.L. Adler and F.L. Denmark (eds), *Violence and the Prevention of Violence*. Westport, Conn.: Praeger, pp. 157–68.

Crew, B.K. (1991) 'Sex differences in criminal sentencing: chivalry or patriarchy?', *Justice Quarterly*, 8: 59–83.

Crowley, M.J., O'Callaghan, M.G. and Ball, P.J. (1994) 'The juridical impact of psychological expert testimony in a simulated child sexual abuse trial', *Law and Human Behavior*, 18 (1): 89–105.

Curry, T.R., Lee, G. and Rodriguez, S.F. (2004) 'Does victim gender increase sentence severity? Further explorations of gender dynamics and sentencing outcomes', *Crime and Delinquency*, 50 (3): 319–43.

Daly, K. (1987) 'Discrimination in the criminal courts: family, gender and the problem of equal treatment', *Social Forces*, 66: 152–75.

Daly, K. (1989) 'Neither conflict nor labeling nor paternalism will suffice: intersections of race, ethnicity, gender and family in criminal court decision', *Crime and Delinquency*, 35: 136–68.

Daly, K. and Bordt, R.L. (1995) 'Sex effects and sentencing: an analysis of the statistical literature', *Justice Quarterly*, 12: 141–75.

Dean, K., Wayne, J.H., Mack, D. and Thomas, K. (2000) 'An examination of happiness, racism, and demographics on judgments of guilt', *Journal of Applied Social Psychology*, 30: 816–32.

Demuth, S. and Steffensmeier, D. (2004) 'The impact of gender and race-ethnicity in the pretrial release process', *Social Problems*, 51 (2): 222–42.

Doise, W., Deschamps, J.C. and Meyer, G. (1978) 'The accentuation of intra-category similarities', in H. Tajfel (ed.), *Differentiation Between Social Groups*. London: Academic Press.

Du Mont, J. Miller, J-L. and Myhr, T (2003) 'The role of "real rape" and "real victim" stereotypes in the police reporting practices of sexually assaulted women', *Violence Against Women*, 9: 466–86.

Eagly, A.H., Makhijani, M.G. and Klonsky, B.G. (1992) 'Gender and the evaluation of leaders: a meta-analysis', *Psychological Bulletin*, 111 (1), 3–22.

Eagly, A.H. and Steffen, V.J. (1986) 'Gender and aggressive behavior: a meta-analytic review of the social psychological literature', *Psychological Bulletin*, 100: 309–30.

Elkins, T.J., Phillips, J.S. and Konopaske, R. (2002) 'Gender-related biases in evaluations of sex discrimination allegations: is perceived threat the key?', *Journal of Applied Psychology*, 87 (2): 280–92.

Elkins, T.J., Phillips, J.S., Konopaske, R. and Townsend, J. (2001) 'Evaluating gender discrimination claims: is there a gender similarity bias?', *Sex Roles*, 44 (1/2): 1.

Engen, R., Gainey, R., Crutchfield, R. and Weis, J. (2003) 'Discretion and disparity under sentencing guidelines: the role of departures and structured sentencing alternatives', *Criminology*, 41: 99–130.

Farnworth, M. and Teske, R.H.C. (1995) 'Gender differences in felony court processing: three hypotheses of disparity', *Women and Criminal Justice*, 62: 23–44.

Farrall, R.A. and Swigert, V.L (1986) 'Adjudication in homicide: an interpretative analysis of the effects of defendant and victim social characteristics', *Journal of Research in Crime and Delinquency*, 23: 349–69.

Farrington, D.P. and Morris, A.M. (1983) 'Sex, sentencing and reconviction', *British Journal of Criminology*, 23: 229–48.

Faulstich, M.E. and Moore, J.R. (1984) 'The insanity plea: a study of societal reactions', *Law and Psychology Review*, 8: 129–32.

Finkel, N. and Groscup, J. (1997) 'Crime prototypes, objectives versus subjective culpability, and a commonsense balance', *Law and Human Behavior*, 21: 209–30.

Fiske, S.T. and Taylor, S.E. (1991) *Social Cognition* (2nd edn). New York: McGraw-Hill.

Forsterlee, L., Fox, G.B., Forsterlee, R. and Ho, R. (2004) 'The effects of a victim impact statement and gender on juror information processing in a criminal trial: does the punishment fit the crime?', *Australian Psychologist*, 39 (1): 57–67.

Franklin, C.A. and Fearn, N.E. (2008) 'Gender, race, and formal court-decision making outcomes: chivalry/paternalism, conflict theory or gender conflict?', *Journal of Criminal Justice*, 36: 279–90.

Frazier, P. and Haney, B. (1996) 'Sexual assault cases in the legal system', *Law and Human Behavior*, 20: 607–28.

Gerdes, E.P., Dammann, E.J. and Heilig, K. (1988) 'Perceptions of rape victims and assailants: effects of physical attractiveness, acquaintance, and subject gender', *Sex Roles*, 19 (3/4): 141–53.

Glick, P. and Fiske, S.T. (1996) 'The ambivalent sexism inventory: differentiating hostile and benevolent sexism', *Journal of Personality and Social Psychology*, 70: 491–512.

Godfrey, B.S., Farrall, S. and Karstedt, S. (2005) 'Explaining gendered sentencing patters for violent men and women in the late-Victorian and Edwardian period', *British Journal of Criminology*, 45: 696–720.

Goldkamp, J.S. and Gottfredson, M. (1979) 'Bail decision making and pretrial detention: surfacing judicial policy', *Law and Human Behavior*, 3: 227–49.

Goodman-Delahunty, J. (1998) 'Approaches to gender and the law: research and applications', *Law and Human Behavior*, 22 (1): 129–43.

Gregory, J. and Lees, S. (1996) 'Attrition in rape and sexual assault cases', *British Journal of Criminology*, 36: 1–36.

Gula, C.A. and Yarmey, A.D. (1998) 'Physical appearance and judgment of status as battered women', *Perceptual and Motor Skills*, 87 (2): 459.

Guthrie, C., Rachlinski, J.J. and Wistrich, A.J. (2001) 'Inside the judicial mind', *Cornell Law Review*, 86: 777–830.

Haegerich, T.M. and Bottoms, B.L. (2000) 'Empathy and jurors' decisions in patricide trials involving child sexual assault allegations', *Law and Human Behavior*, 24: 421–48.

Hall, J.A. and Carter, J.D. (1999) 'Gender-stereotype accuracy as an individual difference', *Journal of Personality and Social Psychology*, 77 (2): 350–59.

Hamilton, D.L. and Sherman, S.J. (1996) 'Perceiving persons and groups', *Psychological Review*, 103 (2): 336.

Hans, V.P. and Vidmar, N. (1982) 'Jury selection', in N.L. Kerr and R.M. Bray (eds), *The Psychology of the Courtroom.* London: Academic Press.

Hedderman, C. (2004) 'Why are more women being sentenced to custody?', in G. McIvor (ed.), *Women Who Offend: Research highlights in social work, 44*. London: J. Kingsley.

Hedderman, C. and Gelsthorpe, L. (eds) (1997) *Understanding the Sentencing of Women*. Home Office Research Study 170. London: Home Office.

Hedderman, C. and Hough, M. (1994) *Does the Criminal Justice System Treat Men and Women Differently?* Home Office Research Study 10. London: Home Office.

Heidensohn. F. (1996) *Women and Crime* (2nd edn). Basingstoke: Macmillan Press Ltd.

Hogg, M.A. and Abrams, D. (1988) *Social Identifications.* London: Routledge.

Howard, J.A. (1984a) 'Societal influences on attribution: blaming some victims more than others', *Journal of Personality and Social Psychology*, 47 (3): 494–505.

Howard, J.A. (1984b) 'The "normal" victim: the effects of gender stereotypes on reactions to victims', *Social Psychology Quarterly*, 47 (3): 270–81.

Jeffries, S., Fletcher, G. and Newbold, G. (2003) 'Pathways to sex-based differentiation in criminal court sentencing', *Criminology*, 41: 329–53.

Jones, C.S. and Kaplan, M.F. (2003) 'The effects of racially stereotypical crimes on juror decision-making and information–processing strategies', *Basic and Applied Social Psychology*, 25 (1), 1–13.

Karamouzis, S.T. and Wood Harper, D. (2007) 'An artificial intelligence system suggests arbitrariness of death penalty', *International Journal of Law and Information Technology*, 16: 1–7.

Katz, C.M. and Spohn, C.C. (1995) 'The effect of race and gender on bail outcomes: a test of an interactive model', *American Journal of Criminal Justice*, 19: 161–84.

Koons-Witt, B.A. (2002) 'The effect of gender on the decision to incarcerate before and after the introduction of sentencing guidelines', *Criminology*, 40: 297–327.

Krahé, B. (1988) 'Victim and observer characteristics as determinants of responsibility attributions to victims of rape', *Journal of Applied Social Psychology*, 18: 50–8.

Krohn, M.D., Curry, J.P. and Nelson-Kilger, S. (1983) 'Is chivalry dead – an analysis of changes in police dispositions of males and females', *Criminology*, 21: 417–37.

Kruttschnitt, C. (1984) 'Sex and criminal court dispositions: the unresolved controversy', *Journal of Research in Crime and Delinquency*, 21: 213–32.

Kruttschnitt, C. and Green, D.E. (1984) 'The sex-sanctioning issue: is it history?', *American Sociological Review*, 49: 541–51.

Kruttschnitt, C. and McCarthy, D. (1985) 'Familial social control and pre-trial sanctions: does sex really matter?', *Journal of Criminal Law and Criminology*, 76: 151–75.

Landsman, S. and Rakos, R.F. (1994) 'A preliminary inquiry into the effect of potentially biasing information on judges and jurors in civil litigation', *Behavioral Sciences and the Law*, 12: 113–16.

Lees, S. (1996) *Carnal Knowledge: Rape on trial*. London: Penguin.

Lerner, M.J. (1980) *The Belief in a Just World: A fundamental delusion*. New York: Plenum.

MacCoun, R.J. (2005) 'Comparing legal fact finders: real and mock, amateur and professional', *Florida State University Law Review*, 32: 511–18.

Mackie, D.M., Hamilton, D.L., Susskind, J. and Rosselli, F. (1996) 'Social psychological foundations of stereotype formation', in C.N. Macrae, C. Stangor, and M. Hewstone (eds), *Stereotypes and Stereotyping*. New York: Guilford.

Masser, B., Lee, K. and McKimmie, B.M. (in press) 'Bad woman, bad victim? Disentangling the effects of victim stereotypicality, gender stereotypicality and benevolent sexism on acquaintance rape victim blame.' *Sex Roles*. University of Queensland.

Mazzella, R. and Feingold, A. (1994) 'The effects of physical attractiveness, race, socioeconomic status, and gender of defendants and victims on judgments of mock jurors: a meta-analysis', *Journal of Applied Social Psychology*, 24: 1315–44.

McKimmie, B., Masters, J., Strub, T., Schuller, R., Terry, D. and Masser, B. (2007) 'Stereotypical and counter-stereotypical defendants: who is he and what was the case against her?' Unpublished manuscript: University of Queensland.

McKimmie, B.M., Newton, C.J., Terry, D.J. and Schuller, R. A. (2004) '"Jurors" responses to expert witness testimony: the effects of gender stereotypes', *Group Processes and Intergroup Relations*, 7(2): 131–43.

McKimmie, B., Terry, D., Schuller, R. and Masters, J. (2006) 'Jury deliberation and the influence of stereotypes', *Australian Journal of Psychology*, 58: Supplement 40.

Mustard, D.B. (2001) 'Racial, ethnic, and gender disparities in sentencing: evidence from the U.S. Federal Courts', *Journal of Law and Economics*, 44: 285–314.

Nagal, S. (1969) *The Legal Process from a Behavioral Perspective*. Homewood, IL: Dorsey Press.

Norton, M.I., Sommers, S.R. and Brauner, S. (2007) 'Bias in jury selection: justifying prohibited peremptory challenges', *Journal of Behavioral Decision Making*, 20: 467–79.

Office of the Director of Public Prosecutions (ACT)(ODPP) and Australian Federal Police (AFP) (2005) *Responding to Sexual Assault: the challenge of change*. Canberra: Office of the Director of Public Prosecutions.

Ogloff, J.R.P. and Vidmar, N. (1994) 'The impact of pretrial publicity on jurors: a study to compare the relative effects of television and print media in a child sex abuse case', *Law and Human Behavior*, 18 (5): 507–25.

Pennington, N. and Hastie, R. (1992) 'Explaining the evidence: tests of the story model for juror decision making', *Journal of Personality and Social Psychology*, 62 (2): 189–206.

Petty, R.E. and Cacioppo, J.T. (1986) 'The elaboration likelihood model of persuasion', in L. Berkowitz (ed.), *Advances in Experimental Social Psychology* (Vol. 19, pp. 123–205). New York: Academic Press.

Quas, J.A., Bottoms, B.L., Haegerich, T.M. and Nysse-Carris, K.L. (2002) 'Effects of victim, defendant, and juror gender on decisions in child sexual assault cases', *Journal of Applied Social Psychology*, 32 (10): 1993–2021.

Quina, K., Wingard, J.A. and Bates, H.G. (1987) 'Language style and gender stereotypes in person perception', *Psychology of Women Quarterly*, 11 (1): 111–22.

Ratneshwar, S. and Chaiken, S. (1991) 'Comprehension's role in persuasion: the case of its moderating effect on the persuasive impact of source cues', *Journal of Consumer Research*, 18 (1): 52–62.

Rodriguez, S.F., Curry, T.R. and Lee, G. (2006) 'Gender differences in criminal sentencing: do effects vary across violent, property, and drug offenses?', *Social Science Quarterly*, 87 (2): 318–39.

Schuller, R.A. and Cripps, J. (1998) 'Expert evidence pertaining to battered women: the impact of gender of expert and timing of testimony', *Law and Human Behavior*, 22 (1): 17–31.

Schuller, R.A., McKimmie, B.M. and Janz, T. (2004) 'The impact of expert testimony in trials of battered women who kill', *Psychiatry, Psychology and Law*, 11 (1): 1–12.

Schuller, R.A. and Rzepa, S. (2002) 'Expert testimony pertaining to battered woman syndrome: its impact on jurors' decisions', *Law and Human Behavior*, 26 (6): 655–73.

Schuller, R.A., Terry, D.J. and McKimmie, B.M. (2001) 'The impact of an expert's gender on jurors' decisions', *Law and Psychology Review*, 25: 59–79.

Schuller, R.A., Terry, D.J. and McKimmie, B.M. (2005) 'The impact of expert testimony on jurors' decisions: gender of the expert and testimony complexity', *Journal of Applied Social Psychology*, 35 (6), 1266–80.

Sherman, J.W., Lee, A.Y., Bessenoff, G.R. and Frost, L.A. (1998) 'Stereotype efficiency reconsidered: encoding flexibility under cognitive load', *Journal of Personality and Social Psychology*, 75(3), 589–606.

Smart, C. (1977) 'Criminological theory: its ideology and implications concerning women', *British Journal of Sociology*, 28: 89–100.

Smith, R.E., Pine, C.J. and Hawley, M.E. (1988) 'Social cognitions about adult male victims of female sexual assault', *The Journal of Sex Research*, 24 (1–4): 101–12.

Smith, V. (1991) 'Prototypes in the courtroom: lay representations of legal concepts', *Journal of Personality and Social Psychology*, 61: 857–72.

Spohn, C.C. (1999) 'Gender and sentencing of drug offenders: is chivalry dead?', *Criminal Justice Policy Review*, 9: 365–99.

Spohn, C.C., Gruhl, J. and Welch, S. (1987) 'The impact of the ethnicity and gender of defendants on the decision to reject or dismiss felony charges', *Criminology*, 25: 175–91.

Spohn, C.C. and Holleran, D. (2000) 'The imprisonment penalty paid by young, unemployed Black and Hispanic male offenders', *Criminology*, 8: 281–306.

Stangor, C., Lynch, L., Duan, C. and Glass, B. (1992) 'Categorization of individuals on the basis of multiple social features', *Journal of Personality and Social Psychology*, 62: 207–81.

Steffensmeier, D.J. (1980) 'Assessing the impact of the women's movement on sex-based differences in the handling of adult criminal defendants', *Crime and Delinquency*, 26 (3): 344–57.

Steffensmeier, D. and Demuth, S. (2000) 'Ethnicity and sentencing outcomes in U.S. federal courts: who is punished more harshly?', *American Sociological Review*, 65: 705–29.

Steffensmeier, D., Kramer, J. and Streifel, C. (1993) 'Gender and imprisonment decisions', *Criminology*, 31 (3): 411–46.

Stern, L.D., Marrs, S., Millar, M.G. and Cole, E. (1984) 'Processing time and the recall of inconsistent and consistent behaviors of individuals and groups', *Journal of Personality and Social Psychology*, 47 (2): 253–62.

Stewart, M., Dobbin, S. and Gatowsky, S. (1996) '"Real rapes" and "real victims": the shared reliance on common cultural definitions of rape', *Feminist Legal Studies*, 4: 159–77.

Strand, E.A. (1999) 'Uncovering the role of gender stereotypes in speech perception', *Journal of Language and Social Psychology*, 18 (1), 86–100.

Swenson, R.A., Nash, D.L. and Roos, D.C. (1984) 'Source credibility and perceived expertness of testimony in a simulated child-custody case', *Professional Psychology: Research and Practice*, 15 (6): 891–98.

Tajfel, H., Sheikh, A.A. and Gardner, A.A. (1964) 'Content of stereotypes and the inference of similarity between members of stereotyped groups', *Acta Psychologica*, 22: 191–201.

Taylor, N. and Joudo, J. (2005) *The impact of pre-recorded video and close circuit television testimony by adult sexual assault complainants on jury decision-making: an experimental study.* Canberra: AIC, Research and Public Policy Series No 68.

Ulmer, J.T., Kurlychek, M.C. and Kramer, J.H. (2007) 'Prosecutorial discretion and the imposition of mandatory minimum sentences', *Journal of Research in Crime and Delinquency*, 44: 427–58.

Vidmar, N. (2005) 'Expert evidence, the adversary system, and the jury', *American Journal of Public Health*, 95: 137–43.

Viki, G.T., Abrams, D. and Masser, B. (2004) 'Evaluating stranger and acquaintance rape: the role of benevolent sexism in perpetrator blame and recommended sentence length', *Law and Human Behavior*, 28 (3), 295–303.

Viki, G.T., Massey, K. and Masser, B. (2005) 'When chivalry backfires: benevolent sexism and attitudes toward Myra Hindley', *Legal and Criminological Psychology*, 10(1): 109–20.

Wayne, J.H., Riordan, C.M. and Thomas, K.M. (2001) 'Is all sexual harassment viewed the same? Mock juror decisions in same- and cross-gender cases', *Journal of Applied Psychology*, 86 (2): 179–87.

Whatley, M.A. and Riggio, R.E. (1993) 'Gender differences in attributions of blame for male rape victims', *Journal of Interpersonal Violence*, 8: 502–11.

Wheeler, G.R. and Wheeler, C.R. (1980) 'Reflections on legal representation of the economically disadvantaged: beyond assembly line justice', *Crime and Delinquency*, 26: 319–32.

Wiener, R., Richmond, T., Seib, H., Rauch, S. and Hackney, A. (2002) 'The psychology of telling murder stories', *Behavioral Science and Law*, 20: 119–39.

Wilczynski, A. (1997) 'Mad or bad? Child-killers, gender and the courts', *British Journal of Criminology*, 37 (3): 419–36.

Wiley, M.G. and Eskilson, A. (1985) 'Speech style, gender stereotypes, and corporate success: what if women talk more like men?', *Sex Roles*, 12 (9): 993–1007.

Williams, M.R., Demuth, S. and Holcomb, J.E. (2007) 'Understanding the influence of victim gender in death penalty cases: the importance of victim race, sex-related victimization, and jury decision making', *Criminology*, 45 (4): 865–91.

Worrall, A. (1981) 'Out of place: female offenders in court', *Probation Journal*, 28: 90–3.

Worrall, A. (1990) *Offending Women: Female lawbreakers and the criminal justice system*. London: Routledge.

Yarmey, A.D. and Kruschenske, S. (1995) 'Facial stereotypes of battered women and battered women who kill', *Journal of Applied Social Psychology*, 25 (4), 338–52.

Chapter 7

'Without fear or favour, prejudice or ill will'[1]: magistrates' sentencing decisions

Pamela Ormerod and Joanna R. Adler

Over 90 per cent of all criminal matters in England and Wales are dealt with in the magistrates' courts (Ministry of Justice (MOJ) 2009a). This chapter focuses on how magistrates make sentencing decisions, from guidance through to process and outcome. It introduces the magistracy and summarises its role in the judicial system. It includes a review of previous empirical work and presents novel research assessing how magistrates approach their sentencing task.

Background: magistrates' roles

A Justice of the Peace (JP), or lay magistrate[2] has a wide range of functions and duties. The office can be traced back to the thirteenth century when powerful local appointees of the Crown helped to administer the law (Skyrme 1979). Gradual changes to the appointment system have opened up the office since then, but not until the twentieth century could women become magistrates.

Currently, local advisory committees, appointed by the Lord Chancellor, advertise to recruit individuals from a cross-section of society. Magistrates should be representative of the communities which they serve and on whose behalf they assist in the administration of justice. No previous legal knowledge is required by appointees and the office is voluntary. Magistrates receive no financial reward for their activity but can claim loss of earnings and out-of-pocket expenses in certain circumstances.

According to judicial statistics (MOJ 2009b) at 1 April 2008 there were 29,419 lay magistrates (50.1 per cent were women), serving within a regional structure of Benches, administered by Her Majesty's Court Service. Individual court hearings usually take place in front of three local justices who constitute the 'bench' for that sitting. The lay magistracy is supplemented by a small cadre of professionally trained, full-time, paid District Judges (DJ) – 134 in April 2008 (MOJ 2009b). DJs were previously called stipendiary magistrates or 'stipes' (Carter 2001). These individuals have legal qualifications, experience – usually as practising solicitors or barristers – and sit alone to determine culpability and sentence. Their powers are essentially identical to those of lay magistrates.

Magistrates are guided and assisted by a legally qualified Legal Adviser [LA] who ensures that court business is undertaken within the statutory legal framework. The LA is responsible for informing and assisting justices in the application of sentencing guidance but s/he is not permitted to take part in the decision-making process (see Carter 2001: 126).

Justices are appointed for their personal qualities, evaluated through interview, against published criteria:

> Good character: to have personal integrity and enjoy the respect and trust of others. Understanding and communication: to be able to understand documents, identify relevant facts, follow evidence and communicate effectively. Social awareness: to appreciate and accept the rule of law. Maturity and sound temperament: to have an awareness and understanding of people and a sense of fairness. Sound judgement: to be able to think logically, weigh arguments and reach a sound decision. Commitment and reliability: committed to serving the community, willing to undergo training and to be in sufficiently good health to undertake your duties on a regular basis. (MOJ 2009c: 9)

They must live or work within 15 miles of the boundary of the commission area so that they have 'a reasonable degree of knowledge of the area'. Candidates must be aged between 18 and 65 years at first appointment. People with certain occupations and their close relatives are precluded from applying, e.g. police officers or parliamentary candidates (MOJ 2009d).

Magistrates receive training on first appointment and throughout their judicial careers (e.g. The Magistrates National Training Initiative

April 2005) and undergo triennial peer appraisal. Appraisal is against a set of role-based competences including the acquisition of skills in structured decision-making. As magistrates gain experience, they may expand their interests into the work of youth panels and family proceedings courts. They will also generally progress from 'winger' positions to that of Chair of the court in which they preside. Lay magistrates exercise their court duties alongside business, professional and/or family responsibilities. They are currently required to sit for a minimum of 26 half-day sittings per annum, more if they join a panel (Magistrates' Association website 2009). The business of the magistrates' courts is varied. According to the Magistrates' Association website (2009), the duties and responsibilities of a magistrate are:

> **Criminal Matters**
> Over 90% of all criminal cases are dealt with by magistrates, either in the adult court, or in the youth court. The work involves, amongst other things, deciding on applications for bail, whether a defendant is guilty or not and passing sentences as appropriate. For a single criminal offence committed by an adult, magistrates' sentencing powers include the imposition of fines, community service orders, probation orders[3] or a period of not more than six months in custody. Magistrates may also sit in the Crown Court with a judge to hear appeals from magistrates' courts against conviction or sentence and proceedings on committal to the Crown Court for sentence.
>
> **Civil Matters**
> Magistrates decide many civil matters, particularly in relation to family work. Specially selected and trained members of the family court panels deal with a wide range of matters, most of which arise from the breakdown of marriage, e.g. making orders for the residence of and contact with children. Proceedings relating to the care and control of children are also dealt with in family proceedings courts. The civil jurisdiction also involves the enforcement of financial penalties and orders such as those in respect of non-payment of council tax.
>
> **Other Duties**
> Members of specialist committees are responsible for appeals against local authority licensing decisions. Magistrates are expected to play a part in the life of the bench and where

> possible, attend bench meetings etc. They may undertake work out of court, as members of committees. They are also expected to deal, at home, with requests for warrants for arrest and search and to take declarations of various kinds.

As with other court proceedings, in magistrates' courts, applications are made, evidence is presented, clarification sought until, armed with the relevant information, decisions can be made. On a finding or admission of guilt, magistrates may request a pre-sentence report (PSR) to assist them in their choice of the most appropriate disposal for a particular offender. This is prepared by the probation service after interviews with the offender and relevant others.

Defendants may be summonsed or charged to appear in court. Offences fall into three categories: summary offences that can *only* be heard in the magistrates' court, indictable offences that *must* be heard in the Crown court because they are so serious, and a band of 'either way' offences which may be heard in the magistrates' court with the agreement of the magistrates and the defendant. In general, the seriousness of the offence is related to the maximum penalties prescribed by parliament. The usual limit of magistrates' sentencing powers is a fine of £5,000 or a custodial period of up to six months for a single offence.

Sentencing guidance has been available for many years, through the Magistrates' Association, in consultation with other bodies, and from appellant courts. From 1999, it was supplemented by that of the Sentencing Advisory Panel (Crime and Disorder Act 1998). With the creation of the Sentencing Guidelines Council (Criminal Justice Act 2003) guidance was put on a statutory basis such that sentencers *must have regard* to it with reasons provided to justify departures from it (see excerpt below).

Guidance is based on the principle of *just deserts* as the penalty must reflect the seriousness of the offence and the personal circumstances of the offender.[4] Magistrates are advised to start the sentencing process by considering all the circumstances of the offence, acknowledging any aggravating or mitigating features, making a judicial assessment of the appropriate seriousness category. The actual or potential harm caused and the culpability of the defendant are relevant. At this stage only, the personal circumstances of the defendant, including guilty pleas or previous responses to penalties, may provide further mitigation that may affect the penalty chosen. The Guidelines indicate how to assess the appropriate starting point for each offence that it deals with. This starting point will be along a range of sentencing options available for a first-time offender, initially pleading not guilty to a particular offence. Reassessments of an individual case are made against this standard, as different factors are taken into account. The overarching guidance from the Sentencing Guidelines Council can be summarised as follows:

1. Identify the offence seriousness in terms of culpability and harm caused and use the guidelines to find the starting point for the range of possible sentences.
    a. Consider both aggravating and mitigating factors to decide whether to add to or reduce sentence from the starting point. Aggravating factors include multiple charges and factors laid down in statute to make an offence more serious, such as racial or religious aggravation or previous convictions.
2. Form a preliminary view of the appropriate sentence, then consider offender mitigation
3. Consider a reduction for a guilty plea
4. Consider ancillary orders, including compensation [ancillary orders could include disqualification of ownership of an animal; an Anti Social Behaviour Order; a Binding Over Order, etc.]
5. Decide sentence and give reasons …
    a. Sentencers must state reasons for the sentence passed in every case, including for any ancillary orders imposed. It is particularly important to identify any aggravating or mitigating factors, or matters of offender mitigation, that have resulted in a sentence more or less severe than the suggested starting point.
    b. If a court imposes a sentence of a different kind or outside the range indicated in the guidelines, it must state its reasons for doing so. The court should also give its reasons for not making an order that has been canvassed before it or that it might have been expected to make. (Summarised from Sentencing Guidelines Council 2008: 15–18)

How do magistrates reach sentencing decisions?

The sentencing guidelines outlined above give a clear framework for sentencing. They also indicate both the amount of information that needs to be processed and the scope for discretion present in sentencing. As such, it is reasonable as psychologists that we ask how magistrates reach their decisions on sentencing. Theoretically, decision-making has been approached from a number of perspectives. These perspectives seek to elucidate both the *process* by which we reach decisions and the *outcomes* of that process. Three categories of model are regularly represented: normative, descriptive and heuristic.

In the *normative* models, the brain functions as an information processing system to make comparative calculations of the significance, likelihood and frequency of events and outcomes. These are factored into a mathematical computation (Van der Pligt 1996), often extremely complex, to predict the choice. They tend to predict the decision that *ought* to be taken (Abelson and Levi 1985), rather than that which may *actually* be made. A *descriptive* approach is more concerned with representing a socio-cognitive process as an expression of thoughts, feelings and emotional reactions. Abelson and Levi (1985) intimate that this approach may explain departures from the 'norm'. *Heuristic processing* represents the variety of short cuts that people use, *good enough* decisions. It may not ensure ideal or thorough deliberation of all circumstances but typically suffices for most purposes, providing a fair representation of what actually may be occurring. It might be mathematical or descriptive in nature.

It should be noted that there is a degree of overlap within the literature. For example, although normative models are explicitly based on mathematical techniques for handling data, a descriptive approach can also lead to models tested through mathematical analyses. Some apparently comprehensive descriptive approaches may subsume heuristics within their cognitive construction. In this way, boundaries become obscured. For a comprehensive overview of decision-making models see, for example, Abelson and Levi (1985) or Semin and Fiedler (1996).

The majority of legal decision-making psychological research has concentrated on jury, rather than judicial, decision-making and most studies have relied on jury-eligible adults or student samples (e.g. Moore and Gump 1995; Pennington and Hastie 1986; Mitchell and Byrne 1973; Kravitz *et al.* 1993). Some studies have involved professional legal decision-makers (e.g. Ebbesen and Konečni 1975; Oswald and Drewniak 1996). A few studies have engaged practising magistrates from England (Kapardis and Farrington 1981; Dhami and Ayton 2001; for example). Differences between professional and lay judges, (Diamond 1990; Hogarth 1971), experts and novices (Carroll and Payne 1977), and the varying approaches of experts with different levels of experience have been observed (Lawrence 1988) and socio-demographic variables have been implicated (Bond and Lemon 1981; Hood 1962; Davis *et al.* 1993).

Several authors have written about the difficulties that need to be addressed in devising a model for legal decision-making. Hawkins (1983) drew attention to the special role of legal discretion in what he suggests is 'an immensely complex matter' (p. 7). He described the legal process as one shaped by 'decisions made in a dynamic, unfolding process ... terminating at various salient points' (p. 7). Lloyd-Bostock (1988) presents sentencing as an 'open' problem-solving task, where the criteria for the 'right' decision are not clear and the moral dimension in sentencing is an additional complication in judging the 'rightness' of a sentence. Limitations on the information available, its probabilistic nature and the time frame, combine with the cognitive capacity of the individual to challenge the intention to reach the 'best' sentencing choice.

Lloyd-Bostock (*ibid.*) raises the importance of the fact that experience gained as a magistrate develops from novice to seasoned practitioner. Representing decision-making as a skill-based task falling somewhere on a continuum according to how automatic it was, she suggests that as legal decision-makers gain experience, the process may become increasingly internally autonomised (cf. Fiske and Taylor 1991). Lloyd-Bostock (1988) suggests that most of the time, sentencing falls around the middle of the automatic spectrum, citing Lawrence and Homel 1986 to proffer 'a patterned expectation which was activated as soon as the charge was read' (Lloyd-Bostock 1988: 63). This is reinforced by judges referring to 'an intuitive process, using terms such as "instinct", "hunch" and "feeling"' (Ashworth *et al.* 1984, cited in Lloyd-Bostock 1988: 63).

We now consider examples of studies that directly explore sentencing decisions made by judges and magistrates (lay and professional). Clearly, magistrates have to decide on acquittal or conviction – the verdict – as well as bail and sentencing decisions. As there is a well-established, easily accessible body of literature on jury verdict decision-making, we have here concentrated on sentencing.

In considering normative or mathematical models of decision-making, the main type of model that has been previously applied to magistrates is attributional, although related models have been applied to jury decision-making (e.g. Fenton and Neil 2000; Pennington and Hastie 1986; Hastie 1993). In the general attribution literature, Anderson (1965) discussed an information integration model for handling cognitive input in the formation of impressions through the consideration of positive and negative attributes that are integrated (normally through summative or weighted averaging) to produce an overall impression. They then influence the creation of schemata that represent knowledge about a concept. From attributes, inferences are made that allow us to ascribe meaning and causality to observed behaviour.

Different models for assigning causal attributions have been developed. Kelley's covariation model (1967, 1973) posited the aspects of consistency, distinctiveness and consensus: with low consistency between observations, an alternative explanation was sought. With high consistency, high distinctiveness and high consensus, an external (situational) attribution was made. High consistency but low distinctiveness and low consensus led to an internal attribution (within the person) as an explanation for the behaviour. An extension of Kelley's model led to the development of Weiner's (1985) attributional theory concerned with the causes and consequences of the attributions made for people's success or failure on a task.

Ewart (1996) adopted Weiner's approach to understand sentencing in English magistrates' courts and the Crown court. Weiner's attributional theory of motivation (Weiner 1985) used the three dimensions of causal locus (internal versus external), stability and controllability to define an activity, the offending behaviour. This theory was applied to predict sentencing outcomes in a sample of both real and hypothetical cases, manipulated in respect of the three dimensions. Following Carroll and Payne (1977), Ewart felt that this particular model replicated factors that sentencers reported taking into account, viz. the degree of responsibility of the defendant (locus), the likelihood of reoffending (stability) and the blameworthiness of the offender (controllability). Further, it could be used to accommodate aggravation and mitigation, both important elements in structured sentencing (Shapland 1981).

Results indicated that the sentencing of some crimes was better represented by an attributional model than others. In explaining this, Ewart (1996) drew on Reitman (1965) to suggest that different models applied in different circumstances. For some offences, the goal state i.e. the appropriate sentence, was well defined, as when the overriding sentencing principle was proportionality, and a 'tariff' approach could be applied. In others, this was less clear because of the particular information about the offence or offender, leading to an alternative choice of model for the decision. The two alternative approaches are represented in Figure 7.1.

This model has the attraction of accommodating many of the relevant legal factors but also alerts us to the possibility that model choice may vary between cases, dependent on the goal-state. Goal-state itself may be related to the type of offence, as Ewart (1996) suggested, or perhaps to the variety of sentencing aims.

Any attributional approach is vulnerable to the Fundamental Attribution Error (Ross 1977). In the sentencing context, this would attach disproportionate culpability to the defendant, over potentially mitigating aspects of the context of the offending behaviour. Further, the 'false consensus effect' (Ross *et al.* 1977) could give rise to sentencing *observers* (the magistrates) distorting the level of deviance of others when determining the seriousness of an offence or the degree of mitigation, thereby producing misleading observations upon which to base model predictions.

McKnight (1981) applied a multi-attributional utility (MAU) model in combination with personal construct theory (Kelly 1955) to identify the causal attributes and their relative importance relevant to the sentencing task. Applying a linear combination representation of these

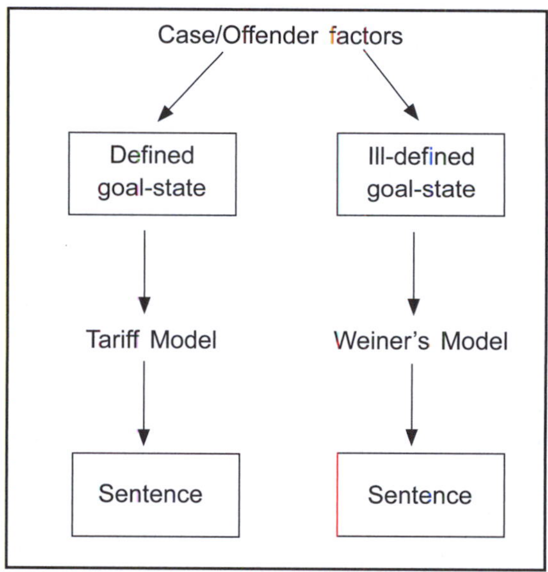

Figure 7.1 After Ewart (1996: 30)

weighted attributes in a MAU model, he collected data to compare nine magistrates' actual sentencing decisions with mathematical predictions. McKnight (1981) reported good correlation between the two, indicating reasonably high predictive power for the model. Apparent 'inconsistency' between participants was explained as a result of the combination of beliefs and values arrived at by subjective construction for each individual. Comparison measurements of group and individual decisions produced 'fair or better' agreement in two of the three cases studied. Indications of sample size and participant tolerance should be noted.

When considering bail (rather than post-verdict) decisions, Konečni and Ebbesen (1982) raised concerns similar to those of Lloyd-Bostock (1988) regarding the extent to which the reasons *provided* for a sentencing decision represented the *actual* reasons for that decision. At interview, judges indicated that they regarded sentencing as a multifaceted, complex task, yet when observed, appeared to base their decisions on relatively few factors: seriousness of offence, prior record of offender, and the recommendation of the probation officer. This was reinforced by later work exploring other judicial decisions (Konečni and Ebbesen 1984; Kunin *et al.* 1992) leading to the conclusion that judicial decision-making was much simpler than reported despite its apparently complex context.

Turning to descriptive models, five approaches have been most widely applied to legal decision-making: *'story' models; anchored narratives; prospect theory; frames of reference;* and *schemata*. Again, sentencing decision-making has been much less frequently explored than jury/verdict decision-making. We have here concentrated on *frames of reference* as previously more clearly applied to sentencing although, no single model of decision-making may be universally applied. Sentencing is an example of a 'difficult' decision and magistrates may each have their own preferred mode for dealing with a problem (Tada 2001).

Lawrence (1988) attempted to model magistrates' sentence decision-making using *frames of reference* that 'define a problem space, set limits on what it contains and focus attention on its features' (p. 231). These frames interact with procedures for making sense of the information magistrates are asked to consider and generating solutions. Lawrence (1988) recruited 15 Australian stipendiary magistrates (i.e. professional practitioners). The data analysed came from magistrates' accounts of their cognitions and the procedure was as naturalistic as possible, with two novices and one experienced magistrate working together (like two wingers and a chair) on three simulated case studies based on real cases; file data were provided, as in a real case. The participants made verbal responses for record and transcription.

Results showed variation between the sentencing decisions of the experienced and novice magistrates. Experts were more willing to regard the defendants as individuals, to be dealt with according to circumstances, whereas the novice worked to a tariff approach. Differences between types of magistrate were apparent, both at the level of objectives brought to a case and inferences made; also, on the sentencing solutions they contemplated. Experience provided the experts with patterns for reducing workloads and led to similar goals and perspectives on different types of offence in this small sample.

Frames of reference fit naturally into the general decision-making literature of schemata and automatic processing. According to Fiske and Taylor (1991), schemata are narrative ways of representing expectations and their effects. A scenario may be more easily understood through scripts that deal with likely sequences of events and a schema that 'fills in the blanks' where ambiguities persist. The more automatic the schema invoked, the more closely the process of accurate consideration blends into a heuristic attempt to reach a 'good enough' understanding.

As the need for accuracy increases and the costs of error can show real adverse implications for other people, Neuberg and Fiske (1987) suggested that automatically cued schemata are replaced by an increased attention to the data. According to Fiske and Taylor (1991), processing moves from a top-down, conceptually driven activity, heavily reliant on organised prior knowledge, to a preference for a bottom-up consideration of the features of a particular scenario. This transition might be replicated for magistrates as they wrestle with cases of increased complexity.

Their model represents a continuum, moving from initial categorisation, organising the information about a person or a situation around the already internalised features of a prototype or by comparison with an exemplar, proceeding to confirmatory categorisation, followed by recategorisation then piecemeal integration. This can be contrasted with the consideration of all the individual pieces of information available, each of which must be evaluated before any understanding of the event is achieved. There was also evidence in the work of Fiske and Taylor (1991) that the use of schemata had implications for how information was encoded, retained in memory and the inferences drawn.

Moving lastly onto heuristic models, these would initially seem to be similar to the schemata in that they allow gaps to be filled through pre-existing knowledge/assumptions made by the decision-maker. Dhami and Ayton (2001) studied the decision-making strategies of English magistrates through an examination of their decisions regarding bail and found results very similar to the Ebbesen and Konečni series reported above. Eighty-one magistrates from 44 courts participated in a postal survey component to the research; and court observations were undertaken. The results compared the predictions of judgement analysis techniques with those of a simple matching heuristic referred to as a fast and frugal model, based on the 'information search, stop and decision-making' format suggested by Gigerenzer and Goldstein (1996). The flowchart in Figure 7.2 shows the decision-making process, as the participant searches the cues to inform his/her decision.

Results showed that the number of cues used in a decision ranged from 1 to 1.67 with a mean of 1.1. Previous convictions and bail record were the most influential cues. In 75 per cent of the decisions, magistrates used only one cue, 21 per cent relied on two, and 3 per cent searched for three cues above the critical value, before making a decision. A comparison with the predictions made using two mathematical compensatory integration models indicated that the

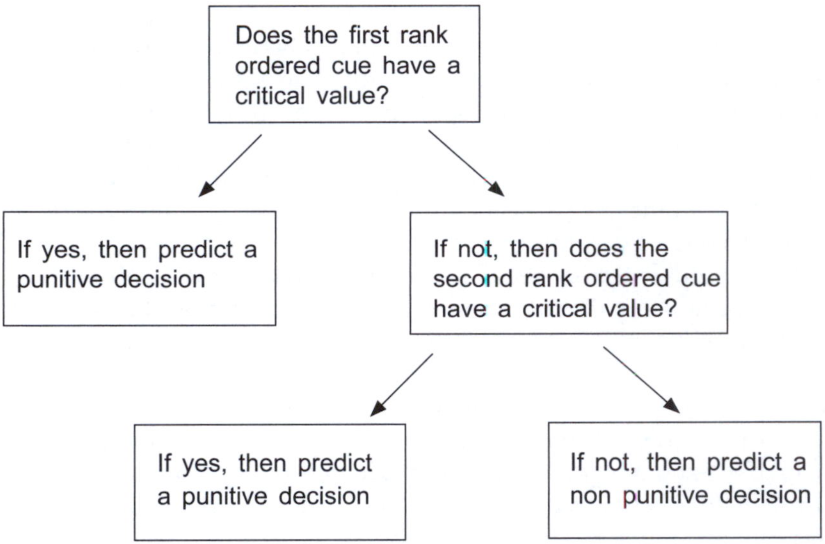

Figure 7.2 Flow chart for the matching heuristic searching up to two cues (Dhami and Ayton 2001)
NB A punitive decision includes the withholding of bail or the imposition of conditions on bail.

matching heuristic, characterised by non-compensatory processing of information, performed at least as well, and in some cases better, than the alternatives. While the model presented an appealingly simple strategy for the resolution of bail decisions, it is more difficult to anticipate how it could be adapted to accommodate the multifaceted choices available to a sentencing Bench.

By positing the model of 'elimination by aspects', Tversky (1972) challenged the assumption of simple scalability in probabilistic analyses of choice. He suggested a staged process of choice with a particular aspect in focus at each stage. As the alternatives are considered, those that do not satisfy this aspect are eliminated. The process proceeds to the next aspect on a weighted consideration, again eliminating alternatives, until only one remains. This appears to be almost a descriptive version of Dhami and Ayton's (2001) later mathematical heuristic. The process can be terminated early if the aspect selected for consideration is weighted so far ahead of other aspects that it permits the early elimination of alternatives. Within the context of the bail study, for example, if the possibility of repeat offending is prioritised, then a consideration of other aspects, such as witness protection, need never be addressed. If no conditions can be imposed to satisfy this concern, the possibility of release will, effectively, be eliminated and a decision made after consideration of a single aspect.

In determining whether an individual will undertake a thorough examination of all the available information, analytical and intuitive decision-making may be distinguished. The former involves slow data processing, with high levels of control and high awareness of that processing while the latter is characterised by rapid, limited consideration of the available material. Individuals differ in their preferred mode (Kokis *et al.* 2002; Sjoberg 2003) and may adapt the process to reflect the particular circumstances and nature of specific decisions. In assessing the implications for justice, we might consider that intuitive and quasi-rational cognition may be more accurate than analytical cognition (Hammond *et al.* 1987) so we should not assume superiority of one approach.

This brings us more directly to explore outcomes. Kapardis and Farrington (1981) and Kapardis (1985) developed and used a sentencing severity scale along with the results of a sentencing exercise, to suggest case features important to predicting sentence. Sentence severity was associated with offence severity. Male offenders of higher social status, with a previous record of offending, attracted more severe punishments but the age, race, plea and prevalence of the offence were not significant. Further, sentencing decisions on real and simulated material were similar and groups were likely to be relatively more severe than individuals, in line with group behaviours such as polarisation and risky shift (Moscovici and Zavalloni 1969).

Relatedly, Corbett (1987) explored magistrates' sentencing in terms of the degree of consensus achieved and did not find support for the idea that the group processes may limit the range of sentences adopted. Corbett (*ibid.*) also looked at the relative proportions of aggravation and mitigation within the reasons given. She found that as the proportion of aggravation increased, the severity of sentencing also increased but there was variation among sentencers about whether material was mitigating or aggravating. In contrast to Shapland (1981) and Fitzmaurice and Pease (1986), this study 'found a fairly linear pattern between favourable and unfavourable observations [made within the reasons given] and sentence severity' (Corbett 1987: 212). When Gilchrist and Blissett (2002) explored magistrates' reasons given in domestic violence cases, they found that extra-legal factors were at play and, again, some confusion was apparent in the interpretation of information as aggravating or mitigating.

Integrating different approaches

Carroll *et al.* (1987) sought to pull together different approaches to sentencing within an organising framework that moved from general concepts to specific outcomes. They looked for analogies between the different features represented in three approaches: individual differences, attitude theory, and attribution theory. Variables identified as relevant to the sentencing task included authoritarianism and locus of control and they found an interrelationship between political ideology and causal attributions.

Another integrated approach was adopted by the first author of this chapter in conducting work for her doctoral thesis (with 82 participants from six Benches of magistrates, three in a major conurbation and three in more rural locations). In her first study, participants received a self-completion questionnaire in three parts. Part 1 placed the individual within defined age bands; assessed their magisterial experience, ethnicity, political affiliation, educational level and employment history. It also contained a compilation of the NEO Five-Factor Inventory (NEO-FFI) (Costa and McCrae 1992) together with other scales, including the original Rotter (1966) scale to measure Locus of Control (LOC). Part 2 sought to derive a sentencing severity scale and Part 3 presented a sentencing exercise of three case vignettes. Participants recorded their sentencing decisions on the 'facts' provided and elucidated reasons for their choices. This material was used to explore how individuals approached the sentencing task – the process; and the severity of the sentencing decision – the outcome.

Who are the magistrates?

Relative to the general population, magistrates do not appear to display any extreme personality characteristics, contrary to their popular image in some quarters (Gifford 1986; Darbyshire 1997). On the elements of the five-factor model, with the possible exception of below average Neuroticism and slightly increased Openness, they were indistinguishable from the general public from whom they are recruited.

None of the five factors demonstrated significant difference for variation in age or gender, and different levels of education (from basic to postgraduate/higher professional training) indicated a significant difference on the measurement of Openness, supporting Costa and McCrae (1992). Different political sympathies also demonstrated significant differences on the dimension of Openness, Liberal Democrat supporters achieving the highest score and Conservatives the lowest.

Although the recruitment criteria might have indicated an enhanced requirement for Conscientiousness, in practice, individuals provided a normal distribution of this attribute. Despite a slight tendency towards internal locus of control, the differences from student means were insufficient to anticipate adverse implications for defendants (see below).

How do magistrates sentence and what affects their choices?

In Part 2, participants were asked to rank order a series of possible sentences to try to construct a sentencing severity scale. In Part 3 of the materials, participants were presented with three vignettes, and the magistrates were asked to indicate an appropriate sentence (*disposal*) for each and to explain their sentencing reasons. A simple algebraic model of sentencing, combining aggravating and mitigating features, assigned positive and negative values respectively and summated, was used to represent aspects of these reasons numerically.

The data provided no strong support for correlations between the five (NEAOC) personality traits tested – Neuroticism, Extroversion, Agreeableness, Openness and Conscientiousness – and the effect they might have on the sentencing process, nor the sentencing outcome. Participants tended to concur although there were modest indications that increasing internal LOC was associated with harsher sentencing and women chose marginally less severe sentences than men. However, even though the mean estimate of seriousness judged by participants was the same for each offence, the mean severity of disposals varied considerably. None of the analyses appeared to support a simple algebraic relationship between the entry point recommended and the interpretation of the case as indicated from the record of aggravating and/or mitigating features, although the amount of aggravation identified appeared influential. In this research, the aggravating and mitigating factors coincided with the Guidance.

There was no predictable relationship with the entry point and the disposal chosen. Disposals seemed to be more closely associated with the sentencing aims and frequently concurred with the sentence proposed in the pre-sentence report (PSR), concordant with Konečni and Ebbesen 1984. The entry point takes into account only the seriousness of an offence and aims to identify proportionate punishment. By contrast, the PSR considers personal information about an offender and may have a specific aim when suggesting sentence. Thus, the sentencing aim emerged as a potentially key determining influence in the sentencing choice, in combination with PSR recommendations. To investigate these findings further, a qualitative approach was employed in a second study with 10 magistrates.

Magistrates' reflections on sentencing

Each magistrate participated in a semi-structured interview lasting one to two hours. The protocol raised aspects of their work including: the effect of training and knowledge; the application of guidance and structured decision-making; sentencing aims; the influence of PSRs and magistrates' relationship with the Legal Advisers. The interplay of individual differences, personality traits or socio-demographic indicators, exerting influence either on the sentencing process or outcome and the role of an individual sitting as either Chair or Winger, were also discussed. Participants were prompted to reflect on actual sentencing dilemmas or difficult choices that they had encountered. The interviews were analysed using Interpretative Phenomenological Analysis (IPA) (Smith and Osborn 2003; Pidgeon and Henwood 1997; Willig 2001). The main themes to emerge were: their willingness and ability to use Guidance and structured decision-making; threats to structured decision-making (such as a failure to reach consensus or having to make decisions that were dissonant with their moral compass); pre- sentence reports, which they were enthusiastic about but emphatically denied using as a short cut to reach their independent decision; the role and influence of the Legal Adviser; personal characteristics (such as agreeableness and conscientiousness) of sentencers and their effect on both process and outcome; group effects on process and outcome (e.g. the impact of strong group cohesion, the role of the chair and co-operative working that could all minimise the impact of processes such as risky shift).

Conclusion

The picture emerges of an increasingly well-trained, accountable body of magistrates that is gender representative. With the capacity to act and think judicially, it is confident in its ability to empathise both with those it serves and those who appear before it. It is versed in structured decision-making and insightful about aspects that may influence it. Continuing improvement in the selection and training of magistrates and consistency of approach to court processes may help reduce the perception of arbitrariness for some defendants. However, it seems unlikely that the personalised reactions to sentencing will ever be wholly overcome. Indeed, it may be one of the strengths of the current system that when a sentence is chosen, the personal characteristics of the sentencer may be differentially engaged.

Notes

1 Extracted from the Judicial Oath sworn by magistrates on appointment.
2 The terms magistrate, lay magistrate, justice and JP refer essentially to the same activity. While JP is a lifetime designation, active service concludes at the age of 70.
3 Now replaced with a single community order that may have requirements attached.
4 www.sentencing-guidelines.gov.uk/docs/SGC%20Magistrates%20Guidelines%20including%20update%201%20%202%20.pdf (accessed May 2009).

References

Abelson, R. and Levi, A. (1985) 'Decision making and decision theory', in G. Lindsey and E. Aronson (eds), *The Handbook of Social Psychology* (3rd edn, Vol. 1, Theory and Method, Ch. 5: 231–309). New York: Random House.

Anderson, N.H. (1965) 'Adding versus averaging as a stimulus combination rule in impression formation', *Journal of Experimental Psychology*, 70: 394–400.

Asch, S.E. (1946) 'Forming impressions of personality', *Journal of Abnormal and Social Psychology*, 41: 258–90.

Ashworth, A., Genders, E., Mansfield, G., Peay, J. and Player, E. (1984) *Sentencing in the Crown Court: Report of an Exploratory Study*. University of Oxford Centre for Criminological Research, Occasional Paper No. 10. Cited in S. Lloyd-Bostock (1988) *Law in Practice: Applications of psychology to legal decision making and legal skills*. London: British Psychological Society and Routledge.

Bond, R.A. and Lemon, N.F. (1981) 'Training, experience and magistrates' sentencing philosophies: a longitudinal study', *Law and Human Behavior*, 5: 123–39.

Carroll, J., Perkowitz, W., Lurigio, A. and Weaver, F. (1987) 'Sentencing goals, causal attributions, ideology and personality', *Journal of Personality and Social Psychology*, 52 (1): 107–18.

Carroll, J.S. and Payne, J.W. (1977) 'Crime seriousness, recidivism risk and causal attributes in judgments of prison term by students and experts', *Journal of Applied Psychology*, 62 (5): 595–602.

Carter, J. (2001) *Magistrates' Companion to the Competences* (2nd edn). Leeds Lawtexts.

Corbett, C. (1987) 'Magistrates' and court clerks' sentencing behaviour: an experimental study', in D.C. Pennington and S.M. Lloyd Bostock (eds), *The Psychology of Sentencing: approaches to consistency and disparity*. Oxford: Centre for Socio-Legal Studies.

Costa, P. and McCrae, R. (1992) *NEO PI-R, Professional Manual, Revised NEO Personality Inventory (NEO PI-R) and NEO Five Factor Inventory (NEO-FFI)*. Odessa, FL: Psychological Assessment Resources.

Darbyshire, P. (1997) 'For the new Lord Chancellor – some causes for concern about magistrates', *Criminal Law Review*, 861–74.

Davis, T., Severy, L., Kraus, S. and Whitaker, M. (1993) 'Predictors of sentencing decisions: the beliefs, personality variables and demographic factors of juvenile justice personnel', *Journal of Applied Social Psychology*, 23 (6): 451–77.

DCA website (2004) www.dca.gov.uk/judicial/ja-arep2004/parttwo.htm#inpost (accessed March 2005).

Dhami, M. and Ayton, P. (2001) 'Bailing and jailing the fast and frugal way', *Journal of Behavioral Decision Making*, 14 (2): 141–68.

Diamond, S. (1990) 'Revising images of public punitiveness: sentencing by lay and professional English magistrates', *Law and Social Inquiry*, 191–221.

Ebbesen, E.B. and Konečni, V.J. (1975) 'Decision making and information integration in the courts: the setting of bail', *The Journal of Personality and Social Psychology*, 32: 805–21.

Ewart, B.W. (1996) 'A social psychological approach to understanding sentencing in the Crown and Magistrates courts', *Issues in Criminological and Legal Psychology*, 26: 23–32.

Fenton, N. and Neil, M. (2000) 'The "jury observation fallacy" and the use of Bayesian Networks to present probabilistic legal arguments', *Mathematics Today, Bulletin of IMA*, 36(6): 180–87.

Fiske, S.T. and Taylor, S.E. (1991) *Social Cognition* (2nd edn). New York: McGraw-Hill.

Fitzmaurice, C. and Pease, K. (1986) *The Psychology of Judicial Sentencing*. Manchester, UK: Manchester University Press.

Gifford, T. (1986) *Where's the Justice? A manifesto for law reform*. London: Penguin.

Gigerenzer, G. and Goldstein, D. (1996) 'Reasoning the fast and frugal way: models of bounded rationality', *Psychological Review*, 103: 650–69.

Gilchrist, E. and Blissett, J. (2002) 'Magistrates' attitudes to domestic violence', *The Howard Journal of Criminal Justice*, 41 (4): 384–63.

Hammond, K.R., Hamm, R.M., Grassia, J. and Pearson, T. (1987) 'Direct comparison of the efficacy of intuitive and analytical cognition in expert judgment', *IEEC Transactions on Systems, Man and Cybernetics*, 17 (5): 753–770.

Hastie, R. (1993) (ed.) *Inside the Juror: The Psychology of Jury Decision Making*. Cambridge: Cambridge University Press.

Hawkins, K.O. (1983) 'Thinking about legal decision making', in J. Shapland (ed.), *Decision Making in the Legal System*, Issues in Criminological and Legal Psychology, No. 5. Leicester, UK: The British Psychological Society for the Division of Criminological and Legal Psychology.

Hogarth, J. (1971) *Sentencing as a Human Process*. Toronto: University of Toronto Press.

Hood, R.G. (1962) *Sentencing in Magistrates' Courts*. London: Stevens.

Julian, J.W. and Katz, S.B. (1968) 'Internal versus external control and the value of reinforcement', *Journal of Personality and Social Psychology*, 8 (1, PT 1): 89–94.

Kapardis, A. and Farrington, D. (1981) 'An experimental study of sentencing by magistrates', *Law and Human Behavior*, 5 (2/3): 107–21.

Kapardis, A. (1985) *Sentencing by English Magistrates as a Human Process*. Nicosia, Cyprus: Asselia Publishers.

Kelley, H.H. (1973) 'The process of causal attribution', *American Psychologist*, 28: 107–28.

Kelley, H.H. (1967) 'Attribution theory in social psychology', in D. Levine (ed.), *Nebraska Symposium on Motivation*. Lincoln, NB: University of Nebraska Press.

Kelly, G.A. (1955) *The Psychology of Personal Constructs*. New York: Norton.

Kokis, J., Macpherson, R., Topiak, M., West, R. and Stanovich, K. (2002) 'Heuristic and analytical processing: age trends and cognitive ability and cognitive style', *Journal of Experimental Child Psychology*, 83 (1): 26–52.

Konečni, V.J. and Ebbesen, E.B. (1984) 'The mythology of legal decision making', *International Journal of Law and Psychiatry*, 7 (1): 5–18.

Konečni, V.J. and Ebbesen, E.B. (eds) (1982) *The Criminal Justice System: a socio-psychological analysis*. San Francisco: Freeman.

Kravitz, D., Cutler, B., and Brock, P. (1993) 'Reliability and validity of the original legal attitudes questionnaire', *Law and Human Behavior*, 17 (6): 661–77.

Kunin, C.C., Ebbesen E.B. and Konečni, V.J. (1992) 'An archival study of decision-making in child custody disputes', *Journal of Clinical Psychology*, 48 (4): 564–73.

Lawrence, J. (1988) 'Expertise on the bench: modelling magistrates' judicial decision-making', in M. Chi, R. Glaser and M.J. Farr (eds), *The Nature of Expertise*. Hillsdale, NJ: Lawrence Erlbaum Associates Inc.

Lawrence, J.A. and Homel, R. (1986) 'Sentencing in magistrates' courts: The magistrate as professional decision-maker', in I. Potas (eds), *Sentencing in Australia: Policies, Issues and Reform*. Canberra: Australian Institute of Criminology.

Lloyd-Bostock, S. (1988) *Law in Practice: Applications of psychology to legal decision making and legal skills*. London: British Psychological Society and Routledge.

Magistrates' Association website (2009) www.magistrates-association.org.uk/ (accessed 8 January 2009).

McKnight, C. (1981) 'Subjectivity in sentencing', *Law and Human Behavior*, 5: 141–47.

Mitchell, H. and Byrne, D. (1973) 'The defendant's dilemma: effects of jurors' attitudes and authoritarianism on judicial decisions', *Journal of Personality and Social Psychology*, 25 (1): 123–29.

MOJ (2009a) www.justice.gov.uk/docs/judicial-court-stats-chapter7pdf (accessed January 2009).

MOJ (2009b) www.justice.gov.uk/docs/judicial-court-stats-chapter9.pdf (accessed January 2009).

MOJ (2009c) *Serving as a Magistrate: A detailed guide to the role of JP*. www.direct.gov.uk/en/CrimeJusticeAndTheLaw/Becomingamagistrate/DG_071396.pdf (accessed March 2009).

MOJ (2009d) www.direct.gov.uk/en/CrimeJusticeAndTheLaw/Becomingamagistrate/index.htm (accessed January 2009).

MOJ (2009e) www.justice.gov.uk/docs/race-equality-scheme.pdf (accessed January 2009).

Moore, P. and Gump, B. (1995) 'Information integration in juror decision making', *Journal of Applied Social Psychology*, 25 (24): 2158–79.

Moscovici, S. and Zavalloni, M. (1969) 'The group as a polarizer of attitudes', *Journal of Personality and Social Psychology*, 12: 125–335.

Neuberg, S.L., and Fiske, S.T. (1987) 'Motivational influences on impression formation: outcome dependency, accuracy-driven attention and individuating processes', *Journal of Personality and Social Psychology*, 53: 431–44.

Oswald, M. and Drewniak, R. (1996) 'Attitude and behavior of male and female judges', in G. Davies, S. Lloyd Bostock, M. McMurran and C. Wilson (eds), *Psychology Law and Criminal Justice*. England: Walter de Gruyter.

Parsons, O. and Schneider, J. (1974) 'Locus of control in university students from Eastern and Western societies', *Journal of Consulting and Clinical Psychology*, 42 (3): 456–61.

Pennington, N. and Hastie, R. (1986) 'Evidence evaluation in complex decision making', *Journal of Personality and Social Psychology*, 51: 242–58.

Phares, E.J. (1971) 'Internal-external control and the reduction of reinforcement value after failure', *Journal of Consulting and Clinical Psychology*, 37 (3): 386–90.

Pidgeon, N. and Henwood, K. (1997) 'Using grounded theory', in N. Hayes (ed.), *Doing Qualitative Research in Psychology*. Hove, England: Psychology Press/Erlbaum (UK) Taylor Francis.

Raven, B.H. (1965) 'Social influence and power', in I.D. Steiner and M. Fishbein (eds), *Current Studies in Social Psychology*. New York: Holt, Rinehart and Winston.

Reitman, W.R. (1965) *Cognition and Thought: An Information Processing Approach*. New York: Wiley.

Ross, L. (1977) 'The intuitive psychologist and his shortcomings', in D. Berkowitz (ed.), *Advances in Experimental Social Psychology*. New York: Academic Press.

Ross, L., Greene, D. and House, P. (1977) 'The "false consensus effect": an egocentric bias in social perception and attribution processes', *Journal of Experimental Psychology*, 13: 279–301.

Rotter, J.B. (1966) 'Generalised expectancies for internal versus external control of reinforcement', *Psychological Monographs*, 80 (Whole No. 609).

Semin, G. and Fiedler, K. (1996) *Applied Social Psychology*. London: Sage.

Sentencing Guidelines Council (2008) *Magistrates' Courts Sentencing Guidelines. Definitive Guideline.* www.sentencing-guidelines.gov.uk/docs/SGC%20Magistrates%20Guidelines%20including%20update%201%20%202%20.pdf (accessed March 2009).

Shapland, J. (1981) *Between Conviction and Sentence: The Process of Mitigation*. UK: Routledge and Kegan Paul.

Sjoberg, L. (2003) 'Intuitive vs. analytical decision making: which is preferred?', *Scandinavian Journal of Management*, 19 (1): 17–29.

Skyrme, T. (1979) *The Changing Image of the Magistracy*. London and Basingstoke: Macmillan Press.

Smith, J. and Osborn, M. (2003) 'Interpretative phenomenological analysis', in J.A. Smith (ed.), *Qualitative Psychology: A practical guide to research methods*, pp. 51–80. Thousand Oaks, CA: Sage Publications, Inc.

Tada, Y. (2001) 'Descriptive meta-model of decision-making', *Dissertation Abstracts International: Section B The Sciences and Engineering*, 61 (8-B): 4442.

Tversky, A. (1972) 'Elimination by aspects: a theory of choice', *Psychological Review*, 79: 281–99.

Van der Pligt, J. (1996) 'Judgement and decision making', in G.R. Semin and K. Fiedler (eds), *Applied Social Psychology*. London: Sage.

Weiner, B. (1985) '"Spontaneous" causal thinking', *Psychological Bulletin*, 97: 74–84.

Willig, C. (2001) *Introducing Qualitative Research in Psychology*. Milton Keynes: Open University Press.

Chapter 8

Eliciting evidence from eyewitnesses for court proceedings

Mark R. Kebbell and Elizabeth A. Gilchrist

Background

Eyewitnesses are central to most court cases (Kebbell and Milne 1998; Zander and Henderson 1993). For example, a witness might state, 'That is the man who robbed me, I'm certain of it!' This is powerful evidence that provides not only information concerning who committed the offence but also the nature of the offence. Research shows that jurors rely heavily on eyewitness accounts to determine whether to convict or to acquit (e.g. Cutler *et al.* 1990). However, research into false convictions, for example where subsequent DNA evidence exonerates a convicted individual, shows that one of the most frequent reasons for a false conviction is erroneous witness evidence (Connors *et al.* 1996; Huff *et al.* 1996). Therefore, it is essential that accurate evidence is presented to a court.

Examination in court

The justice system used in most of the English-speaking world to elicit evidence is 'adversarial'. A central premise of this system is that a person is innocent unless proven guilty or they admit guilt. In adversarial systems, a trial does not establish whether the accused is innocent but whether the prosecution evidence is sufficient, 'beyond reasonable doubt', to prove guilt to the jury (Davies *et al.* 1995). The principal way in which the guilt of the accused is established is through verbal witness evidence in court.

Evidence-in-chief occurs first and is supposed to be a relatively open account of what the witness saw, elicited by the lawyer who called the witness. The open nature of the account is to prevent the lawyer from biasing the witness, who is already assumed to be favourable to the lawyer who called him or her (Evans 1995; Murphy and Barnard 1994; Stone 1995). Cross-examination follows evidence-in-chief and is conducted by the opposing lawyer. If a witness is called by the prosecution, cross-examination is conducted by the defence and vice versa. In his popular guide to advocacy, Evans (1995) identifies four broad objectives of lawyers' cross-examination. These are: laying the foundation; putting your case; eliciting extra and useful facts; and discrediting the evidence.

The lawyer is not allowed to comment on matters that have not been touched on during evidence, so laying the foundation and putting your case involves asking questions concerning the case that test the cross-examining lawyer's alternative explanation of events. Eliciting extra and useful facts concerns the cross-examining lawyer attempting to elicit evidence that is favourable to his or her case. However, arguably the most important aspect of cross-examination, as identified by Evans, is discrediting the evidence and he points out, 'it is not a procedure which is aiming to find out the truth' (p. 150). Re-examination sometimes occurs when the lawyer who conducted evidence-in-chief wishes to ask additional questions about information that was provided in cross-examination.

In sum, the aim of examining witnesses in court is for evidence to be elicited so the jury can determine if the evidence is sufficient beyond reasonable doubt to establish guilt. To achieve this aim, the jury must try to determine the accuracy of the evidence provided by the witnesses.

Factors having an impact on witness accuracy

A number of factors impact on a witness's ability to give accurate evidence. These include factors such as how long a crime lasted, how long ago the crime occurred, if the witness was intoxicated and a host of other factors (for a review, see Kebbell and Wagstaff 1999), none of which is under the control of the Criminal Justice System. However, one factor that is under the influence of the Criminal Justice System, and that is crucial to the accuracy and completeness of eyewitness testimony, is the type of question asked (Clifford and George 1996; Fisher *et al.* 1987; Memon and Vartoukian 1996). Open questions (e.g. 'describe your attacker'), closed questions (e.g. 'what colour was his shirt?'), and yes/no questions (e.g. 'was the colour of his shirt red?') can have a dramatic influence on the accuracy of witness answers (Clifford and George 1996; Davies *et al.* 2000; Fisher *et al.* 1987; Hutcheson *et al.* 1995; Memon and Vartoukian 1996; Memon *et al.* 1998; Memon *et al.* 1994; Milne and Bull 1999). People tend to provide the most accurate answers (i.e. where the proportion of correct to incorrect information is greatest) to open questions. The more closed questioning strategies, mentioned above, can reduce the accuracy although they can add detail. As a general proposition, as questions become ever more specific, responses become less accurate (Kebbell and Wagstaff 1999).

The influence of these questions can be understood in terms of the relative demands of the questions. For more open questions, the task is to tell the questioner what the witness *can* remember. For more specific, closed questions, however, the task changes to one of providing the interviewer with what he or she *wants* the witness to remember. One result of this is that witnesses tend to provide less accurate answers to specific questions because they fill memory gaps with distorted or inaccurate material. In other words, they may become suggestible to the demands of the interviewer (Gudjonsson 1992; Kebbell and Wagstaff, 1999). Answers to 'yes or no' questions may be particularly inaccurate because of a general tendency to answer questions with a 'yes' (Gudjonsson 1990, 1992).

Suggestibility (the tendency to provide the answer believed to be required by the questioner) may also be a particular problem with leading questions. Leading questions suggest the response required (e.g. 'Did you see the man's red jumper?', which suggests that the man wore a red jumper). Witnesses are more suggestible to leading questions than neutrally worded questions (e.g. Loftus 1979; Loftus and Zanni 1975). For example, in a classic study by Loftus and Palmer (1974), participants were shown a film of a car accident. Later they were asked, 'About how fast were the cars going when they smashed into each other?' Alternative versions of the questions used the words 'collided', 'bumped', 'hit', or 'contacted'. Although the words all refer to the coming together of two objects, they differ in what they imply about the speed and force of the impact. Participants who received the 'smashed' version estimated the speed at 40.8 mph compared with participants given the 'contacted' version who estimated the speed at 30.8 mph, on average. Clearly, the implication of this is that if witnesses are questioned using inappropriate strategies, their accuracy is likely to suffer.

Research by Kebbell *et al.* (2004) investigated the frequency of the above question types in the examination of 16 alleged victims of rape, sexual assault and assault from the general population. The trials were held at eight different English courts from 1994 to 1999. The frequency of open and closed questions, questions that were leading, and questions that could be answered with a 'yes' or 'no' were documented. In evidence-in-chief: 30 per cent of questions were open; 14 per cent were closed; 51 per cent could be answered with a yes or no; and 3 per cent were leading. In cross-examination, the frequency of the different question types was significantly different from evidence-in-chief: only 16 per cent of questions were open and 4 per cent were closed. There was a significant increase in yes or no questions and leading questions, when compared with evidence-in-chief, making up 87 per cent and 25 per cent of the questions in cross-examination respectively (questions could be coded into more than one category, see also Kebbell *et al.* 2003).

Overall, these results show that the constraining nature of questioning in court, even in evidence-in-chief, is likely to result in many of the problems that have previously been identified concerning police interviewing (Fisher *et al.* 1987; Kebbell and Hatton 1999). That is, the pattern of questioning is likely to break the concentration of an eyewitness, impairing his or her ability to remember information. The use of such constraining questioning also means that the examination takes the form of the lawyer asking a question and the witness giving a brief answer, the lawyer asking another closed question, and so on. This format allows only a short time between a question's answer and the next question, giving little opportunity for the witness to elaborate an answer. Also, and importantly, the format ensures that the evidence is directed by the lawyer rather than the witness so the only information that is elicited is that which is requested. Therefore, if the lawyer forgets to ask a certain question, or does not realise that certain information is important, no information in that area is elicited for the jury. The large number of leading, potentially suggestive questions asked in cross-examination is also disturbing because of the substantial literature showing that they can lead to inaccurate answers (Loftus and Zanni 1975; Loftus *et al.* 1978).

Problems for witnesses are not confined to constraining and leading questions. Questions involving negatives, double negatives, and multiple questions can also pose difficulties to witnesses (Danet 1980; Kebbell and Johnson 2000; Perry *et al.* 1995). Negatives are questions involving the word 'not' (e.g. 'Did the man *not* tell you to be quiet?').

Double negatives are questions involving using the word 'not' twice (e.g. 'Did John *not* say that he would *not* go to the shops?'). These may cause problems because witnesses may have difficulty understanding the question. For instance, evidence from child witness studies show that with respect to children, 'don't know' responses often are given to questions that are not understood. However, if the question is put to them in a simplified form, they often know the answer (Brennan and Brennan 1988; Perry *et al.* 1995). Alternatively, and additionally, instead of saying 'I don't know', witnesses may be tempted to 'guess' the right answer. Kebbell *et al.* (2004) found that negatives accounted for 2 per cent of questions asked in evidence-in-chief and 15 per cent of questions asked in cross-examination. For double negatives, the frequency was much less, less than 1 per cent for both evidence-in-chief and cross-examination, indicating this form of questioning is unlikely to pose regular problems for witnesses.

Multiple questions are those involving two or more parts that have different answers (e.g. 'At 11 o'clock were you in the bar? Was John at the garage?'). Again, in experimental simulations, these kinds of question cause eyewitnesses problems because they may fail to understand the question and usually only give one answer to the last question rather than an answer to both questions (Brennan and Brennan 1988; Kebbell and Johnson 2000; Perry *et al.* 1995). Kebbell *et al.* (2004) found 2 per cent of questions asked in evidence-in-chief were multiple questions compared with 6 per cent in cross-examination. A number of researchers have identified other types of question that lawyers frequently use in court that create difficulties for eyewitnesses. Lawyers may ask questions with advanced vocabulary and/or legal terminology (e.g. 'Was the perpetrator of the crime occluded by any vehicles?') and with complex syntax making them difficult to process (e.g. 'At any time before or after she cried did the vehicle move either forwards or backwards?') (Danet 1980; Kranat and Westcott 1994; Perry *et al.* 1995; Walker 1993; Westcott 1995). Kebbell and Johnson (2000) investigated the effect of the confusing questions often used by lawyers in court. Participants viewed a videotaped film and were individually questioned about the event a week later. Half the participants were asked questions using six categories of confusing question (negatives, double negatives, leading, multiple-questions, complex syntax and complex vocabulary). The remaining half were asked for the same information using simply phrased equivalents. Confusing questions reduced witness accuracy from 76 per cent in the simply phrased condition to 56 per cent in the confusing lawyers' questions condition (see also Perry *et al.* 1995).

Other lawyers' strategies in cross-examination are more subtle, less clearly defined and documented. These include the techniques of 'pining out', 'prefatory remarks', and 'slippery slopes' (Carson 2000; Cooke 1990; Evans 1995). The process of 'pining out' under cross-examination gets the witness to commit him or herself to a position before the advocate comes to the main focus of the argument. For example, the lawyer may get the witness to state that they are not shy then point out that the witness did not tell anyone about the offence until much later, so discrediting their testimony (see Westcott and Page 2002).

Another method that might be used during cross-examination is the prefatory remark. With this technique the lawyer makes a statement prior to asking a question. If the witness fails to make a comment on the statement it appears that he or she agrees with the statement. For example, the lawyer may say, 'I am sure we all agree you don't get into a man's car you've just met at a nightclub without expecting some sexual element, so could you please tell the court when you got into the car with Mr Smith?' Lawyers may also use the 'slippery slope' approach. Here the lawyer tries to redefine the witness's comments to make the lawyer's account seem more likely. The following example illustrates this.

Lawyer In your statement, you say my client is definitely the robber?
Witness Yes.
Lawyer So my client might be the robber?
Witness Yes.
Lawyer So, let me get this clear, you feel that there is the possibility that he is the robber?
Witness Yes.

Of course lawyers may additionally resort to more direct approaches to discredit witness evidence. For example, they may attack the witness's integrity, innocence, and portray the witness as responsible for the crime (Westcott and Page 2002). All these factors are likely to have an impact on witness credibility, an issue to which we now turn.

Witness credibility

The literature reviewed so far shows that many of the questioning strategies adopted by lawyers can have an adverse influence on witnesses' answers. The implication of this is that evidence distorted or constrained by lawyers' questions might result in miscarriages of justice; either false convictions or, alternatively, false acquittals could occur. However, this problem might not be as damaging as it first appears. Jurors and other triers of fact rely heavily on witness confidence to judge the accuracy of evidence (Cutler *et al.* 1990; Cutler *et al.* 1988; Fox and Walters 1986; Leippe *et al.* 1992; Lindsay *et al.* 1989). So a witness who says, 'I'm absolutely certain that the man had a gun' is more likely to be perceived as accurate than the witness who says, 'I think he may have had a gun'. If witnesses' accuracy is impaired by lawyers' questions but confidence in those inaccurate answers is also reduced, then false convictions would be unlikely.

Conversely, the implications for miscarriages of justice are less positive if eyewitness accuracy is low but eyewitnesses are highly confident in their inaccurate answers. Research shows a reasonable, positive confidence–accuracy relationship can be produced (e.g. Kebbell *et al.* 1996; Lindsay *et al.* 1998; Sporer *et al.* 1995 although this issue is controversial, see Elliott 1993; Kassin *et al.* 1994). However, research also shows that confidence–accuracy relationships can be distorted easily (e.g. Luus and Wells 1994; Shaw and McLure 1996). Leippe (1980) suggests this is because the integrative, cognitive processes used to report memory and to report confidence are often unconscious and can be independent of each other. Thus, eyewitness accuracy can be reduced while confidence remains high (e.g. Wells *et al.* 1981) or confidence can be increased or decreased while memory remains the same (e.g. Luus and Wells 1994).

In the previously mentioned study by Kebbell and Johnson (2000), where lawyers' confusing questions were compared with simplified alternatives, mock witnesses were also required to give confidence judgements for each answer they provided on a 10-point Likert scale from 'pure guess' (1) to 'absolutely certain' (10). The difference between confidence regarding correct and incorrect answers in the simplified condition was 3.03 compared with only 1.59 when confusing lawyers' questions were used. This implies that using confusing questions is likely to reduce still further jurors' ability to discriminate between accurate and inaccurate answers.

In the few studies where the effectiveness of cross-examination has been directly tested, its efficacy in terms of enhancing jurors' ability to discriminate between accurate and inaccurate witnesses has not been good. Wells *et al.* (1979) showed mock witnesses a staged theft of a calculator. Witnesses were then required to identify the 'thief' from photo-spreads. Mock jurors were unable to distinguish between accurate and inaccurate witnesses subjected to cross-examination, although interestingly, asking leading questions in cross-examination improved jurors' accuracy (see also Zanjac and Hayne 2003).

Of course, some witnesses may be deliberately lying and cross-examination also has the aim of uncovering this deceit. Consequently, it is worth discussing the effectiveness of cross-examination for detecting deception. Detection of deception in forensic environments has attracted considerable attention (e.g. Vrij 2000) and there are a number of reasons why deception should be detectable. For example, those who are deceiving are likely to experience cognitive and emotional processes that may influence their verbal and non-verbal responses (Vrij 1998). Nevertheless, an extensive literature now indicates that when required to discriminate between honest and deceiving experimental participants, people are not able to discriminate reliably at above chance between those who are deceiving and those who are telling the truth. The reason for this appears to be that cues to nervousness are often confused with cues for deceit (for reviews see Vrij 1998, 2000). However, these studies have not included cross-examination as a factor.

In what is, to our knowledge, the only study to look at the influence of cross-examination on the detection of deception (Kebbell *et al.* 2002) 20 mock defendants stole a wallet while 20 mock defendants did not. All defendants were subsequently cross-examined concerning whether they had stolen the wallet. The 20 who had stolen the wallet were required to lie and say they did not. The cross-examinations of the deceitful and honest defendants were shown to mock jurors. Jurors were unable to determine at a level greater than chance whether defendants were honest or deceitful. However, Kebbell *et al.* (2002) did find that defendants who had stolen the wallet rated themselves as significantly less credible than those who did not, suggesting an important role of cross-examination may be to discourage lying in court even if it is unlikely to expose deceit directly to jurors.

Thus far, it has been implied that all witnesses should be questioned in a manner that may elicit complete and accurate accounts in a similar manner to the way that police interviews should be conducted (see Milne and Bull 1999); for instance, with open-ended, specific questions and very few leading questions, as has been advocated for child witnesses (Davies *et al.* 2000). However, important distinctions exist between police interviews of eyewitnesses and lawyers' questioning of eyewitnesses in court. Specifically, the police are interested in constructing a complete, accurate description of the critical event. By comparison, once the case reaches the courtroom, lawyers question witnesses for the purpose of convincing the jury or judge that their side of the argument is correct. If an accurate recollection does not serve the purpose of convincing the jury, then it does not further the lawyer's cause. It may even militate against the lawyer's argument. As a result, lawyers are not necessarily interested in eliciting complete, accurate recollections.

Nevertheless, it may be in a lawyer's best interests to elicit a complete and accurate account in evidence-in-chief for several reasons. Firstly, as Bell and Loftus showed, jurors perceive more complete and detailed accounts to be more credible (Bell and Loftus 1989). Secondly, a complete and accurate account in evidence-in-chief will mean less inaccurate and contradictory statements that will be able to be challenged in cross-examination. Thirdly, an initial accurate recall attempt may improve witness memory for an event and inoculate against the distorting and damaging effects of leading questions asked in cross-examination (Geiselman *et al.* 1986). Thus, the potential negative impact of the questioning used in cross-examination may be compounded by poor questioning in evidence-in-chief. At this point, it is worthwhile asking the question, 'Why do lawyers attempt to constrain witnesses' responses in evidence-in-chief?' One reason could be that they are trained with the maxim, 'You should never ask a question to which you do not know the answer' (Evans 1995: 118). Further, they are trained to believe that an accurate and complete account of events might damage their case (Evans 1995; Murphy and Barnard 1994). However, this may not necessarily be correct. For instance, if a defendant is guilty, then obtaining a complete and accurate account from a prosecution witness is potentially more likely to result in a conviction than eliciting an incomplete, inconsistent and distorted account that may raise doubts in the jury's or judge's minds, and leave the witness open to damaging cross-examination. Thus, an important point is the frequency of a defendant's guilt. If most defendants are innocent, there might be some advantage for a prosecution lawyer to distort a prosecution witness's account to secure more convictions. However, the strict criteria needed before a prosecution is brought by the Crown Prosecution Service in England and Wales (Rose 1996) and the high numbers of convictions suggest that the majority of defendants in Crown courts are guilty (Home Office 1995). Thus, an open evidence-in-chief designed to maximise the completeness and accuracy of a witness's evidence might be more likely to lead to just convictions. However, while changing to a more open form of evidence-in-chief may be in a lawyer's best interests, a less distorting cross-examination is often not in an opposing lawyer's best interests and lawyers are likely to be reluctant to change. Thus, the combative nature of an adversarial criminal justice system with a 'rigorous' cross-examination relying on closed, constraining and leading questions seems to a large extent unavoidable (Bartlett and Memon 1995; McEwan 1995).

Nevertheless, many of the problems associated with cross-examination identified here have little to do with challenging, testing the evidence and suggesting alternatives. For example, the use of multiple questions, negatives, complex vocabulary and syntax achieves none of these aims but may unfairly discredit the witness because of the confusion they create. It is difficult to see how justice is served by asking witnesses multiple questions using language they do not understand. Many of these problems can be minimised through appropriate intervention by the judge who is obliged not only to have regard to the need to ensure a fair trial for the defendant, but also to the reasonable interests of other parties to the court process (for a detailed discussion see O'Kelly *et al.* 2003). This is particularly true of vulnerable witnesses who are obliged to relive the ordeal to which they have allegedly been subjected (see Carson 1995; Davies and Noon 1991; Sanders *et al.* 1997; Home Office 1999; Westcott 1995). It is the judge's duty to do everything possible to minimise the trauma suffered by other participants (Murphy 1997). The Court of Appeal has also sanctioned the stopping of cross-examination which is repetitive and in which the witness becomes extremely distressed (*R.* v. *Brown* 1998). The judge has a great deal of power. The following examples show how judges can intervene to ensure the 'best' evidence is elicited from witnesses, in these instances involving people with learning disabilities.

Lawyer Did you get the impression that Andrew was being gregarious, sort of a party person at that time?
Judge Did you think he was getting friendly with everybody, was he?
Lawyer As you went into the kitchen, he picked up the wrench to defend himself against you? Because you have attacked Terry in the past, have you not?
Judge Can we perhaps get an answer to the first question? Did Terry pick up the wrench to defend himself from you?
Lawyer Alan thought you had something in your hand.
Judge That is not a question.

> *Lawyer* All right, but my question is a slightly different one. Did you feel upset when you arrived at the discotheque? Well, let me put this to you. You appeared your normal, happy self when you got there and in no way distressed because nothing had happened.
> *Judge* You must separate these questions. You cannot have a multiple question.
> *Lawyer* And exactly the same question for the second time that you have told the court about. Is the answer still yes? Do you want me to put the question another way? Mohamed, is it right that on the second occasion, the day after, when you were washed by that same man, you did not mind him washing your penis and your genitals. Is that right?
> *Judge* Mr Power, I know you are cross-examining and you have a right to put that. I wonder if it is helpful to say: 'On the second occasion, did you mind him washing you there?', rather than putting the negative, and he can answer yes or no to that.

The clear implication of this is that judges should be advised of the issues concerning confusing questions we have outlined here, to ensure simple questions are asked in language the witness understands. Increasingly, the importance of appropriate questioning is being appreciated (e.g. Home Office 2002) and 'special measures' used for 'vulnerable witnesses'.

Special measures for vulnerable witnesses

Recently a range of special measures have been adopted for vulnerable witnesses in different countries such as in England and Wales, Australia and some parts of the United States (see Chapter 10 of this volume for a detailed discussion of the special measures that have been introduced in England and Wales). The definition of vulnerable varies from jurisdiction to jurisdiction but typically includes individuals deemed vulnerable because of their own characteristics (e.g. children, people with intellectual disabilities) or the crime they may have been the victim of (e.g. hate crime, rape). One such measure is the use of closed circuit television (CCTV) which means the vulnerable witness does not have to give evidence in a crowded courtroom. Many people find talking in public stressful even when the subject is trivial, so discussing a crime such as one's own rape is likely to be more stressful still. Provision of evidence via CCTV reduces this worry. Furthermore, the witness does not have to meet the defendant directly, a major cause of concern for witnesses (Epstein *et al.* 1997; Mackey *et al.* 1992). However, it is also of concern that evidence given by such means should still be effective, and research by Hamlyn *et al.* (2004) has demonstrated that this can be the case. Ninety-eight per cent of those surveyed having given video evidence felt that they had the opportunity to say all they wished compared with only 53 per cent of those who gave evidence in open court.

As well as the in-court experience, the delay between witnessing or being the victim of a crime and giving evidence in court can be particularly upsetting for prospective witnesses and adds to psychological distress and the potential for intimidation (Kebbell and Wagstaff 1999; Maynard 1994). For example, testifying in a trial was one of four significant predictors of PTSD symptoms in adult survivors of child rape, and having a civil lawsuit pending was one of three predictors of depression among adult victims (Epstein *et al.* 1997; Mackey *et al.* 1992). The prior videotaping of evidence has recently become available for many vulnerable witnesses to give an initial account in court via a pre-recorded videotape of their evidence. This has several advantages, as well as reducing stress potentially for the witness. As the evidence is given as soon as a potential crime is disclosed this means memory decay is minimised. Also, the interviewer's questioning can be observed and potentially leading and distorting questions may be identified. The fact that this evidence is elicited with open questions by individuals trained in investigative interviewing, and often subject to legal regulations to ensure they are not too leading, means that evidence elicited in this way is likely to be particularly accurate.

Conclusions

Psychological research has identified ways in which evidence can be enhanced potentially, and this information is increasingly being used by the criminal justice system. However, a great deal still needs to be done to ensure that the appropriate measures are implemented effectively and perhaps most critically, that they work. Future work should, in particular, be aimed at how measures aimed at improving evidence in court influence decision-making earlier in the criminal justice system, such as witnesses' decisions to come forward, guilty suspects' decisions to confess or deny during police interviews, as well as issues that arise later on such as defendants' decision to plead guilty or not guilty and jurors' decision making. This is an ongoing collaborative opportunity for psychology and law to work together to help witnesses provide accurate evidence and achieve justice.

References

Bartlett, D. and Memon, A. (1995) 'Advocacy', in R. Bull and D. Carson (eds), *Handbook of Psychology in Legal Contexts*. Chichester: John Wiley and Sons.

Bell, B.E. and Loftus, E.F. (1989) 'Trivial persuasion in the courtroom: the power of (a few) minor details', *Journal of Personality and Social Psychology*, 56: 669–79.

Brennan, M. and Brennan, R.E. (1988) *Strange Language: child victims under cross-examination* (3rd edn). Wagga Wagga, NSW: Charles Sturt University–Riverina.

Carson, D. (1995) 'Regulating the examination of children', *Expert Evidence*, 4: 2–9.

Carson, D. (2000) 'Developing witness skills'. Unpublished manuscript, University of Southampton.

Clifford, B.R. and George, R. (1996) 'A field evaluation of training in three methods of witness/victim investigative interviewing', *Psychology, Crime and Law*, 2: 231–48.

Connors, E., Lundregan, T., Miller, N. and McEwan, T. (1996) *Convicted by Juries, Exonerated by Science: Case studies in the use of DNA evidence to establish innocence after trial*. Alexandria, VA: National Institute of Justice.

Cooke, D.J. (1990) 'Do I feel lucky? Survival in the witness box', *Neuropsychology*, 4: 271–85.

Cutler, B.L., Penrod, S.D. and Dexter, H.R. (1990) 'Juror sensitivity to eyewitness identification evidence', *Law and Human Behavior*, 14: 185-91.

Cutler, B.L., Penrod, S.D. and Stuve, T.E. (1988) 'Juror decision making in eyewitness identification cases', *Law and Human Behavior*, 12: 41–55.

Danet, B. (1980) 'Language in the legal process', *Law and Society Review*, 14: 445–564.

Davies, G.M. and Noon, E. (1991) *An Evaluation of the Live Link for Child Witnesses*. London: Home Office.

Davies, G.M., Westcott, H.L. and Horan, N. (2000) 'The impact of questioning style on the content of investigative interviews with suspected child abuse victims', *Psychology, Crime and Law*, 6: 81–97.

Davies, M., Croal, H. and Tyrer, J. (1995) *Criminal Justice. An introduction to the criminal justice system in England and Wales*. London: Longman.

Elliott, R. (1993) 'Expert testimony about eyewitness identification: a critique', *Law and Human Behavior*, 17: 423–37.

Epstein, J.N., Saunders, B.E. and Kilpatrick, D.G. (1997) 'Predicting PTSD in women with a history of childhood rape', *Journal of Traumatic Stress*, 10: 573–88.

Evans, K. (1995) *Advocacy in Court: a beginner's guide* (2nd edn). London: Blackstone.

Fisher, R.P., Geiselman, R.E. and Raymond, D.S. (1987) 'Critical analysis of police interview techniques', *Journal of Police Science and Administration*, 15.

Fox, S.G. and Walters, H.A. (1986) 'The impact of general versus specific expert testimony and eyewitness confidence upon mock-juror judgement', *Law and Human Behavior*, 10: 215–28.

Geiselman, R.E., Fisher, R.P. Cohen, G. and Holland, H.L. (1986) 'Eyewitness responses to leading and misleading questions under the cognitive interview', *Journal of Police Science and Administration*, 14: 31–9.

Gudjonsson, G.H. (1990) 'The relationship of intellectual skills to suggestibility, compliance and acquiescence', *Personality and Individual Differences*, 11: 227–31.

Gudjonsson, G.H. (1992) *The Psychology of Interrogations, Confessions and Testimony*. Chichester: Wiley.

Gudjonsson, G.H. and Clarke, N.K. (1986) 'Suggestibility in police interrogation: a social psychological model', *Social Behaviour*, 1: 83–104.

Hamlyn, B., Phelps, A., Turtle, J. and Sattar, G. (2004) *Are Special Measures Working? Evidence from surveys of vulnerable and intimidated witnesses*. London: Home Office Research Study 283.

Home Office (1995) *Digest: Information on the Criminal Justice System in England and Wales*. London: HMSO.

Home Office (1999) *Youth and Criminal Evidence Act*. London: HMSO.

Home Office (2002) *Achieving Best Evidence. Guidance for Vulnerable or Intimidated Witnesses, including Children*. London: Home Office.

Huff, C.R., Rattner, A. and Sagarin, E. (1996) *Convicted But Innocent: Wrongful conviction and public policy*. London: Sage.

Hutcheson, G., Baxter, J., Telfer, K. and Warden, D (1995). Child witness statement quality: question type and errors of omission. *Law and Human Behavior*, 6: 631–48.

Kassin, S.M., Ellsworth, P.C. and Smith, V.L. (1994) 'Déjà vu all over again. Elliott's critique of eyewitness experts', *Law and Human Behavior*, 18: 203–10.

Kebbell, M.R., Brodie, S., Muspratt, S., Patterson, L., Quartermaine, R., Riola, V. and Stevenson, J. (2002) 'The usefulness of cross-examination in detecting deception'. Unpublished manuscript James Cook University.

Kebbell, M.R., Deprez, S. and Wagstaff, G.F. (2003) 'The examination and cross examination of alleged rape-victims and defendants in court', *Psychology, Crime and Law*, 9: 1–13.

Kebbell, M.R. and Hatton, C. (1999) 'People with mental retardation as witnesses in court', *Mental Retardation*, 3: 179–87.

Kebbell, M.R., Hatton, C. and Johnson, S.D. (2004) 'Witnesses with intellectual disabilities in court: what questions are asked and what influence do they have?', *Legal and Criminology Psychology*, 9: 1–13.

Kebbell, M.R. and Johnson, S.D. (2000) 'The influence of lawyers' questions on witness confidence and accuracy', *Law and Human Behavior*, 24: 629–41.

Kebbell, M.R. and Milne, R. (1998) 'Police officers' perception of eyewitness factors in forensic investigations: a survey', *The Journal of Social Psychology*, 138: 323–30.

Kebbell, M.R. and Wagstaff, G.F. (1999) *Face Value? Factors that influence eyewitness accuracy*. London: Police Research Group, Home Office.

Kebbell, M.R., Wagstaff, G.F. and Covey, J.A. (1996) 'The influence of item difficulty on the relationship between eyewitness confidence and accuracy', *British Journal of Psychology*, 87 (4): 653–62.

Kranat, V.K. and Westcott, H.L. (1994) 'Under fire: lawyers questioning children in criminal Courts', *Expert Evidence*, 3: 16–24.

Leippe, M.R. (1980) 'Effects of integrative and memorial processes on the correspondence of eyewitness accuracy and confidence', *Law and Human Behavior*, 4: 261–74.

Leippe, M.R., Manion, A.P. and Romanczyk, A. (1992) 'Eyewitness persuasion: how well do fact finders judge the accuracy of adults' and children's memory reports', *Journal of Personality and Social Psychology*, 63: 181–97.

Lindsay, D.S., Read, J.D. and Sharma, K. (1998) 'Accuracy and confidence in person identification. The relationship is strong when witnessing conditions vary widely', *Psychological Science*, 9: 215–18.

Lindsay, R.C.L., Wells, G.L. and O'Connor, F.J. (1989) 'Mock juror belief of accurate and inaccurate eyewitnesses: a replication and extension', *Law and Human Behavior*, 13: 333–39.

Loftus, E.F. (1979) *Eyewitness Testimony*. London: Harvard University Press.

Loftus, E.F., Miller, D.G. and Burns, H.J. (1978) 'Semantic integration of verbal information into a visual memory', *Journal of Experimental Psychology: Human Learning and Memory*, 4: 19–31.

Loftus, E.F. and Palmer, J.C. (1974) 'Reconstruction of automobile destruction: an example of the interaction between language and memory', *Journal of Verbal Learning and Verbal Behavior*, 13: 585–89.

Loftus, E.F. and Zanni, G. (1975) 'Eyewitness testimony: the influence of the wording of a question', *Bulletin of the Psychonomic Society*, 5: 86–8.

Luus, C.A.E. and Wells, G.L. (1994) 'The malleability of eyewitness confidence: co-witness and perseverance effects', *Journal of Applied Psychology*, 79: 714–23.

Mackey, T., Sereika, S.M., Weissfeld, L.A., Hacker, S.S., Zender, J.F. and Heard, S.L. (1992) 'Factors associated with long-term depressive symptoms of sexual assault victims', *Archives of Psychiatric Nursing*, 6: 10–25.

Maynard, W. (1994) Witness Intimidation: Strategies for Prevention. *Home Office Crime Prevention and Detection Series Paper No. 55*. London: Home Office.

McEwan, J. (1995) 'Adversarial and inquisitorial proceedings', in R. Bull and D. Carson (eds), *Handbook of Psychology in Legal Contexts*. Chichester: Wiley.

Memon, A., Holley, A., Milne, R., Koehnken, G. and Bull, R. (1994) 'Towards understanding the effects of interviewer training in evaluating the cognitive interview', *Applied Cognitive Psychology*, 8: 641–59.

Memon, A. and Vartoukian, R. (1996) 'The effects of repeated questioning on young children's eyewitness testimony', *British Journal of Psychology*, 87: 403–15.

Memon, A., Vrij, A. and Bull, R. (1998) *Psychology and Law: truthfulness, accuracy and credibility*. London: McGraw-Hill.

Milne, R. and Bull, R. (1999) *Investigative Interviewing: psychology and practice*. Chichester: Wiley.

Murphy, P. (ed.) (1997) *Blackstone's Criminal Practice* (7th edn). London: Blackstone.

Murphy, P. and Barnard, D. (1994). *Evidence and Advocacy* (4th edn). London: Blackstone Press.

O'Kelly, C.M.E., Kebbell, M.R., Hatton, C. and Johnson, S.D. (2003) 'When do judges intervene in cases involving people with learning disabilities?', *Legal and Criminological Psychology*, 8: 229–40.

Perry, N.W., McAuliff, B.D., Tam, P., Claycomb, L., Dostal, C. and Flanagan, C. (1995) 'When lawyers question children. Is justice served?', *Law and Human Behavior*, 19: 609–29.

Regina v. *Brown* (1998) *Criminal Appeal Reports*, 2: 364.

Rose, D. (1996) *In the Name of the Law*. London: Jonathan Cape.

Sanders, A., Creaton, J., Bird, S. and Weber, L. (1997) *Victims with Learning Disabilities: Negotiating the Criminal Justice System*. Oxford: Centre for Criminological Research, University of Oxford.

Shaw, J.S. III and Mc Clure, K.A. (1996) 'Repeated post event questioning can lead to elevated levels of eyewitness confidence', *Law and Human Behavior*, 20: 629–53.

Sporer, S.L., Penrod, S.D., Read, J.D. and Cutler, B.L. (1995) 'Choosing, confidence, and accuracy: a meta-analysis of the confidence–accuracy relation in eyewitness identification studies', *Psychological Bulletin*, 118: 315–27.

Stone, M. (1995) *Cross-examination in Criminal Trials* (2nd edn). London: Butterworths.

Vrij, A. (1998) 'Nonverbal communication and credibility', in A. Memon, A.Vrij and R. Bull (eds), *Psychology and Law: truthfulness, accuracy and credibility*. Maidenhead: McGraw-Hill.

Vrij, A. (2000) *Detecting Lies and Deceit*. Chichester: Wiley.

Walker, A.G. (1993) 'Questioning young children in court: a linguistic case study', *Law and Human Behavior*, 17: 58–81.

Wells, G.L., Ferguson, T.J. and Lindsay, R.C.L. (1981) 'The tractability of eyewitness confidence and its implications for triers of fact', *Journal of Applied Psychology*, 66: 688–96.

Wells, G.L., Lindsay, R.C.L. and Ferguson, T.J. (1979) 'Accuracy, confidence, and juror perceptions in eyewitness identification', *Journal of Applied Psychology*, 64: 440–8.

Westcott, H.L. (1995) 'Children's experience of being examined and cross-examined: the opportunity to be heard?', *Expert Evidence*, 4: 13–19.

Westcott, H.L. and Page, M. (2002) 'Cross-examination, sexual abuse and child witness identity', *Child Abuse Review*, 11: 137–52.

Zander, M. and Henderson, P. (1993) 'Crown Court study', *Royal Commission on Criminal Justice. Research studies, 19*. London: HMSO.

Zanjac, R. and Hayne, H. (2003) 'I don't think that's what really happened: the effect of cross-examination on the accuracy of children's reports', *Journal of Experimental Psychology Applied*, 9: 187–95.

Chapter 9

The ageing eyewitness

Rachel Wilcock

Eyewitness evidence plays a vital role in our criminal justice system; however, it is not always accurate (Huff *et al.* 1986). Thus, psychologists have investigated different factors that may influence the accuracy of eyewitness evidence, and research shows that one factor (among many) that reliably affects eyewitness performance is age of the witness (Wilcock *et al.* 2008). The vast majority of research investigating the effect of age on eyewitness performance has focused on comparing children and young adults. This is somewhat surprising bearing in mind that many countries have ageing populations. For example, in the UK, in 2006 there were 11.3 million people of state pensionable age. This is projected to rise to 12.7 million by 2020 and 15 million by 2031 (ONS 2008). One of the implications of this is that older adults may be more likely to witness crime and be involved in the Criminal Justice System (Rothman *et al.* 2000). Additionally, older adults may also be victims of crime. Thornton *et al.* (2003) found that in 2001/2 there were 19,400 reported cases of distraction burglary where the victim was aged 60 years and over. In light of these factors, researchers have recently become interested in examining the performance of older adult witnesses, being those aged 60 and over.

Research does indeed indicate that there are differences between older and younger witnesses in the information they are able to give. In research using a mock witness paradigm where participants (or mock witnesses) viewed a simulated crime event and their memory for the event was later tested, older mock witnesses had a poorer memory than younger mock witnesses for details relating to the perpetrator, the victim, what happened, and the environment in which the mock crime occurred (Yarmey 1982; Yarmey and Kent 1980; Yarmey *et al.* 1984). When the findings of these three studies were averaged, Yarmey (2000) found that overall older adults (mean age 70 years) were 20 per cent less accurate in free recall, 13 per cent less accurate in cued recall, and 15 per cent less complete in their descriptions of the perpetrator than younger adults (mean age 21 years).

There are also qualitative differences in recall between younger and older adults. For example, Yarmey *et al.* (1984) showed mock witnesses a crime event which involved the perpetrator carrying a knife. In this case, 80 per cent of younger witnesses reported the knife, compared with just 20 per cent of older witnesses. The same event included an 11-year-old girl who had long hair worn in a ponytail, and 75 per cent of older witnesses misidentified the girl as a boy, whereas no younger witnesses made that mistake. Worryingly, both of these findings relate to central aspects of a crime that would be very important for a police investigation. Further research has also found that other crucial details relating to the physical characteristics of a perpetrator as well as details relating to what they were wearing are more likely to be absent in older witnesses' accounts compared with younger witnesses' accounts (Brimacombe *et al.* 1997).

In addition to older witnesses being less accurate than younger witnesses there is some debate that they may also be more suggestible than younger witnesses. Susceptibility to suggestion has mostly been tested using a standard misinformation paradigm. Participants view an event and after a delay are subject to some incorrect information (referred to as misinformation) about the event which may be contained in questions asked of participants, or that they read in a newspaper article, or that emerges when discussing the event with a co-witness. Participants are then tested to see whether they have taken on the misinformation or not. Evidence from the cognitive ageing literature suggests that older witnesses may be more susceptible to misinformation because they are more likely to make source monitoring errors (Hashtroudi *et al.* 1989). Source monitoring refers to identifying where information was learnt, for example, (a) did a person experience an event and therefore the information comes directly from that experience or (b) did they hear about an event from another person, dream, or imagine it? In the eyewitness context, after a person has witnessed a crime they may learn new information about it (which could be either accurate or inaccurate) via other witnesses, by reading a newspaper report of the crime, or through information mistakenly being introduced during a police interview. If the witness is an older adult, it is more likely that she or he will make a mistake in his or her source monitoring and when recounting the crime, may include new information that was learnt subsequently to the crime.

Research adopting the misinformation paradigm has revealed mixed findings with regard to older adults. Some studies show that older adults are more likely to be suggestible than younger adults (e.g. Cohen and Faulkner 1989; Karpel *et al.* 2001; Loftus *et al.* 1992; Mitchell *et al.* 2003). Furthermore, some of this research shows that older adults are more likely to be extremely confident that their answers (containing misinformation) are correct. However, other studies have found older adults to be no more suggestible than younger adults (e.g. Bornstein *et al.* 2000; Coxon and Valentine 1997; Dodson and Krueger 2006; Gabbert *et al.* 2003; Searcy *et al.* 2000).

One reason that could explain why we see mixed findings with regard to suggestibility in older adults could be due to differences in the way in which the research is conducted and/or the nature of the sort of misinformation that is given to participants. For example, Mueller-Johnson and Ceci (2004) found that whether or not older adults took on board misinformation about a live event involving a massage of participants' back, neck and shoulders, depended on the nature of the suggestibility. For example, for some suggestions including where on their body they had been massaged, older adults were more suggestible than younger adults. However, for other suggestions such as what the massage therapist had been wearing, younger adults were more suggestible than older adults. Further research is required before drawing any firm conclusions about the extent to which older adults are likely to be suggestible. One way in which we can reduce the chances of misinformation being taken on board during the investigative process is by conducting good interviews, and it is to this that we now turn.

Interviewing

The 'cognitive interview' (CI) is widely used by police forces as a method for improving witnesses' recall of events. It is a memory-enhancing interview technique devised using principles from cognitive psychology and includes four mnemonic instructions (Geiselman *et al.* 1984) including: 1) *report everything* – here witnesses are encouraged to report everything without editing out details even if they think they are of little consequence; 2) *mental reinstatement of context* – witnesses are asked to picture in their minds the physical context, i.e. what was the environment like, and the personal context, i.e. how were they feeling at the time of the crime they witnessed; 3) *change temporal order* – after a witness has recalled the event in the order that comes naturally to them, they will be instructed to recall the event in a different order, for example, from the very end of what they witnessed backwards through to the beginning of the event; 4) *change perspective* – once witnesses have been through their accounts of what happened they will be instructed to go through the accounts of what happened, from the perspective of someone else who was present at the event. (For more details of the four mnemonic instructions and theories behind them, see Milne and Bull, in press.) In addition to the four mnemonic instructions, the enhanced cognitive interview (ECI) also included some new memory-enhancing techniques as well as principles from the social psychology of communication (Fisher and Geiselman 1992). A meta-analysis of 50 studies investigating the effectiveness of the CI/ECI found that they reliably increased event information recalled by young adults and children (Koehnken *et al.* 1999). However, only a handful of published studies have examined the effectiveness of the CI with elderly witnesses.

Mello and Fisher (1996) were the first to investigate the effectiveness of the CI for older adults. Using a mock witness paradigm, younger and older mock witnesses were interviewed either with a standard police interview, a CI, or a modified CI. The modified CI was the same as the CI but the opening free recall was limited and the change perspective instruction was omitted because older adults may have difficulty with both these aspects of the interview. In addition, the modified CI was slowed down even further and questions were reworded for simplicity. The results revealed no significant difference in performance between the modified CI and the CI. However, the CI led to more information compared with the standard police interview. Even more encouragingly, the advantage of the CI over the standard police interview was greater for older witnesses than younger witnesses. In the most recent investigation, Wright and Holliday (2007) used a mock witness paradigm study to examine the performance of young adults (17–31 years), young-old adults (60–74 years) and old-old adults (75–95 years) using the different interviewing approaches. There was a significant effect of age group with young adults performing better than young-old adults who in turn performed better than old-old adults. There was also a significant effect of interview condition for correct details for all age groups with the ECI being most beneficial, followed by the modified CI (which omitted change perspective), followed by the structured interview. Thus it appears that the CI may be beneficial for older adults; however, two studies have not found such beneficial effects.

In a further two studies investigating older adults, both of which utilised the mock witness paradigm, Milne *et al.* (2000) found that the CI did not lead to a significant increase in correct information compared with a structured interview. The authors also found large individual differences in their sample, which they believed may have contributed to the non-significant effect. Similarly McMahon (2000) found the CI to be no more effective than the structured interview in eliciting correct information for older witnesses.

With these mixed findings, it is unclear whether the beneficial effect of the CI for young adults translates to older adults. Possible reasons that could explain the different results are the methods used in the research. For example, some studies used a modified CI and the modifications themselves differed between the studies (Mello and Fisher 1996; Wright and Holliday 2007). Other reasons for different results could be due to the sample; with the exception of Wright and Holliday (2007), the studies had a smaller than ideal sample size. Additionally, one study recruited their older participants from an institute which offered educational courses for older adults (Mello and Fisher 1996) who may not be representative of the older population as a whole. At present, on the basis of this small amount of research, we are not able to draw a conclusion as to whether the CI is beneficial for older adults and further research is urgently needed.

One other piece of research that also considered interviewing older adults has taken a slightly different approach (Wilcock and Bull 2006). Rather than seeing whether the CI as it stands is suitable for older adults, we have investigated adapting some elements of the CI specifically for older adults. Milne and Bull (2002) found that some of the mnemonic recall instructions were more beneficial than others. For example, a combination of *report everything* and *context reinstatement (CR)* were the most useful for children and young adults. However, older adults have a different memory profile from young adults and children. Hence, these recall instructions may also vary in effectiveness for older witnesses. For example, the *change perspective and change temporal order* instruction may not be beneficial because it requires witnesses to perform two different mental operations simultaneously, cognitive demands that are taxing for older adults (Herman and Coyne 1980).

In light of the differences in older adults' memories, Wilcock and Bull (2006) left out both *change perspective* and *change temporal order* and concentrated instead on the remaining two mnemonic instructions, *report everything* and *CR*. However, instead of testing their effectiveness as they are normally used in the CI, both instructions were adapted for older adults. Research shows that older adults are less likely to recall contextual details than younger adults (Schacter *et al.* 1998). Thus the *CR* instruction in this study was supplemented by photographs taken of the event location which allowed older participants to have a physical form of CR in front of them. The *report everything* instruction was modified to make it clear to participants that the interviewer was very interested in what they had to say, that they felt sure the participant had a good memory for the event. This is in response to the belief held by some older adults that they have poorer memories compared with younger adults (Hertzog and Hultsch 2000) and that police officers have a negative opinion of older adults' memory abilities and so they may consequently give shorter and less detailed accounts (Wright and Holliday 2005, see below for more details). Results revealed that the adapted component interviews led to significantly more correct information, but also to a small but significant increase in incorrect information than the original component interviews. There was no significant difference in accuracy rate between the adapted and original interviews. This study was conducted with a small sample and needs replication but researchers may need to consider developing an interview strategy that specifically takes into account the likely effects of cognitive ageing when interviewing older adult witnesses.

After an interview takes place and a suspect has been apprehended a witness may be asked to attend an identification parade. Next we will review the accuracy of older witnesses' identification evidence before examining research that investigates aiding older witnesses' identification performance.

Identification

Some of the early research that was discussed above with reference to mock older witnesses' verbal accounts of a crime event, also investigated their ability to identify the crime perpetrator from photographic line-ups. Generally in research investigating line-up performance, experimenters include a target present (TP) line-up where the 'perpetrator' is present as well as a target absent (TA) line-up where the 'perpetrator' is absent. Thus a TA line-up equates to a real-life situation in which the police suspect in a line-up is innocent. These early studies found there was no effect of age group on correct identifications of the perpetrator from TP line-ups (Yarmey and Kent 1980; Yarmey *et al.* 1984). However, Yarmey *et al.* (1984) also found that older witnesses made substantially more false identifications from both TP and TA line-ups. More recently, Searcy *et al.* (1999) showed younger (18–30 years) and older (60–80 years) mock witnesses a video-recorded re-enactment of a real crime involving two perpetrators. Older witnesses were significantly more likely to make false identifications than younger witnesses on both line-ups, regardless of whether the line-up was TP or TA. This finding has been replicated in a number of subsequent studies (Memon and Bartlett 2002; Rose *et al.* 2005; Searcy *et al.* 2000; Wilcock *et al.* 2005, 2007). It appears that in general, older witnesses demonstrate poorer identification performance.

Other related research has investigated different factors that may influence the age effect on line-up performance. For example, the studies discussed above have generally shown the perpetrator in the mock crime event for a short period of time and have asked participants to identify him/her after a short delay, typically less than an hour. Memon *et al.* (2003) found that length of exposure to the perpetrator's face (either 12 seconds or 45 seconds) had a significant effect on older witnesses' identification performance. Longer duration of exposure led to more accurate line-up performance in terms of correctly identifying the perpetrator, correctly rejecting a target absent line-up, and making fewer false identifications. In a further study, the delay between seeing the mock crime event and viewing the line-ups was manipulated to be either 45 minutes or a week. There was a larger effect of age group for those participants who experienced the week delay (Memon *et al.* 2003).

All of the above studies have considered the older participant group as one large group; however, Memon *et al.* (2004) report one study investigating the identification abilities of young-old mock witnesses aged between 60 and 68 years and old-old mock witnesses aged between 69 and 81 years. They found significant differences between these two groups of older witnesses, in that 75 per cent of the old-old witnesses made false identifications from a target absent line-up compared to just 13 per cent of the young-old witnesses. This would suggest that witnesses who could be classified as old-old may be particularly prone to making false identifications.

One study has investigated the effect of showing mug shots prior to the line-up on older witnesses' identification performance. With young adults there is substantial evidence that if witnesses view mug shots prior to a line-up, they may be less accurate on the line-up both in terms of a reduction in accurate identifications and an increase in false alarm rates (Deffenbacher *et al.* 2006). Older adults who are known to make more source monitoring errors (Hashtroudi *et al.* 1989) and who may be more likely to rely on gist when remembering faces rather than specific verbatim details (Koutstaal and Schacter 1997) may in particular be prone to the mug shot exposure effect. Memon *et al.* (2002) asked participants to view a crime event on videotape and then look at a mug shot album to see if they could identify the perpetrator. They found that older mock witnesses were more likely to make a choice from both the mug shot album and the line-up than younger mock witnesses. In the subsequent line-up, one of the already seen mug shots was included (the 'critical foil'). If a witness had made a choice from the mug shot album, he or she was more likely to falsely identify the critical foil as the perpetrator (regardless of whether she or he had chosen the critical foil from the mug shot book or another suspect's mug shot). Memon *et al.* suggested that participants who chose from the mug shot book and then chose the critical foil in the line-up, were likely to be responding due to a feeling of familiarity for the face rather than being able to recall the specific details of the face.

Another factor over which there has been considerable debate is the extent to which confidence of the witness in the identification decision and the accuracy of the decision are related. (For a review of this topic in relation to young adults see Brewer (2006).) It is an important topic because evidence given by a confident witness is more likely to be believed by jurors than evidence given by a less confident witness (Wells *et al.* 1979). Some research has examined the relationship between eyewitness confidence and older witnesses' line-up accuracy. Scogin *et al.* (1994) examined young (18–35 years), young-old (59–74 years) and old-old (75–94 years) adults' performance on a photographic line-up task having viewed a crime shown on videotape. They found no significant correlation between line-up accuracy and self-ratings of confidence in any age group, meaning that even if an older witness is extremely confident of having correctly identified the perpetrator, this does not necessarily mean a correct identification. Other researchers have also found no correlation to exist between confidence and line-up accuracy in older adults (Adams-Price 1992; Memon *et al.* 2002, 2003; Wilcock *et al.* 2007). Researchers have also considered whether older adults are generally as confident about their line-up decisions as younger adults. Some research suggests they are less confident than younger adults (Memon *et al.* 2002; Memon *et al.* 2003; Rose *et al.* 2003), while other research has found no difference between the two groups (Adams-Price 1992; Searcy *et al.* 1999). At present, there is insufficient evidence to be able to draw a firm conclusion about older adults' confidence in their identification decisions or the relationship between confidence and line-up accuracy for this older age group.

One key issue that researchers have focused on within the confidence–accuracy area is the effect of witnesses receiving feedback after they have made a line-up decision and the effect of that feedback on their subsequent confidence. Wells and Bradfield (1998) found that if a line-up administrator told mock witnesses who had made false identifications (after viewing a target absent line-up), 'Good, you identified the actual suspect', they were significantly more certain that their identification was accurate compared with those who had received no feedback. This effect is very robust and has been replicated in many studies with young adult mock witnesses (Bradfield Douglass and Steblay 2006). Neuschatz *et al.* (2005) investigated whether the post-identification feedback effect found in young adults translates to older adults. They found that older adults were as susceptible as younger adults to the effects of feedback from a line-up administrator. Therefore, as with young witnesses, if confidence is used as a guide to accuracy of older witnesses' performance, then the confidence rating taken immediately after the identification should be used rather than asking witnesses for a confidence rating at a later point in time. This overcomes the problem of inflated ratings of confidence due to feedback being given in a courtroom and jurors being persuaded by the identification evidence of overly confident witnesses.

In the research that has been reviewed thus far examining older witnesses' identification performance, investigators have largely been looking at the differences between younger and older adults. Whilst much of the research evidence shows that there are age-related reductions in eyewitness performance, it may be more helpful to develop methods for aiding the performance of older witnesses, and it is to this issue that we now turn.

Aiding identification performance

A substantial body of research has demonstrated the importance of non-biased line-up instructions given just prior to witnesses viewing a line-up, which inform them that the perpetrator *may or may not* be present in the line-up. For example, Malpass and Devine (1981a) were the first to demonstrate that failure to warn witnesses that the culprit may or may not be in the line-up (biased instructions) resulted in 78 per cent of witnesses making false identifications from a target-absent (TA) line-up, while maintaining a high level of hits in the target-present (TP) line-up. With the warning that the perpetrator may not be in the target-absent line-up (non-biased instructions) the false identification rate fell to 33 per cent. More recently, Steblay (1997) conducted a meta-analysis of 18 studies which confirms that after witnesses receive biased line-up instructions a higher level of choosing ensues. Nowadays the importance of giving witnesses non-biased line-up instructions is recognised in several countries. Thus, informing the witness that the perpetrator may or may not be present in the line-up has been required of police forces in England and Wales since 1986 (Zander 1990) and, more recently, has been recommended by the Attorney General in the USA (Wells *et al.* 2000).

Possibly one factor which could explain why older adults are more likely to make false identifications than younger adults could relate to their memory for non-biased line-up instructions. Indeed, Rose *et al.* (2003) found a significant effect of age group on reported memory for line-up instructions in that 91 per cent of young adults said they remembered the instructions compared with only 75 per cent of the older adults. However, these results were based on a simple 'yes/no' question. In a follow up study, Rose *et al.* (2005) asked younger and older participants to tell the experimenter 'as much as you can remember about the lineup instructions given to you prior to the lineup' and again found a significant effect of age on recall of the line-up instructions. Sixty-eight per cent of younger participants were able to recall the instructions correctly compared with only 46 per cent of older participants. Further, and even more worryingly, those participants who failed to remember the line-up instructions made significantly more false identifications than those participants who correctly remembered the instructions.

In light of these findings, more recent research has focused on developing methods to try to increase older witnesses' memory for the non-biased line-up instructions. Wilcock *et al.* (2005) attempted to enhance the non-biased line-up instructions by giving a fictitious example of a case of false identification and briefly reviewing a DNA exoneration case before giving participants the standard non-biased line-up instructions. Though the enhanced line-up instructions led to significantly better memory concerning the possibility the perpetrator may or may not have been present in the line-up for older participants, their memory of them was not as good as young adults in the control condition who had not received the enhanced line-up instructions. Thus, the enhanced line-up instructions had no significant effect on line-up performance.

Other researchers have successfully reduced the rate of false identifications in young adults when viewing a TA line-up by asking them three questions prior to the line-up. Dysart and Lindsay (2001) devised three questions: (1) 'How clear a memory do you have for the face of the criminal?' (2) 'How confident are you that you will be able to select the criminal if you see a photograph of him in a line-up?' (3) 'How confident are you that you will realise that the guilty person is *not* in the line-up if you are shown a line-up with only innocent people in it?' The final question clearly illustrates the fact that instead of a witness's task being to make an identification, if the police have an innocent suspect, then their task would be to reject the line-up. Memon and Gabbert (2003a) found that the same 'pre-identification' questions had no beneficial effect for older adults. One further study that also investigated the effectiveness of pre-identification questions found that they successfully reduced false identifications made by older adults viewing a TA line-up, although there was also a slight reduction in the number of correct identifications, of the perpetrator from a TP line-up (Wilcock and Bull in press). Whilst it is desirable to reduce false identifications, this should not be at the expense of a reduction in correct identifications of the perpetrator.

In the same study, Wilcock and Bull investigated a different method of illustrating the standard non-biased line-up instructions by giving older mock witnesses a practice target absent line-up. Prior to the line-up for the perpetrator shown in a videotaped mock crime event, half of the mock witnesses were shown a practice line-up composed of famous female faces and they were asked to identify the Queen's face (which was absent). They then received standard non-biased line-up instructions. The practice line-up led to significantly fewer false identifications across three TA line-ups, while maintaining the same rate of correct identifications from three TP line-ups (compared with mock witnesses who just received the standard non-biased line-up instructions). The practice line-up appears to be helpful for older witnesses, though further research would be needed to replicate the effect before a firm conclusion could be drawn.

Other research has also focused on procedures that can be implemented prior to the line-up to aid the performance of witnesses.

Evidence from studies conducted using young adult participants shows that context reinstatement (CR) instructions (see above for details) can lead to greater identification accuracy (e.g. Cutler *et al.* 1987; Gwyer and Clifford 1997; Malpass and Devine 1981b; O'Rourke *et al.* 1989). Thus far, just three studies have investigated whether the beneficial effect of CR instructions might translate to older witnesses. Searcy *et al.* (2001) and Memon *et al.* (2004) found that the cognitive interview containing CR instructions compared with a structured interview had no effect on the number of false identifications made by older adults. Similarly, Memon *et al.* (2002) found CR instructions failed to reduce the rate of false identifications made by older adults after exposure to mug shots. However, as mentioned above, verbal recall of contextual details often shows age-related deficits (Schacter *et al.* 1998) so possibly a different form of CR would be beneficial for older adults. Wilcock *et al.* (2007), instead of using standard CR instructions, examined the effect of photographic context reinstatement on line-up accuracy. That is, older participants viewed a series of photographs taken at the scene of the mock crime event and of objects in the crime event. They then used these photographic cues to aid mental reinstatement of context. Photographic context reinstatement led to significantly fewer false identifications made by older mock witnesses on one of two line-ups that they viewed. Further research investigating whether some form of context reinstatement could aid the performance of older adults on line-ups is warranted.

The final area of research examining possible methods for enhancing older witnesses' performance has focused on line-up presentation methods. Most of the research examining the performance of older witnesses has used simultaneous line-ups (where all faces are shown together). Despite this, substantial amounts of research have demonstrated that showing members of a line-up one at a time in a sequential fashion substantially reduces the number of false identifications made by witnesses viewing target absent line-ups (Steblay *et al.* 2001). Three out of four studies examining simultaneous versus sequential line-up presentation have found that, as with young adults, sequential line-up presentation reduces the rate of false identifications made by older adults viewing target absent line-ups (Memon and Gabbert 2003a; Rose *et al.* 2005; Wilcock *et al.* 2005). However, all four studies also found a reduction in correct identifications of the perpetrator from target present line-ups (Memon and Gabbert 2003a,b; Rose *et al.* 2005; Wilcock *et al.* 2005). Again, as stated above, it is important to reduce the rate of false identifications made by older adults but this should not be at the expense of reducing the rate of correct identifications of the perpetrator.

Although some research has investigated possible methods to aid the performance of older witnesses there is a real need for more research to be conducted. At present we are not in a position to recommend to the police any particular method of showing line-ups or procedure that will improve the accuracy of older adult witnesses.

Perceptions of older eyewitnesses

Whilst it is important to review the performance of older adult witnesses, as has been done thus far in this chapter, it is also crucial to examine how older witnesses are perceived, because their credibility as witnesses in the eyes of jurors will dictate how much weight is given to their evidence in court. Brimacombe *et al.* (1997) found that mock jurors rated the testimony given by older adults as less able to competently describe the perpetrator, less competent and less confident than younger witnesses. In a second study where the age of the witnesses giving testimony was concealed, mock jurors still rated the older witnesses' testimony as less credible than the testimony given by the younger witness. The authors concluded that the content of the testimony rather than the age of the witness guided mock jurors' judgements of credibility. However, in a more recent study, participants rated the testimony of a 79-year-old and completed two standard measures of ageism. Those participants who had a negative view of older adults were more likely to rate the witness's testimony less favourably (Mueller-Johnson *et al.* 2007). In a further study, which examined police officers' views of older witnesses, police officers were reported to lack confidence in dealing with older witnesses and they perceived older witnesses to be less reliable and thorough than younger witnesses (Wright and Holliday 2005). Overall these studies suggest that older witnesses are perceived to be less credible by potential jurors and those involved in the investigative process. This is a worrying finding because perceptions guide behaviour and if older witnesses were to pick up on behavioural cues that they are not being taken seriously, they in turn may not demonstrate their full potential as a witness.

Conclusions

Overall the evidence shows that older adults tend to be poorer witnesses than younger adults in terms of their verbal accounts, in interview situations, and also when viewing identification line-ups. Whilst it is important from both a psychological and practical perspective to be aware of the likely effect of age group on witness performance, it is more interesting to consider what can be done to aid the performance of this group of witnesses. Thus far researchers have examined the utility of existing investigative practices used with younger witnesses, for older witnesses. This may not be the best approach because older witnesses are likely to have different needs from younger witnesses. With regard to interviewing, we need to design a protocol that is specifically developed in light of the cognitive ageing literature to enable any resulting interview technique to be focused on the needs of older adults. With regard to identification, we must develop a robust technique for ensuring that older witnesses remember the non-biased line-up instructions, which may aid their line-up performance. A further area for research which thus far has received scant attention in this country is training members of the criminal justice system in order that they are better informed about the needs of older witnesses and so they are better able to communicate effectively with this group. The number of older witnesses is only going to increase and we are not yet in a position of knowing how best to help them fulfil their potential as valuable witnesses.

References

Adams-Price, C. (1992) 'Eyewitness memory and aging: predictors of accuracy in recall and person recognition', *Psychology and Aging*, 7: 602–8.

Bornstein, B.H., Witt, C.J., Cherry, K.E. and Greene, E. (2000) 'The suggestibility of older witnesses', in M.B. Rothman, B.D. Dunlop and P. Entzel (eds), *Elders, Crime, and the Criminal Justice System. Myth, perceptions, and reality in the 21st century* (pp. 149–62). New York: Springer Series on Life Styles and Issues in Aging.

Bradfield Douglass, A. and Steblay, N. (2006) 'Memory distortion in eyewitnesses: a meta-analysis of the post identification feedback effect', *Applied Cognitive Psychology*, 20: 859–69.

Brewer, N. (2006) 'Use and abuses of eyewitness identification confidence', *Legal and Criminological Psychology*, 11: 3–23.

Brimacombe, C.A.E., Quinton, N., Nance, N. and Garrioch, L. (1997) 'Is age irrelevant? Perceptions of young and old adult eyewitnesses', *Law and Human Behavior*, 21: 619–34.

Cohen, G. and Faulkner, D. (1989) 'Age differences in source forgetting: effects on reality monitoring and on eyewitness testimony', *Psychology and Aging*, 4: 10–17.

Coxon, P. and Valentine, T. (1997) 'The effects of the age of eyewitnesses on the accuracy and suggestibility of their testimony', *Applied Cognitive Psychology*, 11: 415–30.

Cutler, B.L., Penrod, S.D. and Martens, T.K. (1987) 'Improving the reliability of eyewitness identifications: putting context into context', *Journal of Applied Psychology*, 72: 629–37.

Deffenbacher, K.A., Bornstein, B.H. and Penrod, S.D. (2006) 'Mugshot exposure effects: retroactive interference, mugshot commitment, source confusion, and unconscious transference', *Law and Human Behavior*, 30: 287–307.

Dodson, C.S. and Krueger, L.E. (2006) 'I misremember it well: why older adults are unreliable eyewitnesses', *Psychonomic Bulletin and Review*, 15: 770–75.

Dysart, J.E. and Lindsay, R.C.L. (2001) 'A pre-identification questioning effect: serendipitously increasing correct rejections', *Law and Human Behavior*, 25: 155–65.

Fisher, R.P. and Geiselman, R.E. (1992) *Memory Enhancing Techniques for Investigative Interviewing: the cognitive interview.* Illinois: Charles C. Thomas.

Gabbert, F., Memon, A. and Allen, K. (2003) 'Memory conformity: can eyewitnesses influence each other's memories for an event?', *Applied Cognitive Psychology*, 17: 533–43.

Geiselman, R.E., Fisher, R.P., Firstenberg, I., Hutton, L.A., Sullivan, A.I., and Prosk, A. (1984) 'Enhancement of eyewitness memory: an empirical evaluation of the cognitive interview', *Journal of Police Science and Administration*, 2: 74–80.

Gwyer, P. and Clifford, B.R. (1997) 'The effects of the cognitive interview on recall, identification, confidence and the confidence/accuracy relationship', *Applied Cognitive Psychology*, 11: 121–45.

Hashtroudi, S., Johnson, M.K. and Chrosniak, L.D. (1989) 'Aging and source monitoring', *Psychology and Aging*, 4: 106–12.

Herman, J.F. and Coyne, A.C. (1980) 'Mental manipulation of spatial information in young and elderly adults', *Developmental Psychology*, 16: 377–88.

Hertzog, C. and Hultsch, D.F. (2000) 'Metacognition in adulthood and old age', in F.I.M. Craik and T.A. Salthouse (eds), *The Handbook of Aging and Cognition* (2nd edn) (pp. 417–67). New Jersey: Lawrence Erlbaum Associates.

Huff, C.R., Rattner, A. and Sagarin, E. (1986) 'Guilty until proven innocent: wrongful conviction and public policy', *Crime and Delinquency*, 32: 518–44.

Karpel, M.E., Hoyer, W.J. and Toglia, M.P. (2001) 'Accuracy and qualities of real and suggested memories: nonspecific age differences', *Journal of Gerontology*, 56B (2): 103–10.

Koehnken, G., Milne, R., Memon, A. and Bull, R. (1999) 'The cognitive interview: a meta-analysis', *Psychology, Crime and Law*, 5: 3–27.

Koutstaal, W. and Schacter, D.L. (1997) 'Gist-based false recognition of pictures in older and younger adults', *Journal of Memory and Language*, 37: 555–83.

Loftus, E.F., Levidow, B. and Duensing, S. (1992) 'Who remembers best? Individual differences in memory for events that occurred in a science museum', *Applied Cognitive Psychology*, 6: 93–107.

Malpass, R.S. and Devine, P.G. (1981a) 'Eyewitness identification: lineup instructions and the absence of the offender', *Journal of Applied Psychology*, 66: 482–89.

Malpass, R.S. and Devine, P.G. (1981b) 'Guided memory in eyewitness identification', *Journal of Applied Psychology*, 66: 343–50.

McMahon, M. (2000) 'The effect of the enhanced cognitive interview on recall and confidence in elderly adults', *Psychiatry, Psychology and Law*, 7: 9–32.

Mello, E. and Fisher, R.P. (1996) 'Enhancing older adult eyewitnesses' memory with the cognitive interview', *Applied Cognitive Psychology*, 10: 403–17.

Memon, A. and Bartlett, J.C. (2002) 'The effect of verbalisation on face recognition in young and old adults', *Applied Cognitive Psychology*, 16: 635–50.

Memon, A., Bartlett, J., Rose, R. A. and Gray, C. (2003) 'The aging eyewitness: effects of age of face, delay and source memory ability', *Journal of Gerontology: Psychological Sciences*, 58: 338–45.

Memon, A. and Gabbert, F. (2003a) 'Improving the identification accuracy of senior witnesses: do pre-lineup questions and sequential testing help?', *Journal of Applied Psychology*, 88: 341–47.

Memon, A. and Gabbert, F. (2003b) 'Unravelling the effect of sequential lineup presentation in culprit present lineups', *Applied Cognitive Psychology*, 17: 703–14.

Memon, A., Gabbert, F. and Hope, L. (2004) 'The ageing eyewitness', in J.R. Adler (ed.), *Forensic Psychology: Debates, concepts, and practice* (pp. 96–112). Cullompton: Willan Publishing.

Memon, A., Hope, L., Bartlett, J.C. and Bull, R. (2002) 'Eyewitness recognition errors: the effects of mugshot viewing and choosing in younger and older adults', *Memory and Cognition*, 30: 1219–27.

Memon, A., Hope, L. and Bull, R. (2003) 'Exposure duration: effects on eyewitness accuracy and confidence', *British Journal of Psychology*, 94: 339–54.

Milne, R. and Bull, R. (in press) (2nd edn) *Investigative Interviewing: Psychology and practice.* Chichester: Wiley.

Milne, R. and Bull, R. (2002) 'Back to basics: a componential analysis of the original cognitive interview mnemonics with three age groups', *Applied Cognitive Psychology*, 16: 1–11.

Milne, R., McAlpine, S. and Bull, R. (2000) *The cognitive interview: Does it enhance older people's recall?* Paper presented at the Biennial Conference of the American Psychology-Law Society, New Orleans.

Mitchell, K.J., Johnson, M.K. and Mather, M. (2003) 'Source monitoring and suggestibility to misinformation: adult age-related differences', *Applied Cognitive Psychology*, 17: 107–19.

Mueller-Johnson, K. and Ceci, S.J. (2004) 'Memory and suggestibility in older adults: live event participation and repeated interview', *Applied Cognitive Psychology*, 18: 1109–27.

Mueller-Johnson, K., Toglia, M.P., Sweeney, C.D. and Ceci, S.J. (2007) 'The perceived credibility of older adults as witnesses and its relation to ageism', *Behavioural Sciences and the Law*, 25: 355–75.

Neuschatz, J.S., Preston, E.L., Burkett, A.D., Toglia, M.P., Lampinen, J.M., Neuschatz, J.S., Fairless, A.H., Lawson, D.S., Powers, R.A. and Goodsell, C.A. (2005) 'The effects of post-identification feedback and age on retrospective eyewitness memory', *Applied Cognitive Psychology*, 19: 435–54.

Office for National Statistics (ONS) (2008) *Population Trends No. 131*. London: HMSO.

O'Rourke, T.E., Penrod, S.D., Cutler, B.L. and Stuve, T.E. (1989) 'The external validity of eyewitness research: generalizing across subject populations', *Law and Human Behavior*, 13: 385–95.

Rose, R.A., Bull, R. and Vrij, A. (2003) 'Enhancing older witnesses' identification performance: context reinstatement is not the answer', *The Canadian Journal of Police and Security Services*, 1: 173–84.

Rose, R.A., Bull, R. and Vrij, A. (2005) 'Non-biased lineup instructions do matter – a problem for older witnesses', *Psychology, Crime, and Law*, 11: 147–59.

Rothman, M.B., Dunlop, B.D. and Entzel, P. (2000) *Elders, Crime, and the Criminal Justice System. Myth, perceptions, and reality in the 21st Century.* New York: Springer Series on Life Styles and Issues in Aging.

Schacter, D.L., Norman, K.A. and Koutstaal, W. (1998) 'The cognitive neuroscience of constructive memory', *Annual Review of Psychology*, 49: 289–318.

Scogin, F., Calhoon, S.K. and D'Errico, M. (1994) 'Eyewitness confidence and accuracy among three age cohorts', *Journal of Applied Gerontology*, 13: 172–84.

Searcy, J.H., Bartlett, J.C. and Memon, A. (1999) 'Age differences in accuracy and choosing in eyewitness identification and face recognition', *Memory and Cognition*, 27: 538–52.

Searcy, J., Bartlett, J.C. and Memon, A. (2000) 'Influence of post event narratives, line-up conditions and individual differences on false identification by young and older eyewitnesses', *Legal and Criminological Psychology*, 5: 219–35.

Searcy, J.H., Bartlett, J.C., Memon, A. and Swanson, K. (2001) 'Aging and line-up performance at long retention intervals: effects of metamemory and context reinstatement', *Journal of Applied Psychology*, 86: 207–14.

Steblay, N.M. (1997) 'Social influence in eyewitness recall: a meta-analytic review of lineup instruction effects', *Law and Human Behavior*, 21: 283–97.

Steblay, N., Dysart, J., Fulero, S. and Lindsay, R.C.L. (2001) 'Eyewitness accuracy rates in sequential and simultaneous lineup presentations: a meta-analytic comparison', *Law and Human Behavior*, 25: 459–76.

Thornton, A., Hatton, C., Malone, C., Fryer, T., Walker, D., Cunningham, J. and Durrani, N. (2003) *Distraction Burglary amongst Older Adults and Ethnic Minority Communities.* Home Office Research Study 269. Development and Statistics Directorate.

Wells, G.L. and Bradfield, A.L. (1998) '"Good you identified the suspect": feedback to eyewitnesses distorts their reports of the witnessing experience', *Journal of Applied Psychology*, 83: 360–76.

Wells, G.L., Lindsay, R.C.L. and Ferguson, T.J. (1979) 'Accuracy, confidence, and juror perception in eyewitness identification', *Journal of Applied Psychology*, 64: 440–48.

Wells, G.L., Malpass, R.S., Lindsay, R.C.L., Fisher, R.P., Turtle, J.W. and Fulero, S.M. (2000) 'From the lab to the police station. A successful application of eyewitness research', *American Psychologist*, 55: 581–98.

Wilcock, R. and Bull, R. (in press) 'Novel lineup methods for improving the performance of older eyewitnesses', *Applied Cognitive Psychology.*

Wilcock, R. and Bull, R. (2006) *Reviewing and Adapting the Cognitive Interview for Use with Older Adults.* Paper presented at the Second International Investigative Interviewing Conference, Portsmouth, UK.

Wilcock, R., Bull, R. and Milne, R. (2008) *Witness Identification in Criminal Cases: Psychology and Practice.* Oxford University Press.

Wilcock, R.A., Bull, R. and Vrij, A (2005) 'Aiding the performance of older eyewitnesses: enhanced non-biased lineup instructions and presentation', *Psychiatry, Psychology, and Law*, 12: 129–40.

Wilcock, R.A., Bull, R. and Vrij, A. (2007) 'Are older witnesses always poorer witnesses? Identification accuracy, context reinstatement, own age bias', *Psychology, Crime, and Law*, 13: 305–16.

Wright, A.M. and Holliday, R.E. (2005) 'Police officers' perceptions of older eyewitnesses', *Legal and Criminological Psychology*, 10: 211–24.

Wright, A.M. and Holliday, R.E. (2007) 'Enhancing the recall of young, young-old and old-old adults with cognitive interviews', *Applied Cognitive Psychology*, 21: 19–43.

Yarmey, A.D. (1982) 'Eyewitness identification and stereotypes of criminals', in A. Trankell (ed.), *Reconstructing the Past. The role of psychologists in criminal trials* (pp. 205–25). Deventer, The Netherlands: Kluwer.

Yarmey, A.D. (2000) 'The older eyewitness', in M.B. Rothman, B.D. Dunlop, and P. Entzel (eds), *Elders, Crime, and the Criminal Justice System. Myth, Perception, and Reality in the 21st Century* (pp. 127–48). Springer Series on Life Styles and Issues in Aging.

Yarmey, A.D., Jones, H.T. and Rashid, S. (1984) 'Eyewitness memory of elderly and young adults', in D.J. Muller, D.E. Blackman and A.J. Chapman (eds), *Psychology and Law* (pp. 215–28). Chichester: Wiley.

Yarmey, A.D. and Kent, J. (1980) 'Eyewitness identification by elderly and young adults', *Law and Human Behavior*, 4: 359–71.

Zander, M. (1990) *The Police and Criminal Evidence Act*. London: Sweet and Maxwell.

Chapter 10

Safeguarding vulnerable and intimidated witnesses at court: are the 'special measures' working?

Graham M. Davies

If the prosecutor's case was to be believed, this was a series of very nasty domestic assaults. Sally, a 30-year-old single parent, had been in a relationship with Jake, a younger man, for some six months. It had always been a stormy relationship and on her birthday Jake was abusive to her, culminating in him getting a knife from the kitchen drawer and threatening to kill himself. Sally wrestled the knife from him and when she called the police, he ran off. The police arrived and advised Sally, by now very frightened, to lock herself in her house. Her daughter was staying with Tom, her father, for the day and now she rang Tom for help while she checked that all the windows were closed. As she finished the phone call, she heard a familiar voice: it was Jake, who had re-entered the house through an open window, and now grappled with her and threw her to the floor. He then dragged her into the bedroom, where she managed to escape, only to be pursued by him with an axe, with which he threatened to kill Tom. He then assaulted her once more before disappearing with the axe and some of his belongings. Now secure in her house, Sally later received a phone call from an apparently crestfallen Jake. He was outside the door: could he come in, just to collect his remaining belongings? Eventually Sally relented, whereupon Jake pushed past her and grabbed her by the throat, threatening to kill her. After collecting his remaining clothes, he left the house with the keys to her car, in which he drove off into the night.

Jake pled not guilty to three charges of assault and at the trial he sat impassively in the glass-fronted dock when Sally was called to give her evidence. In answer to the prosecutor's gentle prompting, Sally talked in general terms about the ups and downs of her relationship with Jake but when the questions focused on the assaults, she faltered and stopped, looking fearfully toward her former partner in the dock. At this point, the judge intervened and directed that screens be brought into the court to shield Sally from sight of Jake while she gave the rest of her evidence, a move to which both prosecution and defence advocates agreed. When the questioning resumed, Sally's testimony was transformed: she gave a very full and detailed account of the alleged assaults. The screens stayed in place during cross-examination. When Jake's counsel suggested that it was *she* who had assaulted *him*, she pointed to her own diminutive size and build compared with Jake and the bruising she had suffered: could she really have been responsible for throwing him onto the floor? When the trial resumed the following day, Jake's counsel changed his client's plea to guilty on all the assault charges.

The use of screens to protect witnesses from sight of the accused during examination and cross-examination at court are just one of a range of Special Measures designed to assist vulnerable witnesses in giving their best evidence at court. This chapter outlines the nature and motivation for the introduction of Special Measures, the research which has been undertaken into their effectiveness, and poses the question whether such measures in themselves are likely to enhance the chances of justice for vulnerable witnesses.

Special Measures

The need for additional legal and procedural safeguards to assist and support vulnerable witnesses at court was spelled out in the Home Office report *Speaking Up for Justice* (1998), the product of an interdepartmental review which had examined barriers to vulnerable or intimidated witnesses having their voices heard in court. The need for action was supported by research which highlighted the very high rates of attrition where vulnerable witnesses were involved, between an initial complaint to the police and any subsequent court case. A study of complainants with learning disabilities by Sanders *et al.* (1997) revealed that over half led to no further action by the police and a conviction rate of just 18 per cent. Similar disturbing figures emerged from research on female complainants of rape, where 31 per cent resulted in no further police action and just 6 per cent resulted in a conviction for rape at court, with a further 7 per cent convicted on lesser charges (Harris and Grace 1999). Among children alleging abuse, a major study by Gallagher and Pease (2000) reported that 76 per cent were recorded as requiring no further action by the police and only 12 per cent produced a conviction at court (see Davies and Westcott 2006 for further details).

The plight of child complainants had already received some attention from the Home Office. The 1988 Criminal Justice Act introduced the use of live television links into the courts to enable children, initially under the age of 14 years (later under 18 years for sexual and violence offences), to testify from outside the courtroom, thus avoiding the need to view an accused or enter the unfamiliar surroundings of the court itself. The 1991 Criminal Justice Act included a clause permitting pre-recorded videotaped interviews with child complainants to be shown at court in place of live examination-in-chief on the day of the trial. The twin advantages of this scheme were to promote the collection of evidence when the alleged events were still fresh in the child's mind and to enable interviews to be conducted by specially trained police officers and social workers in less formal surroundings, rather than by barristers at court. After a predictably cautious reception from the courts, these two innovations rapidly became established features of cases involving child complainants, particularly of sexual abuse (Davies and Pezdek 2010).

The success of these innovations with children paved the way for more ambitious and wide-ranging variations in procedure (termed Special Measures) embodied in the 1999 Youth Justice and Criminal Evidence Act which sought to assist vulnerable and intimidated witnesses of all ages to give their best evidence. The groups to which the Act applies are:

- children under 17 years of age;
- witnesses with a physical disability or disorder;
- witnesses with a learning disability or mental disorder;
- distressed witnesses (including victims of sexual offences); and
- witnesses in fear of intimidation.

Sally, as a victim of domestic violence, qualified for Special Measures as a distressed witness. Normally, an application to use Special Measures is made to the presiding judge prior to the trial, though there is provision for the granting of Special Measures on the day of the trial and, exceptionally, during the trial itself, as occurred in Sally's case. Application can be made for one or more of the following Special Measures, depending upon an assessment of the needs of the particular witness:

- screens – to ensure that the witness does not see the defendant;
- live TV link – allowing a witness to give evidence from outside the court via CCTV;
- video-recorded evidence-in-chief – a pre-recorded formal interview with the witness;
- clearing the public gallery of the court to allow evidence to be given in private;
- removal of wigs and gowns by court officials during the taking of evidence;
- communication aids, such as alphabet or symbol boards, for witnesses with communication difficulties; or
- intermediaries to assist the witness in communicating with counsel and the court.

A final measure – the use of pre-recorded videotaped cross-examination – was included in the original Act but has not yet been implemented, largely due to legal resistance and logistical problems. The use of intermediaries was first piloted in selected areas before being launched nationally in 2008 (Plotnikoff and Woolfson 2007a). However, the remaining measures have been available to the courts since the Act became law in 2002 and their effectiveness was the subject of two major Home Office-sponsored reviews. Hamlyn *et al.* (2004) contacted and questioned some 552 witnesses identified as vulnerable about their experiences at court before the onset of the new Act and a further 552 after the Act had been implemented. The principal focus of Burton *et al.* (2006) was on tracking cases through the legal process to see if vulnerable witnesses were being successfully identified and receiving the assistance the Act was designed to provide.

Vulnerable or intimidated witnesses

The size of the problem

Speaking Up for Justice (Home Office 1998) estimated that perhaps 9 per cent of all witnesses – 50,000 defence witnesses and 160,000 appearing for the prosecution annually – could be categorised as vulnerable or subject to intimidation. Hamlyn *et al.* (2004) studied two samples of vulnerable witnesses: one from prior and the other subsequent to the Act coming into force. The post-Act sample gives an indication of the type and range of vulnerable witnesses identified by the courts.

The largest group (70 per cent) consisted of witnesses experiencing or being in fear of intimidation. A further 42 per cent were young people under the age of 17, 13 per cent had an illness or disability which might prevent them giving best evidence unaided, 15 per cent were alleged victims of sexual offences and 7 per cent were described as having a learning disability (note some of these categories overlap – a person with a learning disability who also fears intimidation – so the totals do not sum to 100 per cent). Just 1 per cent of all those identified were defence witnesses, who were meant to be covered by the new legislation. The constitution of the vulnerable group showed little change from the period prior to the Act, except for a small rise in the number of juveniles. However, Burton *et al.* (2006) concluded that the numbers of vulnerable witnesses being recorded by the police and the courts were a gross underestimate of the problem. Telephone interviews with witnesses suggested that while most child witnesses were being readily identified, other less readily identifiable groups, such as those with physical or mental disabilities or those in fear and distress, were frequently missed by all agencies. Based on their interview data and using conservative assumptions, Burton *et al.* estimated that some 24 per cent of all witnesses met the criteria for vulnerability.

Witness intimidation

Intimidated witnesses are not necessarily vulnerable, but there is evidence that vulnerable witnesses are more at risk of intimidation than the general population (Fyfe 2001). Hamlyn *et al.* provide some useful insights into the scope of the problem. Witnesses reported that intimidation came principally from defendants (36 per cent) or their family (21 per cent). The police became involved in around two thirds of instances and their action was sufficient to stop the problem in 33 per cent of cases. The Witness Service (69 per cent) and Witness Support (59 per cent) also stepped in to provide support, chiefly prior to a court appearance. Witness intimidation constitutes a major and under-researched feature of the legal system. Hamlyn *et al.*'s data provide some reassuring information on those witnesses who went to court, but tell us little about those who were dissuaded from giving evidence as a result of intimidation and who therefore do not appear in the survey.

Experiences prior to trial

Hamlyn *et al.* (2004) provide a useful snapshot of the experiences of vulnerable and intimidated witnesses subsequent to the Act. According to their figures, nearly half of their respondents experienced a change in the date of their court hearing, 28 per cent of the changes being due to the defence being unready. Postponement of hearings is endemic in the UK legal system and a significant source of additional stress for already anxious witnesses (Plotnikoff and Woolfson 2004). On the more positive side, 35 per cent of witnesses reported that they had been escorted to court by a supporter provided by agencies such as Witness Support and the Witness Service or the police. When they reached court, 23 per cent waited an hour or less to give their evidence, but a similar number had to wait four hours or more. The privacy of a special waiting room was available to 95 per cent of prosecution witnesses, but 44 per cent still managed to encounter the defendant while moving around the court building. There is limited value in elaborate shielding procedures in the courtroom in cases of alleged intimidation if the defendant and the witness meet elsewhere on the day. Separate entrances, catering facilities and toilets for witnesses and defendants are still a rarity, even in recently refurbished courtrooms.

Experience at court

According to Hamlyn *et al.* (2004), some 68 per cent had met the prosecutor prior to giving their evidence, a step now endorsed by the official *Witness Charter* (Office for Criminal Justice Reform 2007a). After examination-in-chief by the prosecution, some 94 per cent were then cross-examined. The job of defence counsel in cross-examination is to test the credibility of witnesses' evidence, frequently through the use of leading questions or suggestions that their statements are suspect and that the witnesses themselves are unreliable, a process normally experienced as stressful by most witnesses (Henderson 2002). Somewhat surprisingly, some 13 per cent of all witnesses reported that they had not expected to be cross-examined. Hamlyn *et al.* report that some 48 per cent of adults and 35 per cent of children were upset 'a lot' by the procedure and a quarter reported being accused of lying to the court. Overall, however, some 66 per cent felt the defence had treated them courteously. The single most positive finding of the Hamlyn *et al.* research was a modest rise in the proportion of witnesses who reported being satisfied with their courtroom experience subsequent to the introduction of Special Measures: an overall increase from 64 to 69 per cent. Greater satisfaction was associated with effective liaison with the police and the prosecutor, being able to give their evidence accurately and low levels of anxiety and distress. But how does each of the individual Special Measures provide psychological support for vulnerable witnesses and impact upon the quality of their evidence?

Special Measures in action

Live TV links and the use of screens

The principal function of both live TV links and the use of screens is to hide the view of the accused from the witness as they give their evidence. Surveys suggest that children certainly find the prospect of giving their evidence in front of an accused a deterrent to testifying (Flin *et al.* 1989) and at least one experimental study demonstrated an inhibiting effect on recall of five- to six-year olds by the presence of an apparent 'offender' when testifying. If the 'offender' was present, just 5 per cent were prepared to state (truthfully) that he had stolen a book, compared with two thirds when testifying in his absence (Peters 1991). While no comparable studies have been conducted with vulnerable adults, there is no reason to believe that the physical presence of an accused is not inhibiting to adults as well, particularly when intimidation has been involved.

There is a continuing debate over the relative effectiveness of screens and TV links as techniques for assisting witnesses. Screens are normally erected around the witness box, but can, as in Sally's case, be erected in front of the defendant. Live TV links normally link a small room within the court building to the courtroom; both are equipped with TV modems which both send and receive pictures and sound. Questions from counsel are relayed to the child, who sits alone except for an usher or other agreed support person to ensure fair play. The child sees whosoever is talking to him or her while the court always sees the child. In addition to modems for the judge, the prosecution and defence counsel, large monitors permit others in the courtroom, including the accused, to observe what is said.

Lawyers tend to favour screens as they find the direct eye contact enables rapport to be more quickly established: communicating effectively via a television link is an acquired skill for both lawyers and witnesses (Doherty-Sneddon and McAuley 2000). Live TV links have an advantage from the witness perspective in that they are spared the need to enter the courtroom.

A number of field studies have examined the relative effectiveness of live TV links and face-to-face testimony for children at court.

Davies and Noon (1991), in an evaluation of the English innovation, compared in-court ratings of children's evidence delivered via the TV link with conventional testimony and reported that witnesses were more consistent and resistant to leading questions when giving their evidence via CCTV, a finding replicated by Doherty-Sneddon and McAuley (2000) in a controlled laboratory simulation. Other evaluations conducted in Scotland (Murray 1995) and Western Australia (O'Grady. 1996) failed to replicate these positive advantages, but the reason for this discrepancy may lie in differences in legislation. In England and Wales, there is a legal presumption ('primary rule') that all child witnesses will use the live TV link, whereas in Scotland and Western Australia at the time of the evaluations, the link was only available on application for children who might not otherwise be able to give their evidence in person, resulting in a user group who were significantly younger and more severely traumatised than those giving evidence in open court (see Davies and Pezdek 2010, for further discussion). While the uniform application of the link in England and Wales has some advantage in ensuring that juries do not draw adverse implications regarding the child's particular fear of an accused, it does mean that some older and more assertive young witnesses may be prevented from fulfilling their wish to confront the accused in open court (Cashmore 2002).

Hamlyn *et al.* (2004) confirmed that virtually all the children surveyed in England and Wales and involved in allegations of sexual abuse testified via the live TV link. The link was also used by 83 per cent of children testifying in other cases, but the corresponding figure for vulnerable adults was only 15 per cent. It would be comforting to think the remaining adults had had access to screens, but in fact screen usage extended to just 8 per cent of the total sample. Given the widespread availability of the TV link, not merely in Crown Court Centres but also in magistrates' courts in England and Wales, it appears that the link is the method of choice for witnesses who fear confrontation with an accused: 80 per cent of users found it helpful in giving their evidence.

Video-recorded evidence-in-chief

Following the 1991 Act, the use of videotaped investigative interviews with child complainants of abuse as a substitute for live examination-in-chief at court has become routine in the English and Welsh courts. When the measure was first introduced, the Home Office published the *Memorandum of Good Practice* (1992), a set of guidelines covering the conduct of these interviews, drafted by a psychologist and a lawyer (Bull 1995). The difficulty for the *Memorandum* interviewer is that such interviews are simultaneously investigative and evidential. They require the interviewer to develop a high degree of social rapport with the child prior to the broaching of the purpose of the interview and to restrict questions to those which are acceptable to the courts. Thus, the *Memorandum* lays a strong emphasis on the value of the child first describing events in their own words and the interviewer subsequently using open-ended prompts rather than questions which are overly specific or leading. This style of interviewing requires considerable practice to first achieve and then maintain the necessary skills; examination of actual recordings of such interviews suggests that many show significant departures from the guidelines (Sternberg *et al*. 2001).

The 1999 Act extended the option of videotaped evidence-in-chief to all groups of vulnerable witnesses who might benefit, as a Special Measure at the discretion of the presiding judge. Given the wider remit of the new legislation, a new set of guidelines appropriate for interviewing adults as well as children was introduced. *Achieving Best Evidence* (Home Office 2002) advised much the same style of interviewing as its predecessor, but included additional guidelines covering the care and support of vulnerable and intimidated witnesses subsequent to interview and at trial. These new guidelines were intended not just for police and social services interviewers but for all those involved in the legal process, including lawyers and judges.

How much use has been made of the new facility by the courts? Hamlyn *et al*. (2004) reported that 95 per cent of child complainants of sexual abuse gave their evidence-in-chief in the form of a videotaped interview. However, only 42 per cent of children giving evidence in other types of case gave their evidence in this way and the take-up among vulnerable adults was just 5 per cent. Those giving their evidence-in-chief on video valued not having to appear in the courtroom (43 per cent) and also found it easier to give sensitive evidence (22 per cent). Equally importantly, 98 per cent of those who gave pre-recorded interviews maintained they had been given the opportunity to say everything they wished, compared with just 53 per cent of those who were taken through their evidence by the prosecutor at court.

Given the apparent advantages for witnesses of all ages of videotaped statements, why is this facility not more widely applied for? The answer may lie in the widespread perception among lawyers and judges that videotaped statements do not have the same emotional impact as statements made in person in the courtroom (Burton *et al.* 2006). There is certainly research evidence that observers perceive those giving videotaped testimony in a less positive light than those who give their evidence in person (Landstrom 2008), but other research suggests that the greater impact of live testimony is reduced or even eliminated when the trial moves to the jury deliberation phase (Davies and Pezdek 2010). There is also the issue of whether live and videotaped statements can ever be equivalent outside of a psychological experiment. As the reactions of witnesses reported by Hamlyn *et al.* demonstrate, most witnesses are better able to give sensitive and full evidence when interviewed soon after the event in an informal setting by a skilled interviewer than when examined months later in front of a crowded courtroom by a barrister (Davies 1994). A belated recognition of this fact is the proposal from the Office for Criminal Justice Reform that the initial videotaped interviews given by alleged adult victims of rape to trained police personnel should automatically be admissible as evidence-in-chief in the same way as those of child complainants (Office for Criminal Justice Reform 2006b).

Wigs, gowns and clearing the gallery

The clearing of the public gallery during the taking of evidence of a sexual or sensitive nature and the removal of formal court dress during the taking of evidence from vulnerable witnesses are both matters which have long lain within the discretion of individual judges to order. Their statutory elevation to Special Measures reflects a belief that they may materially contribute to the giving of good evidence. Cases of a sexual nature have always attracted their fair share of prurient spectators. Witnesses can also be intimidated by the noisy presence in the gallery of a defendant's friends and family. However, Hamlyn *et al.*'s data suggest that judges are reluctant to use this measure: just 10 per cent of respondents reported gallery clearing. It seems for most judges that the right of the public to be informed trumps any privacy sought by witnesses describing disturbing experiences.

The implicit psychological rationale for the removal of wigs and gowns in the Crown court is presumably to reduce the social distance between court personnel and their clients in much the same way as police interviewers wear civilian clothing when video-interviewing children. Children, at least, might be expected to be less forthcoming and more suggestible when questioned by interviewers wearing uniforms (Powell *et al.* 2000). Hamlyn *et al.*'s survey suggests that dress change occurred in just 15 per cent of all cases, though the figure was higher for cases involving child complainants (25 per cent). The general issue of whether judges and barristers should cling to their traditional raiment was raised by the then Lord Chancellor, Lord Irvine, who reported that two thirds of the public were in favour of change, but resistance in some parts of the judiciary quashed the initiative (Dyer 2003).

Communication aids and intermediaries

The available Special Measures include provision for the use of communication aids such as language or symbol boards. Hamlyn *et al.* record no instance of their use throughout their survey but they did report demand for intermediaries from both child and adult witnesses. The role of the intermediary under the Act extends from the investigation stage through to trial. At the investigative stage, intermediaries can assist by explaining questions to the witness in terms they understand and explaining the answers, but without changing the substance of the evidence. Prior to trial, they can accompany the witness on familiarisation visits to the court and any pre-trial meetings. At trial, they can perform a similar service to assist the judge and the lawyers involved. The involvement of an intermediary at trial is at the discretion of the presiding judge and each must swear on oath to communicate a true account of what the witness has said (O'Mahony 2008/9).

The Intermediary Special Measure was the subject of a two-year pathfinder project involving pilots in some six criminal justice areas (Plotnikoff and Woolfson 2007a). At the end of the evaluation there were over 70 trained and registered intermediaries in England and Wales of whom the great majority were speech and language therapists but at least one was a chartered forensic psychologist (O'Mahony 2008/9). During the pilot period there were 206 requests for assistance of which the largest group (57 per cent) concerned witnesses with impairments of intelligence or social functioning. Some 61 per cent of clients were adults and the remainder children. Only 14 per cent of children were referred for intermediaries on the basis of their age alone. The great majority of intermediaries were employed during the investigative and pre-trial phases and few had appeared at court by the end of the pathfinder period. Almost all users reported finding the intermediaries of value. Plotnikoff and Woolfson (2007a) quote one judge as saying: 'Overall, the intermediary worked very well. She was strong and intervened when questions became too complex. Her interventions did not come too often but they were invaluable. The intermediary would be very welcome in any court I sat in' (p. 60). As a result of the success of the pathfinder project, the intermediary scheme was rolled out throughout England and Wales in 2008 and the Scottish Government has launched a consultation on introducing a similar scheme north of the border (Criminal Justice Directorate 2007).

Are Special Measures enough to ensure justice for vulnerable victims?

There is no doubt that the Special Measures provision embodied in the 1999 legislation continues to have a positive influence on the quality of evidence and personal welfare of vulnerable witnesses. Hamlyn *et al.*'s survey found that while vulnerable witnesses as a group were less satisfied with the legal process than those not so classified, 76 per cent of children and 64 per cent of vulnerable adults were satisfied with their treatment and 70 per cent of these would be prepared to give evidence again. Around a third of all witnesses said they would not have been able to give their evidence but for the availability of Special Measures. However, the figures for the sample as a whole reveal that only a minority (44 per cent) would consider going to court on another occasion.

Child respondents to an NSPCC survey suggested that there were many other continuing concerns around the legal process which were not covered by the current Special Measures legislation. These included pre-trial delay, a lack of information and concerns over case progress and a lack of personal involvement in taking decisions over what Special Measures were appropriate (Plotnikoff and Woolfson 2004). A study examining the conduct and progress of trials involving allegations of rape also revealed that Special Measures had not halted the high attrition rates and very low rates of conviction in such trials and that adult and child complainants alike still felt poorly treated by the criminal justice system (Kelly *et al.* 2005).

The Crown Prosecution Service, the Home Office, the Department of Constitutional Affairs and now the Ministry of Justice have responded to such criticisms by setting up an interdepartmental organisation – the Office for Criminal Justice Reform – to orchestrate actions which cross traditional departmental boundaries. This Office has been responsible for a stream of consultation papers, proposing new standards of care and target setting. Indeed, the danger is that the sheer volume of recent initiatives will cloud and confuse the police and the courts without necessarily resolving basic problems. Some schemes, however, have already made a solid contribution to the welfare and concerns of witnesses.

Following the *No Witness No Justice* initiative (Office for Criminal Justice Reform 2006a), the CPS and the police set up Witness Care Units that now cover virtually all the Crown Court Centres in England and Wales. They are designed to provide a single point of contact for all victims and witnesses who are likely to be called in a trial, to conduct a needs assessment, and to keep witnesses informed of the progress and outcome of the case. A pilot study in five criminal justice areas showed an increase in witness attendance of 20 per cent and a 17 per cent drop in ineffective trials caused by the witness withdrawing their statement (Office for Criminal Justice Reform 2006a).

The *Witness Charter* (Office for Criminal Justice Reform 2007a) set out fresh standards for the different agencies within the criminal justice system to achieve for all witnesses, including the vulnerable and intimidated. This placed responsibility for identifying vulnerable witnesses squarely with the police and not the CPS (Standards 3 and 4). The new Charter did not appear to have taken account of the concerns expressed in Burton *et al.*'s survey that the police were not necessarily adept at identifying many types of vulnerability, a point recently repeated in yet another government department document (Department of Health 2008). Standard 8 of the Charter covers witness intimidation and pledges that the police will deal promptly with any complaints. Little further research appears to have been conducted on the problem, though the second edition of *Achieving Best Evidence* (Office for Criminal Justice Reform 2007b) contains greatly expanded guidance on how officers can combat this particular menace and reassure witnesses. The Charter acknowledged concerns, but offered little more than good intentions on listing and delay, though witnesses identified as vulnerable are to receive priority as regard times and dates (Standard 13). There is provision for supporters from the Witness Service to attend court with witnesses when required (Standard 19) and to accompany witnesses into the live TV link room or the courtroom with the permission of the presiding judge or magistrate. Finally, Standard 29 pledges that 'your lawyer' will intervene if questioning in cross-examination is 'unfair, offensive or oppressive' (p. 14); interestingly, the role of the judge or magistrate in safeguarding witnesses in these circumstances is omitted (see below). In 2008, the Office for Criminal Justice Reform issued a clarifying directive to court staff on how the standards demanded by the Charter were to be interpreted and the court's role in fulfilling them (Office for Criminal Justice Reform 2008).

Other documents have dealt specifically with the problems of child witnesses. In 2005, the Crown Prosecution Service launched a consultation on a Children's Charter, which morphed into *Children and Young People* (Crown Prosecution Service 2006), an accessible summary of existing policy on children as victims and defendants, containing many good intentions but no new concrete initiatives. Rather more specific guidance emerged from *Improving the Criminal Trial Process for Young Witnesses* (Office for Criminal Justice Reform 2005), a consultative document containing 31 recommendations to improve the legal process for children as witnesses. One of its more controversial recommendations was a limited revival of the proposal to permit video-recorded cross-examination in cases where a vulnerable person would not otherwise be available as a witness. It also recommended greater flexibility as to how children gave their evidence at court: the more mature and assertive should be permitted to give their evidence live at court, rather than through the live TV link. It also recommended that witnesses be permitted to testify via the link from more distant locations (another town or country; a hospital bed). Another recommendation dealt with magistrates and judges being more active in controlling inappropriate cross-examination: it seems that contrary to the Witness Charter, this *is* a matter for the presiding court officer, at least for children. Plotnikoff and Woolfson (2007a) had noted that 48 per cent of their sample of children did not understand some of the questions they were asked by advocates, 80 per cent had problems with some aspect of questioning, but only 9 per cent remembered the presiding judge or prosecutor intervening to help. A major section is given over to the need for specialist support for young witnesses up to and including trial. It appears that current support is patchy and haphazard and the promised national scheme has not yet materialised (Plotnikoff and Woolfson 2007b). It is evident that the recommendations of the Office for Criminal Justice Reform have raised as many questions as answers and in July 2008 it was announced in the House of Lords that the Government's response had been delayed due to the sheer volume of comments that the outline proposals had provoked.

Conclusions

Giving evidence in court is inevitably a stressful process for all those who are called as witnesses. Indeed, lawyers will argue that a degree of stress is a useful tool in ensuring that witnesses speak the truth: a distant relative of the 'trial by ordeal' that preceded our contemporary legal system (Henderson 2002). However, for many vulnerable and intimidated witnesses, that stress can be so overwhelming that they are either unable to take the stand or fail to give their best evidence. Special Measures have certainly assisted many such witnesses to tell their story at court, but it is evident that the problems of the vulnerable and intimidated do not stop at the courtroom door: there are difficulties both before the court hearing and afterwards, not least in coming to terms with any adverse verdict. The past decade has seen a major focus both in legislation and resources in 'Rebalancing the Criminal Justice System in favour of the Law-Abiding Majority', to quote part of the title of yet another Government report on the problem (Office for Criminal Justice Reform 2006b). If sheer volume of reports and exhortations were enough, the problem would have been solved by now. Perhaps the problems that vulnerable witnesses face are symptoms of an adversarial legal system that needs fundamental re-examination: not so much a rebalancing, more a different set of scales.

Note

The origins of this chapter lie in an invited address to the Division of Forensic Psychology Annual Conference in 2006. The account of the case of Sally and Jake is authentic, although names and some minor details have been changed to protect the identities of those involved.

References

Bull, R. (1995) 'Interviewing children in legal contexts', in R. Bull and D. Carson (eds), *Handbook of Psychology in Legal Contexts* (pp. 235–46). Chichester: Wiley.

Burton, M., Evans, R. and Sanders, A. (2006) *Are Special Measures for Vulnerable and Intimidated Witnesses Working? Evidence from the criminal justice agencies*, Online Report 01/06. London: Home Office.

Cashmore, J. (2002) 'Innovative procedures for child witnesses', in H. Westcott, G.M. Davies and R. Bull (eds), *Children's Testimony: A Handbook of Psychological Research and Forensic Practice* (pp. 203–18). Chichester: Wiley

Criminal Justice Directorate (2007) *The Use of Intermediaries for Vulnerable Witnesses in Scotland*. Edinburgh: Criminal Justice Directorate

Crown Prosecution Service (2005) *Children's Charter: draft for consultation*. London: Crown Prosecution Service.

Crown Prosecution Service (2006) *Children and Young People: CPS policy on prosecuting criminal cases involving children and young people as victims and witnesses*. London: Crown Prosecution Service.

Davies, G.M. (1994) Editorial. 'Live Links: Understanding the message of the medium', *Journal of Forensic Psychiatry*, 5: 225–7.

Davies, G.M. and Noon, E. (1991) *An Evaluation of the Live Live Link for Child Witnesses*. London: Home Office.

Davies, G.M. and Pezdek, K. (2010) 'Children as witnesses', in G. Towl and D. Crighton (eds), *A Textbook of Forensic Psychology*. Chichester: Wiley-Blackwell.

Davies, G.M. and Westcott, H.L. (2006) 'Preventing the withdrawal of complaints and psychological support for victims', in M.R. Kebbell and G.M. Davies (eds), *Practical Psychology for Forensic Investigations and Prosecutions* (pp. 183–202). Chichester: Wiley

Department of Health (2008) *Safeguarding Adults: a consultation on the review of the 'No Secrets' guidance*. London: Department of Health

Doherty-Sneddon, G. and McAuley, S. (2000) 'Influence of video mediation on adult-child interviews: implications for the use of the live link with child witnesses', *Applied Cognitive Psychology*, 14: 379–92.

Dyer, C. (2003) 'Majority verdict finds against wigs', *The Guardian*, 9 May. Available at www.guardian.co.uk/2003/may/09/claredyer/print (accessed 10 October 2008).

Flin, R., Stevenson, Y. and Davies, G.M. (1989) 'Children's knowledge of court proceedings', *British Journal of Psychology*, 80: 285–97.

Fyfe, N.R. (2001) *Protecting Intimidated Witnesses*. Aldershot: Ashgate.

Gallagher, B. and Pease, K. (2000) 'Understanding the attrition of child abuse and neglect cases in the criminal justice system'. Unpublished Report to the Economic and Social Research Council (R000236891).

Hamlyn, B., Phelps, A., Turtle, J. and Sattar, G. (2004) *Are Special Measures Working? Evidence from surveys of vulnerable and intimidated witnesses*. Home Office Research Study 283. London: Home Office.

Harris, J. and Grace, S. (1999) *A Question of Evidence? Investigating and prosecuting rape in the 1990s*. Home Office Study 196. London: Home Office.

Henderson, E. (2002) 'Persuading and controlling: the theory of cross-examination in relation to children', in H.L. Westcott, G.M. Davies and R.H.C. Bull (eds), *Children's Testimony: A Handbook of Psychological Research and Forensic Practice* (pp. 279–94). Chichester: Wiley.

Home Office (1992) *The Memorandum of Good Practice on Video Recorded Interviews with Child Witnesses for Criminal Proceedings*. London: Home Office.

Available at www.homeoffice.gov.uk/rds/prgpdfs/brf115.pdf (accessed 10 October 2008).

Home Office (2002) *Achieving Best Evidence in Criminal Proceedings: Guidance for Vulnerable or Intimidated Witnesses, including Children*. London: Home Office Communication Directorate. Available at www.cps.gov.uk/Publications/docs/Achieving_Best_Evidence_FINAL.pdf (accessed 27 January 2010).

Home Office (1998) *Speaking Up for Justice: report of the interdepartmental working group on the treatment of vulnerable and intimidated witnesses in the criminal justice system*. London: Home Office.

Kelly, L., Lovett, J. and Regan, L. (2005) *A Gap or a Chasm? Attrition in reported rape cases*. Home Office Research Study 293. London: Home Office

Landstrom, S. (2008) *CCTV, Live and Videotapes*. Gothenburg, Sweden: University of Gothenburg.

Murray, K. (1995) *Live Television Live Link: an evaluation of its use by child witnesses in Scottish criminal trials*. Edinburgh: Her Majesty's Stationery Office.

Office for Criminal Justice Reform (2005) *Improving the Criminal Trial Process for Young Witnesses*. London: Office for Criminal Justice Reform.

Office for Criminal Justice Reform (2006a) *No Witness No Justice: the national victim and witness care programme*. London: Office for Criminal Justice Reform.

Office for Criminal Justice Reform (2006b) *Rebalancing the Criminal Justice System in favour of the Law-Abiding Majority: cutting crime, reducing reoffending and protecting the public*. London: Office for Criminal Justice Reform.

Office for Criminal Justice Reform (2007a) *The Witness Charter: standards of care for witnesses in the criminal justice system*. London: Office for Criminal Justice Reform.

Office for Criminal Justice Reform (2007b) *Achieving Best Evidence in Criminal Proceedings: guidance on interviewing victims and witnesses, and using special measures*. London: Office for Criminal Justice Reform. Available at www.cps.gov.uk?publications/docs/Achieving_Best_Evidence_FINAL_pdf (accessed 27 January 2010).

Office for Criminal Justice Reform (2008) *Implementing and Complying with the Witness Charter: operational guidance for CPS staff and managers*. London: Office for Criminal Justice Reform.

O'Grady, C. (1996) *Child Witnesses and Jury Trials*. Perth, Western Australia: Ministry of Justice.

O'Mahony, B. (2008/9) 'The role of the registered intermediary in the criminal justice system', *Forensic Update*, 96 (Winter, 2008/9): 7–11.

Peters, D.P. (1991, April) 'Confrontational stress and children's testimony: some experimental findings'. Paper presented at the Biennial Meeting of the Society for Research in Child Development, Seattle, WA

Plotnikoff, J. and Woolfson, R. (2004) *In Their Own Words: the experiences of 50 young witnesses in criminal proceedings*. London: NSPCC.

Plotnikoff, J. and Woolfson, R. (2007a) *The 'Go Between': evaluation of intermediary pathfinder projects*. London: Home Office. Available at: www.justice.gov.uk/publications/research120607a.htm (accessed 10 October 2008).

Plotnikoff, J. and Woolfson, R. (2007b) *Evaluation of Young Witness Support: examining the impact on witnesses and the criminal justice system*. London: Home Office. Available at: lexiconlimited.co.uk/PDF%20files/Young_Witness_Study_Report.pdf (accessed 10 October 2008).

Powell, M., Wilson, C. and Croft, C. (2000) 'The effect of uniform and prior knowledge on children's event reports and disclosure of secrets', *Journal of Police and Criminal Psychology*, 15: 27–40.

Sanders, A., Creaton, J., Bird, S. and Weber, L. (1997) *Victims with Learning Disabilities: negotiating the criminal justice system*. Oxford: University of Oxford Centre for Criminological Research.

Sternberg, K.J., Lamb, M.E., Davies, G.M. and Westcott, H.L. (2001) 'The "Memorandum of Good Practice": theory versus practice', *Child Abuse and Neglect*, 25: 669–81.

Section 3

Serious and Persistent Offending

In the wider context of forensic psychology, there are some issues that are well established in the discipline and have a substantial body of literature spanning many years. In contrast, the topics in this section consider some very specific manifestations of offending which are not always commonly represented in the literature, or indeed within forensic psychology texts. These topics are included as they are particularly significant given their consequences for victims and society. While all crime has adverse effects for victims, society, and often the offenders and their social groups, the types of criminality addressed in this section can have particularly negative outcomes, either in terms of the number of victims or the nature of the victimisation, be they psychological or physical.

The first two chapters in this section on life course persistent offending and stalking are the original chapters from the first edition of this text by Alex Piquero and Terrie Moffitt and Lorraine Sheridan and Graham M. Davies. The authors were not able to update these chapters fully but were willing for us to include the valuable original versions, with updated readings as supplementary material. The final two chapters, from Margaret Wilson and Lucy Lemanski and from Agnieszka Golec de Zavala and Joanna R. Adler, address terrorism and genocide, both issues of significant international importance to which forensic psychology is able to offer valuable insights.

Chapter 11

Life-course persistent offending*

Alex R. Piquero and Terrie E. Moffitt

Of all facets of crime, perhaps none has received as much research attention as age. The relationship between age and crime is one of the most well-documented (Quetelet 1831; Hirschi and Gottfredson 1983) and contentious (Steffensmeier *et al.* 1989; Britt 1992) of all criminological findings. Researchers studying the relationship between age and crime have typically observed that the aggregate pattern is such that criminal activity tends to peak in the late teens (in early cohorts) through the mid twenties (in contemporary cohorts), then declines throughout adulthood.

At the same time that the relationship between age and crime has been reproduced, it raises the question of the degree to which the *aggregate* pattern displayed in the age/crime curve is similar to – or different from – the pattern of *individual* careers and whether conclusions about individuals can be validly drawn from aggregate data (Piquero *et al.* 2003). For example, how far does the observed

Note from the editors

*When compiling this second edition, we were mindful of the need to balance new chapters with certain core areas of work from the first edition. There were two chapters where the authors had too many other commitments, and were unable to produce a new chapter for this collection. However, we are grateful to them for allowing us to continue to use their initial chapters and thank them for providing us with materials to update them. We thus present this chapter, as it was initially prepared for the first edition but with an updated readings list at the end. We hope that the reader will find these new readings useful additions to what remains a comprehensive chapter on life-course persistent offending.

peak of the aggregate age/crime curve reflect changes within individuals as opposed to changes in the composition of offenders? In other words, is the peak in the age/crime curve a function of active offenders committing more crime, or is it a function of more individuals actively offending at those peak years?

Farrington (1986) suggests that the aggregate peak age of offending primarily reflects variations in prevalence, and not frequency. If this is the case, then it suggests that although the majority of offenders are dropping out of a life of crime, some small select group remains criminally active well into adulthood. This notion of persistence, recognised by proponents of the criminal career paradigm as being one of the key dimensions of the criminal career (Blumstein *et al.* 1986), has been the subject of much empirical attention (Dean *et al.* 1996; Huesmann *et al.* 1984; Paternoster *et al.* 1997), yet has not received much theoretical attention; that is, until the past decade.

In this essay, we examine the ability of one particular theory, Moffitt's (1993) developmental taxonomy, to account for persistence in criminal activity. Her theory takes as its starting point the aggregate age-crime curve, and from it, explains the stability of criminal activity as a function of a particular group of offenders, termed life-course persistent, whose offending proclivities begin early in life and continue throughout the life-course. Herein, we review (1) the underlying theoretical arguments articulated in Moffitt's theory, (2) the research completed on her theory to date, and (3) the challenges levelled against Moffitt's developmental taxonomy. Finally, we conclude with the identification of a number of unanswered research questions that will likely offer a number of important future research directions.

Moffitt's developmental taxonomy

Moffitt's taxonomy proposes two primary types of offenders, each of whom possesses a unique set of factors that cause criminal and antisocial activity, as well as a different patterning of criminal and antisocial activity over the life-course. A third group of individuals, the abstainers, is a small, select group who refrain from antisocial and criminal activity throughout the life-course.

The first group of offenders in Moffitt's theory, adolescence-limited, restricts their offending activity to the adolescent stage of life, occurring between puberty and when they attain adult social roles. The set of factors underlying adolescence-limited delinquency consists of the maturity gap and the peer social context. The maturity gap reflects the youngsters' experience of dysphoria during the relatively role-less years between their biological maturation and their access to mature privileges and responsibilities, while the peer social context reflects the observation that similarly-situated adolescents biologically and socially 'grow up' together, and as a result, look to each other for support during the time period when they are not allowed to be adults. During the adolescent time period, delinquent coping is appealing and involvement in delinquency surfaces as a way to demonstrate autonomy from parents and teachers, win affiliation with peers, and hasten social maturation. Because adolescence-limited delinquency is typically social in nature, the offending manifestations constitute group-oriented activities and relatively minor and status-oriented offences, but not necessarily instrumental violence. Importantly, because their pre-delinquent development is normal, most adolescence-limited delinquents have the characteristics they need to desist from crime when they age into real adult roles, such as healthy personalities and cognitive abilities such as reading skill. They are able to return gradually to a more conventional lifestyle. For a select few adolescence-limited delinquents, their recovery may be delayed because of snares, which are experiences that can compromise the ability to make a successful transition to adulthood. Examples of such snares include a criminal record, incarceration, drug and alcohol addiction, truncated education, and (for girls) unwanted pregnancy.

In contrast, the second group of offenders, the life-course persistent, begins their antisocial activity early in the life-course, offends more while active, commits all sorts of crimes, including violence, and is very unlikely to desist from criminal activity in adulthood. Because peer influence is not a necessary condition for life-course persistent delinquency, some of the crimes engaged in by life-course persistent offenders are committed without the assistance of others, often referred to as 'lone offending'. According to the taxonomy, the child's risk for life-course persistent offending emerges from inherited or acquired neuro-psychological variation, initially manifested as subtle cognitive deficits, difficult temperament, or hyperactivity. The environment in which the child is reared is also an important contributory factor as inadequate parenting, disrupted family bonds, poverty, etc. tend to compromise effective parenting efforts and in many cases exacerbate the child's vulnerabilities. The environmental risk domain expands beyond the family as the child ages, to include poor relations with people such as peers and teachers. Over the first two decades of development, transactions between individual and environment gradually construct a disordered personality with hallmark features of physical aggression and antisocial behaviour persisting to mid-life. The taxonomy anticipates that antisocial behaviour will infiltrate multiple adult life domains including illegal activities, employment, marriage or family life, and intimate victimisation. As could be expected, this infiltration diminishes the possibility of reform such that life-course persistent offenders have few (if any) opportunities for prosocial behaviour and opportunities for change. Fortunately, Moffitt anticipates that membership in this group is quite small, about five to eight per cent of the population.

How do race and gender fit into the taxonomy?

Moffitt's original statements asserted that the theory would describe the behaviour of females as well as it describes the behaviour of males. In particular, Moffitt (1994: 39–40) notes:

> The crime rate for females is lower than for males. In this developmental taxonomy, much of the gender difference in crime is attributed to sex differences in the risk factors for life-course persistent antisocial behaviour. Little girls are less likely than little boys to encounter all of the putative links in the causal chain for life-course persistent antisocial development. Research has shown that girls have lower rates than boys of symptoms of nervous system dysfunction, difficult temperament, late verbal and motor milestones, hyperactivity, learning disabilities, reading failure, and childhood conduct problems … Most girls lack the personal diathesis elements of the evocative, reactive, and proactive person/environment interactions that initiate and maintain life-course persistent antisocial behaviour.
>
> Adolescence-limited delinquency, on the other hand, is open to girls as well as to boys. According to the theory advanced here, girls, like boys, should begin delinquency soon after puberty, to the extent that they (1) have access to antisocial models, and (2) perceive the consequences of delinquency as reinforcing … However, exclusion from gender-segregated male antisocial groups may cut off opportunities for girls to learn delinquent behaviours … Girls are physically more vulnerable than boys to risk of personal victimization (e.g., pregnancy, or injury from dating violence) if they affiliate with life-course persistent antisocial males. Thus, lack of access to antisocial models and

> perceptions of serious personal risk may dampen the vigour of girls' delinquent involvement somewhat. Nonetheless, girls should engage in adolescence-limited delinquency in significant numbers ...

In sum, Moffitt's taxonomy anticipates that (a) fewer females than males would become delinquent (and conduct disordered) overall, and that (b) within delinquents, the percentage who are life-course persistent would be higher among males than females. Following from this, (c) the majority of delinquent females will be of the adolescence-limited type, and further, (d) their delinquency will have the same causes as adolescence-limited males' delinquency.

Regarding race, Moffitt (1994:39) hypothesises that:

> In the United States, the crime rate for Black Americans is higher than the crime rate for Whites. The race difference may be accounted for by a relatively higher prevalence of both life-course persistent and adolescence-limited subtypes among contemporary African Americans. Life-course persistent antisocials might be anticipated at elevated rates among Black Americans because the putative root causes of this type are elevated by institutionalised prejudice and by poverty. Among poor Black families, prenatal care is less available, infant nutrition is poorer, and the incidence of exposure to toxic and infectious agents is greater, placing infants at risk for the nervous system problems that research has shown to interfere with prosocial child development. To the extent that family bonds have been loosened and poor Black parents are under stress, ... and to the extent that poor Black children attend disadvantaged schools ... for poor Black children, the snowball of cumulative continuity may begin rolling earlier, and it may roll faster downhill. In addition, adolescence-limited crime is probably elevated among Black youths as compared to White youths in contemporary America. If racially-segregated communities provide greater exposure to life-course persistent role models, then circumstances are ripe for Black teens with no prior behaviour problems to mimic delinquent ways in a search for status and respect. Moreover, Black young people spend more years in the maturity gap, on average, than Whites because ascendancy to valued adult roles and privileges comes later, if at all. Legitimate desirable jobs are closed to many young Black men; they do not shift from having 'little to lose' to having a 'stake in conformity' overnight

> by leaving schooling and entering the world of work. Indeed, the biological maturity gap [i.e., puberty] is perhaps best seen as an instigator of adolescence-onset delinquency for Black youths, with an economic maturity gap maintaining offending into adulthood.

In sum, Moffitt anticipates that, due to elevated levels of the risk factors for both life-course persistent and adolescence-limited crime, African-Americans will be somewhat more prevalent than White Americans in both offending typologies.

Research on Moffitt's taxonomy

A number of studies have sought to examine the viability of Moffitt's developmental taxonomy, and in particular have assessed some of the key hypotheses underlying the taxonomy. Before we review these research efforts, it is helpful at this point to recall the original hypotheses underlying the two offending groups. For life-course persistent antisocial activity, the predictors should include 'health, gender, temperament, cognitive abilities, school achievement, personality traits, mental disorders (e.g. hyperactivity), family attachment bonds, child-rearing practices, parent and sibling deviance, and socio-economic status, but not age' (Moffitt 1993: 695). For adolescence-limited antisocial activity, the taxonomy anticipates that 'individual differences should play little or no role in the prediction of short-term adolescent offending careers. Instead, the strongest predictors of adolescence-limited offending should be peer delinquency, attitudes toward adolescence and adulthood reflecting the maturity gap [such as desire for autonomy], cultural and historical contexts influencing adolescence, and age' (Moffitt 1993: 695).

What do we know about life-course persistent offending?

A number of the hypotheses associated with life-course persistent offending have been examined with data from the Dunedin Multidisciplinary Health and Development Study, a 30-year longitudinal study of a birth cohort of 1,000 New Zealanders. In general, these studies have examined childhood predictors measured early in life and examined their relation to criminal and antisocial activity measured via self-report, informants such as mothers, teachers and friends, and official records. These efforts have consistently shown that life-course persistent offending is differentially predicted by individual risk factors including under-controlled temperament, neurological abnormalities and delayed motor development at age three, low intellectual abilities, reading difficulties, poor scores on neuropsychological tests of memory, hyperactivity, and slow heart rate (see Bartusch *et al.* 1997; Moffitt and Caspi 2001; Moffitt *et al.* 1994, 1996). In addition, life-course persistent offending is also differentially predicted by parenting risk factors including teenaged single parents, mothers with poor mental health, mothers who were observed to be harsh or neglectful, as well as experiences of harsh and inconsistent discipline, much family conflict, many changes of the primary caretaker, low family SES, and rejection by peers in school (Moffitt and Caspi 2001).

Importantly, the main findings regarding life-course persistent offending uncovered with the Dunedin data have also been observed in other samples from different countries (see review in Moffitt 2001). For example, using data from the Philadelphia portion of the National Collaborative Perinatal Project (NCPP), Tibbetts and Piquero (1999) examined how the biosocial interaction of low birth weight and disadvantaged environment predicted early onset offending. Their results indicated that the biosocial interaction was significantly related to early onset of offending. Piquero and Tibbetts (1999) examined the interaction between pre/perinatal disturbances and disadvantaged familial environment in distinguishing between involvement in non-violent and violent offending. Their analysis indicated that, consistent with Moffitt's expectation, the biosocial interaction was predictive of violent but not non-violent offending (see also Arseneault *et al.* 2002). Piquero (2001) used the Philadelphia data to examine how neuropsychological variation, using cognitive test scores, was related to three different manifestations of life-course persistent offending (*early onset, chronic offending, and seriousness offending*) by age 18. His results indicated that poor neuropsychological test scores were predictive of all three measures of life-course persistent offending in a manner consistent with Moffitt. Gibson *et al.* (2001) extended Piquero's analysis and found that neuropsychological risk also combines with poor familial environments to predict early onset of offending. Finally, Kratzer and Hodgins (1999) used data from a Swedish cohort to study how cognitive abilities related to offending from childhood to age 30. Their results indicated that early start offenders (i.e., life-course persistent offenders) committed more crimes and a greater diversity of crimes than other offending groups. Childhood problems and low global scores of intelligence distinguished these offenders from other offender types as well as non-offenders.

Several recent studies have tested expectations from Moffitt's theory with criminal populations. For example, in a study of 4,000 California Youth Authority inmates followed into their thirties, Ge and his colleagues (2001) found results consistent with Moffitt's theory. For example, significantly more early starters than later starters continued offending past age 21, past age 25, and past age 31. In addition, early onset and low cognitive ability were significant predictors of offending that continued into the thirties. Piquero *et al.* (2004) used another sample of California Youth Authority inmates to study how neuropsychological variation was related to the length of an offender's criminal career and found that a risk contrast, comprising low cognitive abilities and disadvantaged environments, was related to career length such that individuals with low cognitive abilities and reared in disadvantaged environments during childhood tended to experience the longest careers. Finally, Piquero and his colleagues (2002) used yet another sample of California Youth Authority parolees to study how changes in life circumstances were related to changes in criminal activity in the twenties. Their analysis indicated that changes in several life circumstances, such as marriage and heroin dependency, were associated with changes in criminal activity such that marriage served to reduce crime while heroin dependency served to increase crime. Interestingly, the effect of local life circumstances also varied across offender typologies, such that the effects were apparent for some typologies but not others.

In sum, studies using a number of different samples from several different countries show that life-course persistent offending has the predicted neuro-developmental correlates as well as showing the importance of a biosocial interaction.

What do we know about adolescence-limited offending?

Unfortunately, much of the research on Moffitt's taxonomy has tended to focus on life-course persistent offending. Still, a few studies have examined adolescent-limited offending, and they are reviewed below.

Using a low SES sample from Minneapolis, Aguilar *et al.* (2000) found that adolescent-onset delinquents experienced elevated internalising symptoms and perceptions of stress at age 16, which may be consistent with Moffitt's assertion that these adolescents experience dysphoria during the maturity gap. Data from the Dunedin study also indicate that the offending of adolescence-limiteds is strongly associated with delinquent peers, as compared with the offending of life-course persistent offenders (Bartusch *et al.* 1997; Moffitt and Caspi 2001). In addition, Caspi and his colleagues (1993) showed that an increase in young teens' awareness of peers' delinquency pre-dates and predicts onset of their own later delinquency. Piquero and Brezina (2001) used data from 2,000 males participating in the Youth in Transition Survey to test the hypothesis that desires for autonomy promoted adolescent-onset offending. They found that the offences committed by adolescence-limited delinquents were primarily rebellious in nature (i.e., not violent), and that this rebellious offending was accounted for by the interaction between maturational timing and aspects of peer activities that were related to personal autonomy.

To be sure, we cannot finish our discussion of adolescence-limited delinquency without reviewing what we know about those adolescents who refrain from delinquency, commonly referred to as abstainers. This is an important issue because, if as the theory says adolescence-limited delinquency is normative, then the existence of teenagers who abstain from delinquency requires explanation.

Moffitt proffers four potential reasons for such abstinence. First, some youths may refrain from antisocial behaviour because they do not sense the maturity gap, and therefore lack the hypothesised motivation for experimenting with crime, or they may skip the maturity gap altogether because of late puberty. Second, some adolescents incur early initiation into adult roles or, at the very least, they have access to prosocial roles. Third, some adolescents encounter few opportunities for mimicking life-course persistent delinquent models. Fourth, and the 'explanation most central to [Moffitt's] theory', is that abstainers are excluded from opportunities to mimic antisocial peers because of some personal characteristic(s) that cause them to be excluded from the delinquent peer groups, which ascend to importance during adolescence (see also Moffitt *et al.* 1996: 419). Thus, under this hypothesis, some adolescents may possess certain personality characteristics that prevent them from being a part of the peer social context during adolescence.

Unfortunately, aside from a few exceptions (Moffitt *et al.* 1996; Shedler and Block 1990), the developmental histories of adolescents who abstain from delinquency have not been examined in great detail. Only one study, in fact, has tested the 'abstainer' hypotheses as articulated by Moffitt. Piquero *et al.* (2005) used data from the National Longitudinal Survey of Youth, a high-risk adolescent sample, to examine the abstainer hypothesis, and their results led to four major conclusions. First, across three different data sets, adolescent abstainers constituted a small group of individuals. Second, the correlates of abstention primarily included situational and social characteristics, with social factors exhibiting central importance. Individuals who were not part of the peer social context and/or who spent less time with peers, were more likely to be abstainers. The results also revealed that many personality characteristics were not directly related to abstention. Third, bearing in mind the importance of access to the peer social context, Piquero *et al.* found that, consistent with Moffitt, several personality, emotional, structural, and situational characteristics were related to involvement in the peer social context. Finally, split-gender analyses revealed more similarities than differences in the correlates of peer social context and abstention. Thus, Moffitt's writings and hypotheses overestimated the importance of personality traits.

In sum, much less is known about the developmental patterning of adolescence-limited offending as well as the causes of abstention. The few studies that have been conducted appear, at first glance, to provide support for some of the key hypotheses put forth by Moffitt.

Outcomes of life-course persistent and adolescence-limited offenders: personality, crime types and persistence

The two offending typologies have been compared on a number of different outcomes. Herein, we focus on three particular outcomes: personality structures, crime types and persistence in crime into adulthood.

Regarding personality, Moffitt (1993: 684) argued that 'Over the years, an antisocial personality is slowly and insidiously constructed as the accumulating consequences of the youngster's behaviour problems prune away options for change'. A few studies have initiated investigations of this issue.

Moffitt and colleagues have employed the Dunedin data to examine the personality issue in great detail. In the first analysis, Moffitt *et al.* (1996) showed that the age-18 personality characteristics of individuals on the life-course persistent path were differentially associated with weak bonds to family, and psychopathic personality traits of alienation, callousness, and impulsivity. In contrast, the adolescence-limited path at age 18 was differentially associated with a tendency to endorse unconventional values, and with a personality trait called social potency. In their assessment of personality traits at age 26, self- and informant reports concurred that the life-course persistent men were more neurotic (stress-reactive, alienated, and aggressive) and less agreeable (less social closeness, more callous), compared with adolescence-limited men.

Ge *et al.* (2001) used personality data from 4,000 California Youth Authority inmates to examine this issue as well. Taxonomy comparison groups were defined as early starters versus later starters, and as chronic adult arrestees versus those arrested less often. The early starter chronic arrestees were distinguished by extreme personality scale scores, in particular low communality, little concern with impression, irresponsibility, low control of emotions, low achievement motivation, low socialisation, low tolerance (hostile, distrustful), and low well-being.

Regarding crime types, several studies have sought to assess Moffitt's (1993: 695) hypothesis that life-course persistent offenders, as compared with adolescence-limited offenders, would engage in a wider variety of offence types, including 'more of the victim-oriented offences, such as violence'. Data from the Dunedin study up to age 18 reports that the life-course persistent path was differentially associated with convictions for violent crimes (Bartusch *et al.* 1997; Moffitt *et al.* 1996), while the adolescence-limited pathway was differentially associated with non-violent offences. In their investigation of neuropsychology and delinquency, Moffitt *et al.* (1994) found that pre-adolescent antisocial behaviour that was accompanied by neuropsychological deficits predicted greater persistence of crime and more violence until age 18. A follow-up of the Dunedin subjects at age 26 reinforced the finding that life-course persistent men, as a group, differed from adolescence-limited men in the realm of violence, including violence against women. For example, life-course persistent men tended to specialise in serious offences, whereas adolescence-limited men specialised in non-serious offences. Moreover, life-course persistent men accounted for five times their proportional share of the cohort's violent convictions, in addition to exhibiting elevated scores on self-reported and official conviction measures of abuse towards women.

Studies using other samples have tended to replicate these findings. For example, using the Philadelphia NCPP data, Piquero

(2001) found that neuropsychological risk was related to several different manifestations of life-course persistent offending such that poor cognitive scores predicted early onset and serious offending by age 18. Research comparing the predictors of violent crime versus non-violent crime indicates that violence is differentially predicted by birth complications (Raine *et al.* 1997), minor physical anomalies (Arseneault *et al.* 2000) and difficult temperament (Henry *et al.* 1994).

Regarding persistence into adulthood, one of the critical hypotheses emanating from Moffitt's typology is that life-course persistent offenders continue their antisocial proclivities into adulthood whereas adolescence-limited offenders desist, and several studies have attempted to address this question (e.g. Dean *et al.* 1996; White *et al.* 2001). Using the age-26 data from the Dunedin study, Moffitt (2003) found that the childhood-onset delinquents were the most elevated on psychopathic personality traits, mental health problems, substance dependence, numbers of children sired, domestic abuse, financial problems, work problems, drug-related crimes and violent crimes. On the other hand, the adolescent-onset delinquents were less extreme but also elevated on property offences and financial problems.

Ge *et al.* (2001) used data on over 4,000 California Youth Authority inmates followed into their thirties to examine issues related to persistence. They found that significantly more early starters than later starters continued offending past age 21, past age 25, and past age 31. Moreover, early onset and low cognitive ability were significant predictors of offending that continued into the thirties.

Piquero and White (2003) followed up the Philadelphia NCPP into the late thirties to study how cognitive deficits related to persistence. Their analysis indicated that cognitive deficits, measured at both ages 7/8 and 13/14, were related to adult convictions through the thirties.

What do we know about gender as it pertains to Moffitt's taxonomy?

Only a handful of studies have explored the role of gender in Moffitt's taxonomy. Moffitt and her colleagues (2001) reported a comprehensive analysis of gender differences in antisocial behaviour. A number of key findings emerged from their effort. First, the male: female difference was very large for the life-course persistent form of antisocial behaviour (10:1) but much smaller for the adolescence-limited form (1.5:1). Second, childhood-onset females had high-risk neuro-developmental and family background, but adolescent-onset females did not, which indicates that females and males on the same trajectories share the same risk factors. In related research, Moffitt and colleagues have found that the delinquency onset of girls is linked to the timing of their own puberty, that delinquent peers are a necessary condition for onset of delinquency among adolescent girls, and that an intimate relationship with an offender promotes girls' antisocial behaviours.

Other studies have also examined potential sex differences in Moffitt's taxonomy. In a study discussed earlier, Tibbetts and Piquero (1999) found that a biosocial interaction comprising low birth weight and disadvantaged environment predicted early onset of offending for males but not females. Fergusson *et al.* (2000), using data from Christchurch, New Zealand, found that a single model described male and female trajectories of antisocial behaviour, and the male to female ratio was 4:1 for early-onset, versus only 2:1 for late-onset subjects. In another study with these data, Fergusson and Horwood (2002) found that an identical five trajectory group applied for both males and females, and that the risk factors associated with trajectory group membership appeared to operate similarly for both males and females. The only sex differences to emerge indicated that females were more likely to exhibit low-risk or early-onset adolescence-limited offending while males were more likely to exhibit chronic offending or later adolescence-limited onset. Kratzer and Hodgins' (1999) study of a Swedish cohort found similar childhood risk factors for males and females in the life-course persistent group, with a male:female ratio of 15:1 for early-onset, and only 4:1 for late-onset. Using data from the second Philadelphia Birth Cohort, Mazerolle and colleagues (2000) reported that early onset signalled persistent and diverse offending for males and females alike.

In sum, most studies indicate that females are seldom childhood-onset or life-course persistent offenders and more commonly follow the adolescence-limited pattern; however, when females do exhibit the risk factors for life-course persistent offending, their pathway is similar to that of males.

What do we know about race as it pertains to Moffitt's taxonomy?

As is the case with gender, only a few studies have explored the race implications of Moffitt's theory. Early research on this issue, with data from the Pittsburgh Youth Study, showed that childhood risk factors (low IQ and impulsive under-control) were associated with life-course persistent offending (early-onset frequent offending and physical aggression) among Black and White males alike (Caspi *et al.* 1994). However, research using the Pittsburgh data has not divided the Pittsburgh delinquents into childhood- versus adolescent-onset comparison groups.

Donnellan *et al.* (2000) examined how race was implicated in Moffitt's taxonomy using data from California Youth Authority inmates. On a number of different measures of cognitive abilities, life-course persistent offenders scored below adolescence-limited offenders. Interestingly, the predicted finding of differential cognitive risk applied to adjudicated Whites and Hispanics but not to adjudicated African-Americans.

Piquero *et al.* (2005) used data from the Baltimore site of the NCPP to study race differences in the life-course persistent pathway. Their analysis showed that several variables helped to explain differences between Whites and Blacks in the level of chronic offending measured to age 33. However, although Black participants had higher mean levels of risk factors than Whites, the developmental processes predicting chronic offending were the same across groups defined by race. Specifically, low birth weight in combination with adverse familial environments predicted chronic offending from adolescence to age 33 among Whites and African-Americans alike, although the effect size reached statistical significance only among African Americans.

Finally, in a study described earlier, Piquero *et al.* (2004) studied how the life-course persistent explanation could account for criminal career length. Specifically, they split their sample of California Youth Authority inmates into White and non-White parolees, and examined how a risk contrast of cognitive abilities and disadvantaged environments related to career length. When the risk contrast was examined across White and non-White parolees, the results indicated that the risk contrast was more important for non-Whites. In particular, the data pointed to three sets of findings across race. First, among those parolees experiencing low risk in the risk contrast (i.e., no cognitive deficits and no disadvantaged environments), career duration was identical among White and non-White parolees (almost 17 years). Second, among non-Whites only, the risk contrast was related to career length such that non-White parolees experiencing cognitive deficits and disadvantaged environments exhibited the longest career lengths (almost 19 years). Third, among White parolees, the risk contrast was not related to career length; among Whites, career lengths varied between 16 and 17 years, regardless of the level of the risk contrast.

In sum, it is too early to tell how Moffitt's race hypotheses square with empirical research. With the exception of Donnellan *et al.* the research, at this time, seems to suggest that the causal process appears more similar than different across race, with the exception that the mean levels of risk factors are higher among non-Whites than Whites.

Challenges to Moffitt's theory

Although some research efforts have produced, at times, somewhat contradictory results to Moffitt's typology (see in particular Aguilar *et al.* 2000), two key challenges have been put forth regarding the viability of Moffitt's taxonomy. The first concerns the number of offender typologies, and the second calls into question the taxonomy's applicability to females.

As originally outlined, Moffitt anticipated the existence of two groups of offenders. Empirical research using advanced statistical models that are designed to isolate relatively homogeneous categories of offenders, however, has uncovered several additional groups of offenders (D'Unger *et al.* 1998; Nagin and Land 1993; Nagin *et al.* 1995). The most prominent of these additional groups is the 'low-level chronic'. Because of their particular pattern of offending, i.e., persistent, but low-level offending from childhood to adolescence and/or from adolescence to adulthood, this group of offenders does not 'fit' into either of Moffitt's offender typologies. Unfortunately, very little light has been shed on the personal characteristics associated with the low-level chronics.

The second challenge put forth against Moffitt's taxonomy concerns the role of gender. Silverthorn and Frick (1999) reviewed the literature on female antisocial/criminal activity and challenged Moffitt's developmental taxonomy. These authors suggest that, although girls' onset of delinquency is delayed until adolescence, there is no analogous pathway in girls to the adolescence-limited pathway in boys. In particular, they argue for a female-specific theory in which all delinquent girls will have the same high-risk causal backgrounds as life-course persistent males, but that their antisocial activity will start in mid adolescence as opposed to early adolescence/late childhood as in Moffitt's life-course persistent conception. Aside from Moffitt and colleagues' (2001) thorough analysis of sex differences in antisocial behaviour, a number of studies have begun to examine the Silverthorn and Frick challenge, and with the exception of results from Silverthorn *et al.* (2001), fail to find support for their challenge (see Fergusson and Horwood 2002; White and Piquero 2003).

The way forward: future research topics

Since the publication of Moffitt's theory, a number of research efforts have attempted to distinguish between the two offender typologies. Although much has been learned, much remains to be explored. Here, we identify a number of future research directions that may help continue the assessment of Moffitt's typology.

The first hypothesis concerns that of 'snares'. Moffitt contends that individuals (especially adolescence-limited offenders) may encounter 'snares', or life events, that lead to continuation of antisocial lifestyles. Examples of such snares include a criminal record, incarceration, addiction, and so on. Moffitt anticipates that these snares should explain variation in the age at desistance from crime during the adult age period, especially among adolescence-limited offenders. Unfortunately, we know little about how snares are implicated in Moffitt's typology.

The second point for future research concerns the varied outcomes associated with membership in each typology. For example, although Moffitt concentrates her discussion of outcomes within the antisocial domain, there is reason to believe that life-course persistent offenders exhibit risk in other domains as well. For example, life-course persistent offenders are believed to select undesirable partners and jobs, and would, in turn, expand their repertoire into domestic abuse and workplace crime, whereas adolescence-limited offenders would get good partners and jobs, in turn desisting from crime (Moffitt 1993: 695). Similarly, it would be reasonable to suspect that the behaviour of life-course persistent offenders would infiltrate multiple life domains such as employment and health. In this regard, Moffitt (2003) has noted that the antisocial lifestyle of life-course persistent offenders is such that it will place them at greater risk in mid-life for poor health, cardiovascular disease, and early mortality.

A third point for future research concerns the continued attention aimed at studying how race and gender are implicated in the developmental taxonomy. Still perilously little is known about race and gender differences (and similarities) within and between the two offender typologies. An interesting hypothesis that has yet to be tested concerns the effect of the maturity gap across race. Moffitt (2003) predicts that the maturity gap will last longer for African-American young men. Because of this, it may be difficult to distinguish the life-course persistent versus adolescence-limited groups on the basis of chronic offending into adulthood. Clearly, this warrants sustained empirical attention.

A fourth hypothesis that has yet to be explored in detail concerns the role of the neighbourhood environment. Although several studies have sought to examine how neighbourhoods are implicated in the developmental taxonomy (see Lynam *et al.* 2000; Moffitt 1997; Piquero *et al.* 2005), researchers have not examined how changing neighbourhood environments may (or may not) matter for expectations derived from the taxonomy.

Fifth, within the context of Moffitt's theory, researchers have not examined closely the role of co- and solo offending over the life-course across the two typologies. Moffitt's theory anticipates that adolescence-limited offenders will tend to be co-offenders, but that life-course persistent offenders will tend to be solo offenders. Unfortunately, data on co-offending is relatively sparse (Warr 2002), but this should not dissuade researchers from assessing this important prediction.

The final point for future research concerns the role of genetics. According to Moffitt's taxonomy, the genetic component of variation in early-onset antisocial behaviour, a marker for life-course persistent offending, may conceal effects of correlations between vulnerability genes and risky environments, and interactions between them as well. Recently, Caspi *et al.* (2002) used the Dunedin data to study why some children who are maltreated grow up to develop antisocial behaviour, whereas others do not. They found that a functional polymorphism in the gene encoding the neurotransmitter-metabolising enzyme monoamine oxidase A (MAOA) moderated the effect of maltreatment, such that maltreated children with a genotype conferring high levels of MAOA expression were less likely to develop antisocial problems. This result is particularly important because it provides some evidence that some genotypes can moderate children's sensitivity to environmental factors. The study also revealed that children with the at-risk genotype did not develop antisocial behaviour unless they were maltreated, showing that social experiences exert strong control over whether genes can influence behaviour. (Boys on the life-course persistent path in the Dunedin sample were particularly likely to have the combination of a maltreatment history and the at-risk MAOA genotype, but because this group was made up of a very small number of individuals, this finding did not attain statistical significance.) We envision much more work on this front, especially into the role that the interplay between genes and environmental experiences plays in crime over the life-course.

Updated readings

Empirical reports

Odgers, C.L., Moffitt, T.E., Broadbent, J.M., Dickson, N., Hancox, R.J., Harrington, H. *et al.* (2008) 'Female and male antisocial trajectories: From childhood origins to adult outcomes', *Development and Psychopathology*, 20(2): 673–716.

Odgers, C.L., Moffitt, T.E., Tach, L.M., Sampson, R.J., Taylor, A., Matthews, C.L. *et al.* (2009) 'The protective effects of neighborhood collective efficacy on British children growing up in deprivation: a developmental Analysis', *Developmental Psychology*, 45(4): 942–57.

Odgers, C., Caspi, A., Broadbent, J.M., Dickson, N., Hancox, B., Harrington, H.L., Poulton, R., Sears, M.R., Thomson, M. and Moffitt, T.E. (2007) 'Conduct problem subtypes in males predict differential adult health burden', *Archives of General Psychiatry*, 64: 476–84.

Odgers, C.L., Milne, B., Caspi, A., Crump, R., Poulton, R. & Moffitt, T.E. (2007) 'Predicting long-term adult prognosis for the conduct-problem boy: can family history help?', *Journal of the American Academy of Child and Adolescent Psychiatry*, 46: 1240–49.

Blokland, A., Nagin, D. and Nieuwbeerta, P. (2005) 'Life span offending trajectories of a Dutch conviction cohort', *Criminology*, 43(4): 919–54.

Reviews

Piquero, A. and Moffitt, T.E. (2005) 'Explaining the facts of crime: how Moffitt's developmental taxonomy replies to Farrington's invitation', in D.P. Farrington (ed.), *Integrated Developmental and Life-Course Theories of Offending: Advances in Criminological Theory*, Vol 14, pp. 51–72. New Brunswick, NJ: Transactions Press.

Moffitt, T.E. (2006) 'Life-course persistent versus adolescence-limited antisocial behavior: a review of research', in D. Cicchetti and D.J. Cohen (eds), *Developmental Psychopathology, 2nd Edition, Vol 3: Risk, disorder, and adaptation*, pp. 570–98. NY: Wiley.

Moffitt, T.E. (2006) 'A review of research on the taxonomy of life-course persistent and adolescence-limited offending', in F.T. Cullen, J.P. Wright and M. Coleman (eds), *Taking Stock: The Status of Criminological Theory*, pp. 502–21. New Brunswick, NJ: Transaction Publishers.

Critique and debate

R.J. Sampson and Laub, J.H. (2005) 'Developmental criminology and its discontents: trajectories of crime from childhood to old age', *special edition of The Annals of the American Academy of Political and Social Science*, volume 602, November 2005.

References

Aguilar, B.L., Sroufe, A., Egeland, B. and Carlson, E. (2000) 'Distinguishing the early-onset/persistent and adolescence-onset antisocial behaviour types: from birth to 16 years', *Development and Psychopathology*, 12: 109–32.

Arseneault, L., Tremblay, R.E., Boulerice, B., Seguin, J.R. and Saucier, J-F. (2000) 'Minor physical anomalies and family adversity as risk factors for adolescent violent delinquency', *American Journal of Psychiatry*, 157: 917–23.

Arseneault, L., Tremblay, R.E., Boulerice, B. and Saucier, J-F. (2002) 'Obstetric complications and adolescent violent behaviours: testing two developmental pathways', *Child Development*, 73: 496–508.

Bartusch, D., Jeglum, R., Lynam, D.R. Moffitt, T.E. and Silva, P.A. (1997) 'Is age important? Testing a general versus a developmental theory of antisocial behavior', *Criminology*, 35: 13–48.

Blumstein, A., Cohen, J., Roth, J.A. and Visher, C.A. (eds) (1986) *Criminal Careers and Career Criminals*, 2 vols. Panel on Research on Criminal Careers, Committee on Research on Law Enforcement and the Administration of Justice, Commission on Behavioral and Social Sciences and Education, National Research Council. Washington, DC: National Academy Press.

Britt, C. L. (1992) 'Constancy and change in the US age distribution of crime: a test of the "Invariance Hypothesis"', *Journal of Quantitative Criminology*, 8: 175–87.

Caspi, A., Moffitt, T.E., Silva, P.A., Stouthamer-Loeber, M., Schmutte, P. and Krueger, R. (1994) 'Are some people crime-prone? Replications of the personality-crime relation across nation, gender, race and method', *Criminology*, 32: 301–33.

Caspi, A., Lynam, D., Moffitt, T.E. and Silva, P.A. (1993) 'Unraveling girls' delinquency: biological, dispositional, and contextual contributions to adolescent misbehavior', *Developmental Psychology*, 29: 19–30.

Caspi, A., McClay, J., Moffitt, T.E., Mill, J., Martin, J., Craig, I.W., Taylor, A. and Poulton, R. (2002) 'Role of genotype in the cycle of violence in maltreated children', *Science*, 297: 851–54.

Dean, C.W., Brame, R. and Piquero, A.R. (1996) 'Criminal propensities, discrete groups of offenders, and persistence in crime', *Criminology*, 34: 547–74.

Donnellan, M.B., Ge, X. and Wenk, E. (2000) 'Cognitive abilities in adolescence-limited and life-course persistent criminal offenders', *Journal of Abnormal Psychology*, 109: 396–402.

Unger, A.V., Land, K.C., McCall, P.L. and Nagin, D.S. (1998) 'How many latent classes of delinquent/criminal careers? Results from mixed poisson regression analyses', *American Journal of Sociology*, 103: 1593–630.

Farrington, D.P. (1986) 'Age and crime', in M. Tonry and N. Morris (eds), *Crime and Justice: An Annual Review of Research, Volume 7*. Chicago: University of Chicago Press.

Fergusson, D.M., Horwood, L.J. and Nagin, D.S. (2000) 'Offending trajectories in a New Zealand birth cohort', *Criminology*, 38: 525–52.

Fergusson, D.M. and Horwood, L.J. (2002) 'Male and female offending trajectories', *Development and Psychopathology*, 14: 159–77.

Ge, X., Donnellan, M.B. and Wenk, E. (2001) 'The development of persistent criminal offending in males', *Criminal Justice and Behaviour*, 28: 731–55.

Gibson, C., Piquero, A.R. and Tibbetts, S.G. (2001) 'The contribution of family adversity and verbal IQ relate to criminal behavior', *International Journal of Offender Therapy and Comparative Criminology*, 45: 574–92.

Henry, B., Moffitt, T.E., Caspi, A., Langley, J. and Silva, P.A. (1994) 'On the remembrance of things past: a longitudinal evaluation of the retrospective method', *Psychological Assessment*, 6: 92–101.

Hirschi, T. and Gottfredson, M.G. (1983) 'Age and the explanation of crime', *American Journal of Sociology*, 89: 552–84.

Huesmann, L.R., Eron, L.D., Lefkowitz, M.M. and Walder, L.O. (1984) 'Stability of aggression over time and generations', *Developmental Psychology*, 20: 1120–34.

Kratzer, L. and Hodgins, S. (1999) 'A typology of offenders: a test of Moffitt's theory among males and females from childhood to age 30', *Criminal Behaviour and Mental Health*, 9: 57–73.

Lynam, D.R., Caspi, A., Moffitt, T.E., Wikstrom, P.-O., Loeber, R. and Novak, S.P. (2000) 'The interaction between impulsivity and neighbourhood context on offending: the effects of impulsivity are stronger in poorer neighborhoods', *Journal of Abnormal Psychology*, 109: 563–74.

Mazerolle, P., Brame, R., Paternoster, R., Piquero, A. and Dean, C. (2000) 'Onset age, persistence, and offending versatility: Comparisons across gender', *Criminology*, 38: 1143–72.

Moffitt, T.E. (1993) 'Life-course-persistent and adolescence-limited antisocial behaviour: a developmental taxonomy', *Psychological Review*, 100: 674–701.

Moffitt, T.E. (1994) 'Natural histories of delinquency', in E. Weitekamp and H.J. Kerner (eds), *Cross-National Longitudinal Research on Human Development and Criminal Behaviour*. Dordrecht: Kluwer Academic Press.

Moffitt, T.E. (1997) 'Neuropsychology, antisocial behaviour, and neighbourhood context', in J. McCord (ed.), *Violence in the Inner City*. Cambridge: Cambridge University Press.

Moffitt, T.E. (2002) 'Life-course persistent and adolescence-limited antisocial behaviour: A research review and a research agenda', in B. Lahey, T.E. Moffitt and A. Caspi (eds), *The Causes of Conduct Disorder and Serious Juvenile Delinquency*. New York: Guilford.

Moffitt, T.E. and Caspi, A. (2001), 'Childhood predictors differentiate life-course persistent and adolescence-limited pathways, among males and females', *Development and Psychopathology*, 13: 355–75.

Moffitt, T.E., Caspi, A.., Dickson, N., Silva, P.A. and Stanton, W. (1996) 'Childhood-onset versus adolescent-onset antisocial conduct in males: natural history from age 3 to 18', *Development and Psychopathology*, 8: 399–424.

Moffitt, T.E., Caspi, A., Rutter, M. and Silva, P.A. (2001) *Sex Differences in Antisocial Behaviour: Conduct Disorder, Delinquency, and Violence in the Dunedin Longitudinal Study*. Cambridge, UK: Cambridge University Press.

Moffitt, T.E., Lynam, D. and Silva, P.A. (1994) 'Neuropsychological tests predict persistent male delinquency', *Criminology*, 32: 277–300.

Nagin, D.S., Farrington, D.P. and Moffitt, T.E. (1995) 'Life-course trajectories of different types of offenders', *Criminology*, 33: 111–39.

Nagin, D.S. and Land, K.C. (1993) 'Age, criminal careers, and population heterogeneity: specification and estimation of a nonparametric, mixed poisson model', *Criminology*, 31: 327–62.

Paternoster, R., Dean, C.W., Piquero, A., Mazerolle, P. and Brame, R. (1997) 'Generality, continuity, and change in offending', *Journal of Quantitative Criminology*, 13: 231–266.

Piquero, A.R. (2001) 'Testing Moffitt's neuropsychological variation hypothesis for the prediction of life-course persistent offending', *Psychology, Crime and Law*, 7: 193–216.

Piquero, A.R. and Brezina, T. (2001) 'Testing Moffitt's account of adolescence-limited delinquency', *Criminology*, 39: 353–70.

Piquero, A.R. and Tibbetts, S.G. (1999) 'The impact of pre/perinatal disturbances and disadvantaged environments in predicting violent crime', *Studies on Crime and Crime Prevention*, 8: 52–70.

Piquero, A.R. and White, N. (2002) 'On the relationship between cognitive abilities and life-course-persistent offending among a sample of African Americans: a longitudinal test of Moffitt's hypothesis', *Journal of Criminal Justice*, 31: 399–409.

Piquero, A.R., Brame, R. and Lynam, D. (2004) 'Studying the factors related to career length through early adulthood among serious offenders', *Crime and Delinquency*, 50: 412–435.

Piquero, A.R., Brame, R., Mazerolle, P. and Haapanen, R. (2002) 'Crime in emerging adulthood', *Criminology*, 40: 137–69.

Piquero, A.R., Brezina, T. and Turner, M.G. (2005) 'Testing Moffitt's theory of delinquency abstention', *Journal of Research in Crime and Delinquency*, 42: 27–54.

Piquero, A.R., Moffitt, T.E. and Lawton, B. (2004) 'Race differences in life-course-persistent offending: our children, their children: race/ethnicity and crime', in D. Hawkins and K. Kempf-Leonard (eds), *Race, Crime, and the Juvenile Justice System*. Chicago: University of Chicago Press.

Piquero, A.R., Moffitt, T.E. and Lawton, B. (2005) 'Race and crime: the contribution of individual, familial and neighborhood risk factors to life-course persistent offending', in D.F. Hawkins and K. Kempf-Leonard (eds), *Our Children, their Children: Confronting Race and Ethnic Differences in American Juvenile Justice*. Chicago: University of Chicago Press.

Piquero, A.R., Farrington, D.P. and Blumstein, A. (2003) 'The criminal career paradigm: background and recent developments', in M. Tonry (ed.), *Crime and Justice: A Review of Research, Volume 30*. Chicago: University of Chicago Press.

Quetelet, A. (1831) *Research on the Propensity for Crime at Different Ages*. Cincinnati, OH: Anderson Publishing Company (1984 edition).

Raine, A., Brennan, P. and Mednick, S.A. (1997) 'Interaction between birth complications and early maternal rejection in predisposing individuals to adult violence: specificity to serious, early-onset violence', *American Journal of Psychiatry*, 154: 1265–71.

Shedler, J. and Block, J. (1990) 'Adolescent drug use and psychological health', *American Psychologist*, 45: 612–30.

Silverthorn, P. and Frick, P.J. (1999) 'Developmental pathways to antisocial behaviour: the delayed-onset pathway in girls', *Development and Psychopathology*, 11: 101–26.

Silverthorn, P., Frick, P.J. and Reynolds, R. (2001) 'Timing of onset and correlates of severe conduct problems in adjudicated girls and boys', *Journal of Psychopathology and Behavioral Assessment*, 23: 171–81.

Steffensmeier, D.J., Allan, E.A., Harer, M.D. and Streifel, C. (1989) 'Age and the distribution of crime', *American Journal of Sociology*, 94: 803–31.

Tibbetts, S.G. and Piquero, A.R. (1999) 'The influence of gender, low birth weight, and disadvantaged environment in predicting early onset of offending: a test of Moffitt's interactional hypothesis', *Criminology*, 37: 843–78.

Warr, M. (2002) *Companions in Crime: The Social Aspects of Criminal Conduct*. Cambridge: Cambridge University Press.

White, H.R., Bates, M.E. and Buyske, S. (2001) 'Adolescence-limited versus persistent delinquency: extending Moffitt's hypothesis into adulthood', *Journal of Abnormal Psychology*, 110: 600–9.

White, N. and Piquero, A.R. (2002) 'An empirical test of Silverthorn and Frick's delayed-onset pathway in girls: evidence of criminal activity from birth to adulthood', unpublished manuscript.

Chapter 12

Stalking*

Lorraine Sheridan and Graham M. Davies

'Stalking' is a nebulous crime, comprising a set of behaviours that are difficult both to define and legislate against. In 1996, a consultation paper produced by the Home Office noted that stalking was not defined in the civil or criminal law in England and Wales, but stated that 'it can be broadly described as a series of acts which are intended to, or in fact, cause harassment to another person' (1.2). While this may be useful in terms of illustrating what is broadly meant by 'stalking', it also highlights the definitional problem: the term may be applied to almost any behaviour, but only some behaviours will constitute stalking, as long as the behaviour is of a repetitive nature. Certainly, repetition, or persistence, is one of the key features of any stalking case and must usually be present to allow for criminal charges to be brought. The persistent nature of stalking behaviours means that they can be particularly difficult to eradicate. The current chapter

Note from the editors

*When compiling this second edition, we were mindful of the need to balance new chapters with certain core areas of work from the first edition. There were two chapters where the authors had too many other commitments, and were unable to produce a new chapter for this collection. However, we are grateful to them for allowing us to continue to use their initial chapters and allowing us to add new materials to the reference section to update them. We thus present this chapter, as it was initially prepared for the first edition but with an updated readings list at the end. We hope that the reader will find the new readings useful additions to what remains a comprehensive chapter on stalking.

will draw on empirical evidence to illustrate the nature of 'stalking' and seek to identify who stalkers and their victims are most likely to be. The legislative history of stalking will be briefly discussed, before outlining the potential benefits and pitfalls associated with both legal sanctions and alternative modes of intervention.

A new crime?

Although stalking was labelled by the British media as 'the crime of the 1990s' (e.g. Daly 1996), it did not represent a new form of deviant behaviour (e.g. Meloy 1999; Mullen *et al.* 2000). Despite many academic articles stating that stalking was first outlawed by California in 1990, it appears that Californian law had an ancient precedent. Book four of the Ancient Roman legal tome *Institutes of Justinianus* (approximately AD 550) contains the passage *Iniuria committitur ... si quis matrem familias aut praetextatum praetextatumve adsectatus fuerit* which roughly translated means that it is prohibited to inflict injury or cause hindrance by following a boy, girl or married woman. Neither is stalking behaviour new to popular fiction. Louisa May Alcott's nineteenth-century novel *A Long Fatal Love Chase* also bears a strong resemblance to many contemporary accounts of stalking. John Fowles' first novel *The Collector* (1963) features a young art student who is obsessively pursued by an inadequate older man. He observes her every activity, moves house in order to be closer to her, and engages in photographic surveillance before finally entrapping her and holding her hostage. What *is* new is the frequency of such behaviour, perhaps encouraged by the greater empowerment and emancipation of women and ready access to mechanisms of surveillance and control, such as mobile phones and e-mail. Stalking is now a criminal act in most countries of the developed world.

Stalking is now widely considered to be a particular form of 'harassment'. In the past it has been linked to various mental conditions, notably De Clerambault's syndrome and erotomania. De Clerambault, a French psychiatrist, first identified a condition in 1927 that he labelled *psychose passionelle*. De Clerambault stated that sufferers were primarily females who laboured under the delusional belief that a man, with whom she may have had little or no contact, returned intense feelings of love for her. The target of affections were usually persons of much higher socio-economic status and likely to be unobtainable to the sufferer, such as a film star or a politician.

Erotomania, a DSM-IV delusional disorder, has the same predominant theme, and research has suggested that diagnoses are primarily given to females (see Bruene 2001; Fitzgerald and Seeman 2002; Kennedy *et al.* 2002; Lloyd-Goldstein 1998). When stalking research burgeoned in the 1990s, it soon became apparent that the modal stalker was male, rather than female, and that women were more likely to be victims of stalking than men. Spitzberg (2002) conducted a meta-analysis of the stalking literature, reporting that across more than 40 samples, 79 per cent of stalkers were male and that 75 per cent of victims were female. It also became clear that stalkers are a heterogeneous, rather than a homogeneous, group (e.g. Budd and Mattinson 2000; Meloy 1999; Mullen *et al.* 2000). Children and adolescents, for instance, have been found to engage in stalking behaviour (McCann 1998, 2000, 2001, 2002).

What is stalking?

Now that the stalking-related literature encompasses more than 160 studies, reports, reviews and books, researchers and practitioners alike are equipped with a more realistic idea of what stalking constitutes than they were when legislation was introduced in the 1990s. Essentially, 'stalking' encompasses an infinite range of behaviours that may be targeted at one individual by another. Some of these behaviours may be considered as sinister in nature and are likely to be already illegal in most Western legal systems. Threatening telephone calls, death threats and physical assaults are prime examples. Other behaviours may be quite innocuous in themselves, but when sufficiently repeated are often likely to provoke feelings of harassment and intimidation in the target. Examples include walking past the target's home or workplace, and sending letters or flowers to the target. An important question that may be raised is: despite this ambiguity, can citizens distinguish reliably between stalking and other forms of socially intrusive behaviour? This has been examined in several related studies by the authors.

Sheridan *et al.* (2001a) asked 348 women aged between 18 and 65 years to read through a list of 42 intrusive behaviours, and select all those that they personally considered to represent stalking behaviours. Participants were asked to think of the behaviours being performed solely by males towards a female 'target'. The 42 behaviours were designed to represent a continuum of likely stalking and non-stalking acts. Examples included: 'Confining the target against her will', 'Repeated excessive unwanted telephone calls – regardless of content', and 'A stranger engaging the target in an unsolicited conversation in a public place: such as at a bus stop'. The results revealed that there was no one behaviour on which there was unanimous agreement within the sample that it did or did not constitute a stalking behaviour. However, 22 of the 42 items saw agreement from at least 70 per cent of the sample that they were constituent of stalking ('stalking' behaviours). Further, 17 behaviours were seen as representative of stalking by less than 50 per cent of the sample ('non-stalking' behaviours).

A cluster analysis was performed on participants' 'yes/no' responses to the 42 intrusive items. This revealed that both the 'stalking' and 'non-stalking' behaviours could be broken down into sub-clusters. The 'stalking' cluster had four sub-clusters. The first of these, containing 17 items, was labelled 'classic' stalking behaviours. This is because these items were virtually identical to those most commonly revealed by the academic research that has recorded the behaviour of stalkers (see Sheridan and Davies 2001, for an overview) including 'Following the target' and 'Constantly watching/spying on the target'. The seven behaviours in the second sub-cluster were given the label of 'threatening' behaviours as five of them had an overtly threatening/violent theme, for instance, 'Death threats' and 'Confining the target against her will'. The third 'stalking' sub-cluster comprised just three items and was labelled 'unpredictable' stalking behaviours as the three behaviours were threatening, but also unpredictable, when compared with the threatening but more controlled acts listed by the previous sub-cluster (e.g. 'Continuously acting in an uncontrolled, aggressive, or insulting manner upon seeing the target out with other men (friends or partners')). The final sub-cluster of 'stalking' behaviours (containing five items) was focused on 'attachment'. That is, means by which a stalker may seek to maintain maximally close contact with a target. Examples include 'A man the target is not involved with moves house closer to where she lives or places she frequents – just to be nearer to her' and 'Often purposefully visiting places he knows that the target frequents'.

The six items in the first sub-cluster of 'non-stalking' behaviours were collectively labelled 'courtship' behaviours. The common characteristic of these activities was that they could reasonably comprise part of the early stages of courtship, such as 'Telephoning the target after one initial meeting', and 'Agreeing with the target's every word (even when she is obviously wrong)'. The second 'non-stalking' sub-cluster contained just two items and was dubbed 'verbally obscene' behaviours, which is self-explanatory. The final sub-cluster (containing eight items) was labelled 'overbearing' behaviours. The common theme among these was that they illustrated ways by which one individual attempts to interfere in the affairs of another, but not to a degree that unequivocally constitutes harassment. Items included: 'Trying to become acquainted with the target's friends in an attempt to get to know her better' and 'Unasked for offers of help: lifts in his car, DIY, etc.'

This study supported previous work (Sheridan *et al.* 2000) and has since been largely replicated in a sample of 210 British males (Sheridan *et al.* 2002), and in a sample of 354 Trinidadian women (Jagessar and Sheridan 2004). Taken together, these research findings demonstrate that diverse groups share common beliefs concerning the type of activities that are and are not constituent of stalking. All four samples were able consistently to classify a range of acts to the extent that identifiable subgroups of stalking and non-stalking behaviours could be formed. So, although people may not personally be able to define stalking exhaustively, there does appear to be a consensus concerning which types of behaviours are acceptable and which are deviant. This suggests that people can reliably distinguish between the courtship behaviour of someone who is 'trying too hard' to secure a date, and the behaviour of someone whose activities reveal disturbing obsessive traits that require intervention. In all four studies, the real-world relevance of the 'stalking' and 'non-stalking' clusters was tested by also conducting a cluster analysis on the sample's *actual* experiences of the same behaviours. In all cases, the sub-clusters generated by participants' perceptions of stalking were found to partially map on to the sub-clusters generated by the same participants' actual experiences of harassing behaviours. Thus, both potential and actual victims shared a sophisticated perspective on exemplars of stalking behaviours that was grounded in the everyday real-world experiences of stalking victims.

The studies described above did not assess the frequency of stalking behaviours. It was pointed out earlier that virtually any seemingly innocuous activity can constitute stalking, as long as it is engaged in repeatedly. Stalking is unlike many other criminal or intrusive activities in that it does not consist of one isolated incident; rather stalking consists of a series of activities that occur over a protracted period. Past research has reported mean stalking episodes of 24 months (Pathé and Mullen 1997), 58 months (Blaauw *et al.* 2002) and as long as 76 months (Sheridan *et al.* 2001b). Hall (1998) reported that 13 per cent of victims in her study had been stalked for more than five years, with one victim being stalked for more than 31 years. Similarly, the British Crime Survey found that 19 per cent of stalking victims had been harassed for over a year (Budd and Mattinson 2000). It is clear that although stalking is a long-term phenomenon, stalker activity may vary in terms of intensity within individual cases. Some victim studies have reported that the frequency with which stalking occurs is variable over time (Blaauw *et al.* 2002; Brewster 1997; Hall 1998; Sheridan 2001). For instance, in Sheridan's (2001) study victims reported that, over time, stalkers decreased the amount of time in which they were proximal to the victim, but that they also became more violent. Only two of 29 long-term stalking victims said that their stalker's activities became less intense over time.

The victims of stalking

Since we can conclude that stalking is not only protracted and repetitive in nature, but also unpredictable, it is particularly important to identify possible risk factors in potential victims. The most obvious risk factor is gender, given that the research has indicated that the majority of victims are female (75 per cent) and that the majority of stalkers are male (79 per cent) (see Spitzberg's 2002 meta-analysis). However, these findings may not be entirely reliable. One possibility is that the stalking of males, and/or stalking by females go largely unrecorded. It has been suggested (Emerson *et al.* 1998; Hall 1998; White *et al.* 2002) that males may be less likely to recognise or report 'stalking' behaviour as problematic, because they feel less threatened by it than would females. Sheridan *et al.* (2002) conducted a population study of 210 British males, asking them to indicate whether they had had personal experience of 42 intrusive behaviours and, if they had, to provide free narrative concerning their 'worst experience'. Males did report substantially less experience of intrusive experiences than did females and just 5 per cent were judged to have suffered 'stalking'. This was significantly less than the figure of 24 per cent obtained by Sheridan *et al.* (2001b) when conducting the same study with a wholly female sample, but it still represents a sizeable portion of the British male population. Of course, the way in which stalking is measured between studies will have an impact upon resultant estimates of its prevalence in a given population. Tjaden *et al.* (2000) found that when male participants were allowed to self-define as victims of stalking, rather than be defined according to a legal definition, prevalence rates almost tripled. This finding would suggest that males are able to recognise themselves as victims of stalking, but it still may be the case that they are not as concerned about it as are female victims. A comparison of male and female stalkers, however, has suggested that the duration of stalking and the incidence of violent acts do not differ according to stalker gender (Purcell *et al.* 2001).

In addition to gender, age has been mooted as a risk factor for stalking, with those aged 18–30 being reported to be most vulnerable (Hall 1998; Purcell *et al.* 2002; Tjaden and Thoennes 1998). The 1998 British Crime Survey found 16–19-year-olds to be most at risk, with 16.8 per cent of this age group reporting a recent incident of stalking. Those outside the 18–30 age range are by no means immune, however. Victims aged two (Sheridan *et al.* 2001b) and six years have been identified (Purcell *et al.* 2002), as have victims aged 76 (Purcell *et al.* 2002) and 82 years (Blaauw *et al.* 2002). Like gender then, age does not provide practitioners with a reliable indicator for predicting who is likely to become a victim of stalking, but both gender and age do offer a rough statistical guide pointing to vulnerable sections of the population. Another possible risk factor is the victim's socio-economic status. Although victims have been found across the socio-economic spectrum, they do appear to be more highly educated than victims of other interpersonal crimes, and similarly, they appear to be in higher-level professions (e.g. Brewster 1997; Hall 1998; Pathé and Mullen 2002; Sheridan *et al.* 2001a). This is not surprising when one considers that some stalkers have been said to be motivated by resentment (Mullen *et al.* 2000), may be erotomanic (see above), and are themselves often of higher social status than other criminal offenders (e.g. Meloy 1999). The British Crime Survey, however, based on a sample of 9,988 persons, found stalking risk to be highest among victims with a relatively low household income (Budd and Mattinson 2000).

Stalking victims are more frequently found among single persons, although married persons and those in other partnerships are not exempt from stalking victimisation. The 1998 British Crime Survey identified single persons as those most likely to experience stalking (Budd and Mattinson 2000), particularly if they were students and living in privately rented accommodation. It must be noted that many risk factors will overlap to a large degree, however, making the identification of key risk factors rather difficult. What is clear is that virtually anyone may become a victim of stalking, but that risks appear to be greater for young single women in high-status occupations. Since 1990, the media has contained numerous stories regarding the stalking of celebrities (see Lowney and Best 1995). Indeed, it may be argued that stalking was first criminalised in response to the media storm that centred around a number of high-profile celebrity cases (e.g. Saunders 1998). Although celebrities are stalked, they form an overall minority of stalking victims, but are more likely than non-celebrities to suffer the attentions of multiple stalkers (e.g. Pathé and Mullen 2002).

A final risk factor that the research has shown to be closely linked to the stalking of female victims is a history of domestic violence. Many studies (e.g. Burgess *et al.* 2001; Logan *et al.* 2002; McFarlane *et al.* 2002; Mechanic *et al.* 2002) have testified to the strong interrelationship that stalking has with domestic violence (see also Baldry 2002; Walker and Meloy 1998). It is clear that domestic violence does not necessarily end along with the conclusion of a relationship, but may continue in the form of stalking. What is certain is that particular groups of society are disproportionately vulnerable to stalking risk, and the most unequivocal risk factor would appear to be a previous history of domestic violence.

The perpetrators of stalking

Given that domestic violence is such an important risk factor for stalking, this would strongly suggest that a high proportion of stalkers were previously in intimate relationships with their victim. Research indicates that this is indeed the case. Meloy (1999) described the 'modal stalker' as male and the 'modal victim' as his female ex-partner. One of the most reliable research findings in relation to stalkers is that the majority of victims had some form of prior contact with their stalker. Spitzberg (2002) suggests that across 47 studies, 77 per cent of stalkers had had some form of prior acquaintanceship with their victim, while just 18 per cent stalked strangers. It is generally agreed that the largest stalker–victim relational sub-group covers ex-intimates, but proportional estimates have been found to vary substantially as the following examples will illustrate.

In a sample of Dutch victims, 67 per cent reported being stalked by an ex-intimate (Blaauw *et al.* 2002), whilst Wallis' (1996) analysis of police records of English and Welsh stalking cases revealed that 38 per cent had been targeted by ex-partners. In the US, Tjaden and Thoennes (1998) conducted telephone interviews with a random sample, finding that of those who reported being a victim of stalking, 59 per cent of women had been stalked by ex-intimates, as had 30 per cent of men. Finally, Pathé and Mullen (1997) found that 29 per cent of their Australian victims revealed they had been stalked by ex-intimates. It is likely that estimates of the extent of ex-intimate stalking vary at least partly as a function of sampling techniques, the discipline of the researcher and the definition of stalking employed. Two things, however, are apparent: first, ex-intimate stalkers represent a significant proportion of all stalkers; second, stalking by non-intimates also has a high prevalence rate. As regards violence, Meloy *et al.* (2001) found that prior sexual intimacy between victim and stalker resulted in at least an 11-fold increase in potential for violence.

As previously indicated, and as is the case with the perpetrators of most crimes of an interpersonal nature, the majority of stalkers recorded by the literature are males. Compared with the general criminal population, however, stalkers tend to be older. Meloy's review of the literature pertaining to stalkers (1996), for instance, found mean stalker ages within individual studies of, for example, 35 and 40 years. Similarly, Mullen *et al.*'s (2000) classification of stalkers indicated that although mean stalker age varied across sub-categories, overall mean age was over 35 years. As regards socio-economic status, stalkers tend to be found more often in professional occupations than most other criminals (e.g. Hall 1998; Sheridan *et al.* 2001a) but they may be found at any point along the socio-economic continuum. Meloy *et al.* (2001) noted that although the 'modal' stalker will have an average or above average IQ, he will be unemployed. Mullen *et al.* (1999) found that 39 per cent of 145 stalkers were unemployed, and that the majority of stalkers were socially incompetent. Taken together, the research findings pertaining to the demographic characteristics of stalkers suggest that although certain demographic trends do exist, a high proportion of stalkers will fall outside these.

The relevant research has suggested that stalkers may or may not be mentally ill, and may or may not have criminal histories. Stalking has been associated with a variety of mental disorders including antisocial, histrionic, borderline and narcissistic personality disorders (e.g. Zona *et al.* 1998), depression (e.g. McCann 2001), delusional disorder, erotomania (see above), sadism (e.g. Boon and Sheridan 2001), schizophrenia (e.g. Mullen and Pathé 1994) and substance abuse disorder (e.g. Zona *et al.* 1998). Clinicians have noted (e.g. Badcock 2002; Farnham *et al.* 2000) that stalkers are likely to be co-morbid for a range of disorders. However, many stalkers have no history of any psychiatric disturbance. Similarly, although a number of studies have identified the most likely criminal histories with which stalkers will present, not all stalkers will have a criminal record. Meloy *et al.* (2001) examined archival data on 59 stalkers, 66 per cent of whom had been violent towards their victims. No significance was found for drug abuse, drug dependency or prior criminal history. Mullen *et al.* (2000), however, found that 30 per cent of their 145 stalkers suffered from delusional disorders.

The research findings covered by this section allow the conclusions that potential stalkers are difficult to identify, and that a victim will first come into contact with their stalker or future stalker in an almost infinite variety of contexts. Some victims may never actually meet their stalker – the victim studies of Hall (1998), Jones (1996) and Sheridan (2001), for instance, have all identified cases where evidence of stalking existed, but the stalker's identity was never established. It is clear that further investigations and meta-analyses are necessary to provide a more adequate picture of the likely characteristics of stalkers. What is also clear is that stalkers should be grouped into various subtypes according to their demographic characteristics, mental state, motivations, and the nature of their victims (see Mullen *et al.* 2000; Boon and Sheridan 2001, for fuller discussions of the benefits of such typologies).

Stopping stalking

Stalking and the law

Several stalker typologies have suggested that different stalker subtypes will display differing responses to various intervention and treatment strategies. Boon and Sheridan (2001) suggest that legal intervention is likely to curtail the activities of their 'infatuation harasser', while their 'sadistic stalker' will only view police intervention as a challenge that he will be able to overcome while still maintaining control of the victim. Similarly, Mullen *et al.* (2000) note that treatment for their sexually deviant 'predatory stalker' will pose a significant challenge for the clinician, while their 'incompetent suitors' will often stop their stalking activities in response to counselling (although they may later reoffend by focusing on a different victim). The law, however, tends to treat stalkers as a more homogeneous group. As has already been noted, stalking is notoriously difficult to define and, across the developed world, the legislatures of different states and countries have adopted somewhat different approaches when framing legislation to outlaw stalking.

Since California first outlawed stalking in 1991, all US States, as well as Australia, Austria, Belgium, Canada, England and Wales, Germany, Ireland, the Netherlands, Switzerland and others have enacted anti-stalking legislation. In the US, 30 States enacted their anti-stalking laws in 1992 alone, and wide variation was seen between States in the 'stalking' actions covered by the new legislation. This variation was thought to at least partly result from a haste to enact legislation in order to appease public concerns, as well as from debates over the lack of constitutionality of anti-stalking and harassment laws. In response, the National Institute of Justice in 1993 was asked by Congress to develop a Model Stalking Code. Wallace and Kelty (1995) distilled the requirements of the Code into the following definition:

> a knowing, purposeful course of conduct directed at a specific person that would cause a reasonable person to fear bodily injury or death to himself or herself or a member of his or her immediate family. (pp. 100–101)

Yet, significant variation is seen between the laws of various States. These differences primarily relate to the type of stalking behaviour that is outlawed, whether or not a threat or intent is required, and also in relation to the reaction required from the victim (US Department of Justice 2002). Most States offer a broad definition of what constitutes stalking, with some offering specific exemplars of stalking behaviour. For instance, in Michigan, stalking is not limited to, but may include: following or appearing in sight of the victim, approaching or confronting the victim in a public place or on private property, appearing at the victim's workplace or residence, entering into or remaining on property owned, leased or occupied by the victim, telephoning the victim, sending mail or electronic communications, and placing an object on the premises of or delivering an object to the victim. Even fewer States provide very narrow definitions of what constitutes unlawful stalking. In Wisconsin, for instance, a stalker must maintain a visual or physical proximity to the victim in order to contravene State law.

Outside the USA, similar variations exist between countries with regard to what legally constitutes stalking or harassment. In England and Wales, a broad approach has been adopted where 'a person must not pursue a course of conduct which amounts to harassment of another, and which he knows or ought to know amounts to harassment of the other' (section 1, Protection from Harassment Act 1997). 'Harassment' is not, in turn, defined. In Ireland, however, a definition of harassment is provided as follows:

> any person who, without lawful authority or reasonable excuse, by any means including by use of the telephone, harasses another by persistently following, watching, pestering, besetting or communicating with him or her, shall be guilty of an offence. (section 10, Non-Fatal Offences Against the Person Act 1997)

Differences are also seen between countries in terms of the inclusion of threat and intent. For instance, no intent is required in England and Wales, where harassment is considered as having occurred

> if a reasonable person in possession of the same information would think the course of conduct amounted to harassment of the other. (section 2)

Conversely, Australia's Capital Territory prescribes that

> A person shall not stalk another person with intent to cause (a) apprehension or fear of serious harm in the other person or a third person; or, (b) serious harm to the other person or a third person. (Australian Capital Territory, Crimes Act 1900, section 34A)

Most countries and states prescribe the inclusion of a credible threat, but as the Hong Kong Law Reform Commission (2000) notes, this can be problematic. The behaviour of many stalkers may appear to be innocuous, such as the sending of unwanted flowers or regularly walking past the victim's place of work. However, these activities may still be threatening to the victim where they are unwanted and where they take place frequently. The Hong Kong Law Reform Commission further notes that stalkers who are familiar with the threat element of a particular anti-stalking law may purposefully refrain from delivering any specific threat, thereby avoiding prosecution. Some legislatures have circumvented this possibility by adopting the 'reasonable person' test. For example, the USA's 1993 Model Stalking Code, as mentioned above. Differences in the compass of stalking laws between countries have raised extensive debates. In Germany, Smartt (2001) notes that the German debate peaked when the stalker of tennis player Martina Hingis was put on trial in Florida. The Australian stalker had harassed his victim at her home in Germany, yet Hingis was unable to curtail his activities via German or Swiss law. A Florida court sentenced the stalker to two years' imprisonment with a further two years' probation and applied an indefinite injunction banning him from contacting Hingis.

Prescriptive versus non-prescriptive legislation

The victims of stalking also play important roles in the way that stalking may be legally defined. Anti-stalking laws frequently require the victim to display negative effects of stalking, or else require that a reasonable person would be likely to experience negative consequences in the same situation (see Finch 2002). These negative effects may take the form of substantial emotional distress (e.g. under Californian law), serious alarm, annoyance, fright, or torment (e.g. District of Columbia), fear for personal safety (e.g. Florida), arousal of fear (e.g. South Australia), or reasonable mental anxiety, anguish, or fear (e.g. Alabama). Blaauw *et al.* (2002) compared five victim studies in an attempt to discover whether stalking behaviours were consistent between samples. Two of the five studies were conducted in the United States, one by Brewster (1997) who interviewed 187 female victims of ex-partner stalkers in Pennsylvania who were recruited through victim service and law enforcement agencies and one by Hall (1998) whose 145 self-defined stalking victims had made themselves known via regional voicemail boxes that had been set up in seven US target cities. In Australia, Pathé and Mullen's (1997) study was based on questionnaires completed by 100 stalking victims who independently contacted the authors or who were referred to the authors' clinic. Two European studies were also included in the comparison. In the United Kingdom, Sheridan *et al.* (2001b) distributed questionnaires among 95 individuals who had contacted a charity concerned with the promotion of personal safety, and in the Netherlands, 261 completed questionnaires were received from members of the Dutch Anti-Stalking Foundation who had all experienced stalking.

Across the five studies, nine distinct stalker behaviours had been recorded and these were: telephone calls, harassing letters, surveillance of the victim's home, following, unlawful entry to the victim's home, destruction or theft of the victim's property, direct unwanted approaches, threats to harm or kill the victim, and physical assaults. Thus, stalking behaviours were found to be consistent between diverse samples from four different countries. Further, most of the nine stalker behaviours were fairly equally distributed across the different studies. For instance, the number of victims reporting that their stalker telephoned them ranged from 78–90 per cent, instances of following ranged from 68–83 per cent, and threats to kill or harm the victim were reported by between 41 and 53 per cent of victims. Blaauw *et al.* (2002) concluded that this consistency suggests that anti-stalking legislation could prescribe a core of behaviours that constitute stalking. However, it may be argued that stalkers may easily circumvent such prescriptive legislation, with the result that some victims would have no legal recourse. A number of authors have noted that the particularly tenacious nature of many stalkers has led to ingenious methods of harassment designed to cause maximal distress in the victim whilst at the same time minimising the offender's chance of getting caught. Prior to the introduction of the Protection from Harassment Act in 1997, Lawson-Cruttenden (1996) reported that the majority of stalkers known to him had sought meticulously to stay within the bounds of criminal law, despite the objectionable or harassing nature of their behaviour. A more measured suggestion may be for anti-stalking legislation to include behaviours such as the nine detailed above as examples of what may constitute illegal stalking in order to inform the police and courts of the nature of stalking crimes.

Given that stalking has been criminalised only relatively recently, it is likely that debates will continue within different jurisdictions as to how best to frame legislation to outlaw stalking and harassment. The questions of how to define stalking (if at all), and the inclusion of stalker intent, threat and impact upon victims will continue to be discussed, as will the fundamental constitutionality of anti-harassment laws. Because a very fine line can exist between excessive courtship behaviour, reasonable communication attempts and harassment, disparities even within legal systems are almost inevitable. Further, as with many criminal activities, technological progress makes amendments to intervention strategies necessary. Many anti-stalking laws are already broad enough to encompass cyberstalking and other technologically aided harassment activities. Other anti-stalking legislation, such as that of California, has been amended to cover stalking via e-mail. In the case of California, the term 'credible threat' has now been extended to include

> that performed through the use of an electronic communication device, or a threat implied by a pattern of conduct or a combination of verbal, written or electronically communicated statements. (US Department of Justice 2002)

Stalker remedies

Legal intervention is not the only manner by which stalkers may be deterred from their harassment campaigns. In terms of treating stalkers, as previously noted, psychotherapeutic intervention may be the most effective course of action for some stalker subtypes, such as delusional stalkers. For other subtypes, however, such as those with a teenage or mid-life 'crush' and certain ex-partner stalkers, police intervention would be more strongly advocated (Boon and Sheridan 2001).

Although there exists no effective treatment for stalking *per se*, many of the psychiatric conditions associated with stalking behaviour (such as personality disorders, depression, substance abuse disorders, delusional disorders and schizophrenia) may respond to relevant interventions (see Kropp *et al.* 2002). An important factor for a clinician faced with a stalker will be the recognition that as a group, stalkers are likely to be co-morbid for a range of disorders. Kropp *et al.* (2002) suggest that in the case of stalkers, 'treatment' will likely have a preventative aim, rather than a solely rehabilitative aim. Because of this, these authors advocate a multidisciplinary approach to case management, with risk assessment forming the basis of their approach. Mullen *et al.* (2000) also suggest that although management of any existing mental disorder is imperative, this should not be the sole task of the clinician – for many stalkers, the stalking is an all-consuming task and stalkers will need to be connected or reconnected with a real social world if successful intervention is to be achieved. It should be noted that because of the serious negative effects that stalking may have on its victims, victims too should be offered counselling or psychotherapeutic help. In the most extensive study of its kind to date, Davis *et al.* (2002) found a strong link between stalking and poor mental and physical health in a sample of 6,563 women and 6,705 men. Both sexes reported a significantly greater likelihood of injury or chronic disease since they were first victims of stalking.

Conclusions

Stalkers engage in a range of harassing behaviours, many of which are common to a majority of stalkers. Although some stalker activities may appear ostensibly harmless, stalkers become a menace when their behaviour is repetitive and unwanted. Although basic similarities exist between some stalkers and between some victims, it would appear that virtually anyone might become a stalker or the victim of a stalker. Anti-stalking legislation takes a blanket approach to outlawing stalking behaviour, embracing a wide range of stalker subtypes – from those who are infatuated with their target and sincerely wish to start a relationship to sadistic stalkers who intend serious harm. In order to help prevent recidivism, treatment regimes should not take a blanket approach, but should be targeted towards specific sub-categories of stalkers. To help protect the public from the lasting damage that may be inflicted by stalkers, a multidisciplinary approach is required where information is shared between the judiciary, police officers, clinicians and academics.

Updated readings

General stalking references

Dennison, S.M. (2007) 'Interpersonal relationships and stalking: identifying when to intervene', *Law and Human Behavior*, 31 (4): 353–67.

Melton, H.C. (2007) 'Predicting the occurrence of stalking in relationships characterized by domestic violence', *Journal of Interpersonal Violence*, 22: 3–25.

Phillips, L., Quirk, R., Rosenfeld, B. and O'Connor, M. (2004) 'Is it stalking? Perceptions of stalking among college undergraduates', *Criminal Justice and Behavior*, 31: 73–96.

Purcell, R., Pathé, M. and Mullen, P.E. (2004) 'When do repeated intrusions become stalking?', *Journal of Forensic Psychiatry and Psychology*, 15 (4): 571–83.

Sheridan, L.P., Blaauw, E. and Davies, G.M. (2003) 'Stalking: knowns and unknowns', *Trauma, Violence and Abuse*, 4: 148–62.

Sheridan, L.P. and Grant, T. (2007) 'Is cyberstalking different?', *Psychology, Crime and Law*, 13 (6): 627–40.

Sinclair, H.C. and Frieze, I.H. (2005) 'When courtship persistence becomes intrusive pursuit: comparing rejecter and pursuer perspectives of unrequited attraction', *Sex Roles*, 52 (11–12): 839–52.

Turmanis, S.A. and Brown, R.I. (2006) 'The stalking and harassment behaviour scale: measuring the incidence, nature, and severity of stalking and relational harassment and their psychological effects', *Psychology and Psychotherapy: Theory, Research and Practice*, 79 (2): 183–98.

Victims of stalking

Dietz, N.A. and Martin, P.Y. (2007) 'Women who are stalked: questioning the fear standard', *Violence Against Women*, 13: 750–76.

Logan, T.K., Shannon, L. and Cole, J. (2007) 'Stalking victimization in the context of intimate partner violence', *Violence and Victims*, 22 (6): 669–83.

Purcell, R., Pathé, M. and Mullen, P.E. (2005) 'Association between stalking victimisation and psychiatric morbidity in a random community sample', *British Journal of Psychiatry*, 187 (5): 416–20.

Roberts, K.A. (2005) 'Women's experience of violence during stalking by former romantic partners: factors predictive of stalking violence', *Violence Against Women*, 11: 89–114.

Perpetrators of stalking

Kinkade, P., Burns, R. and Fuentes, A.I. (2005) 'Criminalizing attractions: perceptions of stalking and the stalker', *Crime and Delinquency*, 51 (1): 3–25.

McEwan, T., Mullen, P.E. and Purcell, R. (2007) 'Identifying risk factors in stalking: a review of current research', *International Journal of Law and Psychiatry*, 30 (1): 1–9.

Rosenfeld, B. (2004) 'Violence risk factors in stalking and obsessional harassment: a review and preliminary meta-analysis', *Criminal Justice and Behavior*, 31 (1): 9–36.

Sheridan, L.P., Gillett, R., Davies, G.M., Blaauw, E. and Patel, D. (2003) '"There's no smoke without fire": are male ex-partners perceived as more "entitled" to stalk than acquaintance or stranger stalkers?', *British Journal of Psychology*, 94 (1): 87–98.

Spitzberg, B.H. and Veksler, A.E. (2007) 'The personality of pursuit: personality attributions of unwanted pursuers and stalkers', *Violence and Victims*, 22 (3): 275–89.

West, S.G and Friedman, S.H. (2008) 'These boots are made for stalking: characteristics of female stalkers', *Psychiatry*, 5 (8): 37–42.

Whyte, S., Petch, E., Penny, C. and Reiss, D. (2008) 'Who stalks? A description of patients at a high security hospital with a history of stalking behaviour', *Criminal Behaviour and Mental Health*, 18 (1): 27–38.

Stalking and the law

Dennison, S.M and Thomson, D.M. (2005) 'Criticisms or plaudits for stalking laws? What psycholegal research tells us about proscribing stalking', *Psychology, Public Policy, and Law*, 11 (3): 384–406.

Kamir, O. (2004) *Every Breath You Take: Stalking narratives and the law*. Ann Arbor: The University of Michigan Press.

McEwan, T.E, Mullen, P.E and MacKenzie, R. (2007) 'Anti-stalking legislation in practice: are we meeting community needs?', *Psychiatry, Psychology and Law*, 14 (2): 207–17.

Purcell, R., Pathé, M. and Mullen, P.E. (2004) 'Stalking: defining and prosecuting a new category of offending', *International Journal of Law and Psychiatry*, 27 (2): 157–69.

Stalking remedies

Malsch, M. (2007) 'Stalking: do criminalization and punishment help?', *Punishment and Society*, 9 (2): 201–09.

Spitzberg, B.H. (2003) 'Stalking and psychosexual obsession: psychological perspectives for prevention policing and treatment', *Applied Cognitive Psychology*, 17 (5): 621–23.

References

Alcott, L.M. (1996) *A Long Fatal Love Chase*. Waterville, ME: Thorndike.

Badcock, R. (2002) 'Psychopathology and treatment of stalking', in J.C.W. Boon and L. Sheridan (eds), *Stalking and Psychosexual Obsession: Psychological Perspectives for Prevention, Policing and Treatment* (pp. 125–39). Chichester: Wiley.

Baldry, A. (2002) 'From domestic violence to stalking: the infinite cycle of violence', in J.C.W. Boon and L. Sheridan (eds), *Stalking and Psychosexual Obsession: Psychological Perspectives for Prevention, Policing and Treatment* (pp. 83–104). Chichester: Wiley.

Blaauw, E., Sheridan, L. and Winkel, F.W. (2002) 'Designing anti-stalking legislation on the basis of victims' experiences and psychopathology', *Psychiatry, Psychology and Law*, 9 (1): 136–45.

Blaauw, E., Winkel, F.W., Arensman, E., Sheridan, L. and Freeve, A. (2002) 'The toll of stalking: the relationship between features of stalking and psychopathology of victims', *Journal of Interpersonal Violence*, 17: 50–63.

Boon, J.C.W. and Sheridan, L. (2001) 'Stalker typologies: a law enforcement perspective', *Journal of Threat Assessment*, 1: 75–97.

Brewster, M.P. (1997) 'An exploration of the experiences and needs of former intimate stalking victims', *Final Report Submitted to the National Institute of Justice*. West Chester, PA: West Chester University.

Bruene, M. (2001) 'De Clerambault's syndrome (erotomania): an evolutionary perspective', *Evolution and Human Behavior*, 22: 409–15.

Budd, T. and Mattinson, J. (2000) *Stalking: Findings from the 1998 British Crime Survey*. London: Home Office.

Burgess, A.W., Harner, H., Baker, T., Hartman, C.R. and Lole, C. (2001). 'Batterers' stalking patterns', *Journal of Family Violence*, 16: 309–21.

Daly, E. (17 December 1996) 'Sweeping penalties in new laws on stalkers', *The Independent*: 9.

Davis K.E., Coker, A.L. and Sanderson, M. (2002) 'Physical and mental health effects of being stalked for men and women', *Violence and Victims*, 17 (4): 429–43.

Emerson, R.M., Ferris, K.O. and Gardner, C.B. (1998) 'On being stalked', *Social Problems*, 45: 289–314.

Farnham, F.R., James, D.V. and Cantrell, P. (2000) 'Association between violence, psychosis and relationship to victim in stalkers', *The Lancet*, 355: 199.

Finch, E. (2002) 'Stalking: a violent crime or a crime of violence?', *Howard Journal of Criminal Justice*, 41 (5): 422–33.

Fitzgerald, P. and Seeman, M.V. (2002) 'Erotomania in women', in J.C.W. Boon and L. Sheridan (eds), *Stalking and Psychosexual Obsession: Psychological Perspectives for Prevention, Policing and Treatment* (pp. 165–79). Chichester: Wiley.

Fowles, J. (1963) *The Collector*. London: Little Brown and Co.

Hall, D.M. (1998) 'The victims of stalking', in J.R. Meloy (ed.), *The Psychology of Stalking: Clinical and Forensic Perspectives* (pp. 113–37). San Diego, CA: Academic Press.

Home Office (1996) *Stalking – the Solutions: A Consultation Paper*. London: HMSO.

Hong Kong Law Reform Commission (October 2000) 'Stalking – The New Offence', in *Stalking*. Hong Kong: Law Reform Commission of Hong Kong.

Jagessar, J.D.H. and Sheridan, L.P. (2002) 'A cross-cultural investigation into stalking', *Criminal Justice and Behaviour*.

Jagessar, J.D.H. and Sheridan, L.P. (2004) 'Stalking perceptions and experiences across two cultures', *Criminal Justice and Behavior*, 31: 97–119.

Jones, C. (1996) 'Criminal Harassment (or stalking)'. See: www.chass.utoronto.ca/~cjones/pub/stalking (accessed June 2002).

Kennedy, N., McDonough, M., Kelly, B. and Berrios, G.E . (2002) 'Erotomania revisited: clinical course and treatment', *Comprehensive Psychiatry*, 43: 1–6.

Kropp, P.R., Hart, S.D., Lyon, D.R. and LePard, D.A. (2002) 'Managing stalkers: coordinating treatment and supervision', in J.C.W. Boon and L. Sheridan (eds), *Stalking and Psychosexual Obsession: Psychological Perspectives for Prevention, Policing and Treatment* (pp. 141–16). Chichester: Wiley.

Lawson-Cruttenden, T. (1996) 'Is there a law against stalking?', *New Law Journal*, 22 March 1996: 418–19.

Lloyd-Goldstein, R. (1998) 'De Clerambault on-line: a survey of erotomania and stalking from old world to the world wide web, in J. Reid Meloy (ed.), *The Psychology of Stalking: Clinical and Forensic Perspectives* (pp. 193–212. San Diego: Academic Press.

Logan, T.K., Leukefeld, C. and Walker, B. (2002) 'Stalking as a variant of intimate violence: implications from a young adult sample', in K.E. Davis and I.H. Frieze *et al.* (eds), *Stalking: Perspectives on Victims and Perpetrators* (pp. 265–91). New York: Springer.

Lowney, K.S. and Best, J. (1995) 'Stalking strangers and lovers: changing media typifications of a new crime problem', in J. Best (ed.), *Images of Issues: Typifying Contemporary Social Problems* (pp. 33–57). New York: Aldine de Gruyter.

McCann, J.T. (1998) 'Subtypes of stalking (obsessional following) in adolescents', *Journal of Adolescence*, 21: 667–75.

McCann, J.T. (2000) 'A descriptive study of child and adolescent obsessional followers', *Journal of Forensic Sciences*, 45: 195–99.

McCann, J.T. (2001) *Stalking in Children and Adolescents: The Primitive Bond.* Washington, DC: American Psychological Association.

McCann, J.T. (2002) 'The phenomenon of stalking in children and adolescents', in J.C.W. Boon and L. Sheridan (eds), *Stalking and Psychosexual Obsession: Psychological Perspectives for Prevention, Policing and Treatment* (pp. 125–39). Chichester: Wiley.

McFarlane, J., Campbell, J.C. and Watson, K. (2002) 'Intimate partner stalking and femicide: urgent implications for women's safety', *Behavioral Sciences and the Law*, 20: 51–68.

Mechanic, M.B., Weaver, T.L. and Resick, P.A. (2002) 'Intimate partner violence and stalking behavior: exploration of patterns and correlates in a sample of acutely battered women', in K.E. Davis and I.H. Frieze *et al.* (eds), *Stalking: Perspectives on Victims and Perpetrators* (pp. 62–88). New York: Springer.

Meloy, J.R. (1996) 'Stalking (obsessional following): a review of some preliminary studies', *Aggression and Violent Behavior*, 1: 147–62.

Meloy, J.R. (1999) 'Stalking: an old behavior, a new crime', *Psychiatric Clinics of North America*, 22: 85–99.

Meloy, J.R., Davis, B. and Lovette, J. (2001) 'Risk factors for violence among stalkers', *Journal of Threat Assessment*, 1: 3–16.

Mullen, P.E. and Pathé, M. (1994) 'The pathological extensions of love', *British Journal of Psychiatry*, 165: 614–23.

Mullen, P.E., Pathé, M. and Purcell, R. (2000) *Stalkers and Their Victims.* Cambridge: Cambridge University Press.

Mullen, P.E., Pathé, M., Purcell, R. and Stuart, G.W. (1999) 'Study of stalkers', *American Journal of Psychiatry*, 156: 1244–49.

Pathé, M. and Mullen, P.E. (1997) 'The impact of stalkers on their victims', *British Journal of Psychiatry*, 170: 12–17.

Pathé, M. and Mullen, P.E. (2002) 'The victim of stalking', in J.C.W. Boon and L. Sheridan (eds), *Stalking and Psychosexual Obsession: Psychological Perspectives for Prevention, Policing and Treatment* (pp. 1–22). Chichester: Wiley.

Purcell, R., Pathé, M. and Mullen, P.E. (2001) 'A study of women who stalk', *American Journal of Psychiatry*, 158: 2056–60.

Purcell, R., Pathé, M. and Mullen, P.E. (2002) 'The incidence and nature of stalking in the Australian community', *Australian and New Zealand Journal of Psychiatry*, 36: 114–20.

Saunders, R. (1998) 'The legal perspective of stalking', in J.R. Meloy (ed.), *The Psychology of Stalking: Clinical and Forensic Perspectives* (pp. 28–49). San Diego: Academic Press.

Sheridan, L. (2001) 'The course and nature of stalking: an in-depth victim survey', *Journal of Threat Assessment*, 1: 61–79.

Sheridan, L. and Davies, G.M. (2001) 'Stalking: the elusive crime', *Legal and Criminological Psychology*, 6: 133–47.

Sheridan, L., Davies, G.M. and Boon, J.C.W. (2001a) 'Stalking: perceptions and prevalence', *Journal of Interpersonal Violence*, 16: 151–67.

Sheridan, L., Davies, G.M. and Boon, J.C.W. (2001b) 'The course and nature of stalking: a victim perspective', *Howard Journal of Criminal Justice*, 40: 215–34.

Sheridan, L., Gillett, R. and Davies, G.M. (2000) 'Stalking: seeking the victim's perspective', *Psychology, Crime and Law*, 6: 267–80.

Sheridan, L., Gillett, R. and Davies, G.M. (2002) 'Perceptions and prevalence of stalking in a male sample', *Psychology, Crime and Law*, 8: 289–310.

Smartt, U. (2001) 'The stalking phenomenon: trends in European and international stalking and harassment legislation', *European Journal of Crime, Criminal Law and Criminal Justice*, 9: 209–32.

Spitzberg, B.H. (2002) 'The tactical topography of stalking victimization and management', *Trauma, Violence and Abuse*, 3: 261–88.

Tjaden, P. and Thoennes, N. (1998) *Stalking in America: Findings from the national violence against women survey*. Washington, DC: National Institute of Justice and Centers for Disease Control and Prevention.

Tjaden, P., Thoennes, N. and Allison, C.J. (2000) 'Comparing stalking victimization from legal and victim perspectives', *Violence and Victims*, 15: 7–22.

US Department of Justice (January 2002) *Legal Series Bulletin 1: Strengthening Anti-Stalking Statutes*. US Department of Justice, Office of Justice Programs, Office for Victims of Crime.

Walker, L.M. and Meloy, J.R. (1998) 'Stalking and domestic violence', in J.R. Meloy (ed.), *The Psychology of Stalking: Clinical and Forensic Perspectives* (pp. 140–59). San Diego, CA: Academic Press.

Wallace, H. and Kelty, K. (1995) 'Stalking and restraining orders: a legal and psychological perspective', *Journal of Crime and Justice*, 18 (2): 99–111.

Wallis, M. (1996) 'Outlawing stalkers', *Policing Today (UK)*, 2 (4): 25–9.

White, J., Kowalski, R.M., Lyndon, A. and Valentine, S. (2002) 'An integrative contextual developmental model of male stalking', *Violence and Victims*, 15: 373–88.

Zona, M.A., Palarea, R.E. and Lane, J.C. Jr. (1998) 'Psychiatric diagnosis and the offender-victim typology of stalking', in J.R. Meloy (ed.), *The Psychology of Stalking: Clinical and Forensic Perspectives* (pp. 70–83). San Diego, CA: Academic Press, Inc.

Chapter 13

Forensic psychology and terrorism

Margaret A. Wilson and Lucy Lemanski

Introduction

In the recent past 'forensic psychology', as an academic discipline, did not exist. There were individuals who conducted research with application to the criminal justice system (CJS), but they were mainly identified as cognitive, social, developmental psychologists, and so on. The same is still largely true of terrorism research. There are a few university centres known for terrorism research, and masters programmes are being established, but individual researchers are usually based in different disciplines, connected through what Mickolus once called the 'invisible college' (Mickolus 1987).

The aim of this chapter is to examine the relationship between forensic psychology and terrorism research; in particular, where the two areas overlap, where they cannot overlap and where they productively might in the future. At the simplest level, we could suggest that acts of terrorism are crimes and their perpetrators offenders, and so open to the same issues relating to police investigation, criminal prosecution, and custodial management. In many areas, where there is research relating to non-terrorist crime and offenders, there is often a parallel literature in relation to terrorists and terrorism. However, there are also some important differences between terrorist and non-terrorist crimes.

In the course of researching this chapter we compiled a list of topics in forensic psychology and matched them to topics in terrorism research. This process revealed some large gaps. Many of these disparities are a result of nothing more complex than data access.

Researchers in forensic psychology are quite aware of the difficulties of gaining access to police investigations and prison records for 'ordinary' offenders. Requests to examine interrogation transcripts or to interview or assess convicted terrorists are even less likely to be successful. Problems with data access would also explain why there is so little empirical work on terrorism in general and why a large component of what there is relates to public attitudes and responses.

In order to understand the relationship between forensic psychology and terrorism research, it is necessary to start with the very messy area of definitions. In 1988 Schmid and Jongman identified over a hundred different definitions of terrorism; given the increase in publications since 9/11, the debate about what constitutes terrorism and who is a terrorist can only have become more complicated. Whether an act of violence is terrorism or not depends on a host of disputed and constantly debated factors, including who the victim is, who the perpetrator is, the motivation for the attack, the nature of the conflict and 'whose side you are on'.

Terrorism, crime and war

The first area of debate can be summarised thus: 'terrorism' is a pejorative word. Whether or not you support the cause seems to nudge perceptions of actual behaviours over boundary lines between terrorism and 'war', 'resistance' or even 'defence'. The reverse shift can also apply to state-sponsored acts, even those conducted by democratically elected Western governments. Horgan (2005) describes the differences between terrorism and war as 'surface dissimilarities'; war takes place between states, and is broadly symmetrical in terms of means, whereas terrorists employ different tactics and strategies, as they lack comparable resources.

For researchers to remain politically neutral, it has been suggested that terms like 'insurgents', 'activists' or 'combatants' can be employed. Heskin (1985) sees these euphemisms as being used to describe terrorism for which there is 'considerable popular sympathy', which depends, of course, on who you ask. Heskin goes on to state that people are likely to judge acts more leniently if they a) perceive the cause to be just, and b) they or their loved ones are not likely to be victims.

In order to avoid judgements about the legitimacy of the cause, or the affiliation of the individuals, Schmid (1993) proposed that we should not define terrorists by any means other than their actions, i.e. that the definition relies entirely on components of the actual behaviour. There are certain acts that are universally agreed to be unacceptable even in war; for example: using chemical and biological weapons; targeting civilian non-combatants; taking civilian hostages and ill-treatment of POWs (Horgan 2005). Central to discussions on the definition of terrorist acts has been the issue of who the victim is, or was intended to be. Most definitions of terrorism agree that attacks targeting non-combatants (i.e. civilians) are acts of terrorism, although there are some complications. For example, attacks on off-duty or unarmed military personnel could be considered attacks on civilians, but many terrorist groups consider them to be legitimate targets.

While terrorism sits on one boundary with war, on its other side is a boundary with crime. For example, members of terrorist groups often engage in non-terrorist crimes such as robbery and extortion, in order to raise funds for terrorist activities. Similarly, those who are not members of terrorist organisations engage in acts that may be characterised as terrorism, such as the Oklahoma bombing, the campaign of the 'Unabomber', or the sniper shootings in the Washington area in 2002. Horgan (2005) argues that it is the distinction between political and personal that distinguishes terrorism from other forms of homicide and violence, where terrorism is essentially a political crime.

However, not all political crimes constitute terrorism. For example, breaking into opposition party offices and stealing evidence to incriminate their leader is clearly not terrorism. Is the scale of the damage a factor here? Would breaking into the opposition leader's house and killing him or her become an act of terrorism? According to most definitions of terrorism, the motive for the act must be to induce some kind of political change. This type of hypothetical assassination may be political and quite possibly the motive would be to provoke change. What is missing is another important constituent of the definition of terrorism, that the mechanism for change induces *fear*.

Definitions are also complicated by those persons towards whom the fear is directed. While the victims of terrorism can be seen as the person or persons physically harmed, terrorism also concerns itself with other 'targets'. The attack on the victims is designed to effect some kind of change, so the message is being delivered to a target whose influence is sought, usually a government. On occasion these two targets are the same, for example when the violence is directed at politicians. Take, for example, the IRA bombing of the Grand Hotel in Brighton in 1984, which was clearly an attempt to assassinate Prime Minister Margaret Thatcher and members of her cabinet. Few would dispute this as an act of terrorism. Assassinations in general are very difficult to place between crime and terrorism. Schmid (2000) claims they are not true acts of terrorism, whereas others propose they be placed along a continuum representing degrees of typicality between homicide and terrorism (Scholes and Wilson 2008).

In between the actual victims and the targets for change there is usually another audience: the general public whose fear of potential victimisation will act as the catalyst for change. Is it the case, then, that terrorism is an act that aims to cause change whereas a crime does not? What then of crimes committed by protestors for various causes, from the non-violent but criminal damage of eco protestors through to deliberate deaths caused by letter bombs directed towards scientists or medical practitioners? Here we have some interesting intermediate cases, where definitions of terrorism become blurred by the severity of the act and, again, sympathy for the cause.

Aside from definitional issues, terrorism research has not examined the selection of victims in any depth and this is an area that could benefit from a forensic psychological perspective. Horgan's (2005) definitional distinction effectively means that for terrorists, the selection of victims is neither 'personal', nor representative of a private dispute with the victim. Yet it is often reported that personal motivations are important in terrorism; certainly, seeking retribution for, and avenging the death of, loved ones is cited among the motivators for terrorist involvement (e.g. Akhmedova and Speckhart 2006). On the other hand, of course, not all crime is 'personal' either. Most typologies of crime involve both expressive emotion-driven variants alongside purely instrumental ones (e.g. Canter 1994). To demonstrate, an arson attack on an enemy's house is personal and expressive, while burning down your own store for the insurance money is instrumental. Assaulting someone in a street robbery who refuses to hand over their money is instrumental; beating up someone who is sleeping with your wife is personal. The complicating issue is that the personal can become political and the political can become personal. So it is possible that both crime and terrorism contain elements of the expressive and instrumental. Here then forensic psychology could be very helpful in understanding terrorist behaviour.

Rational choice

Rational choice models of crime are particularly relevant in understanding what motivates terrorist action. Like studies of criminal behaviour, the 'rational actor' has also been a theme for terrorism research, although it was met with some hostility in earlier days (Enders and Sandler 2006). Although mental disorder has been dismissed as a way of understanding terrorism (discussed later), the 'irrationality debate' has re-emerged in association with the religious fundamentalism typified by some as 'new terrorism'. Proponents of new terrorism claim that terrorist activity has substantially changed over the past decade or so, and that the phenomenon is characterised by different motivations, diverse organisational structures, and larger-scale, more destructive acts (see Crenshaw 2006 for a review). Crenshaw (2006) concludes, however, that motivations have not changed and that it is not necessary to throw away our old knowledge in favour of the new.

It is true that there have been some large-scale mass casualty incidents recently but do they signify a genuine change in strategy? Here is a public debate forensic psychologists are familiar with – for example, are there more child molesters today than in our parents' time, or do we just hear about them more? It would appear that injuries and deaths per terrorist incident have indeed increased over time, but they seem to be related to the increased ease in manufacturing explosives and the prevalence of suicide bombings. Ackerman and Asal (forthcoming) are currently conducting empirical work on what distinguishes mass casualty terrorism from other forms. This research may help identify whether there are any systematic differences that justify a new classification and go beyond stating that incidents are becoming more lethal.

In terrorism research, a large proportion of the rationality theories have been developed and tested by economists, but there is a clear overlap here with forensic psychology. Take, for example, Routine Activity Theory, which states that crimes can only take place where there is (a) a motivated offender, (b) the absence of a capable guardian and (c) a suitable target (Cohen and Felson 1979), and further, that offenders only commit a crime if the balance of costs and benefits is in their favour (Cornish and Clarke 1986). In crimes such as burglary, this analysis is easy to illustrate, where burglars report their cost–benefit strategies, such as targeting a wealthy-looking, unoccupied house that is not overlooked by neighbours (see, for example, Bennett and Wright 1984). In Stevens' (1994) study of victim selection in predatory rape, 66 per cent of incarcerated offenders report having selected their victims on the basis that they were 'easy prey', that is, perceived to be vulnerable.

Similar perspectives have been argued in terrorism research. For example, hostage taking is a high-risk, high-cost strategy, the pay-off being media attention. Suicide bombs are more 'effective' in terms of loss of life but come at a cost to the organisation. Sandler and colleagues break down the costs and benefits of terrorist strategies and, using empirical data, demonstrate highly rational switches in terrorist behaviour, for example in response to target hardening (see Enders and Sandler 2006). In this respect we can see that civilian populations in shopping centres, for example, are 'easy prey' compared with personnel in military barracks. However, there is a further complication in cost–benefit analysis for terrorists which involves public reaction, and brings us back to the choice of victim. There is a catch-22 here for terrorists, as arbitrary civilian targets may be needed in order to cause fear and as the 'agents for change' discussed above, but attacks on such targets result in loss of sympathy for the cause, and it is well established that terrorism requires the support of the 'conflict community' (see for example McCauley and Moskalenko 2008).

At first glance, it might seem that these issues are just not relevant to forensic psychology. We do not typically judge crimes by the victim or the motivation, do we? Clearly we do; plenty of studies have shown that the CJS operates around some large disparities that relate to perceptions of the victim and the offender. Aspects of the victims' background do alter jurors' perceptions and consequently CJS outcomes (Wilson and Scholes 2009). We also intuitively account for motivations and are more lenient where there was lack of malicious intent (encapsulated in our manslaughter versus murder charges). So perhaps these issues are relevant and what we know from forensic psychology could productively be transferred into terrorism research.

Predictability and profiling

In the rational choice perspectives we see a congruence in approaches between the economists and the forensic psychologists in terrorism research. We both believe in predictability that can be demonstrated through empirical analysis. There are still some who question the rational actor model on the grounds that it cannot predict idiosyncratic responses. However, it certainly has to be the case that prediction based on probabilities is better than no prediction at all. Just like detectives benefiting from the prioritisation of suspects based on the most likely offender profiles for a crime (e.g. Canter 1994), those managing a terrorist hostage-taking incident can benefit from knowing the most likely outcomes of this type of incident in the past (Wilson 2000).

In the early days of forensic psychology, models identifying types of offender behaviour were developed as a precursor to 'offender profiling' (see for example Canter 1994). These analyses would typically identify groups of co-occurring behaviours that showed stability over large samples of data. A particularly stable finding from stranger rape serves as an example. Three broad behavioural styles exist in stranger rape, identifiable not as types of offender, but features of the offence. The drive for practical input to criminal investigation meant that the main focus of this finding would be whether there was a statistical relationship between the type of behaviour displayed and features of the offender's background, allowing prediction of who might be responsible. Forensic psychology then set about a (still ongoing) debate over whether statistical analysis or clinical experience had the most value in contributing to 'offender profiling'.

Ideas of profiling also emerged in early terrorism research and a number of 'profiling' style papers were published claiming to identify common factors in the backgrounds of various groups of terrorists. For example, Hubbard (1971) constructed a list of common features of skyjackers based on interviews with captured offenders that included items such as being protective of a younger sister and having a first sexual experience with an older woman. These types of studies have been extensively criticised on methodological and even 'moral' grounds, but purely on a practical basis, profiling terrorists has been widely dismissed (at least by academics) and as Victoroff (2006) states, 'to focus on capturing and killing terrorists is unlikely to eliminate the problem and, in many political circumstances, quite likely to be counter-productive. If a population supports terrorism, an inexhaustible supply of new terrorists will emerge' (Victoroff 2006: 8).

There is, however, agreement that terrorist actors are likely to be young and male, although such 'base line' characteristics are of little use to either the security services or the police in terms of profiling: all those involved in crime and violent offences are more likely to be male. In parallel to the forensic psychological literature, because of this base line, terrorism researchers have focused disproportionate interest on female activists. In forensic psychology, the rationale is that certain female offenders, such as sex offenders, have different treatment needs to male offenders. In terrorism research it is claimed that, in many cultures, women (e.g. as potential suicide bombers) can move about more freely and attract less attention from the security services. However, it seems likely that the attention given to female offenders in both arenas derives from the theory of 'double deviance' (Lloyd 1995).

Although the numbers of women receiving custodial sentences are increasing, it is indisputable that there are more male offenders in prison than females. Female offenders are considered unusual. Not only have they acted illegally, and as offenders have become 'deviants', but females are also perceived to have transgressed inherent gender roles, and have therefore become 'doubly deviant'. Double deviance theorists claim that this dual transgression of societal codes places female offenders at greater risk of public disapproval.

Comparably, in the terrorism literature, female terrorists are frequently perceived differently from their male counterparts. Female terrorists are often seen as subordinates acting under the influence of commanding males. Many women get involved in terrorism as a product of their relationships with particular men, but it is important to remember that male terrorists become involved through their relationships with other men as well. Alternatively, female terrorists are sometimes portrayed as suffering from a psychological 'syndrome', or mental instability in much the same way that early terrorism researchers perceived male terrorists (see, for example, Pearlstein 1991; de Cataldo Neuberger and Valentini 1996). There are therefore obvious parallels between the perception of the female terrorist in terrorism research and the female offender in traditional forensic psychology.

Crime, terrorism and mental disorder

The causes of crime have been a central interest in forensic psychology over the years, and a range of 'explanations' have been proposed and debated in the literature. Equally, the causes of terrorism have received similar attention, and the same range of explanations has been suggested for terrorist behaviours. Both fields have wrestled with the proportionate influence of biological and environmental factors, including the relative contributions made by mental disorders, personality traits, genetic predisposition, environmental influence, socio-economic status, education, goal-frustration, etc. Therefore, like crime, involvement in terrorism has generated a continuum of explanations from individual to societal level 'causes' which are interrelated. As far as poverty and lack of education are concerned, they do not *cause* terrorism, any more than they cause crime (Krueger and Maleckova 2006). Nonetheless, these stereotypes are pervasive in the public perception of terrorism as well as other violent crimes; take, for example, the way that the media express surprise when rapists, serial killers and bombers alike are found to be well educated or hold down professional jobs. Much of the reporting on the attempted bombings of London and Glasgow in 2007 focused on the fact that the men were 'doctors', and the television coverage of the attempted bombing of the US airliner on Christmas Day 2009 was broadcast from outside the suspect's prestigious central London apartment, highlighting his university education and that his father was a wealthy businessman.

As noted previously in this chapter, a great deal of early psychological research on terrorism was concerned with the individual qualities of the terrorists themselves. Many initial publications were dedicated to the pursuit of a mental diagnosis for 'the terrorist', in order to establish what kind of psychological disorder could account for their actions. But as discussed in relation to definitions of terrorism, it is only the perception of the legitimacy of the act that calls into question the person's motive. To illustrate, most people would not ask what sort of mental disorder characterises those who join the armed forces. Silke (2006b) points out that within many communities, recruits to 'terrorist' organisations are not seen as particularly peculiar or deviant, but instead the decision is perceived similarly to that of joining the military or law enforcement. Whilst the decision to join is not necessarily approved of, local communities can be 'sympathetic and understanding' (Silke 2006b: 50). Although the idea of a terrorist personality remains appealing to some academic researchers, and the mental disorder hypothesis thrives in the media, several authors have reviewed the available literature on the psychological make-up of individual terrorists (e.g. Crenshaw 1986; Horgan 2003; Silke 2003), only to conclude that there is little systematic evidence that terrorists are typically anything but 'normal'. Although the theory of the terrorist personality has been widely discredited, it is perhaps fair to say that no large-scale studies of captured terrorists using psychometric assessment have been conducted, or at least not published (Horgan 2003).

Forensic psychology has a similar problem, whereby the field deals frequently with crimes that the general public struggle to reach consistent conclusions about. Such 'inexplicable' crimes as child abuse, paedophilia, rape and homicide generate contradictory reactions. Often the public cannot reconcile whether the offender is mentally disturbed (after all, 'there must be something wrong with them') with the notion that if the offender is indeed mentally disordered, the case represents diminished responsibility and requires a sentence for treatment, rather than retribution.

Pathways into terrorism

If terrorist perpetrators are not mentally disordered, then we have to look to another area of forensic psychology to provide some clues to their actions. Borum (2004) claims that there are three distinct types of motivational force behind terrorist acts: perceived injustice, identity and the need for belonging. With respect to perceived injustice, Silke (2003) warns that, 'in the wrong circumstances most people could either come to support a terrorist group or possibly even consider joining one. If you, your loved ones and your community were discriminated against, persecuted by the authorities, intimidated, injured or killed, then terrorism may seem an appropriate and justified response' (Silke 2003: 51).

Here, Silke illustrates the difficulties in assessing the motivational drive behind terrorism when perceived from an isolated point of view. On the other hand, researchers who have first-hand experience interviewing terrorists have found that in many cases, issues concerning social identity and belonging account for young people's early involvement in terrorist organisations, often more than any genuine and sincere identification with the cause *per se* (see, for example, Alonso 2006 on recruits to ETA and the IRA). Theories of group processes in psychology, and their application in forensic psychology, may help to interpret recruitment in terrorist organisations. There is a large literature available in forensic psychology concerning gang membership, which is relevant to terrorism research.

Feinstein (2006) observes that belonging to a group is a natural part of transition into adulthood; benefits of gang membership include enjoyment, protection, status and power, as well as the excitement members find in violence. The 'adrenalin buzz' that Feinstein refers to can also be conceptualised as a propensity for risky behaviours. Ryan *et al.* (2007) found that substance use and inclination towards risk-seeking behaviours were directly associated with gang involvement. It is often cited that individuals become involved in gangs as a result of insecure identity and low self-esteem (Wang 1994).

There is also a strong influence of 'family' within gangs. It has been established that parental support can play a protective role against gang membership (e.g. Crosnoe *et al.* 2002). Indeed, it has been found that many members have no other family, therefore the gang provides the loyalty, recognition, understanding and emotional support that is otherwise lacking (Vigil 1988, cited in Rubel and Turner 2000). The influence of family and friends in recruitment and retention to terrorist organisations is also important. In terrorism research, McCauley and Moskalenko (2008) attribute the success of personal influence to 'love', a strong sense of affiliation or loyalty felt for close associates, that hooks many individuals into a terrorist movement. Therefore, both criminal offenders and terrorist actors evidence strong familial links in their 'pathways' into illegal behaviour.

What role can belonging and identity play for a suicide bomber? For communities involved in serious conflict, having a suicide bomber in the family can be seen as quite prestigious, given the absolute sacrifice for the cause. Posthumously, suicide terrorists may be seen as 'martyrs', and families of suicide terrorists in some groups even receive a 'death benefit' of financial compensation and other material advantages. As such, in terms of social identity, suicide terrorists become revered after death, and their families respected (see Hoffman 2006). Aside from the media stereotyping of 'brainwashing', and the promise of '72 virgins in paradise', most researchers who manage to interview actual and potential suicide terrorists and their families report more personal and practical motivations for choosing martyrdom. Suicide terrorists are frequently bereaved, often suffering losses of entire families through conflict (for example, see Akhmedova and Speckhart 2006 on Chechnya, and Ali 2008 on Iraq), and consequently seek to avenge the dead and ensure that any surviving relatives are financially supported. Direct parallels can be drawn here with forensic psychology in relation to those who have lost loved ones as a result of crime and subsequently seek retribution.

Although a gang-related perspective can account for involvement in terrorism, this must be considered against an alternative mechanism; the oft-cited influence of 'charismatic leaders'. Again, despite the media propagation of this hypothesis, there is no published empirical evidence that demonstrates how the qualities or personality of a leader can directly influence potential recruits to terrorism. Indeed, individuals are more often drawn into terrorism by the social influence of family and friends, as discussed above, than the authority or magnetism of any 'cult leader' (Crenshaw 2006). Nonetheless, if future research does reveal evidence for this type of conversion, then forensic psychological research in cult membership may be valuable. Numerous crimes have been committed in the name of cult affiliation: the Sarin gas attack that left 12 passengers dead and many injured was the work of the Tokyo cult 'Aum Shinrikyo'. Group psychology, conformity and identity surface again here in relation to years of sociological and psychological research into cults, but what is the influence of specific leaders? Meloy (1988) found that the leaders of cults, particularly violent ones, are often sadistic or sexual psychopaths; and superficiality, glibness and charm are established, enduring traits of the psychopath. Here, too, forensic psychological research on 'grooming' behaviours may be a productive area for further study.

Falling somewhere in between the psychology of gangs and the psychology of cults is an area that is currently receiving a considerable amount of attention both from the security services and from the academic community. 'Radicalisation' is conceived of as the process by which people, groups or whole communities move from support for a cause through to engaging in violent terrorist action. It has been modelled in the form of a pyramid (or in earlier days, a 'wedding cake') representing the smaller number of people at each level who engage in increasingly active support for a cause. McCauley and Moskalenko (2008) set out the potential psychological mechanisms of radicalisation including individual and group influences along with processes affecting people en masse. It is frequently reported that involvement in terrorism is a gradual process through which people become increasingly engaged over time, and the pyramid can be seen as a stage theory, through which a person moves 'upwards' until they become an activist. However, in order not to imply a stage theory, and in recognition of the possibility of 'sudden conversions', McCauley has recently advocated gradations through the pyramid and a central core of extremist violence (modelled as a 'volcano') that represents a route to violent action at any point (McCauley 2008). As discussed above, while acknowledging the possibility of 'charismatic leaders' influencing previously non-radical individuals to engage in terrorism, it is thought this form of 'short cut' through the pyramid is rare.

It is now the task for psychologists to establish what does happen and, importantly, under which circumstances. Meanwhile other researchers are concerned with measuring radicalisation and devising de-radicalisation programmes. Here forensic psychology can contribute an extensive literature on desistence, commonly referred to as 'What Works' (after McGuire 1985).

Fear of crime and fear of terrorism

The majority of considered definitions of terrorism incorporate not only actual acts of violence, but the *threat* of violence as well. This definitional nuance accounts for the express intention of terrorism to instil fear in a target audience as the mechanism for political change, discussed above. Fear, however, is not similarly central to most other crimes, and the majority of personally motivated crimes are not driven by a desire to terrorise. Nonetheless, non-terrorist crimes *do* cause fear, and a large literature has been dedicated to this phenomenon.

Despite the wealth of research on fear of crime in forensic psychology, it remains a complex and contentious concept. There has been an interest in the influence of individual differences in the experience of fear, and studies have suggested that women and the elderly are most likely to have elevated fear of crime, in contrast to their actual likelihood of victimisation (e.g. Rountree and Land 1996). This is known as the victim–fear paradox, as research reveals that young males are actually most at risk of crime in general. The tendency for some individuals to feel at risk more than others should not apply in the same way in terrorism. Instead, terrorism relies on the indiscriminate proliferation of fear, as it is essential that everyone in the target audience feels as if they are a potential victim. Nonetheless, it is clear that some people do react to terrorism with more fear than others (Gray and Wilson 2009). Studies of responses to terrorism in general, as well as people's reactions to specific terrorist events, might benefit from further psychological analysis of the consequences of terrorist acts, that extend beyond risk perception and have implications for travel behaviour as well as more 'mundane' activities such as shopping and leisure pursuits.

The role of the media

The media can have a significant effect on perceptions of both crime and terrorism, and we have already noted that some media sources tend to perpetuate certain stereotypes. Even more seriously, it has been suggested that the media has played a role in promoting both crime and terrorism as, periodically, television, film and video games are held responsible for inspiring specific violent crimes, as well as adversely influencing general levels of violence. Research on the effects of TV violence has a long history and there is an extensive literature with compelling evidence both for and against transference to real life. Regardless of whether or not crime in the visual media negatively influences behaviour generally, some studies have suggested that individuals can, and do, 'borrow' ideas from media sources. Surette (2002), for example, reports that over a quarter of his sample of serious and violent juvenile offenders actually attempted to commit a crime they had 'seen, read or heard about in the media'.

Such a process of modelling and imitation might be able to account for the 'contagion effect' of some crimes that receive a lot of media attention (Felson 1996). Indeed, crimes that receive a lot of publicity, such as airline hijackings, civil disorders, bombings and political kidnapping, can occur in spates, which may suggest that 'copycats' learn and reproduce behaviours (Felson 1996). Similarly, specific terrorism research has identified certain 'contagion' effects that may occur as a result of media influence, including the repeat of successful tactical approaches by organisations, as well as tactical imitation by others (Hayes 1982; Oots 1986).

From terrorism research, it is evident that perpetrators learn in a variety of ways, including from each other (Silke 2003). However, it is questionable whether highly publicised crimes like hijackings and bombings genuinely occur in waves, or if these 'spates' of attacks are actually products of developing media interest. For example, Fishman (1978) illustrated how 'crime waves' might actually be fallacies constructed by the media, and are sometimes not evidenced in, or even implied by, crime statistics. He found that the start of the 1976 'crime wave' against the elderly in New York City began with the reporting of a double homicide of two elderly sisters, the murder and rape of an elderly woman and the release of a juvenile who assaulted a senior citizen. The media created a theme of 'crimes against the elderly', and media reports increased, despite the fact that homicides against the elderly had decreased by 19 per cent from the previous year.

Investigation into various aspects of the media has proved popular for terrorism researchers in recent years. Unlike other types of crime, terrorism has an additional, unique relationship with the media; a number of academics have suggested that without media coverage terrorism could not function at all. If acts of terrorism were not reported, it would be impossible for terrorists to reach a wider audience in order to instil fear and communicate demands, thereby failing to influence potential victims as required. As such, some authors have suggested that the media actually works to encourage and even facilitate terrorism (see Martin 1985).

Conclusions

This chapter has provided an overview of how some of the major areas in forensic psychology relate to those in terrorism research. Forensic psychology is often observed to draw influence and knowledge from a wide range of disciplines, including psychology, criminology, sociology and law. Terrorism research has developed as a truly interdisciplinary field, benefiting from academic input from a diverse set of arenas such as political science, psychology and economics. Although each field has developed independently over the years, we have seen some considerable overlap in ideas and research. Due to the multidisciplinary nature of terrorism research, it might be difficult to distinguish expressly psychological contributions, although this chapter has identified the parallels that exist between current forensic psychological theory and the concepts that are important in the terrorism literature.

We have illustrated that there are indeed similarities, where principles of forensic psychology can be, and have been, applied to terrorist actions. Such wide applicability suggests that terrorists probably do share some similar characteristics with the 'average' offender, for example in terms of mental stability (as opposed to mental instability) and demographic attributes such as gender and age.

We have seen, however, that there are some important differences between 'terrorists' and the 'average offender'. Crucially, terrorists strive for a distinctive set of goals, and utilise fear through means of threats and violence in order to achieve these aims. Although perpetrators of non-terrorist crimes might be equally goal-oriented and rational, they generally seek personal, individual benefits rather than political change at a societal level. The motivations and mechanisms for terrorism are therefore qualitatively different from those of other crimes that forensic psychology addresses. Perhaps then, the most useful way to perceive the terrorist actor is as an offender of a conceptually and qualitatively different nature. It is important then, to ask questions about terrorism that are influenced by questions in forensic psychology, but to apply them with caution and the recognition that the solutions to terrorism are different from the solutions to crime.

This review has also demonstrated that terrorism research itself is now at a stage in its development where it can provide reciprocal knowledge to forensic psychology. Despite the differences between terrorists and other criminal offenders, the process of comparing compatible disciplines alone can help establish gaps in the research in either field, and can offer initial ideas or starting points from which to explore untouched areas. Although forensic psychology and terrorism research are established fields in their own right, they draw from many different disciplines and, as such, can offer novel perspectives on each other that may previously have been missed.

References

Ackerman, G. and Asal, V. (forthcoming) *Understanding and Combating Mass Casualty Terrorism.* National Consortium for the Study of Terrorism and Responses to Terrorism, University of Maryland, USA.

Akhmedova, K. and Speckhart, A. (2006) 'A multi-causal analysis of the genesis of suicide terrorism', in J. Victoroff (ed.) (2006) *Tangled Roots: Social and Psychological Factors in the Genesis of Terrorism.* Oxford: IOS Press.

Ali, F. (2008) 'From Mothers to Martyrs'. Paper presented at the 31st Annual Scientific Meeting of the International Society of Political Psychology, Paris, 9–12 July 2008.

Alonso, R. (2006) 'Individual motivations for joining terrorist organizations: a comparative qualitative study on members of ETA and IRA', in J. Victoroff (ed.) (2006) *Tangled Roots: Social and Psychological Factors in the Genesis of Terrorism.* Oxford: IOS Press.

Bennett, T. and Wright, R. (1984) *Burglars and Burglary*. Aldershot: Gower.

Borum, R. (2004) *Psychology of Terrorism.* Tampa FL: University of South Florida.

Canter, D. (1994) *Criminal Shadows*. London: Harper Collins.

Cohen, L.E. and Felson, M. (1979) 'Social change and crime rate trends: a routine activity approach', *American Sociological Review*, 44: 588–608.

Cornish, D.B. and Clarke, R.V. (eds) (1986) *The Reasoning Criminal: Rational Choice Perspectives on Offending*. New York: Springer.

Crenshaw, M., (1986) 'The psychology of political terrorism', in M.G. Hermann (ed.), *Political Psychology: Contemporary Problems and Issues*. (pp. 379–413). London: Jossey-Bass.

Crenshaw, M. (2000) 'The psychology of terrorism: An agenda for the 21st century', *Political Psychology*, 21 (2): 405–20.

Crenshaw, M. (2006) 'Have motivations for terrorism changed?', in J. Victoroff, (ed.) (2006) *Tangled Roots: Social and Psychological Factors in the Genesis of Terrorism.* Oxford: IOS Press.

Crosnoe, R., Erickson, K.G. and Dornbusch, S.M. (2002) 'Protective functions of family relationships and school factors on the deviant behavior of adolescent boys and girls: reducing the impact of risky friendships', *Youth and Society*, 33: 515–44.

de Cataldo Neuberger, L. and Valentini, T. (1996) *Women and Terrorism.* New York: St Martin's.

Enders, W. and Sandler, T. (2006) *The Political Economy of Terrorism.* Cambridge: Cambridge: University Press.

Feinstein, J. (2006) *Working with Gangs and Young People: A Toolkit for Resolving Group Conflict.* London: Jessica Kingsley Publishers.

Felson, R.B. (1996) 'Mass media effects on violent behavior', *Annual Review of Sociology*, 22: 103–28.

Fishman, M. (1978) 'Crime waves as ideology', *Social Problems*, 25: 531–43.

Gray, J.M. and Wilson, M.A. (2009) 'The relative risk perception of travel hazards', *Environment and Behavior*, 41 (2): 185–204.

Hayes, R.E. (1982) *The Impact of Government Activity on the Frequency, Type and Targets of Terrorist Group Activity.* McLean, VA: Defense Systems, Inc.

Heskin, K. (1985) 'Political violence in Northern Ireland', *Journal of Psychology*, 119 (5): 481–94.

Hoffman, B. (2006) *Inside Terrorism: Revised and Expanded Edition.* New York: Columbia University Press.

Horgan, J. (2003) 'The search for the terrorist personality', in A. Silke (ed.), *Terrorists, Victims and Society: Psychological Perspectives on Terrorism and its Consequences.* London: John Wiley and Sons Ltd.

Horgan, J. (2005) *The Psychology of Terrorism.* New York: Routledge.

Hubbard, D.G. (1971) *The Skyjacker: His Flights of Fancy*. New York: Macmillan.

Krueger, A.B., and Maleckova, J. (2006) 'Education, poverty and terrorism: Is there a causal connection?', *Journal of Economic Perspectives*, 17: 119–44.

Lloyd, A. (2005) *Doubly Deviant, Doubly Damned: Society's Treatment of Violent Women.* London: Penguin.

Martin, L.J. (1985) 'The media's role in international terrorism', *Terrorism: An International Journal*, 8 (2): 127–46.

McCauley, C. (2008) 'Models and Measures of Political Radicalization'. Paper presented at the 31st Annual Scientific Meeting of the International Society of Political Psychology, Paris, 9–12 July 2008.

McCauley, C., and Moskalenko, S. (2008) 'Mechanisms of political radicalization: pathways toward terrorism', *Terrorism and Political Violence*, 20: 415–33.

McGuire, J. (1985) *What Works: Reducing Reoffending: Guidelines from Research and Practice*. Chichester: John Wiley and Sons.

Meloy, J.R. (1988) *The Psychopathic Mind: Origins, Dynamics, and Treatment.* Northvale, NJ: Aronson.

Mickolus, E.F. (1987) 'Comment – Terrorists, governments, and numbers: Counting things versus things that count', *Journal of Conflict Resolution,* 31 (1): 54–62.

Oots, K.L. (1986) *A Political Organisation Approach to Transnational Terrorism.* Westport, CT: Greenwood Press.

Pearlstein, R.M. (1991) *The Mind of the Political Terrorist.* Wilmington, DE: Scholarly Resources Inc.

Rountree, P.W. and Land, K.C. (1996) 'Perceived risk versus fear of crime: empirical evidence of conceptually distinct reactions in survey data', *Social Forces,* 74 (4): 1353–76.

Rubel, N.M. and Turner, W.L. (2000) 'A systematic analysis of the dynamics and organization of urban street gangs', *American Journal of Family Therapy,* 28: 117–32.

Ryan, L.G., Miller-Loessi, K.M. and Nieri, T. (2007) 'Relationships with adults as predictors of substance use, gang involvement, and threats to safety among disadvantaged urban high-school adolescents', *Journal of Community Psychology,* 35 (8): 1053–71.

Schmid, A.P. (1993) 'Defining terrorism: the response problem as a definition problem', in A.P. Schmid and R.D. Crelinsten (eds), *Western Responses to Terrorism.* London: Frank Cass.

Schmid, A.P. (2000) 'Terrorism and the use of weapons of mass destruction: from where the risk?', (2000) in M. Taylor and J. Horgan (eds) (2000) *The Future of Terrorism.* London: Frank Cass.

Schmid, A. and Jongman, A. (1988) *Political Terrorism: A New Guide to Actors, Authors, Concepts, Data Bases, Theories and Literature.* New Brunswick, NJ: Transaction Books.

Scholes, A. and Wilson, M. (2008) 'Defining political assassinations: how are they different from other homicides?', *European Association of Psychology and Law,* Maastricht, The Netherlands.

Silke, A. (2006a) 'The role of suicide in politics, conflict, and terrorism', *Terrorism and Political Violence,* 18 (1): 35–46.

Silke, A. (2006b) 'Becoming a terrorist', in A. Silke (ed.), *Terrorists, Victims and Society* (2nd edn). Chichester: Wiley.

Silke, A. (2003) *Terrorists, Victims and Society: Psychological Perspectives on Terrorism and its Consequences.* London: John Wiley and Sons Ltd.

Stevens, D. (1994) 'Predatory rapists and victim selection techniques', *Social Science Journal,* 31 (4): 421–33.

Surette, R. (2002) 'Self-reported copycat crime among a population of serious and violent juvenile offenders', *Crime and Delinquency,* 48 (1): 46–69.

Vigil, J.D. (1988) *Barrio Gangs.* Austin, TX: University of Texas Press.

Victoroff, J. (2006) 'Managing terror: the devilish traverse from a theory to a plan', in J. Victoroff (ed.) (2006) *Tangled Roots: Social and Psychological Factors in the Genesis of Terrorism.* Oxford: IOS Press.

Wang, A.Y. (1994) 'Pride and prejudice in high school gang members', *Adolescence*, 29 (114): 279–91.

Wilson, M.A. (2000) 'Toward a model of terrorist behavior in hostage-taking incidents', *Journal of Conflict Resolution*, 44: 403–24.

Wilson, M.A. and Smith, A. (1999) 'Roles and rules in terrorist hostage taking', in D. Canter and L. Alison (eds), *The Social Psychology of Crime: Groups, teams and networks*. Ashgate: Aldershot.

Wilson, M.A. (2003) 'The psychology of hostage-taking', in A. Silke (ed.), *Terrorists, Victims and Society* (2nd edn). Chichester: Wiley.

Wilson, M.A. and Scholes, A. (2009) 'The typical rape: factors affecting victims' decision to report', in T. Gannon and J. Wood (eds), *Public Opinion and Criminal Justice*. Cullompton: Willan Publishing.

Chapter 14

Aetiology of genocide

Agnieszka Golec de Zavala and Joanna R. Adler

> Evil that arises out of ordinary thinking and is committed by ordinary people is the norm, not the exception ... Great evil arises out of ordinary psychological processes. (Staub 1989: 126)

Genocide is one of a number of crimes against humanity. These are defined in international law as acts against people which degrade their human dignity. Such acts are tolerated or actively pursued by state authorities. Destexhe 1995 (quoted on the BBC website) says:

> Genocide is a crime on a different scale to all other crimes against humanity and implies an intention to completely exterminate the chosen group [...]. Genocide is therefore both the gravest and greatest of the crimes against humanity. (news.bbc.co.uk/1/hi/world/africa/3853157.stm)

In this chapter, we will first provide some historical and definitional context of genocide for the reader; we will then move on to discuss how psychology can be brought to bear in discussing such heinous state crimes. This chapter is a more in-depth consideration of matters we first considered in Adler and Golec de Zavala (2010).

Defining genocide

The systematic extinction of the Armenian population by the Turkish State lasted about five years, took a toll of around 1,500,000 deaths and met almost no reaction from the international community at that time. Twenty years later, in 1939, Adolf Hitler outlined his plans for the attack on Poland to the German High Command:

> our war aim does not consist in reaching certain lines, but in the physical destruction of the enemy. Accordingly, I have placed my death-head formations in readiness – for the present only in the East – with orders to them to send to death mercilessly and without compassion, men, women, and children of Polish derivation and language. Only thus shall we gain the living space [*lebensraum*] which we need. Who, after all, speaks today of the annihilation of the Armenians? (Berenbaum 2004; or see www.teachgenocide.org/background/hitler.htm, accessed December 2009)

The Turkish actions in Armenia are also thought to have inspired Hitler in his plans for the annihilation of European Jewry.

In an attempt to classify acts such as the systematic slaughter of the Armenians, Raphael Lemkin proposed the term 'genocide', built of a classical Greek word *genos* (race, tribe) and Latin word *cide* (killing). This term was coined to designate purposeful destruction of a nation or an ethnic group. In 1933, Lemkin proposed to the Legal Council of the League of Nations that genocide as a *crime of barbarity* should be treated as a crime against international law and prosecuted accordingly.

After the Second World War and during the Nuremberg trials, when 24 leading Nazi officials were charged with *crimes against humanity*, the word genocide was used in the indictment although only as a descriptive term. In 1948, the Convention on the Prevention and Punishment of the Crime of Genocide (Article II) defined genocide as

> any of the following acts committed with intent to destroy, in whole or in part, a national, ethnic, racial or religious group, as such: (a) Killing members of the group; (b) Causing serious bodily or mental harm to members of the group; (c) Deliberately inflicting on the group conditions of life calculated to bring about its physical destruction in whole or in part; (d) Imposing measures intended to prevent births within the group; (e) Forcibly transferring children of the group to another group.

The Convention came into effect in 1951 and established genocide as an international crime which the signatory nations should prevent and punish. However, the international law on the crime of genocide was not enforced until after the 'ethnic cleansing' in former Yugoslavia and the Rwandan genocide of 1994.

International law is difficult to uphold and the crime of genocide is not uncontroversial. Problems seem particularly to arise in relation to establishing genocidal intent ('intent to destroy') and in precise identification of those to charge. Popular outrage about mass killings and 'ethnic cleansing' are not sufficient. The international community may stand by unless, and until, it formally recognises such actions as a genocide. Only if that is possible are the signatories to the Convention obliged to intervene.

Thus, as we write this, many Zimbabweans are starving and suffering from preventable, life-threatening diseases; the death toll in Darfur has reached at least 400,000 and the complex situation in the Democratic Republic of Congo seems also to be outside the parameters of the Convention. Yet, there are historically recognised genocides including *Holodomor*, the orchestrated famine of the Ukraine in the 1930s;[1] the Khmer Rouge mass killings in Cambodia during the 1970s; the one hundred days of mass killings in Rwanda in 1994 and the ethnic cleansing in Bosnia–Herzegovina in the 1990s.

Part of the debate around genocide concerns the legal definition used within the Convention on the Prevention and Punishment of the Crime of Genocide. There, the focus is on physical aspects of genocide and is more narrow than the initial proposal from Lemkin (1944). Lemkin meant the term to include 'a coordinated plan of different actions aiming at the destruction of essential foundations of the life of national groups, with the aim of annihilating the groups themselves'. Therefore, genocidal actions should not be limited to mass killings but also 'disintegration of the political and social institutions, of culture, language, national feelings, religion, and the economic existence' of social groups. People become the victims of genocide because they are members of a social group, not because they possess certain individual characteristics. Similarly, Harff and Gurr (2003) define genocide as state-sanctioned deaths of people defined in terms of their 'communal characteristics, i.e., ethnicity, religion or nationality'.

In this chapter, we will consider genocide in this broader way; as we consider the aetiology and possible prevention of genocide drawing on applied psychology. We will discuss common socio-psychological processes that lie beyond genocides, framing them within the legal context. This discussion should help us to understand why it is difficult to attribute blame for collective crimes and determine genocidal intent.

Psychological explanations for genocide

The atrocities committed during genocides are purposeful, systematic and planned; they are cold-blooded, frequently repulsive and unbelievable. First reports of atrocities committed in the German concentration camps during the Second World War provided by the escaped prisoners were not deemed credible. In 1943, the information about people being gassed was first made public in the Netherlands yet it was rejected as war propaganda. This reaction could be related to Just World Theory which predicts that we need to believe in a just and predictable world in which bad things happen to bad people and people who do bad things are evil (Lerner and Simmons 1966). Genocide shatters the belief in a just and orderly world.

One of the first attempts to explain the participation in genocides like the Holocaust was the theory that looked at stable, individual characteristics of perpetrators. A number of scientists launched the search for a 'fascist mentality' (e.g. Adorno *et al.* 1950) or 'authoritarian character' (Fromm 1942): an individual mindset of obedience and propensity for evil. However, numerous studies since then have shown that genocides are not perpetrated by evil people with extraordinary characteristics. Rather, they have been carried out by quite different and ordinary individuals in extra-ordinary social circumstances that bear certain similarities (Staub 1989; Smith 2009; Zimbardo 2004). Thus, genocide should be seen as a societal product (Darley 1992), the result of an interaction of various social forces. Analysing the most important and common characteristics of different genocides may help us to understand the underlying social and psychological processes and possibly predict or help to work against future genocides.

Social conditions that make divisions between social groups salient

As a crime committed in the name of a group, genocide occurs when the social climate emphasises divisions between social groups. Such social climate is likely in times of increased feelings of insecurity and uncertainty, when people tend to turn to their groups for support and reassurance. Genocides occur also in times of rapid social change or economic hardship (Staub 1989). In such conditions, people tend to look for handy, simple (and rarely accurate) explanations of the worsening situation; explanations that would make their world orderly and predictable again. Such simplistic explanations tend to stigmatise one social group and designate it as guilty of the experienced hardship (Staub 1989). Usually, the choice of the group is not accidental. Typically, there is long-lasting animosity towards this group and it is perceived as a threat. The experienced frustration is focused and vented in persecution of the stigmatised group. In other words, one social group is scapegoated. In Nazi Germany, pre-existing anti-Semitism was fanned and enflamed during the economic crisis of the 1920s and 1930s. In Turkey, Armenians were characterised as economic threats to Turks when the state institutions failed during 1915. Blaming another group for the causes of sacrifice and suffering endured by members of an in-group is cognitively and emotionally easier and more beneficial for cohesiveness and mobilisation of that in-group than understanding complex social, historical and economic processes that lead to that suffering.

Genocides occur also in the context of intractable inter-group conflicts or long-term, institutionalised discrimination (Coleman 2003; Staub and Bar-Tal 2003). The sources of inter-group conflicts can lie in competition for scarce resources including, for example, land or distribution of privileges and goods. In this situation, genocides are committed when one group aims at taking possession of resources belonging to another group by physically eliminating the former proprietors. In Rwanda, for example, tribal delineations reinforced by colonial powers and a prolonged conflict over land and possessions resulted in a series of massacres and wars. In 1994, a predictable genocide took place. Preceded by racist propaganda and overt preparations for killings, the political elite used long-standing racial and economic divisions while the country suffered from the effects of drought, lack of trade and civil war (Human Rights Watch (HRW) 1999). Similarly, mass killings and deliberate attempts to wipe out competing ethnic groups in Bosnia–Herzegovina were perpetrated in the midst of the war as individual states competed for control of the former Yugoslavia in the first half of the 1990s.

The controversial resources can be also symbolic (e.g. values, beliefs, opinions) (Sherif 1966). Conflict may also result from frustrated basic human needs of one of the groups. When the basic human needs – such as feeling secure, justly treated, being in control of one's own fate, developing a positive identity or being autonomous but connected with others – are not satisfied in a constructive way, individuals and groups seek their satisfaction in destructive ways (Staub 1999; see also Burton 1987). The tangible origins of intractable conflicts or long-lasting prejudice are often unknown or lost. What matters is the division between social groups and spiralling inter-group animosity. The conflict is perceived as irreconcilable. The division between groups is central in individual and public lives (Staub and Bar-Tal 2003).

When social divisions are salient

According to Social Identity Theory (Tajfel and Turner 1986) and Social Categorization Theory (Turner *et al.* 1987), people function differently when they think about themselves and others as individuals than when they think about themselves and others as members of social groups. In social contexts that emphasise divisions between social categories, people tend to think about themselves and others as representatives of groups defined as 'us' versus 'them' (Sumner 1906; Tajfel and Turner 1986). Similarities between members of the own group (the in-group) and differences between the members of the own group and members of the other group (the out-group) are stressed (Deschamps and Doise 1978; Turner 1982). Individual characteristics that are shared with other members of the in-group are emphasised in the self-image (e.g. Biernat *et al.* 1996) and the own group is clearly favoured (Tajfel and Turner 1986). In-group favouritism is often (however, not always; see, for example, Brewer and Brown 1998) followed by out-group derogation (Tajfel and Turner 1986) and a tendency to ascribe less human features and emotions (infrahumanisation) to out-group's members (e.g. Haslam 2006; Leyens *et al.* 2000). As social divisions deepen and people become more threatened and protective of their group, their thoughts may become more emotionally charged. Understanding nuance and complexity of situations diminishes, giving way to dichotomous reasoning (Castano 2008; Golec 2002; Suedfeld and Tetlock 1977). Evil characteristics are ascribed to the out-group, it is treated as uniform (e.g. Castano *et al.* 2002), and the out-group members are perceived as similar to each other in representing all the evil features. Differences between groups are essentialised, i.e. treated as being rooted in the very nature of the members of the groups. The out-group is deeply devalued, seen as a threat to well-being or even continued existence of the in-group, and can be characterised as anything between an obstacle to achieving ideal and desirable social arrangements and a mortal enemy. As the collective understanding of the inter-group situation loses its complexity, the escalation begins: actions of one group against the other are reciprocated with more ferocity and it is extremely difficult to break this vicious exchange (e.g. Coleman *et al.* 2007).

Malicious group identifications

The tendency to differentiate between in-groups and out-groups (e.g. Turner 1982) and the tendency to identify with in-groups seem to be universal (Sidanius 1993). Yet, some forms of in-group attachment seem to be more malicious than others. However, the tendency to derogate other groups is not necessarily related to positive in-group identification. Early on, Adorno *et al.* (1950) distinguished between uncritical, aggressive and discriminatory pseudo-patriotism and critical attachment to national values, i.e. genuine patriotism. Later, Kosterman and Feshbach (1989) empirically differentiated between two forms of national attachment: competitive nationalism, i.e. the belief in the superiority of one's nation; and patriotism, i.e. positive attachment to the nation. In a similar vein, Schatz *et al.* (1999) describe uncritical, blind patriotism and open and mature constructive patriotism. Only the pseudo-patriotic, uncritical attachment to the nation and nationalism are related to discrimination of other groups and competitive or even hostile attitudes towards other nations.

Roccas *et al.* (2006) introduced a concept of in-group glorification: treating any social in-group as superior and more worthy than other groups that results in derogation of out-groups. Golec de Zavala *et al.* (2009) proposed the concept of narcissistic group identification or collective narcissism, i.e. an emotional investment in an unrealistic belief about the unparalleled greatness of an in-group. The belief in a grandiose image of an in-group is underlain by unacknowledged doubts about the group's greatness and a need for continual external validation. Narcissistic in-group attachment is related to a tendency to react with aggression to perceived lack of proper acknowledgement of the in-group by others (Golec de Zavala *et al.* 2009).

In sum, the more people uncritically identify with and idealise their in-group, the more they are likely to hate and hurt members of other groups without feeling guilty or even acknowledging the moral dimension of their actions. Those who identify with a group in such a malicious way are more likely to promulgate genocidal politics and acts (see Roccas *et al.* 2006; Castano 2008). Importantly, genocides are also likely to be perpetrated in a social climate that emphasises malicious forms of in-group identification through education, propaganda, social politics or norms (e.g. Staub 1989, 1999).

Malicious social contexts

In social contexts that promote malicious in-group identification and spread antagonism, prejudiced perception of a stigmatised group is strengthened by support of the social environment both among peers, and within social institutions (Staub and Bar-Tal 2003). Prejudiced perceptions justify discrimination and harm against members of the stigmatised group and related discriminatory behaviour. Prejudice, discrimination and dehumanisation of the out-group become normative. Such a societal climate enhances moral disengagement from wrongdoings against the out-group.

Bandura (1999) describes four ways in which people disengage from the moral significance of their actions: firstly, the perception of violent actions against members of a stigmatised group is altered and reinterpreted. For example, unlawful imprisonment of the innocent can be reconstructed as protection of the social order; killing other people, as duty. Such acts are ostensibly justified by widespread ideology and supported by the authority of social institutions, which give us the second way to disengage. Institutionalised discrimination is epitomised by the Nuremberg laws of 1935. These laws deprived German Jews of their citizenship, were based on pseudoscientific theories of racial superiority and facilitated the persecution of Jews in Hitler's Germany.

Another strategy of moral disengagement is minimising and misconstruction of the negative effects of the actions for the victims. Euphemistic labels are used to make such consequences abstract (e.g. 'casualties of war'). The plans to exterminate millions of European Jews in Nazi Germany were known as the 'final solution to the Jewish question'. One can also avoid judging the morality of one's own actions when individual responsibility is displaced to authority figures and dissolved between unidentified others who commit similar acts.

Finally, in order to alleviate the ethical gravity of committed atrocities and disengage feelings of guilt, perpetrators devalue, delegitimise and dehumanise the victims (e.g. Bar-Tal 1998). Thus, ironically, victims are blamed for their predicaments (see Brock and Buss 1962), which is often reinforced by the need to hold on to the belief in the just world (Lerner and Simmons 1966). Even bystanders are driven to look for flaws in victims, to account for violence that is committed against them, whether they know that the victim's condition was caused by someone else or not. In the documentary *Shoah,* the last Delegate of the Polish Government in Exile to occupied Poland describes his visits to Warsaw's ghetto. One of the most emotionally charged memories is his own involuntary tendency to think about victims, members of his own nation, now dirty, starving, naked, dying on the streets of the ghetto, as inhuman. 'They were not people,' he says and cries, helplessly acknowledging his automatic reactions to the observed horrors. This is the reaction of a bystander. How much stronger could this be in an active perpetrator?

For most people it is not easy to hurt or kill another human being. It is not something that decent people do. According to Cognitive Dissonance Theory (Festinger 1957), in order to save their self-esteem and reduce the dissonance stemming from the discrepancy between beliefs ('I am a decent person') and acts ('I am hurting another human being'), new beliefs are introduced that diminish the discrepancy. Thus, victims are treated as inhuman and deserving the degrading treatment. Victims are dehumanised, excluded from the human community. Infamously, one of the perpetrators of the My Lai Massacre in South Vietnam in 1968, where American soldiers killed an estimated 500 civilians, was quoted saying, 'I would say that most people in our company didn't consider the Vietnamese human' (http://news.bbc.co.uk/1/hi/world/asia-pacific/7298533.stm).

Bar-Tal (1998) describes several ways in which 'the other' can be dehumanised. One way is bestialisation, i.e. ascribing animal or demonic features to all the members of the stigmatised social group. In Rwanda, members of the Tutsi tribe were called 'cockroaches', the propaganda in Nazi Germany portrayed Jews as an 'inferior race'. Another way consists of attributing to all the members of the group, traits that are considered extremely negative and unacceptable. Another form of dehumanisation is comparing the stigmatised group to groups that are considered violators of pivotal social norms (e.g. murderers or terrorists). Yet another way is labelling the group by names of groups that traditionally serve as an example of negativity (e.g. Vandals, Nazis or Communists) (Bar-Tal 1998; Opotow and McClelland 2007).

The worse the treatment the stigmatised group meets, the deeper is its dehumanisation. Castano and Giner-Sorolla (2006) experimentally demonstrated that dehumanisation of the victims serves the role of psychological defence mechanism for the perpetrators. People who learn that their group committed atrocities against another group tend to see the victims as less likely to experience typical human emotions. And those who see victims as less human feel less collective guilt for perpetrated actions. The protective function of dehumanisation is best described by the survivor of concentration camps who notices: 'the degradation imposed on the prisoners was not a matter of cruelty, but a necessary process: for those operating the gas chambers not to be overwhelmed by distress, victims had to be reduced to sub-human object beforehand' (in Castano 2008). This mechanism leads to a vicious circle of increased violence because when the victim is seen as not human and deserving the cruel treatment further hatred and acts of cruelty seem necessary. Thus, atrocities once committed against a group bring new atrocities in the future. It was observed by Broder (1986, cited in Ray 1988), 'the Germans will never forgive us [the Jews] for Auschwitz'.

Social organisations

The sheer existence of inter-group conflict or even deepest prejudice *per se* is not likely to result in genocide. Mass killing requires efficient organisation of many people. The forces that help unify their actions include justifying ideology and organisations that socialise and 'train' individuals to be capable of autonomous, systematic, mass killings and of reproducing killing structures (Darley 1992). Social organisations and institutions spread the 'ideology of antagonism' (Staub 1989; see also Castano 2008) to justify stigmatising and discrimination of designated social groups. In Rwanda the government (composed predominantly of members of the Hutu people) spread negative propaganda against Tutsis. Pseudoscientific bases indicating genetic superiority of Hutu over Tutsi people were propagated just as they were in Nazi Germany before the Second World War. In 1938, Jaensch, a psychologist and a member of the Nazi party, published a book in which he described a genetic anti-type – liberal, eccentric unreliable and undesirable to the German pure race. The anti-type was represented by all unsupportive of the Nazi regime, Jews and 'Orientals'. Such pseudoscientific theories were central to Nazi discriminatory ideology and politics. Propaganda, 'the cognitive conditioning of hate' (Zimbardo 2004) is used on multiple levels, through multifarious social structures: schools, social institutions, families.

People's attitudes and beliefs are transformed by social processes. Individuals socialised to believe and act on an ideology of antagonism learn to commit atrocities against other human beings incrementally. They come to believe that the other can be hurt, is to be hurt and that they can inflict hurt themselves (e.g. Staub 1989, 1999; Zimbardo 2004). Each step brings small changes in beliefs, attitudes and world views that are mediated through the above-mentioned cognitive dissonance reduction processes: adjustment of beliefs and attitudes to actions for the sake of consistency (Festinger 1957). People also adjust their attitudes and preferences observing their own behaviour (Bem 1972). Through both processes, the attitudinal changes on an individual level make repeating and engaging in even more hostile actions more likely. The injustice, hostilities and atrocities become routine as individuals become habituated, desensitised and less emotionally involved in their perpetration. Discrimination against stigmatised groups is strengthened gradually, allowing collective dissonance reduction (Zimbardo 2004) and desensitising the whole society.

Organisations that prepare people to kill others do not require everybody to realise their goals with equal zeal. There are those who internalise the hostile ideology and believe that killing others is actually moral. These people would be individually more prone to prejudice (e.g. Adorno *et al*. 1950; Altemeyer 1988; Sidanius and Pratto 1999) and/or more exposed to the antagonistic ideology, like members of Hitlerjugend (Hitler Youth), a paramilitary organisation of the Nazi party in 1930s Germany. This organisation educated and prepared young German boys to fight for the Third Reich and exercise their anti-Semitic zeal from the age of 10. In battle, Hitlerjugend divisions consisting of teenagers had a reputation for particular cruelty and fanaticism (e.g. Hughes and Johnson 2004).

Others involved in genocides act on behalf of their group, not necessarily believing in the ideology devaluing the other, but believing that they protect the in-group. Many act through compliance, obedience and conformity. Testimonies of the My Lai Massacre (the so-called My Lai Tapes) mention soldiers who did not want to obey the order to kill Vietnamese civilians yet they did so, crying while firing bullets.[2] Drawing on the testimony of five rank-and-file Hutu killers from Rwanda, Smith (2009) demonstrates how clearly they believed that the Tutsis were their enemies and that they had to fight to save their own people as 'an act of liberation'.

In his testimony, Adolf Eichmann said that he regarded his work, organising and managing deportations and the extermination of European Jews, as a way of building his career. He did not particularly identify with Nazi ideals. He used his organisational skills to fulfil the orders of his superiors and did not reflect much on the moral meaning of his actions and their consequences. Hannah Arendt, in her book *Eichmann in Jerusalem* (1963), coins the phrase 'banality of evil' to emphasise that the worst crimes can be committed by ordinary people. Again, the testimonies cited by Smith (2009) show just how mundane the recruitment to genocide can be, and how previously law-abiding citizens can become brutal, machete- and club-wielding killers.

Genocide is more likely in societies of strong hierarchical structure where obedience to authority is highly valued and where there is no significant political opposition (e.g. Staub 1989). Obedience to orders provides an illusion that someone else takes the responsibility for the committed acts.[3] Milgram's (1974) experiments conducted in 18 variations with more than 1,000 participants demonstrated great human potential (on average, 65 per cent of participants following the 'orders' of the authority) for performing acts believed to seriously harm or kill another human being.

Finally, there are also bystanders who contribute to the possibility of genocide by inaction. Genocides can happen because of passive bystanders (individuals, groups or organisations) who do not protest when an ideology of antagonism prevails and genocidal politics are introduced. If they do not protest in the beginning of the process, they are unlikely to protest at its culmination, when the atrocities are committed. Inaction signifies support. It silences possible protest and defence for the victims. Inaction tells perpetrators that the acts can go unpunished or are implicitly approved. A new social norm is set: perpetrators, victims and bystanders learn that this is now an acceptable and soon, a normative behaviour for this social group. According to the process of informative social influence, in situations that can be seen as ambiguous and not clear (harming an individual or punishing a member of an 'evil' group), the behaviour of others is used as guidance (Sherif 1954). In the Milgram studies mentioned above, compliance dropped to 10 per cent when participants observed a peer refusing to administer the electric shock.

Performing the act

Triggering event

After societal and psychological preparations, the genocidal actions such as destruction of property, imprisonment, mass killings are triggered by mostly symbolic events, used as excuses. Usually, the triggers bring disproportional reactions. For example the assassination of Ernst von Rath, a junior diplomat of the German Embassy in Paris, was used as a trigger for Kristallnacht in November 1938 – the pogrom of German Jews that opened the systematic extermination of Jews in Germany (Gilbert 1987). In Rwanda, the assassination of the president, Juvenal Habyarimana, catalysed the genocide that started hours after his aeroplane was shot down and lasted for about three months (HRW 1999).

Deindividuation

As mentioned above, when an organisation kills, individual responsibility is psychologically diluted and diminished (Darley 1992). Bureaucratic organisation partials, fragmentises and routinises genocidal actions, deprives each particular act of its ethical meaning (Kelman and Hamilton 1989). But someone finally commits the killings. As we described above, individuals who commit the killings during genocides can use various methods to disengage from the moral meaning of their actions. Deindividuation is another psychological process that breaks the social (or even hereditary) limits and facilitates mass killings. Organised mass killings in genocidal contexts are usually committed in groups when individuals remain anonymous and unlikely to be recognised outside the events. People may act in crowds or execute a partial role in the process. When they feel deindividuated – deprived of their individuality and normal sense of self-control – they become more responsive to the goals and desires normative for the crowd or for the role they are performing (Zimbardo 1969, 2004). In both cases, they are more likely to perform more extreme acts than if they were acting alone. The very act of committing mass killings lessens the inhibitions and makes perpetration of further atrocities more likely. Those who commit them do not feel they were 'themselves' when perpetrating the acts (see Smith 2009).

Is prevention possible?

As we have already outlined, societal and psychological changes that lead to genocides take place gradually, generally through small increments. Where there is weak or no political opposition and no culture of critical social reflection, entire societies with their institutions, organisations and structures may slip into genocidal climate without acknowledging or overtly declaring their stance. However, the warning signs are there and can be noticed. Stanton (1996) summarised much of the material we have discussed here and more, in terms of his *8 Stages of Genocide*, stages that are used by Genocide Watch to create a list of countries at different levels of risk (or actual incidence) of genocide. There are a number of organisations set up to monitor, report, raise awareness and help to prevent genocide; these include: Genocide Watch (www.genocidewatch.org); Prevent Genocide International (www.preventgenocide.org); The United States Holocaust Memorial Museum (www.ushmm.org/conscience); Survivors' Rights International (www.survivorsrightsinternational.org) and the Aegis Trust (www.aegistrust.org). It cannot therefore be said that genocide is unpredictable, or unpreventable. Thus it is that Allbright and Cohen (2008) called on the then incoming American President Barack Obama to 'demonstrate at the outset of his presidency that preventing genocide is a national priority', arguing that: 'preventing genocide and mass atrocities is not an idealistic addition to our core foreign policy agenda. It is a moral and strategic imperative.'

Allbright and Cohen also point out the governmental difficulties and risks that have to be taken to challenge genocide while it is building up, but what about after the event? After genocide occurs, there are both national and international responses. Gacacas in Rwanda were set up as a society of about 10 million tried to bring to justice approximately 800,000 people alleged to have participated in the 1994 genocide. They fit into many restorative justice approaches yet they are limited in efficacy and bring with them their own issues of justice.[4] The International Criminal Tribunals for Rwanda and the former Yugoslavia are still bringing forward prosecutions, and hearing cases. The very complexity of the material that they are considering is one more reason why it may be difficult to establish how far the responsibility for genocidal acts goes. Debates over culpability can become mired in questions around who should be deemed the superior who orders the killings. Similarly, the Tribunals could not practically be expected to hear cases of the majority of rank-and-file killers – the person most likely to perform the genocidal acts. If heard at all, their cases rely on national responses.

When we hold perpetrators liable for their actions, should those who committed atrocities with zeal and involvement be treated in the same way as perpetrators who killed with tears in their eyes? Should people be charged for their acts if they believed them to be right, e.g. as sacrifice in the name of their social group, and were supported in this belief by their environment, society and legal system? As Haslam and Reicher (2008) put it: 'People do great wrong, not because they are unaware of what they are doing, but because they consider it to be right.' Ultimately the question becomes which actions should be prosecuted? Genocide is a collective, societal crime. It cannot happen without support of the state structures and institutions on all levels. These questions are often considered philosophical rather than legal or psychological. However, they mark the controversies around the law on genocide. If we forensic psychologists are really to say that we have a role in understanding and preventing criminal behaviour, then we have to have a role in understanding and preventing genocide, this most heinous of crimes with effects that reach forward across international boundaries and across generations.

Notes

1 *Holodomor* was pre Convention on the Prevention and Punishment of the Crime of Genocide, so the international community was not legally obliged to intervene.
2 www.trutv.com/library/crime/notorious_murders/mass/lai/there_6.html (accessed May 2008).
3 Under international law, the existence of illegal orders may be called in mitigation but cannot be used to excuse criminal responsibility of an individual who followed them.
4 e.g. www.hrw.org/en/news/2007/05/29/rwanda-gacaca-trial-condemns-activist-prison

References

Adler, J.R. and Golec de Zavala, A. (2010) 'Genocide', in J.M. Brown and E.A. Campbell (eds), *The Cambridge Handbook of Forensic Psychology*. Cambridge: Cambridge University Press, pp. 502–510.

Adorno, T.W., Frenkel-Brunswik, E., Levinson, D.J. and Sanford, R.N. (1950) *The Authoritarian Personality*. New York: Harper.

Allbright, M.K. and Cohen, W.S. (21 December 2008) 'Never again for real', *New York Times*.

Altemeyer, B. (1988) *Enemies of Freedom: Understanding Right-Wing Authoritarianism*. San Francisco: Jossey-Bass Publishers.

Bandura, A. (1999) 'Moral disengagement in the perpetration of inhumanities', *Personality and Social Psychology Review* [Special Issue on Evil and Violence], 3: 193–209.

Bar-Tal, D. (1998) 'The rocky road toward peace. Societal beliefs functional to intractable conflict in the Israel school textbooks', *Journal of Peace Research*, 35: 723–42.

Bem, D.J. (1972) 'Self-perception theory', in L. Berkowitz (ed.), *Advances in Experimental Social Psychology* (Vol. 6: 1–62). New York: Academic Press.

Berenbaum, M. (2004) 'Case study III: the Holocaust', in S. Totten (ed.), (2004) *Teaching About Genocide: Issues, Approaches and Resources.* Charlotte, NC: Information Age Publishing.

Biernat, M., Vescio, T.K. and Green, M.L. (1996) 'Selective self-stereotyping', *Journal of Personality and Social Psychology*, 71: 1194–1209.

Brewer, M.B. and Brown, R.J. (1998) 'Intergroup relations', in D.T. Gilbert, S.T. Fiske and G. Lindzey (Dir.), *The Handbook of Social Psychology*. New York: McGraw-Hill.

Brock, T.C. and Buss, A.H. (1962) 'Dissonance, aggression, and evaluation of pain', *Journal of Abnormal and Social Psychology*, 65: 197–202.

Burton, J.W. (1987) *Resolving Deep-rooted Conflict: A Handbook.* Lanham (Maryland) and London: University Press of America.

Castano, E. (2008) 'On the perils of glorifying the in-group: intergroup violence, in-group glorification, and moral disengagement', *Social and Personality Psychology Compass*, 2 (1): 154–70.

Castano, E. and Giner-Sorolla, R. (2006) 'Not quite human: infra-humanization as a response to collective responsibility for intergroup killing', *Journal of Personality and Social Psychology*, 90: 804–18.

Castano, E., Yzerbyt, V., Paladino, M. and Sacchi, R. (2002) 'I belong, therefore, I exist: ingroup identification, ingroup entitativity, and ingroup bias', *Personality and Social Psychology Bulletin*, 28: 135–43.

Coleman, P. (2003) 'Characteristics of protracted, intractable conflict: toward the development of a metaframework – I. Peace and conflict', *Journal of Peace Psychology*, 9: 1–37.

Coleman, P.T., Vallacher, R., Nowak, A. and L. Bui-Wrzosinska (2007). *Intractable Conflict as an Attractor: Presenting a Dynamical-Systems Approach to Conflict, Escalation, and Intractability.* Paper presented at the International Association for Conflict Management Meetings.

Darley, J. (1992) 'Social organization for the production of evil', *Psychological Inquiry*, 3: 199–217.

Deschamps, J.-C. and Doise, W. (1978) 'Crossed category memberships in intergroup relations', in H. Tajfel (ed.), *Differentiation Between Social Groups* (pp. 141–58). Cambridge: Cambridge University Press.

Destexe, A. (1995) *Rwanda and Genocide in the Twentieth Century*. New York: New York University Press.

Festinger, L. (1957) *A Theory of Cognitive Dissonance*. Stanford, CA: Stanford University Press.

Fromm, E. (1942) 'Character and the social process', Appendix to *Fear of Freedom*. Oxford: Routledge.

Gilbert, M. (1987) *The Holocaust: A History of the Jews during the Second World War*. Glasgow: Fontana/Collins.

Goldhagen, D.J. (1996) *Hitler's Willing Executioners: Ordinary Germans and the Holocaust*. New York: Knopf.

Golec, A. (2002) *Konflikt polityczny: myslenie i emocje* (Political conflict: Thinking and Feeling). Warszawa: Wydawnictwo Akademickie 'Dalog'.

Golec de Zavala, A., Cichocka, A., Eidelson, R. and Jayawickreme, N. (2009) 'Collective narcissism and its social consequences', *Journal of Personality and Social Psychology*, 97 (6): 1074–96.

Harff, B. and Gurr, T.R. (2003) *Ethnic Conflict in World Politics* (2nd edn). Jackson, TN: Westview Press.

Haslam, N. (2006) 'Dehumanization: an integrative review', *Personality and Social Psychology Review*, 10: 252–64.

Haslam, S.A. and Reicher, S.D. (2008) 'Questioning the banality of evil', *The Psychologist*, 21 (1): 16–19.

Hughes, M. and Johnson, G. (2004) *Fanaticism and Conflict in the Modern Age*. New York: Routledge.

Human Rights Watch (HRW) (1999) *Leave None to Tell the Story. Genocide in Rwanda*. www.hrw.org/reports/1999/rwanda/ (accessed 4 October 2006).

Jaensch, E.R. (1938) *Der Gegentypus. Psychologisch-anthropologische Grundlagen deutscher Kulturphilosophie, ausgehend von dem was wir überwinden wollen. (Zeitschrift für angewandte Psychologie und Charakterkunde)*. Leipzig: Barth.

Kelman, H.C. and Hamilton, V.L. (1989) *Crimes of Obedience: Toward a Social Psychology of Authority and Responsibility*. New Haven, CT: Yale University Press.

Kosterman, R. and Feshbach, S. (1989) 'Toward a measure of patriotic and nationalistic attitudes', *Political Psychology*, 10: 257–74.

Lemkin, R. (1933) *Les Actes Constituant un Danger Général (Interétatique) Considérés Comme Délits de Droit des Gens*. Paris: A. Pedone. Translated by J.T. Fussell as *Acts Constituting a General (Transnational) Danger Considered as Offences Against the Law of Nations*. www.preventGenocide.org/lemkin/madrid1933-english.htm (accessed 20 December 2007).

Lemkin, R. (1944) 'Chapter IX: Genocide a new term and new conception for destruction of nations', in *Axis Rule in Occupied Europe: Laws of Occupation – Analysis of Government – Proposals for Redress*. Washington, DC: Carnegie Endowment for International Peace.

Lerner, M.J. and Simmons, C.H. (1966) 'The observer's reaction to the 'innocent victim': compassion or rejection?', *Journal of Personality and Social Psychology*, 4: 203–10.

Leyens, J.Ph., Paladino, P.M., Rodriguez, R.T., Vaes, J., Demoulin, S., Rodriguez, A.P. and Gaunt, R. (2000) 'The emotional side of prejudice: the role of secondary emotions', *Personality and Social Psychology Review*, 4: 186–97.

Milgram, S. (1974) *Obedience to Authority; An Experimental View*. New York: Harper and Row.

Opotow, S. and McClelland, S.I. (2007) 'The intensification of hating: a theory', *Social Justice Research*, 20 (1): 68–97.

Ray, J.J. (1988) 'Racism and personal adjustment: testing the Bagley hypothesis in Germany and South Africa', *Personality and Individual Differences*, 9 (3): 685–86.

Roccas, S., Klar, Y. and Liviatan, I. (2006) 'The paradox of group-based guilt: modes of national identification, conflict vehemence, and reactions to the in-group's moral violations', *Journal of Personality and Social Psychology*, 91: 698–711.

Schatz, R.T., Staub, E. and Lavine, H. (1999) 'On the varieties of national attachment: blind versus constructive patriotism', *Political Psychology*, 20 (1): 151–74.

Sherif, M. (1954) 'Socio-cultural influences in small group research', *Sociology and Social Research*, 39: 1–10.

Sherif, M. (1966) *In Common Predicament: Social Psychology of Intergroup Conflict and Cooperation*. Boston: Houghton-Mifflin.

Sidanius, J. (1993) 'The psychology of group conflict and the dynamics of oppression: a social dominance perspective', in S. Iyengar and W. McGuire (eds), *Explorations in Political Psychology*. Durham, NC: Duke University Press.

Sidanius, J. and Pratto, F. (1999) *Social Dominance*. New York: Cambridge University Press.

Smith, S. (2009) 'Massacre at Murambi: the rank and file killers of genocide', in N. Loucks, S. Smith-Holt and J.R. Adler (eds), *Why We Kill: Understanding Violence Across Cultures and Disciplines*. Cullompton: Willan Publishing.

Stanton, G.H. (1996) 'The 8 stages of genocide: a briefing paper for the United States State Department [Electronic Version]. Retrieved 30 December, 2008 from www.genocidewatch.org/aboutgenocide/8stagesofgenocide.html.

Staub, E. (1989) *The Roots of Evil: The Origins of Genocide and Other Group Violence*. New York: Cambridge University Press.

Staub, E. (1999) 'The roots of evil: social conditions, culture, personality, and basic human needs', *Personality and Social Psychology Review*, 3: 179–92.

Staub, E. and Bar-Tal, D. (2003) 'Genocide, mass killing and intractable conflict: roots, evolution, prevention and reconciliation', in D.O. Sears, L. Huddy and R. Jervis (eds), *Oxford Handbook of Political Psychology* (pp. 710–51). New York: Oxford University Press.

Suedfeld, P. and Tetlock, P.E. (1977) 'Integrative complexity of communications in international crises', *Journal of Conflict Resolution*, 21: 169–84.

Sumner, W.G. (1906) *Folkways*. New York: Ginn.

Tajfel, H. and Turner, J.C. (1986) 'The social identity theory of intergroup behavior', in S. Worchel and W.G. Austin (eds), *Psychology of Intergroup Relations* (pp. 7–24). Chicago: Nelson-Hall Publishers.

Turner, J.C. (1982) 'Towards a cognitive redefinition of the social group', in H. Tajfel (ed.), *Social Identity and Intergroup Relations*. Cambridge: Cambridge University Press.

Turner, J.C., Hogg, M.A., Oakes, P.J., Reicher, S.D. and Wetherell, M. (1987) *Rediscovering the Social Group: A Self-categorization Theory*. Oxford: Basil Blackwell.

Zimbardo, P.G. (1969) 'The Human Choice: Individuation, reason and order versus deindividuation, impulse and chaos', *Nebraska Symposium on Motivation*, 17: 207–307.

Zimbardo, P. (2004) 'A situationist perspective on the psychology of evil: understanding how good people are transformed into perpetrators', in A. Miller (ed.), *The Social Psychology of Good and Evil: Understanding Our Capacity for Kindness and Cruelty*. New York: Guilford.

Section 4

Treatment as Intervention

In the opening chapter of this book, we highlighted the needs for forensic psychologists to maintain an ethical and professional stance when working with incarcerated individuals. This is particularly important when considering the treatment and criminogenic needs of offenders with histories of drug and alcohol misuse and for those offenders with a mental illness, learning difficulty or indeed personality disorder.

This fourth section of the book looks at treatment approaches and diversionary schemes in place for these disparate groups of offenders. In Chapter 15, Alex Lord revisits his own work and that of others to explore the management of those offenders deemed to be Dangerous and Severe Personality Disordered. In looking at the ethical and treatment challenges posed by this programme, Alex also shows just how successful interdisciplinary teams can be in tackling such difficult areas of work.

In another forensic mental health contribution, Lara Arsuffi takes us through ways to implement anger control programmes with forensic inpatient groups. Chapter 16 moves from consideration of the history of anger management programmes through discussion of appropriate management and treatment strategies with reference to the programme that she has designed and that is gradually being adopted. Lastly, in Chapter 17, Nicholas LeBoutillier and Beverly Love consider the impact of diversionary schemes and other interventions that have been introduced to tackle offenders whose criminal behaviours are associated with substance misuse. Their chapter shows how the interventions have evolved and draws on Home Office case studies and a variety of empirical studies to evaluate their impact and efficacy.

Chapter 15

Treatment of offenders classified as having Dangerous and Severe Personality Disorder

Alex Lord

Background

Prior to the introduction of the concept of 'Dangerous and Severe Personality Disorder' (DSPD) in 1999, forensic mental health practice in the UK was already using concepts of severity and dangerousness as the basis for detention in secure psychiatric hospitals. The International Classification of Diseases (World Health Organisation (WHO) 1992) defines personality disorder in a way that emphasises 'a severe disturbance' of the individual's character leading to persistent, pervasive and problematic behaviours. Dissocial/antisocial personality disorder includes very low frustration tolerance, 'disregard for social norms, rules and obligations' and a low threshold for aggression and violence (WHO 1992).

By the late 1990s, a political impetus had emerged for a review of the provision of services to individuals with marked personality disorders who were considered to pose a high risk of violent and sexual offending. It became increasingly apparent that a significant number of these individuals were being detained in prisons and forensic units. Singleton *et al.* (1998) found that 78 per cent of UK male remand prisoners had symptoms of personality disorder with 63 per cent possessing the antisocial subtype. This compares with an antisocial personality disorder rate of 2–3 per cent in the UK population as a whole (National Institute for Mental Health in England 2003).

The debate about treatment was initially driven by high-profile cases of recidivist offenders whose prison sentences had expired and who were deemed to be 'untreatable' under the 1983 Mental Health Act, making them ineligible for secure psychiatric treatment. Scepticism about the treatability of these offenders was fuelled by a few outcome studies suggesting that individuals rated highly on the Hare Psychopathy Checklist–Revised (PCL-R) may reoffend at higher rates than others, even when rated as having performed well in treatment (e.g. Seto and Barbaree 1999). Coid (1998) questioned whether the goal of detention with such individuals should be treatment, management or control. He argued that mental health practitioners may be best deployed in assessment, regime advice and staff support where custodial staff provide an 'ameliorating influence' through positive role modelling and boundaried treatment of those detained.

This chapter will consider the development of the DSPD concept, debates surrounding its assessment, treatment issues and the challenges posed to staff working in this area.

The development of DSPD

The UK Home Office and Department of Health published a White Paper entitled 'Reforming the Mental Health Act' (December 2000) aimed at including 'Dangerous and Severe Personality Disorder' (DSPD) within new legislation. Due to scepticism about treating it as a clinical disorder, DSPD became a 'working title' for an initiative with three core elements (Bell *et al.* 2003: 12):

1 a new legal framework to include provisions for managing those who pose a risk to others as a result of mental disorder – in this case a personality disorder;

2 development of new specialist services for those assessed as being dangerous and severely personality disordered (DSPD);

3 a research programme to build a sound evidence-base on which decisions on the further expansion of services will be based.

Reactions to these proposals within the psychiatric community were extremely mixed. On the one hand, there were early advocates for DSPD including Keitch (2003: 8) who stated:

> I discovered very quickly that this challenging and sometimes frustrating group had real mental health needs that had not

previously been addressed, often due to the lack of dedicated resources rather than lack of interest in, or disregard for, their needs ...'

In contrast, Gunn (2000) dismissed DSPD as a peculiarly English 'disease' that had been 'invented' by politicians. Haddock *et al.* (2001) found from a survey of forensic psychiatrists in the UK that the overwhelming majority (75 per cent) held negative opinions about DSPD, many with ethical concerns about using medical diagnoses as the basis for indefinite detention. Haddock *et al.* (2001) noted that some respondents even felt that co-operating with DSPD risked breaching their Hippocratic oath. Only 20 per cent of respondents were prepared to work in a DSPD service.

With respect to detaining high-risk offenders, emphasis subsequently shifted to new indeterminate sentences in the 2003 Criminal Justice Act rather than a more radical reform of the Mental Health Act (DSPD Programme 2005a). A greater consensus has emerged concerning the need to provide treatment for individuals with pronounced antisocial personality disorder traits who are repeatedly convicted of committing violent acts. Despite his reservations about using diagnosis to extend preventative detention, Gunn (2000) acknowledged that it would be wrong to divert government attention from a group of mentally disordered offenders who have traditionally failed to attract treatment resources.

DSPD selection criteria and assessment issues

The overwhelming majority of the 3,000–4,000 people estimated to meet the DSPD criteria are already in custody (Tyrer 2007). The long-term plan (DSPD Programme 2005a) for high-secure DSPD services is for there to be a total of 300 places with the following distribution across HM Prison Service and NHS: HMP Whitemoor (84 places); HMP Frankland (80 places); Broadmoor Hospital (70 beds); and Rampton Hospital (70 beds). The admission guidelines (DSPD Programme 2005a: 15) are as follows:

- a PCL-R [Hare Psychopathy Checklist – Revised] score of 30 or above (or the PCL-SV [Hare Psychopathy Checklist: Screening Version] equivalent); or
- a PCL-R score of 25–29 (or the PCL-SV equivalent) plus at least one DSM-IV [Diagnostic and Statistical Manual of the American

Psychiatric Association – Version IV] personality disorder diagnosis other than antisocial personality disorder; or

- two or more DSM-IV personality disorder diagnoses [other than antisocial personality disorder].

These criteria are described as being only guidelines for admission to DSPD services as the most important factor is linking the 'pathology' to the individual's offending behaviour. This functional link makes sense as it is conceivable that some individuals may have moderate levels of antisocial traits but a personality disorder subtype that has never been associated with violent behaviour. However, Aldhous (2007) quotes Coid as stating that there is 'no accepted way of establishing that link'. Inter-rater reliability is difficult to attain in case formulations linking risk and criminogenic needs (Ward *et al.* 2000). As elsewhere, it would be best improved by generating alternative hypotheses, triangulating evidence, using manualised procedures, being aware of judgement biases and linking the formulation to an evidence-based theory (Kuyken 2006).

While formulation may be improved by research on the relationship between specific personality disorders and offending behaviour (Alwin *et al.* 2006), personality disorder diagnosis is far from unproblematic (Tyrer *et al.* 2007). Noting that studies of personality disorder diagnosis often show low inter-rater and test-retest reliability, Tyrer *et al.* (2007) argue that personality is better understood in terms of dimensions that capture normal as well as pathological variations. This, they argue, is likely to have implications for therapy where the global description of a 'personality disorder' would be replaced by 'personality function' in which an individual possesses dimensions that are more or less adaptive across situations and over time.

Even when personality disorder is diagnosed, on DSPD, the decision whether to send an individual to a prison or hospital unit is decided on a 'case by case basis' (DSPD Programme 2005a). The DSPD Programme guide (2005a) states rather vaguely that a hospital disposal will reflect the presence of 'mental health treatment needs' (these are not specified) and, more controversially (on p. 10), when 'an individual is near the end of their sentence and is likely to require continued detention under mental health legislation in order to complete treatment'. It explains that, in practice, a hospital rather than prison DSPD referral should only be made in the first instance if the individual has less than 12 months to serve and that this should have been identified earlier in their sentence. It is already not uncommon for prisoners to be referred to secure psychiatric hospitals in the last few weeks of their sentence with often highly deleterious effects on their mood and subsequent engagement in treatment (Maden 2007). Non-compliance with assessment and treatment is regarded in the guide as a motivational treatment target but is not in itself grounds for refusing referral to a DSPD unit.

Assessing psychopathy in relation to DSPD

Maden (2007) contends that DSPD could not exist without a standardised and reliable diagnostic instrument such as the PCL-R. He argues that prior to the common usage of the PCL-R, the greatest problem in this area of forensic psychiatry had been attempting to diagnose antisocial personality disorder independently of criminal behaviour. The PCL-R is sufficiently codified and manualised for it to be usable in clinical practice and amenable to evaluative research.

Even though the PCL-R may be useful in forensic assessments, Cooke *et al.* (2007) argue that it does confound personality disorder and criminal behaviour. They suggest that psychopathy can be meaningfully understood in terms of three factors (interpersonal style, deficient affective experience and impulsive/ irresponsible behavioural style) where criminal behaviour is a second-order factor. In support of their argument, they note that Cleckley (who influenced Hare's original thinking concerning the PCL-R) did not regard antisocial behaviour as present in all cases, noting that when it was present, the more interesting question concerned the lack of a clear motivation for such behaviour. It will be interesting to see from future research on DSPD populations whether the full PCL-R or the three-factor derivation can be linked differentially to outcomes such as compliance with treatment and recidivism.

A practical challenge in using the PCL-R as part of DSPD assessments is how to produce fully reliable ratings on those who refuse to co-operate at all with the assessment process. While it is essential that PCL-R ratings are corroborated by file data, it is important not to rely on isolated entries and, wherever possible, traits such as glibness and shallow affect need to be assessed in interview by trained assessors (Hare 1998). Hare also notes that when the PCL-R is used in legal proceedings, there is a marked tendency for ratings by defence witnesses to be lower. While Hare recommends obtaining at least two independent PCL-R ratings and averaging if necessary, contrary expert testimony on PCL-R in adversarial legal reviews may militate against such a straightforward resolution.

Assessing risk in relation to DSPD

It was suggested earlier in this chapter that formulating a link between psychopathy, personality disorder and offending behaviour is far from unproblematic (Ward *et al.* 2000). The DSPD Programme guide (2005a) notes that risk of offending is assessed by a combination of structured judgement protocols concerning historical and dynamic risks (such as the Violence Risk Scale (VRS), Wong *et al.* 2007) and actuarial measures such as Static-99. The VRS includes six static risk variables and 20 dynamic variables that are rated in terms of need for treatment and readiness for treatment. While the VRS is based on interviews and rigorous observation, Wong *et al.* acknowledge that there are considerable reinforcements to 'talk the talk' and express a willingness to change.

Hart *et al.* (2007) note that, regardless of methodology, risk assessment is inherently unreliable in terms of its capacity to make concrete predictions about future violence. They contend that, rather than claiming to predict risk in statistical terms, structured protocols help to clarify judgements about the salience of particular risk factors and the imminence/ severity of likely outcomes in order to facilitate and prioritise decisions about case management.

Noting that actuarial risk assessment instruments often form a significant role in detainability and discharge decisions, Hart *et al.* (2007) argue that there are two potential problems with this procedure. Firstly, at the group level, the construction sample used to estimate risk might be unrepresentative of the population as a whole, particularly if it were to be used in a different societal or cultural context. Szmukler (2003) demonstrates that an actuarial risk assessment tool based on an average sensitivity of 0.52 would be wrong in 92 per cent of cases with a typically low base rate for violence of 5 per cent.

Secondly, the application of group-derived risk predictions to individual cases is highly unreliable. Knowing the rate of violence in a given sample may well be useful for estimating prevalence rates in a comparable group but it cannot be applied meaningfully to a randomly selected individual. Reviewing two popular actuarial instruments (the VRAG and Static-99), Hart *et al.* (2007) conclude that, in individual case estimates, variations are so great as to render them 'virtually meaningless'.

Szmukler (2003) raises a further concern surrounding the interpretation of any attempt to predict risk. Since no risk assessment procedure is perfect, there is a political and ethical question about what rate of false positive predictions is socially acceptable. This principle can be applied to DSPD which, in terms of its assessment procedures, has the potential to detain some people unnecessarily. Equally, DSPD assessments have the potential to produce false negatives in which dangerous offenders are either not detained at all or are discharged prematurely.

Szmukler argues that targeting risk assessments solely at people with a mental disorder violates the principle of fairness. While it is increasingly accepted that the mentally disordered and particularly those with personality disorder pose an elevated risk of violence (Hodgins 2007), many of these are not routinely violent. Equally, Szmukler argues that there are many dangerous individuals in society who might be detained 'in the public interest' who do not possess a mental disorder. It is arguably fairer to assess the risk of anyone behaving in a violent manner (particularly if they have done so in the past) and this may be the rationale for extending indefinite detention for recidivist violent offenders in the 2003 Criminal Justice Act.

In an attempt to explore the effectiveness of DSPD criteria and other risk-related measures, the Prisoner Cohort Study analysed 1,396 men serving determinate sentences for violent or sexual offences (Coid *et al.* 2007). Of their sample, about 15 per cent fulfilled the criteria for DSPD and they found that they were significantly more likely than others to reoffend violently after release. They also found an overlap in 70 per cent of cases between DSPD eligibility and qualifying for indeterminate sentencing under the 2003 Criminal Justice Act. This demonstrates that, even prior to their incorporation in risk formulations, the DSPD criteria (psychopathy and personality disorder) are useful means of identifying high-risk individuals who require targeted interventions.

Providing treatment to individuals meeting DSPD criteria

D'Silva *et al.* (2004) reviewed studies attempting to treat high PCL-R scorers and found that the evidence regarding treatment outcomes was inconclusive due to a lack of methodologically rigorous research. Hare (1998) argues that treatment outcomes with high PCL-R scorers have generally been inconclusive because, until recent years, there had been no attempt to divert such individuals from traditional therapeutic interventions into customised treatment programmes.

Hare (1998) suggests that programmes need to allow for the tendency of high PCL-R scorers to dissimulate and manipulate rather than depending on traditional attempts to increase victim empathy or distress about causing harm. Rather than appealing to the conscience of such individuals, it makes more sense to appeal to enlightened self-interest by controlling their impulses and developing pro-social strategies. Abracen *et al.* (2008) believe that particular attention should be paid to the exacerbating effects of sexual deviance and substance misuse when treating and evaluating outcomes with high PCL-R scorers.

The DSPD Programme guide (2005a) suggests that while treatment services may vary between DSPD units, they should adhere to the following common principles and goals:

- Focusing on offending behaviour by addressing criminogenic and mental health issues;
- Applying evidence-based treatment models that are open to evaluation;
- Providing flexible and individualised treatment plans that are regularly reviewed;
- Involving the client in producing transparent treatment plans with shared ownership of treatment outcomes.

Maden (2007) argues that, in terms of models of treatment, DSPD has been particularly influenced by the Violence Risk Programme (VRP). It is instructive to compare the phases of VRP (Wong *et al.* 2007) with those described in Livesley's (2005) framework for treating personality disorder in general (see Table 15.1).

There are striking similarities between the VRP and Livesley's (2005) treatment phases. In addition, Livesley places great emphasis on process strategies that encourage collaboration, consistency within treatment, strengthening the therapeutic alliance through validation and constantly maintaining the client's motivation to change. This is particularly important for personality-disordered offenders who need to receive a combination of preparatory work, support (including boundary management) and aftercare (Alwin *et al.* 2006).

Hogue *et al.* (2007) present an overview of the DSPD Unit at Rampton Hospital. As well as acknowledging the influence of Livesley's framework on treating personality disorder, the paper places great emphasis on individualised case formulation regarding

Table 15.1 A comparison of programmes for violence reduction and treatment of personality disorder

Wong *et al.*'s (2007) Violence reduction programme	Livesley's (2005) Framework for treating personality disorder
1. Engaging resistant or ambivalent clients in treatment with techniques such as motivational interviewing	1. Safety and Managing Crises – stabilising behaviour harmful to self and others 2. Containment – enabling engagement in therapy
2. Orientating clients towards change and action by acquiring the skills to restructure thoughts, feelings and behaviours associated with violence	3. Control and Regulation – teaching impulse control and self-management 4. Exploration and Change – cognitive therapy and schema change
3. Action and maintenance of change through skills generalisation and relapse prevention prior to community reintegration	5. Integration and Synthesis – practice and generalisation

treatment needs and risk-related behaviour. Their patients are encouraged to develop emotion regulation and distress tolerance skills (developed by Linehan 1993) to minimise therapy-interfering behaviours and programme dropout during the challenging process of schema change and modifying core beliefs. A central tenet of Hogue *et al.*'s (2007) approach is that everything possible should be done to prevent iatrogenic effects, i.e. the initial case formulation should review the individual's history of treatment responses, making predictions about potential adverse reactions with a plan to minimise deterioration such as harm to self and others.

Hogue *et al.* (2007) explain that their treatment interventions are offered through a process of gradually engaging their patients in working towards more productive and less risky 'good lives' (e.g. Ward and Stewart's (2003) concept of encouraging achievable goals for sexual offenders). Although it may be difficult to achieve in practice with high-risk, personality-disordered offenders, they aim to offer treatment in a safe 'motivational milieu', dealing with therapy-interfering behaviours and using what they term a 'non-threatening collaborative stance'. Within this treatment philosophy, they list specific treatment interventions including:

- an orientation group;
- coping skills work, insight/engagement work and Dialectical Behavior Therapy (Linehan 1993);
- 'men talking' group regarding masculinity and relationships;
- chromis programme (in conjunction with HM Prison Service) for high-risk violent offenders;
- sexual offending and healthy sexual functioning programmes;
- substance misuse programme;
- therapy for trauma (a common antecedent of personality disorder).

While it is too early for DSPD outcome studies, Wong *et al.* (2007) cite four evaluations of the VRP and similar programmes. Although not based on DSPD criteria, the studies suggest that personality-disordered offenders can make significant reductions in their dynamic risk factors, relative rates of violent recidivism and violent institutional misconduct. However, since 'treatment' in DSPD essentially focuses on risk reduction rather than fully ameliorating the underlying mental disorder, it may be difficult to define tangible outcomes that would reliably meet the admission criteria of less secure units (Duggan 2007).

Potential iatrogenic effects of treatment and responsivity issues

In group psychotherapy, it has been known for some time that the espoused benefits of therapy are not always borne out in practice (Nitsun 1996). Nitsun has observed that individuals may be reluctant to join therapy groups and, when they do, they sometimes become demoralised and frustrated, leading to destructive behaviour and dropping out that threatens the effectiveness and very existence of the group.

Jones (2007) presents a comprehensive critique of how interventions for personality-disordered offenders, like any form of medical treatment, have the potential to make patients worse as well as better. Such individuals may offend more after treatment because they resent being coerced into therapy and they have better victim access and detection avoidance skills. Their sadistic interests, if present, and alternative means of offending may be reinforced and they may develop social skills for faking empathy in treatment evaluations. He argues that, just as motivated clients learn to inoculate themselves against undesired outcomes such as stress and violence, unmotivated clients may use therapy to reinforce their antisocial beliefs, learning how to defend them and feeling emboldened by the fact that they have neither been detected nor modified.

Even motivated individuals who have 'failed' numerous interventions may start to feel stigmatised and betrayed, undermining their self-efficacy and confidence in treatment. This is perhaps the most relevant iatrogenic effect with a DSPD population because this process that Jones (2007) calls 'learned aversion to change' may actually undermine further engagement in treatment and reinforce maladaptive schemas, thereby increasing risk. Jones (2007) notes that personality-disordered offenders may respond in different ways to attempts to create dissonance in cognitive therapy. While some individuals use the emotional distress resulting from dissonant feedback to initiate change, personality-disordered offenders may be particularly prone to four negative outcomes:

1 Facile changes in beliefs, leading to over-malleable or shallow 'chameleon schema';
2 Emotion dissipation behaviour such as therapist-directed anger which prevents schema change and may be problematic in its own right;
3 Increased tolerance of dissonance becoming even more impervious to treatment;
4 Avoidance of new information and increased likelihood of using denial as a coping strategy.

Lord and Willmot (2004) found that denial in sexual offenders is not so much a stable trait as a situationally reinforced state, enabling some individuals to relinquish denial in contexts such as treatment programmes while simultaneously maintaining a degree of denial to protect self-esteem and avoid negative reinforcement with peers and significant others. Unlike treatment programmes that emphasise enhancing low self-esteem in offenders (e.g. Marshall *et al.* 1999), there is also a need to recognise the potential for maladaptively elevated self-esteem (i.e. narcissism) to cause 'threatened egotism' and subsequent violence when an insult is perceived (Bushman and Baumeister 1998).

Farr and Draycott (2007) note that motivating DSPD clients to make sustained changes in their offending behaviour is a challenging process because it ultimately depends on reorientating their internal goals. They argue that behaviour changes that are predominantly motivated by the coercive nature of incarceration are likely to be less stable and enduring than shifts in internal goals. Consequently, they have developed a 'Considering Change' 24-session cognitive-behavioural programme that aims to teach patients how to evaluate themselves accurately, to modify their cognitive distortions that justify remaining in denial and to manage expectations in order to minimise obstacles to sustained behaviour change. The programme is explicit about the likelihood of treatment resistance and relapse, regarding psychopathic traits as a potential strength in that patients are invited to seek novelty and a sense of control by acquiring skills to attain their goals and move towards their ideal self (or away from their feared self). While their preliminary evaluation indicated some shifts in attitudinal stages of change and reduced hopelessness, Farr and Draycott (2007) suggest that sustaining behaviour change requires follow-up motivational work as people with psychopathic traits may be less engaged (and more demotivated about maintaining change) once the novelty of change has subsided.

Thornton and Blud (2007) present a conceptual discussion of how traits within the four facets of PCL-R may interfere with or undermine treatment. Like Jones (2007), they hypothesise that high PCL-R scorers could be more likely to offend due to increasing social competence, modelling antisocial behaviours and manipulating therapists and risk assessments. Noting that treatment outcomes may be particularly poor for those who score highly on all four facets (particularly the interpersonal and affective facets), Thornton and Blud (2007) propose tailoring treatment in the following ways:

1 Not focusing on criminogenic needs that are unlikely to change reliably (such as victim empathy);
2 Targeting treatment-interfering behaviours;
3 Gaining collateral information for progress evaluations;
4 Training staff in boundary maintenance and manipulation avoidance;
5 Using more reliable assessment methods that are more behavioural and depend less on self-report;
6 Appealing to common motivations such as self-interest and control rather than altruistic or emotional values;
7 Linking pro-social behaviour to positive outcomes in treatment and avoiding rewarding antisocial behaviour;
8 Ensuring that antisocial behavioural lapses do not preclude treatment;

9 Considering variations in co-morbid deficits such as executive functioning and learning style;
10 Testing out learning and supporting relapses in antisocial behaviour through graded exposure to the community and gradual reduction of supervision.

Reducing supervision only gradually is consistent with Alwin *et al.*'s (2006) conclusion that 'aftercare' is essential for maintaining behavioural improvements in personality-disordered offenders. The NHS is currently piloting services (DSPD Programme 2005a) in medium-security, community and hostel provision in line with the National Institute for Mental Health in England (2003) recommendation that personality disorder should be 'no longer a diagnosis of exclusion'. There is also provision for a pilot of DSPD services for women in a prison-based unit although Logan (2003) has questioned whether violence risk assessment, psychopathy and personality disorder treatment are comparable in female offenders. Although not applying the full DSPD high-security admission criteria, these units share a similar philosophy with an emphasis on evaluated assessment and treatment with better integration of services around public protection and care pathways.

Potential effects of working on DSPD and relevant staff skills

The DSPD Programme guide recognises (2005a: 19–20) that some individuals are likely to be 'disruptive, difficult to manage and ... highly resistant to participating in therapeutic activity', noting that this is often linked to risk and should only lead to permanent removal from the unit 'in the most extreme cases'. While it encourages temporary removal and liaison with the central DSPD unit, it implicitly recognises that this state of affairs can have an impact on staff morale as the document also requires DSPD units to monitor staff sickness and turnover.

Lord (2003) argues that, if facilities managing personality-disordered individuals are not managed with particular attention to process issues and staff–patient dynamics, there is a great danger of a negative cycle emerging in which therapeutic engagement and therapeutic milieu become difficult to sustain. Trinder (1997) found that staff who work constantly with oppositional clients may become disillusioned and no longer believe that they can rehabilitate their clients, developing a form of 'learned helplessness'. Therapeutic staff may produce overly positive or negative reports on progress either to accelerate or hijack discharge in a process described as 'therapeutic nihilism' (Jones 1997). Some individuals with severe personality disorders are likely to exploit these doubts through acts of non-compliance or violence because they themselves may be ambivalent about their need for treatment. This, in turn, may lead to tensions between staff involved in therapeutic endeavours and those more concerned with security and control.

In such circumstances, Yalom's (1995) goals of therapeutic treatment such as altruism, the instillation of hope and interpersonal learning may be difficult to attain, both from the perspectives of patients and staff. This can lead to staff 'burnout' in which therapists and others experience emotional exhaustion and a reduced sense of personal accomplishment in their work (Maslach and Jackson 1981). Most relevant of all when attempting to treat personality-disordered offenders, Maslach and Jackson's (1981) model includes the notion of 'depersonalisation' in which therapists may experience negative or callous attitudes both to their clients and colleagues.

Carr-Walker *et al.* (2004) compared the attitudes of prison officers working in a DSPD prison unit with psychiatric nurses in a high-security hospital DSPD unit. They found that the prison officers were generally more positive towards individuals with personality disorder, expressing greater liking for them and more interest in working with them. In contrast, nurses tended to be more fearful, angry, frustrated and helpless, with less optimism regarding treatment of personality-disordered offenders. In their conclusion, Carr-Walker *et al.* (2004) speculate that this difference may have been influenced by the nature and degree of experience of working with personality-disordered offenders (the personality disorder label and specialist units may have been relatively new to most prison officers) as well as the culture of the respective organisations.

To date, there has been rather more research on the effects of working therapeutically with sexual offenders than working with personality-disordered offenders. However, these studies are arguably still relevant as Craissati *et al.* (2008) have shown that 37 per cent of their community sexual offender sample had personality disorder traits while Firestone *et al.* (1998) found a prevalence rate as high as 52 per cent in their inpatient sample. Clarke and Roger (2002) proposed a useful model of the staff impact of working with sexual offenders that emphasised an interaction of dispositional factors, such as age, experience and coping style, with dynamic variables such as health, stressful life events and perceived support. Shallow and Brown (2004) have argued that therapists have to reconcile a 'personal–professional dialectic' between their feelings about their clients and the challenge (and potential rewards) of engaging them in therapy. Clarke and Roger (2007) suggested that three key factors may shape the impact on staff of this type of work: negative reactivity to offenders; ruminative vulnerability; and organisational dissatisfaction. Ennis and Horne (2003) found in a study of sexual offender therapists that psychological distress did not correlate with total hours of client contact or therapeutic supervision but peer support acted as a significant protective factor.

Dollard and Winefield (1998) found that correctional officers who perceived themselves to be working in environments that were highly demanding and over which they felt they had little control were experiencing high levels of psychological distress. This level of distress tended to be even higher if the officers perceived themselves to be receiving low social support from colleagues and managers. In a study that replicated this finding amongst psychiatric nurses working in a secure hospital, Bonham (2003) found that perceived support at work was highly negatively correlated with psychological distress.

Lord (2003) reviewed literature from different traditions relevant to staff skills necessary for working with personality-disordered offenders. The papers reviewed included therapist skills related to cognitive-behavioural therapy (Beck and Freeman 1990; Freeman and Jackson 1998; Millon and Davis 2000), working with prisoners in therapeutic communities or secure units (Jones 1997; Losel 1998; McGurk and Fludger 1987), working with sexual offenders (Marshall *et al.* 1999) and competencies for psychiatric nurses (Sainsbury Centre 2001). Despite the diverse nature of this literature, there was a commonality of skills being proposed, perhaps reflecting the idiosyncratic challenge of managing and engaging in treatment of individuals with personality difficulties. The outcome is summarised in Table 15.2.

There is a need for further research into skills and coping strategies in staff working with personality-disordered offenders. However, it is evident that staff require specialist training and supervision as well as closer collaboration between forensic and general mental health services (Alwin *et al.* 2006). It is encouraging that the DSPD Programme guide (2005a) recognises the need for integrated, multidisciplinary teamwork, a management culture of 'trust and openness' and provision for all staff to have regular access to supervision and a staff support service. However, the attainment of these aspirations will need to be audited regularly on each unit.

Table 15.2 A summary of the core staff skills required in working with personality-disordered offenders

1. Realistic motivation and orientation to treatment
Being clear about one's motivation for undertaking this type of work and avoiding the extremes of wanting to 'cure' personality-disordered clients or presuming that these individuals will never change.

2. Emotional resilience/appropriate coping skills and styles
The ability to withstand the emotional reactions displayed and invoked by these individuals as well as having coping skills such as detachment and problem-solving, and eliciting emotional support rather than avoiding issues.

3. Self-insight/receptiveness to supervision and feedback
Awareness of one's beliefs, emotions and behaviour towards personality-disordered clients as well as an active willingness to seek feedback and make changes, if necessary.

4. Clear personal and interpersonal boundaries
An appreciation and application of personal/professional limits regarding issues such as disclosure and recognising/resisting attempted boundary violations by clients.

5. Conflict resolution and ability to challenge non-confrontationally
The ability to work with emotionally labile and, at times, confrontational individuals in a respectful, assertive and solution-focused manner that avoids 'win–lose' outcomes (in either direction).

6. Empathy and ability to build rapport
Perspective-taking and communicating understanding of the client's interpretation of and emotional reaction to a current or past situation while actively collaborating in helping the client to reformulate their thoughts and behaviours.

Conclusions

In this chapter it has become apparent that DSPD services are offering a range of treatment facilities and programmes that were previously not so readily available to personality-disordered offenders. Categorising individuals with DSPD poses the profound ethical and practical challenge of producing a reliable assessment of psychopathy and personality disorder and linking these to hypothesised risks of violence. While the prisoner cohort study has suggested that the DSPD criteria are targeting a significant proportion of high-risk offenders, it is possible that some of these are being detained longer than necessary, others are failing to be assessed and at least some treatment resources are being diverted from high-risk offenders who are not personality disordered.

Nonetheless, within DSPD, there is a growing body of knowledge concerning the criminogenic and clinical needs of this surprisingly poorly understood and under-researched group of offenders. There is an emerging consensus that particular attention must be paid to individualised formulation of risk and need leading to the provision of responsive, boundaried treatment with case-by-case planning to improve motivation, boundary management and generalisation of pro-social skills. In parallel, there is a growing realism about the risk of iatrogenic effects caused by learned aversion to treatment, manipulation of staff and unintended consequences such as developing skills that might be applied to antisocial ends. A particular challenge to the managers of DSPD units will be supporting staff in anticipating these negative outcomes while dealing with effects on staff such as therapeutic nihilism and burnout.

DSPD services have provided scope for forensic psychologists to practise in highly integrated treatment regimes. The benefits of having planned and systematic interventions will need to be weighed against arguably reduced latitude for individual discretion or 'clinical pluralism' (Morris 2003). The willingness to pilot personality-disorder services in less secure units and the community is an encouraging indication of the heterogeneity of the approach to expanding and evaluating services for people with this highly demanding form of mental disorder (DSPD Programme 2005b).

Acknowledgements

I would like to thank Derek Perkins for commenting on a draft of this chapter and to acknowledge Stuart John-Chuan and Adrian Coxell for drawing my attention to relevant papers.

References

Abracen, J., Looman, J. and Langton, C.M. (2008) 'Treatment of sexual offenders with psychopathic traits: recent research developments and clinical implications', *Trauma, Violence, and Abuse*, 9 (3): 144–66.

Aldhous, P. (2007) 'Violent, antisocial, beyond redemption?', *New Scientist*, 2599: 8–9.

Alwin, N., Blackburn, R., Davidson, K., Hilton, M., Logan, C. and Shine, J. (2006) *Understanding Personality Disorder: A report by the British Psychological Society*. BPS: Leicester.

Beck, A.T. and Freeman, A.T. (1990) *Cognitive Therapy of Personality Disorders*. New York: Guilford Press.

Bell, J., Campbell, S., Erikson, M., Hogue, T., McLean, Z., Rust, S. and Taylor, R. (2003) 'An overview: DSPD programme concepts and progress. Dangerous and Severe Personality Disorder (DSPD)', *Issues in Forensic Psychology*, 4: 11–23.

Bonham, A. (2003) 'A test of the demand-control/support model in a secure psychiatric hospital'. Unpublished MSc dissertation, University of Surrey.

Bushman, B.J. and Baumeister, R.F. (1998) 'Threatened egotism, narcissism, self-esteem, and direct and displaced aggression: does self-love or self-hate lead to violence?', *Journal of Personality and Social Psychology*, 75 (1): 219–29.

Carr-Walker, P., Bowers, L., Callaghan, P., Nijman, H. and Paton, J. (2004) 'Attitudes towards personality disorders: comparison between prison officers and psychiatric nurses', *Legal and Criminological Psychology*, 9: 1–13.

Clarke, J. and Roger, D. (2002) 'Working therapeutically with sex offenders: the potential impact on the psychological well-being of treatment providers', *Issues in Forensic Psychology*, 3: 82–96.

Clarke, J. and Roger, D. (2007) 'The construction and validation of a scale to assess psychological risk and well-being in sex offender treatment providers', *Legal and Criminological Psychology*, 12: 83–100.

Coid, J. (1998) 'The management of dangerous psychopaths in prison', in T. Millon, E. Simonsen, M. Birket-Smith and R.D. Davis (eds), *Psychopathy, Anti-social, Criminal and Violent Behavior*. New York: Guilford Press.

Coid, J., Yang, M., Ullrich, S., Zhang, T., Roberts, A., Roberts, C., Rogers, R. and Farrington, D. (2007) 'Predicting and understanding risk of re-offending: the Prisoner Cohort Study', Research Summary No. 6. London: Ministry of Justice.

Cooke, D.J., Michie, C. and Skeem, J. (2007) 'Understanding the structure of the Psychopathy Checklist – Revised', *British Journal of Psychiatry*, 190: ss 39–50.

Craissati, J. Webb, L. and Keen, S. (2008) 'The relationship between developmental variables, personality disorder, and risk in sex offenders', *Sexual Abuse: A Journal of Research and Treatment*, 20 (2): 119–38.

Dollard, M.F. and Winefield, A.H. (1998) 'A test of the demand-control/support model of work stress in correctional officers', *Journal of Occupational Health Psychology*, 3 (3): 243–64.

D'Silva, K., Duggan, C. and McCarthy, L. (2004) 'Does treatment really make psychopaths worse? A review of the evidence', *Journal of Personality Disorders*, 18 (2): 163–77.

DSPD Programme (2005a) *Dangerous and Severe Personality Disorder (DSPD) High Secure Services for Men: Planning and Delivery Guide*. DSPD Programme, Department of Health, Home Office, HM Prison Service.

DSPD Programme (2005b) *Forensic Personality Disorder – Medium Secure and Community Pilot Services: Planning and Delivery Guide*. DSPD Programme, Department of Health, Home Office, HM Prison Service.

Duggan, C. (2007) 'To move or not to move – that is the question! Some reflections on the transfer of DSPD patients in the face of uncertainty', *Psychology, Crime and Law*, 13 (1): 113–21.

Ennis, L. and Horne, S. (2003) 'Predicting psychological distress in sex offender therapists', *Sexual Abuse: A Journal of Research and Treatment*, 15 (2): 149–57.

Farr, C. and Draycott, S. (2007) '"Considering change" – a motivational intervention with DSPD offenders', *Issues in Forensic Psychology*, 7: 62–9.

Firestone, P., Bradford, J.M., Greenberg, D.M. and Larose, M.R. (1998) 'Homicidal sex offenders: psychological, phallometric, and diagnostic features', *Journal of American Academy Psychiatry and Law*, 26 (4): 537–52.

Freeman, A. and Jackson, J. (1998) 'Cognitive behavioural treatment of personality disorders', in N. Tarrier, A. Wells and G. Haddock (eds), *Treating Complex Cases: The Cognitive Behavioural Therapy Approach*. Chichester: Wiley.

Gunn, J. (2000) 'A millennium monster is born', *Criminal Behaviour and Mental Health*, 10: 73–6.

Haddock, A.W., Snowden, P.R., Dolan, M., Parker, J. and Rees, H. (2001) 'Managing dangerous people with severe personality disorder: a survey of forensic psychiatrists' opinions', *Psychiatric Bulletin*, 25: 293–96.

Hare, R.D. (1998) 'The Hare PCL-R: some issues concerning its use and misuse', *Legal and Criminological Psychology*, 3: 99–119.

Hart, S.P., Michie, C. and Cooke, D.J. (2007) 'Precision of actuarial risk assessment instruments: evaluating the "margins of error" of group v. individual predictions of violence', *British Journal of Psychiatry*, 190: ss 60–65.

Hodgins, S. (2007) 'Persistent violent offending: what do we know?', *British Journal of Psychiatry*, 190: ss 12–14.

Hogue, T., Jones, L., Talkes, K. and Tennant, A. (2007) 'The peaks: a clinical service for those with dangerous and severe personality disorder', *Psychology, Crime and Law*, 13 (1): 57–68

Home Office and Department of Health (2000) *Reforming the Mental Health Act*.

Jones, L. (1997) 'Developing models for managing treatment integrity and efficacy in a prison-based TC: the Max Glatt Centre', in E. Cullen, L. Jones and R. Woodward (eds), *Therapeutic Communities for Offenders*. Chichester: Wiley.

Jones, L. (2007) 'Iatrogenic effects with personality disordered offenders', *Psychology, Crime and Law*, 13 (1): 69–79.

Keitch, I. (2003) 'Foreword. Dangerous and Severe Personality Disorder (DSPD)', *Issues in Forensic Psychology*, 4: 8–10.

Kuyken, W. (2006) 'Evidence-based case formulation: is the emperor clothed?', in N. Tarrier (ed.), *Case Formulation in Cognitive Behaviour Therapy. The Treatment of Challenging and Complex Cases*. London: Routledge.

Linehan, M.M. (1993) *Cognitive-Behavioral Treatment of Borderline Personality Disorder*. New York: Guilford Press.

Livesley, W.J. (2005) 'Principles and strategies for treating personality disorder', *Canadian Journal of Psychiatry*, 50: 442–50.

Logan, C. (2003) 'Women and Dangerous and Severe Personality Disorder: assessing, treating and managing women at risk. Dangerous and severe Personality Disorder (DSPD)', *Issues in Forensic Psychology*, 4: 41–53.

Lord, A. (2003) 'Working with personality-disordered offenders', *Forensic Update*, 73: 31–9.

Lord, A. and Willmot, P. (2004) 'The process of overcoming denial in sexual offenders', *Journal of Sexual Aggression*, 10 (1): 51–61.

Losel, F. (1998) 'Treatment and management of psychopaths', in D.J. Cooke, A.E. Forth and R.D. Hare (eds), *Psychopathy: Theory, Research and Implications for society*. Dordrecht: Kluwer.

Maden, A. (2007) 'Dangerous and severe personality disorder: antecedents and origins', *British Journal of Psychiatry*, 190: ss 8–11.

Marshall, W.L., Anderson, D. and Fernandez, Y. (1999) *Cognitive Behavioural Treatment of Sexual Offenders*. Chichester: Wiley.

Maslach, C. and Jackson, S.E. (1981) 'The measurement of experienced burnout', *Journal of Occupational Behaviour*, 2: 99–113.

McGurk, B. and Fludger, N. (1987) 'The selection of prison officers', in B. McGurk, D.M. Thornton and M. Williams (eds), *Applying Psychology to Imprisonment: Theory and Practice*. London: HMSO.

Millon, T. and Davis, R. (2000) *Personality Disorders in Modern Life*. Chichester: Wiley.

Morris, M. (2003) 'Clinical pluralism: a model of practice for DSPD treatment teams. Dangerous and Severe Personality Disorder (DSPD)', *Issues in Forensic Psychology*, 4: 65–75.

National Institute for Mental Health in England (2003) *Personality Disorder: No longer a diagnosis of exclusion*. London: Department of Health.

Nitsun, M. (1996) *The Anti-Group: Destructive Forces in the Group and their Creative Potential (International Library of Group Psychotherapy and Group Processes)*. Routledge.

Sainsbury Centre for Mental Health (2001) *The Capable Practitioner: A framework and list of the practitioner capabilities required to implement the National Service Framework for Mental Health*. London: Sainsbury Centre.

Seto and Barbaree (1999) 'Psychopathy, treatment behavior, and sex offender recidivism', *Journal of Interpersonal Violence*, 14 (12): 1235–48.

Shallow, C. and Brown, J. (2004) 'The personal–professional dialectic', *Forensic Update*, 73: 31–9.

Singleton, N., Meltzer, H. and Gatward, R. (1998) *Psychiatric Morbidity Among Prisoners: Summary Report*. Office for National Statistics.

Szmukler, G. (2003) 'Risk assessment: "numbers" and "values"', *Psychiatric Bulletin*, 27: 205–7.

Thornton, D. and Blud, L. (2007) 'The influence of psychopathic traits on response to treatment', in H. Herve and J.C. Yuille (eds), *The Psychopath: Theory, Research and Practice*. Lawrence Erlbaum Associates.

Trinder, H. (1997) 'Stress, coping styles and well-being among the staff of a high security prison facility'. Unpublished MSc dissertation, University of Leicester.

Tyrer, P. (2007) 'An agitation of contrary opinions', *British Journal of Psychiatry*, 190: ss 1–2.

Tyrer, P., Coombs, N., Ibrahimi, F., Mathilakath, A., Bajaj, P., Ranger, M., Rao, B. and Din, R. (2007) 'Critical developments in assessment of personality disorder', *British Journal of Psychiatry*, 190: ss 51–9.

Ward, T. and Stewart, C.A. (2003) 'The treatment of sex offenders: risk management and good lives', *Professional Psychology, Research and Practice*, 34 (4): 353–60.

Ward, T., Nathan, P., Drake, C.R., Lee, J.K.P. and Pathe, M. (2000) 'The role of formulation-based treatment for sexual offenders', *Behaviour Change*, 17: 251–64.

Wong, S.C.P., Gordon, A. and Deqiang, G. (2007) 'Assessment and treatment of violence-prone forensic clients: an integrated approach', *British Journal of Psychiatry*, 190: ss 66–74.

World Health Organisation (1992) *ICD-10 Classification of Mental and Behavioural Disorders*, Geneva.

Yalom, I.D. (1995) *The Theory and Practice of Group Psychotherapy* (4th edn). New York: Basic Books.

Chapter 16

Anger control group work with forensic psychiatric inpatients: theories and practical applications

Lara Arsuffi

> Anyone can be angry; that is easy. But to be angry with the right person, at the right time, for the right reason, to the right degree and under the right circumstances, that is not easy and is not within everyone's power.
>
> Aristotle, *Nicomachean Ethics*

Before reviewing the effectiveness of anger management group interventions with forensic inpatients, this chapter will briefly summarise current conceptualisations of anger and aggression and will make an argument supporting the provision of anger control treatment to this population. It will also describe a recent anger control group programme which is currently being piloted in two medium secure units in London. Difficulties with conducting research in this area and practice issues encountered during treatment provision will also be touched upon. It is hoped that readers interested in setting up, delivering and evaluating anger control group treatment with this population will find this chapter useful in increasing their awareness of the actual and potential contributions of applied psychological services, in assisting problem-solving and decision-making and in aiding the formulation of policy and its implementation.

Psychological theories of anger and aggressive behaviour

There are competing psychological theories of aggression, each providing potential insights into the build-up and display of aggression. One clear division that emerges from the literature is the question of whether violent behaviour results from factors that are beyond the perpetrator's control, or whether they are acts of free will and, therefore, largely preventable (Linsley 2006). Biological theories of aggression suggest that brain chemicals (serotonin and noradrenaline), certain areas of the brain (the limbic system and cerebral cortex), the male sex hormone androgen and genetic make-up (an extra Y chromosome) play an important role in regulating aggressive impulses (Hollin 1992; Owens and Ashcroft 1995; Harper-Jaques and Reimer 1998; Jeffrey 1979).

In challenging the then commonly held belief that human beings were essentially good, Freud viewed aggression as an innate instinctual urge that could be expressed when a person was provoked or abused (Davidson *et al.* 2001). Fromm believed that aggression is a genetically programmed response designed as a defence mechanism to protect the person against (real or perceived) threats (Fromm 1973). The frustration-aggression hypothesis proposes that aggression is the response to the frustration of goal-directed behaviour by an outside source. Goals may include basic needs such as food, sleep, sex, love and recognition. Aggression is triggered by the blocking of the goal, is accompanied by high arousal (i.e. anger), and manifests itself in the form of an immediate and impulsive response to the source of frustration, provocation or threat (Berkowitz 1990).

In contrast to biological and instinct theories, social learning theory focuses on aggression as a learnt behaviour (Bandura 1973). The social learning view of aggression is that emotional arousal, stemming from an aversive experience, motivates aggression. Whether aggression or some other response actually occurs depends on what consequences people have learnt to expect. For example, if a person has received a reward (money, sexual gratification) due to a deviant aggressive act, s/he will be conditioned towards committing that act again. Cognitive theorists (Mischel and Shoda 1995) propose that an aggressive response is influenced by cognitive processes such as judgements, self-esteem and expectations. In a situation where an individual's behaviour is perceived as a threat or dangerous, the recipient's reaction will be intensified.

Drawing from cognitive-behavioural principles, Novaco (1975) conceptualises anger as an affective stress reaction which may have positive as well as negative functions and does not always result in aggressive behaviour. Novaco (1975) places stress, understood as a state of imbalance between environmental demands and the response capabilities of the person to cope, as occupying a central role in his proposed model of anger. Particular external events may not be viewed as equally stressful by different individuals. Hence, in Novaco's (1975) framework of anger, it is the individual's perception of such external events and of his/her coping mechanisms that affect the experience of anger. Anger is construed as involving both physiological arousal and a cognitive labelling of that arousal as anger, or a semantically proximate term, such as annoyed, irritated, enraged or provoked. Further, anger is determined by expectations that one has regarding events and one's response to them, as well as by the appraisal of their meaning during and following the experience. More specifically, when one's experience is discrepant from expectations, arousal accompanies a disturbance of equilibrium, as the person seeks to adjust to the demands of the situation. Expectations for desired outcomes that do not occur result in aversive arousal that must be labelled as anger. Another way in which expectations influence anger arousal is with regard to the anticipation of aversive events based on previous and current appraisals. When one expects an antagonistic experience and the appraisal of the event in question is anger-inducing, anger more readily occurs (Novaco 1975).

Using this framework: physiologically, anger consists of sympathetic arousal, increased muscle tension, release of adrenal hormones, and other elements of Cannon's 'flight or fight response' (Deffenbacher 1999). Cognitively, clinical anger involves biased information processing involving (1) an exaggerated sense of violation and being wronged, (2) attack, revenge or retribution, (3) blame, (4) externalisation, (5) denigration and minimisation of the source of anger, (6) overgeneralised and often inflammatory labelling (Deffenbacher 1999). Associated with these cognitive processes is an inclination to act in an antagonistic or confrontational manner towards the source of the provocation (Novaco 1994). Physiological, cognitive and behavioural responses rapidly interact with each other with often reinforcing properties (Deffenbacher 1999).

Finally, information-processing models (Huesmann 1998) also highlight the importance of cognitions, particularly how people evaluate the consequences of their actions, and how these fit in with their existing mental scripts that guide individuals to choose actions, based on past experiences and learned consequences. Emotion plays a significant role in the choice and enactment of an aggressive script. For example, if someone expects to be ridiculed by his/her peers and to lose status for choosing to walk away from a provocative situation, and the person experiences a raised heart rate and increased sweating, s/he might interpret this as evidence that s/he is getting angry, access anger cognitions, and choose a script found to have been successful in the past, such as behaving aggressively to maintain status amongst the peer group and diffuse feelings of anger (Huesmann 1998).

The latter highlights how the focus has recently shifted from describing aggression by its nature to understanding its motivation (Raine *et al.* 2006; Tremblay *et al.* 2007), that is, the function it serves for the individual; for example, it might be an effective method by which to deal with conflict. In addition, it has been recognised that aggression can be adaptive and carry benefits to the perpetrators, who can be classified into one of three categories: reactive aggressors, proactive aggressors and mixed-motive aggressors (Ireland 2008). Reactive violence can be described as an uncontrolled form of aggression that occurs in the context of a provocation (real or perceived), frustration or threat, and can be understood within the frustration-aggression hypothesis. Proactive aggression (referred to also as planned, instrumental or predatory violence) is explained by the social learning model. Mixed-motive aggression is based on the notion that motivation can change over time (Ireland 2008). It has been assumed that proactive aggressors are not characterised by emotional regulation difficulties (e.g. anger) like their reactive counterparts. This assumption, however, has not been supported by developmental research (Dodge and Coie 1987) which found that anger correlated with both types of violence.

Identifying main effect or univariate predictors for aggression is a complex task as many factors, interacting together, may be involved in triggering violent behaviour (Monahan *et al.* 2001). Previous literature has highlighted risk factors including: delusional threat symptoms (Stompe *et al.* 2004), psychopathy (Heilbrun *et al.* 1998; Rice and Harris 1997), interpersonal style (Doyle and Dolan 2006), impulsiveness (Barratt 1994) and others (see Monahan *et al.* 2001).

Anger does not always lead to violent behaviour and violence can occur without an antecedent anger emotion (Monahan *et al.* 2001; Howells *et al.* 2005). However, anger dyscontrol has been emphasised as a salient characteristic of violent offenders (Howells *et al.* 2004; Novaco *et al.* 2000; Blackburn 1993), whose behaviours are aetiologically related to frustration, poor impulse control, interpersonal problems and inadequate coping abilities (Howells *et al.* 1997; Kroner and Reddon 1995; Stermac 1986).

Friedman and Booth-Kewley (1987) defined anger as an immediate emotional arousal to a given or perceived situation and aggression as the actual or intended harming of others. Anger is believed to play several roles in aggression (Huesmann 1998; Berkowitz 1990). It may

(1) reduce inhibitions and increase the chances that a person will use aggression as a means of expression; (2) it can provide a justification for aggressive retaliation by interfering with moral reasoning and judgement; (3) it energises behaviour by increasing arousal levels; and (4) anger primes aggressive thoughts, scripts, and associated expressive-motor behaviours. The nature of the relationship between anger and violent crime is complex, but literature suggests that anger is frequently experienced prior to the commission of an offence (Zamble and Quinsey 1997) and offenders report elevated levels of anger (Rice *et al.* 1990), higher than non-violent offenders (Howells *et al.* 2005).

In addition to its associations with offending behaviour, anger appears to be a particularly important emotion in residential settings, linked with adjustment and disciplinary problems and physical assaults on care staff (Howells *et al.* 2005). Evidence has been accumulating to suggest that recorded violence and aggression in healthcare settings are increasing (Linsley 2006). For example, in 2000, the Department of Health conducted a national survey into the reported incidences of violence and aggression in NHS trusts (Department of Health 2001). A total of 84,273 violent or abusive incidents were reported. This was an increase of 24,000 over the previous year 1998–9. In 2001 they conducted a follow-up survey which showed a further 13 per cent increase (Health Services Commission 2003). In 2002–03, the number had risen again, with the average number of incidents for NHS mental health and learning disability trusts being almost two and a half times the average for all trusts, despite evidence that staff working in mental health units were much less likely to report verbal abuse (Health Services Commission 2003). In 2004, the Commission for Health Improvement conducted a survey which showed that 15 per cent of respondents (N = 203,911) had experienced physical violence at work in the previous year, usually from patients or their relatives (Commission for Health Improvement 2004).

Epidemiological studies point strongly to anger as a risk factor for violence among various forensic and civil populations (Taylor *et al.* 2002; Monahan *et al.* 2001; Cornell *et al.* 1999; Novaco and Renwick 1998; Novaco 1994; Kay *et al.* 1988; Craig 1982). Consequently, anger management interventions may be beneficial to forensic inpatients, to reduce the risk of future violence towards others, whether healthcare staff or members of the community, and to provide them with more adaptive skills to express negative feelings like anger, rather than expressing it inappropriately via aggressive behaviour.

Engaging forensic inpatients in treatment presents many challenges to clinicians. Some patients may feel coerced into treatment, affecting their willingness to participate collaboratively in the therapeutic process. Other patients, by contrast, may comply passively with treatment, hoping to get a 'good report'. Others may be too ill and paranoid (Arsuffi 2007). In addition, forensic psychiatric inpatients typically present with multiple problems, including a difficult childhood history, concentration difficulties, negative symptoms of mental illness, and cognitive deficits (Arsuffi 2007; Dudeck *et al.* 2007; Dernevik *et al.* 2002). These and other variables (e.g. personality characteristics, social support, therapeutic mindedness, interpersonal skills, age, ethnicity, socio-economic level, etc.) are widely recognised as critical factors mediating the success of treatment (Brown 1996; Bonta 1995; Van Voorhis 1997; Kennedy 1999). The responsivity principle states that styles and modes of treatment must be closely matched to the preferred learning style and abilities/characteristics of the offender (Andrews *et al.* 1986) as treatment effectiveness depends on effective matching as well as intensity of intervention (Bonta 1995). Ignoring responsivity factors may undermine treatment gains, waste resources, increase recidivism and consequently decrease public safety (Kennedy 2000).

Outcomes of different anger management studies

Novaco (1975) developed an anger management therapeutic approach, based on cognitive-behavioural elements, that focuses on developing a client's competence to respond to stressful events so that maladaptive emotions and concomitant cognitions are reduced and behavioural adaptation achieved. This treatment approach aims to identify and modulate cognitive, behavioural and physiological responses to provocation through various treatment techniques, which include, among others, physiological monitoring, relaxation training, assertiveness training, cognitive restructuring, reappraisal and self-instruction. Anger is not viewed as inherently problematic but becomes so because of its intensity, frequency or, most importantly, its behavioural effects (aggression, hostility, provocation). Novaco's (1975) therapeutic strategy does not attempt to inculcate the suppression of anger. Far from emotion suppression, the therapy attempts to minimise the maladaptive effects of anger and to maximise its adaptive functions, and to provide clients with cognitive and behavioural coping skills (Novaco 1975).

The vast amount of research about the effectiveness of anger management programmes has found overall beneficial outcomes with effect sizes ranging from 0.6 to 0.9 (Del Vecchio and O'Leary 2004). However, 73 per cent of these studies have been carried out on college students and thus the results may not be generalisable to other ages, educational levels or occupations (Del Vecchio and O'Leary 2004). There are a few studies that have evaluated the effectiveness of anger management treatment with offenders detained in psychiatric institutions and these will now be reviewed. Comparisons between studies are difficult as different methods of data collection are often employed. They have obtained mixed results, which limit generalisations and their findings need to be replicated with more rigorous designs and larger sample sizes.

Arsuffi (2007) assessed the effectiveness of two short-term cognitive-behavioural interventions with forensic psychiatric inpatients detained in a British medium secure unit. Eight patients attended eight one-hour sessions of a structured, anger management, cognitive-behavioural programme, delivered by two qualified clinical psychologists and one social therapist. Data were collected using patients' self-reports and observations of ward behaviour, at pre group, post treatment and two-month follow up. The experimental group was compared with a similar control group, consisting of patients who were referred to and were suitable for treatment, but had refused to attend the group. Statistical analyses indicated that patients participating in anger management did not overall have significantly different levels of subjective anger relative to the controls. In addition, no significant differences were observed in ward behaviour ratings, although the incidents of assaultiveness and emotional lability in the treatment group decreased in the expected direction. It was concluded that the overall impact of treatment was small and non-significant compared with the control group.

Arsuffi (2007) further investigated the relationship between treatment outcome and the strength of the therapeutic alliance between facilitators and group participants. Correlational analyses suggested that the stronger the relationship measured at week three of treatment by the Working Alliance Inventory (Horvath and Greenberg 1989) the more likely were patients at follow-up to self-report a lower disposition to express anger when criticised by others or treated unfairly, to express angry feelings towards people or objects in the environment, and to self-report feelings of depression, suggesting that a stronger therapeutic relationship with group facilitators might have a positive impact on treatment outcome. These findings should be interpreted with the caveat reminder that the sample consisted of eight patients only.

McMurran *et al.* (2001) evaluated the progress of four male, legally detained personality disordered offenders in an English medium secure unit who attended a structured, cognitive-behavioural programme consisting of 15 two-and-a-half-hour sessions to control angry aggression. Four staff members were involved in the delivery of the programme. The first six sessions were facilitated as a demonstration by a qualified clinical psychologist, and the remaining sessions were facilitated by a qualified nurse, a health care assistant and an assistant psychologist, with the qualified clinical psychologist as an observer.

Data were collected using several assessment methods: psychometric tests; ward behaviour ratings completed by nurses; and self-monitoring ratings completed by patients every time an anger experience occurred. At post group, the psychometric tests of anger and aggression, STAXI (Spielberger 1986) and Buss-Durkee Hostility Inventory (Buss and Durkee 1957), showed improvements, although non-significant, for three patients. No change in behaviour occurred over time for any patient, with staff and patient ratings concurring. However, aggressive behaviour was low at the start and remained low throughout, as one might expect in such a highly controlled environment, with an absence of disinhibitors such as alcohol and drugs and fewer 'real-life' provocations to anger. Five months after the end of the treatment, information gained from clinical records indicated that two patients were showing no anger or aggression problems and one, who had been discharged, returned to drug use (McMurran *et al.* 2001). The authors (McMurran *et al.* 2001) concluded by stating that a more rigorous experimental design was needed to replicate their study and test the results.

Similarly *et al.* (1997) evaluated a cognitive-behavioural anger treatment based on the stress inoculation procedure developed by Novaco (1975) with four mentally disordered patients in a maximum security forensic hospital in Scotland. The patients had a history of serious violence and suffered from a mental illness. The intervention consisted of a five-session preparatory phase followed by a 20-session treatment procedure administered by two highly trained forensic clinical psychologists.

The rationale for the preparatory phase was that patients, as prospective participants in anger management, often lack a number of prerequisites for optimal involvement in a self-regulatory, coping skills intervention. For example, they may lack the ability to identify emotions and to differentiate them in type and degree of intensity. They are likely to have rudimentary self-monitoring skills and to have had limited training in applying relaxation induction. Particularly in a forensic setting, they may be likely to be very guarded about self-disclosure and to be quite ambivalent about earnestly engaging in treatment and assessment (Renwick *et al.* 1997). Hence the preparatory phase was constructed to 'prime the patient motivationally' as well as to establish some basic skills of emotion identification, self-monitoring, communication and arousal reduction skills. It also sought to build trust in the therapists and the goals of the treatment programme, providing an atmosphere conducive to personal disclosure and to the active collaboration required by the therapeutic approach (Renwick *et al.* 1997).

Assessment of treatment efficacy was obtained by clinical staff at programme completion. Each patient's consultant psychiatrist, key worker and day-care worker evaluated gains during a structured interview, followed by a behaviour rating scale. Based on the clinical and empirical data, the results reflected noteworthy gains in emotional competence, in anger management and in social-behavioural competencies. Further, at the time of writing, three out of the four patients were recommended for discharge. However the authors themselves stressed that controlled clinical trials were needed to replicate these preliminary positive findings (Renwick *et al.* 1997).

Hilton and Frankel (2003) described a structured, cognitive-behavioural, anger management programme implemented in a British medium secure unit (MSU) with male forensic inpatients (N = 6). Inclusion criteria included the following: (1) patients had problems with anger control, rather than instrumental aggression; (2) they were not actively psychotic at the start of the programme; (3) their cognitive functioning was of sufficient level to enable them to cope with the content of the programme; and (4) patients were motivated to engage in the programme and change their behaviour. The programme involved 13 sessions and one follow-up session, covering a range of skills, such as self-monitoring, coping, and preparing for high-risk situations. The programme was highly interactive to keep patients engaged, increase their retention of the information and enhance their learning experience. In order to achieve these, role-plays and interactive tasks were introduced early in the programme to aid concentration and attention. It ran once a week for two hours.

Evaluation of treatment effectiveness was carried out on two levels. Patients completed psychometric tools (the STAXI and three questionnaires respectively assessing impulsivity, locus of control and emotional coping skills) pre and post group. In addition, after each session, the facilitators recorded specific details about each group member's participation. These recordings were used to write overall qualitative reports detailing each group member's progress. Overall, on a qualitative level, all patients benefited from the group. Facilitators noted evidence of learning and good participation from all group members. On a quantitative level, the evaluation did not produce consistently positive results. Due to the limited information provided by the authors in this paper, it is difficult to evaluate treatment effectiveness and make comparisons with other anger management group programmes.

A less recent study (Stermac 1986) evaluated the efficacy of a short-term cognitive-behavioural anger management intervention with 40 forensic Canadian inpatients. The participants had a wide forensic history, ranging from mischief to first-degree murder. To qualify for the study, they had to have average verbal IQ and be free of psychosis. They were randomly assigned to six one-hour anger management treatment sessions or to a psycho-educational intervention of equivalent length. The groups were comparable on several demographic variables such as: age; diagnosis; level of education attained; occupation; previous psychiatric and criminal histories and current index offences. Patients were assessed pre and post intervention with two self-report measures and one visual motor task designed to evaluate anger, coping strategies and impulsivity. The outcome measures were the Novaco Provocation Inventory (Novaco 1975), the Coping Strategies Inventory (Tobin *et al.* 1982) and the Porteus Mazes-Vineland Revision (Porteus 1965) respectively.

The psycho-educational condition was designed to provide basic information on psychiatry, psychology and law and was run on rotation by psychiatrists, psychologists and social workers. The anger management condition was based upon cognitive-behavioural and stress inoculation principles and was facilitated by a qualified psychologist and a psychology graduate student. The results of the study demonstrated that, following treatment, experimental participants reported significantly lower levels of anger than did control participants. In addition, they reported a greater use of cognitive restructuring strategies and less use of self-denigration strategies (Stermac 1986). However, no follow up was carried out; thus it is unclear if these changes were maintained. Further, due to the absence of ward behaviour measures, it is also not known to what extent the self-reported changes in anger management following treatment were reflected in behavioural differences on the wards during anger-related situations.

In summary, studies evaluating structured anger control group interventions with mentally disordered offenders detained in psychiatric hospitals are mostly based on a cognitive-behavioural approach to intervention. Comparisons and generalisations are difficult due to small sample sizes, lack of comparable data, and methodological limitations, such as convenience sampling methods, several studies lacking a comparison group (thereby allowing for the potential of a Hawthorne effect, (Landsberger 1958) and lack of robust participant randomisation. Each of the reviewed studies is open to bias. Such issues are, however, difficult to avoid as researchers often have access only to small patient populations and deliver the intervention themselves, making large studies, with 'blinding' of conditions, difficult. In addition, randomised trials do not come without downfalls when working with people whose risk needs to be reduced. For example, patients who need treatment the most and/or who are more motivated to attend may be randomised in the control group; hence having to wait several months before receiving treatment, which may decrease their motivation to engage. While waiting for treatment, patients may be transferred to another hospital which may not provide the treatment they need. Or patients may be hospitalised for longer, waiting to receive treatment, which raises further ethical questions. It also has financial implications for the already overstretched health budgets.

The Triple C (Cool, Calm and Composed) Programme

Because forensic psychiatric inpatients typically present with multiple problems, short-term (i.e. six to 12 sessions) cognitive-behavioural programmes may be too brief in promoting lasting and significant behavioural change (Arsuffi 2007). Following interviews with colleagues working in six medium secure units in the UK and a review of evidence-based anger management interventions drawing from dialectical behaviour therapy, cognitive behaviour therapy and social learning principles, Arsuffi designed the Triple C Programme. This comprises 30 one-and-a-half-hour sessions (see Table 16.1), with a strong skill-based component and repetition of learning points to accommodate patients with poor academic backgrounds and limited life-skills. Further, drawing on literature suggesting that a stronger therapeutic alliance with group facilitator(s) is related to positive outcomes (Arsuffi 2007; Rondeau *et al.* 2001; Tuttman 1997; Abouguendia *et al.* 2004), the first five sessions are a preparatory phase to support the development of an alliance between patients and facilitators and to provide patients with basic skills of emotion recognition and self-monitoring, as recommended by Renwick *et al.* (1997).

The Triple C Programme is based on the central assumption of the risk-need-responsivity model (e.g. Gendreau 1996; Andrews and Bonta 1998; McGuire 2001), which states that the best way to reduce recidivism is to teach offenders adaptive ways to manage aspects of their lives linked to offending. Specifically, the programme aims to address criminogenic needs such as maladaptive regulation and expression of anger and other negative emotional states (e.g. stress), low frustration threshold, poor impulse control, limited social skills (e.g. social perspective taking, problem-solving) and cognitive deficits (e.g. poor critical reasoning), which have been linked to violent offending. For example, offenders who lack self-control tend towards being action oriented, responding without stopping to think about the consequences and not fully analysing a situation. Unsophisticated critical reasoning may lead to cognitive distortions such as externalisation of blame, overgeneralisations, misattributions and catastrophising, which are likely to raise arousal levels in anger-inducing situations. Lack of social perspective taking would lead to offenders being non-empathic, misreading social situations. Inadequacies in social problem-solving could lead to a limited ability to recognise the possibility that problems will develop, an inability to generate solutions, and being unable to visualise step-by-step means to achieve goals. These deficits might also lead to increased arousal levels in stressful situations.

The anger control programme addresses the criminogenic needs listed above by:

- teaching patients skills directly related to the problem behaviour such as assertiveness; goal setting; self-control; perspective-taking; relaxation; interpersonal problem-solving and positive self-talk;
- teaching both cognitive and behavioural techniques to have an impact on offenders' thinking, i.e. challenge cognitive distortions likely to increase arousal levels; improve flexibility; enhance reflection; develop consequential thinking; promote a more sophisticated moral reasoning; encourage generalisation to everyday situations, etc;
- using role-plays to give participants many chances to practise the skills and providing them with immediate feedback and guidance;

Table 16.1 Outline of Triple C Programme's contents

(1) Introduction	(16) Helping others
(2) Being angry is OK	(17) Dealing with someone else's anger
(3) Understanding our and others' feelings	(18) Assertiveness skills
(4) Controlling the physical feelings of anger	(19) Keeping out of arguments
(5) Why coping with angry feelings?	(20) Setting effective goals
(6) Being in control of our mind	(21) Dealing with group pressure
(7) Increasing our strength to tolerate distress	(22) Understanding others' points of view
(8) The ABC of anger	(23) Responding effectively to failure
(9) Reducing anger	(24) Dealing with provocations
(10) Reducing anger provoking thoughts	(25) The anger connection
(11) Resisting peer pressure	(26) How to decrease anger in difficult situations
(12) Creating coping thoughts	(27) What do we do that may make people angry with us?
(13) Understanding the feelings of others	(28) Blocks to coping in real life
(14) Thinking ahead	(29) What have we learnt from coming to this group?
(15) Getting ready for a difficult conversation	(30) Final evaluation and celebration

- utilising a range of culturally appropriate and tangible exercises to match most patients' learning styles, and by using concrete rewards as motivators for engagement in treatment;
- repetition and reinforcement of learning points, to accommodate patients with limited life-skills and cognitive and dysexecutive deficits;
- based on previous research (Arsuffi 2007), providing an adequate dose of treatment.

It is important to evaluate the effectiveness of anger management groupwork with forensic inpatients to ensure that treatment needs (the need to reduce the risk of future violence) are being met. Data are currently being collected by an independent researcher pre, post group and at two-month follow-up using self-report, behavioural and clinical data. The evaluation hypotheses are that patients participating in the Triple C programme would show significantly decreased levels of anger, measured by self-report psychometric questionnaires (i.e. STAXI and NAI (Novaco Anger Inventory) and by observations of behaviour on the wards (recorded by nursing staff in the Ward Anger Rating Scale), relative to a similar control group. Data screening and analyses have not yet been completed because additional groups are currently being run in order to build sample size and run meaningful statistical analyses. The overall, final results would be used to modify the whole anger control programme.

Initial data suggest that service users are enjoying the programme, as demonstrated by the overall low attrition rate. Multidisciplinary staffs delivering the intervention are of the opinion that it is generally beneficial to group participants, as it provides them with skills to cope more adaptively during arousing situations. Preliminary statistical data have found a significant difference between experimental ($N = 4$) and control ($N = 5$) group on anger reaction, as measured by the STAXI, at post group ($F = 10.573$; $p = .014$), suggesting that patients who attended the group were less likely to express anger when criticised or treated unfairly by others.

In addition, a positive significant correlation ($r = 0.966$; $p < 0.05$) has been found between clients' self-reported strength of the therapeutic alliance, as measured at week three of treatment by the Working Alliance Inventory (Horvath and Greenberg 1989), with anger control, suggesting that the stronger the relationship the more likely were patients at post group to self-report a higher ability to control their angry feelings. Further, a significant negative correlation has been found between the strength of the alliance and anger expression at post group (r = –.975; p = .025), suggesting that the stronger the therapeutic relationship, the less likely were participants to self-report expressing their angry feelings. Again, these findings should be interpreted with caution, given the small sample size.

Alongside this quantitative evaluation, data are also collected qualitatively to examine change using the patients' perceptions of therapy and the change process. For example, each session is appraised at the end by participants completing anonymous evaluation forms (see Table 16.2) and a confidential focus group is facilitated during the last session. The focus group approach has been chosen because it has been applied previously to examine change in various settings. For example, Miller *et al.* (2006) used focus groups to explore perceptions about therapeutic effectiveness in terms of psychological change amongst HMP Dovegate therapeutic community residents. Focus groups were found to be an especially productive research method. Hence the use of an end-treatment focus group to explore the effectiveness of the Triple C Programme from the patients' point of view.

One of the strengths of the Triple C Programme is that, during treatment development, patient motivation and treatment responsivity were considered. Treatment responsivity is addressed by using different exercises (i.e., role-plays, video discussions, filming patients

Table 16.2 Format of confidential evaluation forms completed by patients at the end of each Triple C session

I found this session useful:

Very 0 … 1 … 2 … 3 … 4 … 5 Not at all

I have enjoyed this session:

A lot 0 … 1 … 2 … 3 … 4 … 5 Not at all

The most important things I have learnt are:

……………………………………………………………………………

My suggestions for improving the session are:

……………………………………………………………………………

while role-playing and playing the tapes back to them, drawings, facilitators' modelling, etc.) to communicate concepts and skills, to match most patients' learning styles, and by delivering the programme over 30 sessions which include a strong skill-based component and repetition of learning points to accommodate patients with poor academic backgrounds and limited life-skills.

Patient motivation to enter treatment is encouraged by having the Patients' Representatives developing leaflets for the programme and distributing them to their peers. The Patients' Representatives are service users who have been elected by their peers to present the views of patients to staff during formal and informal meetings. Patients' Representatives also speak about the intervention during community meetings and collect names from interested patients. Suitable patients, who do not spontaneously volunteer for treatment but are referred by their multidisciplinary team, are subsequently approached separately by a staff member they have a good relationship with and motivational interviewing is used to encourage their attendance at the groups. Concrete rewards are also used as motivators. For example, refreshments are offered and patients are provided with folders in which they place the sessions' handouts.

Patients are all from different ethnic backgrounds; they typically grew up in deprived and dangerous social environments (i.e. inner city London, gang culture) and are currently residing on low and medium secure psychiatric wards where the overt expression of anger and aggression meets certain social roles and serves a function (Averill 1982), that is, by being overtly angry and aggressive (or not), patients attain a social position amongst their community (peers and staff) and achieve a goal (e.g. increased feelings of self-worth, protection from a perceived danger). For example, during the programme, more than one participant disclosed that walking away from a provocative situation on the ward might lead to the person being viewed as a wimp by the other patients and may encourage bullying. Similarly, another participant commented that on the streets of London 'you want to hit first not to get hit'; and in an evaluation form a client commented that one of his learning points was that 'when people are calm it doesn't mean that they are scared', suggesting that, prior to participating in the group, he might have believed that being calm was associated with being fearful.

The programme attempts to modify patients' social norms and encourage adaptive expression of anger and aggression by using real-life scenarios that are relevant to the participants, namely, moral reasoning exercises about gang culture; being subject to peer pressure to steal or hit; and role-plays about being stopped and searched by the police; having a disagreement with a drug dealer; not receiving one's benefit cheque on time. These aim to encourage people to recognise the negative outcomes associated with certain ways of behaving. However, during the end of treatment focus group, participants suggested that the examples and role-plays used in the group could have been more 'real life' to their own experiences. One of the ways this could be achieved would be to draw up a list of commonly shared anger-provoking situations through the pre-group interviews. By making exercises more culturally appropriate, we may be in a stronger position to promote second-order change as opposed to first-order change (Ecker and Hulley 1996).

There are several advantages to running group interventions with psychiatric forensic inpatients. First of all, the group provides an opportunity to explore implications of behaviour with people who are perceived as similar. By hearing their peers' experiences and discovering that they have reacted to situations in ways very similar to their own responses, patients may feel validated and their motivation to engage in treatment might increase. They may also learn from each other and might support one another in changing behaviour, in the group and on the wards. In addition, from a service point of view, groupwork maximises staff resources in an already stretched NHS system, with several patients at once accessing treatment to reduce risk, rather than waiting to be seen individually by a clinician with limited resources because of a heavy caseload.

But is groupwork the best way to increase anger control in psychiatric forensic inpatients, given that they are such a heterogeneous population with multiple needs? Some people might not be suitable for groupwork; they may be better suited for individual treatment, during which the intervention can be tailored to the specific formulation of each patient, e.g. adapting interventions for people with cognitive deficits or examining issues relevant to intimate relationships for people who engage in domestic violence. A way to accommodate both clients' idiosyncrasies and the demands of a busy clinical setting might be to identify which parts of a groupwork programme apply to everyone and which parts do not. The programme could then be offered in a modular way with all patients attending the part that applies to everyone, then being split into subgroups who attend different modules according to their needs.

Conclusions

This chapter detailed current psychological formulations of anger and aggression and how these are applied in clinical settings to reduce forensic inpatients' future risk of maladaptive expression of anger via aggressive behaviour. Difficulties with conducting research in this area and practice issues encountered during treatment provision have also been briefly touched upon. Based on the limited research to date and on qualitative evaluations of current and previous pilots, the following recommendations might be considered when providing anger control interventions to similar populations:

- It is essential to develop a therapeutic alliance to maximise treatment outcome. This might be achieved by having individual sessions with patients before the group to explicitly discuss and agree goals. Further, one-to-one sessions in between group sessions could be useful to address patients' concerns and support practice of strategies. Finally, post-group booster sessions might be useful to maintain or reinforce learning.
- There are many benefits in having a large multidisciplinary facilitator team, including communication of psychological knowledge and skills to other professions, more comprehensive formulations of patients' needs, and greater opportunities for reinforcement of patients' newly acquired skills on the wards.
- Training ward staff in the same techniques taught to patients is also likely to maintain consistency of approaches and maximise learning.
- Patient motivation and treatment readiness and responsivity must be addressed to reduce attrition rates, inform future group programmes and maximise treatment outcomes. These can be achieved by involving patients in programme development, advertisement and recruitment, by using motivational interviewing with patients prior to treatment implementation, by utilising a range of culturally appropriate and tangible exercises to match most patients' learning styles, and by using concrete rewards as motivators for engagement in treatment.
- More thorough suitability assessments for anger treatment are needed to inform group programmes (e.g. is patients' violent behaviour related to anger control problems? Are patients impulsive, over controlled or are they using violence instrumentally?).

- Programmes must be planned of sufficient intensity and length to meet individual needs. In particular, they must be designed with a strong, client-led, skill-based component and repetition and reinforcement of learning points, to accommodate patients with limited life-skills, cognitive deficits and dysfunctional executive functions.
- Ongoing evaluations and more controlled clinical trials are needed to continue building the limited research literature in this area of inpatient treatment. There is also the need for agreement on common outcome measures and development of networks to improve sample sizes. The team led by Arsuffi is trying to achieve this by piloting the Tripe C Programme in different sites, with the same client group, using the same outcome measures.

References

Abouguendia, M., Joyce, S.A., Piper, W. and Ogrodniczuk, J.S. (2004) 'Alliance as a mediator of expectancy effects in short-term group psychotherapy', *Group Dynamics*, 8 (1): 3–12.

Andrews, D.A. and Bonta, J. (1998) *The Psychology of Criminal Conduct* (2nd edn). Cincinnati, OH: Anderson Publishing Co.

Andrews, D.A., Kiessling, J.J., Robinson, D. and Mickus, S. (1986) 'The risk principle of case classification: an outcome evaluation with young adult probationers', *Canadian Journal of Criminology*, 28: 377–84.

Arsuffi, L. (2007) 'Anger management groupwork: a controlled study with British forensic psychiatric inpatients in a medium secure unit', *Forensic Update*, 89: 16–24.

Averill, J.R. (1982) *Anger and Aggression: An Essay on Emotion*. New York: Springer-Verlag.

Bandura, A. (1973) *Aggression: A Social Learning Analysis*. New York: Holt.

Barratt, E.S. (1994) 'Impulsiveness and aggression', in J. Monahan and H.J. Steadman (eds), *Violence and Mental Disorder: Developments in Risk Assessment*. The University of Chicago Press.

Berkowitz, L. (1990) 'On the formation and regulation of anger and aggression: a cognitive-neoassociationistic analysis', *American Psychologist*, 45: 494–503.

Blackburn, R. (1993) *The Psychology of Criminal Conduct: Theory, Research and Practice*. Chichester: Wiley.

Bonta, J. (1995) 'The responsivity principle and offender rehabilitation', *Forum on Corrections Research*, 7 (3): 34–7.

Brown, M. (1996) 'Refining the risk concept: decision context as a factor mediating the relation between risk and programme effectiveness', *Crime and Delinquency*, 42: 435–55.

Buss, A.H. and Durkee, A. (1957) 'An inventory for assessing different kinds of hostility', *Journal of Consulting Psychology*, 21: 343–9.

Commission for Health Improvement (2004) *Commission for Health Improvement NHS Staff Survey*. London: Commission for Health Improvement.

Cornell, D.G., Peterson, C.S. and Richards, H. (1999) 'Anger as a predictor of aggression among incarcerated adolescents', *Journal of Consulting and Clinical Psychology*, 67: 108–15.

Craig, T.J. (1982) 'An epidemiological study of problems associated with violence among psychiatric inpatients', *American Journal of Psychiatry*, 139: 1262–6.

Davidson, R.J., Scherer, K. and Goldsmith, H.H. (2001) *Handbook of Affective Sciences*. Oxford: Oxford University Press.

Deffenbacher, J.L. (1999) 'Cognitive-behavioural conceptualisation and treatment of anger', *JCLP/In Session: Psychotherapy in Practice*, 55 (3): 295–309.

Del Vecchio, T. and O'Leary, K.D. (2004) 'Effectiveness of anger treatments for specific anger problems: a meta-analytic review', *Clinical Psychology Review*, 24: 15–34.

Department of Health (2001) *2000/2001 Survey of Reported Violence or Abusive Incidents, Accidents Involving Staff and Sickness Absence in NHS Authorities in England*. London: Department of Health.

Dernevik, M., Grann, M. and Johansson, S. (2002) 'Violent behaviour in forensic psychiatric patients: risk assessment and different risk-management levels using the HCR-20', *Psychology, Crime and Law*, 8: 93–111.

Dodge, K.A. and Coie, J.D. (1987) 'Social information processing factors in reactive and proactive aggression in children's peer groups', *Journal of Personality and Social Psychology*, 53: 1146–58.

Doyle, M. and Dolan, M. (2006) 'Evaluating the validity of anger regulation problems, interpersonal style, and disturbed mental state for predicting inpatient violence', *Behavioural Sciences and the Law*, 24: 783–98.

Dudek, M., Spitzer, C., Stopsack, M., Freyberger, H.J. and Barnow, S. (2007) 'Forensic inpatients, male sexual offenders: the impact of personality disorder and childhood sexual abuse', *Journal of Forensic Psychiatry and Psychology*, 18 (4): 494–506.

Ecker, B. and Hulley, L. (1996) *Depth Oriented Brief Therapy*. San Francisco: Jossey-Bass.

Friedman, H. and Booth-Kewley, S. (1987) 'The disease-prone personality: a meta-analytic view of the construct', *American Psychologist*, 42: 539–55.

Fromm, E. (1973) *The Anatomy of Human Destructiveness*. Harmondsworth: Penguin.

Gendreau, P. (1996) 'Offender rehabilitation: what we know and what needs to be done', *Criminal Justice and Behaviour*, 23: 144–61.

Harper-Jaques, S. and Reimer, M. (1998) 'Biopsychosocial management of aggression and violence', in M.A. Boid and M.A. Nihart (eds), *Psychiatric Nursing*. New York: Lippincott-Raven.

Health Services Commission (2003) *A Safer Place to Work: Protecting NHS Hospital and Ambulance Staff from Violence and Aggression*. London: The Stationery Office.

Heilbrun, K., Hart, S., Hare, R., Gustafson, D., Nunez, C. and White, A. (1998) 'Inpatient and post discharge aggression in mentally disordered offenders: the role of psychopathy', *Journal of Interpersonal Violence*, 13: 514–27.

Hilton, N. and Frankel, A. (2003) 'Therapeutic value of anger management programmes in a forensic setting', *British Journal of Forensic Practice*, 5 (2): 8–15.

Hollin, C.R. (1992) *Criminal Behaviour*. London: Farmer Press.

Horvath, A.O. and Greenberg, L.S. (1989) 'Development and validation of the Working Alliance Inventory', *Journal of Counselling Psychology*, 36 (2): 223–33.

Howells, K., Day, A., Williamson, P., Bubner, S., Jauncey, S., Parker, A. and Heseltine, K. (2005) 'Brief anger management programs with offenders: outcomes and predictors of change', *Journal of Forensic Psychiatry and Psychology*, 16 (2): 296–311.

Howells, K. Day, A. and Wright, S. (2004) 'Affect, emotions and sex offenders', *Psychology, Crime and Law*, 10: 179–95.

Howells, K., Watt, B., Hall, G. and Baldwin, S. (1997) 'Developing programs for violent offenders', *Legal and Criminological Psychology*, 2: 117–28.

Huesmann, L.R. (1998) 'The role of social information processing and cognitive schema in the acquisition and maintenance of habitual aggressive behaviour', in R.G. Green and E. Donnerstein (eds), *Human Aggression: Theories, Research, and Implications for Social Policy*, pp. 73–109. San Diego, CA: Academic Press.

Ireland, J.L. (2008) 'Conducting individualised theory-driven assessments of violent offenders', in J.L. Ireland, C.A. Ireland and P. Birch (eds), *Violent and Sexual Offenders: Assessment, Treatment and Management*. Cullompton: Willan Publishing.

Jeffrey, C.R. (1979) *Biology and Crime*. London: Sage Publications.

Kay, S.R., Wolkenfeld, F. and Murrill, L.M. (1988) 'Profiles of aggression among psychiatric inpatients. II: covariates and predictors', *Journal of Nervous and Mental Disease*, 176: 547–57.

Kennedy, S. (1999) 'Responsivity: the other classification principle', *Corrections Today*, 6 (1): 48.

Kennedy, S. (2000) 'Treatment responsivity: reducing recidivism by enhancing treatment effectiveness'. Correctional Service Canada. http://www.csc-scc.gc.ca/text/rsrch/compendium/2000/chap_5_e.shtml

Kroner, D.G. and Reddon, J.R. (1995) 'Anger and psychopathology in prison inmates', *Personality and Individual Differences*, 18: 783–8.

Landsberger, H.A. (1958) *Hawthorne Revisited*. Ithaca, NY: Cornell University.

Linsley, P. (2006) *Violence and Aggression in the Workplace: A Practical Guide for All Healthcare Staff*. Abingdon: Radcliffe Publishing.

McGuire, J. (2001) 'What works in correctional intervention? Evidence and practical implications', in G.A. Bernfeld, D.P. Farrington and A.W. Leschied (eds), *Offender Rehabilitation in Practice: Implementing and Evaluating Effective Programs*, pp. 25–43. Chichester: Wiley.

McMurran, M., Charlesworth, P., Duggan, C. and McCarthy, L. (2001) 'Controlling angry aggression: a pilot study intervention with personality disorders offenders', *Behavioural and Cognitive Psychotherapy*, 29: 473–83.

Miller, S., Sees, C. and Brown, J. (2006) 'Key aspects of psychological change in residents of a prison therapeutic community: a focus group approach', *Howard Journal*, 45 (2): 116–28.

Mischel, W. and Shoda, Y. (1995) 'A cognitive-affective system theory of personality: re-conceptualising situations, dispositions, dynamics, and invariance in personality structure', *Psychological Review*, 102: 246–68.

Monahan, J., Steadman, H.J., Silver, E., Applebaum, P.S., Clark-Robbins, P., Mulvey, E.P., Roth, L.H., Grisso, T. and Banks, S. (2001) *Rethinking Risk Assessment: The MacArthur Study of Mental Disorder and Violence*. Oxford: Oxford University Press.

Novaco, R.W. (1975) *Anger Control: The Development of an Experimental Treatment*. Lexington, KY: Lexington.

Novaco, R.W. (1994) 'Anger as a risk factor for violence among the mentally disordered', in J. Monahan and H. Steadman (eds), *Violence and Mental Disorder*, pp. 21–59. Chicago: University of Chicago Press.

Novaco, R.W., Ramm, M. and Black, L. (2000) 'Anger treatment with offenders', in C.R. Hollin (ed.), *Handbook of Offender Assessment and Treatment*, pp. 281–96. John Wiley and Sons Ltd.

Novaco, R.W. and Renwick, S.J. (1998) 'Anger predictors of the assaultiveness of forensic hospital patients', in E. Sanavio (ed.), *Behaviour and Cognitive Therapy Today: Essays in Honour of Hans J. Eysenck*, pp. 199–208. Pergamon.

Owens, R.G. and Ashcroft, J.B. (1995) *Violence: A Guide for the Caring Professions*. London: Croom.

Porteus, S.D. (1965) *Porteus Maze Test: The Development and Evaluation of an Experimental Treatment*. Lexington, MA: D.C. Heath.

Raine, A., Dodge, K., Loeber, R., Gatzke-Kopp, L., Lynam, D., Reynolds, C., Stouthamer-Loeber, M. and Liu, J. (2006) 'The reactive-proactive aggression questionnaire: differential correlates of reactive and proactive aggression in adolescent boys', *Aggressive Behaviour*, 32: 159–71.

Renwick, S.J., Black, L., Ramm, M. and Novaco, R.W. (1997) 'Anger treatment with forensic hospital patients', *Legal and Criminological Psychology*, 2: 103–16.

Rice, M. and Harris, G. (1997) 'The treatment of mentally disordered offenders', *Psychology, Public Policy, and Law*, 3: 126–83.

Rice, M.E., Harris, G.T., Quincey, V.L. and Cyr, M. (1990) 'Planning treatment programmes in secure psychiatric facilities', in D.N. Weisstub (ed.), *Law and Mental Health: International Perspectives* (vol 5: 162–230). New York: Pergamon.

Rondeau, G., Brodeur, N., Brochu, S. and Lemire, G. (2001) 'Dropout and completion of treatment among spouse abusers', *Violence and Victims*, 16 (2): 127–43.

Spielberger, C.D. (1986) *State Trait Anger Expression Inventory: STAXI Professional Manual*. Florida: Psychological Assessment Resources, Inc.

Stermac, L.E. (1986) 'Anger control treatment for forensic patients', *Journal of Interpersonal Violence*, 1 (4): 446–57.

Stompe, T., Ortwein-Swoboda, G. and Schanda, H. (2004) 'Schizophrenia, delusional symptoms, and violence: the threat/control override concept re-examined', *Schizophrenia Bulletin*, 30 (1): 31–45.

Taylor, J.L., Novaco, R.W., Gillmer, B. and Thorne, I. (2002) 'Cognitive-behavioural treatment of anger intensity among offenders with intellectual disabilities', *Journal of Applied Research in Intellectual Disabilities*, 15 (2): 151–65.

Tobin, D.L., Holroyd, K. and Reynolds, R. (1982) *The Assessment and Treatment of Coping: Psychometric Development of the Coping Strategies Inventory*. Paper presented at the American Association for the Advancement of Behaviour Therapy.

Tremblay, R.E., Mihic, L., Graham, K. and Jelley, J. (2007) 'Role of motivation to respond to provocation, the social environment, and trait aggression in alcohol-related aggression', *Aggressive Behaviour*, 33: 389–411.

Tuttman, S. (1997) 'Protecting the therapeutic alliance in this time of changing health-care delivery systems', *International Journal of Group Psychotherapy*, 47 (1): 3–16.

Van Voorhis, P. (1997) 'Correctional classification and the responsivity principle', *Forum on Corrections Research*, 9 (1): 46–50.

Zamble, E. and Quinsey, V.L. (1997) *The Criminal Recidivism Process*. Cambridge: Cambridge University Press.

Chapter 17

Developments in treatment for drug misuse offenders[1]

Nicholas LeBoutillier and Beverly Love

Introduction

> Occasional drug use is not the principal cause of Britain's drug problems. The bulk of drug-related harm (death, illness, crime and other social problems) occurs among the relatively small number of people that become dependent on Class A drugs, notably heroin and cocaine.
>
> (Reuter and Stevens 2007: 7)

The treatment of drug misusing offenders is a prominent issue, clouded in media commentary about the rights of those who are estimated to commit up to half of the United Kingdom's acquisitive crimes (HMG 2008). The aim of this chapter is to provide the reader with an overview of developments in the treatment for drug misusing offenders. Initially, however, a general review of drugs and crime will be conducted. This will be followed by a background review of the development of treatment services in the United Kingdom and consideration of recent progress in treatments for drug misusing offenders. There is an additional section which will consider the issue of mental health and substance misuse, sometimes referred to as dual diagnosis or co-morbidity.

The methods used to define and classify drugs depend upon the need to understand use and misuse. Whilst a biopsychological approach categorises according to psychopharmacological effect, a legal classification categorises on the basis of perceived health and social risk. Julien (2005) largely classifies drugs according to their psychopharmacological effects. Alcohol, barbiturates, benzodiazepines, and second-generation anxiolytics are defined as *sedative-hypnotic drugs*; cocaine, amphetamine, caffeine and nicotine are collectively referred to as *psychostimulants*. Similarly, other drugs are defined on the basis of their *biological* (e.g. anti-depressants) and *therapeutic* (e.g. gingko) treatment potential. A final umbrella group of drugs is defined according to their *abuse properties* (e.g. cannabis). Alternatively, a series of UK legislative procedures has resulted in a legal system that classifies drugs on the basis of their risk to the individual and society. Here, drugs are grouped into Classes A, B, and C where guideline penalties are suggested for possession and dealing. Alongside these are other controlled substances such as inhalants, alcohol and tobacco that have age, purpose and location restrictions.

This classification system forms part of a long history of UK legislative acts dating back to the 1860s and passing through distinct phases (Reuter and Stevens 2007). Reuter and Stevens (2007) note that the first attempt to regulate the access and sale of substances occurred through the Pharmacy Act (1868). This resulted in the restriction of the sale of poisons and dangerous substances to pharmacies. During this period there were very few controls on drug use; both heroin and cocaine were freely available without prescription and were often sold as a panacea. For example, Coca-Cola originally contained extracts from the coca plant and was popularised as a health and energy-providing tonic (Maisto *et al.* 1995). The second phase, occurring from the 1920s to the 1960s, referred to by Reuter and Stevens (2007) as *Creating a National System*, saw the introduction of a series of Acts restricting the sale and use of opium, cocaine, morphine and heroin to dependent users. This phase also resulted in the criminalisation of cannabis possession. The third phase, *Increasing Control*, occurred as a result of both the increase in heroin prescribing by general practitioners and the introduction and widespread use of cannabis, amphetamine and LSD (Reuter and Stevens 2007). This was a tightening up and formalisation of the national system with key legislative acts (e.g. the Misuse of Drugs Act 1971) imposing penalties for the possession and sale of illicit substances. Reuter and Stevens' final phase, *Integrating Criminal Justice and Health*, occurred from the early 1990s onwards. This resulted in both an increase in the powers available to the authorities (e.g. Anti-Social Behaviour Act 2003) and the establishment of links between the punitive and treatment processes (e.g. the Criminal Justice Act 1991).

The United Kingdom has the highest number of dependent drug users and one of the highest rates of recreational drug use in Europe

(Reuter and Stevens 2007). A recent British Crime Survey (2006) showed that 34.9 per cent of the 16–59-year-old people sampled reported lifetime use of an illicit substance with 13.9 per cent stating that they had tried a Class A drug. Self-reported use in the past year showed that cannabis was the most frequently used drug (8.9 per cent), followed by cocaine (2.4 per cent), Ecstasy (1.6 per cent), amphetamine (1.3 per cent), amyl nitrate (1.2 per cent), and hallucinogens (1.1 per cent). When the figures are calculated for people aged between 16–24, self-reported use rates increase to 45.1 per cent with 16.9 per cent reporting Class A drug use. Observation of past year use shows that 21.4 per cent reported using cannabis; this is followed by cocaine (5.9 per cent), Ecstasy (4.3 per cent), amyl nitrate (3.9 per cent), hallucinogens (3.4 per cent), and amphetamines (3.3 per cent); see Roe and Man (2006) for full details on self-reported drugs use in England and Wales.

Defining drug misusing offenders

Drug misusing offenders are often described as those offenders whose drug misuse is 'problematic' rather than recreational. Problematic drug misuse involves 'dependency, regular excessive use and involves risky behaviour towards self and others, including offending behaviour' (Advisory Council on the Misuse of Drugs 1988, adapted by Edmunds *et al.* 1999). The offending behaviour often involves acquisitive crime, which some suggest funds the drug dependency, known as the 'economic' model of drug-related crime (Brochu 2001). The two drugs (and their derivatives) most commonly associated with these 'crime-spree' scenarios are opium (heroin, morphine) and cocaine (crack); this association is linked to the notion that these drugs are the most likely to lead to dependence. A recent estimate suggests that there are 327,000 regular users of these drugs in the United Kingdom, with 281,000 opiate users and 193,000 crack-cocaine users (HMG 2008). Hammersley *et al.'s* (2003) analysis of young offenders and drug use found that the type of offence most commonly linked to substance use was theft (92 per cent of cohort). This was followed by wilful damage (80 per cent), shoplifting (80 per cent), fighting/disorder (71 per cent), buying stolen goods (70 per cent) and selling stolen goods (70 per cent). The proposed economic cost of drug misuse offending in the UK is £15.4 billion (HMG 2008). A general estimate of the US costs of all types of substance use in 2002 was $430 billion with $170 billion of that cost linked to alcohol use and $138 billion linked to cigarette smoking (cited in Julien 2005).

As noted, the popularised link between drugs and offending posits the individual as an addict committing crimes to fund his/her habit; the *economic necessity* hypothesis. However, recent reviews of research into the link between drugs and crime have challenged this model (Albery *et al.* 2003; Pudney 2002; Seddon 2000). For example, Pudney's (2002) study of the sequence of initiation into crime and drugs showed that criminal and truanting activities preceded drug taking *per se*, occurring up to four years prior to the age of onset for drugs associated with the economic necessity model: crack cocaine and heroin. Thus, research and review materials tend to proffer a complex interaction between drug taking and other criminal activities that also requires the consideration of tobacco, alcohol, family circumstances, deprivation and schooling. Albery *et al.* (2003) cite five potential links between drugs and crime. These are:

1 The act of taking drugs is a criminal act;
2 Drug-taking may lead to other forms of crime;
3 Non-drug-taking crimes may lead to drug-taking;
4 There is a complex interaction between drug-taking and other crimes;
5 There are associated causes that lead to both non-drug-taking and drug-taking crimes.

The link is further compounded through the inevitability of a *drug causes crime* scenario, suggesting the likelihood of an eventual causal relationship arising from drug dependence (Bennett and Holloway 2005). Further, the statistics also indicate that young males are most likely to commit crimes (14–18 years old) at the same age that they are also likely to try drugs. Finally, statistics on the numbers of prisoners who have drug misuse problems further obscure the association. For example, Penfold *et al.'s* (2005) study of current prisoners and prison staff in six prisons in the UK suggested that heroin, crack cocaine and cannabis use were prevalent.

However we choose to understand the association between drug misuse and criminal behaviour, interventions and treatments are justified on the basis that: there is clear evidence that drug misusers are likely to engage in 'crime-spree' behaviours; drug misuse increases the likelihood of offending; and, as a group, drug misusers have higher levels of contact with the criminal justice system (McSweeney *et al.* 2008).

The development of intervention and treatment programmes

> Treatment can be defined in general terms as the provision of one or more structured interventions designed to manage health and other problems as a consequence of drug abuse and to improve or maximize personal social functioning. (UNDOC 2003, Chapter II: 2)

An observation of the history of interventions and treatments for drug misuse shows cycles of tolerance and prohibition (Blume 2000). The earliest forms of intervention occurred as a response to opium dependence and were largely administered by general practitioners (GPs). A well-known example is the British Model, whereby until the 1960s GPs were free to prescribe heroin and cocaine to those they diagnosed as dependent. The patients then picked up the drugs from their pharmacy. As this practice resulted in a minority of GPs overprescribing, the procedure was stopped in 1967 (the Dangerous Drugs Act) and thousands of people were referred to newly established specialist Drug Dependency Units (Farrell *et al.* 1998).

In the 1960s an increase in illicit drug use occurred as the drug culture in the USA became popular in the UK. Consequently, many of the early treatments and interventions were based upon those that had been developed in the USA. The earliest examples of these were Christian-based programmes and therapeutic communities. The most accessible and easily transferable model was the 12-step programme (or Minnesota Method) that had been adapted from Alcoholics Anonymous (AA) to Narcotics Anonymous (NA). These programmes adopted a disease-based model of alcohol and drug dependence with a spiritual method of sustained recovery. As can be seen below, the first seven steps focus upon an acknowledgement of the addiction and a desire to withdraw from drug-taking. The final five steps resolve to maintain the changes in behaviour and to rectify the problems that the person has previously caused through their behaviours. These steps are the focus of anonymous meeting groups.

The 12 Steps (Alcoholics Anonymous 2001)

1. We admitted we were powerless over alcohol – that our lives had become unmanageable;
2. Came to believe that a Power greater than ourselves could restore us to sanity;

3 Made a decision to turn our will and our lives over to the care of God *as we understood Him;*
4 Made a searching and fearless moral inventory of ourselves;
5 Admitted to God, to ourselves, and to another human being the exact nature of our wrongs;
6 Were entirely ready to have God remove all these defects of character;
7 Humbly asked Him to remove our shortcomings;
8 Made a list of all persons we had harmed, and became willing to make amends to them all;
9 Made direct amends to such people wherever possible, except when to do so would injure them or others;
10 Continued to take personal inventory and when we were wrong promptly admitted it;
11 Sought through prayer and meditation to improve our conscious contact with God *as we understood Him*, praying only for knowledge of His Will for us and the power to carry that out;
12 Having had a spiritual awakening as the result of these steps, we tried to carry this message to alcoholics, and to practise these principles in all our affairs.

Therapeutic communities also emerged during this period. The aim of this approach was to provide an asylum for drug users where peers are encouraged to both support each other in abstinence and confront each other in doubt. Two similar approaches emerged: first the user-oriented and democratic, UK-based, Maxwell Jones model such as the Phoenix House Project; and second, the USA-based Synanon approach, such as the Richmond Fellowship Crescent House Project (Dale-Perera 1998). Finally, this period also witnessed the development of non-statutory street-based agencies offering informal advice, counselling and information to drug users (Dale-Perera 1998).

The 1970s and 1980s saw further developments in the treatment of drug users. The Misuse of Drugs Act (1971) established clear penalties for drug users and dealers. Drug workers and drug teams were established, those who worked with drug users came together to form integrated units and SCODA (Standing Conference on Drug Abuse) was established to bring together non-statutory services (Dale-Perera 1998). There was also an increase in substitute opiate prescribing for heroin users with a tendency to prescribe oral rather than injecting methadone (Farrell *et al.* 1998). The most important factor occurring during this period was the emergence of HIV/

AIDS in the mid to late 1980s. This threatened to reach epidemic proportions in those who injected drugs and led to a rise in harm reduction procedures. As the threat of HIV/AIDS exceeded the danger of drug using, outreach projects that focused upon helping hard-to-reach users were developed; similarly, needle-exchange schemes that supplied clean injecting equipment and safe disposal units were set up (Dale-Perera 1998). Finally, the use of drug rooms was piloted in the Netherlands. The policies, interventions and treatments in the 1980s were characterised by a general rhetoric supporting hard-line abstinence policies (e.g. Nancy Reagan's 'Just Say No!' campaign from 1984 onwards)[2] set against local-level implementations of harm reduction procedures designed to minimise the spread of infectious diseases.

In Britain, the early 1990s showed a dramatic change in drug policy. Harm prevention and reduction merged into an integrated whole and there was a specific emphasis upon developing a consistent policy with measurable outcomes such as the Home Office's Drug Harm Index (DHI). The Criminal Justice Act (1991) refocused the debate with the formal introduction of treatment as a condition of probation. This was followed by the Government's *Tackling Drugs Together* proposal that required the police to introduce drug strategies, and later by the Crime and Disorder Act (1998) which required Drug Treatment and Testing Orders (DTTO). Coupled with these initiatives was the short-lived introduction of a 'drug czar' (Keith Hellawell), the development of a National Treatment Agency and national and local information (FRANK) and communication (Connexions) programmes. These more recent developments emphasise abstinence, treatment and harm reduction in a unified package of services aimed at reducing drug misuse offending.

From the *ad hoc* developments in the 1960s, interventions and treatments have proliferated, targets have been set and achieved on the number of people receiving help (HMG 2008), points of access have been varied to include the hard-to-reach clients and there have been transitions in services. Prior to providing an overview of the English and Welsh present system of services, a brief review of the types of treatment available will be given. Stevens *et al.* (2006) provide a thorough overview of the different types of treatment available to problem drug users. These include: low threshold; detoxification; pharmacotherapies; talking therapies; and alternative therapies. The following summary will adopt this classification.

Low threshold services are those that provide simple and efficient ways of reducing problem drug use threats. They include drop-in services, needle exchange, targeted delivery of health care, outreach services, and drug consumption rooms (Stevens *et al.* 2006). Drop-in services provide basic lifeline assistance such as food, clothing and shelter, as well as advice on employment, health and welfare. These services may act as vital communication points that maintain the contact between problem drug users and the services provided to assist them back into society. As noted, needle exchange services arose from the fears of HIV/AIDS and more recently, hepatitis B and C. They provide users with the paraphernalia required to avoid these infectious diseases: needles, syringes, spoons, filters, water, citric acid and condoms. Initial fears that these services would increase drug use proved to be unfounded and considerable research has shown that they play an important role in reducing blood-borne diseases in drug users; see Gibson *et al.'s* (2001) meta-review of research.

> Multiperson use of needles and syringes contributes to a considerable illness burden in both developed and developing countries. Use of nonsterile syringes can occur within the context of illicit drug injection and is associated with transmission of blood-borne pathogens, including HIV, hepatitis B virus (HBV) and hepatitis C virus (HCV), human Tcell lymphotropic viruses, and even malaria. Syringe sharing, or even reuse of syringes by the same person, increases the risk of endocarditis, cellulitis, and abscesses. (Strathdee and Vlahov 2001: 1)

To provide a targeted healthcare delivery service, it is necessary to set up clinics close to areas of high drug use. They may provide professional or peer assistance, shelter, or medical services to *hard-to-reach* groups such as the homeless, sex workers and other vulnerable groups (Stevens *et al.* 2006). The most controversial low threshold service is the drug consumption room. Like most of these interventions, the rooms emerged in the late 1980s from the need to protect injecting users from infectious diseases. Reviews of the use of safe rooms show that they provide a range of services that reduce needle sharing and assist in the welfare and education of high-risk users (Kerr *et al.* 2005; Kimber *et al.* 2005).

The second category of treatments listed by Stevens *et al.* (2006) are detoxification procedures. The aim of a detoxification programme is to decrease the drug user's physical and psychological dependence on a drug. This is a difficult procedure as detoxification leads to a host of withdrawal symptoms (e.g. pain, fever and craving). Consequently, users are often placed on substitute drugs that are less harmful but mimic some of the effects of the drug (e.g. methadone as a replacement for heroin) or they are given drugs that block the effects of the to-be-withdrawn substance (e.g. naltrexone decreases the effect of heroin). These procedures are carefully introduced and monitored (the maintenance programme) and are coupled with psychological and social counselling. A successful programme removes dependence while limiting the amount of trauma to the individual. In the past two decades, there has been a development of ultra-rapid opioid detoxification (UROD) programmes which combine the antagonist effects of naloxone and naltrexone with the analgesic and sedative effects of anaesthetics. The purpose of these four-to-six-hour detoxification procedures is to remove the intolerable effects of dependence as quickly as possible (see Kaye *et al.* 2003). UROD is not a magic bullet, as the effects of withdrawal persist, but the aim is to set them at manageable levels so they can be dealt with on a symptom-to-symptom basis.

For detoxification to succeed, the drug user must be highly motivated to come off the drug. Unfortunately, the level of commitment needed is too high for every dependent user to succeed and in these circumstances an alternative pharmacotherapeutic may be adopted. This involves the prescribed replacement of the harmful drug with a less dangerous alternative. Following the withdrawal of L-alpha acetylmethadol (LAAM) in 2004, the main drugs used to substitute opiate dependence are methadone and buprenorphine. Controversially, dexamphetamine may be used to treat cocaine dependence; however, due to potentially dangerous side effects this should be done in conjunction with continued medical examination (Stevens *et al.* 2006). The importance of pharmacotherapies to both the individual and society is highlighted by Julien's review of the treatment of opiate dependence:

> Opioid dependence is a brain-related medical disorder (characterized by predictable signs and symptoms) that can be effectively treated with significant benefits for the patient and for society. However, society must make a commitment to offer effective treatment for opioid dependence to all who need it. Everyone dependent on opioids should have access to methadone, LAAM, or buprenorphine maintenance therapy in a methadone clinic or in a physician's office. (2005: 494)

Reviews of the use of substitute drugs to treat drug misusing offenders have shown that they are effective in reducing both drug misuse and acquisitive offending (Hammersley *et al.* 1989).

Therapeutic communities (TC) have been an integral feature of drug treatment and intervention for the past 40 years. The emergence of the HIV/AIDS epidemic reframed the treatment process towards a harm reduction approach that sat awkwardly beside the abstinence ideology of the TC (Broekaert 2006). Residential rehabilitation is particularly problematic because it is both an expensive and selective form of treatment. These projects were developed through the belief that substance dependent individuals are capable of removing drugs from their lives. In the first decade of the twenty-first century, they are adapting to social and economic needs. As Broekaert states in his review of the future of the TC in Europe:

> The drug-free TC extended its approach to other target groups, such as prisoners, mothers and children, adolescents, dually diagnosed residents, methadone maintained clients, chronic abusers and mental health patients. TC treatment, methadone programmes and harm reduction methods have been integrated. Brief interventions have been introduced that utilize family and social network support. The TC movement has adopted post-modern approaches that advocate the introduction of shorter programmes, de-institutionalization, outreach and community-based interventions. (2006: 1678)

Many of the contemporary talking therapies are based upon an eclectic mixture of humanistic, behavioural and cognitive approaches. Stevens *et al.* (2006) highlight three types of therapy (motivational interviewing; cognitive behavioural approaches; and community reinforcement and contingency contracting) that have all been successfully applied to substance-dependent individuals. Motivational interviewing is a non-coercive, goal-directed, client-centred counselling technique aimed at identifying and focusing upon ambivalence. It is normally applied to addictive behaviours but may be used in other circumstances (Rollnick and Miller 1995). The key to motivational interviewing is to encourage the client to recognise that there is conflict in their lives. It neither aims to diagnose the source of the conflict nor to offer specific advice on how to change the behaviours. In this respect, it differs from traditional methods that seek change through confrontation.

Motivational interviewing may be used as an early assessment approach in a structured prevention programme that includes cognitive behavioural therapy (CBT) and community reinforcement and contingency contracting. CBT is a general approach premised by the notion that thoughts, behaviours and emotions are fundamentally entwined in the individual. CBT works in the present to change problematic thoughts and behaviours. Its aim is to provide drug misusing offenders with the skills and strategies to avoid offending behaviours. The effectiveness of CBT is dependent upon the implementation services that assist the opportunity for change. These reinforcements and contingencies include: family counselling; providing drug-free social networks; improving job opportunities and implementing positive reward programmes such as token economies (Stevens *et al.* 2006).

Dual diagnosis and drug misusing offenders

The term dual diagnosis will be discussed in relation to the co-occurrence of a mental health problem with drug misuse, although there are several other definitions of the term. There is no direct evidence of a link between dual diagnosis and drug misusing offending but there is considerable indirect support for the importance of future investigation. Research has focused upon three key associations: drug misuse and mental health; prisons and mental health; and offending and dual diagnosis. These are discussed below.

Findings in the UK indicate that mental health disorders for those with drug misuse problems are higher than for the general population (Department of Health 2002). For example, Strathdee *et al.* (2002) found that 93 per cent of clients in drug misuse services indicated mild to moderate mental health problems: depression (41 per cent); generalised anxiety and panic attacks (55 per cent). Weaver *et al.* (2002) found that nearly 75 per cent of clients of drug services had mental health problems: depression and/or anxiety disorder (68 per cent); severe anxiety (19 per cent); mild (40.3 per cent) and severe (26.9 per cent) depression. Finally, Marsden *et al.* (2000) found that 29 per cent of opiate-dependent clients in drug treatment services had anxiety and 26 per cent had depression.

The Social Exclusion Unit *Reducing Re-offending* Report (2002) found that male (x 14) and female (x 35) prisoners were more likely to have a mental health disorder than the general population (despite legislative diversionary procedures). The SEU report found that approximately 70 per cent of prisoners had two or more mental health disorders and that 40 per cent of male prisoners and 63 per cent of female prisoners had a neurotic disorder. The Institute of Psychiatry found that 66 per cent of prisoners on remand had a mental health disorder and

39 per cent of sentenced prisoners had mental health disorders. (IOP 1998, cited in Bird 1998). Bird (1998) also found that 55 per cent of prisoners had some form of neurotic disorder and that most prisoners had a high prevalence of depression and general worry. Strathdee *et al.*'s (2002) study of primary care services found that those with an indication of dual diagnosis were at greater risk of criminal behaviour than those with no dual diagnosis. For example, 62 per cent of patients in forensic services had a dual diagnosis. Research also shows that those with dual diagnosis were at greater risk of offending behaviour (Banerjee *et al.* 2002; Tessler and Dennis 1989).

In combination, this research shows the importance of understanding the link between drug misuse, mental health, and offending; especially as those with a dual diagnosis have problems accessing help for either their drug or mental health problem or both (Department of Health 2002; Mind 2007; Social Exclusion Unit 2002; Banerjee *et al.* 2002). The Department of Health (2002) suggests this is because mental health and drug treatment services have developed separately and consequently there are few services that deal with both problems concurrently. Wanigaratne *et al.* (2005) suggest that addressing a drug misuser's mental health can have beneficial effects on her/his drug taking behaviour. They also claim that the psychological health of clients on any drug treatment programme should be a key outcome measure of the efficacy of that programme (see also Wilke 2004; Bean and Nemitz 2004).

We now turn to an overview of how the UK Government has integrated treatments and interventions to address the needs of substance misusing offenders. Please note that there are some additional, related approaches taken in Scotland and Northern Ireland, to those in England and Wales, due to greater legislative autonomy.

The UK Government's response to drug misusing offenders

> Despite some methodological limitations, recent studies seeking to assess the impact of the Drug Interventions Programme (DIP) have reported some successes in terms of delivering improved rates of engagement with drug treatment and sustaining high rates of retention. (McSweeney *et al.* 2008: 6)

The Drug Interventions Programme (DIP) began in April 2003 as a UK Government (Home Office) initiative to tackle Class A drug misuse and the associated acquisitive crime. During the early development of DIP there was little evidence, either in the UK or the rest of the world, from which to draw a macro-level national programme of support and help for drug misuse offenders. Consequently, an indirect evidence-base and policy context was drawn from the following documents: Social Exclusion Unit *Reducing Re-offending* Report (2002), Hiller *et al.*, cited by Fox 2002, *Through The Prison Gate* (Morgan and Owers 2001), *Justice For All White Paper* (Home Office 2002a) and the *Updated Drug Strategy* (Home Office 2002b). From these documents, the following areas were identified as key to reducing reoffending and drug-taking behaviour: education and training; employment; drugs and alcohol rehabilitation; mental and physical health; attitudes/life skills; housing; debt and benefits; and family networks.

We now turn to considering some examples of intervention. Each of the cases presented below is taken directly from the file of case studies from the Drug Interventions Programme, compiled by the DIP Strategic Communications Team in 2008 (see link below). We are grateful for permission to include these case studies.

The aim of the DIP was to develop throughcare and aftercare procedures that ensured a continuity of treatment and intervention from the drug misusers' point of arrest, to sentencing, release from prison or community service and integration back into the community. In order to achieve this, the procedures are managed by Criminal Justice Integrated Teams (CJITs) outside prisons and Counselling, Assessment, Referral, Advice and Throughcare (CARAT) workers inside prisons.

Appropriate individuals are referred (predominantly by Criminal Justice System agencies) to CJITs who firstly assess the individual's needs (see example success stories). CJIT workers then help the individual to access the appropriate range of interventions from the previously noted areas. CJITs use a multi-agency approach to work closely with those involved in providing the interventions. For example, they may seek support from Jobcentre Plus, education services, GPs, local mental health teams, drug treatment services and housing services.

The Drug Interventions Programme also consists of a range of coercive interventions including drug testing on arrest and charge, required assessment, conditional cautioning and restrictions on bail. Some of these are available across England and Wales and some are only available in specific areas. The idea is that the different elements of DIP together provide an opportunity to offer a drug misusing offender treatment and support at every stage of the criminal justice process. The aim is to draw as many problematic drug misusing

Example DIP success story: Brian (pseudonym), male, 37

Intervention: CARAT (Counselling, Assessment, Referral, Advice and Throughcare) services in prison; probation supervision and community treatment; police monitoring via Prolific and other Priority Offender (PPO) scheme[3]

Case and outcome: Brian had a total of 46 previous convictions spanning a 20-year period and was responsible for 125 criminal offences including burglary, theft, fraud, assault, drugs and firearms offences. He served several prison sentences and his last saw him released in July 2007. He had PPO (Prolific and other Priority Offender) status for several years and had caused the local community much harm and distress. Brian had a long history of Class A drugs misuse and had a heroin and crack cocaine addiction for several years. He first tested positive on arrest in July 2004.

DIP measures have been taken since this time and the police team have continually enforced treatment conditions when in force and offered treatment through DIP treatment providers at other times. As a result Brian has not been arrested since July 2007 and has been in drug treatment since his last release from prison. He is prescribed methadone through local drug services and has engaged in the 12-step programme. Brian has not taken illegal drugs in all that time. He is now being removed from the PPO list and his whole attitude to life is being changed. His health is much improved and he has recently completed a sponsored run in aid of charity.

Source: http://drugs.homeoffice.gov.uk/publication-search/dip/dip-success-stories-2008 (accessed September 2009)

offenders as possible, including those on the fringes of offending, into treatment and support and to maximise their engagement and retention in that support.

DIP also has strong connections with Counselling, Assessment, Referral, Advice and Throughcare (CARAT) workers in prisons who provide the link for drug misusing offenders from prison to community-based support to further help maximise retention in treatment. Some of the DIP measures offer offenders the choice to take up drug treatment and support in order to address their drug-related offending. Whilst this may be viewed as a coercive route into

Example DIP success story: Danielle (pseudonym), female 27

Intervention: restriction on bail; debt and benefit management; housing support; Tier 3 prescribing; alcohol intervention; one-to-one sessions; crisis intervention; motivational interviewing; solution focus therapy; education, training and employment support.

Case and outcome: Danielle had been using heroin, crack and alcohol daily for seven years. During that time there were only two days when she had not used. When she signed up to DIP in September 2007, following her arrest, she was testing positive for opiates and cocaine. Danielle was also injecting in her neck and drinking heavily. She attended her follow-up assessment and met her case manager with whom she discussed her needs and the support she required.

Leading up to her court appearance in November 2007, Danielle was engaging with her case worker and regularly attending her appointments. In court she was bailed on condition she engaged with DIP. At that time Danielle owed £7,000 in housing benefits and was also in arrears with her gas, water, electricity and TV licence but, despite these problems, she completed her bail without any breaches and made the decision to continue to engage with DIP voluntarily. Her case worker referred Danielle to the DIP housing manager, who managed to get her housing arrears cancelled. Her case worker then dealt with all Danielle's other outstanding bills, getting them 'quashed', and organised for her to start afresh, paying her bills weekly.

To help with Danielle's drinking problem she completed a 'drink diary', which involved daily logging of everything she drank, and then the following week, she aimed to reduce on the previous week's intake.

When Danielle told her case worker that she was interested in 'getting back into computers' she was put in touch with a local college and attended an open day at the college where she is now undertaking a computer course. Just three months after her arrest, Danielle was testing negative and continues to do so. She attributes her success to DIP and, of course, her case worker.

Source: http://drugs.homeoffice.gov.uk/publication-search/dip/dip-success-stories-2008 (accessed September 2009) drug treatment, there is research to support its effectiveness (Skodbo *et al.* 2007).

Evidence suggests that DIP is having an impact on reducing drug misuse and the associated crime. Since DIP began, drug-related crime has reduced by a fifth; furthermore, over 4,500 drug misusing offenders enter treatment each month (http://drugs.homeoffice.gov.uk/drug-interventions-programme/strategy/impact-and-success/ accessed November 2009). Research which examined the DIP's impact found that drug misusing offenders reduced their offending by 26 per cent after they had been identified and maintained contact with the DIP. Nearly half of the cohort had reductions in offending by up to 79 per cent. Twenty-five per cent of the cohort maintained a similar level of offending and 28 per cent showed increased levels of offending (Skodbo *et al.* 2007). However, establishing a direct cause and effect was not possible as no control group was used. Further research, which evaluated the Aftercare element of DIP, showed that a sample of participants on six CJIT caseloads significantly reduced their Class A drug misuse. Furthermore, acquisitive offending reduced by 34 per cent for those who had been on the caseload for between 11 and 13 weeks (Love 2007).

Conclusion

The aim of this chapter is to inform the reader of a range of issues related to treatments and interventions for drug misusing offenders. The increase in drug use in the past 50 years has caused considerable disruption to UK society, ruining lives, families and communities. Whilst initial *ad hoc* reactions from legislators had little impact upon the problems, recent coherent and inclusive policies have shown some successes. It is essential that these policies continue to be informed by researchers in the social sciences. It is also important that the appropriate drug treatment services are available to tackle those substances being abused and causing the most harm to individuals, communities, victims and the families of those affected.

Further exploration of the prevalence of dual diagnosis among offending populations is necessary. The relationship between different types of drug misuse including poly-drug misuse and different types of mental ill health among both community and prison-based offenders is required. The efficacy of addressing mental health and dual diagnosis issues in drug treatment programmes also warrants attention.

Whilst it is outside the scope of this chapter, it is equally important to ensure that preventative measures are targeted at the next generation of potential problematic drug misusing offenders. This includes the children of drug misusing parents and the younger siblings of drug misusing offenders, which forward thinking programmes already address.

Notes

1 Comments and views expressed by the authors in this chapter are those of the authors and are not necessarily those of the Home Office or Civil Service (nor do they necessarily reflect Government policy).
2 www.npr.org/templates/story/story.php?storyId=9252490 (accessed December 2009).
3 The Prolific and Other Priority Offender programme aligned with the Drug Interventions Programme in 2007 to ensure the highest crime causing individuals (with drug misuse issues) are identified and targeted for supervision and interventions to offer them the opportunity to change their offending behaviour or face a swift return to the courts. www.crimereduction.homeoffice.gov.uk/ppo/ppominisite01.htm

References

Albery, I.P., McSweeney, T. and Hough, M. (2003) 'Drug use and criminal behaviour: indirect, direct or no causal relationship?', in J.R. Adler (ed.), *Forensic Psychology. Concepts, Debates and Practice*. Cullompton: Willan Publishing.

Alcoholics Anonymous (2001) *Chapter 5: How It Works (fourth edition)*. Alcoholics Anonymous World Services. www.aa.org/bigbookonline/en_BigBook_chapt5.pdf.

Banerjee, S., Clancy, C. and Crome, I. (2002) *Co-existing Problems of Mental Disorder and Substance Misuse (Dual Diagnosis): An Information Manual*. London: The Royal College of Psychiatrists' Research Unit.

Bean, P. and Nemitz, T. (eds) (2004) *Drug Treatment: What Works*. London: Routledge.

Bennett, T. and Holloway, K. (2005) *Understanding Drugs, Alcohol and Crime*. Maidenhead: Open University Press.

Bird, L. (for the Mental Health Foundation) (1998) 'The prevalence of mental health problems in the prison setting'. *Updates*, 1, 3.

Blume, J. (2000) 'Treatment of drug misuse in the new century', *Western Journal of Medicine*, 172 (1): 4–5.

Brochu, S. (2001) *The Relationship Between Drugs and Crime*. Montreal: University of Montreal, cited in T. Bennett and K. Holloway (2005)

Understanding Drugs, Alcohol and Crime. Maidenhead: Open University Press.

Broekaert, E. (2006) 'What future for the Therapeutic Community in the field of addiction? A view from Europe', *Addiction*, 101: 1677–8.

Dale-Perera, A. (1998) 'Drug services', in G.V. Stimson, C. Fitch and A. Judd (eds), *Drug Use in London*. London: Leighton Print.

Department of Health (2002) *Mental Health Policy Implementation Guide Dual Diagnosis Good Practice Guide*. DoH publications No. 27767. London: Department of Health.

Edmunds, M., Hough, M., Turnbull, P.J. and May, T. (1999) *Doing Justice to Treatment: Referring Offenders to Drug Services*. Home Office, DPAS Paper 2. London: Home Office.

Farrell, M., Sheridan, J., Griffiths, P. and Strang, J. (1998) 'Substitute opiate prescribing and pharmacy services', in G.V. Stimson, C. Fitch and A. Judd (eds), *Drug Use in London*. London: Leighton Print.

Fox, A. (2002) 'Aftercare for drug using prisoners: lessons from an international study', *Probation Journal*, 49 (2): 120–9.

Gibson, D.R., Flynn, N.M. and Peralec, D. (2001) 'Effectiveness of syringe exchange programs in reducing HIV risk behavior and HIV seroconversion among injection users', *AIDS*, 15: 1329–41.

Hammersley, R., Forsyth, A., Morrison, V. and Davies, J.B. (1989) 'The relationship between crime and opioid use', *British Journal of Addiction*, 84: 1029–43.

Hammersley, R., Marsland, L. and Reid, M. (2003) *Substance Use by Young Offenders: the impact of normalisation of drug use in the early years of the 21st century*. Home Office Research Study 261. London: Home Office.

HM Government (2008) *Drugs: Protecting Families and Communities. The 2008 drug strategy (first edition).* drugs.homeoffice.gov.uk/publication-search/drug-strategy/drug-strategy-2008-2018.

Home Office (2002a) *Justice For All White Paper*. London: Home Office.

Home Office (2002b) *Updated Drug Strategy*. London: Home Office, Drugs Strategy Directorate, www.drugs.gov.uk/publication-searchdrugs-strategy/updated-drug-strategy-2002.pdf

Hough, M. (1996) *Drugs Misuse and The Criminal Justice System: A Review of The Literature*. DPI Paper 15. London: Home Office.

IOP (1998) *Health Advisory Committee For The Prison Service Review*. London: The Stationery Office.

Julien, R.M. (2005) *A Primer of Drug Action (tenth edition)*. New York: Worth Publishers.

Kaye, A.D., Gevirtz, C., Bosscher, H.A., Duke, J.B., Frost, E.A.M., Richards, T.A. and Fields, A.M. (2003) 'Ultra rapid opiate detoxification: a review', *Canadian Anaesthesiologists' Society*, 50: 663–71.

Kerr, T., Tyndall, M., Li, K., Montaner, J. and Wood, E. (2005) 'Safer injecting facility use and syringe sharing in injection drug users', *The Lancet*, 366: 316–18.

Kimber, J., Dolan, K. and Wodak, A. (2005) 'Survey of drug consumption rooms: service delivery and perceived public health and amenity impact', *Drug and Alcohol Review*, 24 (1): 21–4.

Love, B. (2007) 'An evaluation of the UK Government's Aftercare DIP and an assessment of participants' psychological health'. Unpublished. Cited by DIP Strategic Communications Team (2007) *Evidence of The Impact of the Drug Interventions Programme – Summaries and Sources* (www.drugs.gov.uk).

Maisto, S.A., Galizio, M. and Connors, G.J. (1995) *Drug Use and Abuse (second edition)*. London: Harcourt Brace College Publishers.

Marsden, J. Gossop, M. Stewart, D. Rolfe, A. and Farrell, M. (2000) 'Psychiatric symptoms among clients seeking treatment for drug dependence – intake data from the National Treatment Outcome Research Study', *British Journal of Psychiatry*, 176: 285–9.

McSweeney, T., Turnbull, P.J. and Hough, M. (2008) *The Treatment and Supervision of Drug-dependent Offenders. A review of the literature prepared for the UK Drug Policy Commission*. London: UK Drug Policy Commission.

Mind (2007) *Understanding Dual Diagnosis*. London: Mind. www.mind.org.uk/Information/Booklets/Understanding/Understanding+dual+diagnosis (Accessed 2007).

Morgan, R. and Owers, A. (2001) *Through the Prison Gate: a joint thematic review by HM Inspectorates of Prisons and Probation*. London: HM Inspectorate of Prisons.

Penfold, C., Turnbull, P.J. and Webster, R. (2005) *Tackling Prison Drug Markets: An exploratory qualitative study*. Home Office Online Report 39/05. London: Home Office.

Pudney, S. (2002) *The Road to Ruin? Sequences of initiation into drug use and offending by young people in Britain*. Home Office Research Study 253. London: Home Office.

Reuter, P. and Stevens, A. (2007) *An Analysis of UK Drug Policy. A Monograph Prepared for the UK Drug Policy Commission*. London: UK Drug Policy Commission.

Roe and Man (2006) *Drug Misuse Declared: findings from the 2005–6 British Crime Survey*. Home Office Statistical Bulletin, 15/06. London: Home Office.

Rollnick S. and Miller, W.R. (1995) 'What is motivational interviewing?', *Behavioural and Cognitive Psychotherapy*, 23: 325–34.

Seddon, T. (2000) 'Explaining the drug–crime link: theoretical, policy and research issues', *Journal of Social Policy*, 29 (1): 95–107.

Skodbo, S., Brown, G., Deacon, A., Cooper, A., Hall, A., Millar, T., Smith, J. and Witham, K. (2007) *The Drug Interventions Programme (DIP): Addressing Drug Use and Offending Through 'Tough Choices'*. Home Office Research Report 2. London: Home Office.

Social Exclusion Unit (2002) 'Reducing Re-offending by Ex-prisoners', London: Office of the Deputy Prime Minister.

Sondhi, A., O'Shea, J. and Williams, T. (2002) *Arrest Referral: Emerging Findings From the National Monitoring and Evaluation Programme*. DPAS18. London: Home Office.

Stevens, A., Hallam, C. and Trace, M. (2006) *Treatment for Dependent Drug Use. A Guide For Policymakers.* The Beckley Foundation Drug Policy Programme, Report Ten.

Strathdee, S.A. and Vlahov, D. (2001) 'The effectiveness of needle exchange programmes: a review of the science and policy', *AIDScience*, 1 (16): 1–31.

Strathdee, G., Manning, V., Best, D., Keaney, F., Bhui, K., Witton, J., Wall, S., McGillivary, L., Marsden, J., Johnson, F., Piek, C. and Wilson-Jones, C. (2002) 'Dual diagnosis in a primary care group (PCG)', National Treatment Agency, November 2004 briefing.

Tessler, R. and Dennis, D. (1989) *A Synthesis of NIMH funded Research Concerning Persons Who Are Homeless and Mentally Ill.* Washington DC: NIMH Division of Education and Service Systems Liaison, cited by Department of Health, National Addiction Centre (2003) *Dangerousness of Drugs: A Guide To The Risks and Harms Associated With Substance Misuse*, January.

Turnbull, P.J. and McSweeney, T. (2000) *Drug Treatment in Prison and Aftercare: A literature review and results of a survey of European countries*. Strasbourg: Council of Europe.

UNDOC (2003) *Drug Abuse Treatment: a Practical Planning and Implementation Guide.* Vienna: United Nations Publication.

Wanigaratne, S., Davis, P., Pryce, K. and Brotchie, J. (2005) *The Effectiveness of Psychological Therapies on Drug Misusing Clients*, National Treatment Agency for Substance Misuse, June, research briefing 11.

Weaver *et al.* (2002) *Co-morbidity of Substance Misuse and Mental Illness Collaborative Study (COSMIC) NTA*, new series August 2004.

Wilke, D.J. (2004) 'Predicting suicide ideation for substance users: the role of self-esteem, abstinence, and attendance at 12-step meetings', *Addiction, Research and Theory*, June, 12 (3): 231–40.

Section 5

Intervention and Prevention

This section concentrates on the prevention of recidivism and attempts to minimise the risk of offending in the first place. It concentrates on community- and society-wide programmes. Intimate partner violence (IPV) leads to death and significant harm to women, children and indeed men. It cuts across society and sexuality and recent government attempts to highlight this insidious crime indicate that it is far from a domestic triviality. In Chapter 18, Elizabeth A. Gilchrist and Mark R. Kebbell have provided a revised, updated and reappraised version of their chapter looking at intervention and the long-term effects of programmes designed to tackle IPV.

Chapter 19 focuses on the other end of the offending spectrum, reassessing attempts to prevent life-course persistent offending. This chapter by Brandon Welsh and David Farrington is based on critical appraisal, using benefit–cost analysis. It clearly links psychological and criminological intervention to social policy. It is an updated case for ongoing intervention to prevent delinquency. To complement this large-scale review, Chapter 20 provides the historical context of political interventions in the family, specifically in parenting. Anthony H. Goodman and Joanna R. Adler have updated their chapter considering the impact of such interventions on parents and their children, and how parenting is situated within offending and child protection arenas. Lastly in this section, Liz A. Dixon and Joanna R. Adler consider hate crimes. Hate crimes can escalate from relatively low-level neighbour disputes, and can include anything from persistent verbal abuse to brutal murders. Their very variety and range pose problems not just for legislators, but also for intervention and management of hate crimes offenders. The behaviours are not new, yet how to work with such offenders is a relatively underdeveloped field as the legal recognition of the harm done by hatred is still in its infancy.

Chapter 18

Intimate partner violence: current issues in definitions and interventions with perpetrators in the UK

Elizabeth A. Gilchrist and Mark R. Kebbell

> Given the unpalatable nature of wife abuse, it is perhaps inevitable that explanations are entangled with political, moral and interdisciplinary issues.
>
> (Blackburn 1993)

Introduction

Since the first edition of this book, there have been many initiatives aimed at reducing the incidence or impact of intimate partner violence. There have been a raft of British Government responses to domestic violence, including the Domestic Violence, Crime and Victims Act 2003 and new assessments and interventions across agencies (e.g. Metropolitan Police Service 2003; National Probation Service 2007) and there is ongoing academic work. Yet, there are still substantial gaps in knowledge and provision.

Many correlates of intimate partner violence have been identified (Gilchrist *et al.* 2003; Finney 2004; MacPherson 2002), and whilst the data are dominated by material collected in North America, there is a growing body of data from the UK (Gilchrist *et al.* 2003; Graham-Kevan and Archer 2003; Bowen *et al.* 2002; Dixon *et al.* 2008; Johnson *et al.* 2006). Despite this, debate and confusion remain as to the nature of intimate partner violence (Johnson 1995); the relationship between intimate partner violence and gender (Graham-Kevan and Archer 2003a; Giles 2005; Dobash and Dobash 2004); the key causal factors leading to IPV (Holtzworth-Munroe *et al.* 1997; Gilchrist *et al.*

2003; McMurran and Gilchrist 2008) and the routes and mechanisms by which these become activated (Norlander and Eckhardt 2005; Gilchrist 2008). Recent consideration of interventions seeking to reduce IPV has provided limited evidence that they can be shown to work (Bowen *et al.* 2008; Bowen *et al.* 2002; Dutton and Corvo 2007; Feder and Wilson 2005; Gondolf 2004) and there are ongoing debates as to whether current interventions focus on appropriate targets (Bowen and Gilchrist 2004; Graham-Kevan 2007; McMurran and Gilchrist 2007) and adopt the most appropriate approaches (Langlands *et al.* 2009).

This chapter focuses on the major issues currently gaining attention: thus definitions of IPV, the role of gender, heterogeneity amongst offenders and typologies of IPV and interventions will be considered. Due to the weight of evidence, the chapter will focus mostly on male-to-female IPV but will consider this critically in the light of more recent empirical studies and theoretical developments.

What's in a name?

Developments in IPV research and practice are mirrored in the changing language used over the decades. 'Battered women' (e.g. Pizzey and Forbes 1974), 'couple violence' and 'family violence' (Healey *et al.* 1998) put the focus on women, the couple or families, rather than on the abusive men. 'Wife batterer' or 'spouse batterer' were preferred in the USA but all these terms were criticised for concentrating on physical violence rather than a wider range of abuses. More recently, terms such as 'abuse', 'abuses' or 'constellation of abuses' (Dobash *et al.* 2000) were seen as being more appropriate than violence. For some, the gender neutral 'spouse abuse' was problematic (Dobash *et al.* 2000) but the alternative, 'wife beating', still put the focus onto married couples. A more fundamental problem is that many of these terms did not fit within criminal justice labels where perpetrators are convicted of violence (direct or indirect), criminal damage or public disorder, rather than abuse.

The term 'domestic violence' has been widely used in the UK. This fails to address the relationship between gender and violence but does 'fit' with the criminal justice system, e.g. the recent Domestic Violence, Crime and Victims Act 2003 and the new 'domestic violence' courts. It has been suggested that domestic/family violence could, and perhaps should, encompass a wider range of protagonists. The current definition of domestic violence does reflect this broad conceptualisation and includes violence between other family members over 18 beyond the adults who are or have been intimate partners. It is defined as:

> Any incident of threatening behaviour, violence or abuse (psychological, physical, sexual, financial or emotional) between adults who are or have been intimate partners or family members, regardless of gender or sexuality. (Home Office 2005)

Previously the Home Affairs Select Committee (1993) had defined domestic violence as:

> Any form of physical, sexual or emotional abuse which takes place within the context of a close relationship. In most cases, the relationship will be between partners (married, cohabiting, or otherwise) or ex-partners.

There was recognition that there was a gendered aspect to this type of violence, noting that

> in most cases, the abuser is male and the victim female and that lifetime prevalence, repeat victimization, injury, fear and threats are higher for women. (Home Affairs Select Committee 1993)

Domestic abuse, domestic violence and intimate partner violence are often used interchangeably (Easton *et al.* (2006). However, it is suggested that IPV may be the term of choice for those who wish to move away from 'politically laden' terms and focus on developing empirically validated theory (Johnson 2005; Saunders 2004) thus it is intimate partner violence on which this chapter will focus.

How much is there?

Intimate partner violence constitutes the largest single type of violence against women and accounts for 25 per cent of all violent crime in the UK (Home Office 2002). More recent research suggests that 45 per cent of women and 26 per cent of men had experienced at least one incident of interpersonal violence in their lifetimes (Walby and Allen 2004) and one in five women will experience IPV across a lifetime (MacPherson 2002). In situations of repeat abuse (more than four incidents) 89 per cent of victims were women (Walby and

Allen 2004). Data from a 'snapshot' survey in September 2000 show that the police in the UK received 1,300 calls reporting incidents of intimate partner violence in one day, and suggest that they would receive around 570,000 calls per year (Stanko 2000). This is less than the official estimate of numbers of intimate partner violence incidents for 1995, which was 6.6 million but implies a far larger hidden figure (Mirrlees-Black 1999).

The level and impact of violence, is also very high; two women per week are killed by their current or former partner (Department of Health 2005) with suggestions that thousands of children either witness or directly experience abuse within their family of origin (Home Office 2005). It is estimated that, in supporting victims across the UK, the 'tangible and intangible costs' could be as much as £23 billion annually (Home Office 2005).

Much early work was broadly descriptive, not focused directly on risk-related concepts (for example Dobash *et al.* 2000), or very general, for example the British Crime Survey generated copious general information about intimate partner violence incidents and victims, but not about perpetrators (Mirrlees-Black *et al.* 1996). More recent work has started to address these problems, e.g. Gilchrist *et al.* (2003) identified risk-relevant characteristics of a sample of male convicted intimate partner offenders. This study identified IPV offenders as a heterogeneous group, with diverse needs. Several characteristics which previous research has linked to risk of IPV were identified. These included 'witnessing domestic violence in childhood, disrupted attachment patterns, high levels of interpersonal dependency and jealousy, attitudes condoning domestic violence and lack of empathy' (Gilchrist *et al.* 2003: 1). Alcohol use was present in 62 per cent of the offences and 48 per cent of the sample were alcohol dependent. However, the study was somewhat limited as it considered only male perpetrators, did not measure risk, nor compare with non-offender controls. Further UK research has considered male and female perpetrators (Graham-Kevan and Archer 2003); types of IPV perpetrator across a range of abuse groups (Johnson *et al.* 2006; Dixon and Browne 2003; and Aldridge and Browne 2003) and more direct risk relevant factors (see below).

Do women do as much as men?

Does the data support a gendered definition of intimate partner violence? There are at least two aspects to this question: 1) there is equivocal evidence on the link between gender and IPV, potentially due to different methodologies; and 2) conceptual debates remain over types of abuse within an intimate relationship. A more gender neutral view indicates women perpetrating as much as men whereas research traditionally associated with feminists demonstrates male-perpetrated abuse towards women.

There are substantial methodological issues around gender symmetry. Those who argue for gender symmetry in IPV tend to base their work on large-scale samples of people not previously identified as victims. The phenomenon is then measured using tools such as the Conflict Tactics Scale (CTS) (Straus 1979), and the results are interpreted as indicating 'gender symmetry' in the violence/abuse. This is then used as a basis for suggesting family therapy as appropriate intervention with a focus on family dynamics and arguments, assuming a neutral backdrop.

The evidence for gender disparity in IPV tends to come from different samples: women who have sought help from various agencies; who have reported their partners to the police; those who have contacted a refuge and so on. The information is then collected using different tools and questionnaires and perhaps using more qualitative methods to try to reflect the complexity of the women's experiences. The data from these types of study identify men as the primary aggressors, little of the female violence as proactive nor initiated by women (Dobash and Dobash 2004). There are ongoing debates as to how far methodology, data analysis and even ideology have affected the pattern of IPV reported. Graham-Kevan has suggested that there has been biased reporting in even official government figures, which maintains a distorted view of IPV as being a problem of male perpetrators and continues to present women as victims (Graham-Kevan 2007).

Commonly used survey tools such as the CTS have been criticised, as they do not include any dimension of frequency of assault, so may under-report the reality of women's experiences, hide the amount of male violence, and not include a measure of outcome of the violence. Hence, the impact of a woman hitting a man and a man hitting a woman are treated as the same, although data from other sources (emergency health care) suggest that when men hit women, women suffer more (Dobash *et al.* 1992; Giles 2005). Further issues from women involved in the Duluth initiative in the US, and from research conducted by Dobash *et al.* (2000) in the UK, suggest that if women are being physically abused within a relationship, this is only one of a 'constellation of abuses'. The coercive, unequal power-sharing, emotionally and socially controlling context of the violence is not reflected.

Recently, Lindhorst and Tajima (2008) reviewed some key features that they argue must be included in a study of IPV (e.g. social context; situational context; social construction of meaning by the survivor; cultural and historical contexts; and the context of systemic oppression) and suggest the potential development of a 'contextualised' survey. It may be that this type of survey will address some of the limitations of previous work, enabling us to partial out the impact of the measurement tool from any sampling influence and clarify whether violence reported by men and women in broad samples is qualitatively similar or different.

It has been suggested that women's violence tends to be reactive rather than proactive, sometimes termed 'violent resistance' (Muftic *et al.* 2007), and still needs to be seen in the context of the woman as victim (Giles 2005; Dobash and Dobash 2004). Busey (1993) identified four types of 'female defendants': self-defending victims, angry victims, mutually combatant women and primary physical aggressors. Combining the two latter categories, where the women could be seen as either equally or more responsible for initiating the violence, this amounted to a maximum of only five per cent of women arrested for intimate partner violence in Denver, supporting the notion that female aggression is primarily reactive. This is further supported by evidence from 'dual arrests' (both male and female partners) following IPV offences that identified many of the female perpetrators as initially having been the complainant, as using violence out of 'frustration, fear or in self-defence' and sharing more characteristics with victims than offenders (Muftic *et al.* 2007: 766). Other data suggest there is more reciprocal violence among women offenders than fear-driven violence. Graham-Kevan and Archer (2005) found that over 50 per cent of the variance in women's use of violence could be explained by their partner's violence, while fear was negatively related to their use of violence. They suggest that research of mutually violent episodes could identify whether women's violence could be in retaliation and point to the need for multiple explanations of women's violence. A comparison of 'sole arrest' and 'dual arrest' females identified a subset of women sharing characteristics with typical male IPV offenders, using violence proactively, having higher prior arrests and rearrest rates (Muftic *et al.* 2007).

In addition to the meaning of the act differing, consequences also vary by gender. Archer (2000) found that if abuse was measured by recording specific acts, using measures such as the CTS (Straus 1979), then women were more likely to self-report being violent, but when the consequences were taken into account, men were more likely to have injured their partners. He also found that when specific samples were considered, e.g. those in refuges, high-risk offenders, there was a large effect size in the male direction (Archer 2000).

Johnson (1995) has suggested that the different results not only derive from different methodologies but reflect two quite distinct phenomena. Violence within an intimate relationship which involved abusive control of partners, initially termed 'patriarchal terrorism' but later 'intimate terrorism', was identified as being the violence researched by feminists. A separate type of violence, 'common couple violence', where inappropriate conflict resolution resulted in violence, was considered by the 'family violence' camp, in more gender neutral terms. This too has been challenged by suggestions that intimate terrorists perhaps reflect the most serious IPV offenders, irrespective of gender (Frieze 2005).

Graham-Kevan and colleagues have conducted a number of studies exploring whether behaviours predicted by the Johnson typology were differentially present in male and female perpetrators. They identified that the majority of male perpetrators did fit an 'intimate terrorism' profile, while more women fitted a 'violent resistance' profile. Also most 'intimate terrorism' was perpetrated by men (87 per cent). This was taken as providing broad support for Johnson's (1999) contention that there are two main types of physical aggression accessed by feminist and family violence researchers but the notion of intimate terrorism being the exclusive preserve of male perpetrators is challenged (Graham-Kevan and Archer 2003; Graham-Kevan 2003b). The separation of these two groups into distinct phenomena is also challenged by recent work. Frye *et al.* (2006) explored the experience of physical assault, controlling behaviours, injury and escalation of violence among urban women and identified that there was little evidence for widespread situational couple violence but that there was evidence for relatively high levels of controlling behaviours and physical assault. However, only a small proportion of women experienced controlling behaviours and escalation of violence and injury which would typify intimate terrorism. Extrapolating from their data, they suggest that rather than conceptualising situational couple violence and intimate terrorism as separate forms of violence we should reconceptualise them as being on a continuum (Frye *et al.* 2006). Along similar lines, Johnson (2005) emphasises the need to be clear about the type of IPV being discussed in any research or policy developments and goes as far as to suggest that 'it is no longer scientifically or ethically acceptable to speak of domestic violence without specifying … the type of violence to which we refer'. This has not been achieved yet but perhaps sets a goal for future work (see below for further consideration of typologies).

Theories and evidence

There are a variety of levels of explanation, which have been proposed to explain intimate partner violence offending. They range from a societal/cultural level to those focusing on individuals and individual pathologies. Previously, research has focused on understanding intimate partner violence in terms of societal structure, at a macrosystemic – society in general – or microsystemic – family – level (Edelson and Tolman 1992), though overlap had been recognised (Dobash *et al.* 2000). Related work includes a range of factors and recognises the heterogeneity within IPV, both in terms of male and female perpetrators and in terms of variation among male perpetrators. Most recent theory posits some level of integrated model. The nested ecological model (Dutton 1985; Edelson and Tolman 1992) identifies five different levels which function together to make intimate partner violence a more or less likely potential outcome and seeks to integrate them. The levels are: individual, microsystem (the immediate situation, e.g. family); mesosystem (interactions between an individual's microsystems); exosystem (structures and systems of society); and macrosystem (group history, culture and ethnicity) (Edelson and Tolman 1992). This model has been conceptualised as an onion with violence at the core and many layers affecting this core; whilst not all subsequent research deals explicitly with all the factors, the recognition of the 'other layers of the onion' is implicit in most work.

Sociocultural explanations tend to argue that intimate partner violence is a product of a patriarchal or an aggressive society that facilitates and supports violence to resolve conflict, or control women. There are studies that suggest structural factors at a societal level may have an effect. For example, studies have identified higher levels of intimate partner violence in societies where women have less access to independent resources and to divorce (Alvazzi del Frate and Patrignani 1995; van Dijk *et al.* 1994), where women have lower status (Bhatt 1998) and in societies where patriarchal attitudes are prevalent (Levinson 1989). Archer (2006) conducted a review of evidence from a range of sources across a number of countries to explore structural factors such as collectivism versus individualism, gender equality and patriarchal attitudes. His findings suggest dominant cultural beliefs about aggression against intimate partners have a strong influence on the amount of male-to-female and female-to-male violence. In countries with low gender equality and beliefs that support a man's right to chastise his partner, there are higher levels of violence against women. However, in countries with more gender equality, there is both lower violence against women and higher victimisation of men. Archer notes that the debate about male victimisation and implication for theory and policy is relevant only in countries relatively high on equality (Archer 2006).

At slightly lower level, whilst victim data suggest that IPV cuts across all social classes and ethnicities within a culture, research within the general sociological framework has linked increased risk of intimate partner violence with lower socio-economic status (Dobash *et al.* 2000; Healey *et al.* 1998); age, cohabiting status and employment (Stets 1995); increased stress or social isolation (Gelles 1997); or that differential access to social support and resources may affect victims' responses to IPV (Gondolf 1988; Foa *et al.* 2000). Interpersonal explanations tend to situate the problem within family interactions, including problematic attachment styles, and there are data which suggest that violence may be linked to structural factors at a family level, for example, cohabiting couples were found to be more likely than daters to use abusive behaviours (Magdol *et al.* 1998). Other researchers have found that there was some relationship between marital conflict styles and later violence by the male partner, although these were mediated by other factors such as the level of aggression in the male partner (Leonard and Senchak 1996).

The coupling of two specific types of individual, rather than the behaviour of any one individual within that family has been identified as problematic, for example, anxious women and dismissive men (Bond and Bond 2004). Recent work by Doumas *et al.* (2008) expanded this area, considering links between attachment style of both partners and male- and female-perpetrated violence, taking violence reciprocity into account. They found a relationship between female attachment anxiety and violence, by both males and females. Additionally, 'miss-pairing' (Doumas *et al.* 2008: 629) of males who were high on avoidant attachment and females high on anxious attachment, linked with violence, and there continued to be a link even when partner violence was partialled out, but only for female attachment and violence. The authors emphasise the need for longitudinal research before any causal conclusions can be drawn, but suggest that assessment of attachment styles of both partners may add utility to risk assessment in treatment (Doumas *et al.* 2008).

One of the most widely cited risk factors at an individual level is the experience, or witnessing, of physical abuse within their family of origin (Reitzel-Jaffe and Wolfe 2001). Stith *et al.* (2000) conducted a meta-analysis and found that growing up in an abusive family was positively correlated to becoming involved in a violent marital relationship. However, this intergenerational transmission of violence may be mediated by harsh parental discipline, ineffective parenting strategies and wider societal influences (Hotaling and Sugarman 1986; Straus and Smith 1990; O'Hearn and Margolin 2000; Simons *et al.* 1995). Ehrensaft *et al.* (2003) identified conduct disorder, exposure to parental violence and power assertive punishment as the strongest family of origin predictor variables of later IPV. They suggest that this supports a social learning based model of IPV such that coercive, power-based responses to conflict are learned and replicated, more so in those with individual tendencies to problematic behaviours (conduct disorder) but not exclusively (Ehrensaft *et al.* 2003).

Various psychopathologies, for example jealousy, poor attachment, poor impulse control and low self-esteem (Gilchrist *et al.* 2003; Eberle 1982), anger and depression (Maiuro *et al.* 1988), alcohol and substance abuse (Easton *et al.* 2000) have also been identified as elevated among intimate partner violence offenders (Dutton 1995). Given various concerns regarding the role of alcohol in excusing IPV, and in potentially blaming the victim, it is interesting to note that a review of this area conducted for the Home Office identified that offender-only drinking was common, but victim-only drinking was not (Finney 2004). Other recent work has suggested that alcohol may be linked with IPV both directly, through 'deviance disavowal' mechanisms, that is drinking to create an acceptable cause for the IPV, or perhaps indirectly by both reflecting poor executive cognitive functioning (ECF) and exacerbating poor cognitive processing (McMurran and Gilchrist 2008).

Interpersonal dependency has been found to be higher in those who are violent towards an intimate partner, than those who are more generally violent (Kane *et al.* 2000). UK work identified witnessing domestic violence in childhood, disrupted attachment patterns, high levels of interpersonal dependency and jealousy, attitudes condoning domestic violence and lack of empathy were all present in a sample of men mandated to IPV treatment in the community (Gilchrist *et al.* 2003). This study also identified heterogeneity of treatment needs amongst IPV offenders.

One important development over the past few years is the increased sophistication of the modelling and measuring of concepts related to IPV (Janghinrichsen-Rohling 2005) such as anger (Norlander and Eckhardt 2005); attitudinal characteristics, e.g. seeing violence as acceptable (Saunders *et al.* 1987) or holding beliefs which condone wife assault (Johnson 1995), and holding restricted definitions of violence (Chamberland *et al.* 2007) but authors stress the importance of trying to untangle implications for general meaning and specific intervention from these studies. Recent work has linked cognition with other IPV risk factors. A study on cognition and IPV based on a sample of over one thousand respondents found that strong expectation of aggressive behaviour following alcohol consumption was the best predictor of subsequent intimate partner violence (Field *et al.* 2004).

In line with increasing sophistication in approach (Janghinrichsen-Rohling 2005) attempts have been made to establish appropriate scales to measure cognitive distortions related to IPV, e.g. a Relational Entitlement and Proprietariness Scale (REPS) which found that up to 22 per cent of the variance in instrumental violence within relationships could be explained by 'Proprietariness' (Hannawa *et al.* 2006). Eckhardt *et al.* (1998) suggested a method using articulated thoughts and simulated situations (ATTS) to measure cognition present in violent relationships under more realistic arousal conditions. When aroused, those in the maritally violent group articulated thoughts that evidenced more global irrational beliefs, specifically they demeaned others, made absolutist demands that others act appropriately and magnified the importance of situation. They evidenced dichotomous thinking, drew arbitrary conclusions, made hostile attributions and evidenced fewer anger controlling statements.

Interestingly, recent research extending this work failed to find a relationship between IPV and articulation of cognitive distortions, finding a stronger link between psychopathology and IPV and that, in response to 'criticism' cues, IPV men tended to respond with anger, whereas men in other groups responded with sadness. Also, there were differences across the group reflecting different personality profiles (Costa and Babcock 2008). Recent work has also suggested that it is not just the beliefs held which must be studied but also the processes by which they come to be activated as this may link distorted thinking with situational factors and anger arousal and may vary with types of offender (Gilchrist 2008).

Recent work has moved beyond single-factor explanations and perhaps the notion of modelling various pathways to IPV offending, identifying the factors that may increase or protect from the risk of IPV, and the creation of an integrated theory whereby the mechanisms that allow these factors to work is becoming more likely. Better evidence indicates that patriarchy may create the conditions under which male-to-female IPV is more likely and this varies by country. Within a culture, we can identify groups at greater risk of perpetrating IPV. At an individual level, we can identify direct and indirect factors linked to IPV. We have moved beyond asking about 'the causal' factors in IPV to consider how various factors interact such that IPV is more or less likely.

Are there different types of intimate partner violence offender?

Typology research is a growing area of investigation and debate. Gondolf (1988) identified three types of batterers: sociopathic, antisocial and typical; Saunders (1992) identified three groups: family only, emotionally volatile and generally violent; Hamberger and Hastings (1986) identified three groups: schizoidal/borderline, narcissistic/antisocial and passive/dependent/compulsive; Tweed and Dutton (1998) identified two groups: instrumental and impulsive offenders; Holtzworth-Munroe and Stuart (1994) initially identified three groups but refined this to four groups on the basis of empirical data (Holtzworth-Munroe *et al.* 2000): family only, low-level antisocial, generally violent, borderline/dysphoric; and Gilchrist *et al.* (2003), using UK data, identified two groups, primarily identifying an antisocial group and an emotionally volatile group. Within a mixed group of convicted and non-convicted men, Dixon and Browne (2003) identified 50 per cent, 30 per cent, and 20 per cent (respectively) of their sample as fitting the profile of family only, generally violent/antisocial, and dysphoric/borderline personality respectively. They also identified that there was a significant difference between the perpetrators mandated to a programme and those attending without a court mandate such that court-referred men were less likely to be categorised into the family-only group.

Further research by Holtzworth-Munroe *et al.* (2000) demonstrated both that subtypes of IPV offender could be identified across different samples, and that differences among the groups remained stable over time. They linked this to stable personality characteristics but also identified that there were difficulties in distinguishing between their generally violent and dysphoric borderline groups. More recent work has also identified that placement of individual perpetrators into groups is less stable (Holtzworth-Munroe and Meehan 2004). From this, Holtzworth-Munroe and colleagues suggest that care should be applied when drawing clinical interpretation from this data as, although we know that antisocial and borderline personality characteristics are relevant for IPV, the specific mechanisms and influence of situational factors are less clear.

There are suggestions that typologies should be broadened to encompass violent families, possibly incorporating reciprocal family violence, hierarchical family violence and paternal family violence (Dixon and Browne 2003), which would link with the expanded definitions of IPV (intimate terrorists, violent resistance and situational couple violence, see earlier). Also, of developing the typologies based on physiological difference, for example, while Gottman *et al.* (1995) suggested there may be two groups of perpetrator who vary in terms of heart rate change, type 1 experiencing accelerated heart rate during violence 'pit bulls', and type 2 experiencing lowered heart rate during violence 'cobras', Mitchell and Gilchrist (2006) have suggested that two groups of perpetrator may differ in terms of the function of the violence: one group perhaps engaging in predatory attack and the other in affective defence, indicative of differences in underlying neural responses. Saunders has suggested that research considering pathways from childhood to different types of offender would be of value. Also, it is suggested that the nested ecological model and the theory of triadic influence may offer more relevant theoretical frameworks (Saunders 2004).

Dobash and Dobash compared lethal and non-lethal violent offenders and found that lethal IP offenders looked more 'conventional' than simple abusers in that they displayed fewer 'offender characteristics' apart from prior IPV, were more likely to be employed, had fewer problems in their backgrounds, they were more likely to have engaged in sexual violence and have used a weapon, they were less likely to have been drunk at the time of the abuse, but more likely to have been possessive in their relationship and to have separated from their partner prior to the violent incident (Dobash *et al.* 2009). This research identified some problems with current typologies and risk assessment which focuses only on the early established notion of ever-increasing frequency and severity of abuse, culminating ultimately in lethal violence (also challenged by Holtzworth-Munroe and colleagues) and identifies a need for continued work to understand the role of possessiveness in lethal IPV and to explore the particular characteristics of the circumstances in which lethal IPV occurs (Dobash and Dobash 2007).

Interventions

A full review of the interventions of the past 10 years is beyond the scope of this chapter. Whilst there are some real positives, some problematic attitudes remain as to how seriously to treat this type of offending and how to deal with the offenders (Gilchrist and Blissett 2002), and there is some evidence that programme content may be less important overall than the fact of treatment and that the treatment effect can be relatively modest (Healey *et al.* 1998; Hanson and Wallace-Carpretta 2000; Kropp and Bodnarchuk 2001). From a psychological perspective, one of the major interventions developed has been that of the IPV perpetrator programme. It is on these programmes that this part of the chapter will focus. Interventions in IPV have been greatly informed by the 'Duluth' model of intervention (Pence and Paymar 1993), although wider cognitive-behavioural perspectives are also employed (see for example Healey *et al.* 1998 or Geffner and Rosenbaum 2001 for alternatives). The Duluth model is a psycho-educational perpetrator group, with concurrent support for women and children. The original group was developed in Duluth, Minnesota and formed part of a co-ordinated community response to intimate partner violence. This group built upon information from women survivors of IPV to develop an educational programme designed to make men aware that they had been socialised into particular views and expectations which led on to feelings of entitlement which in turn linked to their use of violence and abuse (Pence and Paymar 1993).

The strength of the Duluth model is that it does not allow victim blaming, minimisation or denial, holds the perpetrator accountable for his actions, recognises the influence of culture on the violence and thereby reflects what the statistics tell us about intimate partner violence. It resonates with women's experiences and makes it clear that there is an element of choice in many men's offending. However, critics suggest that it overemphasises the gendered aspect of IPV; fails to address women's violence; does not take personality disorder into account and fails to respond to the heterogeneity identified by the typology research (Graham-Kevan 2007b; Dutton and Corvo 2007). The Duluth model may also be criticised for not incorporating what we know about effective methods of enabling and encouraging change into the model, for assuming that men will change purely through exposure to new ideas, and for assuming that it is culturally driven attitudinal problems which drive offending for all men (Graham-Kevan 2007a). The Duluth camp is also criticised for failing to use rigorous evaluation of outcomes, for failing to consider alternative interventions and of using flawed science to support their approach (Dutton and Corvo 2007).

In the UK, a range of approaches has been adopted, although with the growing importance of programme accreditation the diversity is narrowing. Scourfield and Dobash (1999) identified that most were broadly psycho-educational interventions based on the Duluth model, although some were more psychodynamic in approach. Bowen *et al.* (2002) also identified a range of approaches in intervention in the UK but identified that the distinction between the cognitive-behavioural groups and the feminist-informed programmes may be less marked in practice than suggested by their theoretical orientation due to programme deliverers making use of both.

The majority of programmes, in the UK at least, hold that men are led into offending through concepts of male entitlement and appropriate gender role behaviour and that, having offended, men minimise and justify their behaviour through common techniques of neutralisation (Sykes and Matza 1957). Even with interventions which hold that cultural beliefs and societal structures are key features in IPV offending, there is some assumption that the thoughts of intimate abusers are relevant to their offending.

Reviews of IPV interventions suggest that the effectiveness of individually focused programmes is limited – even to zero impact overall (Washington State Institute for Public Policy 2006). The 'what works' debate in the UK has identified cognitive-behavioural programmes as being more effective and that there are certain 'quality' aspects of intervention which also affect outcome (McGuire 1985). In terms of measuring effectiveness of tackling intimate partner violence, the debates have mirrored the general debate, suffering from similar limitations in terms of experimental rigour and issues such as definitions of success, appropriate follow-up periods and appropriate measures of change (Harper and Chitty 2005).

But, there are also further debates about what should be the appropriate outcome for an intimate partner violence programme: can reduction of violence be enough? Does it make any difference if the abuse only occurs once every six months rather than once every month? Is cessation of physical violence enough? If a man stops beating his partner, but the threat is always there, is her quality of life enhanced? Can programmes aim to transform offenders into 'accountable men'? Can one justify imposing one particular set of standards and beliefs, which go well beyond 'no violence', on individuals from a range of cultures and backgrounds? There have been ongoing debates as to appropriate evaluation for IPV programmes and claims that there has been poor science applied which has skewed findings (Dutton and Corvo 2007). The majority of evaluations have at best employed a quasi-experimental design (Dobash and Dobash 2000). Also, the majority of participants in domestic violence offender programmes have been court referred and face alternative sanctions if they do not complete the programme, so are a skewed sample (Fagan 1996). There is no random allocation of participants to treatment and no treatment conditions as it has been considered that this would be unethical and few true experiments have been conducted. Certainly few have achieved a high rating on the Scientific Methods Scale which assesses methodological standards in crime prevention (Harper and Chitty 2005). These issues have posed real questions when establishing the efficacy of interventions.

There are bigger questions about whether simple outcome evaluations are appropriate. Bowen and Gilchrist (2004) suggested that adopting a comprehensive evaluation framework might explore the match between the problem and the intervention, the integrity of the programme delivery and the costs involved, similarly to the cost-based evaluation conducted by the Matrix Knowledge Group (2007) and would be more meaningful than a consideration of outcome (Bowen and Gilchrist 2004).

Hamberger and Hastings (1993) conducted a broad review of published studies evaluating interventions with perpetrators of intimate partner violence and suggest that it is almost impossible to say whether these programmes work. They identified problems with small sample sizes, non-random assignment to groups, no control groups, attrition, inadequate specification, differential follow-ups and outcome measures, inappropriate statistical analyses and lack of treatment of anomalous findings. The studies provided variable information about effects of treatment, some identifying recidivism rates for both treated and untreated groups, some identifying only recidivism rates for treated offenders, and some did not report the effects in this way. It appeared that certain programmes could claim complete cessation, while others found more modest improvements with completers' recidivism rate of between 33–41 per cent and the drop-outs' rate of between 46–48 per cent (Hamberger and Hastings 1993: 209). Edelson (1996) reported that success rates varied from between 53 to 85 per cent. Gondolf (1997) initially found that the recidivism rates for those completing programmes were similar to those for men who drop out at the start (Gondolf 1997, in Healey *et al.* 1998). Gondolf's (2004) more recent review suggested an 18 per cent difference between the programme completers and those who had received less than three months of counselling. They calculated that, even using a conservative analysis, their programmes had achieved a 0.44–0.64 effect size. Conversely, Harrell (1991) found that those undertaking batterer intervention actually relapsed at a higher level than those in the control group.

The measurement and design of the study does appear to have a significant effect on the strength of effect size found but the majority of evaluations have found 'modest but statistically significant reductions in men participating in batterer interventions' (Healey *et al.* 1998: 8). This concurs with a review by Edelson and Tolman, who concluded that the percentage of successful outcomes ranges from 53 to 85 per cent and suggested that as this is across different programmes, and different evaluation methods, there is some favourable evidence for perpetrator programmes (Edelson and Tolman 1992). Babcock and LaTaillade (2000) calculated the effect sizes of IPV programmes as varying from between 0.02 and 0.54. The effect sizes of quasi- and true experimental evaluations were small when police reports of reoffending were used (d = 0.32), and smaller still when partner report was used within a true experimental design (d = 0.11) (Babcock and LaTaillade 2000). A more recent systematic review of 10 experimental and quasi-experimental studies identified that official reports would indicate that the programmes have a small but significant effect on reducing reoffending (d = 0.26); however, there was no effect (d = 0) when victim reports were used to measure outcome, and quasi-experimental designs which compare treated with those rejected or rejecting treatment showed a large positive significant effect (by our calculation, approximately d = 0.75). This was, however, attributed more to pre-existing differences amongst those in the group rather than being seen as an effect of the group (Feder and Wilson 2005). Recent UK research suggests that treatment dropouts differ in their characteristics and risk level from those who do not (Bowen and Gilchrist 2006) and it is possible that this is what has the effect on recidivism rather than completion or otherwise of an offending behaviour programme. Also offender characteristics such as high interpersonal dependency and high previous contact with police have been found to predict recidivism more than treatment completion (Bowen *et al.* 2005).

These programmes may have a small consistent effect on some measures, (Feder and Wilson 2005; Babcock *et al.* 2004; Dobash *et al.* 1996; Gondolf 1997) but there are few data to suggest that any one particular approach has greater impact. Perhaps we are attempting to address the wrong question and, given the heterogeneity in IPV offending, we should focus less on establishing whether groups 'work' and more on 'which groups work best for which type of perpetrator?' Also, how to engage more participants in evaluation; how to maintain the input of victims; and reconsider using experimental designs (Feder and Wilson 2005). We also need to focus more on understanding what is it about the effective programmes that facilitates change. If therapeutic alliance is as relevant as content, this has important implications for future developments (Bowen and Gilchrist 2004).

It may be that the focus on 'deficits' and failure to employ a 'strengths-based' approach may also explain why many IPV programmes suffer from high attrition rate and why many of the perpetrators evidence limited motivation to engage with the programme, particularly when attendance is court-mandated (Bowen and Gilchrist 2004). Langlands *et al.* (2009) suggest that applying a Good Lives Model to interventions with IPV offenders may allow individualised assessment and treatment; could incorporate aspects of both feminist and CBT interventions and harness the perpetrators' motivations to achieve positive goals to the rehabilitation process in a way which is likely to maintain them in treatment more effectively (Langlands *et al.* 2009).

Conclusions

Recent research on IPV has explored and enhanced the models applied to IPV. It has investigated and challenged claims for gender symmetry or disparity in IPV, resulting in an expansion of the range of definition of subtypes of IPV behaviours, of subgroups of IPV offenders, and a greater recognition that applying multifactorial models and perhaps a pathways approaches to theory development in this area might be beneficial. Interventions with perpetrators continue to be important although they may only have a small treatment effect and there are ongoing concerns about how to deal with attrition, evaluation, and whether 'one size fits all' programmes are appropriate given the noted heterogeneity in IPV perpetrators.

There have been significant developments in the IPV field over the past few years. There is greater interdisciplinarity and greater scientific rigour; there is real movement towards including situational and cultural pathways into different types of IPV offending and a helpful complexity is developing across the field. Further work that focuses on the mechanisms through which risk factors are translated into violence and which addresses heterogeneity in all its forms will be the next step.

References

Aldridge, A. and Browne, K. (2003) 'Perpetrators of spousal abuse', *Trauma, Violence and Abuse*, 4 (3): 265–76.

Alvazzi del Frate, A. and Patrignani, A. (1995) *Women's Victimisations in Developing Countries*. Rome: UNICRI.

Andrews, D.A. and Bonta, J. (1994) *The Psychology of Criminal Conduct*. Vancouver: Anderson Publishing Co.

Archer, J. (2000) 'Sex differences in aggression between heterosexual partners: a meta-analytic review', *Psychological Bulletin*, 126 (5): 651–80.

Archer, J (2006) 'Cross-cultural differences in physical aggression between partners: a social-role analysis', *Personality and Social Psychology Review*, 10 (2): 133–52.

Austin, J.B. and Dankwort, J. (1999) 'Standards for batterer programs: a review and analysis', *Journal of Interpersonal Violence*, 14 (2): 152–68.

Babcock, J.C., Green, C.E. and Robie, C. (2004) 'Does batterers' treatment work? A meta-analytic review of domestic violence treatment outcome research', *Clinical Psychology Review*, 23: 1023–53.

Babcock, J.C. and LaTaillade, J.J. (2000) 'Evaluating interventions for men who batter', in J.P. Vincent and E.N. Jouriles (eds), *Domestic Violence: Guidelines for Research Informed Practice*. London: Jessica Kingsley Publishers.

Bhatt, R.V. (1998) 'Domestic violence and substance abuse', *International Journal of Gynaecology and Obstetrics*, 63: ss 25–31.

Blackburn, R. (1993) *The Psychology of Criminal Conduct: Theory, Research and Practice*. London: Wiley.

Bond, S.B. and Bond, M. (2004) 'Attachment styles and violence within couples', *Journal of Nervous and Mental Disease*, 192: 857–63.

Bowen, E., Brown, L. and Gilchrist, E. (2002) 'Evaluating probation based offender programmes for domestic violence perpetrators: a pro-feminist approach', *Howard Journal*, 41 (3): 221–36.

Bowen, E. and Gilchrist E. (2004) 'Comprehensive evaluation: a holistic approach to evaluating domestic violence offender programmes', *International Journal of Offender Therapy and Comparative Criminology*, 48: 215–34.

Bowen, E. and Gilchrist, E. (2006) 'Predicting dropout of court-mandated treatment in a British sample of domestic violence offenders', *Psychology, Crime and Law*, 12 (5): 573–87.

Bowen, E., Gilchrist, E. and Beech, A. (2005) 'An examination of the impact of community-based rehabilitation on the offending behavior of male domestic violence offenders and the characteristics associated with recidivism', *Legal and Criminological Psychology*, 10: 189–209.

Bowen, E., Gilchrist, E. and Beech, A. (2008) 'Change in treatment has no relationship with subsequent re-offending in UK domestic violence sample: a preliminary study', *International Journal of Offender Therapy and Comparative Criminology*, 1–17.

Busey, T. (1993) 'Women defendants and reactive survival syndrome', *The Catalyst*, Winter: 6–7.

Chamberland, C., Fortin, A. and Laporte, L. (2007) 'Establishing a relationship between behavior and cognition: violence against women and children within the family', *Journal of Family Violence*, 22: 383–95.

Costa, D. and Babcock, J. (2008) 'Articulated thoughts of intimate partner abusive men during anger arousal: correlates with personality disorder features', *Journal of Family Violence*, 23: 395–402.

Cunningham, A., Jaffe, P.G., Baker, L., Dick, T., Malla, S., Mazaheri, N. and Poisson, S. (1998) *Theory Derived Explanations of Male Violence Against Female Partners: Literature Update and Related Implications for Treatment and Evaluation*. London: London Family Court Clinic.

Department of Health (2005) *Responding to Domestic Abuse*. London: Department of Health.

Dixon, L. and Browne, K. (2003) 'The heterogeneity of spouse abuse: a review', *Aggression and Violent Behavior*, 8 (1): 107–30.

Dixon, L., Hamilton-Giachristis, C. and Browne, K.D. (2008) 'Classifying partner femicide', *Journal of Interpersonal Violence*, 23 (1): 74–93.

Dobash, R., Cavanagh, K., Dobash, R. and Lewis, R. (2000) 'Domestic violence programmes: a framework for change', *The Probation Journal*: 18–29.

Dobash, R.E. and Dobash, R.P. (2000) 'Evaluating criminal justice interventions for domestic violence', *Crime and Delinquency*, 46 (2): 252–70.

Dobash, R.E. and Dobash, R.P. (2007) 'Lethal and nonlethal violence against an intimate female partner', *Violence Against Women*, 13 (4): 329–53.

Dobash, R.P. and Dobash, R.E. (2004) 'Women's violence to men in intimate relationships', *British Journal of Criminology*: 1–26.

Dobash, R.E., Dobash, R.P. and Cavanagh, K. (2009) '"Out of the blue": men who murder an intimate partner', *Feminist Criminology*, 4: 194–225.

Dobash, R.P., Dobash, R.E., Cavanagh, K. and Lewis, R. (1999) 'A research evaluation of British programmes for violent men', *Journal of Social Policy*, 28 (2): 205–33.

Dobash, R., Dobash, R., Lewis, R. and Cavanagh, K. (2000) *Changing Violent Men*. London: Sage.

Dobash, R.P., Dobash, R.E., Wilson, M. and Daly, M. (1992) 'The myth of sexual symmetry in marital violence', *Social Problems*, 39 (1): 71–91.

Doumas, D., Pearson, C., Elgin, J. and McKinley, L. (2008) 'Adult attachment as a risk factor for intimate partner violence: the "mispairing of partners" attachment styles', *Journal of Interpersonal Violence*, 23: 616–34.

Dutton, D. (1995) *The Domestic Assault of Women*. California: Sage.

Dutton, D.G., Bodnarchuk, M., Kropp, P.R., Hart, S.D. and Ogloff, J. (1997) 'Wife assault treatment and criminal recidivism: an 11-year follow-up', *International Journal of Offender Therapy and Comparative Criminology*, 41: 9–23.

Dutton, D.G. (1985) 'An ecologically nested theory of male violence towards intimates', *International Journal of Women's Studies*, 8 (4): 404–13.

Dutton, D. and Corvo, K., (2007) 'The Duluth Model: a data-impervious paradigm and a failed strategy', *Aggression and Violent Behavior*, 12 (6): 658–67.

Easton, C., Swan, S. and Sinha, R. (2000) 'Motivation to change substance abuse among offenders of domestic violence', *Journal of Substance Abuse Treatment*, 19: 1–5.

Easton, C., Neavins, T. and Mandel, D. (2006) 'Aggression, violence and domestic abuse', in J. Grant and N. Potenza (eds) (2006) *Textbook of Men's Mental Health*. USA: American Psychiatric Publishing Inc.

Eberle, P.A. (1982) 'Alcohol and abusers and non-users: a discriminant analysis of differences between two subgroups of batterers', *Journal of Health and Social Behaviour*, 23: 260–71.

Eckhardt, C., Barbour, K. and Davison, G. (1998) 'Articulated thoughts of maritally violent and nonviolent men during anger arousal', *Journal of Consulting and Clinical Psychology*, 66 (2): 259–69.

Edelson, J.L. (1996) 'Controversy and change in batterers' programs', in J.L. Edelson and Z.C. Eisikovits (eds), *Future Interventions with Battered Women and Their Families* (pp. 154–69). Thousand Oaks, CA: Sage.

Edelson J.L. and Tolman R.M. (1992) *Intervention for Men Who Batter: An ecological approach*. California: Sage.

Ehrensaft, M., Cohen, P., Brown, J., Smailes, E., Chen, H. and Johnson, J. (2003) 'Intergenerational transmission of partner violence: a 20 year prospective study', *Journal of Consulting and Clinical Psychology*, 71 (4): 741–53.

Fagan, J. (1996) 'The criminalization of domestic violence: promises and limits.' Research report, National Institute of Justice, Washington, DC.

Feder, L. and Wilson, D. (2005) 'A meta-analytic review of court-mandated batterer intervention programs: can courts affect abusers' behavior?', *Journal of Experimental Criminology*, 1: 239–62.

Field, C., Caetano, R. and Nelson, S. (2004) 'Alcohol and violence related cognitive risk factors associated with the perpetration of intimate partner violence', *Journal of Family Violence*, 19 (4): 249–53.

Finney, A (2004) *Alcohol and Intimate Partner Violence: key findings from the research*. Findings No. 216. London: Home Office.

Foa, E., Cascardi, M., Zoellner, L. and Feeny, N. (2000) 'Psychological and environmental factors associated with partner violence', *Trauma, Violence and Abuse*, 1 (1): 67–91.

Frieze, I.H. (2005) 'Female violence against intimate partners: an introduction', *Psychology of Women Quarterly*, 29: 229–37.

Frye, V., Manganello, J., Campbell, J., Walton-Moss, B. and Wilt, S. (2006) 'The distribution of and factors associated with intimate terrorism among a population-based sample of urban women in the United States', *Journal of Interpersonal Violence*, 21: 1286–1313.

Geffner, R. and Rosenbaum, A. (eds) (2001) *Domestic Violence Offenders: Current Interventions, Research and Implications for Policies and Standards*. New York: Haworth Press.

Gelles, R. (1997) *Intimate Violence in Families*. California: Sage.

Gilchrist, E. (2008) 'Implicit thinking and intimate partner violence', *Scottish Journal of Criminal Justice Studies*, 14: 46–62.

Gilchrist, E. and Blissett, J. (2002) 'Magistrates' attitudes to domestic violence and sentencing options', *The Howard Journal*, 41 (4): 347–62.

Gilchrist, E., Johnson, R., Takriti, R., Beech, A., Kebbell, M. and Weston, S. (2003) *Domestic Violence Offenders: Characteristics and offending related needs*. Findings No. 217. London: Home Office.

Giles, J. (2005) '"Woman bites dog" – making sense of media and research reports that claim women and men are equally violent', *New Zealand Medical Journal*, 118 (1225): 1–8.

Gondolf, E.W. (1988) 'Who are those guys? Towards a behavioural typology of men who batter', *Violence and Victims*, 3: 187–203.

Gondolf, E.W. (1997) 'Batterers' programs: what we know and what we need to know', *Journal of Interpersonal Violence*, 12 (1): 83–98.

Gondolf, E.W. (2004) 'Evaluating batterer counseling programs: a difficult task showing some effects and implications', *Aggression and Violent Behavior*, 9: 605–31.

Grottman, J.M., Jacobson, N.S., Rushe, R.H., Shortt, J.W., Babcock, J., LaTaillade, J.J. and Waltz, J. (1995) 'The relationship between heart rate reactivity, emotionally aggressive behavior, and general violence in batterers', *Journal of Family Psychology*, 9 (3): 227–48.

Graham-Kevan, N. (2007) 'Distorting intimate violence findings: playing with numbers', *European Journal of Criminal Policy Research*, 13: 233–34.

Graham-Kevan, N. (2007) 'Domestic violence: research and implications for batterer programmes in Europe', *European Journal of Criminal Policy Research*, 13: 213–25.

Graham-Kevan, N. and Archer, J. (2003) 'Patriarchal terrorism and common couple violence: a test of Johnson's predictions in four British samples', *Journal of Interpersonal Violence*, 18: 1247–70.

Graham-Kevan, N. and Archer, J. (2005) 'Investigating three explanations of women's relationship aggression', *Psychology of Women Quarterly*, 29: 270–77.

Hamberger, L.K. and Hastings, J.E. (1993) 'Court mandated treatment of men who assault their partner: issues, controversies and outcomes', in N.Z. Hilton (ed.), *Legal Responses to Wife Assault: Current Trends and Evaluation*. London: Sage.

Hamberger, L.K., Lohr, J.M., Bonge, D. and Tollin, D.F. (1996) 'A large sample empirical typology of male spouse abusers and its relationship to dimensions of abuse', *Violence and Victims*, 11 (4): 277–91.

Hannawa, A., Spitzberg, B., Wiering, L. and Teranishi, C. (2006) '"If I can't have you, no one can": development of a relational proprietariness scale (REPS)', *Violence and Victims*, 21 (5): 539–60.

Hanson, R.K. and Wallace-Carpretta, S. (2000) *A Multi-site Study of Treatment for Abusive Men. User Report 2000–05*. Ottawa: Department of the Solicitor General of Canada.

Harper, G. and Chitty, C. (2005) *The Impact of Corrections on Re-offending: a review of what works* (3rd edn). Home Office Research Study 291. London: Home Office.

Harrell, Adele V. (1991) 'Evaluation of court-ordered treatment for domestic violence offenders.' Final report, Grant 90-12L-E-089, State Justice Institute. Washington, DC: The Urban Institute.

Healey, K., Smith, C. with O'Sullivan, C. (1998) 'Batterer intervention: program approaches and criminal justice strategies', *Issues and Practices in Criminal Justice Series*. Washington, DC: US Department of Justice.

Holtzworth-Munroe, A., Bates, L., Smultzer, N. and Sandin, E. (1997) 'A brief review of the research on husband violence', *Aggression and Violent Behavior*, 2: 65–99.

Holtzworth-Munroe, A., Meeham, J.C., Herron, K., Rehman, U. and Stuart, G.L. (2000) 'Testing the Holtzworth-Munroe and Stuart (1994) batterer typology', *Journal of Consulting and Clinical Psychology*, 68 (6): 1000–19.

Holtzworth-Munroe, A. and Meehan, J. (2004) 'Typologies of men who are maritally violent: scientific and clinical implications', *Journal of Interpersonal Violence*, 19 (12) 1369–89.

Holtzworth-Munroe, A. and Stuart, G.L. (1994) 'Typologies of male batterers: three subtypes and the differences among them', *Psychological Bulletin*, 116 (3): 476–97.

Home Affairs Select Committee (1993) *Government Policy Around Domestic Violence*. London: Crime Police Strategy Unit.

Home Office (1999) *Living Without Fear*. London: Central Office of Information.

Home Office (2002) *Crime Reduction Programme: Violence Against Women Initiative*, www.crimereduction.gov.uk

Home Office (2005) *Domestic Violence: a national report*. London: Home Office.

Hotaling, G.T. and Sugarman, D.B. (1986) 'An analysis of risk markers in husband to wife violence: the current state of knowledge', *Violence and Victims*, 1 (2): 101–24.

Janghinrichsen-Rohling, J. (2005) 'Top 10 Greatest "Hits": important findings and future directions for intimate partner violence research', *Journal of Interpersonal Violence*, 20: 108–18.

Johnson, M. (1995) 'Two forms of violence against women', *Journal of Marriage and the Family*, 57: 283–94.

Johnson, M.P. (1999) 'Two types of violence against women in the American family: identifying intimate terrorism and common couple violence.' Paper presented at the annual meeting of the National Council on Family Relations, November 1999, Irvine, CA.

Johnson, M.P. (2005) 'Domestic violence: it's not about gender – or is it?', *Journal of Marriage and Family*, 67 (5): Research Library Core, 1126.

Johnson, R., Gilchrist E., Beech, A., Weston, S., Takriti, R. and Freeman, R. (2006) 'A psychometric of UK domestic violence offenders', *Journal of Interpersonal Violence*, 211 (10): 1270–85.

Kane, T.A., Staiger, P.K. and Ricciardelli, L.A. (2000) 'Male domestic violence, attitudes, aggression and interpersonal dependency', *Journal of Interpersonal Violence*, 15 (1): 16–29.

Kropp, P.R. and Bodnarchuk, M. (2001) *Evaluation of Three Assaultative Men's Treatment Programs–Summary Report*. Vancouver: The British Columbia Institute Against Family Violence.

Kropp, P.R. and Hart, S.D. (2000) 'The spousal assault risk assessment (SARA) guide: reliability and validity in adult male offenders', *Law and Human Behaviour*, 24 (1): 101–17.

Langlands, R., Ward, T. and Gilchrist, E. (2009) 'Applying the good lives models to male perpetrators of domestic violence', in P. Lehman and C.A. Simmons (eds), *Strengths Based Batterer Intervention: A New Paradigm in Ending Family Violence*. New York: Springer Verlag.

Leonard, K.E. and Senchak, M. (1996) 'Prospective prediction of marital aggression within newly wed couples', *Journal of Abnormal Psychology*, 105: 369–80.

Levinson, D. (1989) *Family in Cross-cultural Perspective*. Beverly Hills: Sage.

Lindhorst, T. and Tajima, E. (2008) 'Reconceptualizing and operationalizing context in survey research on intimate partner violence', *Journal of Interpersonal Violence*, 23 (3), March: 362–88.

Magdol, L., Moffitt, T.E., Caspi, A. and Silva, P.A. (1998) 'Developmental antecedents of partner abuse: a prospective-longitudinal study', *Journal of Abnormal Psychology*, 107 (3): 375–89.

Matrix Knowledge Group (2007) *The Economic Case For and Against Prison*. London: Matrix Knowledge Group.

MacPherson, S (2002) *Domestic Violence: Findings From The 2000 Scottish Crime Survey*. Edinburgh: Scottish Executive Central Research Unit.

Maiuro, R., Cahn, T., Vitaliano, P., Wagner, B. and Zegree, J. (1988) 'Anger hostility and depression in intimate partner violent versus generally violent assaultative men and non-violent control subjects', *Journal of Consulting and Clinical Psychology*, 56: 17–23.

McGuire, J. (1985) *What Works: reducing reoffending guidelines from research and practice*. Chichester: John Wiley and Sons.

McMurran, M. and Gilchrist, E. (2008) 'Anger control and alcohol use: appropriate interventions for perpetrators of domestic violence?', *Psychology, Crime and Law,* 14 (20): 107–16.

Metropolitan Police Service (2003) *MPS Risk Assessment Model for Domestic Violence Cases*. London: Metropolitan Police.

Millon, T. (1994) *Millon Clinical Multiaxial Inventory*–III. Minneapolis, MN: National Computer Systems.

Mirrlees-Black (1999) *Domestic Violence: findings from a new British Crime Survey self-completion questionnaire*. Home Office Research Study 191. London: Home Office.

Mirrlees-Black, C., Mayhew, P. and Percy, A. (1996) *The 1996 British Crime Survey: England and Wales*. Home Office Statistics Bulletin. London: HMSO.

Mitchell, I. and Gilchrist, E. (2006) 'Domestic violence and panic attacks–common neural mechanisms?', *Legal and Criminological Psychology,* 11: 267–82.

Morran, D. (2002) Personal communication, 12 November.

Muftic, L., Bouffard, J. and Bouffard, L. (2007) 'An exploratory study of women arrested for intimate partner violence: violent women or violent resistance?', *Journal of Interpersonal Violence*, 11: 753–74.

MVA (2000) *Violence in Scotland: Findings from the 2000 Scottish Crime Survey*. Edinburgh: Scottish Executive Central Research Unit.

National Probation Service (2007) *Domestic Violence Interventions News Special*. London: Home Office.

Norlander, B. and Eckhardt, C. (2005) 'Anger, hostility and male perpetrators of intimate partner violence: a meta analytic review', *Clinical Psychology Review*, 25: 119–52.

O'Hearn, H.G. and Margolin, G. (2000) 'Men's attitudes condoning marital aggression: a moderator between family of origin abuse and aggression against female partners', *Cognitive Therapy and Research*, 24 (2): 159–74.

Pence, E. and Paymar, M. (1993) *Education Groups for Men Who Batter: The Duluth Model*. New York: Springer.

Pizzey, E. and Forbes, A. (1974) *Scream Quietly or the Neighbours Will Hear*. Harmondsworth: Penguin.

Reitzel-Jaffe, D. and Wolfe, D.A. (2001) 'Predictors of relationship abuse among young men', *Journal of Interpersonal Violence*, 16 (2): 99–115.

Saunders, D.G. (1992) 'A typology of men who batter: three types derived from cluster analysis', *American Journal of Orthopsychiatry*, 62: 264–75.

Saunders, D. (2004) 'The place of a typology of men who are maritally violent within a nested ecological model: a response to Holtzworth-Munroe and Meehan', *Journal of Interpersonal Violence*, 19: 1390–5.

Saunders, D.G. (1996) 'Feminist-cognitive-behavioral and process psychodynamic treatments for men who batter: interactions of abuser traits and treatment model', *Violence and Victims*, 4: 393–414.

Saunders, D.G., Lynch, A.B., Grayson, M. and Linz, D. (1987) 'The inventory of beliefs about wife beating: the construction and initial validation of a measure of beliefs and attitudes', *Violence and Victims*, 2 (1): 39–57.

Scourfield, J.B. and Dobash, R.P. (1999) 'Programmes for violent men: recent developments in the UK', *Howard Journal*, 38 (2): 128–43.

Simons, R.L., Wu, C., Johnson, C. and Conger, R.D. (1995) 'A test of various perspectives on the intergenerational transmission of domestic violence', *Criminology*, 33 (1): 14–171.

Stanko, E. (2000) *A Day to Count*, www.domesticviolencedatasource.org

Stets (1995) 'Modelling control in relationships', *Journal of Marriage and the Family*, 57 (2): 487–501.

Stith, S.M., Rosen, K.H., Middleton, K.A., Busch, A.L., Lundeberg, K. and Carlton, R.P. (2000) 'The intergenerational transmission of spouse abuse: a meta-analysis', *Journal of Marriage and Family*, 62: 640–54.

Straus, M.A. (1979) 'Measuring intrafamily conflict and violence: the conflict tactics scales', *Journal of Marriage and the Family*, 41: 75–88.

Straus, M. and Gelles, R. (eds) (1990) *Violence in American Families*. New Brunswick, NJ: Transaction Publishers.

Straus, M. and Smith, C. (1990) 'Violence in Hispanic families in the United States: incidence rates and structural interpretation', in M. Straus and R. Gelles (eds), *Physical Violence in the American Family*. Garden City, NJ: Anchor Press.

Sykes, G.M. and Matza, D. (1957) 'Techniques of neutralization: a theory of delinquency', *American Sociological Review*, 22: 664–70.

Tolman, R.M. and Bennett, L.W. (1990) 'A review of the quantitative research on men who batter', *Journal of Interpersonal Violence*, 5 (1): 87–118.

Tweed, R.G. and Dutton, D.G. (1998) 'A comparison of impulsive and instrumental subgroups of batterers', *Violence and Victims*, 13 (3): 217–30.

van Dijk, J., Mayhew, P. and Killias, M. (1994) *Experiences of Crime Across the World*. Deventer: Kluwer.

Walby, S. and Allen, J. (2004) *Domestic Violence, Sexual Assault and Stalking: Findings from the British Crime Survey*. London: Home Office Research, Development and Statistics Directorate.

Waltz, J., Babcock, J.C., Jacobson, N.S. and Gottman, J.M. (2000) 'Testing a typology of batterers', *Journal of Consulting and Clinical Psychology*, 68 (4): 658–69.

Washington State Institute for Public Policy (2006) *Evidence Based Adult Corrections Programs: What Works and What Does Not*. Olympia: Washington State Institute for Public Policy, January.

Wolfus, B. and Bierman, R. (1996) 'An evaluation of a group treatment program for incarcerated male batterers', *International Journal of Offender Therapy and Comparative Criminology*, 40 (4): 318–33.

Chapter 19

Effective programmes to prevent delinquency

Brandon C. Welsh and David P. Farrington

The main aim of this chapter is to summarise briefly some of the most effective programmes for preventing delinquency and later offending whose effectiveness has been demonstrated in high-quality evaluation research. Only programmes with outcome measures of delinquency, antisocial behaviour, or disruptive child behaviour are included; programmes were not included if they only had outcome measures of risk factors such as low IQ or poor parenting. Some of the programmes did not have a direct measure of delinquency, because this would have required a long-term follow-up. However, there is considerable continuity between disruptive child behaviour and juvenile delinquency (e.g., Farrington 2009). Therefore, programmes that have immediate effects on disruptive child behaviour are likely to have long-term effects on delinquency and later offending.

Within the constraints of this chapter, it is not feasible to present an exhaustive or systematic review of interventions to prevent crime (see Welsh and Farrington 2006). Systematic reviews are much more rigorous than more traditional narrative reviews of the literature. Whereas traditional reviews rarely include detailed information about why studies were included or excluded, systematic reviews provide explicit and transparent information about the criteria used for including or excluding studies. Systematic reviews focus on studies that have the highest methodological quality and use the most rigorous methods possible to combine results from different studies statistically to draw conclusions about what works. These reviews contain methods and results sections and are reported with the same level of detail that characterises high-quality reports of original research. They include detailed summary tables of key features of studies such as design, sample sizes and effect sizes.

We will describe some of the most important and best-evaluated programmes, with special reference to programmes that have carried out a benefit–cost analysis. The conclusion from the Perry Preschool Programme (discussed later) that, for every dollar spent on the intervention, 17 dollars were saved in the long term (Schweinhart *et al.* 2005) proved particularly convincing to policy-makers. The monetary costs of crime are enormous (Welsh *et al.* 2008). Dubourg *et al.* (2005) estimated that they totalled £36 billion in England and Wales in 2003–04. There are tangible costs to victims, such as replacing stolen goods and repairing damage, and intangible costs that are harder to quantify, such as pain, suffering and a reduced quality of life. There are costs to the government or taxpayer for police, courts, prisons, crime prevention activities, and so on. There are also costs to offenders; for example, those associated with being in prison or losing a job.

To the extent that crime prevention programmes are successful in reducing crime, they will have benefits. These benefits can be quantified in monetary terms according to the reduction in the monetary costs of crime. Other benefits may accrue from reducing the costs of associated social problems such as unemployment, divorce, educational failure, drug addiction, welfare dependency, and so on. That offending is part of a larger syndrome of antisocial behaviour (Farrington *et al.* 2006; West and Farrington 1977) is good news, because the benefits of a crime prevention programme can be many and varied. The monetary benefits of a programme can be compared with its monetary costs to determine the benefit-to-cost ratio. Surprisingly, few benefit–cost analyses of crime prevention programmes have ever been carried out (Aos *et al.* 2004; Farrington and Welsh 2007; Greenwood 2006).

This chapter is organised around two main categories of programmes to prevent delinquency: (1) individual and family programmes, and (2) peer, school and community programmes.

Individual and family programmes

Four types of programmes are particularly successful: parent education (in the context of home visiting), parent management training, child skills training, and preschool intellectual enrichment programmes (Farrington and Welsh 2007). Generally, the programmes are targeted on the risk factors of poor parental child-rearing, supervision or discipline (general parent education or parent management training), high impulsivity, low empathy and self-centredness (child skills training), and low intelligence and attainment (preschool programmes).

General parent education

The best-known home visiting programme (and the only one with a direct measure of delinquency) is the Nurse–Family Partnership carried out in the semi-rural community of Elmira, New York, by David Olds and his colleagues (1998). This programme was designed with three broad objectives: (1) to improve the outcomes of pregnancy; (2) to improve the quality of care that parents provide to their children; and (3) to improve the women's own personal life course development (completing their education, finding work, and planning future pregnancies) (Olds *et al.* 1993: 158).

The programme enrolled 400 women prior to their 30th week of pregnancy. Women were recruited if they had no previous live births and had at least one of the following high-risk characteristics prone to health and developmental problems in infancy: under 19 years of age, unmarried, or poor. The women were randomly assigned to receive home visits from nurses during pregnancy, or to receive visits both during pregnancy and during the first two years of life, or to a control group who received no visits. Each visit lasted about one and a quarter hours and the mothers were visited on average every two weeks. The home visitors gave advice about prenatal and postnatal care of the child, about infant development, and about the importance of proper nutrition and avoiding smoking and drinking during pregnancy.

The results of this experiment showed that the postnatal home visits caused a significant decrease in recorded child physical abuse and neglect during the first two years of life, especially by poor, unmarried, teenage mothers; 4 per cent of visited versus 19 per cent of non-visited mothers of this type were guilty of child abuse or neglect (Olds *et al.* 1986). This last result is important, partly because children who are physically abused or neglected have an enhanced likelihood of becoming violent offenders later in life (Widom 1989). In a 15-year follow-up (13 years after programme completion), which included 330 mothers and 315 children, significantly fewer experimental compared with control group mothers were identified as perpetrators of child abuse and neglect (29 per cent versus 54 per cent), and, for the higher risk sample only, significantly fewer treatment mothers in contrast to the controls had alcohol or substance abuse problems or were arrested (Olds *et al.* 1997). At the age of 15, children of the higher risk mothers who received prenatal or postnatal home visits or both had incurred significantly fewer arrests than their control counterparts (20 as opposed to 45 per 100 children; Olds *et al.* 1998).

Several benefit–cost analyses show that the benefits of this programme outweighed its costs for the higher risk mothers. The most important are by Greenwood *et al.* (2001; see also Karoly *et al.* 1998) and Aos *et al.* (2004). Greenwood *et al.* measured benefits to the government or taxpayer (welfare, education, employment and criminal justice), not benefits to crime victims consequent upon reduced crimes. Aos *et al.* measured a somewhat different range of benefits to the government (education, public assistance, substance abuse, teen pregnancy, child abuse and neglect, and criminal justice), as well as tangible benefits to crime victims. Both reported that, for every dollar spent on the programme, the benefits were about three to four times greater; $4.06 according to Greenwood *et al.* and $2.88 according to Aos *et al.*

In order to test the generalisability of the results of the Elmira study, two urban replications are currently under way: one in Memphis, Tennessee (Olds *et al.* 2004a), and the other in Denver, Colorado (Olds *et al.* 2004b). Early follow-up results of both replications (four and two years after programme completion, respectively) show continued improvements on a wide range of outcomes for both nurse-visited mothers and their children compared with their control counterparts.

Preschool programmes

The most famous preschool intellectual enrichment programme is the Perry project carried out in Ypsilanti (Michigan) by Lawrence Schweinhart and David Weikart (1980). This was essentially a Head Start programme targeted at disadvantaged African American children. A sample of 123 children were allocated (approximately at random) to experimental and control groups. The experimental children attended a daily preschool programme, backed up by weekly home visits, during two years, usually covering ages three to four. The aim of the 'plan-do-review' programme was to provide intellectual stimulation, to increase thinking and reasoning abilities, and to increase later school achievement.

This programme had long-term benefits. Berrueta-Clement *et al.* (1984) showed that, at age 19, the experimental group was more likely to be employed, more likely to have graduated from high school, more likely to have received college or vocational training, and less likely to have been arrested. By age 27, the experimental group had accumulated only half as many arrests on average as the controls (Schweinhart *et al.* 1993). Also, they had significantly higher earnings and were more likely to be home-owners. More of the experimental women were married, and fewer of their children were born out of wedlock.

The most recent follow-up of this project, at age 40, which included 91 per cent of the original sample, found that the programme continued to make an important difference in the lives of the participants (Schweinhart *et al.* 2005). Compared with the control group, experimental participants had significantly fewer lifetime arrests for violent crimes (32 per cent v. 48 per cent), property crimes (36 per cent v. 58 per cent), and drug crimes (14 per cent v. 34 per cent), and were significantly less likely to be arrested five or more times (36 per cent v. 55 per cent). Improvements were also recorded in many other important life course outcomes. For example, significantly higher levels of schooling (77 per cent v. 60 per cent graduating from high school), better records of employment (76 per cent v. 62 per cent), and higher annual incomes were reported by the programme group compared to the controls. A benefit–cost analysis at age 40 found that the Perry project produced just over $17 benefit per dollar of cost, with 76 per cent of this being returned to the general public – in the form of savings in crime, education and welfare, and increased tax revenue – and 24 per cent benefiting each experimental participant. Desirable results were also obtained in other preschool evaluations (Campbell *et al.* 2002; Reynolds *et al.* 2001).

Day care programmes

One of the very few prevention experiments beginning in pregnancy and collecting outcome data on delinquency was the Syracuse (New York) Family Development Research Programme of Ronald Lally and his colleagues (1988). The researchers began with a sample of pregnant women (mostly poor African American single mothers) and gave them weekly help with child-rearing, health, nutrition and other problems. In addition, their children received free full-time day care, designed to develop their intellectual abilities, up to age five. This was not a randomised experiment, but a matched control group was chosen when the children were aged three.

Ten years later, about 120 treated and control children were followed up to about age 15. Significantly fewer of the treated children (2 per cent as opposed to 17 per cent) had been referred to the juvenile court for delinquency offences, and the treated girls showed better school attendance and school performance. However, the benefit-to-cost ratio of this programme was only 0.3 according to Aos *et al.* (1999). This was largely because of the cost of the programme ($45,000 per child in 1998 dollars, compared with $14,000 for Perry and $7,000 for Elmira); providing free full-time day care up to age five was very expensive. Against this, it is important to note that the early findings of Aos *et al.* (1999) tend to underestimate the benefit-to-cost ratio.

Desirable results were also obtained in a day care intervention in Houston by Johnson and Walker (1987) but not by McCarton *et al.* (1997) in the large-scale Infant Health and Development Program. This project, implemented in eight sites across the United States, had encouraging results at age three; however, the experimental and control children were not significantly different in behaviour problems at age eight.

Parent management training

Perhaps the best-known method of parent training was developed by Gerald Patterson (1982) in Oregon. Parents were trained to notice what a child is doing, monitor behaviour over long periods, clearly state home rules, make rewards and punishments contingent on the child's behaviour, and negotiate disagreements so that conflicts and crises did not escalate. His treatment was shown to be effective in reducing child stealing and antisocial behaviour over short periods, in small-scale studies (Patterson *et al.* 1982, 1992).

Carolyn Webster-Stratton and Mary Hammond (1997) evaluated the effectiveness of parent training and child skills training with about 100 Seattle children (average age five) referred to a clinic because of conduct problems. The children and their parents were randomly allocated to receive either (a) parent training, (b) child skills training, (c) both parent and child training, or (d) to a control group. The skills training aimed to foster prosocial behaviour and interpersonal skills using video modelling, while the parent training involved weekly meetings between parents and therapists for 22–24 weeks. Parent reports and home observations showed that children in all three experimental conditions had fewer behaviour problems than control children, both in an immediate and in a one-year follow-up. There was little difference between the three experimental conditions, although the combined parent and child training condition produced the most significant improvements in child behaviour at the one-year follow-up.

Stephen Scott and his colleagues (2001) evaluated the Webster-Stratton parent training programme in London. About 140 children aged three to eight who were referred for antisocial behaviour were allocated to receive parent training or to be in a control group. The programme was successful. According to parent reports, the antisocial behaviour of the experimental children decreased, while that of the control children did not change. Since this programme is relatively cheap (£571 per child for a 12-week programme), it is likely to be cost-effective.

Frances Gardner and her colleagues (2006) evaluated the success of the Webster-Stratton programme in Oxfordshire. Over 70 children, aged two to nine, referred for conduct problems, were randomly assigned to receive parent training or to be in a waiting-list control group. Follow-up parent reports and observations again showed that the antisocial behaviour of the experimental children decreased compared with the controls. Other studies also show that parent training is effective in reducing children's antisocial behaviour (e.g. Long *et al.* 1994; Mason *et al.* 2003; see also the systematic review by Piquero *et al.* 2009).

Skills training

One of the most successful early skills training programmes that measured the effects on crime is the Montreal Longitudinal-Experimental Study of Richard Tremblay and his colleagues (1995, 1996). This programme combined child skills training and parent training. Tremblay *et al.* (1996) identified disruptive (aggressive/hyperactive) boys at age six (from low socio-economic neighbourhoods in Montreal) and randomly allocated over 300 of these to experimental or control conditions.

Between ages seven and nine, the experimental group received training designed to foster social skills and self-control. Coaching, peer modelling, role playing and reinforcement contingencies were used in small group sessions on such topics as 'how to help', 'what to do when you are angry', and 'how to react to teasing'. Also, their parents were trained using the parent management training techniques developed by Patterson (1982). Parents were taught how to provide positive reinforcement for desirable behaviour, to use non-punitive and consistent discipline practices, and to develop family crisis management techniques.

By age 12 (three years after treatment), the experimental boys committed significantly less burglary and theft, were significantly less likely to get drunk, and were significantly less likely to be involved in fights than the controls. Also, the experimental boys had significantly higher school achievement (McCord *et al.* 1994; Tremblay *et al.* 1992). At every age from 10 to 15, the experimental boys had significantly lower self-reported delinquency scores than the control boys. Interestingly, the differences in delinquency between experimental and control boys increased as the follow-up progressed. Boisjoli *et al.* (2007) showed that fewer experimental boys had a criminal record by age 24. Also, there were differences between experimental and control boys in trajectories of delinquency (Vitaro *et al.* 2001) and of aggression, vandalism and theft (Lacourse *et al.* 2002). Unfortunately, no benefit–cost analysis of this programme has yet been carried out. A small number of other studies also show that skills training is effective in reducing delinquency (e.g., Jones and Offord 1989; see also the systematic review by Lösel and Beelmann 2006).

Peer, school and community programmes

Three types of programmes are particularly successful: school-based parent and teacher training, school-based anti-bullying curricula, and multi-systemic therapy (MST). Generally, the programmes are targeted on the risk factors of poor parenting and poor school performance (school-based parent and teacher training), bullying (school-based anti-bullying) and intrapersonal (e.g. cognitive) and systemic (family, peer, school) factors associated with antisocial behaviour (MST).

Peer programmes

There are no outstanding examples of effective intervention programmes for delinquency or later offending based on peer risk factors. The most hopeful programmes involve using high-status conventional peers to teach children ways of resisting peer pressure; this has been effective in reducing drug use (Tobler *et al.* 1999). Also, in a randomised experiment in St. Louis, Ronald Feldman and his colleagues (1983) showed that placing antisocial adolescents in activity groups dominated by prosocial adolescents led to a reduction in their antisocial behaviour (compared with antisocial adolescents in antisocial groups). This suggests that the influence of prosocial peers can be harnessed to reduce offending. However, putting antisocial peers together can have harmful effects (Dodge *et al.* 2006).

The most important intervention programme whose success seems to be based mainly on reducing peer risk factors is the Children at Risk programme (Harrell *et al.* 1999), which targeted high-risk youths (average age 12) in poor neighbourhoods of five cities across the United States. Eligible youths were identified in schools, and over 670 were randomly assigned to experimental or control groups. The programme was a multiple-component community-based prevention strategy targeting risk factors for delinquency, including case management and family counselling, family skills training, tutoring, mentoring, after-school activities and community policing. The programme was different in each neighbourhood.

The initial results of the programme were disappointing (Harrell *et al.* 1997), but a one-year follow-up showed that (according to self-reports) experimental youths were less likely to have committed violent crimes and used or sold drugs (Harrell *et al.* 1999). The process evaluation showed that the greatest change was in peer risk factors. Experimental youths associated less often with delinquent peers, felt less peer pressure to engage in delinquency, and had more positive peer support. In contrast, there were few changes in individual, family or community risk factors, possibly linked to the low participation of parents in parent training and of youths in mentoring and tutoring (Harrell *et al.* 1997: 87). In other words, there were problems of implementation of the programme, linked to the serious and multiple needs and problems of the families. No benefit–cost analysis of this programme has yet been carried out, but its relatively low cost ($9,000 per youth) and its targeting of high-risk youths suggest that its benefits may possibly outweigh its costs.

School programmes

One of the most important school-based prevention experiments was carried out in Seattle by David Hawkins and his colleagues (1991). They implemented a multiple-component programme combining parent training, teacher training and child skills training. About 500 first grade children (aged six) in 21 classes in eight schools were randomly assigned to be in experimental or control classes. The children in the experimental classes received special treatment at home and school which was designed to increase their attachment to their parents and their bonding to the school. Also, they were trained in interpersonal cognitive problem-solving. Their parents were trained to notice and reinforce socially desirable behaviour in a programme called 'Catch them being good'. Their teachers were trained in classroom management, for example to provide clear instructions and expectations to children, to reward children for participation in desired behaviour, and to teach children prosocial (socially desirable) methods of solving problems.

This programme had long-term benefits. O'Donnell *et al.* (1995) focused on children in low income families and reported that, in the sixth grade (age 12), experimental boys were less likely to have initiated delinquency, while experimental girls were less likely to have initiated drug use. In a later follow-up, Hawkins *et al.* (1999) found that, at age 18, the full intervention group (receiving the intervention from grades one to six) admitted less violence, less alcohol abuse and fewer sexual partners than the late intervention group (grades five to six only) or the controls. A benefit–cost analysis of the programme by Aos *et al.* (2004) found that for every dollar spent on the programme, more than $3 was saved to government and crime victims.

Another important school-based prevention experiment was carried out by Israel Kolvin and his colleagues (1981) in Newcastle upon Tyne. They randomly allocated 270 junior school children (aged seven to eight) and 322 secondary school children (aged 11 to 12) to experimental or control groups. All children had been identified as showing some kind of social or psychiatric disturbance or learning problems (according to teacher and peer ratings). There were three types of experimental programmes: (a) behaviour modification/reinforcement with the seniors, 'nurture work', teaching healthy interactions with the juniors; (b) parent counselling/teacher consultations with both; and (c) group therapy with the seniors, play groups with the juniors.

The programmes were evaluated after 18 months and after three years using clinical ratings of conduct disturbance. Generally, the experimental and control groups were not significantly different for the juniors, although there was some tendency for the nurture work and play group conditions to be better behaved than the controls at the three-year follow-up. For the seniors, those who received group therapy showed significantly less conduct disturbance at both follow-ups, and there was some tendency for the other two programmes also to be effective at the three-year follow-up. Many other school-based prevention experiments have also been successful in reducing antisocial behaviour (Gottfredson *et al.* 2006; Wilson and Lipsey 2007).

School bullying, of course, is a risk factor for offending (Farrington 1993). Several school-based programmes have been effective in reducing bullying. The most famous of these was implemented by Dan Olweus (1994) in Norway. It aimed to increase awareness and knowledge of teachers, parents and children about bullying and to dispel myths about it. A 30-page booklet was distributed to all schools in Norway describing what was known about bullying and recommending what steps schools and teachers could take to reduce it. Also, a 25-minute video about bullying was made available to schools. Simultaneously, the schools distributed to all parents a four-page folder containing information and advice about bullying. In addition, anonymous self-report questionnaires about bullying were completed by all children.

The programme was evaluated in Bergen. Each of the 42 participating schools received feedback information from the questionnaire, about the prevalence of bullies and victims, in a specially arranged school conference day. Also, teachers were encouraged to develop explicit rules about bullying (e.g. do not bully, tell someone when bullying happens, bullying will not be tolerated, try to help victims, try to include children who are being left out) and to discuss bullying in class, using the video and role-playing exercises. Also, teachers were encouraged to improve monitoring and supervision of children, especially in the playground. The programme was successful in reducing the prevalence of bullying by half.

A similar programme was implemented in 23 Sheffield schools by Peter Smith and Sonia Sharp (1994). The core programme involved establishing a 'whole-school' anti-bullying policy, raising awareness of bullying and clearly defining roles and responsibilities of teachers and students, so that everyone knew what bullying was and what they should do about it. In addition, there were optional interventions tailored to particular schools: curriculum work (e.g. reading books, watching videos), direct work with students (e.g. assertiveness training for those who were bullied) and playground work (e.g. training lunch-time supervisors). This programme was successful in reducing bullying (by 15 per cent) in primary schools, but had relatively small effects (a 5 per cent reduction) in secondary schools.

Ttofi and Farrington (2009) completed a systematic review of the effectiveness of anti-bullying programmes in schools. They found 59 high-quality evaluations of 30 different programmes. They concluded that, overall, anti-bullying programmes were effective. The results showed that bullying and victimisation were reduced by about 20–23 per cent in experimental schools compared with control schools.

Community programmes

There are a few types of community-based programmes that are successful. Mentoring is one example. Big Brothers Big Sisters (BBBS) of America is a national youth mentoring organisation that was founded in 1904 and is committed to improving the life chances of at-risk children and teens. One BBBS programme brought together unrelated pairs of adult volunteers and youths, aged 10 to 16. Rather than trying to address particular problems facing a youth, the programme focused on providing a youth with an adult friend. The premise behind this is that the 'friendship forged with a youth by the Big Brother or Big Sister creates a framework through which the mentor can support and aid the youth' (Grossman and Tierney 1998: 405). The programme also stressed that this friendship needs to be long lasting. To this end, mentors met with youths on average three or four times a month (for three to four hours each time) for at least one year.

An evaluation of the BBBS programme, by Grossman and Tierney (1998), took place at eight sites across the United States and involved randomly assigning more than 1,100 youths to the programme or to a control group that did not receive mentoring. At programme completion, it was found that those youths who received the intervention, compared with their control counterparts, were significantly (32 per cent) less likely to have hit someone, initiated illegal drug use (46 per cent less), initiated alcohol use (27 per cent less), or truanted from school (30 per cent less). The experimental group members were also more likely (but not significantly) than the controls to do better in school and have better relationships with their parents and peers. A benefit–cost analysis of this programme by Aos *et al.* (2004) found that for every dollar spent on the programme more than \$3 was saved to the government and crime victims.

A systematic review and meta-analysis of 18 mentoring programmes by Jolliffe and Farrington (2008) concluded that this was an effective approach in preventing delinquency. The weighted mean effect size was d = .21, corresponding to a significant 10 per cent reduction in delinquency. Mentoring was more effective in reducing offending when the average duration of each contact between mentor and mentee was greater, in smaller scale studies, and when mentoring was combined with other interventions.

One of the most important community-based treatment programmes is Multi-Systemic Therapy (MST), which is a multiple component programme (Henggeler *et al.* 1998). The particular type of treatment is chosen according to the particular needs of the youth; therefore, the nature of the treatment is different for each person. The treatment may include individual, family, peer, school and community interventions, including parent training and child skills training. The treatment is delivered in the youth's home, school and community settings.

Typically, MST has been used with juvenile offenders. For example, in Missouri, Charles Borduin and his colleagues (1995) randomly assigned 176 juvenile offenders (mean age 14) either to MST or to individual therapy, focusing on personal, family and academic issues. Four years later, only 29 per cent of the MST offenders had been rearrested, compared with 74 per cent of the individual therapy group. According to Aos *et al.* (2001), the benefit-to-cost ratio for MST is very high, largely because of the potential cost savings from targeting chronic juvenile offenders. For every dollar spent on this programme, $13 were saved in victim and criminal justice costs.

Unfortunately, disappointing results were obtained in a large-scale independent evaluation of MST in Canada by Alan Leschied and Alison Cunningham (2002). Over 400 youths who were either offenders or at risk of offending were randomly assigned to receive either MST or the usual services (typically probation supervision). Six months after treatment, 28 per cent of the MST group had been reconvicted, compared with 31 per cent of the control group, a non-significant difference. Therefore, it is not totally clear how effective MST is when it is implemented independently, although it was successful in a Norwegian evaluation (Ogden and Hagen 2006). Two recent meta-analyses of the effectiveness of MST reached contradictory conclusions. Nicola Curtis and her colleagues (2004) found that it was effective, but Julia Littell (2005) reported that it was not. Nevertheless, MST is a promising intervention technique, and it is being used in the UK (Jefford and Squire 2004).

Communities That Care

In the interests of maximising effectiveness, what is needed is a multiple-component community-based programme including several of the successful interventions listed above. Many of the programmes reviewed in this chapter are of this type. However, Communities That Care (CTC) has many attractions (Farrington 1996). Perhaps more than any other programme, it is evidence-based and systematic: the choice of interventions depends on empirical evidence about what are the important risk and protective factors in a particular community and on empirical evidence about 'what works' (Sherman *et al.* 2006). CTC is supported at the local level across the United States, at the last count in several hundred communities (Harachi *et al.* 2003). It has also been implemented in over 20 sites in England, Scotland and Wales, and in Australia, Canada and the Netherlands (Flynn 2008; France and Crow 2001; Utting 1999). While the effectiveness of its individual components is clear, there are promising signs – based on a large-scale randomised controlled trial in the United States – that the overall CTC strategy is also effective (Hawkins *et al.* 2008).

CTC was developed as a risk-focused prevention strategy by David Hawkins and Richard Catalano (1992), and it is a core component of the US Office of Juvenile Justice and Delinquency Prevention's (OJJDP) Comprehensive Strategy for Serious, Violent and Chronic Juvenile Offenders (Wilson and Howell 1993). CTC is based on a theory (the social development model) that organises risk and protective factors. The intervention techniques are tailored to the needs of each particular community. The 'community' could be a city, a county, a small town, or even a neighbourhood or a housing estate. This programme aims to reduce delinquency and drug use by implementing particular prevention strategies that have demonstrated effectiveness in reducing risk factors or enhancing protective factors. It is modelled on large-scale community-wide public health programmes designed to reduce illnesses such as coronary heart disease by tackling key risk factors (e.g. Farquhar *et al.* 1985; Perry *et al.* 1989). There is great emphasis in CTC on enhancing protective factors and building on strengths, partly because this is more attractive to communities than tackling risk factors. However, it is generally true that health promotion is more effective than disease prevention (Kaplan 2000).

CTC programmes begin with community mobilisation. Key community leaders (e.g. elected representatives, education officials, police chiefs, business leaders) are brought together, with the aim of getting them to agree on the goals of the prevention programme and to implement CTC. The key leaders then set up a Community Board that is accountable to them, consisting of neighbourhood residents and representatives from various agencies (e.g. school, police, social services, probation, health, parents, youth groups, business, church and media). The Community Board takes charge of prevention on behalf of the community.

The Community Board then carries out a risk and protective factor assessment, identifying key risk factors in that particular community that need to be tackled and key protective factors that need enhancing. This risk assessment might involve the use of police, school, social or census records or local neighbourhood or school surveys. After identifying key risk and protective factors, the Community Board assesses existing resources and develops a plan of intervention strategies. With specialist technical assistance and guidance, they choose programmes from a menu of strategies that have been shown to be effective in well-designed evaluation research.

The menu of strategies listed by Hawkins and Catalano (1992) includes prenatal/postnatal home visiting programmes, preschool intellectual enrichment programmes, parent training, school organisation and curriculum development, teacher training, and media campaigns. Other strategies include child skills training, anti-bullying programmes in schools, situational prevention, and policing strategies. The choice of prevention strategies is based on empirical evidence about effective methods of tackling each particular risk factor, but it also depends on what are identified as the biggest problems in the community. While this approach is not without its challenges and complexities (e.g. cost, implementation, establishing partnerships among diverse agencies), an evidence-based approach that brings together the most effective prevention programmes across multiple domains offers the greatest promise for reducing crime and building safer communities.

Conclusions

High-quality evaluation research shows that many programmes are effective in reducing delinquency and later offending, and that in many cases the financial benefits of these programmes outweigh their financial costs. The best programmes include general parent education, parent management training, pre-school intellectual enrichment programmes, child skills training, teacher training, anti-bullying programmes, mentoring and MST. While most is known about programmes for boys, there are also effective interventions designed specifically for girls (Hipwell and Loeber 2006).

High-quality experimental and quasi-experimental evaluations of the effectiveness of crime reduction programmes are needed in the United Kingdom. Most knowledge about the effectiveness of prevention programmes, such as child skills training, parent training and preschool intellectual enrichment programmes, is based on American research.

There have been many commendable UK crime prevention initiatives in recent years. In September 2006, the UK government announced an action plan for 'social exclusion', which is a general concept including antisocial behaviour, teenage pregnancy, educational failure and mental health problems (Cabinet Office 2006). This action plan emphasised early intervention, better coordination of agencies, and evidence-based practice (systematically identifying what works and rating evaluations according to methodological quality: see Farrington 2003). It proposed home visiting programmes targeting at-risk children from birth to age two, implemented by midwives and health visitors, inspired by the work of David Olds (Olds *et al.* 1998). It proposed that teenage pregnancy 'hot spots' would be targeted with enhanced social and relationship education and better access to contraceptives. It proposed multi-agency and family-based approaches to tackle behavioural and mental health problems in childhood, including treatment foster care (Chamberlain and Reid 1998) and MST (Henggeler *et al.* 1998). It also proposed interventions for adults with chaotic lives, mental health problems and multiple needs, to try to get more of them into employment.

Since the mid-1990s, there has been increasing emphasis on early intervention and evidence-based practice in the UK (Sutton *et al.* 2004 2006). In 1995 Child and Adolescent Mental Health (CAMHS) teams were established in every part of the country to provide support for children and young people who were experiencing a range of emotional and behavioural difficulties. The services fall within the remit of the Department of Health and practitioners typically employ a wide range of theoretical approaches.

The major government initiative for preschool children is called Sure Start (www.surestart.gov.uk). The first Sure Start centres were established in 1999 in disadvantaged areas, and there are now over 800 Sure Start programmes in the UK. These centres provide early education and parenting programmes, integrated with extended childcare, health and family support services. The services are supposed to be evidence-based. Widely used parenting programmes include *The Incredible Years* (Webster-Stratton 2000), *Triple-P* (Sanders *et al.* 2000) and *Strengthening Families, Strengthening Communities* (Steele *et al.* 1999). A National Academy for Parenting Practitioners has been established.

It is very difficult to evaluate large-scale national programmes such as Sure Start. The main evaluation so far compared outcomes for 150 Sure Start areas and 50 non-Sure Start areas (Sure Start-to-be) by assessing a random sample of families with a nine-month-old child or with a three-year-old child in each locality (Melhuish *et al.* 2005). The results showed that, for three-year-old children, with non-teenage mothers (86 per cent of the sample), the children showed greater social competence and had fewer behaviour problems, and there was less negative parenting in the Sure Start areas than in the control group areas. However, among teenage mothers (14 per cent of the sample), in the Sure Start areas the children showed less social competence, had lower verbal ability and had more behaviour problems than in the control areas.

Sure Start programmes are currently being developed into Children's Centres, to cover every part of the UK. Typically, these will be service hubs, offering and coordinating information to support children and their parents. One of their implicit objectives is to reduce conduct disorder and aggressiveness among young children through the provision of parenting programmes. The Centres also contribute to the strategic objectives of *Every Child Matters*, the major government policy document (Chief Secretary to the Treasury 2003; www.everychildmatters.gov.uk). This applies to all children from birth to age 19 and aims to improve educational achievement and reduce the levels of ill health, teenage pregnancy, abuse and neglect, crime and antisocial behaviour.

In 1999 the Home Office supported a national initiative intended to prevent children's future antisocial or criminal behaviour by working with children aged eight to 13, together with their families. Projects entitled On Track were set up in 24 local authorities and practitioners were required to employ a limited number of approaches to supporting families, including behaviour management, promoting home–school liaison, play therapy and parenting packages. The Department for Children, Schools and Families has now assumed responsibility for taking forward all work with children aged from 0–19. It has invited bids from 15 local authorities to provide parenting support focusing on children aged eight to 13, requiring that those bidding for funding shall use one of the three parenting packages mentioned above.

While all of these initiatives are commendable, what is largely missing in the UK at present is risk-focused primary prevention delivered at an early age and designed to reduce later offending and antisocial behaviour (Farrington and Welsh 2007). Consideration should be given to implementing a multiple-component risk-focused prevention programme such as CTC more widely throughout Great Britain. This integrated programme could be implemented by existing Crime and Disorder Partnerships. However, they would need resources and technical assistance to conduct youth surveys and household surveys to identify key risk and protective factors for both people and places. They would also need resources and technical assistance to measure risk and protective factors, to choose effective intervention methods, and to carry out high-quality evaluations of the effectiveness of programmes in reducing crime and disorder.

The focus should be on primary prevention (offering the programme to all families living in specified areas) not on secondary prevention (targeting the programme on individuals identified as at risk). Ideally, the programme should be presented positively, as fostering safe and healthy communities by strengthening protective factors, rather than as a crime prevention programme targeting risk factors. Cost–benefit analyses of the effectiveness of prevention programmes should be given some priority, and a standard how-to-do-it manual should be developed.

Nationally and locally, there is no agency whose primary mandate is the prevention of crime. For example, the very worthwhile intervention programmes being implemented by Youth Offending Teams are overwhelmingly targeted on detected offenders. Therefore, a national agency should be established with a primary mandate of fostering and funding the early prevention of crime.

This national agency could provide technical assistance, skills and knowledge to local agencies in implementing prevention programmes, could provide funding for such programmes, and could ensure continuity, coordination, and monitoring of local programmes. It could provide training in prevention science for people in local agencies, and could maintain high standards for evaluation research. It could also act as a centre for the discussion of how policy initiatives of different government agencies influence crime and associated social problems. It could set a national and local agenda for research and practice in the prevention of crime, drug and alcohol abuse, mental health problems, and associated social problems. National crime prevention agencies have been established in other countries, such as Sweden (Andersson 2005) and Canada (Sansfaçon and Waller 2001).

The national agency could also maintain a computerised register of evaluation research and, like the National Institute of Clinical Excellence, advise the government about effective and cost-effective crime prevention programmes. Medical advice is often based on systematic reviews of the effectiveness of health care interventions organised by the Cochrane Collaboration and funded by the National Health Service. Systematic reviews of the evaluation literature on the effectiveness of criminological interventions should be commissioned and funded by government agencies.

Crime prevention also needs to be organised locally. In each area, a local agency should be set up to take the lead in organising risk-focused crime prevention. In Sweden, 80 per cent of municipalities had local crime prevention councils in 2005 (Andersson 2005). The local prevention agency could take the lead in measuring risk factors and social problems in local areas, using archival records and local household and school surveys. It could then assess available resources and develop a plan of prevention strategies. With specialist technical assistance, prevention programmes could be chosen from a menu of strategies that have been proved to be effective in reducing crime in well-designed evaluation research. This would be a good example of evidence-based practice.

Recent promising developments in the UK, such as Sure Start and Every Child Matters, have clearly been influenced by recent research on childhood risk factors and risk-focused intervention strategies. The time is ripe to expand these experimental programmes into a large-scale, evidence-based, integrated national strategy for the reduction of crime and associated social problems, including rigorous evaluation requirements.

References

Andersson, J. (2005) 'The Swedish National Council for Crime Prevention: a short presentation', *Journal of Scandinavian Studies in Criminology and Crime Prevention*, 6: 74–88.

Aos, S., Phipps, P., Barnoski, R. and Lieb, R. (1999) *The Comparative Costs and Benefits of Programs to Reduce Crime* (version 3.0). Olympia, Washington: Washington State Institute for Public Policy.

Aos, S., Phipps, P., Barnoski, R. and Lieb, R. (2001) *The Comparative Costs and Benefits of Programs to Reduce Crime* (version 4.0). Olympia, Washington: Washington State Institute for Public Policy.

Aos, S., Lieb, R., Mayfield, J., Miller, M. and Pennucci, A. (2004) *Benefits and Costs of Prevention and Early Intervention Programs for Youth.* Olympia, Washington: Washington State Institute for Public Policy.

Berrueta-Clement, J.R., Schweinhart, L.J., Barnett, W.S., Epstein, A.S. and Weikart, D.P. (1984) *Changed Lives: The Effects of the Perry Preschool Program on Youths Through Age 19*. Ypsilanti, Michigan: High/Scope Press.

Boisjoli, R., Vitaro, F., Lacourse, E., Barker, E.D. and Tremblay, R.E. (2007) 'Impact and clinical significance of a preventive intervention for disruptive boys', *British Journal of Psychiatry*, 191: 415–19.

Borduin, C.M., Mann, B.J., Cone, L.T., Henggeler, S.W., Fucci, B.R., Blaske, D.M. and Williams, R.A. (1995) 'Multisystemic treatment of serious juvenile offenders: long-term prevention of criminality and violence', *Journal of Consulting and Clinical Psychology*, 63: 569–87.

Cabinet Office (2006) *Reaching Out: An Action Plan for Social Exclusion.* London: Cabinet Office.

Campbell, F.A., Ramey, C.T., Pungello, E., Sparling, J. and Miller-Johnson, S. (2002) 'Early childhood education: young adult outcomes from the Abecedarian project', *Applied Developmental Science*, 6: 42–57.

Chamberlain, P. and Reid, J.B. (1998) 'Comparison of two community alternatives to incarceration for chronic juvenile offenders', *Journal of Consulting and Clinical Psychology*, 66: 624–33.

Chief Secretary to the Treasury (2003) *Every Child Matters*. London: The Stationery Office.

Curtis, N.M., Ronan, K.R. and Borduin, C.M. (2004) 'Multisystemic treatment: a meta-analysis of outcome studies', *Journal of Family Psychology*, 18: 411–19.

Dodge, K.A., Dishion, T.J. and Lansford, J.E. (eds) (2006) *Deviant Peer Influences in Progams for Youth: Problems and Solutions*. New York: Guilford.

Dubourg, R., Hamed, J. and Thorns, J. (2005) *The Economic and Social Costs of Crime against Individuals and Households, 2003/4*. London: Home Office (Online Report 30/05).

Farquhar, J.W., Fortmann, S.P., MacCoby, N., Haskell, W.L., Williams, P.T., Flora, J.A., Taylor, C.B., Brown, B.W., Solomon, D.S. and Hulley, S.B. (1985) 'The Stanford five-city project: design and methods', *American Journal of Epidemiology*, 122: 323–34.

Farrington, D.P. (1993) 'Understanding and preventing bullying', in M. Tonry and N. Morris (eds), *Crime and Justice*, vol. 17 (pp. 381–458). Chicago: University of Chicago Press.

Farrington, D.P. (1996) *Understanding and Preventing Youth Crime*. York: Joseph Rowntree Foundation.

Farrington, D.P. (2003) 'Methodological quality standards for evaluation research', *Annals of the American Academy of Political and Social Science*, 587: 49–68.

Farrington, D.P. (2009) 'Conduct disorder, aggression and delinquency', in R.M. Lerner and L. Steinberg (eds) *Handbook of Adolescent Psychology* (3rd edn). Hoboken, NJ: Wiley.

Farrington, D.P., Coid, J.W., Harnett, L., Jolliffe, D., Soteriou, N., Turner, R. and West, D.J. (2006) *Criminal Careers up to age 50 and Life Success up to age 48: New Findings from the Cambridge Study in Delinquent Development*. London: Home Office (Research Study No. 299).

Farrington, D.P. and Welsh, B.C. (2007) *Saving Children from a Life of Crime: Early Risk Factors and Effective Interventions*. Oxford: Oxford University Press.

Feldman, R.A., Caplinger, T.E. and Wodarski, J.S. (1983) *The St. Louis Conundrum*. Englewood Cliffs, NJ: Prentice-Hall.

Flynn, R.J. (2008) 'Communities That Care: A comprehensive system for youth prevention and promotion, and Canadian applications to date', in R. Hastings and M. Bania (eds), *Towards More Comprehensive Approaches to Prevention and Safety. IPC Review*, vol. 2 (pp. 83–107). Ottawa, Canada: Institute for the Prevention of Crime, University of Ottawa.

France, A. and Crow, I. (2001) *CTC – The Story So Far*. York: Joseph Rowntree Foundation.

Gardner, F., Burton, J. and Klimes, I. (2006) 'Randomized controlled trial of a parenting intervention in the voluntary sector for reducing child conduct problems: outcomes and mechanisms of change', *Journal of Child Psychology and Psychiatry*, 47: 1123–32.

Gottfredson, D.C., Wilson, D.B. and Najaka, S.S. (2006) 'School-based crime prevention', in L.W. Sherman, D.P. Farrington, B.C. Welsh and D.L. MacKenzie (eds), *Evidence-Based Crime Prevention*, revised edition (pp. 56–164). New York: Routledge.

Greenwood, P.W. (2006) *Changing Lives: Delinquency Prevention as Crime-Control Policy*. Chicago: University of Chicago Press.

Greenwood, P.W., Karoly, L.A., Everingham, S.S., Houbé, J., Kilburn, M.R., Rydell, C.P., Sanders, M. and Chiesa, J. (2001) 'Estimating the costs and benefits of early childhood interventions: nurse home visits and the Perry Preschool', in B.C. Welsh, D.P. Farrington and L.W. Sherman (eds), *Costs and Benefits of Preventing Crime* (pp. 123–48). Boulder, CO: Westview Press.

Grossman, J.B. and Tierney, J.P. (1998) 'Does mentoring work? An impact study of the Big Brothers Big Sisters program', *Evaluation Review*, 22: 403–26.

Harachi, T.W., Hawkins, J.D., Catalano, R.F., Lafazia, A.M., Smith, B.H. and Arthur, M.W. (2003) 'Evidence-based community decision making for prevention: two case studies of Communities That Care', *Japanese Journal of Sociological Criminology*, 28: 26–37.

Harrell, A.V., Cavanagh, S.E., Harmon, M.A., Koper, C.S. and Sridharan, S. (1997) *Impact of the Children At Risk Program: Comprehensive Final Report, Vol. 2*. Washington, DC: The Urban Institute.

Harrell, A.V., Cavanagh, S.E. and Sridharan, S. (1999) *Evaluation of the Children at Risk Program: Results 1 Year after the End of the Program*. Washington, DC: National Institute of Justice.

Hawkins, J.D. and Catalano, R.F. (1992) *Communities that Care*. San Francisco: Jossey-Bass.

Hawkins, J.D., Catalano, R.F., Kosterman, R., Abbott, R. and Hill, K.G. (1999) 'Preventing adolescent health risk behaviors by strengthening protection during childhood', *Archives of Pediatrics and Adolescent Medicine*, 153: 226–34.

Hawkins, J.D., von Cleve, E. and Catalano, R.F. (1991) 'Reducing early childhood aggression: results of a primary prevention program', *Journal of the American Academy of Child and Adolescent Psychiatry*, 30: 208–17.

Hawkins, J.D., Brown, E.C., Oesterle, S., Arthur, M.W., Abbott, R.D. and Catalano, R.F. (2008) 'Early effects of Communities That Care on targeted risks and initiation of delinquent behavior and substance abuse', *Journal of Adolescent Health*, 43: 15–22.

Henggeler, S.W., Schoenwald, S.K., Borduin, C.M., Rowland, M.D. and Cunningham, P.B. (1998) *Multisystemic Treatment of Antisocial Behavior in Children and Adolescents*. New York: Guilford.

Hipwell, A.E. and Loeber, R. (2006) 'Do we know which interventions are effective for disruptive and delinquent girls?', *Clinical Child and Family Psychology Review*, 9: 221–55.

Jefford, T. and Squire, B. (2004) 'Model practice', *Young Minds Magazine*, 71: 20–21.

Johnson, D.L. and Walker, T. (1987) 'Primary prevention of behavior problems in Mexican-American children', *American Journal of Community Psychology*, 15: 375–85.

Jolliffe, D. and Farrington, D.P. (2008) *The Influence of Mentoring on Reoffending*. Stockholm, Sweden: National Council for Crime Prevention.

Jones, M.B. and Offord, D.R. (1989) 'Reduction of antisocial behaviour in poor children by non-school skill development', *Journal of Child Psychology and Psychiatry*, 30: 737–50.

Kaplan, R.M. (2000) 'Two pathways to prevention', *American Psychologist*, 55: 382–96.

Karoly, L.A., Greenwood, P.W., Everingham, S.S., Hoube, J., Kilburn, M.R., Rydell, C.P., Sanders, M. and Chiesa, J. (1998) *Investing in Our Children: What We Know and Don't Know about the Costs and Benefits of Early Childhood Interventions*. Santa Monica, CA: Rand Corporation.

Kitzman, H., Olds, D.L., Henderson, C.R., Hanks, C., Cole, R., Tatelbaum, R., McConnochie, K.M., Sidora, K., Luckey, D.W., Shaver, D., Engelhardt, K., James, D. and Barnard, K. (1997) 'Effect of prenatal and infancy home visitation by nurses on pregnancy outcomes, childhood injuries, and repeated childbearing: a randomized controlled trial', *Journal of the American Medical Association*, 278: 644–52.

Kolvin, I., Garside, R.F., Nicol, A.R., MacMillan, A., Wolstenholme, F. and Leitch, I.M. (1981) *Help Starts Here: The Maladjusted Child in the Ordinary School*. London: Tavistock.

Lacourse, E., Cote, S., Nagin, D.S., Vitaro, F., Brendgen, M. and Tremblay, R.E. (2002) 'A longitudinal-experimental approach to testing theories of antisocial behaviour development', *Development and Psychopathology*, 14: 909–24.

Lally, J.R., Mangione, P.L. and Honig, A.S. (1988) 'The Syracuse University Family Development Research Program: long-range impact of an early intervention with low-income children and their families', in D.R. Powell (ed.), *Parent Education as Early Childhood Intervention: Emerging Directions in Theory, Research and Practice* (pp. 79–104). Norwood, NJ: Ablex.

Leschied, A. and Cunningham, A. (2002) *Seeking Effective Interventions for Serious Young Offenders: Interim Results of a Four-year Randomized Study of Multisystemic Therapy in Ontario, Canada*. London, Ontario: London Family Court Clinic.

Littell, J.H. (2005) 'Lessons from a systematic review of effects of Multisystemic Therapy', *Children and Youth Services Review*, 27: 445–63.

Long, P., Forehand, R., Wierson, M. and Morgan, A. (1994) 'Does parent training with young noncompliant children have long-term effects?', *Behavior Research and Therapy*, 32: 101–7.

Lösel, F. and Beelmann, A. (2006) 'Child social skills training', in B.C. Welsh and D.P. Farrington (eds), *Preventing Crime: What Works for Children, Offenders, Victims, and Places* (pp. 33–54). New York: Springer.

Mason, W.A., Kosterman, R., Hawkins, J.D., Haggerty, K.P. and Spoth, R.L. (2003) 'Reducing adolescents' growth in substance use and delinquency: randomized trial effects of a parent-training prevention intervention', *Prevention Science*, 4: 203–12.

McCarton, C.M., Brooks-Gunn, J., Wallace, I.F., Bauer, C.R., Bennett, F.C., Bernbaum, J.C., Broyles, R.S., Casey, P.H., McCormick, M.C., Scott, D.T., Tyson, J., Tonascia, J. and Meinert, C.L. (1997) 'Results at age 8 years of early intervention for low-birth-weight premature infants: the Infant Health and Development Program', *Journal of the American Medical Association*, 277: 126–32.

McCord, J., Tremblay, R.E., Vitaro, F. and Desmarais-Gervais, L. (1994) 'Boys' disruptive behavior, school adjustment, and delinquency: the Montreal Prevention Experiment', *International Journal of Behavioral Development*, 17: 739–52.

Melhuish, E., Belsky, J. and Leyland, A. (2005) *Early Impacts of Sure Start Local Programmes on Children and Families: Report of the Cross-Sectional Study of 9 and 36 Months Old Children and Their Families.* London: The Stationery Office.

O'Donnell, J., Hawkins, J.D., Catalano, R.F., Abbott, R.D. and Day, L.E. (1995) 'Preventing school failure, drug use, and delinquency among low-income children: long-term intervention in elementary schools', *American Journal of Orthopsychiatry*, 65: 87–100.

Ogden, T. and Hagen, K.A. (2006) 'Multisystemic treatment of serious behaviour problems in youth: sustainability of effectiveness two years after intake', *Child and Adolescent Mental Health*, 11: 142–9.

Olds, D.L., Henderson, C.R., Chamberlin, R. and Tatelbaum, R. (1986) 'Preventing child abuse and neglect: a randomized trial of nurse home visitation', *Pediatrics*, 78: 65–78.

Olds, D.L., Henderson, C.R., Phelps, C., Kitzman, H. and Hanks, C. (1993) 'Effects of prenatal and infancy nurse home visitation on government spending', *Medical Care*, 31: 155–74.

Olds, D.L., Eckenrode, J., Henderson, C.R., Kitzman, H., Powers, J., Cole, R., Sidora, K., Morris, P., Pettitt, L.M. and Luckey, D. (1997) 'Long-term effects of home visitation on maternal life course and child abuse and neglect: fifteen-year follow-up of a randomized trial', *Journal of the American Medical Association*, 278: 637–43.

Olds, D.L., Henderson, C.R., Cole, R., Eckenrode, J., Kitzman, H., Luckey, D., Pettitt, L., Sidora, K., Morris, P. and Powers, J. (1998) 'Long-term effects of nurse home visitation on children's criminal and antisocial behavior: 15-year follow-up of a randomized controlled trial', *Journal of the American Medical Association*, 280: 1238–44.

Olds, D.L., Kitzman, H., Cole, R., Robinson, J., Sidora, K., Luckey, D.W., Henderson, C.R., Hanks, C., Bondy, J. and Holmberg, J. (2004a) 'Effects of nurse home-visiting on maternal life course and child development: age 6 follow-up results of a randomized trial', *Pediatrics*, 114: 1550–9.

Olds, D.L., Robinson, J., Pettitt, L.M., Luckey, D.W., Holmberg, J., Ng, R.K., Isacks, K., Sheff, K.L. and Henderson, C.R. (2004b) 'Effects of home visits by paraprofessionals and by nurses: age 4 follow-up results of a randomized trial', *Pediatrics*, 114: 1560–8.

Olweus, D. (1994) 'Bullying at school: basic facts and effects of a school based intervention programme', *Journal of Child Psychology and Psychiatry*, 35: 1171–90.

Patterson, G.R. (1982) *Coercive Family Process*. Eugene, OR: Castalia.

Patterson, G.R., Chamberlain, P. and Reid, J.B. (1982) 'A comparative evaluation of a parent training program', *Behavior Therapy*, 13: 638–50.

Patterson, G.R., Reid, J.B. and Dishion, T.J. (1992) *Antisocial Boys*. Eugene, OR: Castalia.

Perry, C.L., Klepp, K-I. and Sillers, C. (1989) 'Community-wide strategies for cardiovascular health: the Minnesota Heart Health Program youth program', *Health Education and Research*, 4: 87–101.

Piquero, A.R., Farrington, D.P., Welsh, B.C., Tremblay, R.E. and Jennings, W.G. (2009) 'Effects of early family/parent training programs on antisocial behavior and delinquency', *Journal of Experimental Criminology*, 5 (2): 83–120.

Reynolds, A.J., Temple, J.A., Robertson, D.L. and Mann, E.A. (2001) 'Long-term effects of an early childhood intervention on educational achievement and juvenile arrest: a 15-year follow-up of low-income children in public schools', *Journal of the American Medical Association*, 285: 2339–46.

Sanders, M.R., Markie-Dadds, C., Tully, L.A. and Bor, W. (2000) 'The Triple P Positive Parenting Program: a comparison of enhanced, standard and self-directed behavioral family intervention for parents of children with early onset conduct problems', *Journal of Consulting and Clinical Psychology*, 68: 624–40.

Sansfaçon, D. and Waller. I. (2001). 'Recent evolution of governmental crime prevention strategies and implications for evaluation and economic analysis', in B.C. Welsh, D.P. Farrington and L.W. Sherman (eds), *Costs and Benefits of Preventing Crime* (pp. 225–47). Boulder, CO: Westview Press.

Schweinhart, L.J., Barnes, H.V. and Weikart, D.P. (1993) *Significant Benefits: The High/Scope Perry Preschool Study Through Age 27*. Ypsilanti, MI: High/Scope Press.

Schweinhart, L.J. and Weikart, D.P. (1980) *Young Children Grow Up: The Effects of the Perry Preschool Program on Youths Through Age 15*. Ypsilanti, MI: High/Scope Press.

Schweinhart, L.J., Montie, J., Zongping, X., Barnett, W.S., Belfield, C.R. and Nores, M. (2005) *Lifetime Effects: The High/Scope Perry Preschool Study Through Age 40*. Ypsilanti, MI: High/Scope Press.

Scott, S., Spender, Q., Doolan, M., Jacobs, B. and Aspland, H. (2001) 'Multicentre controlled trial of parenting groups for child antisocial behaviour in clinical practice', *British Medical Journal*, 323: 194–6.

Sherman, L.W., Farrington, D.P., Welsh, B.C., and MacKenzie, D.L. (eds) (2006) *Evidence-Based Crime Prevention*, revised edition. New York: Routledge.

Smith, P.K. and Sharp, S. (1994) *School Bullying*. London: Routledge.

Steele, M., Marigna, M.K., Tello, J. and Johnson, R. (1999) *Strengthening Multi-Ethnic Families and Communities: A Violence Prevention Parent Training Program*. Los Angeles, CA: Consulting and Clinical Services.

Sutton, C., Utting, D. and Farrington, D.P. (eds) (2004) *Support From the Start: Working with Young Children and Their Families to Reduce the Risks of Crime and Antisocial Behaviour*. London: Department for Education and Skills (Research Report 524).

Sutton, C., Utting, D. and Farrington, D.P. (2006) 'Nipping criminality in the bud', *The Psychologist*, 19: 470–5.

Tobler, N.S., Lessard, T., Marshall, D., Ochshorn, P. and Roona, M. (1999) 'Effectiveness of school-based drug prevention programs for marijuana use', *School Psychology International*, 20: 105–37.

Tremblay, R.E., Vitaro, F., Bertrand, L., LeBlanc, M., Beauchesne, H., Boileau, H. and David, L. (1992) 'Parent and child training to prevent early onset of delinquency: the Montréal Longitudinal-Experimental study', in J. McCord and R.E. Tremblay (eds), *Preventing Antisocial Behavior: Interventions from Birth Through Adolescence* (pp. 117–38). New York: Guilford.

Tremblay, R.E., Pagani-Kurtz, L., Masse, L.C., Vitaro, F. and Pihl, R.O. (1995) 'A bimodal preventive intervention for disruptive kindergarten boys: its impact through mid-adolescence', *Journal of Consulting and Clinical Psychology*, 63: 560–8.

Tremblay, R.E., Mâsse, L.C., Pagani, L. and Vitaro, F. (1996) 'From childhood physical aggression to adolescent maladjustment: the Montreal Prevention Experiment', in R.D. Peters and R.J. McMahon (eds), *Preventing Childhood Disorders, Substance Use, and Delinquency* (pp. 268–98). Thousand Oaks, CA: Sage.

Ttofi, M.M. and Farrington, D.P. (2009) 'What works in preventing bullying? Effective elements of anti-bullying programmes', *Journal of Aggression, Conflict and Peace Research*, 1 (1): 13–24.

Utting, D. (ed.) (1999) *A Guide to Promising Approaches*. London: Communities that Care.

Vitaro, F., Brendgen, M. and Tremblay, R.E. (2001) 'Preventive intervention: assessing its effects on the trajectories of delinquency and testing for mediational processes', *Applied Developmental Science*, 5: 201–13.

Webster-Stratton, C. (2000) *The Incredible Years Training Series*. Washington, DC: Office of Juvenile Justice and Delinquency Prevention.

Webster-Stratton, C. and Hammond, M. (1997) 'Treating children with early-onset conduct problems: a comparison of child and parent training interventions', *Journal of Consulting and Clinical Psychology*, 65: 93–109.

Welsh, B.C. and Farrington, D.P. (eds) (2006) *Preventing Crime: What Works for Children, Offenders, Victims, and Places*. New York: Springer.

Welsh, B.C., Loeber, R., Stevens, B.R., Stouthamer-Loeber, M., Cohen, M.A. and Farrington, D.P. (2008) 'Costs of juvenile crime in urban areas: a longitudinal perspective', *Youth Violence and Juvenile Justice*, 6: 3–27.

West, D.J. and Farrington, D.P. (1977) *The Delinquent Way of Life*. London: Heinemann.

Widom, C.S. (1989) 'The cycle of violence', *Science*, 244: 160–6.

Wilson, S.J. and Lipsey, M.W. (2007) 'School-based interventions for aggressive and disruptive behavior: update of a meta-analysis', *American Journal of Preventive Medicine*, 33 (2S): 130–43.

Wilson, J.J. and Howell, J.C. (1993) *A Comprehensive Strategy for Serious, Violent, and Chronic Juvenile Offenders*. Washington, DC: Office of Juvenile Justice and Delinquency Prevention.

Chapter 20

Parenting projects, justice and welfare

Anthony H. Goodman and Joanna R. Adler

In the previous chapter, Brandon Welsh and David Farrington provided a wide-ranging review of the best demonstrated, most cost-effective ways of preventing offending. Here, we consider parenting training programmes in more depth, seeking to provide an analysis of parenting programmes within a specific political context and to explore people's experiences on those programmes. These two chapters have some similarities in terms of policy implications. We also think it likely that context-specific, multifaceted programmes, set within a better run system of crime prevention and far improved social policies, offer the best hope. Yet we have concerns about how such policies will be effected and their implications for the individuals targeted.

Parental skills training has found a place on the political agenda, with resources to match. This chapter provides an appraisal of what has been a major initiative of the British Labour Government; an initiative that brought the State into the very heart of the family in order to deal with parents deemed to be failing their children and society at large. The attempt has been made to engage with the parents/guardians of young people who either offend, fail to attend school, or in some way bring their nominal caregivers to the attention of the authorities as 'poor parents'.

Many parents are indeed worried, if not desperate, about the welfare and future of their children and some have appreciated the imaginative way that parenting programmes assist them to engage more constructively in raising their children. However, it is essential that intervention is sensitive to familial context and allows parents to express feelings about their interactions with officialdom. We also contend that, as Cieslik and Pollock warn:

> The focus on 'problem youth' misrepresents the majority of young people's lives, fuelling the mediazed moral panics ... This in turn contributes to the development of often authoritarian and punitive social policy initiatives such as curfews, school exclusion and workfare type welfare programmes. (2002: 15)

As far as offending behaviour is concerned, parents are seen as part of the solution because they have been posited as part of the problem. Poor parenting can be seen as a reliably replicated predictive factor in delinquency studies, both longitudinal and cross-sectional (for example, Farrington 1995; Kolvin *et al.* 1988; West 1982; Wilson 1987). Parental neglect and inappropriate parenting are associated both with young people's psychological distress and with offending behaviour in males (Chambers *et al.* 2001) and in females (Chesney-Lind and Shelden 1998).

Keeping children within the family, but trying to 'improve' that family, seems to be more sensible than removing children to situations of care that may themselves be harmful (Bessant and Hil 1998; Haapasalo 2000). A rationale for supporting parents was laid down by the UK Home Office, in the draft guidance issued on Parenting Orders made under the Crime and Disorder Act 1998:

> Parenting is a challenging job. Helping parents to develop good parenting skills is an effective way of ensuring that problems in a child or young person's behaviour or development are not allowed to grow unchecked into major difficulties for the individual, their family and the community. The Government is therefore aiming to increase the parenting support available to all parents. (Home Office 1998a: 1)

The Government decided that supporting parents should not be entirely voluntary but needed a coercive underpinning by way of statutory order. This New Labour policy can thus be seen as a return to the 30-year-old Conservative notion of the 'cycle of deprivation' promulgated by Sir Keith Joseph. His thesis was that children who were not given adequate care, principally consistent love and guidance, would in turn become inadequate parents, producing the next generation of deprived children (Holman 1978).

While the Conservatives were thus concentrating on the family, the Left were setting those families firmly within a societal context. Cohen argued for a minimalist approach from Government, 'a commitment to do less harm, rather than more good' (1979a). He drew heavily on Foucault to argue that the State was reproducing a complicated system of classification that had typified nineteenth-century penitentiaries. Cohen linked this to three aspects of community control that he called blurring, widening and masking. *Blurring* refers to an erosion of the boundaries of social control, with the implicit assumption that (new) community alternatives are less costly and more humane than custody. However, intensive community programmes may make it difficult to demarcate between the home and the institution. Concomitantly, *widening* refers to the expansion of the social control network. When instituted, community orders and the like are proffered as alternatives to custody. Yet when sentencing patterns are assessed, these programmes tend to be used for offenders at the 'shallow' end of offending, rather than at the heavy end, thereby extending the reach of judicial sanctions. Finally, *masking* is the process whereby interventions that are intended as benevolent endeavours are instead intrusive, with the threat of custody for failure to comply. Cohen's conclusion was that it was important to eradicate the socio-economic, demographic and structural inequalities that were incompatible with a moral society. This was important for all, not just offenders (Cohen 1979b).

In the same year, Donzelot produced a book, the title of which made his viewpoint clear – *The Policing of Families*. He regarded the intervention of professionals or 'technicians' as intrusive and controlling:

> … the family appears as though colonised. There are no longer two authorities facing one another: the family and the apparatus, but a series of concentric circles around the child: the family circle, the circle of technicians and the circle of social guardians. (1979: 103)

More recently, Petersen (1995) returned to much the same arena, making the case that policies such as Juvenile Intensive Probation Supervision (USA) or the Intensive Supervision and Surveillance Programme (England) ignore the societal context of delinquent activity. This, in turn, resulted in greater disempowerment of young people and greater empowerment of a few key players, deemed to know best. This was later echoed in *The Psychologist*: 'It is easier to pathologise the poor and disadvantaged rather than to think about how to provide resources to help people meet their aspirations' (Lewis 2002: 511).

On the other side of this debate are those such as Walters and White (1988) who argue strongly against the cult of 'disresponsibility'. This theme seems to have been picked up in England and Wales, where there have been more White Papers, Commissions and Bills before Parliament regarding crime, justice and delinquency over the past 30 years than ever before. The introduction to *No More Excuses*, one such White Paper, asserted that:

> For too long we have assumed that young offenders will grow out of their offending if left to themselves. The research shows that this does not happen. An excuse culture has developed within the youth justice system. It excuses itself for its inefficiency, and too often excuses the young offenders before it, implying that they cannot help their behaviour because of their social circumstances. (Home Office 1997: Preface)

The history of youth justice: the move from welfare to a justice model

During the nineteenth century, the State formalised intervention. By 1866, vagrant children could be sent to industrial schools and by 1894, there were over 17,000 children in industrial schools and 4,800 young delinquents in reformatories (Morris *et al*. 1980). The Children Act of 1908 established juvenile courts, separating young offenders from their adult counterparts. The Criminal Justice Act 1933 united industrial schools and reformatories, and section 44 stated that:

> ... every court, in dealing with a child or young person who is brought before it, either as an offender or otherwise, shall have regard to the welfare of the child or young person and shall in a proper case take steps for removing him from undesirable surroundings or for securing that proper provision is made for his education and training. (Criminal Justice Act 1933)

More than 20 years later, the Ingleby Committee (Home Office 1960) was still trying to integrate the notions of punishment and welfare. It recommended raising the age of criminal responsibility to 14, with younger children being subject to care, protection or control proceedings.

The Children and Young Persons Act of 1963 set the age of criminal responsibility at 10 years, where it has remained. It concentrated on widening and defining the responsibilities of local authorities towards children and reflects the continuing tensions between punishment and welfare. It explicitly identified the family as a major cause of delinquency. In 1965, the Home Office, under the Labour Government, published the White Paper *The Child, the Family and the Young Offender.* Alongside the 1968 Home Office publication *Children in Trouble*, it laid great stress on the fact that juvenile delinquents are children in states of deprivation. In 1979, Conservative junior ministers were contrasting bored youngsters who slip into crime with the deliberate totally uncaring or violent and identifiable minority for whom a deterrent sentence is justified, i.e. the 'depraved' young offender.

The 1965 White Paper had recommended a revolutionary resolution to the justice versus welfare debate by abolishing the Juvenile Court, raising the age of criminal responsibility to 16 years and introducing family councils, comprising social workers and suitably experienced people, to deal with offenders and non-offenders after issues of guilt and innocence had been resolved.

> The maturing local authority childcare service undoubtedly represented the latest generation of 'child savers'. Their view was that delinquency was a symptom of emotional disturbance, created by a troubled family background and that, crudely speaking, criminal prosecution and punishment merely hid these causal factors, as well as failing to provide the necessary services to deal with them. (Thorpe *et al.* 1980: 5)

These radical changes were not made, due to strong opposition from the police, magistrates, lawyers and probation officers. In 1968, *Children in Trouble* expressed the view that influences on a boy's behaviour were located in his 'genetic, emotional and intellectual factors, his maturity, and his family, school, neighbourhood and wider social settings' (1968: para. 6). This White Paper was turned into statute, the 1969 Children and Young Persons Act. The Juvenile Court was retained but limited in its operation. Power shifted from magistrates to social workers and Intermediate Treatment was introduced as a preventative measure. It marked a shift towards treatment and grafted a welfare approach on to a punitive system as Detention Centres and Borstals were retained. In doing so, it was not accepted in either Left or Right commentary.

The 1980 White Paper *Young Offenders* completed the swing to control (Home Office 1980). In 1968 'much behaviour by children [had been] part of the process of growing up, but some has more deep-seated causes' (Home Office 1968). By 1980, children were not referred to, instead: 'the Government share[d] the general public concern about the level of juvenile offending' (Home Office 1980: para. 34). The 'short, sharp, shock' was introduced but later demonstrated to have had no significant effect on reconviction rates (Newburn, 2002).

The 1982 Criminal Justice Act gave back power to the judiciary, who would decide where young offenders should be placed, via care orders with residential requirements. It allowed conditions to be inserted into supervision orders and introduced community service for juveniles, a sanction not contingent upon social work. Borstal was abolished and custodial sentences were normally of determinate length. Punitive, Intensive Intermediate Treatment Schemes were funded by the Home Office and provided by the voluntary sector. The combination of both the White Paper and the Criminal Justice Act 1982

> attacked the root of the social welfare perspective underlying the 1969 Act ... Both documents represented a move away from treatment and lack of personal responsibility to notions of punishment and individual parental responsibility ... from the belief in the 'child in need' to the juvenile criminal – what Tutt called the 'rediscovery of the delinquent'. (Gelsthorpe and Morris 1994: 972)

The 1988 Criminal Justice Act replaced Detention Centres with Young Offenders' Institutions. This was a pragmatic decade in terms of juvenile penal policy, also marked by an increasing use of the caution and decrease in custody for young offenders. The right to legal aid for young offenders facing possible incarceration, and the requirement that the reason for jailing young offenders had to be given in open court helped to encourage restraint by sentencers.

Drawing in the parents: the legal context of children and parenting

The 1990 White Paper *Crime, Justice and Protecting the Public* marked a major change by advocating a tripartite approach. For children under the age of 10, responsibility rested completely with the parent. For those aged between 10 and 15, parents were expected to exercise some supervision over them and to know their children's whereabouts. Children aged 16 and 17 were to be regarded as at an intermediate stage between childhood and adulthood, with reduced parental responsibility. The White Paper also advocated financial accountability of parents for the actions of their children.

This drawing in of parents (and guardians) was formalised in the Criminal Justice Act 1991, when parents could be bound over in the sum of £1,000 to 'take proper care and exercise proper control over the child' (s. 58). The effect of this was examined by Drakeford (1996) who found discrepancies in how the Act was implemented and that bind overs were used most heavily on mothers in court, as opposed to both the mother and father or father alone. Parents interviewed in the small study felt that the imposition of the bind over had led to 'embitterment and erosion of productive family functioning' (1996: 254). The 1991 Act was reinforced in the Criminal Justice and Public Order Act 1994 when minors' parents or guardians could themselves be made the subject of a bind over to ensure that the offenders complied with their sentence requirements. Yet, as Drakeford and McCarthy pointed out, parents are not eligible for legal representation and both the 1991 and 1994 Acts

> require those parents targeted to control behaviour which is not specified, by means which are equally unspecific. With both Orders there exists the potential for a criminal sanction, in terms of a fine, should parents fail to 'take responsibility' for their children. (2000: 98)

The Crime and Disorder Act (CDA) 1998, gives four circumstances when a parenting order can be made:

(a) When a Child Safety Order is made in respect of a child;
(b) When an Anti-Social Behaviour Order or Sex Offender Order is made in respect of a child or young person;
(c) When a child or young person is convicted of an offence; or
(d) When a person is convicted of an offence under section 443 (failure to comply with school attendance order) or section 444 (failure to secure regular attendance at school of registered pupil) of the Education Act 1996. (CDA 1998, Section 8)

The parenting order can last for up to 12 months and may include attendance at counselling or guidance sessions. Failure to comply with a parenting order is not an arrestable offence but, on conviction, can lead to a £1,000 fine. In addition, the court can impose any sentence available for a non-imprisonable offence (Home Office 1998a).

A child safety order, available for children under 10 at the time of the order, is expected to last for three months but can be for up to a year. It can be made in four possible circumstances: when a child under the age of 10 commits an act which, had they been 10 or over would have constituted an offence; that the order is necessary to *prevent* the young person committing such an act (our emphasis); that the child has broken a local child curfew scheme (introduced in the same Act); finally, that the child has acted in a way 'that caused or was likely to cause harassment, alarm or distress' to people outside of the child's household (Home Office 1998b). The child safety order is consistent with the government's emphasis on early intervention and blurs the boundaries between social services and youth offending teams. The child safety order may be supervised by a local authority social worker or by a member of the youth offending team. Until then, children under 10 would have been worked with by local authority social services, not staff with an offending label. Should the order be breached for non-compliance, then a care order could be substituted, under the Children Act 1989.

Parents have expressed worries about the possibility of losing their children when social services become involved. They worried about being seen as failed parents or being pushed into unsatisfactory, short-term accommodation. Parents sometimes felt disempowered after professionals became involved (Department of Health 2000). The 'accessibility and quality of the initial response from social services' was seen as a source of concern by other agencies who looked to social services to provide leadership in the context of children in need of safeguarding. 'Duty systems were found to be impersonal and unresponsive ... operating tight criteria for accepting referrals' (Department of Health 2002: 46–7). Even if concerned parents overcome their anxiety about the risk of approaching social services, they are liable to find unhelpful responses as they do not demonstrate a crisis level of need. Despite this, an earlier document stated: 'Parents ... require and deserve support. Asking for help should be seen as a sign of responsibility rather than as a parenting failure' (Department of Health 1999: 1). If these words are to be meaningful, then a system of non-stigmatising support, that can be triggered well before major family crisis, needs to be instigated. Indeed, the most recent government green paper acknowledges this in its very title *Support For All* (DCSF 2010).

Parenting projects in practice

In 1999, the Youth Justice Board for England and Wales funded 42 pilot parenting projects that were independently evaluated. Each project developed in its own way, responding to local need and initiative. The projects were evaluated between June 1999 and December 2001. Two approaches that were found to be useful were the Webster-Stratton programme (see previous chapter) and the Hilton Davies model for working with isolated and vulnerable parents. In the latter approach, one-to-one work is used, not only to address parenting issues but to deal with social and welfare issues. This multi-agency type approach requires patience and tact but, above all, respect and empathy for the parents (Coleman *et al.* 1999). Webster-Stratton's techniques were mentioned in the previous chapter and the Policy Research Bureau's findings are similar to those in the United States. As the title of the Brestan and Eyberg (1998) paper asserts, they considered 82 studies over 29 years, based on 5,272 children and adolescents. They found that there were two types of intervention that could be deemed 'well established': social modelling type video-based programmes first elucidated by Webster-Stratton and others (Webster-Stratton and Herbert 1994) and parent-training programmes based on Patterson and Gullion's (1968) ideas (considered further in the previous chapter). In terms of efficacy of the interventions (whether well established or not), they found that just under 25 per cent of the studies reviewed provided limited support for the interventions (Brestan and Eyberg 1998).

The sample in the evaluation of the English pilot schemes was 96 per cent white British, 81 per cent female and 49 per cent lone parents. The findings demonstrated that few projects engaged with the young people, focusing instead on the parents. Projects tended to be either 'preventative' (working with a wide group of parents) or 'therapeutic' (targeting 'higher tariff' parents in crisis) (Ghate and Ramella 2002). Most projects took a long time to move from inception to practice and typically offered a mixture of one-to-one and group work. Interventions could start from crisis intervention and move to more structured work.

Findings from the evaluation were encouraging with improved parent/child communication, supervision and monitoring; less conflict; better relationships; more influence; and better coping with the pressures of parenting. This was irrespective of whether the parent was on a statutory parenting order or if contact was voluntary. There were high levels of need for both emotional and practical support (Ghate and Ramella 2002).

It was apparent that overwhelmingly it was the mothers who were seen by the project staff. One major complaint by mothers was that they had been made to feel like criminals in the courtroom, as if they had offended, not their children. As a consequence of this, project staff had to work hard in the early stages of contact with the parent/guardian to overcome the negative feelings engendered by the court experience. It was also difficult for the parents to acknowledge that they had developed dysfunctional relationships with their children, or to accept that they had to relearn how to deal with conflicts. Through observing parenting groups and interviewing parents, it became clear that helpful coping and management strategies could indeed be taught without resorting to violence or rejection. The essential premise on which such schemes are founded is that, as Feldman pointed out:

> Parenting is a learned skill like any other, 'instinct' is not enough. The current emphasis is on techniques and resources, and in general on the current family situation in which parents and children interact ... There is an increasing interest in the direction of effect being two-way: as well as parents influencing their offspring, children influence the way their parents behave towards them. (1993: 188)

As the Government acknowledged in the Child Safety Orders guidance document, research by Graham and Bowling (1995) found that a number of factors have been identified as related to the onset of offending. These English findings mirror those of many previous studies that have included parenting as only one of a number of psycho-social risk (and protective) factors in delinquency (Chambers *et al.* 2001; Fergusson and Horwood 1998; Harris and Mertlich 2003; Holtzworth Munroe *et al.* 1997). The Home Office concentrated on relationships with parents and family attachment; parental supervision; parent and sibling criminality; truancy; exclusion from school; and association with delinquent peers. As Golombok comments:

> We must also remember that relationships between children and their parents do not take place within a social vacuum. Parents who are in conflict, or who have psychological problems themselves are less able to be effective mothers or fathers to their child. The social circumstance of the family, and the neighbourhood in which the family lives, also makes a difference to the quality of family life. Poverty, and the social disadvantages that accompany it, is one of the most detrimental and pernicious influences faced by children today. (2000: 102)

In other studies of the backgrounds of the most seriously, repeatedly offending youth, their family situations have been found to be multi-problematic: disruptive, out of control, socially and criminally deviant. Different patterns of family problems were associated with different patterns of delinquent activity, even at the less serious levels (Gorman-Smith *et al.* 1998). Similarly, Smith and Stern concluded that the relationship between family life and offending is not a straightforward correlation and delinquency must be tackled in the proper familial and societal context (Smith and Stern 1997). Beyond parenting styles, other important considerations could include: peer activities; parental employment; school attainment and attendance; substance use; the personality or mental health of the child; gang membership; ethnicity; family nationality; and so on (e.g. Gavazzi *et al.* 2003; Moffitt *et al.* 2002). For example, there is evidence that substance abusing mothers have themselves experienced a higher incidence of childhood abuse. Their substance reliance not only affects the way that they are perceived (and possibly copied) by their children but can affect their physical and psychological abilities to parent (Alison 2000).

Multi-systemic programmes or those taking an 'ecological' approach to school and family intervention (as discussed in the previous chapter) thus seem promising (e.g. Borduin 1999; Dishion and Kavanagh 2000). This appears particularly to be the case when dealing with violent youth, where the 'most effective treatment and prevention' interventions are those that 'simultaneously address the multiple factors related to youth violence' (Kashani *et al.* 1999: 200). Family intervention can have an impact, even if this is the only official sanction. Meta-analysis has shown that successful intervention significantly reduces the time spent in institutions by children with conduct disorder and or delinquent engagement (Woolfenden *et al.* 2002).

A sound theoretical foundation for a parenting programme is a good start, but is by no means sufficient, particularly if the individual is lost within the multiplicity of approaches. If we return to the English Pilot Projects, some mothers reported problems with their mental health; substance abuse; offending; chaotic home life; and issues of neglect. There were others who did not have these experiences, yet were not successfully controlling their children. This brings us to a consideration of the children themselves, many of whom had special educational needs, were poor or non-school attendees, had behavioural problems and were at risk of eviction because of nuisance. In many instances, the relationship between the parents and the statutory services had degraded, with a high level of distrust on both sides.

Some of the histories of the parents are a testimony to their resilience and care for their family. They should certainly not be labelled irresponsible. One mother was so desperately worried about her teenage daughter that she described taking another young child under her arm as she went round the streets at midnight trying to find her. Her interview highlights levels of loneliness and isolation but also her tenacity in trying to hold her family together. This mother was taught some useful techniques to engage with her child without losing her temper. By the end of her group sessions, they appeared to be working. Many parents expressed regret that the group process was too short. These concerns can be considered in the light of findings from the Syracuse Family Development Programme where 'enriched day care' was given over a five-year period (Little and Mount 1999; and see previous chapter).

One final observation is that when these 'problem families' were engaged, with a 'fresh pair of eyes', the outlook of the statutory agencies was challenged to the benefit of the parent and family. A family that is labelled as problematic can find themselves prevented from accessing support. The intervention of the parenting project worker forced the organisations to reappraise what they were doing with such families.

The research on the parenting projects in England and Wales (Ghate and Ramella 2002) is encouraging but it ran for a very short time, therefore any conclusions drawn from it must be tentative. Yet it is impressive that the projects had succeeded in working with a high number of such disaffected families. This was irrespective of whether contact was voluntary or on an imposed parenting order. The accessibility of the project workers was most important and positively commented on by parents. They were seen as being neutral and different from previous officials. All the workers had been engaged as part of the pilot projects and were therefore not directly identified as being part of an existing formal agency.

Parental responsibility and child protection

There is a central incongruity at the heart of the Crime and Disorder Act 1998, around the concept of responsibility. The Act abolishes *doli incapax*, thereby effectively implying that from the age of 10, children have sufficient maturity to know right from wrong and are sufficiently rational to know the consequences of their actions. Parental authority decreases as the child grows older and the Gillick judgement points out that this parental authority must yield to the child when they are intellectually able to make up their own mind (Jones and Bell 2000). Thus the loss of *doli incapax* is incompatible with holding the parent responsible for the wrongdoing of the child. Jones and Bell consider the continuing responsibility of the parent as 'problematic' but this has not stopped parents or, more accurately, mothers from being sent to prison for the non-attendance of their children at school.

These parenting issues must be set within the proper context of the need to protect children, as well as that of holding their parents more widely accountable. It is difficult to think of protecting children and young people without recalling the tragedy of Victoria Climbié, the young girl who was brutally killed by her great-aunt and partner. The subsequent report by Lord Laming (2003) led to the Children Act 2004, and the *Every Child Matters: Change for Children* (DES 2004) programme which has five key areas to improve for children: being healthy, staying safe, enjoying and achieving, making a positive contribution, and achieving economic well-being. In addition, further papers were published that concentrated on particular problems such as the problems for young people when their parents took drugs, an area of increasing interest, discussed further below (Chatwin 2008).

The aim of Every Child Matters was to join up the various government departments in thematic initiatives. In 2006, the Respect Action Plan was announced with the intention to roll out Family Intervention Projects (FIPs). These are aimed at addressing 'anti-social behaviour, youth crime, school absenteeism, drug and alcohol addiction, domestic violence, poor mental health and inter-generational disadvantage' (DCSF 2009: 1).

The commitment to expanding State intervention into families was underlined when the Respect Action Plan was built on in the Children's Plan (2007) and the Children's Plan One Year On (December 2008[1]). The Youth Crime Action Plan (2008[2]) stated that all local authorities would receive funding for FIPs targeted on youth crime, with 32 FIPs targeting child poverty funded in the 2008 Budget. The DCSF report (2009) presented information on families that had been offered support through a FIP to reduce antisocial behaviour (ASB). The take-up rate was quoted as 2,225 out of a possible 2,229 (up until 31 March 2009) and the quoted results were given for families who had stayed the course of the programme (699 families having completed, with 990 still engaged during the report write-up). This attrition rate should be considered in conjunction with the much less publicised refusal rate of 16 per cent, as 367 families refused to engage at different stages of the FIP. The published conclusions are thus based on the results for the 699 families who had completed to that point, and these 'show overwhelmingly positive improvements across a wide range of measures' (2009: 1) with a 68 per cent drop in housing enforcement actions and families with four or more ASB problems declining from 46 per cent to 6 per cent. Other significant improvements were with education and learning problems, truancy, poor school behaviour, child protection concerns, mental health problems, domestic violence and family drug and alcohol problems.

Referrals came from a number of agencies, including housing, local ASB teams, social services and the police. In this way it took a similar path to the previous Youth Inclusion Support Programmes (YISPs) that had been paid for through the Children's Fund. Of the families that took up the FIP 69 per cent were single parent, the majority were large families, 89 per cent were white, around a quarter had at least one member with a disability and/or included one or more children with special educational needs.

The most common FIP intervention was outreach or floating support, on average for just over a year and with initial average provision of nine hours per week (direct contact) decreasing to six hours per week. Interventions were described as focusing on challenging ASB (69 per cent), one-to-one parenting support (65 per cent), supporting children into education (54 per cent), providing meaningful activities for parents and children (52 per cent), help to avoid eviction (45 per cent) and other more general supportive measures. In general support was given directly by the FIP but it could be provided by others, almost always statutory agencies.

In November 2007 the National Academy for Parenting Practitioners (NAPP) was established to train and support practitioners working with parents. Three of the academy's main aims, set out in the *Strategic Plan 2008–2010*, are to

- create, commission and deliver training for practitioners providing support and training to parents on parenting skills;
- promote and provide appropriate support for those who have undertaken training to enable to implement effectively; and
- gather and evaluate the best quality evidence, using it to refine programmes. (NAPP 2008: 5)

The academy has ambitious plans 'to deliver or commission training for over 4,000 expert practitioners in evidence based programmes' (*ibid*: 2) as well as developing training in general for the less experienced and providing 'support and advice' to local authorities. After embarking on a process of 'scoping the gaps' the NAPP concluded that there were considerable needs for practitioner training and training options that were underpinned by qualifications. The £30m provided by the DCSF to NAPP over the period 2007–2010 means that parenting training will be given a high priority over this time with 'strategic commissioning' of 150 courses of training in evidence-based parenting programmes with 3,400 places. This is linked to the five outcomes of Every Child Matters and will be integral to children's services and the Youth Justice Board (YJB).

The YJB published in 2009 *National Specification for Substance Misuse* which drew on the 2008 Drug Strategy and the reform of children's services in the wake of Every Child Matters. The Strategy has four key objectives:

- A greater emphasis on family support;
- Mainstreaming drug and alcohol prevention work;
- Improving the treatment system for young people;
- Building an evidence base of what works. (YJB 2009: 10)

For young people, there is to be a specialist assessment which has to be recorded. This fully involves the young person but also the family is to be 'routinely involved in young people's substance misuse work where this is applicable and appropriate [with their consent]' (*ibid.*: 30). Assessments should also 'routinely, but sensitively, explore issues of parental substance misuse' (*ibid.*: p.21). Youth offending, parenting and substance misuse are thus to be systematically explored as part of the assessment process within youth offending teams, linking in with the potential to order parenting programmes.

Conclusion

It can be seen that supporting parents has been 'mainstreamed' with an assumption that this must be a positive development. The danger is that the notion of parenting and constructive use of support and advice to parents becomes subsumed within the context of punishment and control. As successive governments 'play to the gallery' in maintaining a populist stance on law and order, it will be very difficult to overcome the stigma involved in being the recipient of a parenting order and the effectiveness of working constructively with parents will be diminished. Surely it will be more constructive to avoid parenting orders becoming part of the culture of punishment.

We welcome the idea of national and local agencies dedicated to crime prevention, yet we hope that the system will not lose sight of the individual, nor that it further stigmatises and disadvantages. Cohen's concepts of masking, widening and blurring are still relevant today in terms of drawing parents into the criminal justice system when previously this would not have been the case. The difficult trick is to be able to support and guide, without being judgemental and blaming. This takes time, patience and resources.

Notes

1 See www.dcsf.gov.uk/childrensplan (accessed December 2009).
2 See www.homeoffice.gov.uk/documents/youth-crime-action-plan (accessed December 2009).

References

Alison, L. (2000) 'What are the risks to children of parental substance misuse?', in F. Harbin and M. Murphy (eds), *Substance Misuse and Child Care. How to Understand, Assist and Intervene when Drugs Affect Parenting.* Lyme Regis: Russell House Publishing.

Bessant, J. and Hil, R. (1998) 'Parenting on trial: state wards and governments' accountability in Australia', *Journal of Criminal Justice*, 26 (2): 145–57.

Borduin, C.M. (1999) 'Multisystemic treatment of criminality and violence in adolescents', *Journal of the American Academy of Child and Adolescent Psychiatry*, 38 (3): 242–9.

Brestan, E.V. and Eyberg, S.M. (1998) 'Effective psychosocial treatments of conduct-disordered children and adolescents: 29 years, 82 studies, and 5,272 kids', *Journal of Clinical Child Psychology*, 27 (2): 180–9.

Chambers, J., Power, K., Loucks, N. and Swanson, V. (2001) 'The interaction of perceived maternal and paternal parenting styles and their relation with the psychological distress and offending characteristics of incarcerated young offenders', *Journal of Adolescence*, 24 (2): 209–27.

Chatwin, C. (2008) 'Parental use of alcohol and illicit drugs. A critical review of recent research', in P. Kennison and A. Goodman (eds), *Children as Victims.* Exeter: Learning Matters.

Chesney-Lind, M. and Shelden, R.G. (1998) *Girls, Delinquency and Juvenile Justice* (2nd edn). London: Wadsworth.

Cieslik, M. and Pollock, G. (eds) (2002) *Young People in Risk Society: The Restructuring of Youth Identities and Transitions in Late Modernity.* Aldershot: Ashgate.

Cohen, S. (1979a) 'How can we balance justice, guilt and tolerance?', *New Society*, 1 March: 475–7.

Cohen, S. (1979b) 'Community control – a new Utopia', *New Society*, 15 March: 609–11.

Coleman, J., Henricson, C. and Roker, D. (11 March 1999) *Parenting in the Youth Justice Context. A Report by the Trust for the Study of Adolescence.* London: Trust for the Study of Adolescence.

DCSF (November 2009) *Anti-social Behaviour Family Intervention Projects Monitoring and Evaluation.* Research Brief DCSF-RBX-09-16. London: DCSF.

DCSF (2010) *Support For All. The families and relationships green paper*. Cm 7787. Norwich: the Stationery Office. http://publications.dcsf.gov.uk/eOrderingDownload/CM-7787.pdf (accessed February 2010).

DES (2004) *Every Child Matters: Change for Children.* London: The Stationery Office.

Department of Health (1999) *Working Together to Safeguard Children.* London: Department of Health.

Department of Health (2000) *Assessing Children in Need and their Families: Practice Guidance.* London: The Stationery Office.

Department of Health (October 2002) *Safeguarding Children: a Joint Chief Inspectors Report on Arrangements to Safeguard Children*. London: Department of Health Publications.

Dishion, T.J. and Kavanagh, K. (2000) 'A multilevel approach to family-centered prevention in schools: process and outcome', *Addictive Behaviors*, 25 (6): 899–911.

Donzelot, J. (1979) *The Policing of Families: Welfare Versus the State.* London: Hutchinson and Co. Ltd.

Drakeford, M. (1996) 'Parents of young people in trouble', *Howard Journal of Criminal Justice*, 35 (3): 242–55.

Drakeford, M. and McCarthy, K. (2000) 'Parents, responsibility and the New Youth Justice', in B. Goldson (ed.), *The New Youth Justice.* Lyme Regis: Russell House Publishing.

Farrington, D.P. (1995) The twelfth Jack Tizard Memorial Lecture: 'The development of offending and antisocial behaviour from childhood: key findings from the Cambridge Study in Delinquent Development', *Journal of Child Psychology and Psychiatry and Allied Disciplines*, 36: 929–64.

Feldman, P. (1993) *The Psychology of Crime.* Cambridge: Cambridge University Press.

Fergusson, D.M. and Horwood, L.J. (1998) 'Exposure to interparental violence in childhood and psychosocial adjustment in young adulthood', *Child Abuse and Neglect*, 22 (5), 339–357.

Gavazzi, S.M. Slade, D., Buettner, C.K. Partridge, C., Yarcheck, C.M. & Andrews, D.W. (2003). 'Toward conceptual development and empirical measurement of global risk indicators in the lives of court', *Psychological Reports*, 92 (2): 599–615.

Gelsthorpe, L. and Morris, A. (1994) 'Juvenile justice 1945–1992', in M. Maguire, R. Morgan and R. Reiner (eds), *The Oxford Handbook of Criminology.* Oxford: Oxford University Press.

Ghate, D. and Ramella, M. (September 2002) *Positive Parenting: The National Evaluation of the Youth Justice Boards Parenting Programme.* London: Policy Research Bureau for the Youth Justice Board.

Golombok, S. (2000) *Parenting: What Really Counts?* London: Routledge.

Gorman-Smith, D., Tolan, P.H., Loeber, R. and Henry, D.B. (1998) 'Relation of family problems to patterns of delinquent involvement among urban youth', *Journal of Abnormal Child Psychology,* 26 (5): 319–33.

Graham, J. and Bowling, B. (1995) *Young People and Crime.* Home Office Research Study 145. London: Home Office.

Haapasalo, J. (2000) 'Young offenders' experiences of child protection services', *Journal of Youth and Adolescence,* 29 (3): 355–71.

Harris, M.A. and Mertlich, D. (2003) 'Piloting home-based behavioral family systems therapy for adolescents with poorly controlled diabetes', *Children's Health Care,* 32 (1): 65–79.

Holman, R. (1978) *Poverty: Explanations of Social Deprivation.* London: Martin Robertson.

Holtzworth Munroe, A., Smutzler, N. and Sandin, E. (1997) 'A brief review of the research on husband violence. 2. The psychological effects of husband violence on battered women and their children', *Aggression and Violent Behavior*, 2 (2): 179–213.

Home Office (1960) *Report on the Committee on Children and Young Persons.* Cmnd 1191 [The Ingleby Report]. London: HMSO.

Home Office (1965) *The Child, The Family and the Young Offender.* Cmnd 2742. London: HMSO.

Home Office (1968) *Children in Trouble.* Cmnd 3601. London: HMSO.

Home Office (1980) *Young Offenders.* Cmnd 8045. London: HMSO.

Home Office (1990) *Crime, Justice and Protecting the Public.* London: HMSO.

Home Office (1997) *No More Excuses – A New Approach to Tackling Youth Crime in England and Wales.* London: Home Office.

Home Office (1998a) *The Crime and Disorder Act Guidance Document: Parenting Order.* London: Home Office.

Home Office (1998b) *The Child Safety Order: Draft Guidance Document.* London: Home Office.

Jones, G. and Bell, R. (2000) *Balancing Acts: Youth, Parenting and Public Policy.* York: York Publishing Services Limited for the Joseph Rowntree Foundation.

Kashani, J.H., Jones, M.R., Bumby, K.M. and Thomas, L.A. (1999) 'Youth violence: psychosocial risk factors, treatment, prevention, and recommendations', *Journal of Emotional and Behavioral Disorders*, 7 (4): 200–10.

Kolvin, I., Miller, F.J., Fleeting, M. and Kolvin, P.A. (1988) 'Social and parenting factors affecting criminal-offence rates: findings from the Newcastle

Thousand Family Study (1947–1980)' *British Journal of Psychiatry*, 152 (80–90).

Laming, Lord (2003) *The Victoria Climbié Inquiry*. London: The Stationery Office.

Lewis, C. (2002) 'The changing family, head to head: should parenting be taught?', *The Psychologist*, 15 (10): 510–12.

Little, M. and Mount, K. (1999) *Prevention and Early Intervention with Children in Need*. Aldershot: Ashgate.

Moffitt, T.E., Caspi, A., Harrington, H. and Milne, B.J. (2002) 'Males on the life-course-persistent and adolescence-limited antisocial pathways: follow-up at age 26 years', *Development and Psychopathology*, 14 (1): 179–207.

Morris, A., Giller, H., Szwed, E. and Geach, H. (1980) *Justice for Children*. London: Macmillan Press Ltd.

National Academy for Parenting Practitioners (2008) *Strategic Plan*. www.parentingacademy.org/UploadedFiles/Strategic_Plan_200810.pdf (accessed December 2009).

Newburn, T. (2002) 'Young people, crime, and youth justice', in M. Maguire, R. Morgan and R. Reiner (eds), *The Oxford Handbook of Criminology* (3rd edn). Oxford: Oxford University Press.

Patterson, G.R. and Gullion, M.E. (1968) *Living with Children: New methods for parents and teachers*. Illinois: Research Press.

Petersen, R.D. (1995) 'Expert policy in juvenile justice: patterns of claims making and issues of power in a program construction', *Policy Studies Journal*, 23 (4): 636–51.

Smith, C.A. and Stern, S.B. (1997) 'Delinquency and antisocial behavior: a review of family processes and intervention research', *Social Service Review*, 71 (3): 382–420.

Thorpe, D., Smith, D., Green, C. and Paley, J. (1980) *Out of Care: The Community Support of Juvenile Offenders*. London: George Allen and Unwin.

Walters, G.D. and White, T.W. (1988) 'Crime, popular mythology, and personal responsibility', *Federal Probation*, 52 (1): 18–26.

Webster-Stratton, C. and Herbert, M. (1994) *Troubled Families–Problem Children*. Chichester: Wiley.

West, D.J. (1982) *Delinquency: its roots, career and prospects*. Cambridge, Mass.: Harvard University Press.

Wilson, H. (1987) 'Parental supervision re-examined', *British Journal of Criminology*, 27: 275–301.

Woolfenden, S.R., Williams, K. and Peat, J.K. (2002) 'Family and parenting interventions for conduct disorder and delinquency: a meta-analysis of randomised controlled trials', *Archives of Disease in Childhood*, 86 (4): 251–6.

Youth Justice Board (2009) *National Specification for Substance Misuse*. London: YJB.

Chapter 21

The challenge of managing prejudice and hate in offending behaviours

Liz A. Dixon and Joanna R. Adler

Hate crime is a global phenomenon as well as a local one. It is characterised by conflicting lifestyles, entrenched and fleeting prejudices, personal and political incidents and events. Other features include legitimate and historical grievances, retaliation and escalation, and an incapacity or unwillingness to engage in dialogue. The impact differs depending on victim–perpetrator profile, the specific impact and response of others. Hate crime ranges from low level antisocial offending to murder, genocide and some forms of terrorism. The role of charismatic leaders is not to be underestimated and media coverage can fuel prejudice and division and foment stereotypes (Nielsen 2002). Britain has long been familiar with the pernicious effects of hate preachers from the far right and is now working to contain espoused violence from Islamic extremists. Whilst we are increasingly recording, prosecuting and intervening in crime behaviours aggravated by racial or religious components, we still lag behind in our responses to hate crimes targeted at the lesbian, gay, transgendered and bisexual members of our society and at those with learning difficulties, mental health problems and disabilities. Indeed, the former Director of Public Prosecutions highlighted responses to disability hate crime as 'a scar on the conscience of criminal justice' (McDonald 2008).

Europe has learnt from international historical hatreds and considered ways to tackle new variants, such as the Organization for Security and Co-operation in Europe's (OSCE) practical guide to passing legislation on hate crimes (OSCE 2009). Partly because different situations pertain in different countries, there is no unified response. Countries approach hate phenomena in a variety of ways with concomitantly different means of responding to hate incidents and hate crime. Some European countries have invested in NGO projects to promote awareness and others have developed programmes to support and empower victims. In Germany, the government works to support community groups that tackle far right hate in particular, given its Nazi legacy. Hall (2005) further contrasts the USA and UK approaches, highlighting the wider remit in the UK, with less discretion for police and prosecution.

This chapter aims to reflect the progress made in addressing hate crime and some of the specific learning points in the professional journey covered over the past 10 years. It will explore the significant progress we have made in addressing offending that is informed by prejudice or hate as the behaviours have been identified and assessed. We will consider some of the psychological implications both for prevention and intervention and outline areas of ongoing development.

Definitions

In considering definitions, we start with that of the Association of Chief Police Officers of England, Wales and Northern Ireland (ACPO).

> Hate crimes and incidents are taken to mean any crime or incident where the perpetrator's prejudice against an identifiable group of people is a factor in determining who is victimised. A victim of hate crime does not have to be a member of a minority or someone who is generally considered to be vulnerable. For example the friends of a visible minority ethnic person, lesbian or refugee may be victimised because of their association. In some cases the perpetrator's perception may be wrong. This can result in a person entirely unconnected with the hate motivation becoming a victim. (Giannasi 2008, taken from the ACPO manual on hate crimes)

This wide-ranging definition facilitates policing that can react to local community needs and could encompass both low-level incidents or more serious offending. Also, a victimised group could be acknowledged as such based on common beliefs, practices, nationality, ethnicity, disability or even which football team they support. Despite its broad base, this approach is limiting in its emphasis on perceived group membership as 'a factor in determining who is victimised' by the perpetrator. The pertinent current legislation takes an even narrower approach to the groups considered, including for example, crimes targeted at lesbian, gay and bisexual people but not transgendered hate crime. However, the legislative framework could also be considered to be broader than that provided by ACPO in its treatment of hate as 'aggravating' without having to be the main motivation. Yet, by deeming hate crime to be an aggravating condition within an offence, thereby attracting an enhanced sentence, it also means that offenders have an active disincentive to acknowledging it as motivation and this can itself pose challenges for treatment.

The ACPO definition we have given above is not the only policing definition. In 2005, the Police Standards Unit published two related definitions that should be used by police in practice. The first is of a hate incident: 'Any hate incident, which may or may not constitute a criminal offence, which is perceived by the victim or any other person, as being motivated by prejudice or hate' and the second is of a hate crime: 'Any hate incident, which constitutes a criminal offence, perceived by the victim or any other person, as being motivated by prejudice or hate'. It is important to note that the police are responsible for collecting and collating data on both incidents and crimes (and that they recognise the potential for overlap) (Home Office and ACPO 2005). This pair of definitions brings forward the perceptions of the victim, witnesses or someone who is otherwise involved, rather than focusing exclusively on the motivations of the offender. It also acknowledges the need for early intervention or prevention of escalation of a hate incident into a hate crime and the different standards of evidence needed for each. For most victims, the distinction between incident and crime is unimportant or even irrelevant, but it is important to understand when interpreting police and other criminal justice agency responses. The means by which hate crime is conceptualised and defined will in turn determine whether it is recognised by statutory authorities and how they respond to it (Jacobs and Potter 1998).

Prevalence and experiences

> Britain has made great progress in recent years towards allowing every citizen to maximise their potential. But we must not be complacent. While prejudice and negative attitudes still exist there is still work to do. And nowhere is this more stark than where prejudice leads to hate crime. (Jacqui Smith, Home Secretary, taken from the foreword to Dick 2008).

British society has a long history of race crime for many years (Bowling 1998) and various government initiatives tried to trigger concern and action with limited success. The death of Stephen Lawrence in 1993 was the third high-profile racist murder within a year in the London borough of Greenwich and led to revolutionary changes in the management of race crime. The campaign and subsequent inquiry (Macpherson 1999) into the failure of the Metropolitan Police to investigate Stephen's murder changed public awareness and raised widespread concern. In the 'post Lawrence' period there have been successful prosecutions for high-profile 'hate' murders including those of Anthony Williams, a black teenager from Liverpool and Jody Dobrowski, a young man targeted for his sexuality and beaten to death on Clapham Common. These cases have demonstrated improved system capacity and expertise. However, the murder of Zahid Mubarek by his racist psychopathic cell mate in HMYOI Feltham and the torture and beating to death of Brent Martin – targeted solely because of his learning difficulties – show how criminal justice agencies need to be ever vigilant. These high-profile murders and a growing awareness of preventative policies and procedures alongside the identification of solutions have increased agency capacity to identify and work with hate crimes.

Given the inconsistency in definition and that systematic, criminal justice approaches are relatively nascent in Britain, it is not entirely surprising to see that the levels reported to the 2007/8 wave of *Crime in England and Wales* (Kershaw *et al.* 2008) mirrored the historic priorities and current policies. It is also worth noting that policing and prosecution authorities have historically dealt with domestic violence (intimate partner violence) and hate crimes in the same units. As such, it is very difficult to unpick the extent of hate crimes and hate incidents, but there are some estimates and limited official statistics available.

The Crown Prosecution Service (CPS 2008) brought around 35,500 cases of hate crime in England and Wales in the three years to March 2008. Of these, the vast majority were for racist and anti-religious hate, over 33,000; just over 2,400 related to homophobic crimes of hate and there were just 183 cases of disability hate crime brought to court. The reported crime figures from Kershaw *et al.* (2008) include crimes aggravated by racial or religious components that are recorded by the police and indicate just under 40,000, in just one of the three years considered by the CPS (with detection rates between 23 and 50 per cent). Kershaw *et al.* also report that 13,337 victims of crimes of violence and of theft described themselves as having a longstanding illness or disability. The low figures for disability-related hate crime prosecutions seem even less representative when considering the findings from Mencap (2000) or MIND (2007), where only 18 per cent of respondents felt safe most or all of the time, 71 per cent reported victimisation in the preceding two years and 41 per cent reported ongoing victimisation.

Another under-representation in recorded crime and prosecution figures is demonstrated by Dick (2008) who reports that 60 per cent of lesbian and gay people have been a victim of any kind of hate incident or crime with a sixth of those being physical assaults. However, 75 per cent of those incidents were not reported to the police and 70 per cent were not reported to any third party until the Gay British Crime Survey was conducted. Outside England and Wales, the Scottish Parliament has lagged behind regarding legislation but the victims' pictures are similar. Although homophobic hate crime is now more likely to be reported than before, Capability Scotland and the Disability Rights Commission report that 73 per cent of disabled respondents reported being frightened or attacked by verbal abuse and intimidation and estimate that 47 per cent 'had experienced hate crime because of their disability' (www.capability-scotland.org.uk/hatecrime.aspx?resource=faqs, accessed June 2009). Sectarian violence is still a real concern in Northern Ireland and is included within the Northern Ireland Executive's definition of hate crime and that used by the Police Service of Northern Ireland (PSNI). The PSNI reports that

> in 2008–2009 there were 771 racist hate crimes, 134 homophobic hate crimes, 35 faith/religion related hate crimes, 1,017 sectarian hate crimes and 28 disability related hate crimes. Over the same period in 2007–2008 there were 757 racist hate crimes, 114 homophobic hate crimes, 62 faith/religion related hate crimes, 1,056 sectarian hate crimes and 42 disability related hate crimes. (www.psni.police.uk/index/news-archive/news-2009/news_releases_june_2009/300609_launch_of_hate_crime_campaign.htm, accessed June 2009)

Here too it has been 'concluded that the annual statistics produced by the PSNI do not reflect the experiences of people with a disability' (Vincent *et al.* 2009) and the PSNI have themselves tried to increase rates of reporting all forms of hate crime (see link above).

Bowling (1998) gives a chronological account of racist crime in Britain over two centuries and highlights periods such as 1958 when murders were so prevalent that there was a self-imposed curfew by black communities in West London. Campaigning bodies for victims likewise worked to highlight how the racist element of antisocial behaviour and criminal acts was minimised by the agencies, the perpetrators and the country at large. The Racial Attacks and Harassment Reports (e.g. Home Affairs Committee 1994; Home Office 1981 and 1989 or House of Commons 1986), a government initiative, tried to raise concern about the prevalence of race crime but it took the Lawrence campaign to raise awareness among the majority white culture of the victims' actual experiences and difficulties in reporting. Bowling (*ibid.*) highlighted the processes involved in the production of race offending, characterising it as a crime with a message and highlighting the dynamic interactions between different parties. He was able to show how limited previous police investigation tools had been in capturing the essence of the crime as they were viewing offences in isolation rather than as part of a continuum. Without a full appreciation of the context of hate crimes, they had failed to reflect the enormity of the crime or the pattern of offending behaviour, to say nothing of victims' experiences. Bowling's research and analysis is illuminating and influenced large parts of the Macpherson Report (1999).

In *We Can't All Be White*, Chahal (1999) documented victims' experiences, including how they adapted their lives to cope with constant targeted attacks. More latterly, the publication of *Crime and Prejudice* by Victim Support (Bell *et al.* 2006) and other reports already mentioned have illustrated the ongoing challenges in reporting hate crime from different sectors in the community (MIND 2007; Dick 2008). The literature shows how hate crime can have a ripple effect, victimises certain communities and hurts more than parallel crimes. It adds to the ferocity of the offence – it does indeed act as an aggravating feature (Garcia and McDevitt 1999). Iganski (2008a) refers to Perry's work from 2001 drawing on ingroup biases that exclude and punish the outgroups. Perry explores the context and structural components where perpetrators of hate target the groups that are demonised or dehumanised by the dominant groups in society (please see below for further consideration of the aetiology of hate crime).

Iganski (*ibid.*) likens the experience of racism and racial harassment to violence against women. All women seem to experience sexism at a certain level; it is the intensity that appears to relate to whether they report it. In the first author's experience working with perpetrators of hate crime in London Probation, we have found that there are nearly always previous incidents in offenders' histories. The victim literature testifies to the frequency of racial harassment preceding the crimes. Many victims fail to report 'mundane' or everyday 'racism' because the experience is so prevalent (e.g. Carroll 1998).

Aetiology

The significance of prejudice as an aggravating feature is explored in most explanations of hate crime. Jacobs and Potter (1998) provide an overview of the challenges faced in singling out hate and prejudice as aggravating features in crime. The ingroup–outgroup theories derived from Tajfel (e.g. Tajfel and Turner 1986) and wider debates on stigma, dehumanisation and societal competition considered by Golec de Zavala and Adler (this volume) are of direct pertinence when considering the aetiology of hate crime offending behaviours. It is worth also noting that amongst others, Brewer (1999) concluded that the desired preferential treatment for members of one's ingroup is a stronger motivator than a direct hatred of an outgroup.

In 1997, the Home Office commissioned Sibbitt to conduct research into perpetrators of racist hate crime. She reported that it was very difficult to find a stereotypical racist perpetrator although different age stratifications did seem to emerge within communities. She writes about perpetrator communities rather than individuals and ties this into her findings that different age groups participate differently in the production of racist incidents and crime. Sibbitt concludes that the elders socialise their prejudices into the younger offenders, who act out these prejudices when offending. More recently, Verkuyten (2007) has found that in pre-adolescent children with high ethnic identification (whether in a majority or minority ethnic group), ingroup favouritism can have at least a momentary self-enhancing effect.

Ray *et al.* (2004) carried out research into racist offending following disturbances in the north of England in cities including Oldham, Rochdale and Bolton, during the summers of 2000 and 2001. Offenders were prepared to admit to violence but did not acknowledge the racism; rather, they appeared to feel slighted. The research highlighted perpetrator shame and envy experienced when faced with black and Asian minority ethnic communities whom they perceive to have more social capital, better economic prospects and where the social capital seems stronger (Ray *et al.* 2004). This shame fuelled the antisocial racist behaviour. Beck (1999) elaborates on the themes of hurt becoming hate and gives an account rooted in cognitive therapy that practitioners have found helpful in explaining why some perpetrators are receptive to extreme ideologies.

Boeckmann and Turpin-Petrosino (2002) edited an edition of the *Journal of Social Issues* dedicated to hate crimes that gives the reader a comprehensive overview of the (US) legal, policy and psychological literature at that time. Of particular relevance to this chapter are the typology proposed by McDevitt *et al.* (2002) and findings that Boeckmann and Turpin-Petrosino summarise as 'the perpetrators' aversion toward the victim not as an individual, but as a representative of a group perceived as possessing a reviled set of characteristics' (Herek *et al.* 2002) with such ideas being increasingly promulgated via the internet (Levin 2002). In the same issue, Turpin-Petrosino (2002) also identifies the importance of looking at informal social networks. Her piece focused on the strategies employed by the Ku Klux Klan and neo-Nazi American hate groups. At the time of writing this chapter, we see the British National Party running youth camps training young people to use knives and guns, promulgating material via MySpace, Bebo and Facebook and producing animated films all aimed at recruiting young people as part of their ostensible 'Racism cuts both ways' campaign and recent gains in elections that saw them representing us at county as well as local level for the first time and sending two representatives to the European Parliament: Andrew Brons (Yorkshire and Humberside) and Nick Griffin (North West).

Iganski (2007) analysed detailed statistics from the London race hate forum over a 10-year period. The data show patterns of targeting and repeat race hate, victimisation hotspots in the areas where people mill together and where everyday conflicts and routine incivilities occur; that is, areas with higher volumes of crime in general not just hate crime. Iganski (*ibid.*) comments on the finding that hate crime is committed on the whole by 'ordinary people rather than bigots' and illuminates the background structural contexts in which hate crime develops. His evaluation of the spatial distribution of race hate in London shows that geography of space and place mediates between the background of structural components of hate crime alongside specific situational incidents. Spatial dynamics, demographics and the strength of community cohesion are presented as risk factors with some forms of hate but not all. These findings are similar to those considered by Putnam (2007) who contextualises the long-term benefits of immigration and diversity by pointing out the need to acknowledge their short-term, negative impacts where they

> tend to reduce social solidarity and social capital. New evidence from the US suggests that in ethnically diverse neighborhoods residents of all races tend to 'hunker down'. Trust (even of one's own race) is lower, altruism and community cooperation rarer, friends fewer. (Putnam 2007: 137)

Criminal justice and policy responses

The overall findings of the Macpherson Inquiry were that the investigation into the death of Stephen Lawrence was marred by institutional racism, professional incompetence and a lack of leadership. The recommendations included that all community agencies needed to consider their responses to prejudice and hate as part of a wider acknowledgement of the pervasiveness of racist attitudes. The report of the Inquiry triggered a series of fundamental changes. Jack Straw, the then Home Secretary, marked it out as a watershed in government policy and thinking. It had a major impact on the criminal justice system, highlighting the reality and impact of institutional racism and prejudice and the consequences of failure to engage with black and minority ethnic communities' staff and victims. The Metropolitan Police Service was overhauled with positive outcomes and policy. There was an energised and committed attitude from the police which effused through related agencies.

Ten years on, Trevor Phillips, chair of the Equality and Human Rights Commission (EHRC) and Jack Straw (then Minister of Justice) suggested that the police are no longer institutionally racist (news.bbc.co.uk/1/hi/uk/7904194.stm, accessed June 2009) and a series of reviews of other institutions also heralded change. The Crown Prosecution Service developed its policies and practices after a critical inquiry in 2000 and has been proactive in investing in diversity matters and issuing guidance including: *Guidance on Prosecuting More Cases of Racist and Religious Violence* (CPS 2005) that was shortly followed by policy and guidance on homophobic, transgendered and disability hate crime (CPS 2007a, b, c and d). The Probation Service was criticised for lack of policies in the *Thematic Inspection Report* (HMIP 2000) and has become more proactive with regard to developing interventions (Dixon 2002). The prison service has been subject to a number of inquiries which highlighted the issues around race relations and developed the Respect Initiative (www.respectonline.org.uk/, accessed December 2009) to promote change and good practice. However, it was the extensive inquiry into the death of Zahid Mubarek (Keith for the House of Commons 2006) which really triggered change such as new cell-sharing assessment, improved training and better communication protocols amongst security, courts, medical services and criminal and community justice agencies.

New legislation to address racist offending was launched and has been subsequently amended to acknowledge other hate-related offending. The changes include relevant parts in all of the following Acts of Parliament: Crime and Disorder Act 1998; Anti-terrorism, Crime and Security Act 2001; Race Relations Act 2002; Racial and Religious Hatred Act 2006; Disability Discrimination Act 2005. Of particular relevance is the Powers of Criminal Courts (Sentencing) Act 2000 that requires courts to consider racial or religious hostility as an aggravating factor when deciding on the sentence for any offence which is not specifically stated under the Crime and Disorder Act 1998; section 146 of the Criminal Justice Act 2003 extended this beyond race and religious motivations. The Equality Act 2010 provides enhanced protection provided against discrimination on the basis of age, disability, gender reassignment, marriage and civil partnership, pregnancy and maternity, race, religious belief, sex or sexual orientation.

In 2002, Burney and Rose suggested that despite some problems with identifying racist hate in high-tariff cases, the law had indeed helped outlaw racist offending and was having a deterrent effect. Statistics have demonstrated significant progress regarding the reporting of incidents (see for example the Runnymede Trust's ongoing quarterly bulletins that started in 1969). Indeed it was the progress on race prejudice that facilitated the widened criminological gaze to consider other forms of prejudice such as homophobic, religious and disability hate crime (Iganski 2008a; Victim Support 2006).

Among several influential contributions, Hewitt has pointed out the importance of assessing policy at the local level. In *Routes of Racism* (1996) he considered the challenges in addressing race crime and evaluated concerted government initiatives aimed at challenging racism. In the more recent *White Backlash* (2005) he astutely chronicles the impact on the local community in Greenwich of those government initiatives. Clumsy anti-racist policies had the effect of ostracising key elements of the community. Hewitt points out that this led to a lack of community engagement which then engendered poor reporting and lack of the support vital to drive agency and government anti-racist initiatives. He manages to convey the sense of distress and outrage of white schoolchildren and their families who felt labelled, overlooked and excluded. One example of this was when their cultural heritages were not included in school corridors and montages. Hewitt identifies different forms of exclusion, economic and social, which led to the backlash. His extensive research revealed that the white non-racist population felt they had been labelled as if they were of the same mind as the sympathisers with the far right policies of Combat 18 (an offshoot of the British National Party, affiliated to Blood and Honour) which had set up office locally. Hewitt highlights the damaging impact on crime of ostracising parts of the community from anti-racist policies that could only have been effective had they been part of a community endeavour.

One of the themes picked up after the initial disturbances in the north of England in 2000 was linked to issues of integration and communication. The term community cohesion was adopted, which gave credibility to the critical importance of including all groups in work to develop good cohesion. Community cohesion should reflect integration that itself aims to stop stereotyping and reduce community tensions between different faith and cultural groups (e.g. Cantle 2001; Ousley 2001). The Race Relations Amendment Act 2000 introduced legislation that instructed all agencies to carry out impact assessment on all their policies to anticipate and thus reduce the potential for exclusion and to promote community integration. The Cantle report (*ibid.*) and other inquiry reports recommended that agencies develop perpetrator programmes to address issues of racist offending.

Interventions

Some would argue that hate crime laws have the effect of prioritising some victims over others (Iganski 1999) and this does seem to have been the case when we look at how hate crimes legislation and interventions have developed in Britain. For example, crimes against people with a learning difficulty, mental illness or other disability and homophobic crimes are still under-reported, under- recorded and their victims are still under-supported (e.g. MIND 2007; Dick 2008; Kershaw *et al.* 2008). There are also thought-provoking debates about how issues of free speech and dangers of punishing it play out in the public arena (e.g. Dixon and Ray 2007; Iganski 2002). Iganski (2002) put together a collection that summarises the issues; he is persuasive in his conclusion that hate crime is unique and the evidence justifies a different approach.

The Macpherson Inquiry (1999) recommended reforming policies of reporting so as to empower victims of race hate crime. MIND (2007) made several recommendations, and highlighted examples of good practice for third party reporting and local outreach to encourage victims of hate crime to come forward. Indeed, victims' groups have traditionally campaigned for action in these areas. In contrast, it took the offending agencies time to believe that they had a part to play and could address racist behaviour in the way that they addressed other offending behaviours. On reflection, it may also be that it took time for agencies to accept that perpetrators had been socialised in their beliefs and were not wholly responsible for the development of prejudice. There was also a feeling that education would enlighten those with distorted cognitions about others. However, as Bowling (1998) highlighted, the issues involve relationships, and an emotional component that needs addressing alongside the cognitive distortions. Schools have had some success in the endeavour to promote tolerance and the citizenship curriculum has helped promote community cohesion initiatives (Cowan *et al.* 2002). In the past decade, schools, NGOs and youth clubs have worked with some success to devise programmes of intervention to develop tolerance and an appreciation of diversity. Lemos (2000) recognised the need that many agencies had in challenging behaviour and devised a subscription website[1] to provide legal materials, case studies and examples of good practice to help disseminate best practice and promote innovative projects across housing and policing agencies.

McGhee has commented on the practitioners who have developed interventions (McGhee 2005); he highlights the importance of engaging in dialogues that help reflection on practice and encourage the use of motivational interviewing techniques to work with denial and resistance. A key theme in this approach is the promotion of positive racial identities that are not defensive attitudes. In common with other interventions and the policing of hate crimes, this method has developed out of one intervention taken with perpetrators of intimate partner violence (see Gilchrist and Kebbell, this volume). Male IPV offenders explore notions of masculinity and are encouraged to develop masculine identities that do not promote domination over women, ownership and violence. They then review their attitude to women and are facilitated in reflecting on their action through new 'lenses' (Bem 1993). With racial offences, perpetrators explore the formation of their own racial or cultural identities, which is a challenge in itself as they can be fragile and undeveloped. This can contribute to some of the negativity to other cultures where they perceive the identity to be stronger, better and richer (Ray *et al.* 2004).

The Probation Service has a particular role to play in addressing hate crime as they are charged with tackling attitudes and reducing the risk of reoffending. There are inherent difficulties in assessing motivation where the crime is attitudinal as denial and minimisation are the norm. The courts' enhanced sentencing powers for crimes of hate can serve as a disincentive to admit to such offending at the outset. Denial can be conscious and unconscious, and there is often a lack of insight which, along with shame and stigma (Ray *et al.* 2004) can act as a barrier to intervention. Those challenging the behaviours need to be aware of their own attitudes around prejudice, race, religion, disability and sexuality. The practitioners' attitudes can influence or even derail the intervention, as they can lead to collusion, so training to manage these dynamics is essential (Dixon 2002).

Initially, the advice from National Probation Service management was predicated on the idea that the offending behaviours could be contained using mainstream interventions. This was challenged and successful interventions have subsequently been developed with specific features (Court 2003; McGhee 2005; Hall 2005). These features include areas highlighted in the preceding paragraph and in the section on aetiology above – exploration of socialisation experiences, strengthening cultural and racial identities which are not based on defensiveness, a focus on the management of peer pressure, the raising of victim awareness, and concern with the particular target group. Toolkits like London Probation's Diversity Awareness and Prejudice Pack (DAPP) challenge perpetrators by focusing on outputs geared to exposing, then managing and containing prejudices. The toolkit builds on practitioner experiences indicating that prejudicial attitudes can vary in potency, intent, impact and motivation.

Racial and other forms of hate tend to occur as an aggravating rather than motivating factor (Burney and Rose 2002; Court 2003) and are treated as such by the courts and subsequent interventions. The McDevitt *et al.* typology (2002) distinguishes between different motivations used within interventions. They identify: thrill seekers, the most common category, who are motivated by the thrill or sense of power that offending can give; reactive offenders, who act on a perceived sense of grievance and act this out in incidents involving the target groups; retaliatory offenders, who hit back, having been on the receiving end of hate; and the relatively rare mission offenders, who target specific groups with premeditation. Practitioners have found that this typology is helpful in making assessment about risk and interventions and they resonate with their experience (Court 2003). With mission offenders, the primary aim is to enhance victim protection as the offending is premeditated and targeted. Work with thrill seekers is often geared at diverting them into prosocial attitudes and working on their capacity to resist peer pressure as this can also drive the offending.

The task of developing interventions for hate offenders drew on a variety of sources and expertise. Criminal justice practitioners working with perpetrators of hate have learned from developments in other targeted offending, namely sex offending and domestic violence (Dixon and Otikpitpki 1999). Iganski (2007) helpfully draws our attention to Kelly (1987), who posits a continuum between the day-to-day sexism of women's everyday experience and the severity of domestic violence which can result in murder. Perry (2001) and Iganski (2008b) speak powerfully about the same dynamics at work in the commission of hate crime, everyday racism that most minority groups experience and then racial attacks. Some of the most vulnerable members of our society can be particularly worried that police and other agencies will not consider the lower level, insidious, repetitive offending to be important, so victims are likely to report more serious crimes only. This in turn has been highlighted as a critical problem in the policing and prosecution of hate-aggravated crime; a problem that is itself worsened by lack of recognition of the signs that an offence is aggravated by racial, religious, disabilist, or homophobic and transgendered hate (Hall 2002, 2006, 2007; Giannasi 2008; Orr 2008).

There is a critical role to be played through multi-agency work assisting in highlighting the subtleties involved and the importance of shared community intelligence. When looking at how to deal with prejudice in presenting behaviour, social housing groups became a key agency as they developed a range of staged sanctions to mark antisocial behaviour and support victims (Lemos 2000). They had to deal with both perpetrators and victims of harassment and faced very similar issues around identification, assessment and risk management. They developed interview proformae to reduce the antagonism that they met when they challenged tenants' prejudices. The challenges involved are similar to those probation practitioners face where offender counter-accusation and denial are common, despite clear evidence on Crown Prosecution papers and witness statements of ferocity of attacks and prevalence of harassment. (Lemos 2000; McDonald 2008; Orr 2008). In drawing upon victims' testimonies to understand the process of offending, policy-makers and those running interventions have also learned more about the role that language plays in escalating behaviours and developing the intent (see 'Aetiology', above).

Those involved with perpetrators work hard to learn about distorted victim perceptions and to assist offenders to develop identities that are more pro-social. If successful, then perpetrators acknowledge that they unconsciously dehumanise the 'other' and the perpetrators may go further in seeing the prejudicial attitude acting as an accelerant where it is as if the aggression is unleashed like a coil. Dixon and Court (2003) testify to the increased ferocity of the attacks in addition to the ripple effect on the community and they highlight the importance of gathering both criminal and community intelligence prior to working with those charged with racially aggravated offences and to have at their disposal 'relevant materials' prior to engaging with the work, in line with the way that we would work with sex offenders or perpetrators of intimate partner violence. Iganski's (2007 and 2008a) local, situational analyses with their focus on context are also helpful to practitioners, demonstrating why they need to work with local communities to gather community intelligence, learn about target groups and available solutions. So it is that professionals involved in the monitoring of hate crime in a community have learned to familiarise themselves with community demographics, community cohesion, the target groups and victims. The worker thus needs to be proactive to prepare for the intervention and concomitant interviews, given community and situational-specific dynamics. It is essential that practitioners assemble available community intelligence and read all the prosecution papers, the most important of which are the witness statements. In this way, workers are victim focused, will avoid collusion, support victims and maximise opportunities to reduce and manage risk.

The need to have flexible intervention is imperative given changing presentations of offending, moving targets and the greater confidence in our capacity to promote change at all stages. Practitioners working with offending agencies, schools and mediation services highlight the importance of visual interventions and these include the use of film, video and photography (e.g. the Heartstone projects, www.heartstone.co.uk/). Another innovation is the growing use of mediation and restorative techniques (Gavrielides *et al.* 2008). One of the more powerful exercises, named the *community project,* in DAPP relies on the practitioners to design a project which will involve the offender in their diversity journey. A senior probation officer in Liverpool used to send offenders down to the docks to walk the slave trade trail and then report back to her on that experience. In Greenwich, offenders go to the Racial Attack Monitoring Unit to meet staff working with victims and are confronted with an emotive photo collage illustrating the cost of racial hatred. The Heartstone project (*ibid.*) helps pupils and offenders to consider different perceptions and elements of their communities in an effort to promote pride and develop concern. It also encourages empathy and awareness, challenges ignorance and denial and facilitates changing the view of events and communities. The perpetrators of prejudice are thus encouraged to progress on their own diversity journey.

In this chapter, we have considered the development of hate crimes and means to tackle them. We pointed to pertinent legislation in England and Wales, highlighting some of the approaches taken elsewhere. We have tried to elucidate some of the complexity of this field. Differential definition, low reporting rates and lack of nuance in interventions have all too frequently failed victims and offenders. However, we hope that we have also demonstrated that as reporting rates, prosecutions and convictions rise, the numbers of interventions made will increase and there will be better scope for dealing with hate crimes more appropriately. As we conclude this chapter, it is worth reiterating the importance of moving beyond criminal justice (Perry 2003) and engaging at the local level. As Hall reminds us, 'We should perhaps take a step back and carefully consider what it is that we are responding to in order to ensure that our efforts are appropriate, effective and above all built upon solid foundations' (2005: 239).

Note

1 www.lemosandcrane.co.uk/raceactionnet/login.php, accessed April 2009.

References

ACPO (Association of Chief Police Officers) (2005) *Hate Crime: Delivering a Better Service. Good practice and tactical guidance*. London: ACPO.

Allport, G.W. (1945/1979) *The Nature of Prejudice*. Reading, MA: Addison-Wesley.

Beck, A.T. (1999) *Prisoners of Hate: The Cognitive Basis of Anger, Hostility and Violence.* HarperCollins.

Bell, Michael and Associates (2006) *Crime and Prejudice. The Support Needs of Victims of Hate Crime: a research report*. London: Victim Support.

Bem, S.L. (1993) *The Lenses of Gender: Transforming the Debate on Sexual Inequality*. London: Yale University Press.

Boeckmann, R.J and Turpin-Petrosino, C. (2002) 'Understanding the harm of hate crime', *Journal of Social Issues*, 58 (2): 207–25.

Bowling B. (1998) *Violent Racism Victimization, Policing and Social Context*. Oxford: Clarendon Press.

Brewer, M.B. (1999) 'The psychology of prejudice: ingroup love and outgroup hate?', *Journal of Social Issues*, 55 (3): 429–44.

Burney, E. and Rose, G. (2002) *Racist Offences: "How is the Law Working?"* Home Office Research Study 244. London: Home Office Research Development and Statistics Directorate.

Cantle, T. (2001) *Community Cohesion: A Report of the Independent Review Team*. London: Home Office.

Carroll, G. (1998) 'Mundane extreme environmental stress and African American families: a case for recognizing different realities', *Journal of Comparative Family Studies*, 29: 271–84.

Chahal, K. and Julienne, L. (1999) *We Can't All Be White. Racist victimisation in the* UK. York: Joseph Rowntree Foundation.

Cowan, G., Resendez, M., Marshall, E. and Quist, R. (2002) 'Hate speech and constitutional protection: priming values of equality and freedom', *Journal of Social Issues*, 58 (2): 247–63.

Court. D. (2003) 'Direct work with racially motivated offenders', *Probation Journal*, 50 (1): 52–8.

CPS (2005) *Guidance on Prosecuting More Cases of Racist and Religious Violence*. London: Crown Prosecution Service, www.cps.gov.uk/publications/prosecution/rrpbcrpol.html (accessed May 2009).

CPS (2007a) *Policy for Prosecuting Cases of Homophobic and Transphobic Crime*. London: Crown Prosecution Service, www.cps.gov.uk/publications/docs/htc_policy.pdf (accessed May 2009).

CPS (2007b) *Guidance on Prosecuting Cases of Homophobic and Transphobic Crime*. London: Crown Prosecution Service, www.cps.gov.uk/publications/docs/htc_guidance.pdf (accessed May 2009).

CPS (2007c) *Policy for Prosecuting Cases of Disability Hate Crime*. London: Crown Prosecution Service, www.cps.gov.uk/publications/docs/disability_hate_crime_policy.pdf (accessed May 2009).

CPS (2007d) *Guidance on Prosecuting Cases of Disability Hate Crime*. London: Crown Prosecution Service, www.cps.gov.uk/publications/docs/disability_hate_crime_guidance.pdf (accessed May 2009).

CPS (2008) *First Annual Hate Crime Report 2007–8*. Available at www.cps.gov.uk/Publications/docs/CPS_hate_crime_report_2008.pdf

Dick, S. (2008). *Homophobic Hate Crime: The Gay British Crime Survey 2008*. London: Stonewall.

Dixon, L. (2002) 'Tackling racist offending: a targeted or generalised approach?', *Probation Journal*, 49 (3): 205–16.

Dixon, L. and Court, D. (2003) 'Developing good practice with racially motivated offenders', *Probation Journal*, 50 (2): 149–53.

Dixon, L. and Otikpitpki, T. (1999) 'Working with racially motivated offenders', *Probation Journal*, 46 (3): 157–63.

Dixon, L. and Ray, L. (2007) 'Current issues and developments in race hate crime', *Probation Journal*, 54 (2): 109–24.

Garcia, L. and McDevitt, J. (1999) *The Psychological and Behavioral Effects of Bias and Non Bias Motivated Assault*. Washington, DC: US Department of Justice, National Institute of Justice.

Gavrielides, T., Parle, L., Salla, A., Liberatore, G., Mavadia, C. and Arjomand, G. (2008) *Addressing Hate Crime Through Restorative Justice And Cross-Sector Partnerships: A London Study*. London: ROTA.

Giannasi, P. (2008) 'Hate Crime. Race for Justice.' Presentation given to the Hate Crimes Symposium. London: Middlesex University. www.mdx.ac.uk/fps (accessed May 2009).

Hall, N. (2002) *Policing Racist Hate Crime in London: Policy, Practice and Experience after the Stephen Lawrence Inquiry*. Research report for the Metropolitan Police Service.

Hall, N. (2005) *Hate Crime*. Cullompton: Willan Publishing.

Hall, N. (2006) 'Proactive anti-racism', *Police Professional*, 49: 21–4.

Hall, N. (2007) *Making Sense of Numbers: The Social Construction of Hate Crime in London and New York*. Vienna: European Monitoring Centre on Racism and Xenophobia.

Herek, G.M., Cogan, J.C. and Gillis, J.R. (2002) 'Victim experiences in hate crimes based on sexual orientation', *Journal of Social Issues*, 58 (2): 319–39.

Her Majesty's Inspectorate of Probation (2000) *Thematic Inspection Report: Towards Race Equality*. London: HMIP. www.justice.gov.uk/inspectorates/hmi-probation/docs/hmiprobthematicracefulldoc-rps.pdf (accessed December 2009).

Hewitt, R. (1996) *Routes of Racism. The social basis of racist attack*. Stoke-on-Trent: Trentham Books.

Hewitt, R. (2005) *White Backlash and the Politics of Multiculturalism*. Cambridge: Cambridge University Press.

Home Affairs Committee (1994) *Racial Attacks and Harassment*. London: HMSO Volumes 1 and 2.

Home Office (1981) *Racial Attacks: Report of a Home Office Study*. London: Home Office.

Home Office (1989) *The Response to Racial Attacks and Harassment. Guidance for statutory agencies Report of the Inter-Departmental Racial Attacks Group*. London: Home Office.

Home Office Police Standards Unit and ACPO (2005) *Hate Crime: Delivering a Quality Service. Good practice and tactical guidance.* www.acpo.police.uk/asp/policies/Data/Hate%20Crime.pdf (accessed May 2009).

House of Commons (1986) *Racial Attacks and Harassment*. Third report from the Home Affairs Committee, Session 1985–86. London: HMSO.

Iganski, P. (1999) 'Why make hate a crime?', *Critical Social Policy*, 19 (3): 386–95.

Iganski, P. (ed.) (2002) *The Hate Debate*. London: Profile.

Iganski, P. (2007) *Evaluation of the London-Wide Race Hate Crime Forum as a model of good practice between statutory criminal justice agencies and the voluntary sector non governmental organisations*. London: London Probation Service.

Iganski, P. (2008a) *Hate Crime and the City*. Bristol: The Policy Press.

Iganski, P. (2008b) 'Criminal law and the routine activity of "hate crime"', *Liverpool Law Review*, 29 (1): 1–17.

Isal, S. (2005) *Preventing Racist Violence: Work with Actual and Potential Perpetrators – Learning from Practice to Policy Change*. The Runnymede Trust. www.runnymedetrust.org/publications/23/167.html (accessed May 2009).

Jacobs, J.B. and Potter, K.A. (1998) *Hate Crime, Criminal Law and Identity Politics*. New York, NY: Oxford University Press.

Keith, B. (2006) Return to an Address of the Honourable the House of Commons dated 29th June 2006 for the Report of The Zahid Mubarek Inquiry ordered by the House of Commons to be printed 29th June 2006. HC 1082-I. London: The Stationery Office. report.zahidmubarekinquiry.org.uk/volume_one.pdf (accessed May 2009).

Kelly, L. (1987) 'The continuum of sexual violence', in J. Hammer and M. Maynard (eds) *Women, Violence and Social Control*. Basingstoke: Macmillan.

Kershaw, C., Nicholas, S. and Walker, A. (eds) (2008) *Crime in England and Wales 2007/8. Findings from the British Crime Survey and Police Recorded Crime*. London: Home Office RDS. www.homeoffice.gov.uk/rds/pdfs08/hosb0708.pdf (accessed May 2009).

Lemos, G. (2000) *Racial Harassment: Action on the Ground*. London/York: Lemos and Crane/Joseph Rowntree Foundation.

Levin, B. (2002) 'From slavery to hate crime laws: the emergence of race and status-based protection in American criminal law', *Journal of Social Issues*, 58 (2): 227–45.

Macpherson, Sir W. (1999) *The Stephen Lawrence Inquiry*. London: The Stationery Office.

McDevitt, J., Levin, J. and Bennett, S. (2002) 'Hate crime offenders and extended typology', *Journal of Social Issues*, 58 (2): 303–18.

McDonald, Sir K. (2008) *Prosecuting Disability Hate Crime*. www.cps.gov.uk/news/articles/dhc_dpp_speech/ (accessed May 2009).

McGhee, D. (2005) *Intolerant Britain: Hate, Citizenship and Difference*. Milton Keynes: Open University Press and McGraw-Hill.

Mencap (2000) *Living in Fear*. www.mencap.org.uk/document.asp?id=1670 (accessed May 2009).

MIND (2007) *Another Assault*. London: Mind, The National Association for Mental Health.

Nielsen, L.B. (2002) 'Subtle, pervasive, harmful: racist and sexist remarks in public as hate speech', *Journal of Social Issues*, 58 (2): 265–80.

Orr, D. (2008) 'We must protect disabled people against this wave of barbaric and hateful crimes: he died in his mother's arms, so badly beaten that his uncle did not at first recognise his face', *The Independent*, 30 January. www.independent.co.uk/opinion/commentators/deborah-orr/deborah-orr-we-must-protect-disabled-people-against-this-wave-of-barbaric-and-hateful-crimes-775617.html (accessed May 2009).

OSCE (Organization for Security and Co-operation in Europe) (2009) *Hate Crime Laws. A Practical Guide.* Warsaw: Office for Democratic Institutions and Human Rights, OSCE.

Ousley, H. (2001) *Community Pride not Prejudice: Making Diversity Work in Bradford*. Bradford: Bradford Vision.

Perry, B. (2001) *In the Name of Hate*. New York: Routledge.

Perry, B. (2003) 'Where do we go from here? Researching hate crime', *Internet Journal of Criminology*. www.internetjournalofcriminology.com/Where%20Do%20We%20Go%20From%20Here.%20Researching%20Hate%20Crime.pdf (accessed November 2007).

Putnam, R.D. (2007) 'E pluribus unum: diversity and community in the twenty-first century. The 2006 Johan Skytte Prize Lecture', *Scandinavian Political Studies*, 30 (2): 137–74.

Ray, L., Smith, D. and Wastell, L. (2004) 'Shame rage and racist violence', *British Journal of Criminology*, 44 (3): 350–68.

Sibbitt, R. (1997) *The Perpetrators of Racial Harassment and Racial Violence.* Research Study 176. London: Home Office.

Tajfel, H. and Turner, J.C. (1986) 'The social identity theory of intergroup behavior', in S. Worchel and W.G. Austin (eds) *Psychology of Intergroup Relations* (pp. 7–24) Chicago: Nelson-Hall Publishers.

Turpin-Petrosino, C. (2002) 'Hateful sirens … who hears their song? An examination of student attitudes toward hate groups and affiliation potential', *Journal of Social Issues*, 58 (2): 281–301.

Verkuyten, M. (2007) 'Ethnic in-group favoritism among minority and majority groups: testing the self-esteem hypothesis among preadolescents', *Journal of Applied Social Psychology*, 37 (3): 486–500.

Victim Support (2006) *Crime and Prejudice. The Support Needs of Victims of Hate Crime: a Research Report*. London: Michael Bell Associates for Victim Support.

Vincent, F., Radford, K., Jarman, N., Martynowicz, A. and Rallings, M.-K. (2009) *Hate Crime against People with Disabilities: A baseline study of experiences in Northern Ireland*, www.ofmdfmni.gov.uk/hate_crime_against_people_with_disabilities__pdf_760kb_.pdf

Section 6

Punishment and Corrections

In Chapter 22, Sarah Marsden opens this section by exploring the broadening out of the reach of the criminal sanction and its purposes. She explores the philosophy of punishment and how it is perceived by wider society. This chapter provides a context for the subsequent chapters by Nancy Loucks and Lisa Marzano wherein we explore in more depth the effects of imprisonment. Those who are incarcerated can be seen as the bedraggled, disempowered and disenfranchised. As such it should not be surprising that we see histories of abuse and trauma alongside women's offending behaviours. Recognition of this led to previous government aims to reduce the numbers of women in prison. In Chapter 23, Nancy Loucks takes us through some of the key issues around women's imprisonment and provides us with an updated and revised version of her chapter in the first edition.

In a new contribution, Lisa Marzano explores in more depth issues around women's and men's self-harming behaviours in prison. She sets these behaviours within previous reviews and looks again at the meaning of the behaviours for the prisoners engaging in them. Estimates that up to a third of prisoners have engaged in self-harm should indicate the extent of this problem. They also point to the kinds of broader issues around coping strategies and institutionalisation that are relevant when considering how to integrate an offender back into society after release.

Chapter 25 is another new contribution, that considers issues of release, reintegration and recidivism. Ros Burnett has provided an account both of policy and impact and considers how realistic our expectations are of prisoners as they approach life beyond the gate.

Once again, our last chapter comes from Graham Towl, this time written as a reflection on his time both working with and managing psychological policy within prisons. His wide-ranging appraisal encompasses mistakes of the past, points to areas currently in need of addressing and provides additional signposts as to how we can develop our profession further.

Chapter 22

What role does punishment play in deterring crime? Practical, theoretical and ethical perspectives

Sarah Marsden

> Deterrence is a principle with much immediate appeal ... but much crime is committed on impulse, given the opportunity presented by an open window or an unlocked door, and it is committed by offenders who live from moment to moment; their crimes are as impulsive as the rest of their feckless, sad or pathetic lives.
>
> (Home Office 1990: 6, cited in Tonry 2004: 34)

Punishment is a concept of great practical and symbolic significance (Garland 2006), about which there are complex and consequential political, sociological and moral debates (Garland 1991). State-sanctioned punishment has evolved considerably down the ages, moving from the gruesome 'blood sanctions' of medieval Europe, to the use of imprisonment and the modern-day penitentiary. The nature of punishment has therefore seen a move from a mother convicted of infanticide being buried alive and impaled, to the present-day focus on loss of freedom as punishment (Langbein 1976). Some argue the decline in public punishment in the seventeenth century has been ascribed to an exhibition of humanitarian thinking; however, others, among them Foucault, argue that the aim was actually one of social control to prevent the pain and revolt of the masses (Foucault 1977; Spierenburg 1998). Some propose that this application of control continues, with contemporary society seeing an integral system of restraints built into its fabric (Rose 2000).

The role of punishment as a deterrent will be approached from two distinct angles. Following an exposition of the theoretical debates surrounding the concept and its operation within the criminal justice system, its function will be assessed via traditional and critical perspectives. The role of punishment in crime reduction will be considered with a view to critically assessing the current state of knowledge with respect to its efficacy, and related pragmatic and ethical dimensions. Discussion will then move on to the evolving discourse surrounding deterrence and punishment.

It will be presented that the traditional conceptualisation of punishment as deterrence is becoming supplemented by an increasingly built-in set of deterrent strategies. The 'responsibilisation' of the population, with an emphasis on risk, and increasingly designed in systems of control, is interpreted as an exhibition of the conceptual emphasis now placed on the prevention of crime. This is arguably a result of the failure of *post hoc* punishment as a sufficient deterrent, and can be related to increasing political homogeneity, where traditional dichotomies of ideology and approach traditionally defined as 'left' and 'right' are being merged, seeing the use of 'warehousing versus correctional reform [and] punishment and stigmatisation versus integration' (O'Malley 1999: 176) leading to an incoherent approach to crime control.

Thus, it will be presented that punishment is being transmuted into an increasingly opaque system of integral preventatives. This leaves the rationalised subject of the discourse deterred without consciousness, but with complicity in its occurrence and the concept that 'walls are terrible, but man is good' (Blouet 1843, cited in Foucault 1977: 239) ultimately inverted. The effect of this will be presented as a redefinition of traditional criteria of punishment and a related impact of net-widening. The corollary of this is a perceptual and administrative shift in the concept of crime, and hence, by definition, an increase in its incidence.

Political and public debate

Debate over punishment as a deterrent has witnessed conflicting opinions emerge in many societal spheres. The complex interaction between politics, policy, public opinion and academic inquiry has seen divergent views promulgated (Ball 1955) ranging across all aspects of the process of punishment. This includes the appropriate degree of punishment, who has the right to dictate it, and to what extent public opinion should be incorporated into decision-making (e.g. Fickling 2006). A further question has revolved around the most appropriate style of intervention (Daly 2002; Nagin 1998) and debates around efficacy (Beyleveld 1979). These concerns are historically embedded, the underlying rationale of punishment having been debated through the centuries (Bentham 1798; Kant 1785). The situating of the academic is also a subject of contemporary debate, with a cross-disciplinary approach called for, combining normative and explanatory theory to address the issue (Braithwaite 2000a).

The importance of punishment as a deterrent concept can be seen in its position as a core principle of governance: '[to] ensure we can protect the public, and turn offenders' lives around in a way that cuts re-offending and makes the country safer' (Home Office 2006: 8). The deterrent potential of punishment is particularly pertinent where crime is high on the public agenda and the results of government intervention are equivocal (Cunliffe and Shepherd 2007). In addition, the psychological effects of victimisation are considerable (Resick 1987), and the concept of punishment as compensation for distress caused is enshrined in the legal framework (Ashworth 1986).

The political rhetoric associated with this debate has been described as ignoble (Tonry 2004). One of the consequences of this can be argued to reflect a process of 'othering' (Garland 1996) and a 'return of the dangerous classes' (Gordon 1994), a term which refers to social outsiders deemed to represent moral failure, positioned beyond the realm of an otherwise cohesive and integrated society (Morris 1994). A factor impacting on this phenomenon may be the emphasis on risk-based policy, which has crucially altered the polemic such that 'punishment loses its privileged status as a strategy to be deployed in the ordering of security' (Shearing 2001: 217). This has been presented as part of the 'managerialism' (Brownlee 1998) inherent in contemporary criminal justice thinking.

Formal punishment is ultimately an expression of state policy, on which the effect of public opinion has been observed internationally (Roberts *et al.* 2002). Arguably, a cyclical process of information dissemination, assimilation and reaction can be deduced. In this conception, the media circulate unrepresentative criminal justice stories, for example, by dedicating disproportionate coverage to extreme offences (O'Connell 1999; Roberts and Doob 1990). Arguably, this contributes to an increasingly castigatory debate on crime control. This has a related impact on public perceptions, the nature of which, whilst not always consistent, are generally argued to be punitive (Cullen *et al.* 2000), although evidence suggests that this is based upon a poorly informed understanding of judicial sentencing (see Gray 2008 for a summary). These are surmised to become incorporated into policy as reflective of the general view, influenced by heightened media attention (Burstein 2003).

A related concern is that public knowledge of criminological matters is frequently inaccurate (Hough and Roberts 1999), and influenced by a public distrust of government (Zimring 2001; Zimring and Johnson 2006). Thus, it is possible to see a cycle perpetuated, resulting in increasingly castigatory measures and government intervention. One potential effect of this has been the burgeoning of a 'surveillance society' (*The Economist* 2007). Arguably, the outcome of these developments is demonstrated in the United Kingdom having a criminal justice system that is amongst the most punitive in the world (Tonry 2004). This can be further seen in the findings that England and Wales have the highest prison population totals in Western Europe (King's College London 2008).

Theoretical approaches to punishment

Punishment has traditionally been codified to encompass a number of elements. It must involve pain or other consequences normally considered unpleasant; it must involve an offence against legal rules; it must be of an actual or supposed offender for their offence; it must be intentionally administered by people other than the offender, and it must be imposed and administered by an authority constituted by a legal system against which the offence is committed (Benn 1958; Flew 1954; Hart 1968). Deterrence in its turn has historically been considered under two rubrics; that of special and general deterrence. The first has the aim of discouraging further acts of delinquency by the individual offender, with general deterrence aiming to encourage civilians not to commit acts of crime for fear of the potential consequences (Von Hirsch and Ashworth 1998).

The philosophical debate surrounding punishment and sanction has seen a variety of approaches proposed. Beccaria's (1764) *Of Crimes and Punishments* was arguably the first exposition of utilitarian thought and was seen as a response to those subject to public sanctions. This encompassed the concept of punishment as deterrence rather than recompense. Crystallised by Bentham, utilitarianism rests on the principle that 'nature has placed mankind under the governance of two sovereign masters, pain and pleasure' (Bentham 1798: 29). Hence, morality should be judged on what conveys the greatest pleasure for the greatest number. Deontological thought is the contra view, most famously espoused by Kant (1785), where punishment is essentially retributive and backward-looking; the offender suffers in proportion to the pain she or he has inflicted under the stipulations of a categorical imperative. Most criminal justice systems are eclectic, drawing from utilitarian and deontological traditions (Walker 1991). British sentencing is guided by 'two main philosophies ... "desert" which emphasises the need to make the punishment fit the crime so as to be "proportionate" and "commensurate"; and "utilitarian" which emphasises the achievement of practical outcomes such as crime reduction' (House of Commons 2002: 8).

Both ideologies have been criticised (see Walker 1991); however, a particular problem for the utilitarian tradition has been that this philosophical orientation could be used to justify punishing the innocent. This is the consequence of an analysis concluding that the greater good is served by punishing an individual who has done no wrong, if it is justified by its potential to maximise social utility. Take the example of someone who has been murdered from a particular ethnic group by someone from a different group. Without a scapegoat to frame for the crime, members of the group to which the victim belonged may act as vigilantes and attack innocent members of the other group. Here it could be argued that there would be greater social utility in framing an innocent person to prevent further violence (Ten 1991).

This debate is a contemporary one of considerable consequence; erosions of standards of evidence in certain circumstances have been reasoned to result in the potential for increased numbers of false convictions and hence the punishing of the innocent (Smilansky 1990). Arguably this has been seen in legislative changes, for example concerning Anti Social Behaviour Order which are subject to civil, not criminal standards of proof (Campbell 2002) and international legal changes relating to terrorist suspects (Welch 2004). It is here at the periphery of the criminal justice system – arguably with a focus on marginalised subjects – that ostensibly utilitarian concepts can be construed as being applied to enhance the power of the state and control over social interaction and autonomy (Brown 2004).

Practical operation of punishment

For state punishment to be set in motion the crime must be reported; this has been presented as a representation of the victim's feeling that public accountability is apposite (Stephenson 1992). Before any punishment can be imposed, it is first necessary for blame to be apportioned to the accused. The model of blame apportionment proposed by Shaver (1986) includes establishing harm done, and identification of a person responsible for its cause, about whom there is sufficient evidence to assess intent. This takes into account mitigation, including distal causes such as mental illness as well as proximate situational ones, such as provocation. Unless a sufficiently persuasive justification for the action in question is presented, blame is attributed and appropriate punishment decided. Internal attribution of blame has been shown to indicate more punitive, retributive attitudes towards disposal in both 'lay people' and criminal justice professionals (Cullen *et al.* 1985).

Historically, sentencing was a matter of substantial judicial discretion which is now characterised by the content, source, authority, style and mechanics of guidance (Von Hirsch and Ashworth 1998). In the United Kingdom, considerations in determining a sentence include punishment, deterrence, rehabilitation, public protection and reparation as aims (Criminal Justice Act 2003). A variety of options are available with respect to punitive sanctions; discharge, fine, community sentence or custodial prison sentence, by far the most common being financial penalties (Home Office 2004). Public opinion about these issues encompasses representations of the victim's needs and those of society, as well as judgements of punishment and social exclusion (Oswald *et al.* 2002). Some have argued that these responses are evolutionarily based, where punishment takes a reparatory role stemming from an evolutionary bias towards moral outrage (Walsh 2000). However, whilst broadly punitive in nature, public opinion has been found to incorporate more progressive approaches to offenders (Cullen *et al.* 2000).

Another important influence in the practice of sentencing is the operation of the 'legal complex' (Rose and Valverde 1991). Increasing guilty pleas via sentence reduction has been argued to result in a form of complicity between defendant and court where the 'system can be tuned to *produce* guilt by providing lesser sanctions … for those that plead guilty' (Indermaur 1996: 18, italics in original). It has also been suggested that the increasing number of offenders receiving custodial sentences is due to the downgrading of charges resulting in greater conviction rates (Millie *et al.* 2003). This is argued to have the related effect of sentencers believing certain crimes are becoming qualitatively worse and hence imposing more punitive sanctions (Millie *et al.* 2003). Thus, some influences on punishment and disposal can be seen as systemically originated and a result of the focus on the efficiency of the process rather than the delivery of justice (O'Malley 1999).

It has been presented that the historically rooted debate over punishment and deterrence has incorporated punitive and rehabilitative aims; and, additionally, that utilitarian principles may be applied to the concept of crime, arguably increasing the scope of deviant behaviour and by definition its incidence. Discussion will now turn from the process, influences and justifications of punishment to its practical role as deterrent and the question of 'what works'. This will encapsulate consideration of the practical, ethical and methodological issues at play in its assessment and application.

'What works?'

'With a few isolated exceptions, the rehabilitative efforts that have been reported so far have had no appreciable effect on recidivism' (Martinson 1974: 25). Although this pronouncement was later modified (Martinson 1979), it can be construed as the prevailing opinion of many criminal justice thinkers (Garland 1991). Alternative views espouse the increase in crime on the occasion of police strikes (Andenaes 1974) as an overarching justification of the success of the criminal justice system. More nuanced evaluation has taken a variety of forms (Welsh and Farrington 2001) and produced conflicting conclusions. For example, consideration has encompassed initiatives such as 'boot camps', which were found to be ineffective in the majority of cases (MacKenzie *et al.* 2001). Ultimate conclusions as to the effectiveness of deterrence range from: 'there exists no scientific basis for expecting that a general deterrence policy … will do anything to control the crime rate' (Beyleveld 1979: 136); to: 'the combined deterrent and incapacitation effect generated by the collective actions of the police, courts, and prison system is very large' (Nagin 1998: 366).

There are a variety of ways in which deterrence may work on individuals, and more broadly on society. It has been reasoned that deterrence can operate by way of preventing recidivism through the temporal or spatial displacement of crime, and through a general stabilisation or reduction of crime rates (Beyleveld 1979). In line with general and special deterrence, this can be seen to operate on those who have not yet committed an offence. This may therefore be operationalised through preventative measures, or via the perceived impact of punishment upon others. Alternatively, deterrence through the infliction of punishment on the individual can be assessed via recidivism rates, with which there are considerable methodological problems (Lloyd *et al.* 1994; Maltz [1984] 2001). One aspect of the deterrent effect found relatively consistently, however, is that certainty as opposed to severity of punishment has the greatest impact upon crime prevention (Von Hirsch *et al.* 1999).

Official figures for England and Wales state that recidivism rates have remained relatively stable over recent years, fluctuating around 55 per cent (Cunliffe and Shepherd 2007). Within this, there has been a considerable increase in the use of community sentences, with an almost inverse decline in the use of fines (Solomon and Rutherford 2007). Statistically, recidivism in those given community orders is asserted to be lower overall (Cuncliffe and Shepherd 2007), with other research indicating that prison does not operate as a deterrent (Burnett and Maruna 2004). However, results from a systematic review of reoffending have been equivocal, with comparisons of different interventions offering no significant differences in recidivism (Villettaz *et al.* 2006). Complex interactions are argued to be present within the social aspect of the prison context, having differential impacts on recidivism (Windzio 2006). For example, it has been found that the more isolated an individual prisoner, the lower the rate of recidivism and the more afraid an individual is of other prisoners, the higher the rate of recidivism (Windzio 2006).

Further work has observed a positive deterrent effect of targeted interventions through the use of 'crackdowns' on particular issues, although considerable decay has been observed (Ross 1982). Another finding is that hypothesised displacement effects have been found to be relatively rare, and that unintended positive crime reduction benefits were seen in areas that were not the subject of 'hot spot' policing (Braga 2001), illustrating the nuanced nature of interventions.

Mediating factors in the offending process are argued to originate from a number of sources (Blackburn 1995). These include a lower perception of risk of apprehension in those who have pro-criminal attitudes and behaviours (Horney and Marshall 1992). The effects of shame have also been considered (Braithwaite 2000b). This argument proposes that societies which communicate shame about crime effectively have lower crime rates and vice versa (Braithwaite 2000b). Also implicated is the salience of informal social controls, such as family and peer sanctions on criminal behaviour (Bazemore 2001). In addition, group processes and defiance based on perceptions of unfairness (Sherman 1993) as well as levels of personal morality and legislative authority (Tryer 1990) are posited as influential.

Perceptual deterrent studies looking at the effect of certainty and severity of punishment have been widely applied to the issue (Paternoster 1987). However, methodological criticisms have been made of their operationalisation; specifically, that the complex psychological processes involved in individual responses to deterrence are not fully recognised in these studies (Williams and Hawkins 1986). Psychometric testing for recidivism has also met with limited success, with measures contributing only a small degree to the prediction of reoffending (Cumberland and Boyle 1997). The outcomes of these studies go some way to illustrating the intricate nature of individual experiences of imprisonment, and the related problem of assessing deterrent effect.

Disagreements about the efficacy of deterrence are argued to stem from the difficulty of assessing its effects (Walker 1991). Issues contributing to this include methodological inadequacies and the difficulty of isolating the appropriate criteria for identifying deterrence effects (Beyleveld 1979). Other views are that deterrence is a variable process affecting individuals differentially (Andenaes 1974). This implies that a micro rather than macro examination is necessary. This may be considered particularly important as it has been presented that reporting aggregates may mask any specific deterrent effect at the individual level (Walker 1991). A further, related issue is that cumulative punishment levels have been found not to impact upon individual conceptualisations of punishment (Kleck *et al.* 2005), casting doubt on the notion and process of general deterrence.

The static nature of reoffending rates indicates that the various interventions applied by the state have a limited impact on recidivism. Further, that any work should be carried out cognisant of differential individual responses and mediating factors on deterrence effects, and that these issues are compounded by problems surrounding effective measurement. A balanced approach to the issue is therefore warranted, incorporating an understanding of the wider impacts of affecting deterrence.

Ethical considerations in the application of punishment

The potential negative effects of attempts to reduce recidivism and offending should be weighed particularly carefully, as they raise the possibility of causing harm. From the application of the death penalty to the wider impacts on offenders and their families, the outcomes of state intervention are highly consequential and deserve careful consideration.

One of the most prevalent explicators of criminal behaviour is that practised by econometricians who base their assessments upon the assumption that 'most potential criminals are sufficiently rational to be deterrable' (Posner 1985: 1285). The decision to commit crime is argued to be the result of a cost–benefit analysis: the potential reward against the probability of being caught and sentenced (Cornish and Clarke 1986). It has been presented that this conceptualisation neglects the social embeddedness of human experience, in addition to the wider social and context effects implicated in human behavioural processes (Norrie 1986). This conceptualisation has also spurred a number of arguments, one of the more controversial of which includes a hypothesised reduction in murders through the application of capital punishment (Ehrlich 1975). Whilst this has been criticised for methodological and conceptual flaws (Brier and Feinberg 1980), the ethical implications of an uncritical acceptance of the foundation of this argument are considerable.

A further issue of ethical concern and one of considerable topicality is prison overcrowding and its effects. A variety of methods to deal with the issue have been proposed, ranging from the building of 'Titan' jails, to a reduction in incarceration (Hough and Solomon 2008). It has been argued that both longer sentences and the propensity to apply incarceration as a punishment (Millie *et al*. 2003) contribute to the considerable prison overcrowding; prisoner numbers now having exceeded the system's capacity (Home Office 2007). Arguably, this illustrates the positioning of one sentencing aim over another; rehabilitative efforts are significantly hampered in a system that may not adequately be able to cater for its wards. This is particularly pertinent where rehabilitative efforts have been seen to be efficacious only where high-risk members of the population are identified, and therapy is focused on criminogenic needs appropriately tailored for the individual (Andrew *et al*. 1990).

Translating debate from America, the possibility of 'armies of ex-prisoners' (Currie 1998: 30) released insufficiently prepared for reintegration into the community is one which makes the role of the psychologist particularly challenging. This is especially salient where the initiation of therapeutic measures may be harmful if curtailed (Howells and Day 2007), thus raising the possibility of ethical practice being brought into conflict with wider structural parameters. These issues also raise questions of attribution of responsibility for failures in rehabilitation. If treatment is designated a part of the prevailing system of punishment, an argument could be made that recidivism as a result of the failure of rehabilitative aims can be ascribed to the state.

Further ethical discussions have surrounded the possible negative psychological effects that prison may induce in its inhabitants – both prisoners and prison officers (Irwin 2005; Light 1991; O'Donnell and Edgar 1999). Historically, the view proposed is that prison induces methods of coping (Richards 1978), with little evidence of long-term harm (Sapsford 1978). However, particular needs have been identified within the prison population that are said to be ill-met by current organisational systems, and research within the field has been criticised as incomplete (Gendreau *et al.* 1999). In particular, the needs of members of ethnic minorities, those with learning difficulties, those in segregation units, as well as other minority groups, are considered ill-addressed (Liebling and Maruna 2004; Miller 1994). Additionally, some of these groups' mental health requirements have been identified as divergent from other elements of the population hence requiring particular attention and resources (Royal College of Psychiatrists 2007).

The background, characteristics and familial responsibilities of particular relevance to the female offender population result in a different set of ethical concerns (Loucks 2004, and see Chapter 23 of this volume). This raises the concomitant issue of unintended punishment inflicted on those not guilty of an offence (Walker 1991). This is particularly pertinent, as the negative effects on children of having care-givers in prison has been highlighted (Boswell 2002; Cadell and Crisp 1997). Thus 'the task of adjudicating who is reformable and who is irredeemable' (Vaughan 2000: 86) is one which conveys acute practical and ethical concerns.

Consideration thus far has been given to the empirical, instrumental effects of punishment as deterrence and its ethical implications. The view taken is that traditional concepts of sentencing and punishment have had only a limited effect on reducing crime. Attention will now turn to the broader role of punishment in deterrence, encompassing discussion of the wider sociology of punishment (Garland 1991).

Governance and punishment

Formal punishment is a responsibility of the state and, as considered in the political and public debates discussed above, it may be considered a 'condensation symbol' for society's concerns (Lyons and Scheingold 2000). This can be considered a powerful motif in the wider socio-political sphere (Garland 1991). Thus the proposal that the ability of the state to protect its citizens against crime, in particular through the use of punishment as deterrence, is a failed project (Garland 1996) is one of considerable salience. This is particularly marked as it has been further posited that the admittance of such a failure would result in a questioning of the legitimacy of the system and its humanitarian corollaries (Currie 1998).

The oscillating discourse surrounding the crime and punishment debate has been presented as contradictory, with conflicting agendas and ideologies revolving around the varying application of discipline, punishment, incapacitation, restitution and reintegration (O'Malley 1999, 2002). A number of explanations for this incoherence have been presented (O'Malley 1999), including that of a 'nostalgia' (Simon 1995) for past methods of punitive action. A further interpretation is that as a consequence of the limits of the sovereign state to successfully address the issue of crime, there is a denial of responsibility. Thus, punishment is used as a show of strength, but may alternatively be conceived as a technique illustrative of weak authority and inadequate controls (Garland 1996).

Explanation has also considered the sometimes uncomfortable amalgam of political orientation and conflicting ideologies. Discourses and practices of the traditional 'left' and 'right' are hereby incorporated into a 'New Right' penality (O'Malley 1999). Thus, the retributive ideologies associated with particular political perspectives are being incorporated with conflicting rehabilitative models. One consequence of this is said to be a cycling through of historically applied remedies (O'Malley 1999; Rose 2000; Simon 1995) in an attempt to address the recurrent problem of crime and punishment. For example: 'incapacitation and warehousing versus reintegration, [and] formal criminalisation versus informal victim/offender settlements' (O'Malley 1999: 176) which are described as at best inconsistent, and at times contradictory (O'Malley 1999).

Criminologies of everyday life

The proposal that deterrent strategies have been insufficiently effective in reducing crime is arguably related to a change in their application and approach, with increasing numbers of people affected by their operation. Thus, it is posited that the site of punishment and deterrence is being subverted via the 'normalisation' of crime (Garland 1996). This shifts the perception of crime from extraordinary to commonplace, with the actor an 'illicit, opportunistic consumer' (*ibid.*: 451) capable of delinquency according to actuarial forms of risk assessment (Garland 1997). Thus, the project of deterrence and the notion of criminal expand. This is based on the subject as a rational actor who makes cost–benefit analyses of risk (Cornish and Clarke 1986) and implies that everyone is a potential criminal. A result of this is argued to be the infliction of punishment upon all as a regulatory strategy (Shearing 2001). This is enacted via related impacts on freedom of determination, movement and society. There is therefore an inversion of punishment's role as deterrent such that it becomes an integral part of daily existence for everyone, as opposed to the intermittent presence of traditional deterrence strategies.

Crime as a risk to be calculated is presented as part of the 'criminologies of everyday life', where deviance as normal invokes 'supply side criminology' (Garland 1996). In this conceptualisation, the number of opportunities to commit crime are reduced by creating disincentives, and enhancing the risks associated with criminality. The result of this is argued to be a 'new penology' (Feeley and Simon 1992) which has as its focus regulation of levels of deviance and risk reduction. As the shift takes place from retributive to risk logic, the conflict between the two systems is argued to be mediated via the practice of restorative justice (Shearing 2001).

The focus on restoring 'a balance between the interests of the victim and the offender' in restorative justice (Miers 2001: 13) has arguably been subverted into a potentially more insidious form of punitive measure. Its attraction has been said to lie in its appeal as a theoretical framework without punishment as a referent (Roach 2000). However, similarities between retributive and restorative justice have been identified and their consequences questioned (Daly 2002). One issue raised is the responsibilisation of the actors through the application of normative estimates of moral reasoning and a lack of appreciation of the social embeddedness of the aetiology of their behaviour. This is argued to result in an attempt at 'moral restructuring through the restorative justice process' (Gray 2005: 954). Thus the endeavour has had the effect of enforcing social norms and informal processes of approbation and control. One example of this would be reintegrative shaming (Braithwaite 1989), which aims to communicate disapproval to a transgressor in a way which encourages them not to commit a similar act again.

The control and responsibilisation implicated with the subversion of the principles of restorative justice are seen on a larger scale in the development of 'governable spaces' (Rose and Valverde 1991). Here, both crime and the potential criminal are strategically controlled and modified (Rose and Valverde 1991). Surveillance is 'designed in'; both into the fabric of technologies and architecture, and also into the processes of human interaction. Thus '[c]ommunity … is itself a *means* of government' (Rose 2000: 329; italics in original) and the 'shadow of the law' (Rose and Valverde 1991: 550) is present in all aspects of life holding the power of sanction.

Alongside these developments is a 'responsibilisation strategy' or 'control society' (Garland 1996; Rose 2000) where accountability is dispersed through individuals, families, communities and wider organisations. This shifts responsibility for crime control away from the state. The result is the invocation of the citizenry in the process of 'target hardening' and risk reduction, resulting in 'governance at a distance' (Garland 1997). Therefore, it may be considered that the site and object of punishment are shifting as a result of the failure of traditional punitive measures. The incorporation of new technologies of control, a mentality of risk, and the translation of the site of responsibility into the community has arguably resulted in overt measures of governmental deterrence being gradually relocated into the community via social and structural processes.

Conclusions

It has been presented that the role of punishment as a deterrent is one upon which many spheres of influence operate, with historical debates gaining contemporary salience through the interaction of government, media and society. Through a historical exposition of rationales of punishment, alternate influences within the criminal justice system were discussed, focusing on a widening conceptualisation of legality and a shift in the criteria involved in the dispensation of justice. Additionally, it was pointed out that structural pressures may result in the downgrading of *a priori* concepts of justice for bureaucratic and administrative aims.

Consideration was then given to the efficacy of punishment as an instrumental crime deterrence strategy, and suggested intervening factors in the process of criminal activity were discussed. The reported evidence, whilst equivocal, suggested that punitive measures imposed by the state have not been successful in combating crime. The concomitant ethical and practical correlates were then examined, highlighting issues resulting from an increasingly punitive system of crime control lacking the necessary infrastructure.

A broader conceptualisation of punishment as deterrence was then discussed, with the argument presented that through a variety of state-led strategies, punishment is arguably being imposed as part of a programme of wider deterrence founded on the premise of risk. Thus it has been reasoned that through the alteration of the discourse and practice of crime control as a result of the traditional system's failure, the concept of punishment has been augmented, and now affects the lives of a much wider population.

To return to the criteria outlined in the exposition (Benn 1958; Flew 1954; Hart 1968) the concept of 'offence' has been widened with increasing spheres of behaviour being determined as illegal. It can also be asserted that the concept of intentionality has been subverted. From comparatively transparent methods of crime control targeted on actual offenders, the argued responsibilisation of the populace via an overarching discourse of individual and group accountability has resulted in a loss of both its intentionality to focus punishment on the offender, and the legitimacy of its being administered via a publicly accountable authority.

Therefore the role of punishment in deterring crime can be presented as mediated through the redefinition of its concept. Due to structural, societal and political influences, the historical notion of punishment has been distended and subverted. The consequent net-widening effect can be envisaged to increase levels of crime due to a widening of its definition, mitigating any deterrent effect it may have, making it ever less likely that:

> Every man, whoever he may be, and however low he may have fallen, requires, if only instinctively and unconsciously, respect to be given to his dignity as a human being. The prisoner is aware that he is a prisoner, an outcast and he knows his position in respect to the authorities, but no brands, no fetters, can make him forget that he is a man. And since he is a human being, it follows that he must be treated as a human being. God knows, treatment as a human being may transform into a man again even one in whom the image of God has long been eclipsed. (Dostoevsky 1861: 249)

References

Andenaes, J. (1974) *Punishment and Deterrence*. Ann Arbor: University of Michigan Press.

Andrew, D.A., Zinger, I., Hoge, R.D., Bonta, J., Gendreau, P. and Cullen, F.T. (1990) 'Does correctional treatment work? A clinically relevant and psychologically informed meta-analysis', *Criminology*, 28 (3): 369–404.

Ashworth, A. (1986) 'Punishment and compensation: victims, offenders and the state', *Oxford Journal of Legal Studies*, 6 (1): 86–122.

Ball, J.C. (1955) 'The deterrence concept in criminology and law', *The Journal of Criminal Law, Criminology, and Police Science*, 46 (3): 347–54.

Bazemore, G. (2001) 'Young people, trouble and crime', *Youth and Society*, 33 (2): 199–226.

Beccaria, M. (1764) *Of Crimes and Punishments* (translated by E.D. Ingraham). Philadelphia: Phillip H. Nicklin.

Benn, S.F. (1958) 'An approach to the problems of punishment', *Philosophy*, 33 (126): 325–41.

Bentham, J. (1798) *Introduction to the Principles of Morals and of Legislation*. London: Payne.

Beyleveld, D. (1979) 'Deterrence research as a basis for deterrence policies', *Howard Journal of Criminal Justice*, 18 (3): 135–49.

Blackburn, R. (1995) *The Psychology of Criminal Conduct*. Chichester: John Wiley and Sons.

Blouet, A. (1843) *Projet de Prisons Cellulaires*. Paris.

Boswell, G. (2002) 'Imprisoned fathers: the children's view', *Howard Journal of Criminal Justice*, 41 (1): 14–26.

Braga, A.A. (2001) 'Effects of hot spots policing on crime', *Annals of the American Academy of Political and Social Science*, 578 (1): 104–25.

Braithwaite, J. (1989) *Crime, Shame and Reintegration*. Cambridge: Cambridge University Press.

Braithwaite, J. (2000a) 'The regulatory state and the transformation of criminology', *British Journal of Criminology*, 40 (2): 222–38.

Braithwaite, J. (2000b) 'Shame and criminal justice', *Canadian Journal of Criminology*, 42 (3): 281–98.

Brier, S.S. and Feinberg, S.E. (1980) 'Recent econometric modelling of crime and punishment', *Evaluation Review*, 4 (2): 147–91.

Brown, A.P. (2004) 'Anti-social behaviour, crime control and social control', *Howard Journal of Criminal Justice*, 43 (2): 203–11.

Brownlee, I. (1998) 'New Labour – new penology? Punitive rhetoric and the limits of managerialism in criminal justice policy', *Journal of Law and Society*, 25 (3): 313–35.

Burnett, R. and Maruna, S. (2004) 'So "prison works", does it? The criminal careers of 130 men released from prison under Home Secretary, Michael Howard', *Howard Journal of Criminal Justice*, 43 (4): 390–404.

Burstein, P. (2003) 'The impact of public opinion on public policy: a review and an agenda', *Political Research Quarterly*, 56 (1): 29–40.

Cadell, D. and Crisp, D. (1997) *Imprisoned Women and Mothers*. Home Office Research Study 162. London: Home Office.

Campbell, S. (2002) *A Review of Anti-social Behaviour Orders*. Home Office Research Study 236. London: HMSO.

Cornish, D.B. and Clarke, R.V.G. (1986) *The Reasoning Criminal: Rational Choice Perspectives on Offending*. New York: Springer-Verlag.

Criminal Justice Act 2003 (2003) Retrieved 3 May 2007, from: www.opsi.gov.uk/acts/acts2003/20030044.htm

Cullen, F.T., Clark, G.A., Cullen, J.B. and Mathers, R.A. (1985) 'Attribution, salience and attitudes toward criminal sanctioning', *Criminal Justice and Behavior*, 12 (3): 305–31.

Cullen, F.T., Fisher, B.S. and Applegate, B.K. (2000) 'Public opinion about punishment and corrections', *Crime and Justice*, 27: 1–79.

Cumberland, A.K. and Boyle, G.J. (1997) 'Psychometric prediction of recidivism: utility of the risk needs inventory', *Australian and New Zealand Journal of Criminology*, 30 (1): 72–86.

Cunliffe, J. and Shepherd, A. (2007) *Re-offending of Adults: Results from the 2004 Cohort*. Home Office Statistical Bulletin 06/07. London: HMSO.

Currie, E. (1998) *Crime and Punishment in America*. New York: Metropolitan Press.

Daly, K. (2002) 'Restorative justice: the real story', *Punishment and Society*, 4 (1): 55–79.

Dostoevsky, F. (1861/1985) *The House of the Dead* (translated by D. McDuff). London: Penguin Books.

Ehrlich, A. (1975) 'The deterrent effect of capital punishment: a question of life and death', *The American Economic Review*, 65 (3): 397–417.

Feeley, M. and Simon, J. (1992) 'The new penology: notes on the emerging strategy of corrections and its implications', *Criminology*, 30 (4): 449–74.

Fickling, D. (2006) 'Blair backs Reid over paedophile sentence', *The Guardian*, 13 June: 1–2.

Flew, A. (1954) 'The justification of punishment', in H.B. Acton (ed.), *The Philosophy of Punishment* (pp. 83–101). London: Macmillan and Co.

Foucault, M. (1977) *Discipline and Punish: the Birth of the Prison* (translated by A. Sheridan). London: Penguin Books.

Garland, D. (1991) 'Sociological perspectives on punishment', *Crime and Justice*, 14: 115–65.

Garland, D. (1996) 'The limits of the sovereign state: strategies of crime control in contemporary society', *The British Journal of Criminology*, 36 (4): 445–71.

Garland, D. (1997) '"Governmentality" and the problem of crime', *Theoretical Criminology*, 1 (2): 173–214.

Garland, D. (2006) 'Concepts of culture in the sociology of punishment', *Theoretical Criminology*, 10 (4): 419–47.

Gendreau, P., Goggin, C. and Cullen, F. (1999) *The Effects of Prison Sentences on Recidivism*. Report to the Corrections Research and Development and Aboriginal Policy Branch. Retrieved 10 May 2007, from www.prisonpolicy.org/scans/e199912.htm

Gordon, D. (1994) *The Return of the Dangerous Classes: Drug Prohibition and Policy Politics*. New York: W.W. Norton.

Gray, J.M. (2008) 'What shapes public opinion of the justice system?', in T. Gannon and J.L. Wood (eds), *The Criminal Justice System and Public Opinion: Myths and Realities*. Cullompton: Willan Publishing.

Gray, P. (2005) 'The politics of risk and young offenders' experiences of social exclusion and restorative justice', *The British Journal of Criminology*, 45 (6): 938–57.

Hart, H.L.A. (1968) *Punishment and Responsibility: Essays in the Philosophy of Law*. Oxford: Oxford University Press.

Home Office (2004) *Criminal Statistics: England and Wales 2003*. London: HMSO.

Home Office (2006) *A Five Year Strategy for Protecting the Public and Reducing Re-offending*. London: HMSO.

Home Office (2007) *Population in Custody Monthly Tables March 2007 England and Wales*. Retrieved 19 May, 2007, from www.homeoffice.gov.uk/rds/pdfs06/prisapr06.pdf

Horney, J. and Marshall, I.H. (1992) 'Risk perceptions among serious offenders: the role of crime and punishment', *Criminology*, 30 (4): 575–94.

Hough, M. and Roberts, J.V. (1999) 'Sentencing trends in Britain', *Punishment and Society*, 1 (1): 11–26.

Hough, M. and Solomon, E. (2008) 'Introduction', in M. Hough, R. Allen and E. Solomon (eds). *Tackling Prison Overcrowding*. Abingdon: The Policy Press.

House of Commons (2002) *The Criminal Justice Bill: Sentencing; Bill 8 of 2002–2003*. House of Commons Research Paper 02/76. Retrieved 15 May 2007, from www.parliament.uk/commons/lib/research/rp2002/rp02-076.pdf

Howells, K. and Day, A. (2007) 'Readiness for treatment in high risk offenders with personality disorder', *Psychology, Crime and Law*, 13 (1): 47–56.

Indermaur, D. (1996) 'Offender psychology and sentencing', *Australian Psychologist*, 31 (1): 15–19.

Irwin, J. (2005) *The Warehouse Prison: Disposal of the New Dangerous Class*. Los Angeles, CA: Roxbury Publishing Company.

Kant, I. (1785/1993) *Groundwork of the Metaphysic of Morals* (translated by H.J. Paton). Abingdon: Routledge.

King's College, London (2008) *World Prison Brief*. Retrieved 30 October 2008 from www.kcl.ac.uk/depsta/law/research/icps/worldbrief/wpb_stats.php?area=all&category=wb_poptotal

Kleck, G., Sever, B., Li, S. and Gertz, M. (2005) 'The missing link in general deterrence research', *Criminology*, 43 (3): 623–59.

Langbein, J.H. (1976) 'The historical origins of the sanction of imprisonment for serious crime', *Journal of Legal Studies*, 5 (1): 35–60.

Liebling, A. and Maruna, S. (2004) 'Introduction', in A. Liebling and S. Maruna, *The Effects of Imprisonment*. Cullompton: Willan Publishing.

Light, S.C. (1991) 'Assaults on prison officers: interactional themes', *Justice Quarterly*, 8 (2): 243–61.

Lloyd, C., Mair, G. and Hough, M. (1994) *Explaining Re-conviction Rates: a critical analysis*. Home Office Research Study 136. London: Home Office.

Loucks, N. (2004) 'Women in prison', in J.R. Adler (ed.), *Forensic Psychology: Concepts, Debates and Practice*. Cullompton: Willan Publishing.

Lyons, W. and Scheingold, S. (2000) *The Politics of Crime and Punishment*. Retrieved 15 May 2007, from www.ncjrs.gov/criminal_justice2000/vol_1/02c.pdf

MacKenzie, D.L., Wilson, D.B. and Kider S.B. (2001) 'Effects of correctional boot camps on offending', *Annals of the American Academy of Political and Social Science*, 578: 126–43.

Maltz, Michael D. ([1984] 2001) *Recidivism*. Originally published by Academic Press, Inc., Orlando, Florida. Retrieved 15 May 2007, from www.uic.edu/depts/lib/forr/pdf/crimjust/recidivism.pdf

Martinson, R. (1974) 'What works? Questions and answers about prison reform', *Public Interest*, 35: 22–35.

Martinson, R. (1979) 'New findings, new views: a note of caution regarding sentencing reform', *Hofstra Law Review*, 7 (2): 242–58.

Miers, D. (2001) *An International Review of Restorative Justice.* Home Office crime reduction series paper 10. London: HMSO.

Miller, H.A. (1994) 'Re-examining psychological distress in the current conditions of segregation', *Journal of Correctional Health Care*, 1 (2): 39–53.

Millie, A., Jacobson, J. and Hough, M. (2003) 'Understanding the growth in the prison population in England and Wales', *Criminal Justice*, 3 (4): 369–87.

Morris, L. (1994b) *Dangerous Classes: the Underclass and Social Citizenship*. Abingdon: Routledge.

Nagin, D.S. (1998) 'Deterrence and incapacitation', in M. Tonry (ed.), *The Handbook of Crime and Punishment* (pp. 345–68). New York: Oxford University Press.

Norrie, M. (1986) 'Practical reasoning and criminal responsibility: a jurisprudential approach', in D.B. Cornish and R.V. Clarke (eds), *The Reasoning Criminal: Rational Choice Perspectives on Offending*. New York: Springer-Verlag.

O'Connell, M. (1999) 'Is Irish public opinion towards crime distorted by media bias?', *European Journal of Communication*, 14 (2): 191–212.

O'Donnell, I. and Edgar, K. (1999) 'Fear in prison', *The Prison Journal*, 79 (1): 90–9.

O'Malley, P. (1999) 'Volatile and contradictory punishment', *Theoretical Criminology*, 3 (2): 175–96.

O'Malley, P. (2002) 'Globalizing risk? Distinguishing styles of neo-liberal criminal justice in Australia and the USA', *Criminal Justice*, 2 (2): 205–22.

Oswald, M.E., Hupfeld, J., Klug, S.C. and Gabriel, U. (2002) 'Lay-perspectives on criminal deviance, goals of punishment, and punitivity', *Social Justice Research*, 15 (2): 85–98.

Paternoster, R. (1987) 'The deterrent effect of the perceived certainty and severity of punishment: a review of the evidence and issues', *Justice Quarterly*, 4 (2): 173–217.

Posner, R. (1985) 'An economic theory of criminal law', *The Columbia Law Review*, 85 (6): 1193–1231.

Resick, P.A. (1987) 'Psychological effects of victimization: implications for the criminal justice system', *Crime and Delinquency*, 33 (4): 468–78.

Richards, M. (1978) 'The experience of long-term imprisonment', *The British Journal of Criminology*, 26 (4): 403–22.

Roach, K. (2000) 'Changing punishment at the turn of the century: restorative justice on the rise', *Canadian Journal of Criminology*, 42 (3): 249–80.

Roberts, P.A. and Doob, A.N. (1990) 'News media influences on public views of sentencing', *Law and Human Behavior*, 14 (5): 451–68.

Roberts, J.V., Stalens, L.J., Indamaur, D. and Hough, M. (2002) *Penal Populism and Public Opinion: Lessons from Five Countries*. New York: Oxford University Press.

Rose, N. (2000) 'Government and control', *The British Journal of Criminology*, 40 (2): 321–39.

Rose, N. and Valverde, M. (1991) 'Governed by law?', *Social and Legal Studies*, 7 (4): 541–51.

Ross, H. L. (1982) *Deterring the Drinking Driver: Legal Policy and Social Control*. Lexington, MA: Heath.

Royal College of Psychiatrists (2007) *Prison Psychiatry: Adult Prisons in England and Wales*. Retrieved 17 May 2007, from www.rcpsych.ac.uk/files/pdfversion/cr141.pdf

Sapsford, R. (1978) 'Life sentence prisoners: psychological changes during sentence', *The British Journal of Criminology*, 18 (2): 128–45.

Shaver, K.G. (1986) *The Attribution of Blame*. New York: Springer-Verlag.

Shearing, C. (2001) 'Punishment and the changing face of the governance', *Punishment and Society*, 3 (2): 203.

Sherman, L.W. (1993) 'Defiance, deterrence, and irrelevance: a theory of the criminal sanction', *Journal of Research in Crime and Delinquency*, 30 (4): 445–73.

Simon, J. (1995) 'They died with their boots on: the boot camp and the limits of modern penality', *Social Justice*, 22 (1): 25–49.

Smilansky, S. (1990) 'Utilitarianism and the 'punishment of the innocent: the general problem', *Analysis*, 50 (4): 256–61.

Solomon, E. and Rutherford, M. (2007) *Community Sentences Digest*. London: Centre for Crime and Justice Studies.

Spierenburg, P. (1998) 'The disappearance of public executions', in T.J. Flanagan, J.W. Marquart and K.G. Adams, *Incarcerating Criminals: Prisons and Jails in Social and Organizational Context* (pp. 2–9). New York: Oxford University Press.

Stephenson, G.M. (1992) *The Psychology of Criminal Justice*. Oxford: Blackwell Publishing.

Ten, C.L. (1991) 'Crime and punishment', in P. Singer (ed.). *A Companion to Ethics* (pp. 366–72). Oxford: Blackwell Publishing.

The Economist (2007) 'Information overload', 40: 15 January.

Tonry, M. (2004) *Punishment and Politics: Evidence and Emulation in the Making of English Crime Control Policy.* Cullompton: Willan Publishing.

Tryer, P. (1990) *Why People Obey the Law.* New Haven: Yale University Press.

Vaughan, B. (2000) 'The civilizing process and the Janus-face of modern punishment', *Theoretical Criminology*, 4 (1): 71–97.

Villettaz, P., Killias, M. and Zoder, I. (2006) *The Effects of Custodial vs. Non-custodial Sentences on Re-offending: a systematic review of the state of knowledge.* University of Lausanne. Retrieved 10 May 2007, from www.campbellcollaboration.org/doc-pdf/Campbell-report-30.09.06.pdf

Von Hirsch, A. and Ashworth, A. (1998) *Principled Sentencing.* Edinburgh: Edinburgh University Press.

Von Hirsch, A., Bottoms, A., Burney, E. and Wikstrom P.O. (1999) *Criminal Deterrence and Sentence Severity. An Analysis of Recent Research.* Oxford: Hart Publishing.

Walker, N. (1991) *Why Punish? Theories of Punishment Reassessed.* Oxford: Oxford University Press.

Walsh, A. (2000) 'Evolutionary psychology and the origins of justice', *Justice Quarterly*, 17 (4): 841–64.

Welch, M. (2004) 'Trampling human rights in the war on terror: implications to the sociology of denial', *Critical Criminology*, 12 (1): 1–20.

Welsh, B.C. and Farrington, D.P. (2001) 'Toward an evidence-based approach to preventing crime', *The Annals of the American Academy of Political and Social Science*, 578 (1): 158–73.

Williams, K.R. and Hawkins, R. (1986) 'Perceptual research on general deterrence: a critical review', *Law and Society Review*, 20 (4): 545–72.

Windzio, M. (2006) 'Is there a deterrent effect of pains of imprisonment?', *Punishment and Society*, 8 (3): 341–64.

Zimring, F.E. (2001) 'Imprisonment rates and the new politics of criminal punishment', *Punishment and Society*, 3 (1): 161–66.

Zimring, F.E. and Johnson, D.T. (2006) 'Public opinion and the governance of punishment in democratic political systems', *The Annals of the American Academy of Political and Social Science*, 605 (1): 265–80.

Chapter 23

Women in prison

Nancy Loucks

Women make up about 4.3 per cent of prison populations worldwide (Walmsley 2006). Most research has therefore focused on men, the majority population. However, it is precisely this minority status and marginalisation that increases the need to recognise women in prison as a distinct group with distinctive needs. A consistent picture of poverty, deprivation, victimisation and marginalisation makes up the basis of every female custodial population studied in every jurisdiction. The 'career' criminals and thrill-seekers common among male prisoners are virtually absent in women's prison, replaced instead by people in custody often through desperate circumstances or lives so chaotic that they fail to comply with community penalties or bail.

This chapter outlines the backgrounds, characteristics and issues surrounding women who end up in custody. Much of the information is based on research in the UK, but an international context is included where appropriate.

Backgrounds of women in custody

Women who end up in custody are distinctive for a number of reasons. Features such as addiction, psychological distress, abuse, poverty and unemployment, while not exclusive to women in custody, characterise the vast majority of them (see for example Byrne and Howells 2002).

Drugs

Drug use is among the most common features of women in custody in many countries. In Scotland, the Inspectorate of Prisons reported that an estimated 98 per cent of women in prison have problems with addiction to drugs (HMIP for Scotland 2005). This rate is higher than in some countries. For example, research among female prisoners in England reported rates of 75 per cent use of illicit drugs in the six months prior to imprisonment (Plugge *et al.* 2006), while a meta-analysis by Fazel *et al.* (2006) found rates of drug abuse and dependence ranging from 30–60 per cent among female prisoners. However, the higher rate in Scotland is comparable to that found in other countries and populations: one US study (Birecree *et al.* 1994), for example, recorded rates of 90 per cent. A project on young offenders in Scotland (Loucks *et al.* 2000) found the rate of prior drug use to be about 95 per cent, with no significant difference in reported experience of drug use between young men and women prior to custody.

Backgrounds of drug use among female prisoners tend to be heavy. Plugge and colleagues in England (2006) found that 38 per cent had injected drugs at some stage, 56 per cent of whom had done so within a month of entry to prison. Their report of 75 per cent illicit drug use in the six months prior to custody compares to a rate of 12 per cent in the previous year amongst the general population. A national survey of prisoners in the United States (Snell and Morton 1994) showed that women in prison used more drugs and used them more frequently than did male prisoners. Prior to custody, 42 per cent of female prisoners used drugs daily, compared with 36 per cent of male prisoners, and more were likely to be under the influence of drugs when they committed their offence (36 per cent compared with 31 per cent).

The available research suggests that few women begin their drug use in prison: in-depth research among female prisoners in Scotland (Loucks 1998) found that only three women did so, and more often than not they simply tried drugs once or twice, usually cannabis. Others began using different drugs in prison, for example where their normal drug of choice was not available, or where they chose to experiment. Drug use most commonly began for the women as teenagers.

Alcohol

Though not as common a problem as illicit drug use among female prisoners, a significant proportion of women in prison show evidence of alcoholism or alcohol-related problems. For example, 23 per cent of female prisoners in Loucks' research in Scotland said they never drank, but 20 per cent said they drank daily outside custody. Based on the AUDIT scale (Fleming *et al.* 1991), 10–15 per cent were addicted to alcohol. This is similar to rates of alcoholism among female prisoners in much of the past research, but a lower rate to that most recently reported in Plugge *et al.* (2006) which found that 42 per cent of female prisoners in England drank alcohol in excess of government guidelines prior to their imprisonment. In the Scottish sample (Loucks 1998), binge drinking was more common than regular heavy drinking. Female binge drinkers tended to combine drink and drugs, and a third had been drinking at the time of their offence, almost all of whom thought this contributed to their offence. These behaviours would not necessarily show up as addiction on clinical scales, nor did most of these women believe they had a problem with alcohol.

In contrast to the findings of previous research among female prisoners (e.g. Kendall 1993, in Canada), few women in Scottish prisons appeared to be cross-addicted to drugs and alcohol. Only one woman in Loucks' research in Scotland was found to be cross-addicted. Her story was important in other ways too, in that it exemplified the dire situation of many women when they enter custody. This woman had a substantial history of all forms of abuse: she grew up in an alcoholic family, ran away from physical and sexual abuse at home and was taken into care, where she was sexually abused by her foster father. She then entered a series of abusive relationships from which she had yet to escape. The following section shows that this woman's story was more often the norm than the exception among women in prison.

Backgrounds of abuse

Another recurring theme throughout the research into women in custody is the finding that so many of the women are victims as well as offenders. Loucks' research in Scotland showed that the vast majority of women in prison had been direct or indirect victims of physical, sexual, or emotional abuse, and often a combination of these: 82 per cent had suffered some form of abuse during their lives, and 67 per cent were directly aware of the abuse of others close to them. The rate of abuse in Scotland is similar to rates found in other female prison populations, such as in Canadian research by Lightfoot and Lambert (1992). A survey of 13,986 male and female prisoners in the United States (Snell and Morton 1994; also Morash *et al.* 1998) showed lower reported rates of abuse among women. Even so, the reported rates for female prisoners in their research (43 per cent) were almost four times higher than the comparable figure for men (12 per cent). More recent research reported 50 per cent of female prisoners having past experience of domestic violence, compared with a quarter of male prisoners, while a third had been victims of sexual abuse, compared with a tenth of male prisoners (Corston 2007). A study of 50 prolific self-harmers in women's prisons in England carried out for the Corston Report found that only 12 of them (24 per cent) had not experienced abuse or rape in the past.

In Loucks' research (1998), most women who reported being victims of abuse said this had taken place throughout their lives (as children, teenagers, and as adults), usually on a daily or virtually daily basis. Many were going back out to violent families or partners and for some, prison was the first 'safe' place they had been (see also Bradley and Davino 2002).

Health

Perhaps unsurprisingly in view of the above, female prisoners suffer more frequent and serious chronic disease, acute illness and injuries; these can be attributed to factors such as poverty, poor nutrition and lack of medical care, but also to drug use (Plugge *et al.* 2006; Anderson *et al.* 2002). Research in the USA has found that women in prison show even higher rates of HIV/AIDS than do men in custody (Zaitzow 2001; Ingram Fogel and Belyea 1999). Ingram Fogel and Belyea (1999), as well as Plugge *et al.* (2006) reported a high proportion of high-risk behaviour among the women, including substance abuse, extensive past or ongoing violent experiences including sexual abuse, a high proportion of multiple partners (including prostitution), and low use of condoms.

Suicidal behaviour and emotional distress

Suicide and self-injury are common experiences for a significant proportion of female prisoners. Loucks (1998) reported that over a third (38 per cent) had attempted suicide at some time in the past. Suicide attempts were more common outside custody than in prison: only seven (24 per cent) of the 29 women who said they had tried to kill themselves had tried it while in prison. One study in Australia (Putnins 2005) found that almost half of women in prison (47 per cent) had attempted to take their own lives at some point.

A notable proportion (17 per cent) had a history of deliberately injuring themselves, separate from those incidents that they considered as suicide attempts. None of the women did this for the first time in prison. Plugge *et al.* (2006) found that 16 per cent of female prisoners in their sample had deliberately harmed themselves without intending suicide in the *month* prior to their imprisonment. This suggests a much higher rate in the longer term. Rates of self-harm appear to be considerably higher in prison among females: in 2005, 56 per cent of all recorded incidents of self-harm in England were for female prisoners, despite women making up only 5 per cent of the prison population (Corston 2007).

A history of treatment for mental health or emotional problems is also a common feature among this group. Research in England and Wales (Singleton *et al.* 1998), for example, showed that 40 per cent of women in custody had received help or treatment for a mental health or emotional problem in the year before they entered custody – double the proportion of male prisoners. Women in prison prior to conviction or sentence contained the highest proportion of prisoners ever admitted to a psychiatric hospital – 22 per cent, including 6 per cent admitted for six months or more and 11 per cent admitted to a secure ward. This compares with 8 per cent of sentenced male prisoners, with 2 per cent admitted for six months or more and 3 per cent in a secure facility. Research in Australia (Dixon *et al.* 2004) reported that 78 per cent of the young females in their sample had three or more mental health problems, while a study in the United States (Timmons-Mitchell *et al.* 1997) reported an average of five diagnosable mental health problems in its sample.

Education, employment and economic circumstances

Education among women in prison is generally limited. Loucks (1998) found that over 90 per cent had left school at age 16 or under. Roughly three-quarters had a history of truancy, half had been suspended at some stage, and a third had been expelled. A subsequent study (Henderson 2001) largely supported these findings, showing that only 14 per cent of women in prison had stayed in school beyond the statutory minimum age (16 in Scotland), and that 61 per cent left school with no qualifications.

Most women in prison in Scotland (80 per cent) are unemployed at the time of their imprisonment (Loucks 1998). Henderson (2001) found that, of those who had been employed, most were employed in unskilled manual work. For those who had held a job at any stage, the longest period of employment was usually less than a year. Because of these features, the main source of income for women in prison tends to be from social welfare services. In Scotland, two-thirds of the women in custody depended on state benefits (Income Support, Incapacity Benefit, Jobseeker's Allowance, and so on) for their main income (Henderson 2001). Almost half of the 179 respondents believed their offence was related to financial need, with a similar proportion saying past offences were the result of a shortage of money.

Characteristics

The backgrounds of women in prison outlined above make them a distinctive population once in prison as well (also Richie 2001). Even a brief glance at offence types, sentences, demographics, and mental health sets female prisoners aside with very different needs from the vast majority of the population in prison.

Offences and sentences

As stated at the outset, women make up a very small proportion of the offending population (17 per cent of all arrests for recorded crime in the UK; Corston 2007) and an even smaller percentage of the prison population (5.5 per cent in England in 2006: *ibid.*). The patterns of women's offending also differ quite substantially from those for men. Offending by women is disproportionately for relatively minor or non-violent offences, such as soliciting and shoplifting, and financial crimes such as fraud, forgery and embezzlement. In the United States, a national survey of almost 14,000 male and female prisoners (Snell and Morton 1994) found that nearly half of all women in prison were serving sentences for non-violent offences and had past convictions only for other non-violent offences. One in three women in prisons in the United States is there for a violent crime, compared with roughly one in every two male prisoners (Chesney-Lind 1997).

Disparities between male and female prisoners in Scotland appear to be less, with roughly equal proportions in prison for violent offences on 30 June 2007 (Scottish Government 2008). Differences were apparent, however, for offences of dishonesty (18 per cent of sentenced women in prison on 30 June 2007, compared with 11 per cent of men) and for 'other' crimes (33 per cent compared with 19 per cent, primarily drug offences – 28 per cent compared with 14 per cent: *ibid.*). Further, the types of offending within offence types appear to differ: research in England found that, despite reported rises in violent offences among girls in the past few years, many of these were at the lower end of the scale in terms of seriousness and resulted in reprimands or warnings rather than convictions (NACRO, cited in Bennett 2008).

International differences are worth noting here: while disparities in offence types differ between men and women, some countries prosecute women for 'moral crimes' that do not apply to men. For example, Anzia (2008) reported that women in Afghanistan can be punished for acts considered to be against the dignity of the family. These include adultery, leaving an abusive partner, premarital relationships, and refusal to marry. Eloping with someone not chosen by the family after a dowry has been paid legally justifies arrest. Further, women who make public accusations of rape may themselves be imprisoned.

Perhaps as a consequence of different patterns of offending, a higher proportion of women are in prison for short sentences. In Scotland in 2007/08, 50 per cent of sentenced female adults and young offenders in custody on a given day were serving sentences of shorter than two years, compared with 30 per cent of their male counterparts (Scottish Government 2008). Further, a higher proportion of the female prison population on a given day – almost a third of those in custody in Scotland – is made up of people not yet convicted or sentenced (32 per cent, versus 21 per cent of male prisoners). Many of these unconvicted and unsentenced women end up without a custodial sentence. In 1998, for example, 525 unconvicted females were held in custody prior to sentencing. Of these, less than half (222 women, or 42 per cent) eventually received a custodial sentence (Scottish Court Services 2000). Despite this, the average daily population of women in prison in Scotland increased by 87 per cent from 1998/99–2007/08 (Scottish Government 2008), with no corresponding change in crime rates. This is a rate over four times greater than the increase in the male prison population, which increased by 20 per cent in the same period (*ibid.*) and the difference cannot be accounted for solely on the basis of the different population starting points.

Demographics

Imprisonment often begins early for women (in Scotland by age 16, and by age 15 in England). Female prison populations are therefore generally young: again in Scotland, roughly two-thirds are under the age of 30, and a fifth are under age 21. Many have been to court or even to prison several times. However, two-thirds of those serving sentences at any given time will never have spent time in custody before. Almost half of this group are first offenders. The majority of women in prison are parents, though in Scotland, only about two-thirds currently had custody of their children (some of whom had adult children).

A disproportionate number of incarcerated women in many countries (e.g. England and the United States) are from ethnic minorities. Indeed, recent surges in female prison populations in many countries have included an even greater proportion of women from ethnic minorities: the Corston Report on women's imprisonment (2007), for example, reported that 28 per cent of female prisoners in the UK are from black and minority ethnic (BME) groups – a rate over three times greater than in the general population. In the United States, Huling (1995) suggests that a higher prevalence of illicit drug use among ethnic minorities is likely to be responsible for much of this, as increasingly harsh punishments for the use and sales of drugs such as crack cocaine have been imposed. However, most users of illicit drugs in the US are white (Substance Abuse and Mental Health Services Administration 1999).

In a number of countries, ethnic minorities and foreign nationals who have been used as drug couriers or 'mules', with and without their knowledge or consent, make up a substantial number of women in prison. The types of problems women in prison face (see 'Issues for women in custody', below) are even more extreme for foreign nationals, who are even further away from children, family, and social and community supports than are the other women.

Psychological distress

As noted above, psychological distress was clearly a common feature of women in custody, perhaps unsurprisingly in light of their extensive histories of suicidal behaviour, mental health problems, addiction and abuse. Levels of hopelessness, based on the Beck Hopelessness Scale (Beck *et al.* 1974), showed clinical levels of hopelessness for a high proportion of women in prison in Scotland (Loucks 1998). Prisoners often score highly for hopelessness using this scale: Zamble and Porporino (1988) found, for example, that a third of their subjects scored '6' or higher (where higher scores indicate higher levels of hopelessness). In Scotland, the *mean* score among women in prison was 6.3.

A recent Prison Survey in Scotland (Scottish Prison Service 2007) noted a number of differences in how male and female prisoners felt about themselves. For example, almost half (48 per cent) of female prisoners reported that they felt useful 'none of the time' or 'rarely', compared with 39 per cent of male prisoners. Similar patterns were evident for feeling relaxed (42 per cent saying 'none of the time' or 'rarely' compared with 27 per cent of male prisoners); dealing with problems well (33 per cent of female prisoners doing this 'none of the time' or 'rarely', compared with 22 per cent of male prisoners); feeling good about themselves (43 per cent saying 'none of the time' or 'rarely', compared with 29 per cent of male prisoners); and feeling confident (45 per cent saying 'none of the time' or 'rarely', compared with 28 per cent of male prisoners).

Distress was also evident from the results of the Hospital Anxiety and Depression Scale (HADS: Zigmond and Snaith 1983) administered during the research in 1997 (Loucks 1998). Just over half of the women in prison in Scotland had scores for depression within the 'normal' range, and only a third had 'normal' scores for anxiety. Over a quarter of women were recorded as having moderate or severe depression, and over a third had such scores for depression.

Research in prisons in England and Wales showed similar patterns. According to Singleton and colleagues (1998), female prisoners were significantly more likely than male prisoners to suffer from a neurotic disorder: while 59 per cent of remand and 40 per cent of sentenced male prisoners in their sample were assessed as having a neurotic disorder, the proportions for women were 76 per cent and 63 per cent respectively. These were most commonly mixed anxiety and depressive disorders. Their research also suggested that psychotic disorders may be more common among female prisoners on remand (21 per cent, as assessed by lay interviews, compared with 9 per cent of male remand prisoners, 4 per cent of male sentenced prisoners, and 10 per cent of female sentenced prisoners).

Issues for women in custody

Issues women face while in prison are in most cases similar to those of men. For example, both groups often have difficulty finding housing and employment upon release, both are separated from children and family, both may be struggling with addiction and the stress of imprisonment, and both may be faced with intimidation and violence while in prison. However, the proportion of male and female prisoners dealing with these issues differs, as does the impact on the two groups. This section outlines such issues in more detail.

Childcare

As noted above, a high proportion of female prisoners have dependent children. Custody of children is generally of more concern for women in prison than it is for men: research in Scotland (Inspectorates of Prisons and Social Work Services 1998) found that only 17 per cent of fathers looked after their children while the mother was in custody. This compares with 87 per cent of mothers who care for the children when the father is in prison. Comparable figures in the United States showed that 25 per cent of the women's children, compared with 90 per cent of children of male prisoners, lived with the other parent during imprisonment (Morash *et al.* 1998). Indeed, research in Canada found that children of mothers in prison are likely to face a number of placements during their mother's incarceration (Centre for Children and Families in the Justice System 2003). The picture in England and Wales was even more extreme, where only 5 per cent of the 8,100 children affected each year by their mother's imprisonment remained in their home and were looked after by the other parent (Wolfe 1999). Potential loss of custody of a child is therefore a very real concern for women who end up in prison.

Visits to women in prison can also be problematic. The low number of women held in custody means that few prisons or Young Offender Institutions exist which hold women. This means that many women will be located at a great distance from their families. Statistics from the Prison Reform Trust in London note that nearly a fifth of female prisoners in England and Wales are held over 100 miles away from their committal court town. In such circumstances, women in prison are less likely than male prisoners to have contact with their children. Research in the United States (Snell and Morton 1994) reported that over half of women with children under age 18 had never received a visit from their children while in prison. This is particularly the case where the women are foreign nationals: one study in England found that only 11 per cent of female foreign nationals had received a visit from their children while in prison (Caddle and Crisp 1997).

The research by Caddle and Crisp also noted a range of psychological effects on children whose mothers are imprisoned. This included problems with behaviour, sleeping, eating, bed-wetting, overall health, and with making and keeping friends. These issues were particularly acute when the children had to move home or go into care. While these problems may occur when the father is imprisoned, problematic behaviour among children has been found to be more common when the mother is taken into custody (Richards and McWilliams 1996).

Housing

As with childcare, housing is another issue which differs for female prisoners. Again, statistics in Scotland show that women are more likely to lose their housing while in custody than are men (Inspectorates of Prisons and Social Work Services 1998). Research in England and Wales noted that a third of female prisoners lose their homes while in prison (Wolfe 1999). Women are more often single parents and have tenancy agreements in their own names; men, in contrast, are more likely to have a partner at home to maintain the tenancy.

Addiction

Some women use custody as an opportunity to withdraw from drugs. However, others continue to abuse licit and illicit drugs. The most recent Prison Survey in Scotland (Scottish Prison Service 2007) found that 33 per cent of women admitted to using illegal drugs in prison during the previous month, primarily heroin (88 per cent of those who said they had used drugs) and cannabis (57 per cent). Drugs use among women in custody tends to differ from their use outside, usually because drugs are less readily available and, similarly, because their drug of choice may not be accessible. Because addiction is such a common feature of female prisoners prior to custody, withdrawal from addiction and its consequences poses tremendous problems for many women in prison. The difficulty of withdrawal for women in prison is usually more than the physical consequences. Rather, withdrawal forces many women to face issues they had blocked out with drugs, often for the first time, such as experiences of abuse and social realities such as poverty and loss of housing or custody of children.

Victimisation and custody

Victimisation has many implications for women in general, but perhaps particularly for those in custody. Increased substance abuse was one possible consequence, where people tried to block out memories of abuse (or, as one woman mentioned, violence from her partner hurt less when she was drunk). A small-scale study in the United States (Chiavaroli 1992) noted that treatment for drug abuse among victims of sexual abuse appeared to be more effective when it addressed both issues. Increased vulnerability during withdrawal from drugs or alcohol was therefore an important problem for victims.

People in custody often have feelings of shame, isolation, or self-blame as a result of their imprisonment, which in turn lowers their self-esteem. This is particularly the case for women who have been victims of abuse, where even standard prison procedures such as body searches or cell searches, and the loss of autonomy which is a basic part of prison life, can trigger feelings of helplessness and frustration common to the experience of abuse itself; in a sense prison 'retraumatises' them, albeit unintentionally, forcing them to relive past abuse.

Finally, prison staff are placed in a difficult position with victim/offenders: to what extent should professional staff in prisons 'open a can of worms' and help women address their past or ongoing abuse? This question is controversial, especially because the majority of the female prison population are short-term prisoners; whether it is safe or even responsible for a prison to start addressing issues which may take years to deal with is a question as yet unresolved. Some women are forced to address past abuse while they are in custody, for example if it is directly relevant to their offence or addiction, but these would primarily be longer-term prisoners who are more likely to have access to ongoing support while in custody.

Bullying

More direct victimisation can also take place in prisons: violence and bullying are not unusual among female prisoners. In Scotland, a quarter of prisoners said they had been bullied at some stage, though not necessarily during their current sentence. Physical assaults were also surprisingly common, with 15.1 per cent of prisoners saying they had been assaulted in a prison. These figures can, however, be misleading, as definitions of bullying and assaults are generally problematic. A recent Prison Survey in Scotland (Scottish Prison Service 2007) reported lower rates of bullying, with 18 per cent of women saying they had been bullied in the prison in the past month and 14 per cent saying they had feared for their safety in that time.

Bullying in women's prisons is often in the form of 'taxing' (where prisoners who are more dominant take things from those who are more vulnerable), intimidation, ostracism and extortion. Physical bullying (assaults, etc.), in contrast, is generally more common among male prisoners. Bullying among female prisoners is often more insidious and therefore more difficult for staff to detect. As a result, some women complained during the research in Scotland that bullying frequently took place in front of staff, but that staff did nothing about it. Often, however, the behaviour was too ambiguous for staff to recognise it as bullying and to take appropriate action.

Bullying among female prisoners in Scotland (see Loucks 2005) is often related to competition for medication. The prison's detoxification programme meant that the vast majority of women were receiving prescription drugs, usually diazepam and dihydrocodeine. Prescriptions were also common for other problems such as mental disorder or poor health, with the result that about 97 per cent of the women were receiving some form of medication in the prison. With the relative shortage of illicit drugs coming into prison, the women would go to extreme measures to get prescription drugs from others. This included threats for people to give others their medication or telling people what to say to the medical staff to get extra. Measures designed to keep people from retaining their medication were being abused: women taking liquid medication would put cotton wool in their mouths to absorb it, or alternatively people would regurgitate their medication to pass on to other people. Despite the problems associated with medication, however, the physical and psychological distress of the vast majority of the women made it a necessary part of prison life.

Suicidal behaviour

Rates of suicide among women in custody are higher than among women in the population at large. One reason is that withdrawal from drugs and the stresses of imprisonment increase the risk of suicide and self-harm among a group already vulnerable to such behaviour (see for example Liebling 1996). Further, women use more lethal methods of suicide in custody than they do outside prison: outside, women are most likely to resort to overdoses or 'cutting up', but inside prison, methods are generally limited to hanging, which is much more likely to be lethal. Men tend to adopt forms of suicide that are more likely to be lethal both in and out of custody (firearms or hanging outside prison, and again hanging inside custody). Among female prisoners in Scotland (Loucks 1998), suicide attempts were more often associated with addiction to alcohol than to drugs. The reason for this is less clear, though it may be because drug use was a feature of such a large proportion of the population. Finally, clinical levels of hopelessness, anxiety, depression, and poor problem-solving were notably high among the women in prison in Scotland – characteristics often related to suicidal behaviour.

What was very clear from Loucks' research in Scotland was that prison seems unlikely in itself to 'cause' suicidal behaviour. It can, however, be the 'last straw' in combination with problems outside. Such problems include the fact that many women will be withdrawing from drugs and will therefore be facing reality, perhaps for the first time in years. This reality can be intolerable, especially where extreme physical and sexual abuse are involved. In prison, women are away from their usual social supports. They may feel failure or shame, perhaps combined with bullying in custody and the loss of autonomy and (for victims of abuse) the retraumatisation that imprisonment can bring.

One question is whether the higher levels of distress among women in prison are all that surprising. Psychometric tests are designed to look at people's response to 'everyday' problems. However, the 'everyday' problems among women in prison are unusually severe compared with the 'average' population outside. If women are wrestling with daily drug use and addiction, daily physical, sexual and emotional abuse, daily financial crises and housing problems, etc., their distress will understandably be high. This is not to say that women or even female offenders outside prison do not experience similar problems. What is clear, however, is that an 'alarmingly high' proportion of women in prison show characteristics (such as the above) associated with risk of suicide (Liebling 1994).

Life events

Previous research has shown a consistent relationship between the number of stressful events in a person's life and that person's emotional and physical health (Holmes and Rahe 1967). That research measured the number of stressful events with a Life Change Scale (also known as the Holmes and Rahe Social Readjustment Rating Scale). With this in mind, the author of this chapter designed a short Prisoner Life Events Scale (PLES: Loucks 1999), developed specially for women in custody, during some research conducted in two women's prisons in England (Loucks 2001). The PLES is a 19-point scale, with an option for additional responses, designed to measure types of events other than custody itself which may influence a person's behaviour and ability to cope while inside.

The results derived from use of the scale showed quite dramatically the stressors that affect women in custody, above and beyond the stress of custody itself. Nearly half the women lost possession of their accommodation outside while they were in prison. Lack of visits from family was also a common concern. A high proportion in both prisons (roughly a third) had a close family member seriously ill while they were in custody. Having a close friend or family member go to prison during their time in custody and formal separation from partners were also common events, as were death or victimisation of family and friends. In total, the women reported an average of 3.0–4.8 such events during their current period of custody.

Using a different scale of life events, research elsewhere reported an average of 10 life events in the year prior to custody (Keaveny and Zauszniewski 1999). The authors reported a positive correlation between the number of life events and levels of depression.

A man's world

The small proportion of women in custody inevitably means that custodial culture is dominated by the needs of men. Programmes and activities in prisons are often designed with the needs and interests of male prisoners in mind (see Carlen 1983; Stern 1998; Sheehan *et al.* 2007). Covington cites an example of the situation in the United States, but arguably the same situation exists in most jurisdictions:

> Despite this growing information on best practices for treating females, male-based programming remains the norm in many settings. Even female-only programs are often merely copies of men's programs, not based on research or clinical experience with women and girls. This problem is especially acute for juveniles. Boys far outnumber girls in the juvenile justice system, so programs are designed with the needs of males in mind, and services for female adolescents simply replicate the male model (Pepi 1998) (Covington 1998: 12–13)

Overall, female offenders are a vastly different group with different needs and problems from male offenders. The criminal justice system seems to have a very different effect on them, so policies and programmes directed towards men will often not be particularly useful (see also Easteal 2001).

Conclusion

Two inquiries into women's offending were conducted in Scotland (Inspectorates of Prisons and Social Work Services 1998) and in England (Wedderburn Committee 2000) specifically to understand

and address the needs of women who end up in prison. The Corston Report in 2007 reiterated the findings of these two inquiries and made 43 recommendations for action, 40 of which the government accepted. The main emphasis of the recommendations from these reports was on ensuring appropriate alternatives to custody for female offenders and on increasing the information available about the women and their needs. Importantly in the 1998 joint Inspectorates' report in Scotland, the recommendations secured a commitment by the government to halving the female prison population within two years and to keeping young women under the age of 18 out of Prison Service custody. The logic behind this was that the problems these women are dealing with are best identified and addressed outside custody, without complicating already difficult circumstances by the fact of imprisonment (also Radosh 2002). This is not to say that serious offending should be ignored, rather that it be prevented through more appropriate targeting of resources for female offenders. Unfortunately, the goals in both countries to reduce the population of female prisoners have failed to meet their targets, and the number of women who enter custody continues to rise. Indeed, rather than decreasing to 100 female prisoners in Scotland, the numbers have trebled to well over 400.

Much of the information above is based on research in Scotland. However, the evidence available internationally shows an almost identical picture of female prisoners in every country (Lemgruber 2001; McIvor 1999; Stern 1998). Women consistently make up a tiny proportion of prisoners. They consistently come from backgrounds of poverty, unemployment, abuse and addiction. They are consistently young, uneducated and unskilled. Most are mothers of young children and are often single mothers. Most have committed a non-violent offence. An inquiry into female offenders in England and Wales (Wedderburn Committee 2000) described female prisoners as 'overwhelmingly, though not exclusively, drawn from a group who share all the characteristics of "social exclusion" '. Overall, it is clear that the problems which female offenders face are unlikely to be solved by imprisonment and are in reality made worse.

References

Anderson, T.L., Rosay, A.B. and Saum, C. (2002) 'The impact of drug use and crime involvement on health problems among female drug offenders', *The Prison Journal*, 82 (1): 50–68.

Anzia, L. (2008) 'Rape, torture and humiliation in women's prisons: a global state of crisis', Women News Network, www.alternet.org/story/99987/

Beck, A.T., Weissman, A.W., Lester, D. and Trexler, L. (1974) 'The assessment of pessimism: the hopelessness scale', *Journal of Consulting and Clinical Psychology*, 42: 861–5.

Bennett, A. (2008) 'Violence by girl offenders has been exaggerated, says Nacro', *Children and Young People Now*, www.cypnow.co.uk/bulletins/Youth-Justice/news/849821/?DCMP=EMC-YouthJustice.

Birecree, E.A., Bloom, J.D., Leverett, M.D. and Williams, M. (1994) 'Diagnostic efforts regarding women in Oregon prison systems – a preliminary report', *Journal of Offenders Therapy and Comparative Criminology*, 38 (3): 217–30, Fall 1994.

Bradley, R.G. and Davino, K.M. (2002) 'Women's perceptions of the prison environment: when prison is "the safest place I've ever been" ', *Psychology of Women Quarterly*, 26 (4): 351–9.

Byrne, M.K. and Howells, K. (2002) 'The psychological needs of women prisoners: implications for rehabilitation and management', *Psychiatry, Psychology and Law*, 9 (1): 34–43.

Caddle, D. and Crisp, D. (1997) *Imprisoned Women and Mothers*. Home Office Research Study 162. London: Home Office.

Carlen, P. (1983) *Women's Imprisonment: A Study in Social Control*. London: Routledge and Kegan Paul.

Centre for Children and Families in the Justice System (2003) *Waiting for Mommy: Giving a Voice to the Hidden Victims of Imprisonment*. Ontario: Centre for Children and Families in the Justice System, London Family Court Clinic.

Chesney-Lind, M. (1997) *The Female Offender: Girls, Women, and Crime*. Thousand Oaks: Sage Publications.

Chiavaroli, T. (1992) 'Rehabilitation from substance abuse in individuals with a history of sexual abuse', *Journal of Substance Abuse Treatment*, 9 (4): 349–54.

Corston, Baroness J. (2007) *The Corston Report: The need for a distinct, radically different, visibly-led, strategic, proportionate, holistic, woman-centred, integrated approach*. Review of women with particular vulnerabilities in the criminal justice system. London: Home Office.

Covington, S.S. (1998) 'Women in prison: approaches in the treatment of our most invisible population', *Women and Therapy*, 21 (1): 141–55.

Dixon, A., Howie, P. and Starling, J. (2004) 'Psychopathology in female juvenile offenders', *Journal of Child Psychology and Psychiatry*, 45 (6): 1150–8.

Easteal, P. (2001) 'Women in Australian prisons: the cycle of abuse and dysfunctional environments', *The Prison Journal*, 81 (1): 73–86.

Fazel, S., Bains, P. and Doll, H. (2006) *Substance Abuse and Dependence in Prisoners: a Systematic Review*. London: Blackwell Publishing.

Fleming, M.F., Barry, K.L. and MacDonald, R. (1991) 'The alcohol use disorders identification test (AUDIT) in a college sample', *The International Journal of the Addictions*, 26 (11): 1173–85.

Henderson, S. (2001) *Women Offenders: Effective Management and Intervention*. Scottish Prison Service Occasional Papers 2001. Edinburgh: Scottish Prison Service.

HM Inspectorate of Prisons for Scotland (2005) *HMP and YOI Cornton Vale: Inspection 2–3 February 2005*. Edinburgh: Scottish Executive.

HM Inspectorates of Social Work Services and Prisons (1998) *Women Offenders – A Safer Way: A Review of Community Disposals and the Use of Custody for Women Offenders in Scotland*. Edinburgh: Social Work Services and Prisons Inspectorate for Scotland.

Holmes, T.H. and Rahe, R.H. (1967) 'The social readjustment rating scale', *Journal of Psychosomatic Research*, 11: 213–18.

Huling, T. (1995) 'African American women and the war on drugs', paper presented at the Annual Meeting of the American Society of Criminology Conference, Boston.

Ingram Fogel, C. and Belyea, M. (1999) 'The lives of incarcerated women: violence, substance abuse, and at risk for HIV', *Journal for the Association of Nurses in AIDS Care*, 10 (6): 66–74.

Keaveny, M. E. and Zauszniewski, J. A. (1999) 'Life events and psychological well-being in women sentenced to prison', *Issues in Mental Health Nursing*, 20 (1): 73–89.

Kendall, K. (1993) *Literature Review of Therapeutic Services for Women in Prison: Companion Volume I to Program Evaluation of Therapeutic Services at the Prison for Women*. Correctional Services of Canada.

Lemgruber, J. (2001) 'Women in the criminal justice system', keynote speech, in N. Ollus and S. Nevala (eds), *Women in the Criminal Justice System: International examples and national responses*. Proceedings of the workshop held at the Tenth United Nations Congress on the Prevention of Crime and the Treatment of Offenders, Vienna, Austria, 10–17 April 2000. Helsinki: HEUNI.

Liebling, A. (1994) 'Suicide amongst women prisoners', *Howard Journal of Criminal Justice*, 33 (1): 1–9.

Liebling, A. (1996) 'Prison suicide: what progress research?', in A. Liebling (ed.), *Deaths in Custody: Caring for People at Risk* (pp. 41–53). London: Whiting and Birch Ltd.

Lightfoot, L. and Lambert, L. (1992) *Substance Abuse Treatment Needs of Federally Sentenced Women: Technical Report No. 2 (Draft)*. Correctional Services Canada.

Loucks, N. (2001) *Evaluation of Improved Regimes for Female Offenders*. London: HM Prison Service for England and Wales, Women's Policy Group, unpublished.

Loucks, N. (1998) *HMPI Cornton Vale: Research into Drugs and Alcohol, Violence and Bullying, Suicides and Self-Injury, and Backgrounds of Abuse*. Scottish Prison Service Occasional Papers, Report No. 1/98. Edinburgh: Scottish Prison Service.

Loucks, N. (1999) 'The Prisoner Life Events Scale'. Unpublished.

Loucks, N. (2005) 'Bullying behaviour among women in prison', in J.L. Ireland (ed.), *Bullying among Prisoners: Innovations in Theory and Research* (pp. 27–43). Cullompton: Willan Publishing.

Loucks, N., Power, K., Swanson, V. and Chambers, J. (2000) *Young People in Custody in Scotland: The characteristics and perceptions of young people held in custody*. Occasional Paper 3/2000. Edinburgh: Scottish Prison Service.

McIvor, G. (1999) 'Women, crime and criminal justice in Scotland', *Scottish Journal of Criminal Justice Studies*, 5 (1): 67–74.

Morash, M., Bynum, T. and Koons (1998) *Women Offenders: Programming Needs and Promising Approaches*. National Institute of Justice.

Pepi, C. (1998) 'Children without childhoods: a feminist intervention strategy utilizing systems theory and restorative justice in treating female adolescent offenders', in J. Harden and M. Hill (eds), *Breaking the Rules: Women in Prison and Feminist Therapy*. New York: Haworth.

Plugge, E., Douglas, N. and Fitzpatrick, R. (2006) *The Health of Women in Prison Study Findings*. Oxford: Department of Public Health, University of Oxford.

Putnins, A.L. (2005) 'Correlates and predictors of self-reported suicide attempts among incarcerated youths', *International Journal of Offender Therapy and Comparative Criminology*, 49 (2): 143–57.

Radosh, P.F. (2002) 'Reflections on women's crime and mothers in prison: a peacemaking approach', *Crime and Delinquency*, 48 (2): 300–15.

Richards, M. and McWilliams, B. (1996) *Imprisonment and Family Ties*. Home Office Research Bulletin 38.

Richie, B.E. (2001) 'Challenges incarcerated women face as they return to their communities: findings from life history interviews', *Crime and Delinquency*, 47 (3): 368–89.

Scottish Court Services (2000) Personal correspondence.

Scottish Government (2008) *Prison Statistics Scotland, 2007/08*. Statistical Bulletin, Crime and Justice Series. Edinburgh: Scottish Government.

Scottish Prison Service (2007) *Tenth Prison Survey 2007: Female Offenders*. Edinburgh: Scottish Prison Service.

Sheehan, R., McIvor, G. and Trotter, C. (2007) 'What does work with women offenders?', in R. Sheehan, G. McIvor and C. Trotter (eds.), *What Works with Women Offenders* (pp. 300–10). Cullompton: Willan Publishing.

Singleton, N., Meltzer, H. and Gatward, R., with J. Coid and D. Deasy (1998) *Psychiatric Morbidity among Prisoners: A survey carried out in 1997 by the Social Survey Division of ONS on behalf of the Department of Health*. London: Office for National Statistics.

Snell, T.L. and Morton, D.C. (1994) *Women in Prison*. Special report. Washington, DC: Bureau of Justice Statistics.

Stern, V. (1998) *A Sin Against the Future: Imprisonment in the World*. London: Penguin Books.

Substance Abuse and Mental Health Services Administration (1999) *National Household Survey on Drug Abuse: Summary Report 1998*. Rockville, MD: Substance Abuse and Mental Health Services Administration.

Timmons-Mitchell, J., Brown, C., Schultz S.C., Wright, Jr, L.W., Webster, S.E., Semple, W. and Flamenbaum-Goldstein, D. (1997) 'Comparing the mental health needs of female and male incarcerated juvenile delinquents', *Behavioral Sciences and the Law*, 15: 195–202.

Walmsley, R. (2006) *World Female Imprisonment List*. London: International Centre for Prison Studies, King's College, London.

Wedderburn Committee (2000) *Justice for Women: The Need for Reform*. Report of the Committee on Women's Imprisonment. London: Prison Reform Trust.

Wolfe, T. (1999) *Counting the Cost: The Social and Financial Consequences of Women's Imprisonment*. Report prepared for the Wedderburn Committee on Women's Imprisonment. London: Prison Reform Trust.

Zaitzow, B.H. (2001) 'Whose problem is it anyway?: Women prisoners and HIV/AIDS', *International Journal of Offender Therapy and Comparative Criminology*, 45 (6): 673–90.

Zamble, E. and Porporino, F.J. (1988) *Coping, Behaviour, and Adaptation in Prison Inmates*. New York: Springer-Verlag.

Zigmond, A.S. and Snaith, R.P. (1983) 'Hospital anxiety and depression scale', *Acta Psychiatrica Scandinavica*, 67: 361–70.

Chapter 24

Self-harm in prisons: dominant models and (mis)understandings

Lisa Marzano

In 2007 alone, over 22,000 incidents of self-harm were recorded in prisons in England and Wales, involving approximately 7,500 prisoners (just under 10 per cent of the average prison population) (Safer Custody Group and Offender Policy Group 2008). Other estimates have suggested that up to 30 per cent of all prisoners have engaged in some form of self-harm during the course of their incarceration, mostly by cutting themselves (Brooker *et al.* 2002). These rates are thought to be between four and 12 times higher than those reported in the general population (Meltzer *et al.* 1999; Towl and Hudson 1997), and are failing to decline (Paton and Jenkins 2005; Safer Custody Group 2007) despite the introduction of several preventative initiatives (see HM Prison Service 2005). In the context of an ever-expanding prison population (de Silva *et al.* 2006), absolute numbers of self-harming incidents – and self-harming prisoners – are likely to increase further.

Clearly, an understanding of the processes that lead to such disproportionately high rates of self-harm, and the implications for practice, are essential. However, to date, there is no agreed theoretical model to account for self-harm in prisons (Towl and Crighton 2008). This may be due to this topic having been 'studied by scholars in a variety of disciplines' and 'subsequently been understood and thus constructed in a variety of ways' (Kilty 2006: 163–4). Arguably, what we 'know' about self-harm in prisons cannot be separated from the ways in which it has been studied, the questions being asked (and those omitted), or the perspectives of those researching it and those being researched. Exploring these is thus an important step in furthering our knowledge and understanding of this phenomenon.

Previous accounts of prisoner self-harm have tended to fall within two main bodies of research. The first, more established, literature has addressed (or perhaps 'buried' (Howard League 1999)) this phenomenon within the broader framework of suicide in prisons (e.g. Borrill *et al.* 2005; Inch *et al.* 1995; Liebling 1992, 1995; Liebling and Krarup 1993). As a known precursor to suicide (Dooley 1990; Owens *et al.* 2002; Topp 1979) (of which prisoners are also disproportionately at risk (Fazel and Benning 2009; Fazel *et al.* 2005)), self-harm has been predominantly researched and 'managed' as a proxy for suicide, rather than as an issue in its own right. By ruling out the idea that self-injury may *not* be a precursor to suicide, this approach may have contributed to obscuring and potentially trivialising alternative meanings and motivations (see also Howard League 2003; Rickford and Edgar 2005).

As the majority of incidents of self-harm in prison appear not to be motivated by suicidal intent, nor to result in death (Safer Custody Group 2007), a second, smaller body of literature has begun to focus on seemingly non-suicidal forms of self-harm, but done so almost exclusively in relation to female prisoners (e.g. Cookson 1977; Cullen 1985; Howard League 2001; Loucks 1997; Snow 1997). Although this issue has been repeatedly shown to be more prevalent among women, both in custody (Corston 2007; Safer Custody Group 2007) and outside (Hawton and Harriss 2008), the over-representation of self-harm among imprisoned men suggests that their needs and motivations in relation to self-harm cannot be overlooked.[1] Ignoring them also risks 'that self-harm becomes sidelined as a "women's problem" and that the distress experienced by these women is belittled' (Howard League 1999: 6; see also Marzano 2007a).

Breaking away from the traditional emphasis on prison suicide, and the traditional (female) gendering of prisoner self-harm, this chapter brings together these two bodies of research within a wider discussion of how self-harm in custody has been understood – and sometimes perhaps misunderstood – in the prison-based literature. Consistent with the Prison Service definition, the term 'self-harm' is used here to describe 'any act where a prisoner deliberately harms themselves, irrespective of the method, intent or severity of any injury' (HM Prison Service 2003: para. 3.1.1). The term 'self-injury' is also employed, with the same meaning. Although 'self-harm' is generally considered to be broader and more inclusive than 'self-injury' (for a discussion of this and other definitional issues see Crighton and Towl 2002), both are common in prisons (Safer Custody Group 2002), and are therefore used interchangeably. For simplicity, these are here referred to as *a* behaviour, although both terms may be used to describe a wide variety of behaviours, ranging from a self-inflicted cut or cigarette burn, to a potentially life-threatening act such as hanging or the swallowing of harmful objects or substances.

The first part of this chapter reviews dominant accounts and conceptualisations of prisoner self-injury, most notably the notions of self-harm as a) an individual 'illness'; b) a symptom of 'prison-induced distress'; c) a means of 'coping' with prison life; and d) a 'manipulative' behaviour. The models presented are not intended to be exhaustive nor mutually exclusive, but to provide an overview and critique of the main concepts and debates in this field of study. The second and final part of the chapter considers how these very tensions and ideas have been (re)produced and reflected in policy, before moving on to discuss their implications for forensic psychological research and practice. Lastly, some suggestions for future studies are made. The focus of this chapter is primarily on England and Wales but, where appropriate and possible, international references are included.

Dominant constructions of prisoner self-harm: a review of the literature

Both in the UK (Ireland 2000; Maden *et al.* 2000; Shea 1993) and abroad (Fotiadou *et al.* 2006; Fulwiler *et al.* 1997; Ivanoff 1992; Lohner and Konrad 2006), most studies focusing on self-harm in prisons have been concerned with prevalence, risk factors and clinical concomitants (for a systematic review see Lohner and Konrad 2007). In turn, this body of research may be located within – and across – two main conceptual paradigms. On the one hand, psychiatric and psychological studies focusing on the 'imported vulnerability' of 'at risk' prisoners; on the other, sociological analyses of the role of imprisonment itself in precipitating self-harm. Both research traditions, and combinations thereof, have been central to how we understand this issue and its enduring prevalence in prisons. Therefore, it is to these, respectively, that the discussion now turns.

Importation models: self-harm as an 'individual illness'

Psychological and psychiatric analyses of self-injury in prison have predominantly focused on identifying the common features of those prisoners most likely to self-harm, i.e. to establish a profile of the 'vulnerable' (Liebling 1992), 'high risk' prisoner, which could assist the prediction and prevention of self-harm in custody. Consistent with community studies, these have suggested that the risk of self-harming is statistically associated with being white, young, coming from disadvantaged social, economic and familial backgrounds, and having experienced or witnessed some form of emotional, physical and/or sexual abuse. Rates of self-injury have also been found to be especially high among prisoners with a history of psychiatric disorder and treatment, a past of alcohol and/or drug dependency, and those convicted for sexual and violent offences, serving long sentences, and with a history of disciplinary infractions. Further risk factors include poor coping and problem-solving skills, previous self-injury, close affiliation with someone with a history of self-harm, and high levels of aggression, impulsivity, anxiety, helplessness and depression (see Crighton and Towl 2002; Livingstone 1997).

The profile of the self-harming prisoner is thus remarkably similar to that of prisoners more generally. 'Prisons collect individuals who find it difficult to cope, they collect excessive numbers of people with mental disorders, they collect individuals who have weak social supports, they collect individuals who, by any objective test, do not have rosy prospects' (Gunn 1994, as quoted in HMCIP 1999: para. 3.11). An important implication of this is that high rates of self-harm in prisons may be viewed as 'demographically representative of the population they contain' (Liebling 1992: 24); in other words, they may be due to the prison population being – or being *selected* to be (Liebling 1995) – disproportionately at risk of self-harm. Whilst this might be a powerful argument for contesting contemporary policies of incarceration, it arguably adds little to our understanding of how to predict or prevent self-harm within custody. Indeed, by (over)emphasising the psychiatric illnesses and/or psychological deficiencies of those who self-injure, but overlooking the environmental correlates of this behaviour, these studies appear to suggest that prisons can do little or nothing to prevent its occurrence.

Some of the 'psy-literature' (Rose 1985) has contributed to creating a picture of prisoner self-harm as 'a complex and difficult to manage clinical problem' (Chowanec *et al.* 1991: 202), 'a symptom of pervasive maladjustment' (*ibid.*: 203) and/or 'of long term personality problems' (Maden *et al.* 2000: 199), including 'severe psychopathology' (*ibid.*; see also Wilkins and Coid 1991). As analyses of self-harm in the community have shown (see e.g. Johnstone 1997), pathologising self-injury risks further stigmatising and alienating individuals, and can be associated with a variety of negative staff attitudes and practices. For instance, 'too often, further inquiry into the reason for the behaviour, in particular into the situational determinants of self-wounding, stops once a diagnosis is made' (Babiker and Arnold 1997: 14). In a prison, the implications of medicalising self-harm may be even more acute, not least because it may leave staff (most of whom are not psychiatrically trained) feeling unprepared and/or unwilling to deal with this issue (Marzano 2007b).

At the same time, this model may be seen to imply that self-injury is irrational, meaningless and a threat to the security of the institution (Kilty 2006). In turn, this can legitimise punitive and tautological responses to self-harm, with prisoners' needs being reconstructed as institutional risk factors to be controlled and (self)governed. Within the actuarial 'risk culture' (Lupton 1999) that permeates the Prison Service (see e.g. Carlen 2002; Rickford and Edgar 2005), this – and the tendency to view all self-harm as a precursor to suicide – can lead to constructing prisoners who self-harm as dangerous and risky, to others and to themselves. As a consequence, their needs can become overridden by security concerns and by the imperative of preventing deaths in custody.

Deprivation models: self-harm as a symptom of 'prison-induced distress'

Dissatisfaction with this individualistic model led sociological researchers to focus on the situational factors that may increase the risk of self-harm in custody. Whilst this potentially problematic emphasis on risk has remained pervasive, attention has shifted away from risky individuals and backgrounds, to risky times, cultures and regimes (for more detailed reviews see Crighton and Towl 2002; Livingstone 1997; Lohner and Konrad 2007). In so doing, researchers were able to show that withdrawing from drugs and alcohol, being transferred to another prison or hospital, receiving bad news and experiencing relationship problems (either inside or outside prison) are all times of high risk, as are nights, early mornings and weekends. Being on remand, serving a life sentence and having no previous experience of imprisonment were also reported to increase prisoners' vulnerability, especially in early periods of custody. Further factors include the lack or avoidance of 'purposeful activities' (HMCIP 2004), being physically and socially isolated (e.g. in segregation or in a single cell) and being bullied by other prisoners or staff. Indeed, the overall social and 'moral climate' (Liebling and Arnold 2004) of a prison has been described as a crucial risk factor for self-harm, particularly in relation to prisoners' perceptions of relationships, safety, care and fairness. In turn, all of these are thought to be affected by overcrowded conditions and associated problems of low staff levels, training and morale, hence perhaps the heterogeneity of self-harm rates across different types of establishments.

Overall these findings suggest that the stresses and 'pains' of imprisonment (Sykes 1958; Toch 1992), although often said in the psychological literature to have negligible long-term effects (see e.g. Bukstel and Kilmann 1980; Richards 1978; Sapsford 1978), are directly implicated in the production and persistence of self-harm in prisons. Adding further strength to this argument is the finding that the prevalence of self-harm increases with time spent in custody (Safer Custody Group 2004). Thus, rather than (or as well as) being a symptom of individual illness, prisoner self-harm has been reconceptualised as an outcome of 'prison-induced distress' (Liebling 1992), a test of the 'health' (HMCIP 1999), 'moral performance' (Liebling and Arnold 2004) and legitimacy of our prisons and criminal justice system (Liebling *et al.* 2005a).

Despite its popularity, this model may be criticised for its insularity in relation to wider discussions on self-harm (within and beyond prisons), and seeming disregard of individual differences and experiences, especially those pre-dating prison. These should be considered, as not all who become exposed to the potentially damaging effects of imprisonment go on to self-harm. Moreover, there is evidence that many of those who do, have a history of self-harm outside prison (Livingstone 1997), and continue to self-injure following release from custody (Howard League 2002).

Combined models: self-harm as a 'coping mechanism'

In view of these limitations, attempts to bridge situational and dispositional models of prisoner self-harm have gained increasing support in recent years. It is now well established that 'prisons expose already vulnerable populations to additional risk' (Liebling *et al.* 2005a: 210) and that self-harm in custody is a complex phenomenon resulting from the dynamic interactions between individuals and their environments (see also Towl and Crighton 2008).

Some studies have embraced this new, 'combined model' (*ibid.*) by focusing on a wider range of individual *and* prison-related factors, and adopting an interactionist (Zamble and Porporino 1988) conceptualisation of risk. In other words, rather than exclusively relying on static, statistically derived factors, this body of research is concerned with how these interact, how they may be mediated or moderated at an individual and institutional level, and their significance in the aetiology of self-harm. In this context, an important finding has been that, whilst there appear to be only 'differences of degree' in the criminal justice histories and background characteristics of prisoners who self-harm and those who do not, their descriptions of prison life differ in marked ways (Liebling 1995). As a result, the ways in which individuals experience and cope with being in prison have come to be seen as key to understanding self-harm in custody. Indeed, the concept of 'coping in prison' – and the associated notion of 'the poor copers' (Liebling 1992, 1995) – have come to exemplify this new paradigm, despite their circularity and somewhat vague definitions.

In some cases, the resulting emphasis on coping styles (e.g. Brown and Ireland 2006; Power *et al.* 1997) has meant focusing once again on the individual differences (read deficiencies) of self-harming prisoners, and *their* inability to deal with prison life – with arguably insufficient attention being paid to the wider system's (in)ability to cope with its growing and vulnerable populations (see also Smith 2000; Thomas *et al.* 2006). In addition, whilst providing a more sophisticated model of prisoner self-harm, this approach holds limited explanatory power. In particular, it fails to explain why prisoners who self-harm are poor copers, what they may be struggling to cope with, or how their limited coping abilities may lead to their self-harming.

Qualitative analyses of prisoner self-injury, however few, have helped to clarify some of these points. By exploring the experiences and motivations of prisoners who self-harm (mostly through semi-structured interviews), these studies have contributed to shifting attention and stigma away from their psychological (dis)functioning, to the feelings and events that may underlie them. In particular, issues of trauma, abuse, powerlessness and neglect have been shown to play an important role in initiating and maintaining this behaviour (Borrill *et al.* 2005; Loucks 1997; Snow 1997, 2002) and its associated symptoms, including drugs and mental health problems, and poor coping skills.

This body of work has also highlighted that self-harming can have a variety of functions and meanings for those who self-injure, thus explaining how it may become a 'coping strategy' (Howard League 2001). Consistent with the wider self-harm literature (Connors 1996; Klonsky 2007), prisoners' self-injury has been found to provide a sense of relief, escape and control over feelings of anxiety, depersonalisation, anger and helplessness, and one's environment (Cullen 1985; Jeglic *et al.* 2005; Loucks 1997; Snow 1997, 2002). Participant-centred accounts have also contributed to reframing self-harm as a way of punishing oneself or others, a means of re-enacting trauma or self-cleansing, distracting oneself from emotional pain or '"speaking" about what are social and political, as well as personal experiences' (Babiker and Arnold 1997: 37). On this basis, self-harming has been described as not only 'a necessary though unhealthy way of responding to [and coping with] distressing and oppressive conditions' (Fillmore and Dell 2000: 9), but also an act of defiance and resistance, a way of regaining some power.

By bringing attention to individuals' apparent reasons for self-injuring, these studies have challenged the notion that self-harm is necessarily meaningless, irrational or 'weak' behaviour (Groves 2004), or that it may inevitably be linked with or lead to suicide. Indeed, self-injury has sometimes been argued to be the very opposite of suicide, and reconceptualised as a survival strategy – albeit perhaps a maladaptive one. This idea has long been celebrated in the feminist (Cresswell 2005; Spandler and Warner 2007) and penal reform literature (Howard League 2001). Not only does it offer a seemingly more sympathetic reading of self-harm than the individual illness model, it also opens up the possibility that this behaviour may be a form of self-care and 'self-soothing' (McAllister 2003), rather than something to be stopped at all costs. Indeed, and despite Prison Service opposition to the principles of 'safe self-harming' and 'harm minimisation', it has often been argued that removing all means to self-injure can be counter-productive, potentially leading to more severe self-harm (see e.g. Pembroke 2007; Shaw and Shaw 2007).

However, it is questionable whether the discourses put forward as positive reconceptualisations of self-harm may actually always 'work' in relation to prisoners, particularly male prisoners. For example the idea of self-harm as an attempt to gain power and demonstrate agency may be viewed more positively when applied to the 'white, suburban, attractive teenage girl [who] persists as the face of self-mutilation' (Brickman 2004: 87) than it would when considered in relation to male offenders. Even with regard to women prisoners, 'it seems to be beyond the scope of correctionalism to view resistance as anything but a threat to the security of the institution' (Kilty 2006: 165).

On the other hand, it is perhaps beyond the scope of perspectives so firmly rooted within a prison reform agenda to acknowledge that, in some instances, resistance may indeed be viewed negatively. The conceptualisation of self-harm as a coping strategy has been criticised for normalising and romanticising this behaviour, and its more 'instrumental' functions. It is to these that the discussion now turns.

Self-harm as a 'manipulative' act

The view that 'conscious manipulation of the environment is a factor in self-injury' (Cookson 1977: 346) is a recurrent, albeit contested, theme in the literature on self-harm in prisons. Whilst most frequently discussed in relation to staff's attitudes towards this behaviour (see e.g. HMCIP 1990; Liebling *et al.* 2005b; Snow 1997), it has also been cited as one of the main motivations behind prisoners' self-harm (Dear *et al.* 2000; Franklin 1988; Jeglic *et al.* 2005; Power and Spencer 1987; World Health Organisation 2000). This argument, although not unique to prisons, marks one of the greatest points of departure between accounts of self-harm in custody and in the community. As suggested by Groves (2004: 55), the manipulative 'diagnosis' 'may be particularly salient in this context', not least because of the 'universal, subcultural obsession of prison staff that frequently they are being manipulated by prisoners' (Harding 1994: 210). The predominance of this discourse in staff's accounts of prisoners' self-harm renders it an especially important one to explore and deconstruct, particularly as there is often no clarification of what is meant by the term, and 'little available guidance for staff on how to construe this behaviour, or on how to manage it' (Bowers 2003: 323; see also Marzano and Adler 2007).

The notion of self-harm as manipulative behaviour is not intended to describe *all* incidents of self-injury in custody. Evidence that some prisoners go to great lengths to conceal their self-inflicted injuries (Rivlin 2006) would counter this argument very quickly. Rather, it has been used to describe a proportion of incidents, thought to be between 24 and 50 per cent of all self-harm in prisons (with lower estimates being based on prisoners' self-reported motives, as interpreted and coded by researchers (see Dear *et al.* 2000; Power and Spencer 1987), and higher ones on data obtained from psychiatric records (see Franklin 1988)). The main argument made for differentiating between these and more 'genuine' forms of self-harm is that failing to manage them differently may 'contribute to a pattern of repetitious behaviour' (Franklin 1988: 214), with the behaviour of 'manipulators' being reinforced by the attention and support received (Jeglic *et al.* 2005).

This claim, based on the assumption of an identifiable subgroup of manipulators, has been criticised on several grounds. Firstly, there is evidence that the majority of those reportedly self-harming for 'manipulative or gain-seeking reasons' (*ibid.*) are nonetheless likely to injure themselves in medically serious ways (Dear *et al.* 2000), and to also self-harm for different purposes (Snow 2002). In relation to such a complex phenomenon, rigid classifications of behaviours, groups and motivations are likely to be artificial, misleading and potentially dangerous.

Secondly, the very idea – and semantics – of there being a manipulative element to self-injury have been described as 'singularly unhelpful' (*ibid.*), particularly in an institutional setting. They may rationalise punitive staff responses (Crighton and Towl 2002) and legitimise the view that self-injury is 'unworthy of attention and/or effective treatment' (Snow 1997: 50). This, in turn, may reproduce the very feelings and circumstances leading to prisoners' self-harming in the first place (Johnstone 1997).

Given the above, 'softer' variations of this theme have been employed, most notably the suggestion that (some) self-harm is a form of 'attention-seeking' and/or carried out for 'instrumental' purposes (e.g. Snow 2002). Nonetheless, these also emphasise the effects of self-harm on others, and its potentially strategic and exploitative nature. In so doing, they too may serve to locate self-injury within a behavioural (Corbett and Westwood 2005) and moral framework that 'condemns self-mutilation and through it, the self-mutilator' (Groves 2004: 56).

Further undermining the validity and reliability of these concepts is evidence of their inconsistent uses and applications. There has been little discussion or agreement as to what actually counts as a manipulative or instrumental motive. For instance, in a study of 'parasuicidal' behaviour among Scottish male young offenders, Power and Spencer (1987) interpreted self-harming to avoid harassment from other prisoners as an 'instrumental motivation'. Under this same category, Snow (2002) included reasons as varied as wanting 'changes in medication' and 'transfer', 'being alone' and 'wanting someone to talk to'. It is questionable whether classifying these motives within broader categories is actually useful and, if so, whether the label instrumental (as opposed to interpersonal or situational) provides an accurate description for any of these alleged motives, or adequately reflects why some would go to such extreme lengths in order to achieve their goals.

It is also worth noting that self-harming behaviours are seemingly more likely to be construed as manipulative when involving Black prisoners, those with an extensive criminal history and, above all, men (Johnson 1973; World Health Organisation 2000). In other words, 'the [alleged] meaning of these acts also varies according to who performs them' (Groves 2004: 56). This, and the popular/populist construction of criminals as rational, immoral actors (see e.g. Cornish and Clarke 1986), suggest that the notion of self-harm as instrumentally motivated may provide a better explanation for the prevalence of this model in the prison literature (compared with accounts of self-harm in the community) than it does for the high incidence of self-injury among prisoners.

Implications for practice

As concluded by Rayner and Warner (2003: 315), 'there are a range of explanations of self-harm that are culturally available and which can be drawn on differentially'. This is perhaps especially the case in the context of prisons, where debates over the vulnerability of its populations, and the likely effects of incarceration, have led to much controversy regarding how this phenomenon can and should be understood. As discussed in this chapter, self-harm in prison has been constructed as a product of individual differences and deficiencies, of prison-induced distress, or – combining both explanations – a strategy employed by vulnerable individuals to cope with the harms and pains of imprisonment. The latter model, currently the most popular, has helped to reframe self-harm as potentially functional and meaningful (albeit maladaptive), but introduced the unhelpful concept of 'the poor copers'. When attention has focused on the interpersonal and instrumental purposes of prisoners' self-harm, even more stigmatising labels have emerged, most notably 'the manipulators' and 'the attention seekers'.

These different conceptualisations of self-harm have clear implications for the ways in which this behaviour is managed and prevented in prisons, not least in relation to the aims and targets of intervention(s), and how accountable staff groups are for their delivery. For instance, prevention strategies may aim to identify individuals at risk through screening all prisoners upon their arrival in custody; reduce their means and opportunities to self-harm through changes to the built environment, cell sharing and regular monitoring by staff; or aim to improve the moral climate of a prison by promoting peer support and closer staff–prisoners relationships. An alternative (or additional) approach may be to treat underlying – or co-morbid – mental health or substance abuse issues, via psychotropic medication, detoxification programmes and/or psycho-social interventions, particularly in the form of problem-solving therapy, counselling and dialectical behavioural therapy. These interventions, singularly, or in combination, may be differentially implemented depending on the level of risk of particular individuals, establishments, situations, or forms of self-injury (for more extensive discussions see Daigle *et al.* 2007; Konrad *et al.* 2007; McArthur *et al.* 1999; Paton and Jenkins 2005). Indeed, assumptions about different types of self-harm – and self-harming prisoners – may influence whether all incidents are treated as precursors to suicide, whether a supportive response is made, or 'a behavioural plan' put into place.

Like the assumptions underlying them, these different ways of 'treating' and preventing self-harm in prison require some attention, as they may have unintended consequences and iatrogenic effects. Although these cannot be fully explored in this context, the following section considers issues and debates that may be of particular relevance to forensic psychologists.

Forensic psychologists and prisoner self-harm: too much involvement or not enough?

Besides some involvement in the training and support of staff, psychologists' main roles in relation to this area of practice have entailed studying self-harming prisoners, and assessing and reducing their level of risk. In turn, this has mostly involved the design and delivery of programmes aimed at improving prisoners' coping skills and social problem-solving (Towl and Crighton 2008). However, despite their stated intentions, these activities may not always be as beneficial or sympathetic as they first appear.

Psychology has mainly constructed itself as a benign discipline (Gergen 1996), but rarely questioned who may benefit from its discourses and practices, and who may not (Henriques *et al.* 1998; Lazard and Marzano 2005). Among others, Burman *et al.* (1996: 5) have argued that, wittingly or unwittingly, psychology has had an important role 'in pathologising those who fail to fit its norms'. In relation to this subject, its predominant emphasis on the coping skills and personal characteristics of prisoners who self-harm (even when considering their interactions with environmental factors) has contributed to individualising – and thus de-politicising – this issue. As discussed earlier in the chapter, this can have the effect of constructing self-harm as a state, trait or illness of particular individuals, while obscuring the role of wider systemic and institutional issues in its aetiology, pathologisation and persistence.

According to Carlen (2007; see also Carlen and Tombs 2006), when individualistic psychological explanations are used to inform in-prison programmes, the consequences can be even more far-reaching. As well as perpetuating unhelpful stereotypes, this 'therapunitive rhetoric' risks bringing further legitimacy to the overuse of imprisonment, by suggesting that – even in the present conditions – prisons are capable of dealing with the complex needs of those in their custody. Although her critique is specifically directed at the growing rehabilitation and 're-integration industries' in women's prisons, it is arguably also relevant to the current context:

> Although in themselves the psychological programmes are most probably harmless [... they] actually cause harm because they suggest to women that they should be able to control their responses to adverse material circumstances over which, in fact, they have no control. (Carlen 2007: 7)

On the other hand, at least in the short term, it is possible that *not* providing such interventions may result in even more harm. Indeed, even if 'imprisonment causes more psychological damage than any in-prison therapy can ever cure' (*ibid*.), it is difficult to view the 'warehousing' of prisoners as anything but deleterious (Cavadino and Dignan 2002). From this perspective, it may seem problematic that forensic psychologists working in prisons have 'increasingly moved away from this area of work in favour of work intended to reduce the risk of re-offending' (Towl and Crighton 2008: 193; see also Towl 2004). Psychological interventions aimed at reducing self-harm remain few, almost exclusively aimed at women prisoners, and poorly evaluated. This is despite recent evidence of their effectiveness in the community (Hawton 2008), and suggestions that addressing the issues underlying prisoners' self-harm may also diminish the likelihood of their reoffending upon release from custody (see e.g. Liebling 1992).

Moving forward? Some tensions and recommendations

Clearly, prisoner self-harm is a complex and multifaceted issue that does not lend itself to a single explanation or definition nor to simple solutions. Indeed, individualistic or institutional solutions may not always even be desirable. In much of the relevant policy and literature this has tended to be constructed as problematic, on theoretical, methodological and practical grounds (see e.g. Crighton and Towl 2002). However, post-structural feminists have suggested that the recognition of multiple versions or constructions of 'truth' in relation to self-harm is potentially liberating and empowering (e.g. Shaw 2002; see also Bordo 1993). It may help to challenge dominant and often stigmatising understandings of this issue, and encourage more flexible responses to people who self-harm. In the words of McAllister (2003: 184), 'opening up self-harm to multiple readings offers hope that individualised, effective responses for clients may be possible'.

There might not be a 'right' way of conceptualising or addressing this issue. Attempts to do so may well be 'impracticable' (Rayner and Warner 2003) and potentially counterproductive. This, however, is not to suggest that we should stop exposing and critiquing unhelpful and (ostensibly) helpful ways of understanding self-harm in prisons, or seeking effective strategies to reduce its alarming incidence.

Some have argued that, regardless of one's perspective, to continue to research and 'regulate' prisoners' self-harm are likely to perpetuate and amplify the 'problem' (Groves 2004). The risk is that of 'reproducing rather than transforming precisely that which is being protested' (Bordo 1993: 177) and that accounts and interventions 'intended to liberate oppressed groups [...] end up simply locking them within different restrictive discourses' (Willig 1999: 9). On the other hand, the dangers of failing to challenge unhelpful practices and discourses may be even greater. This may reinforce their hegemony, and further hide and normalise the needs and distress of which self-harm is a symptom, and the arguably poor health and moral performance of our prisons and criminal justice system. Although it is perhaps useful to de-pathologise prisoners' self-harm, to de-problematise and normalise this issue – and its potentially fatal consequences – seem both unethical and counterproductive.

Further suggestions for future studies

Whilst we arguably do not need to stop researching this area, we do perhaps need to start doing so in different and more 'participatory' ways. Over the past three decades, descriptive and 'predictive' analyses of prisoner self-harm have abounded, despite their limited explanatory power. In contrast, particularly in relation to male self-injury, there have been few published studies on the motivations and experiences of those who harm themselves in custody, or on the impact of their behaviour on other prisoners and staff. Investigating how the latter groups view and respond to self-injury may also contribute to a more systemic and relational understanding of this issue, and help to counter the notion that vulnerable prisoners are an isolated problem to be addressed. For this very reason, it may be useful to increase our understanding of the links (if any) between self-harming in prison and in the community. Given the disadvantaged backgrounds of most persons in custody, and the disempowering effects of imprisonment, the question of why there are not even more prisoners harming themselves may also provide some interesting insights.

In an environment where the 'self-harm problem' is seemingly pervasive and enduring, 'resolution' (Sinclair and Green 2005) of self-injury is also an especially useful area to explore. Both in prisons and outside, most studies have focused on what may initiate and maintain the behaviour, with fewer attempts being made to understand (particularly from a phenomenological perspective) why and how people may come to stop self-harming. In this context, a participant-centred approach can – and arguably should – inform the development of policy and practice in important ways. The question of why it has not already done so, despite years of campaigning and growing consensus regarding what strategies may contribute to reducing self-harm in custody (see e.g. Konrad *et al.* 2007), warrants further attention.

As contended by Frater (2008: 845) in relation to prison suicides, 'the risk factors are known, but public policy is lagging behind'. Arguably, rather than to keep raising the same criticisms and suggestions against a system that has indeed incorporated these in its official rhetoric (e.g. HM Prison Service 2001; Safer Custody Group 2001), we need to start asking why these continue to fail, and in whose interest. Nobody has made this point more eloquently than Foucault (1977: 271–2):

> If the prison-institution has survived for so long, with such immobility, if the principle of penal detention has never seriously been questioned, it is no doubt because this carceral system was deeply rooted and carried out very precise functions [...] Perhaps one should reverse the problem and ask oneself what is served by the failure of the prison: what is the use of these different phenomena that are continually being criticized [...]

As concluded by Groves (2004: 53), 'self-mutilation must, on some level, be construed as a failure of the prison'. In the longer term, it is perhaps this wider failure, and its functions, 'successes' and normalisation, that we need to expose and critique.

Note

1 Gender-specific issues are too long and complex to debate fully in this context. However, for interesting discussions see Brickman (2004), Bowen and John (2001), Loucks (this volume) and Taylor (2003).

References

Babiker, G. and Arnold, L. (1997) *The Language of Injury: Comprehending Self-Mutilation*. Leicester: The British Psychological Society.

Bordo, S. (1993) *Unbearable Weight: Feminism, Western Culture, and the Body*. London: University of California Press.

Borrill, J., Snow, L., Medlicott, D., Teers, R. and Paton, J. (2005) 'Learning from near misses: interviews with women who survived an incident of severe self-harm', *Howard League Journal*, 44: 57–69.

Bowen, A.C.L. and John, A.M.H. (2001) 'Gender differences in presentation and conceptualisation of adolescent self-injurious behaviour: implications for therapeutic practice', *Counselling Psychology Quarterly*, 14 (4): 357–79.

Bowers, L. (2003) 'Manipulation: description, identification and ambiguity', *Journal of Psychiatric and Mental Health Nursing*, 10: 323–8.

Brickman, B.J. (2004) '"Delicate" cutters: gendered self-mutilation and attractive flesh in medical discourse', *Body and Society*, 10 (4): 87–111.

Brooker, C., Repper, J., Beverley, C., Ferriter, M. and Brewer, N. (2002) *Mental Health Services and Prisoners: A Review*. Sheffield: Mental Health Task Force.

Brown, S.L. and Ireland, C.A. (2006) 'Coping style and distress in newly incarcerated male adolescents', *Journal of Adolescent Health*, 38 (6): 656–61.

Bukstel, L.H. and Kilmann, P.R. (1980) 'Psychological effects of imprisonment on confined individuals', *Psychological Bulletin*, 85: 469–93.

Burman, E. (1997) 'Minding the gap: positivism, psychology, and the politics of qualitative methods', *Journal of Social Issues*, 53 (4): 785–801.

Burman, E., Aitken, G., Alldred, P., Allwood, R., Billington, T., Goldberg, B., Gordo-López, A.J., Heenan, C., Marks, D. and Warner, S. (eds) (1996) *Psychology Discourse Practice: From Regulation to Resistance*. London: Taylor and Francis.

Carlen, P. (2002) 'Governing the governors: telling tales of managers, mandarins and mavericks', *Criminal Justice*, 2 (1): 27–49.

Carlen, P. (2007) 'The Women's Imprisonment and Re-Integration Industries.' Paper delivered on 21 February 2007, Middlesex University, London.

Carlen, P. and Tombs, J. (2006) 'Reconfigurations of penality: the ongoing case of the women's imprisonment and reintegration industries', *Theoretical Criminology*, 10 (3): 337–60.

Cavadino, M. and Dignan, J. (2002) *The Penal System: An Introduction* (3rd edn). London: Sage.

Chowanec, G.D., Josephson, A.M., Coleman, C. and Davis, H. (1991) 'Self-harming behaviour in incarcerated male delinquent adolescents', *Journal of the American Academy of Child and Adolescent Psychiatry*, 30 (2): 202–7.

Connors, R. (1996) 'Self-injury in trauma survivors: 1. Functions and meanings', *American Journal of Orthopsychiatry*, 66 (2): 197–206.

Cookson, H.M. (1977) 'A survey of self-injury in a closed prison for women', *British Journal of Criminology*, 17 (4): 332–47.

Corbett, K. and Westwood, T. (2005) '"Dangerous and Severe Personality Disorder": a psychiatric manifestation of the risk society', *Critical Public Health*, 16 (2): 121–33.

Cornish, D.B. and Clarke, R.V. (eds) (1986) *The Reasoning Criminal: Rational Choice Perspectives on Offending*. New York: Springer-Verlag.

Corston, Baroness (2007) *The Corston Report: A review of women with particular vulnerabilities in the criminal justice system*. London: Home Office.

Crighton, D. and Towl, G. (2002) 'Intentional self-injury', in G. Towl, L. Snow and M. McHugh (eds), *Suicide in Prisons*. Oxford: BPS Blackwell.

Cresswell, M. (2005) 'Self-harm "survivors" and psychiatry in England, 1988–1996', *Social Theory and Health*, 3: 259–85.

Cullen, J.E. (1985) 'Prediction and treatment of self-injury by female young offenders', in D.P. Farrington and R. Tarling (eds), *Prediction in Criminology*. Albany: State University of New York Press.

Daigle, M.S., Anasseril, E.D., Dear, G.E., Frottier, P., Hayes, L.M., Kerkhof, A., Konrad, N., Liebling, A. and Sarchiapone, M. (2007) 'Preventing suicide in prisons, Part II: International comparisons of suicide prevention services in correctional facilities', *Crisis*, 28 (3): 122–30.

Dear, G.E., Thomson, D.M. and Hills, A.M. (2000) 'Self-harm in prison: manipulators can also be suicide attempters', *Criminal Justice and Behavior*, 27 (2): 160–75.

de Silva, N., Cowell, P., Chow, T. and Worthington, P. (2006) *Prison Population Projections 2006–2013, England and Wales*. Home Office Statistical Bulletin, 11/06. London: Home Office.

Dooley, E. (1990) 'Prison suicide in England and Wales: 1972–1987', *British Journal of Psychiatry*, 151: 218–21.

Fazel, S., Benning, R. and Danesh, J. (2005) 'Suicides in male prisoners in England and Wales, 1978–2003', *The Lancet*, 366: 1301–2.

Fazel, S. and Benning, R. (2009) 'Suicides in female prisoners in England and Wales, 1978–2004', *British Journal of Psychiatry*, 194: 183–4.

Fillmore, C. and Dell, C.A. (2000) *Prairie Women, Violence, and Self-Harm*. Winnipeg: The Elizabeth Fry Society of Manitoba.

Fotiadou, M., Livaditis, M., Manou, I., Kaniotou, E. and Xenitidis, K. (2006) 'Prevalence of mental disorders and deliberate self-harm in Greek male prisoners', *International Journal of Law and Psychiatry*, 29: 68–73.

Foucault, M. (1977) *Discipline and Punish: The Birth of the Prison.* (translated by A. Sheridan). Harmondsworth: Penguin.

Franklin, R.K. (1988) 'Deliberate self-harm – self-injurious behaviour within a correctional mental health population', *Criminal Justice and Behavior*, 15 (2): 210–18.

Frater, A. (2008) 'Deaths in custody: the risk factors are known, but public policy is lagging behind', *British Medical Journal*, 336: 845–56.

Fulwiler, C., Forbes, C., Santangelo, S. and Folstein, M. (1997) 'Self-mutilation and suicide attempt: distinguishing features in prisoners', *Journal of the American Academic of Psychiatry and the Law*, 25 (1): 69–77.

Gergen, K.J. (1996) 'Social psychology as social construction: the emerging vision', in C. McGarty and A. Haslam (eds), *The Message of Social Psychology: Perspectives on Mind in Society*. Oxford: Blackwell.

Groves, A. (2004) 'Blood on the walls: self-mutilation in prisons', *Australian and New Zealand Journal of Criminology*, 37 (1): 49–64.

Harding, M. (1994) 'What can we learn from suicide and self-injury?', in A. Liebling and T. Ward (eds), *Deaths in Custody: International Perspectives*. London: Whiting and Birch Ltd.

Hawton, K. and Harriss, L. (2008) 'The changing gender ratio in occurrence of deliberate self–harm across the lifecycle', *Crisis*, 29: 4–10.

Hawton, K. (2008) 'Evidence-based clinical care for deliberate self-harm patients.' Paper delivered on 28 August 2008, 12th European Symposium on Suicide and Suicidal Behaviour, Glasgow.

Henriques, J., Hollway, W., Urwin, C., Venn, C. and Walkerdine, V. (1998) *Changing the Subject: Psychology, Social Regulation and Subjectivity.* London: Routledge.

HMCIP (1990) *Review of Suicide and Self-Harm.* London: HMSO.

HMCIP (1999) *Suicide Is Everyone's Concern: A Thematic Review by HM Chief Inspector of Prisons for England and Wales.* London: HMSO.

HMCIP (2004) *Expectations: Criteria for Assessing the Conditions in Prisons and the Treatment of Prisoners*. London: HMCIP.

HM Prison Service (2001) *Prevention of Suicide and Self-Harm in the Prison Service: An Internal Review.* London: HMSO.

HM Prison Service (2003) *Prison Service Order 2700: Suicide and Self-Harm Prevention*. London: HMSO.

HM Prison Service (2005) *Prison Service Order 18/2005: Introducing ACCT (Assessment, Care in Custody and Teamwork) – the Replacement for the F2052SH (Risk of Self-Harm)*. London: HMSO.

Howard League (1999) *Scratching the Surface: The Hidden Problem of Self-Harm in Prisons*. London: The Howard League for Penal Reform.

Howard League (2001) *Suicide and Self-Harm Prevention: Repetitive Self-Harm Amongst Women and Girls in Prison.* London: The Howard League for Penal Reform.

Howard League (2002) *Suicide and Self-Harm Prevention: Following Release from Prison*. London: The Howard League for Penal Reform.

Howard League (2003) *Suicide and Self-Harm Prevention: The Management of Self-Injury in Prison*. London: The Howard League for Penal Reform.

Inch, H., Rowlands, P. and Soliman, A. (1995) 'Deliberate self-harm in a young offenders Institution', *Journal of Forensic Psychiatry*, 6 (1): 161–71.

Ireland, J.L. (2000) 'A descriptive analysis of self-harm reports among a sample of incarcerated adolescent males', *Journal of Adolescence*, 23 (5): 605–13.

Ivanoff, A. (1992) 'Background risk factors associated with parasuicide among male prison inmates', *Criminal Justice and Behavior*, 19 (4): 426–36.

Jeglic, E.L., Vanderhoff, H.A. and Donovick, P.J. (2005) 'The functions of self-harm behaviour in a forensic population', *International Journal of Offender Therapy and Comparative Criminology*, 49 (2): 131–42.

Johnson, E. (1973) 'Felon self-mutilation: correlates of stress in prison', in B. Danto (ed.), *Jail House Blues* (pp. 237–72) Michigan: Epic Publications.

Johnstone, L. (1997) 'Self-injury and the psychiatric response', *Feminism and Psychology*, 7 (3): 421–6.

Kilty, J.M. (2006) 'Under the barred umbrella: is there room for a women-centred self-injury policy in Canadian corrections?', *Criminology and Public Policy*, 5 (1): 161–82.

Klonsky, E.D. (2007) 'The functions of deliberate self-injury: a review of the evidence', *Clinical Psychology Review*, 27: 226–39.

Konrad, N., Daigle, M.S., Daniel, A.E., Dear, G.E., Frottier, P., Hayes, L.M., Kerkhof, A. and Liebling, A. and Sarchiapone, M. (2007) 'Preventing suicide in prisons, Part I. Recommendations from the International Association for Suicide Prevention Task Force on Suicide in Prisons', *Crisis*, 28 (3): 113–21.

Lazard, L. and Marzano, L. (2005) 'Changing the story: an examination of strategies for resisting sexism and racism', *Psychology of Women Section Review*, 7 (1): 21–9.

Liebling, A. (1992) *Suicides in Prison*. London: Routledge.

Liebling, A. (1995) 'Vulnerability and prison suicide', *British Journal of Criminology*, 35 (2): 173–87.

Liebling, A. and Arnold, H. (2004) *Prisons and Their Moral Performance: A Study of Values, Quality and Prison Life*. Oxford: Clarendon Press.

Liebling, A. and Krarup, H. (1993) *Suicide Attempts and Self-Injury in Male Prisons*. London: Home Office Research Planning Unit.

Liebling, A., Durie, L., Stiles, A. and Tait, S. (2005a) 'Revisiting prison suicide: the role of fairness and distress', in A. Liebling and A. Maruna (eds), *The Effects of Imprisonment*. Cullompton: Willan Publishing.

Liebling, A., Tait, S., Durie, L., Stiles, A. and Harvey, J. (2005b) *An Evaluation of the Safer Locals Programme: Final Report*. Cambridge: Cambridge Institute of Criminology, Prison Research Centre.

Livingstone, M. (1997) 'A review of the literature on self-injurious behaviour amongst prisoners', *Issues in Criminological and Legal Psychology,* 28: 21–35.

Lohner, J. and Konrad, N. (2006) 'Deliberate self-harm and suicide attempt in custody: distinguishing features in male inmates' self-injurious behaviour', *International Journal of Law and Psychiatry*, 29 (5): 370–85.

Lohner, J. and Konrad, N. (2007) 'Risk factors for self-injurious behaviour in custody: problems of definition and prediction', *International Journal of Prisoner Health,* 3 (2): 135–161.

Loucks, N. (1997) *HMPI Corton Vale: Research into Drugs and Alcohol, Violence and Bullying, Suicides and Self-Injury and Backgrounds of Abuse.* Edinburgh: Scottish Prison Service.

Lupton, D. (1999) *Risk*. London: Routledge.

Maden, A., Chamberlain, S. and Gunn, J. (2000) 'Deliberate self-harm in sentenced male prisoners in England and Wales: some ethnic factors', *Criminal Behaviour and Mental Health*, 10: 199–204.

Marzano, L. (2007a) 'Is my work "feminist" enough? Tensions and dilemmas in researching male prisoners who self-harm', *Feminism and Psychology*, 17: 295–301.

Marzano, L. (2007b) 'Self-Harm in a Men's Prison: Staff's and prisoners' perspectives.' Unpublished PhD thesis, Middlesex University, London.

Marzano, L. and Adler, J. (2007) 'Supporting staff working with prisoners who self-harm: a survey of support services for staff dealing with self-harm in prisons in England and Wales', *International Journal of Prisoner Health*, 3: 268–82.

McAllister, M. (2003) 'Multiple meanings of self-harm: a critical review', *International Journal of Mental Health Nursing*, 12: 177–85.

McArthur, M., Camilleri, P. and Webb, H. (1999) 'Strategies for managing suicide and self-harm in prisons', *Trends and Issues in Crime and Criminal Justice*, 125: 1–6.

Meltzer, H., Jenkins, R., Singleton, S., Charlton, J. and Yar, M. (1999) *Non-Fatal Suicidal Behaviour amongst Prisoners*. London: Office for National Statistics.

Owens, D., Horrocks, J. and House, A. (2002) 'Fatal and non-fatal repetition of self-harm'. *British Journal of Psychiatry*, 181: 193–9.

Paton, J. and Jenkins, R. (2005) 'Suicide and suicide attempts in prisons', in K. Hawton (ed.), *Prevention and Treatment of Suicidal Behaviour: From Science to Practice* (pp. 307–34). Oxford: Oxford University Press.

Pembroke, L. (2007) 'Harm minimisation: limiting the damage of self-injury', in H. Spandler and S. Warner (eds), *Beyond Fear and Control: Working with Young People Who Self-Harm*. Ross-on-Wye: PCCS Books.

Power, K.G., McElroy, J. and Swanson, V. (1997) 'Coping abilities and prisoners' perceptions of suicidal risk management', *The Howard Journal*, 36 (4): 378–92.

Power, K.G. and Spencer, A.P. (1987) 'Parasuicidal behaviour of detained Scottish young offenders', *International Journal of Offender Therapy and Comparative Criminology*, 31: 227–34.

Rayner, G. and Warner, S.J. (2003) 'Self-harming behaviour: from lay perceptions to clinical practice', *Counselling Psychology Quarterly*, 16 (4): 305–29.

Richards, B. (1978) 'The experience of long-term imprisonment', *British Journal of Criminology*, 18 (2): 162–9.

Rickford, D. and Edgar, K. (2005) *Troubled Inside: Responding to the Mental Health Needs of Men in Prison*. London: Prison Reform Trust.

Rivlin, A. (2006) 'Suicide and Parasuicide at a Therapeutic Community Prison for Men.' Unpublished MPhil thesis, Oxford University, Oxford.

Rose, N. (1985) *The Psychological Complex: Psychology, Politics and Society in England, 1869–1939*. London: Routledge and Kegan Paul.

Safer Custody Group (2001) *Preventing Suicides and Making Prisons Safer for All Who Live and Work There*. London: HMSO.

Safer Custody Group (2002) *F213SH Self-Harm Form: Senior Managers Briefing Pack*. London: HMSO.

Safer Custody Group (2004) *Recorded Self-Harm in the Prison Service*. Research Briefing 2. London: HMSO.

Safer Custody Group (2007) *Reported Self-Harm in Prisons in 2006*. (Internal report).

Safer Custody Group and Offender Policy Group (2008) *Monthly Self-Harm Report – June 2008*. (Internal report).

Sapsford, R.J. (1978) 'Life-sentence prisoners: psychological changes during sentence', *British Journal of Criminology*, 18 (2): 128–45.

Shaw, S.N. (2002) 'Shifting conversations on girls' and women's self-injury: an analysis of the clinical literature in historical context', *Feminism and Psychology*, 12 (2): 191–219.

Shaw, C. and Shaw, T. (2007) 'A dialogue of hope and survival', in H. Spandler and S. Warner (eds), *Beyond Fear and Control: Working with Young People Who Self-Harm*. Ross-on-Wye: PCCS Books.

Shea, S.J. (1993) 'Personality characteristics of self-mutilating male prisoners', *Journal of Clinical Psychology*, 49 (4): 576–85.

Sinclair, J. and Green, J. (2005) 'Understanding resolution of deliberate self harm: qualitative interview study of patients' experiences', *British Medical Journal*, 330 (7500): 1112–15.

Smith, C. (2000) ' "Healthy prisons": a contradiction in terms?', *The Howard Journal of Criminal Justice*, 39 (4): 339–53.

Snow, L. (1997) 'A pilot study of self-injury amongst women prisoners', *Issues in Criminological and Legal Psychology*, 28: 50–9.

Snow, L. (2002) 'Prisoners' motives for self-injury and attempted suicide', *British Journal of Forensic Practice*, 4 (4): 18–29.

Spandler, H. and Warner, S. (eds) (2007) *Beyond Fear and Control: Working with Young People Who Self-Harm*. Ross-on-Wye: PCCS Books.

Sykes, G. (1958) *The Society of Captives.* Princeton, NJ: Princeton University Press.

Taylor, B. (2003) 'Exploring the perspectives of men who self-harm', *Learning in Health and Social Care*, 2 (2): 83–91.

Thomas, J., Leaf, M., Kazmierczak, S. and Stone, J. (2006) 'Self-injury in correctional settings: "pathology" of prisons or of prisoners?', *Criminology and Public Policy*, 5 (1): 193–202.

Toch, H. (1992) *Mosaic of Despair: Human Breakdowns in Prison.* Washington: American Psychological Association.

Topp, D.O. (1979) 'Suicide in prison', *British Journal of Psychiatry*, 134: 24–37.

Towl, G. (2004) 'Psychological services in Her Majesty's Prison and Probation Services', in J.R. Adler (ed.), *Forensic Psychology: Concepts, Debates and Practice*. Cullompton: Willan Publishing.

Towl, G. and Crighton, D. (2008) *Psychology in Prisons* (2nd edn.). Chichester: Wiley-Blackwell.

Towl, G. and Hudson, D. (1997) 'Risk assessment and management of the suicidal', *Issues in Criminological and Legal Psychology*, 28: 60–4.

Wilkins, J. and Coid, J. (1991) 'Self-mutilation in female remanded prisoners: an indicator of severe psychopathology', *Criminal Behaviour and Mental Health*, 27: 247–67.

Willig, C. (ed.) (1999) *Applied Discourse Analysis: Social and Psychological Interventions*. Buckingham: Open University Press.

World Health Organisation. (2000) *Preventing Suicide: A Resource for Prison Officers.* Geneva: WHO.

Zamble, E. and Porporino, F.J. (1988) *Coping, Behaviour, and Adaptation in Prison Inmates.* New York: Springer-Verlag.

Chapter 25

Post-corrections reintegration: prisoner resettlement and desistance from crime

Ros Burnett

There are many examples of persistent offenders who move on from a life of crime to become law-abiding, trusted citizens, and who seem unlikely to become involved in criminal activity ever again. This is the heart-warming, reassuring ending that we in criminal justice occupations surely all aspire towards: the reformed person whose offending is in the past and who in society is now imperceptibly one of us. The statistics on recidivism, however, and inquiries into the effects of imprisonment and the problems typically faced by returning prisoners, show that the road from leaving prison to integration within the community is often long and faltering.

The stage immediately following release is known to be the most problematic for ex-prisoners and much of the literature on 'resettlement' is rightly focused on this early period of 're-entry' (as it is termed in America) into the community. Correspondingly, this chapter begins with a brief overview of resettlement policy, particularly as it pertains to England and Wales and the initial post-custody re-entry period.

The second part of the chapter turns to research on desistance from crime and the process by which individuals may progress from a criminal past to a law-abiding future. In this, it will distinguish between 'primary' and 'secondary' desistance; a conceptual division to differentiate those who have paused their offending from those whose non-offending is accompanied by 'the role or identity of a "changed person"' (Maruna *et al.* 2004: 274). For psychologists and mental health professionals, often working at the 'heavy end' of assessing risk and treating disordered criminal conduct, notions of reform and the ending of criminal careers may seem remote, but desistance research provides insight into how qualitative changes might occur sooner.

In discussing this change process, the final section of the chapter will centre on two, related, critical factors in sustained desistance and reintegration: (1) agency and linked self-factors; and (2) how people in positive relationship to the offender, including penal professionals, can nurture those self-factors. These go to the heart of debates in research and policy concerned with whether it is the person who needs to change or their social conditions.

Developments in resettlement work

Policy background to resettlement

Given the extraordinarily high number of people imprisoned in recent years, it is not surprising that the resettlement of prisoners has become a prominent issue in criminal justice. In America, the interest shown at national and state level in 'prisoner re-entry' has been 'nothing short of remarkable' (Travis 2007: 84). In England and Wales, resettlement has recently been 'rediscovered' (Hedderman 2007: 9). Following years of neglect,[1] we have seen its 'elevation … to a position of relatively high priority in penal policy' (Maguire and Raynor 2006: 22) spurred on by a Social Exclusion Unit inquiry (SEU 2002), a joint inspectorate report (HMCI Probation and Prisons 2001) and political promises to reduce crime. Conversely, however, stringent licence conditions and recall provisions arguably make it harder for ex-prisoners to resettle.

On a strategic level, an elaborate network of services, action plans and policies for improving provision exist for those leaving prison. The SEU (2002) report on reoffending by ex-prisoners identified the need for a unified rehabilitation strategy to address factors associated with reoffending, particularly among the neglected categories of young adults, short-term prisoners, women and BME groups. The Home Office largely adopted its recommendations for a long-term, cross-departmental approach to meeting resettlement needs, and introduced a national action plan to reduce reoffending, with seven 'pathways' to improve access to: accommodation; education, training and employment; healthcare; drug treatment; financial benefits; children and family support; thinking and behaviour programmes

(Home Office 2004). Local action plans reveal the elaborate regional infrastructures that have been set up to support re-entry, including collaboration with the voluntary sector and faith groups (e.g. London Resettlement Board 2007).

The main vehicle for carrying forward this rehabilitation framework was the integration of the Prison and Probation Services into the National Offender Management Service (NOMS). A National Offender Management Model (NOMM) was introduced. Phase 2 of this model was implemented in autumn 2006 for high-risk prisoners sentenced from December 2006, requiring the setting up of offender management units in prisons, and close liaison with outside probation services, in order to provide a 'seamless experience to offenders and promote community reintegration upon release' (HMI Probation 2008: 19).

The plight of the returning prisoner

The necessity of this complex of strategies and 'through-the-gate' interventions is evident from surveys of the multiple disadvantages suffered by the 'typical' prisoner. The prison population is 'overwhelmingly drawn from the economically disadvantaged and politically powerless' and they 'tend to have experienced many forms of social exclusion, suffer mental health problems, have a history of substance abuse, experience learning difficulties and are prone to self harm and suicide' (Jewkes 2007: 197). Such high vulnerability, publicised by the SEU, continues to be found in more recent inquiries (for example, United Kingdom Drug Policy Commission (UKDPC) 2008; Prison Reform Trust 2008).

Re-entry is particularly challenging for short-term prisoners, who are less likely to receive pre- and post-release support and interventions. Probation and prison resources are increasingly focused on more serious offenders even though these short-term prisoners form the majority of adults sent to prison. Given the numerous problems they face, this neglect helps to create a 'revolving doors' pattern of reoffending and reincarceration (HMI Probation and HMI Prison 2001; Home Affairs Committee 2005).

Peak rates for reoffending or breaching licence conditions occur during the period immediately following release, and deaths from accidents or suicide are relatively high in the first few weeks (National Research Council 2007). Imprisonment also often results in the loss of accommodation, employment and disrupts family relationships, augmenting any problems prisoners had prior to sentence. Thus, many leave prison impoverished, with substance abuse issues and without employment, family support and adequate housing. They also have to contend with stigmatisation and the institutional barriers erected against anyone with a prison record, and any help they received in prison may be undercut by having to return to disadvantaged communities.

Resettlement in practice

Given this almost Sisyphean task for returning prisoners, and the high recidivism and reincarceration rates, aspirations of 'turning over a new leaf' might seem fanciful. How is sustained reintegration possible, and do any resettlement interventions help to reduce reoffending? Since the rescuing of the 'rehabilitative ideal' from nearly three decades of scepticism, there is now evidence that some interventions aimed at reducing reoffending can make an impact if properly targeted and implemented; though, admittedly, much of this comes from efficacy pilots, and it is tantalisingly difficult to replicate in everyday practice (McGuire 2002; Wormith *et al.* 2007; see also Section 6 of this volume). Prison-based programmes, here and elsewhere, include some commendable 'through-the-gate' initiatives specifically concerned with resettlement, though with mixed results (Seiter and Kadela 2003; Wilson and Davis 2006), and more rigorous evaluations are needed (Petersilia 2004).

A challenging title given to an earlier American paper was *But They All Come Back* (Travis 2000). The recent policy attention given to resettlement in England and Wales makes clear that we have recognised this problem; however, there is a gap between the rhetoric and reality of resettlement practice (Hedderman 2007). Among obstacles to implementation are the twin perils of overcrowding and underspending. The annual report of the Chief Inspector of Prisons notes that, while there are isolated examples of promising and innovative resettlement practice, overall performance in resettlement work, especially in training prisons, has declined during a period of 'unprecedented pressure' (HMI Prisons 2008: 5).

Following cuts and retraction on planned services, inspectors found 'staff who are increasingly frustrated at the gap between what is expected and what is deliverable' (HMI Prisons 2008: 6) – and more of such 'efficiency savings' are planned. While the effect of overcrowding on prison resources is well known, numbers under probation service supervision, including ex-prisoners on licence, have also expanded hugely, stretching the Service beyond capacity. In these 'straitened circumstances' (Hedderman 2007: 20) integrity of implementation is unlikely to be achieved.

Another strain comes from tensions between the resettlement aims of sentence planning and 'national standards for supervision [which] steer practitioners to prioritise short term risk control over longer reintegration aims' (Hedderman 2007: 20). Ironically, although rehabilitation practice has renewed credibility and legitimacy, this 'new rehabilitationism' is more focused on offending behaviour than on the whole person, and the objective is to prevent reoffending and so increase community security, rather than rehabilitation of the individual as an end in itself (Raynor and Robinson 2005).

Recent trends and paradigm shifts in resettlement

Recent developments in resettlement in the UK to some extent mirror and are influenced by the US re-entry movement, hailed as a 'new model' in which services 'reach behind the prison walls' and 'corrections and parole become more a broker of institutional arrangements and less the punitive agents of the criminal justice system' (Travis 2007: 85). The idea of 'through-care' with a community focus is not so new in the UK for those with longer memories, though its revival within the present system is more elaborate if less welfare based.

Other trends and developments in England and Wales embrace: rediscovery of the importance of family ties (Codd 2007); provision that is tailored for groups of prisoners with distinct needs (e.g. females, ethnic minorities and foreign nationals, older prisoners, mentally disordered); and much greater involvement of voluntary sector services and faith groups (Crow 2006; Hucklesby and Hagley-Dickinson 2007). Generally, practice lags behind policy, though there are some impressive examples of initiatives in operation and further advanced; for instance, PS Plus, which is essentially orientated towards increasing prisoners' employment prospects; and the South West Integration (Swing) model of resettlement (see Hucklesby and Hagley-Dickinson 2007).

A risk-based approach, centring on dynamic factors that correlate highly with recidivism, remains the dominant model in offender management and resettlement policy. This Risks-Needs-Responsivity (RNR) framework, developed by Andrews and Bonta (2006) and their colleagues is, deservedly, regarded as the 'reigning paradigm in rehabilitation theory and practice' (Ward and Maruna 2007: 19), being the most fully developed and rigorously supported. The crisis of spiralling prison populations, however, has prompted rethinking about what works best, or what else might help, to slow the 'revolving door'.

In the UK, as elsewhere, there are movements towards resettlement provision that: is holistic and multi-agency; is restorative (inclusive and supportive, as well as reparative and redemptive); applies the principles of therapeutic jurisprudence; makes greater use of positive incentives to encourage compliance; and is strengths-based as well as needs-based.

Strengths-based interventions (e.g. Maruna and LeBel 2003; Burnett and Maruna 2006), though not mutually exclusive with the RNR model, de-emphasise the faults and failings of individuals and focus more on what they can do for others and on their own behalf, and their psychological well-being. One strengths-based approach which is theoretically well elaborated – the Good Lives Model (GLM) – is gathering momentum in practice (see Ward and Maruna 2007). Its guiding assumption is that all people strive towards the attainment of primary human goods; namely, 'experiences, activities, or states of affairs that are strongly associated with well-being and higher levels of personal satisfaction and social functioning' (2007: 21). Law-breaking is one outcome when people perceive that legally acceptable routes are closed to them. Rather than focusing on deficits, interventions should therefore focus on assisting people to reach what they want for themselves legitimately, thereby reducing their perceived need to offend. Thus, interventions should focus on people's 'approach', not 'avoidance', goals (Ward and Maruna 2007).

To varying extents, paradigm shifts towards restorative justice, therapeutic jurisprudence, and strengths-based approaches, claim a different ethos – one of moral inclusion, forgiveness, and welcoming support from the community. State services, in contrast, have been characterised as risk-based, narrowly concerned with individual pathologies, cognitive-behavioural deficits and programmes to correct thinking and behaviour patterns. Such contrasts can be exaggerated, but perhaps an incontrovertible difference is that the purpose of the former is the well-being and productive life of the individual while the purpose of the latter is reduction of reoffending. Strengths-based approaches, focusing on positive psychology, individual value and the principle of social exchange, fit well into a desistance paradigm for resettlement.

Desistance from crime

With a soaring prison population, funding cuts, 'back-end sentencing' policies (Travis 2007) which return people to prison for breaching licence conditions rather than for reoffending, and high proportions of unsupported short-term prisoners, resettlement policy itself seems to be caught in a 'revolving door'. In this context, discussion of sustained desistance and the termination of criminal careers may seem purely 'academic' to forensic psychologists and frontline staff working with chronic or serious offenders. Given the difficulties facing exiting prisoners, the barriers against reintegration can seem insuperable. Some prisoners themselves take this view, even finding consolations in the prospect of returning to prison (see Howerton *et al.* 2009) and seeing themselves as 'doomed to deviance' (Maruna 2001). However, uncertainties and setbacks are endemic in efforts to change and, in assessing individuals' future potential, we can take heart from desistance research.

The duration of criminal careers

Even the most chronic offenders generally stop. Longitudinal research shows wide variability in career lengths which cannot be predicted from static variables and people's histories (Ezell and Cohen 2005). There is a strong linear decline in residual career length as people age, and criminal convictions continue until later life only for a very small percentage.

Farrington (2003), using data from the Cambridge Study of Delinquent Development, found the mean estimate of career length to be 10.4 years. Scholars analysing data on a sample of nearly 2,000 of 'California's most serious youthful offenders' found an average overall career length of approximately 17 years (Ezell 2007: 10). Importantly though, they found wide variability, which 'should not be overlooked as it seriously hampers the ability to prospectively predict a given offender's career length' (Ezell 2007: 29). A quarter of the sample had convictions for less than 13 years, and, applying Moffitt's (1993) dual typology, some better fitted the trajectories of 'adolescent limited' patterns than 'life-course persistent' patterns despite their criminal histories being indicative of the latter. These findings alone justify work with even the most incorrigible/persistent offenders, and validate the need for fully resourced resettlement services including properly skilled criminal justice practitioners. It seems that change is always possible, and therefore we need a better understanding of why and how.

The study of desistance from crime

The study of 'desistance' from crime, concerned with 'the process of ending a period of involvement in offending behaviour' (Farrall and Calverley 2006: 1), is a relatively new field of criminological research. Criminal career research had previously given more attention to 'onset' and 'persistence' or 'recidivism'. As a field of inquiry, it has expanded massively over the past two decades and features increasingly in policy discussion. The concept of 'desistance' is used to denote both periods of non-offending and the end of criminal careers – in the vernacular, 'going straight' and 'giving it up'. The usually gradual, intermittent process it involves explains the differential use of the concept within the literature to refer to lulls and crime-free gaps as well as the projected termination of offending.

While qualitative studies tend to contrast 'desisters' with 'persisters' to explore differences in their crime career narratives, respondents' accounts, and alternative measures, indicate that most cannot be definitively categorised as one or the other. They vacillate in a grey terrain between persistence and desistance, in which criminal behaviour remains a possibility (Piquero 2004). For example, the Oxford study of recidivism (Burnett 2000, 2004a) found that the majority of 130 male property offenders, when interviewed close to their release date, were uncertain whether they would reoffend. While 80 per cent wanted to 'go straight', only 25 per cent thought they definitely would. Ambivalence about which course they would follow was reflected in alternative imagined outcomes. Optimally, they would acquire a good job and settle comfortably in a happy relationship. Prospects of not getting there or 'losing it', however, or being tempted into low-risk crimes of acquisition, were other imagined scenarios. When interviewed again during the six months following release, 60 per cent self-reported that they had reoffended. These patterns suggest divided intention to either desist or to reoffend, depending on the arising dynamics of their circumstances.

The study of desistance aims to elucidate the interplay between the different dimensions involved in change: including life-course transitions, subjective factors, objective factors, and ageing. Qualitative researchers particularly focus on the subjective dimension to understand better how individuals make sense of objective variables in this complex interaction. While desistance scholars concur that successful withdrawal from criminal activity is the outcome of person–structure–maturation interactions, there are disagreements about whether the main initiating factors are structural or subjective (Maruna 2001; Farrall 2002; Giordano *et al.* 2002; Laub and Sampson 2003; LeBel *et al.* 2008).

An overview of key desistance theories and studies would require another chapter (for recent reviews see Farrall and Calverley 2006; Kazemian 2007). Here, I draw upon specific theories and findings selectively in order to explore two emergent themes in discussions of successful resettlement: (1) the role of 'self-factors', including agency/autonomy/self-determination and, more generally, mental processes such as perceptions, values and emotions; and (2) the role of 'relationship', including family support, mentoring, staff relational skills and working alliances.

Adopting a desistance framework in rehabilitative and resettlement agendas

Gaps remain in desistance research (see Kazemian 2007). How the process applies to different groups according to gender, race, and offence type requires further investigation. Also, 'the importance of the social environment for stability and change in individuals' crime involvement has been highly undervalued by the majority of criminology's developmental and life-course theories' (Wikström and Treiber 2009: 416). Further, we need to specify the mechanisms involved in change and continuity, and to clarify conceptually key variables such as 'agency'. Nevertheless, a desistance paradigm provides useful insights for rehabilitative and resettlement agendas.

While there are some tensions between desistance research and investigations of 'what works', in other respects they converge (Maguire and Raynor 2006; Ward and Maruna 2007). The differences are, arguably, overstated as a by-product of distinguishing new insights, but such reframing can reinvigorate policy and practice – and one can discern this effect occurring in desistance research to theoretical directions in rehabilitation and resettlement policy. The desistance movement shifts the emphasis away from 'what works to what helps' (Ward and Maruna 2007: 12). Because quantitative criminal career research shows that most persistent offenders eventually stop irrespective of rehabilitative interventions, a desistance focus is on events that occur in the 'natural environment' and away from the criminal justice system (Farrall 2002). As this field of study has expanded, however, desistance theory has progressed from being somewhat dismissive of rehabilitative intervention to joining forces with rehabilitation researchers (Ward and Maruna 2007).

Desistance theorists propose that an understanding of desistance should be the starting place for developing rehabilitative approaches. McNeill (2006: 55), for example, advocates that 'desistance is the process that offender management exists to promote and support; [and] that approaches to intervention should be embedded in understandings of desistance'. While this desistance paradigm can include interventions to address risks and needs, these should be developed with regard to the individual's strengths, and should be 'subordinated' within a 'more broadly conceived role' for the key worker who would co-develop with the desister an individualised plan to assist and support desistance (p. 57). This model would 'require the worker to act as an advocate providing a conduit to social capital as well as a "treatment" provider building human capital' (p. 57). The notion of 'secondary desistance' assumes subjective reconstruction and the development of a new role identity; and therefore sustained desistance will be facilitated by 'encouraging offenders to make good through restorative processes and community service (in the broadest sense)' (p. 57) and by forms of inclusion,[2] such as certification of non-offender status (Maruna and LeBel 2003), thereby facilitating the 'progressive and positive reframing of their identities' (McNeill 2006: 57).

The 'self' and 'relationship' in the process of desistance

Agency and self-factors

The most compelling theories of secondary desistance take an 'agentic view of desistance' (Giordano *et al.* 2002: 992) and emphasise ex-offenders' development of a 'replacement self' (Maruna 2001). In Maruna's theory of narrative self-change, the desisters' explanations of how they 'recovered' involve some help or opportunity to find the 'real me' (2001: 88) within themselves and 'to accomplish what he or she was "always meant to do"...' (p. 87). These 'redemption scripts' include themes of: realising what really matters to them; gaining a sense of some control over their future; and ambitions 'to be productive and to give something back to society, particularly the next generation' (p. 88). Similarly, Giordano *et al.*'s (2002) theory of cognitive transformation is concerned with a 'new or refashioned identity' (p. 1001) and a 'transformation in the way the actor views the deviant behaviour or lifestyle itself' (p. 1002). Prior, related, steps in this change process are a 'general cognitive openness to change' (p. 1000) and then appropriate responsiveness to events and opportunities that arise ('hooks for change' p. 1000; 'catalysts for lasting change', p. 992) such as employment and new relationships.

Laub and Sampson (2003), in their social bonding theory of desistance, question whether such cognitive shifts and redefinition of self-concept are necessary as channels for desistance. Based on an extensive longitudinal study following up respondents to the age of 70, they argue that offenders renounce crime primarily as a result of social attachments developed in stable marriages, employment, or military experience, and that becoming a non-offender occurs almost by default, because they have invested themselves in these different activities which become valuable to them. Gradually, with a new daily routine that provides 'both structure and meaningful activity' (2003: 144) they become motivated to remain crime-free, making the 'commitment to go straight without even realizing it' (2003: 147).

The notion of creative self-reconstruction and re-evaluation of what matters as a necessary part of becoming a non-offender is a recurring theme in desistance studies. Some accounts imply a sudden, conscious decision to give up crime. For example, Leibrich (1993: 236) observes that respondents 'reached a point of inner conflict which had to be resolved'. Studies of acquisitive crime suggest a slow 'burn-out' as former thieves come to recognise that offending had ultimately proved unrewarding and counterproductive (Shover 1996; Burnett 2000, 2004a). Whether self-identity changes occur intrinsically within the process of becoming a non-offender or afterwards, all theories implicate the role of agency and studies report that ex-offenders, asked who or what helped them move away from crime, nearly always respond that primarily they did it themselves.

There are differences though in the extent to which people see themselves as having agency – that is, the 'power to make things happen intentionally through both habitual and deliberate choices' (Wikström and Treiber 2009: 407). Indeed, persisters' narratives often express powerlessness in influencing events (e.g. Maruna 2001). This is likely to be born out of their negative experiences as well as individual differences, and the causal importance of the agency/self dimension in desistance should therefore be understood in relation to social constraints and situational pressures which influence choices. Further, while agency involves reasoning and decision-making, we should not underestimate the role of emotions 'in general and immediate preferences for action', nor overlook that agency is itself partly 'driven by habitual, unconscious mechanisms as well as (and probably more frequently than) deliberate mechanisms' (Wikström and Treiber 2009: 397).

Allowing for such variability and limitations, human agency (or the related concepts of 'autonomy' and 'self-determination') has consistently featured as important in studies of desistance; though its conceptual elements and how it comes into play need to be more systematically explored (Bottoms *et al.* 2004; LeBel *et al.* 2008). It is agentic change to which analysts refer when they argue that resettlement work should prioritise ex-prisoners' 'own efforts' in resisting involvement in offending (Crow 2006: 39), and should include – as well as practical support – 'skilled and systematic work with offenders in relation to thinking, attitudes and motivation' (Lewis *et al.* 2007: 49).

Personal relationships and relationships with criminal justice workers

Any discussion of these self factors is incomplete without discussion of others in relationship to that self, not least because our views of self are partly reliant on the views of significant others (see Maruna *et al.* 2006). More generally, those 'self-factors' that shape choice and habits of behaviour – emotions, attitudes, beliefs, values and so forth – are developed and modified in the context of human relationships. Forming a close relationship is one of the main variables associated with change in desistance trajectories, though explanations vary as to the mechanisms involved. As noted above, Laub and Sampson (2003) suggest that 'good marriages' work through a process of informal social control. Giordano *et al.* (2007: 1641), meanwhile, suggest that such 'positive emotional connections' effect a changed view of self and a repositioning of values and priorities. The relationship is experienced as 'extremely rewarding and fulfilling and replaces drug use and crime as a source of positive meanings. Eventually, this facilitates a more other-directed worldview, one that is a significant part of her identity transformation' (2007: 1641).

Clearly, only the deepest and most personal relationships will effect profound changes of this nature. To a lesser degree and in different ways, however, there is considerable overlap between the supportive, influence processes involved in personal relationships and those in a 'therapeutic alliance' between the ex-offender and professional workers in contact with them (Burnett 2004b). The desisting sample in Maruna's study often observed that having 'someone who believed in' them was powerful in enabling them to break out of the 'cycle of crime and imprisonment' (2001: 87). While the impact of this on self-concept is likely to be more pronounced if it emanates from a romantic partner or family member, for someone without close relationships, this sense of another having faith in them and recognising their potential might come from professionals such as probation officers or psychologists.

Acknowledgement of the benefits of such interpersonal support is evident in the recommendation of numerous policy and research reports that there should be 'continuity' of contact with key professional workers. For example, the evaluation of the Resettlement Pathfinders found that contact with the same mentor before and after release was associated with lower reconviction rates (Lewis *et al.* 2007). Ironically, the joining together of the prison and probation services to create seamless sentences seems to have jeopardised the prospects for continuity of face-to-face contact with key workers, even though on paper there is provision for this. The introduction of contestability and networks of services and sectors has further fragmented services, creating a 'pass the parcel' approach (Robinson 2005). These circumstances 'make the generalized establishment of close supportive relationships an unlikely prospect' (Maguire and Raynor 2006: 29).

The transformative or therapeutic benefits of a working relationship with a trusted professional, by whom the individual feels understood and supported, have long been recognised. The mainstay of traditional probation practice was the use of an 'officer–offender relationship' to help individuals improve their social circumstances and avoid reoffending (Burnett and McNeill 2005). Although 'counselling' fared badly in meta-analytical reviews of 'what works', it has remained an axiom of professional wisdom among community justice practitioners that supportive relationships (through befriending, advising, motivating, modelling and brokering of services) can be pivotal in desistance (Burnett 2004b).

Interestingly, in clinical psychology, where specific interventions and methods are used, such relationship processes, together with 'client factors', are termed 'non-specific factors' or 'extra-treatment factors', meaning they are not intrinsic to treatment itself. Yet, despite these marginalising labels, they have emerged repeatedly in comparative studies as at least as important as the interventions themselves in contributing to effective outcomes (Hubble *et al.* 1999; Norcross 2002).Though still under-researched in a criminal justice context, the value of practitioner skills and motivational work is now recognised in RNR models of rehabilitation (Dowden and Andrews 2004) and within desistance research (Ward and Maruna 2007), and there is growing interest in understanding how relationships 'work' to assist personal change and reintegration.

These desister–practitioner relationships play on and are sustained by loyalty, empathy and positive regard. Rex (1999: 380), for example, found that probation officers' empathy, care, professionalism and commitment were 'crucial in preparing probationers to take quite directive guidance from supervisors'. The evaluators of the Resettlement Pathfinders suggest that continuity matters because 'offenders are more likely to keep appointments with and take advice from somebody they know and in whom they have some confidence [and] the challenging of discrepancy and the maintenance of motivation are also easier in the context of a relationship' (Lewis *et al*. 2007: 49). As in all relationships, people are more responsive to criticism and challenge from someone they respect, and who appears to care about their present and future well-being.

Motivational interviewing, developed by clinical psychologists, provides a theoretically elaborated practice model of the therapeutic value of comparable, though more formal, relationship processes in the mental health field (Miller and Rollnick 2002) and in criminal justice settings (McMurran 2002). The leading authorities on the concept of motivational interviewing define it as a directive, person-centred counselling style, helping clients to explore and resolve ambivalence about the problematic behaviour (Miller and Rollnick 2002).

The person or their social opportunities?

Yet, contrary to research which finds supervisory relationships to be of value in desistance, Farrall's (2002) study, following the progress of 199 people on probation, found that meetings with probation officers were largely seen by probationers as irrelevant to desistance efforts.[3] Based on their accounts about what did make a difference, Farrall argued that interventions to address the way people think are inappropriate because, even when motivated to desist, people still need to have social connections and opportunities in order to be included and to participate in society. He therefore proposed that services aimed at reducing reoffending should be concerned with sources of social capital rather than with building human capital. This argument returns us to the abiding question of whether it is individuals or their circumstances which need to change in order to promote desistance. Although it is generally conceded that both need to be addressed as part of a holistic approach, debate continues on where the emphasis should be.[4]

The findings of the Resettlement Pathfinders provide a recent source of empirical data (Clancy *et al*. 2006; Lewis *et al*. 2007) which, together with the thinking which it stimulated (Raynor 2004; Maguire and Raynor 2006), are helpful towards resolving this debate. The best results were obtained within the offending-focused probation sector pathfinders, in comparison to welfare-focused voluntary sector pathfinders. The probation-led projects also used a cognitive-motivational programme (FOR-a-Change) which began prior to release and was based on the principles of motivational interviewing.

The investigators concluded that resettlement should address thinking, beliefs and motivation, as well as practical needs, in the context of a 'through-the-gate' supportive relationship with skilled and motivated staff (Maguire and Raynor 2006; Lewis *et al.* 2007). Based on comparison of probation sector and voluntary probation sector models of resettlement applied in different pathfinders, and the 'implicit criminologies of resettlement' which they respectively embrace, Raynor (2004: 222) proposed that an 'offender responsibility' model of desistance has more to offer for effective resettlement practice than an 'opportunity deficit' model. Whereas the 'opportunity deficit' model sees offenders as 'victims of circumstances' whose offending resulted from 'lack of some resource or blockage of some opportunity' (Raynor 2004: 222), the responsibility model 'recognises that social, environmental and personal problems are real, but tends to treat them as challenges or obstacles which confront offenders with choices about how to respond' (2004: 223).

Concluding thoughts

Following a short review of recent developments in resettlement policy, this chapter has discussed reintegration of prisoners in the light of research on desistance, with particular attention to the roles of personal agency and the supportive, potentially transformative, roles of significant others who have relationships with them, including the 'therapeutic alliance' that may be formed with mentors and other professionals. Although conditions on other levels, notably their social structural circumstances and the situational contexts in which they find themselves, are also critical to understanding and achieving successful reintegration, it is especially relevant for forensic psychology and mental health professionals to be appreciative of 'self-restorative forces' (Toch 1997: 97) and the relationship-based elements of assisted desistance (Rex 1999; Burnett and McNeill 2005; McNeill *et al.* 2005).

Discussions of 'secondary desistance', involving the reconstruction of self into a prosocial member of society who, in some accounts, wants to 'make good' through useful employment, parenting and caring, or writing a book so that others can learn from their mistakes (Maruna 2001), can seem idealistic when set against research findings on the recidivism of released prisoners and barriers against access to a non-offending lifestyle (Burnett 2004a; Farrant 2006). Farrall and Calverley raise the question: 'Do they always, as Maruna's sample members seem to suggest, develop into "desistance missionaries", spreading the gospel of "reform", or are some of them "ordinary people" now worrying about getting to work on time, paying bills and getting dinner ready?' (2006: 14). No doubt their neighbours, and criminal justice practitioners, will happily settle for the latter – even though the generativity theory is surely no exaggeration. Wanting to give something to others and to 'make a mark' are natural human proclivities and Maruna's theory of redemption brilliantly illuminates that theme in desisters' narratives and sees its value for interventions. The conceptual distinction between primary desistance and secondary desistance, however, simplifies the observed variety of desistance trajectories which includes different patterns of intermittency, continuation and cessation. Many will fall into that 'vast middle ground of offending between the end points of persistent offending and desisting' (Laub and Sampson 2003: 197) where they may be ambivalent about giving up crime or just struggling to get through each day.

These betwixt-and-between individuals are likely to be the ones with whom staff are working in our currently demoralised, overstretched and under-resourced offender management system. Critics of resettlement policy have highlighted failures of implementation and the need for multifaceted, properly resourced services. The inadequacy of resettlement provision is abundantly evident in the rates of reoffending and in the churn of repeat imprisonment. However, the practical necessities of material resources for returning prisoners tend to sideline more obvious elements of assistance, such as empathic support and person-centred approaches. While ideally this would be provided in the context of a working alliance built on continuity and collaborative sentence planning, even one-off worker–offender interactions can be conducted according to the same therapeutic, strengths-based principles. Another way of looking at this is that simple truths (like the value of showing interest, talking and caring) can be overlooked in the labyrinth of multi-agency strategies and the bureaucracy of performance monitoring.

Notes

1 See Maguire *et al.* (2000) and Crow (2006) for useful reviews of provision for discharged prisoners in the past.
2 Importantly, McNeill (2006) additionally argues, this final step is ethically necessary. It is what is owed to former offenders by way of making good to *them* in the context of a society in which injustice has been suffered by them.
3 Though in a later follow-up study, there was some retrospective valuing of input by probation officers (Farrall and Calverley 2006).
4 Disagreement often hinges on different political and ideological positions regarding social inequality, human rights and whose interests should be prioritised, and on different theoretical assumptions about how people change.

References

Andrews, D.A. and Bonta, J. (2006) *The Psychology of Criminal Conduct* (4th edn). Cincinnati, OH: Anderson.

Bottoms, A., Shapland, J., Costello, A., Holmes, D. and Muir, G. (2004) 'Towards desistance: theoretical underpinnings for an empirical study', *Howard Journal*, 43 (4): 368–89.

Burnett, R. (2000) 'Understanding criminal careers through a series of in-depth interviews', *Offender Programs Report*, 4 (1): 1–15.

Burnett, R. (2004a) 'To re-offend or not to re-offend? The ambivalence of convicted property offenders', in S. Maruna and R. Immarigeon (eds), *After Crime and Punishment: Pathways to Offender Reintegration* (pp. 152–180). Cullompton: Willan Publishing.

Burnett, R. (2004b) 'One-to-one ways of promoting desistance: in search of an evidence base', in R. Burnett and C. Roberts (eds), *What Works in Probation and Youth Justice: Developing Evidence-Based Practice* (pp. 180–97). Cullompton: Willan Publishing.

Burnett, R. and Maruna, S. (2006) 'The kindness of prisoners: strengths-based resettlement in theory and in action', *Criminology and Criminal Justice*, 6 (1): 83–106.

Burnett, R. and McNeill, F. (2005) 'The place of the officer–offender relationship in assisting offenders to desist from crime', *Probation Journal*, 52 (3): 2211–42.

Clancy, A., Hudson, K., Maguire, M., Peake, R., Raynor, P., Vanstone M and Kynch, J. (2006) *Getting Out and Staying Out: Results of the Prisoner Resettlement Pathfinders.* Bristol: Policy Press.

Codd, H. (2007) 'Prisoners' families and resettlement: a critical analysis', *Howard Journal*, 46 (3): 255–63.

Crow, I. (2006) *Resettling Prisoners: A Review.* London: University of Sheffield and NOMS.

Dowden, C. and Andrews, D. (2004) 'The importance of staff practice in delivering effective correctional treatment: a meta-analysis'. *International Journal of Offender Therapy and Comparative Criminology*, 48: 203–14.

Ezell, M.E. (2007) 'Examining the overall and offense-specific criminal career lengths of a sample of serious offenders', *Crime and Delinquency*, 53 (1): 3–37.

Ezell, M.E., and Cohen, L.E. (2005) *Desisting from Crime: Continuity and Change in Long-term Crime Patterns of Serious Chronic Offenders*. Oxford: Oxford University Press.

Farrall, S. (2002) *Rethinking What Works With Offenders: Probation, Social Context and Desistance From Crime*. Cullompton: Willan Publishing.

Farrall, S. and Calverley, A. (2006) *Understanding Desistance From Crime: Theoretical Directions in Resettlement and Rehabilitation*. Berkshire: Open University Press.

Farrant, F. (2006) *Out for Good: The Resettlement Needs of Young Men in Prison*. London: Howard League for Penal Reform.

Farrington, D.P. (2003) 'Key results from the first forty years of the Cambridge Study in Development', in T.P. Thornberry and M.D. Krohn (eds), *Taking Stock of Delinquency: An Overview of Findings from Contemporary Longitudinal Studies* (pp. 137–84). New York: Plenum.

Giordano, P.C., Cernkovich, S.A. and Rudolph, J.L. (2002) 'Gender, crime, and desistance: toward a theory of cognitive transformation', *American Journal of Sociology*, 107: 990–1064.

Giordano, P.C., Schroeder, R.D. and Cernkovich, S.A. (2007) 'Emotions and crime over the life course: a neo-Meadian perspective on criminal continuity and change', *American Journal of Sociology*, 112 (6): 1603–61.

Hedderman, C. (2007) 'Rediscovering resettlement: narrowing the gap between policy rhetoric and practice reality', in A. Hucklesby and L. Hagley-Dickinson (eds), *Prisoner Resettlement: Policy and Practice*. Cullompton: Willan Publishing.

HMCI Probation and HMCI Prisons (2001) *Through the Prison Gate: A Joint Thematic Review*. London: HMSO.

HMCI Prisons (2008) *Annual Report 06/07*. London: TSO.

HMI Probation (2008) *Annual Report 2007–08*. London: HMI Probation. Available at: http://inspectorates.justice.gov.uk/hmiprobation/

Home Affairs Committee (2005) *Rehabilitation of Prisoners*. First Report of Session 2004–05, Volume I. London: TSO.

Home Office (2004) *Reducing Re-Offending: National Action Plan*. London: Home Office.

Howerton, A., Burnett, R., Byng, R. and Campbell, J. (2009) 'The consolations of going back to prison: what 'revolving door' prisoners think of their prospects', *Journal of Offender Rehabilitation*, 48 (5): 439–61.

Hubble, M.A., Duncan, B.L. and Miller. S.D. (eds) (1999) *The Heart and Soul of Change: What Works in Therapy*. Washington, DC: American Psychological Association.

Hucklesby, A. and Hagley-Dickinson, L. (eds) (2007) *Prisoner Resettlement: Policy and Practice*. Cullompton: Willan Publishing.

Jewkes, Y. (2007) 'Prisoners', in Y. Jewkes (ed.) *Handbook on Prisons* (pp. 197–9). Cullompton: Willan Publishing.

Kazemian, L. (2007) 'Desistance from crime: Theoretical, empirical, methodological, and policy considerations', in L. Kazemian and D. Farrington (eds), *Journal of Contemporary Criminal Justice*, 23 (1) (special issue on desistance).

Laub, J.H. and Sampson, R.J. (2003). *Shared Beginnings, Divergent Lives: Delinquent Boys to Age 70*. Cambridge, MA: Harvard University Press.

LeBel, T., Burnett, R., Maruna, S. and Bushway, S. (2008) 'The "chicken and egg" of subjective and social factors in desistance from crime', *European Journal of Criminology*, 5 (2): 131–59.

Leibrich, J. (1993) *Straight to the Point: Angles on Giving up Crime*. Otago, New Zealand: University of Otago Press.

Lewis, S., Maguire, M., Raynor, P., Vanstone, M. and Vennard, J. (2007) 'What works in resettlement? Findings from seven Pathfinders for short-term prisoners in England and Wales', *Criminology and Criminal Justice*, 7 (1): 33–53.

London Resettlement Board (2007) *London Reducing Re-offending Action Plan 2007–2009*. London: Ministry of Justice, NOMS and the Government Office for London. www.gos.gov.uk/497417/docs/247610/LondonRRAP.pdf (accessed 20 December 2008).

Maguire, M. and Raynor, P. (2006) 'How the resettlement of prisoners promotes desistance from crime: or does it?' *Criminology and Criminal Justice*, 6 (1): 19–38.

Maguire, M., Raynor, P., Vanstone, M. and Kynch, J. (2000) 'Voluntary after-care and the Probation Service: a case of diminishing responsibility', *Howard Journal of Criminal Justice*, 39 (3): 234–48.

Maruna. S. (2001) *Making Good: How Ex-convicts Reform and Rebuild their Lives*. Washington, DC: American Psychological Association.

Maruna, S. and LeBel, T.P. (2003). 'Welcome home? Examining the reentry court concept from a strengths-based perspective', *Western Criminology Review*, 4 (2): 91–107.

Maruna, S., LeBel, T., Mitchel, N. and Naples, M. (2004) 'Pygmalion in the reintegration process: desistance from crime through the looking glass', *Psychology, Crime and Law*, 10: 271–81.

McGuire, J. (2002) 'Integrating findings from research reviews', in J. McGuire (ed.), *Offender Rehabilitation and Treatment: Effective Programmes and Policies to Reduce Re-offending*. Chichester: Wiley and Sons.

McMurran, M. (ed.) (2002) *Motivating Offenders to Change: A Guide to Enhancing Engagement in Therapy*. Chichester: Wiley.

McNeill, F. (2006) 'A desistance paradigm for offender management', *Criminology and Criminal Justice*, 6 (1): 39–62.

McNeill, F., Batchelor, S., Burnett, R. and Knox, J. (2005) *21st Century Social Work. Reducing Re-offending: Key Practice Skills*. Edinburgh: The Scottish Executive.

Miller, W.R. and Rollnick, S. (eds.) (2002) *Motivational Interviewing* (2nd edn). New York: Guilford.

Moffitt, T.E. (1993) 'Adolescence-limited and life-course-persistent antisocial behavior: a developmental taxonomy', *Psychological Review*, 100: 674–701.

National Research Council (2007) *Parole, Desistance from Crime, and Community Integration*. Report of the Committee on Community Supervision and Desistance from Crime, National Research Council. Washington, DC: National Academy Press. www.nap.edu/catalog/11988.html

Norcross, J.C. (ed.) (2002) *Psychotherapy Relationships that Work: Therapist Contributions and Responsiveness to Patients*. Oxford: Oxford University Press.

Petersilia, J. (2004). 'What works in prisoner reentry? Reviewing and questioning the evidence', *Federal Probation*, 68 (2): 4–8.

Piquero, A. (2004) 'Somewhere between persistence and desistance: The intermittency of criminal careers', in S. Maruna and R. Immarigeon (eds), *After Crime and Punishment: Pathways to Offender Reintegration* (pp. 102–25). Cullompton: Willan Publishing.

Prison Reform Trust (2008) *Bromley Briefings Prison Factfile*, December 2008. London: Prison Reform Trust.

Raynor, P. (2004) 'Opportunity, motivation and change: some findings from research on resettlement', in R. Burnett and C. Roberts (eds), *What Works in Probation and Youth Justice* (pp. 217–33). Cullompton: Willan Publishing.

Raynor, P. and Robinson, G. (2005) *Rehabilitation, Crime and Justice*. Basingstoke: Palgrave.

Rex, S. (1999) 'Desistance from offending: experiences of probation', *Howard Journal*, 38 (4): 366–83.

Robinson, G. (2005) 'What works in offender management?', *Howard Journal*, 44 (3): 307–18.

Seiter, R.P. and Kadela, K.R. (2003) 'Prisoner reentry: what works, what does not, and what is promising', *Crime and Delinquency*, 49 (3): 360–88.

Shover, N. (1996) *Great Pretenders: Pursuits and Careers of Persistent Thieves*. Boulder, CO: Westview Press.

Social Exclusion Unit (2002) *Reducing Re-offending by Ex-prisoners*. London: SEU.

Toch, H. (1997) *Corrections: A Humanistic Approach*. New York: Harrow and Heston.

Travis, J. (2000) *But They All Come Back: Rethinking Prisoner Reentry*. Washington, DC: US Department of Justice, National Institute of Justice.

Travis, J. (2007) 'Reflections on the reentry movement', *Federal Sentencing Reporter*, 20 (2): 1–4.

UKDPC (2008) *Reducing Drug Use, Reducing Reoffending: Are programmes for problem drug-using offenders in the UK supported by the evidence?* London:

United Kingdom Drug Policy Commission. Available at www.ukdpc.org.uk/reports (accessed 20 December 2008).

Ward, T. and Maruna, S. (2007) *Rehabilitation: Beyond the Risk Paradigm*. London and New York: Routledge.

Wikström, P.-O. and Treiber, K. (2009) 'What drives persistent offending: the neglected and unexplored role of the social environment', in J. Savage (ed.), *The Development of Persistent Criminality*. Oxford: Oxford University Press.

Wilson, J. and Davis, R. (2006) 'Good intentions meet hard realities: an evaluation of the Project Greenlight reentry program', *Criminology and Public Policy*, 5 (2): 303–38.

Wormith, J.S., Althouse, R., Simpson, M., Reitzel, L.R., Fagan, T.J. and Morgan, R.D (2007) 'The rehabilitation and reintegration of offenders: the current landscape and some future directions for correctional psychology', *Criminal Justice and Behavior*, 34 (7): 879–92.

Chapter 26

Psychology in the National Offender Management Service for England and Wales

Graham Towl

Introduction

In this chapter coverage is given of the prevalence and growth of psychological practice in prisons along with some questions for reflection upon about this stage in the development of the discipline in UK prison and probation services. The historically significant change with the advent of the statutory regulation of practitioner psychologists in the UK from 2009 is also touched upon. But perhaps most potentially contentiously the 'elephant in the living room' within forensic psychology in particular, in the current period (2008–10) are the challenging training arrangements for forensic trainees. These are assessed with some ideas for improvements. Regrettably, the experience of trainees for the past five years has been that it takes an unnecessarily long time to qualify as a forensic psychologist in the UK. However, readers are reminded that any such discussions about training arrangements are best viewed as a commentary at a particular point in time in the development of such training arrangements. Given the recent history of relatively rapidly changing training requirements, and the new role of the Health Professions Council, prospective trainees would be well advised to get the most up-to-date information from their relevant professional and institutional bodies. The situation with forensic psychology is given a high level of focus because these are the largest single group of applied psychologists working directly in prisons. However, one significant change in recent years, as discussed below, is the advent of a greater variety of applied psychologists working with offenders who are in prisons or community-based services.

The 2003 strategic framework for psychological services in prisons and probation is covered with some thoughts about its successes and limitations. This is followed by some further reflections upon forensic psychology in the National Offender Management Service (NOMS) and the final section reaffirms the need for forensic psychologists to be more clearly focused upon existing and emerging ethical issues in the field. Hopefully, there will be food for thought with the sharing of perspectives which follow.

From 2000 to 2005 there was an unprecedented growth in the numbers of psychological staff working in prisons and probation. Indeed it has been observed that this was a booming era for forensic psychology in the UK (Farrington 2003). The numbers of psychologists and psychological assistants working in prisons more than doubled during this period, peaking at about 1,000 staff. In probation services, the numbers of directly employed staff went from one or two up to over 30 (Towl and Crighton 2005).

Marked increases in psychological staffing within prisons have also been seen with staff employed through the National Health Service (NHS) and private healthcare providers including clinical, counselling, health and forensic psychologists. Educational psychologists have also been on the increase in providing valuable services under the auspices of local authorities to imprisoned children and young people. Although such services are relatively recent, they are nonetheless important.

End of a booming era of growth for forensic psychology?

Since 2005, the booming era of growth within forensic psychology (from about 1998–2005) has largely been brought to a standstill. The precise reasons for the growth and subsequent flattening of staff numbers (in NOMS) may be contentious and contested. The British Psychological Society's (BPS) Division of Forensic Psychology (DFP) has had a pivotal role in these developments, partly because it maintains a monopoly on training requirements.[1] The process whereby trainee forensic psychologists work towards qualification has changed over recent years (and months). In the past (the 1980s) it had taken two or three years for a trainee to become qualified. Currently it is virtually unheard of for a forensic psychologist to qualify within three years of their initial graduation. Many have spent over four years in postgraduate training and are still not deemed qualified. This is both regrettable and totally unnecessary. It is perhaps especially regrettable given the very high levels of interest and development within the discipline. The expansion of postgraduate (and undergraduate) forensic psychology courses has been a real strength and achievement in the development of the profession in the UK.

Employers, and the largest single employer of forensic psychologists is the prison service, have played a role in contributing to bringing the growth to a standstill. First, as with other grades of staff, there have been repeated pressures to cut costs and improve efficiencies. Second, and perhaps most importantly, there appears to have been a narrowing of the roles of forensic psychologists for both trainees and qualified staff. The restricted practice of deeming particular posts only suitable for qualified forensic psychologists has also contributed to recruitment and retention problems of qualified staff. This can operate at two levels: one, it can contribute to an increasing narrowing of the roles of forensic psychologists; and, two, other qualified psychologists can be excluded from even applying for some posts. In turn, this makes maintaining an adequate level of supervision for trainees more challenging. Parallels can perhaps be drawn with the NHS where clinical psychologists dominate that professional market in much the same way as forensic psychologists do in prisons. There are similar results to such poor employment practices: unnecessary staff shortages and most importantly a too frequent failure to provide services to those who need them. Also, services in prisons are heavily dependent upon clinical work undertaken by forensic trainees, and such organisational arrangements require high levels of supervision and support to be in place.

Prison managers and policy-makers often conflate 'psychology' with 'psychologists'. The most obvious and widespread example of this is in the application of manualised groupwork-based interventions, commonly referred to in prison parlance as 'programmes' (Crighton and Towl 2008). Although these interventions are psychologically based in terms of their theoretical underpinnings they clearly do not need to be facilitated by psychologists. This is one potential benefit of such a manualised approach. There are, of course, disadvantages to such a 'treatment' approach, and many of these have been ably documented elsewhere (e.g. Thomas-Peter 2006a, 2006b).

In recent years the work of forensic psychologists has increasingly become influential in policy and practice. But there remain significant problems within the profession, particularly with regard to the supervised practice element of the training arrangements. The context of the problem lies with the Division of Forensic Psychology – which makes the rules for training requirements and employers, in this case NOMS, which provides salaries, training costs and opportunities to undertake germane supervised work. If the difficulties are not adequately addressed, for example, with the provision of clear and achievable training routes, then the boom years of forensic psychology may well be over. There will simply not be enough qualified staff coming through, which will result in a reduction in the number of trainees appointed and supervised and ultimately a contraction of this area of the workforce. However, with the advent of Statutory Regulation through the Health Professions Council comes the opportunity to broaden and develop the debate about appropriate training and qualification standards in (forensic) psychological practice.

The potentially good news is that much of the above is within the hands of the profession in terms of learning from our mistakes and better shaping the future for the application of forensic psychology in the UK. In which case, there is reason to be optimistic about the possible futures of the forensic psychology profession in NOMS in the UK.

Historic changes

As alluded to above, a historic milestone in the development of the registration of practitioner psychologists in the UK took place in July 2009. The milestone involves the introduction of the statutory regulation of psychologists. Until then, anyone might have referred to themselves as a psychologist; the title was not protected in law in the ways that titles were protected for a medical or nursing practitioner, who would need to demonstrate their qualifications, registration and continued maintenance of each. The new regulatory arrangements are administered by the Health Professions Council (HPC). At the time of publishing, this development has had little direct impact on the training of forensic psychologists. However, as the relationship between the profession and its regulator evolves, this development is likely to afford those involved with the organisation of the training and supervision of psychological staff with a greater flexibility in the demonstration of the relevant knowledge and skills required for independent practice and qualification.

During the current period of intra-professional flux in forensic psychology practitioner education, other applied psychologists will increasingly provide psychological services in prisons and probation. This may well bring a welcome eclecticism with improved breadth and depth of theoretical development and delivery of such services. However, on the other hand, it is perhaps unfortunate that at this point of high demand for (forensic) psychological services in prisons and probation, as a profession, we struggle to get 'fit for purpose' organisational arrangements in place for the training of the next generation of forensic psychologists. At the most basic level, there need to be clear start and end dates for training (as is the case in other areas of psychology, e.g. clinical). At the supervised practice stage (as currently configured), training may also benefit from a marked reduction in the paper-based outputs required of trainees. As mentioned above the advent of the HPC should give the discipline an opportunity to look at some of these arrangements afresh. It is anticipated that there may be an increased range of training 'providers' in competition with those accredited through the Division of Forensic Psychology of the BPS.

It may be that those considering work in the forensic field in the future may choose another applied psychology specialism as their route into such work. Eventually, it may be that all those on an applied psychology route start with a generic training and subsequently specialise. Such issues and futures are currently a matter of sometimes vigorous debate within the BPS but this is not merely an intra-professional, parochial matter. The Improving Access to Psychological Therapies (IAPT) policy in health serves as an illustration of what can be achieved when public services focus on improved access to services rather than on precisely who delivers which particular service. There will, of course, be parallels within offender management services. A growth in staff other than psychologists delivering psychological services is to be anticipated. Psychologists need to influence and shape some of this growth. Psychologists are well placed to play pivotal roles in the design, quality control and evaluation of such potential interventions. Below, consideration is given of the immediate history of some of the central developments in psychological services in prisons and probation using the 2003 strategic framework as a signpost of the changes.

The 2003 strategic framework for psychological services in prisons and probation

The strategic framework for psychological services in prisons and probation set the agenda for service provision at the beginning of the twenty-first century (HM Prison Service and the National Probation

Service 2003; Towl 2004). However, it is perhaps timely to revisit the organisation and development of services with a view to focusing upon what would be professionally and practically desirable over the coming five to ten years. At the time of writing, public services including prisons and probation have moved from a period of being relatively awash with funds to a tightening on central government public spending, given government commitments for the British taxpayer to contribute at unprecedented levels to the subsidising of the failing UK private sector in banking and finance. It is perhaps ironic that what some may view as a process tantamount to corporate white-collar crime in the banking industry will have the indirect result of a relative reduction in budgets to address crime and reduce reoffending! The advent of economic recession with probable increases in unemployment may well contribute to an increase in some crimes over the coming period. But let us briefly look more closely at lessons learnt from the 2003 framework and how we may use these to inform future directions.

What lessons may be learnt from the 2003 strategy? First, it provided a useful framework for service developments; with a number of regions drawing upon it in the strategic planning process for local service improvements in the development and delivery of psychological services. It was also successful in ensuring that psychology and psychologists heightened their profile within and outside the organisation. Much good-quality work was undertaken. Qualified staff received generous increases in their minimum pay. Between 2000 and 2005, training and supervision arrangements for trainees were much improved, resulting and reflected in the markedly improved retention figures from 2001–2004 (HM Prison Service and the National Probation Service 2003). Much went right. However, it was perhaps less successful in contributing to a widening of the roles of forensic psychologists. Also, another major problem was that there was a failure on the part of prison managers to develop senior practitioner roles in the field, which may well have contributed to the loss of some of the stronger clinicians. The progressive downgrading of geographical area based posts also may have played a part in the losses of some highly competent staff. These two developments have contributed to an impoverishment of future practice and training with the often unnecessary loss of high-calibre staff.

Perhaps the key weakness of the framework was my own failure to engage actively with offenders themselves as part of the consultation process in the development of the strategy. This was a mistake. Psychologists, other staff and interest groups within and beyond the organisation were consulted but this was not enough.

Moving back to the apparent narrowing of the roles of forensic psychologists, in terms of applied psychology across the piece, there was a broadening of services provided, with the introduction of a greater range of applied psychologists not seen on a similar scale previously (Towl 2004). Let us look briefly at the range of applied psychologists engaged in work with offenders to give a flavour of the potential depth and breadth of such work.

Clinical psychologists are employed through the NHS and there has been a growth in such services especially perhaps since the NHS took over prison health services from the previous in-house arrangements (Cinamon and Bradshaw 2006; Crighton 2005). Clinical psychologists do work with offenders addressing mental health needs and with those experiencing learning difficulties. There has perhaps been more focus on those with mental health needs but there is an increasing recognition of the potential importance of working effectively with those with identified (and not identified) learning disabilities or difficulties. As is the case with a number of other applied psychologists, clinical psychologists in prisons and with probation services often undertake forensic work. For example, clinical psychologists may help children and young people and indeed adult offenders with their problems in managing their anger. Anger management groupwork and individual work has long been a stalwart of psychology in prisons.

Counselling psychologists also undertake clinical work with offenders. Some are directly employed by the prison service and others are employed through the NHS to work with offenders. Some counselling psychologists focus upon the vulnerabilities of offenders rather than their perceived risk of harm to others. So, for example, a counselling psychologist may help a prisoner to address his or her feelings and self-image despite challenging life histories often characterised by multiple deprivations including neglect and abuse.

Educational psychologists appear to be undertaking increasing amounts of work with Young Offender Teams (YOTs) and also work in Young Offender Institutions (YOIs). This is vital work. This is an area that still requires much further development, but a start has been made with some encouraging developments. Offenders tend, as a group, to be educationally disadvantaged. It is crucial that the learning needs of offenders are addressed. This is important not just in terms of personal development and relationships, which are important, but also so that prisoners may improve their chances of gaining and maintaining successful employment. Children who go to prison often have not been successfully 'parented'; in the absence of such guidance and role models, without intervention and support, sadly many will simply return to prison shortly after having being released.

Health psychologists are starting to make their presence recognised within the NHS. Indeed their clinical focus on 'health' rather than 'illness' should arguably underpin much of the fundamental work undertaken within the NHS. A similar public health based model could be applied to work with offenders, and not just in relation to their offending. Health psychologists have increasingly started to undertake work within prisons, some directly employed by the prison service and some through the NHS. Prisoners, like other members of the public, can have multiple health needs. It is well documented that prisoners have a range of mental and physical health needs. Perhaps the single most important area where health psychologists could have an impact upon saving lives (and this can surely make a claim for inclusion under public protection) is in the introduction of smoking cessation programmes in prisons for prisoners and staff. Again, it is perhaps worth observing that this is an area of public protection not routinely focused upon within the forensic field. Yet there are disproportionately high numbers of regular smokers among offender populations. Smoking cessation interventions have the potential to save lives.

Occupational psychologists have worked for the Home Office and prison service for a relatively long period of time and although their numbers have not grown dramatically, their influence has perhaps been understated. In particular, the work undertaken in prison officer and middle and senior manager selection and promotion has had some potentially far-reaching effects in terms of everyday prison life. One real strength of the input of occupational psychologists in this area of work has been in addressing issues of racism and sexism at the point of recruitment, sometimes deselecting candidates on such grounds. This is important given the history of insularity, institutionalised racism and sexism which is deeply entrenched within prisons. Staff selection and development are fascinating fields to engage with a potentially substantial long-term impact in building therapeutic capacity and compassion within the coercive context of prisons.

Forensic psychologists are the most prevalent type of practitioner psychologist employed by the prison service. As has been noted above, the public sector prison estate, as part of the National Offender Management Service is, by far, the largest single employer of forensic psychologists. Some probation services employ forensic psychologists too, but the majority do not. Others 'buy in 'psychological services through the NHS or private healthcare sector. It is uncertain why probation services have tended to resist the appointment of psychological staff. There are, of course, some notable exceptions, where probation-based psychological services are thriving and much valued. All too often the work of forensic psychologists can be unduly manualised with the widespread prevalence of 'programmes'. This is not only professionally undesirable (because of an undue proceduralisation and prescriptive approach to the roles of forensic psychologists) but also in terms of any commitment to an evidence-based approach, with significant resources going into this still largely experimental area with mixed empirical findings (Thomas-Peter 2006a, 2006b; Towl and Crighton 2007; Crighton and Towl 2008) as to their efficacy. In the case of sex offender treatment, no UK studies have demonstrated a statistically significant reduction in sex offender reconviction rates using a randomised evaluation design (Kenworthy *et al.* 2003, Crighton and Towl 2007). Problems with the appropriate allocation of prisoners to such groupwork may also have contributed to some of the disappointing empirical findings in UK prisons in this area in recent years (Crighton and Towl 2008). One key professional vulnerability with this large-scale investment of psychological resources in such an experimental area is that studies may fail to show effectiveness, which ultimately may persuade the Treasury to cease such investments.

The work of forensic psychologists has not widened as much as had been intended in the 2003 strategic framework. It is uncertain whether or not this is because forensic psychological staff have been attracted to highly manualised work with offenders or because of local (and perhaps regional or national) management directives to undertake such work. Indeed this may well reflect the broader development of managerialist approaches within public services sometimes known as New Public Management (NPM) which has, among other aspects, a focus upon the measurement of activities (Towl 2008; Towl and Crighton 2008). Of course, the introduction of other types of applied psychologists as mentioned above may also have indirectly contributed to the narrowing of the roles of some forensic psychologists.

Risk assessment remains a key area of work within forensic psychological practice (Towl and Crighton 1996; Crighton and Towl 2008). This area will increasingly come into public focus with the consequences of the sustained use of Indeterminate Public Protection sentences which have added markedly to the numbers of imprisoned indeterminate sentenced prisoners. Increasingly, psychologists will be called upon to undertake timely, accurate and fair risk assessment for this group of offenders. There may well also be pressure to design and deliver new types of interventions to address relevant prisoner needs for this group. Since the launch of the strategic framework in 2003, the demands for risk assessments have been on the increase, and will continue to increase for the immediately foreseeable future. There is clearly much that forensic psychologists can contribute.

Reflections upon 'psychology' in prisons and probation

Arguably the most striking inequality in the distribution of psychological services within NOMS is the massive over-resourcing of services in prisons in comparison with a dearth of such services in the probation arm of NOMS. Indeed the impact of this is further exacerbated when the evidence for the efficacy of psychologically based interventions is considered. In general, psychologically based interventions designed to reduce the risk of reoffending of participants appear to be more likely to be effective in a probation (community) setting rather than a prison setting. If psychologists are to have their maximum impact within NOMS, then there needs to be a radical reallocation of psychological resources within NOMS from the prisons arm to the probation arm. Such an approach may also contribute to improving the confidence of sentencers in the value of community based sentences although will not be uncontroversial in an era of cuts to more traditional aspects of probation services.

If public protection is a key aim, then there would also need to be a significant shift of such intervention-based resources within prisons from the high-security estate to the young offender estate (Crighton and Towl 2008). Imprisoned children and young people, in comparison with adults, on average, go on to commit more offences subsequent to their release. In economic terms, there will be a greater return on financial investments aimed at reducing the risk of reoffending with children and young people than with adults. This is so, if we assume similar levels of efficacy for such interventions across both groups. Work purportedly aimed at reducing the risk of reoffending with 'accredited programmes' in the high-security prisons is unlikely to be effective in meeting this aim nor is it likely to be cost-effective. This is partly because prisoners assigned to such 'programmes' are unlikely to be released for many years. This gives rise to both practical and empirical problems if we wish to adopt an evidence-based approach to our work. Even a two-year reconviction-based follow-up study to test whether or not the programme had been effective could take 10–15 years to complete. Even if the study showed a positive effect in reducing the reconviction rates, we would need to satisfy ourselves (and others) that the effect was not due to other factors over the intervening 10–15 year period. Also prisoners at the early stages of long sentences may psychologically be better served in coming to terms with their sentence. A number may be appealing their sentences and this needs to be respected too, and not be routinely and unprofessionally dismissed as probable 'denial'. Useful work could potentially be done with prisoners in assisting them in supporting their psychological well-being despite the difficult circumstances of incarceration. Working with prisoners to reduce their risk of reoffending is important and central work, but it is not the only focus that psychologists should have in their work with prisoners. Psychologists can forget the importance of kindness and consideration when working with prisoners. This can be partly related to the explicitly coercive nature of prisons. Psychologists are by no means immune to the processes of institutionalisation.

Of course, much that can be offered to the public that would serve to reduce reoffending, or indeed crime, is more a matter of social policy than criminal justice policy alone. Perhaps psychologists need to have a better understanding of, and be more vocal about, such matters. An example may illustrate this point. In recent years there has been a great deal of discussion and debate within forensic psychology about risk assessment. Various risk assessment 'tools' have come onto the market, some more aggressively marketed than others. The field has been awash with such developments reflected in publications, conference papers and their sometimes widespread usage. One underpinning 'risk factor' for premature death (including violent death), major illness and crime is poverty. Indeed it would perhaps be interesting to reflect upon whether or not poverty in the UK accounts for more premature death than the totality of UK homicides. Some will assert that this is not a forensic matter, but I contend that it is. Lower socio-economic groups are significantly overrepresented in convicted offender populations. Yet forensic psychologists often continue to act as if the public is best protected by the development of ever more sophisticated risk assessment tools to be used with those who have already been convicted for violence. Surely, students of forensic psychology should be in a position to appreciate well-established links between social and economic disadvantage and convictions for crimes. The parallel to this is of course an understanding of social and economic advantage and its links with a lower probability of conviction for crimes. Often what is missing from debates about risk assessment within forensic psychology is a broader consideration of justice. This includes viewing the 'offenders' as potential perpetrators of harm as well as potential victims of harms, but above all as members of the public themselves. Psychologically, this can be challenging. Risk assessments are not merely matters of empirical accuracy but also of justice, equity and fairness.

The nature and context of the risk assessments undertaken by forensic psychologists can result in an undue focus upon the individual at the expense of a full consideration of environmental factors which may impact upon the risk of reoffending. This potential professional bias can be illustrated using the example of suicide in prisons. While imprisoned (whether held on remand or sentenced) members of the public have an inflated risk of completing suicide. By far the single most powerful predictor of suicide in prison is the temporal propinquity to the reception point in a given prison for an individual prisoner. This effect is far more significant, empirically, than any mental illness diagnostic category. In short, what is most statistically powerful in prediction terms is a readily identifiable environmental factor (Towl and Crighton 2000). One implication of this finding is that, on average, moving a prisoner from one prison to another will result in an increased risk of suicide. Thus, as with crime, there are some powerful environmental and social factors which require understanding and acknowledgement if psychologists are to work most ethically and effectively in NOMS. One implication of this may be that we could test the hypothesis that the postcode to which the individual offender is discharged may have as much of an impact on his or her risk of reoffending as, say, the index offence. Indeed, there remain a number of interesting hypotheses for testing within the discipline and there is much to do and learn from, which continues to make the world of forensic psychology so fascinating.

Future directions

One pervasive theme in this chapter on the development of forensic psychology in prisons and probation in the UK is the need to look afresh at the social and ethical context of our work. What is clear from the past decade or so of developments is that underpinning all our work there needs to be a clear and coherent sense of ethical practice.

This will be the key foundation for much of forensic psychological practice for the foreseeable future.

So, what should we do differently? As part of the Health Professions Council (HPC) we will have the opportunity to learn from other professionals in terms of both their mistakes and achievements. Perhaps especially for those working in prisons, it is worth giving a particular mention to the publication *Inside Time*, a prisoner-based newspaper which is produced monthly. In recent years and months a number of issues have been raised within its pages that have called into question the practices of some psychologists working in prisons. Overall, such contributions have made a valuable contribution to debates about the ethics of particular practices among psychologists in prisons. The British Psychological Society has, in recent years, provided some excellent sets of ethical guidance. It is a privilege to have access to such materials in informing our thinking about the ethics of our practice.

Despite some of the intra-professional setbacks (perhaps especially with the training arrangements) and limitations described in this chapter, financial investment in psychological methods has never been so high. There is much for psychologists to contribute and very high levels of need within offender populations. Thus, there is the potential for us to ensure tangible benefits from the application of psychological methods with those in high need. What could be more professionally challenging and satisfying than that?

Acknowledgements

I would like to acknowledge and thank Professor David Crighton and Ms Derval Ambrose for their helpful comments upon an earlier draft of this chapter. Thank you both.

Note

1 This monopoly position has, to date, been barely affected by statutory registration of psychologists and the move towards Health Professions Council (HPC) regulation as the HPC only directly regulates programmes that lead to a full qualification. At the time of writing (January 2010), there is only one provider of forensic psychology training accredited by the HPC (as a doctoral route), with all other provision remaining unchanged, and under the auspices of the BPS.

References

Cinamon, J. and Bradshaw, R. (2006) 'Prison health in England', *British Journal of Forensic Practice*, 7 (4): 8–13.

Crighton, D.A. (2005) 'Applied psychological services', *British Journal of Forensic Practice*, 7 (4): 49–55.

Crighton, D.A. and Towl, G.J. (2007) 'Experimental interventions with sex offenders: a brief overview of their efficacy', in *Evidence Based Mental Health*, 10: 35–7.

Crighton, D.A. and Towl, G.J. (2008) *Psychology in Prisons*, 2nd edn. Oxford: BPS Blackwell, Oxford.

Farrington, D.P. (2003) 'Foreword',in G.J. Towl (ed.), *Psychology in Prisons*. Oxford: BPS Blackwell.

HM Prison Service and the National Probation Service (2003) *Driving Delivery: A strategic framework for psychological services in HM Prison Service and the National Probation Service*. London: Home Office.

Kenworthy, T., Adams, C.E., Bilby, C., Brooke-Gordon, B. and Fenton, M. (2003) 'Psychological interventions for those who have sexually offended or are at risk of offending', *The Cochrane Database of Systematic Reviews*, issue 4, art. no. CD004858.

Thomas-Peter, B.A. (2006a) 'The needs of offenders and the process of changing them', in G.J. Towl (ed.), *Psychological Research in Prisons*. Oxford: BPS Blackwell.

Thomas-Peter, B.A. (2006b) 'The modern context of psychology in corrections: influences, limitations and values of "What Works?" ', in G.J. Towl, (ed.), *Psychological Research in Prisons*. Oxford: BPS Blackwell.

Towl, G.J. and Crighton, D.A. (1996) *Psychology for Forensic Practitioners*. London: Routledge.

Towl, G.J. and Crighton, D.A. (2000) 'Risk assessment and management', in G.J. Towl, L. Snow and M.J. McHugh (eds), *Suicide in Prisons*. Oxford: BPS Blackwell.

Towl, G.J. (2004) 'Applied psychological services in HM Prison Service and the National Probation Service', in A. Needs and G.J. Towl *Applying Psychology to Forensic Practice*. Oxford: BPS Blackwell.

Towl, G.J. and Crighton, D.A. (2005) 'Applied psychological services in the National Probation Service for England and Wales', in D.A. Crighton and G.J. Towl *Psychology in Probation Services*, Oxford: BPS Blackwell.

Towl, G.J. and Crighton, D.A. (2007) 'Psychological services in English and Welsh prisons', in R.K. Ax and T.J. Fagan (eds), *Corrections, Mental Health and Social Policy: International Perspectives*, Illinois: Thomas.

Towl, G.J. and Crighton, D.A. (2008) 'Psychologists in prisons', in J. Bennett, B. Crewe and A. Wahidin (eds), *Understanding Prisons Staff*. Cullompton: Willan Publishing.

Towl, G.J. (2008) 'Introduction and Overview', in G.J. Towl, D.P. Farrington, D.A. Crighton and G. Hughes, *Dictionary of Forensic Psychology*. Cullompton: Willan Publishing.

Concluding remarks

It is a challenging time to be working as a forensic psychologist. For people embarking upon their career, there seems to be a difficult process to complete training and an uncertain career path to follow. Yet, that uncertainty itself reflects the diversity of jobs and careers available to those who are interested in forensic psychology. There is ongoing debate as to what makes something psychological in the first place, and whether forensic psychological approaches are the only ones appropriate within forensic settings. There is also debate about where to take the discipline in the coming years. There is much potential to influence policy, practice and indeed to challenge and address offending behaviour.

The first edition of this book counselled against complacency. We would reiterate here that we need to do more as psychologists to evaluate our own efficacy, to hold ourselves accountable and to ensure that our voices are heard. Whether we like it or not, recidivism rates are still one of the means by which our efficacy is judged and as we move into more high-profile and contentious arenas, the risks and vulnerabilities of people who can be victimised become ever more salient.

We need to continue to engage with the system that we seek to describe, understand and facilitate. We need to engage with other practitioners and policy-makers in ways that are meaningful to them, but we need to engage with them in an ever evaluative and self-appraising manner. Wherever our debates may ultimately take us, the challenges for us are to be rigorous, professional, ethical, yet accessible and useful to the forensic field.

Index